International Political Economy

Interests and Institutions in the Global Economy

Second Edition

Thomas Oatley
University of North Carolina at Chapel Hill

PEARSON
Longman

New York   San Francisco   Boston
London   Toronto   Sydney   Tokyo   Singapore   Madrid
Mexico City   Munich   Paris   Cape Town   Hong Kong   Montreal

Acquisition Editor: Edward Costello
Senior Marketing Manager: Elizabeth Fogarty
Production Manager: Denise Phillip
Project Coordination, Text Design, and Electronic Page Makeup: WestWords, Inc.
Cover Designer/Manager: Wendy Ann Fredericks
Cover Photo: © Jane Sterrett/Stock Illustration Source
Manufacturing Buyer: Roy Pickering
Printer and Binder: R.R. Donnelley & Sons
Cover Printer: Phoenix Color Corporation

Library of Congress Cataloging-in-Publication Data

Oatley, Thomas
    Political economy : interests and institutions in the global economy /
    Thomas Oatley.— 2nd ed.
        p. cm.
    Includes bibliographical references and index.
    ISBN 0-321-35566-0
    1. International economic relations. 2. International finance. 3. Globalization. I. Title.

HF1359.O249 2005
337—dc22

                                                                            2005007736

Please visit our website at *http://www.ablongman.com*

ISBN 0-321-35566-0

3 4 5 6 7 8 9 10—DOC—08 07 06

Brief Contents

Detailed Contents

Preface

This book emerged from a certain frustration that has arisen from my effort to find suitable material for use in teaching international political economy (IPE) to advanced undergraduates. I have found that available edited volumes assume that undergraduates have considerable background in economic theory, in the relationship between economic and political processes, and in the history of the international economic system. In my experience, however, few undergraduates taking their first course in international political economy have such a background. And while available texts do an excellent job providing the substantive context by describing the creation and evolution of the postwar international economic system, most do a much less thorough job presenting many of the theories used by today's scholars of international political economy. What was lacking, I believed, was a text that set forth the historical and contemporary context of the modern international economic system and explained the core theories of international political economy. In brief, I thought that there was a considerable gap between the way available texts present IPE to undergraduates and how the field practices IPE as a scholarly endeavor.

This book is intended to fill that gap. It differs from existing textbooks in three principal ways. First, it has a more extensive discussion of economic concepts and theories than most IPE textbooks have. This reflects my belief that it is impossible to understand how the international economic system operates without some background in economic principles and theories. In addition, I believe that without a knowledge of how economic processes affect groups within society, it is impossible to understand why interest groups desire certain policies and why governments adopt specific policies. Every chapter contains an explicit discussion of some body of economic literature that has particular relevance to the issue under consideration. In presenting these theories, I emphasize the underlying intuition and make no attempt to describe the formal theoretical structure that supports these theories. In each instance, I stress the connections between the economic theory being discussed and the issue under consideration. It is my hope that bringing out these connections will provide an introduction to international economics sufficient to allow students to make sense of the international economic system.

Second, the book has a more extensive discussion of domestic politics than most other IPE textbooks have. The last 15 years have brought an explosion of studies that focus on the domestic politics of trade and exchange-rate policy. Indeed, it is hard to find a scholarly work on any aspect of international political economy that does not acknowledge the importance of domestic politics. Few existing textbooks incorporate this literature, and most provide only a cursory and rather unsystematic discussion of domestic politics. I dedicate more than one quarter of the book to the domestic politics of trade and exchange rates. In addition, the chapters on developing countries draw heavily on explanations based in domestic politics, to make sense of the trade and development strategies adopted by developing countries in the postwar period.

Finally, but hardly least important, I place little emphasis on the three traditional schools of international political economy that structure many of the current textbooks: mercantilism, liberalism, and Marxism. My decision to de-emphasize the traditional schools is based in part on two weaknesses in these schools. First, each presents a coherent, but largely self-contained, interpretive framework that focuses on one aspect of the international political economy and neglects many others. As a consequence, these frameworks often force students to adopt an "either–or" mentality when study-ing international political economy. Either global market-based capitalism is a good thing that raises global welfare, as liberals claim, or it is an exploitative system that ben-efits firms at the expense of workers, as Marxists claim. Either the international politi-cal economy is essentially cooperative, as the liberals emphasize, or it is essentially conflictual, as nationalists and Marxists emphasize. In most instances, the international political economy fails to fit wholly into any one of these three frameworks. Interna-tional economic transactions can raise social welfare, but they also often promote an unequal distribution of the gains. Countries sometimes engage in economic coopera-tion, but also sometimes become embroiled in economic conflict. Thus, rather than using three traditional schools that offer self-contained perspectives on, and that focus solely on, one aspect of the international political economy while neglecting others, this book develops an approach that can incorporate all of these aspects.

The second weakness of the three traditional schools is that they are often more useful for evaluating foreign economic policy outcomes than for explaining foreign eco-nomic policy decisions. Each traditional school offers an elaborate framework that tells us how governments should behave. Mercantilists argue that governments should intervene in markets, while liberals argue that governments should not intervene in markets. Marxists argue that capitalism should be replaced by socialism. None are good at telling us why governments adopt one set of foreign economic policies rather than another. Governments do intervene in the market for reasons that have little to do with national security, and they liberalize trade in areas that mercantilists would question. Marxism is better at offering explanations, but there are many instances in which sim-ple class conflict between labor and capital fails to account for the policies that firms and labor pursue or that governments adopt. For example, capitalist firms are impor-tant actors in the international economy, and they play a large role in shaping govern-ment policy. Yet, not all firms have identical interests. In fact, some firms clearly gain from globalization, but others clearly lose. Nor can workers be treated as an undifferen-tiated group. As is the case with firms, some workers lose from globalization, whereas others clearly benefit. The complexities of international economic exchange cannot, therefore, be reduced to a simple Marxist framework that emphasizes class conflict between labor and capital. For these reasons, students of international political econ-omy have increasingly turned away from theoretical explanations based explicitly on the three traditional schools of political economy. These historical perspectives continue to shape public and scholarly debates about the role of the market, about the relative gains of labor and firms in a capitalist economy, and about the state's proper role in the econ-omy. They have played a much less important role during the last 15 years, however, in shaping the explanatory theories that students of international political economy have developed to explain the foreign economic policies that governments adopt.

I use an analytical framework based on the interaction between interests and institutions. This approach allows me to draw heavily on contemporary scholarship. In addition, it allows me to develop several distinct explanations covering a large number of countries; all of the explanations start from the same point: governments' foreign economic policies reflect the interaction between societal interests and political institutions. The result, I hope, is a book that bridges the gap between international political economy as practiced by scholars and international political economy as presented to undergraduates.

New to the Second Edition

This second edition embodies many changes, some large and some small, that I think yield a much better book. Three large changes are most readily apparent. The most evident is a shift from the 9 long chapters of the first edition to 16 shorter chapters in the second edition. The greater number of chapters reflects a repackaging, rather than a doubling, of content. I have split each of the original chapters in half to sharpen each chapter's focus and make the material more accessible to students. I also have added a new feature to each chapter. This "Policy Analysis and Debate" feature encourages students to explore policy options in the contemporary global economy. Each issue asks students to consider the merits and demerits of alternative approaches to an important contemporary policy issue, encourages them to advocate and defend a specific policy, and provides references to online and published research to help formulate their position. Finally, the book offers a new concluding chapter on the consequences of and controversies over globalization. This chapter begins by defining what globalization is and then examines the debate about its impact on global poverty and income distribution, working conditions in the developing world, and the environment.

I have also made a number of smaller changes. I have added a more extensive discussion of trade theory in Chapter 3. I present a partial-equilibrium approach to explain the notion of "gains from trade," and I present the standard $2 \times 2 \times 2$ general equilibrium model to explain comparative advantage. I then carry over the general equilibrium model into the discussion in Chapter 4 of factor price equalization and the domestic politics of trade. I have also included a more structured discussion of balance-of-payments adjustment in Chapter 10 and a longer discussion of the African debt crisis and the Heavily Indebted Poor Countries Initiative in Chapter 15. Most chapters have been rewritten and in some cases reorganized in order to make the material more accessible. Finally, I have updated the examples, as well as the tables and figures, where it was appropriate and useful to do so.

Thanks

No book such as this is the work of a single person. I have benefited immensely from the advice and support of a large number of people. A few deserve special mention. Eric Stano of Longman Publishers supported this project from its initial conceptualization to the final production of the first edition. I am grateful for his encouragement and his patience as the project evolved through its many iterations. Ed Costello, who took over from Eric as the book moved toward its second edition, gently encouraged me to consider a more profound revision than I wished to undertake and graciously provided the time necessary to complete it. His advice and assistance were invaluable. Roland Stephen went well beyond the call of duty as a friend and colleague in entertaining my questions, providing suggestions about how to improve the text and using early versions of the book in his class at North Carolina State University. Eric Reinhardt at Emory University and Jeffry Frieden at Harvard University each offered comments based on their experience with using the text in their courses that I think helped me improve the second edition.

Numerous reviewers provided detailed comments that vastly improved the book in so many ways. It is no light burden to write a thoughtful and constructive review of a book, and I thank them all for taking the time to do so. My thanks, therefore, go to Ali R. Abootalebi, University of Wisconsin, Eau Claire; Francis Adams, Old Dominion University; Katherine Barbieri, University of South Carolina; Charles H. Blake, James Madison University; Charles Boehmer, University of Texas at El Paso; Terry D. Clark, Creighton University; Linda Cornett, University of North Carolina at Asheville; Charles R. Dannehl, Bradley University; Robert A. Dayley, Albertson College of Idaho; Mark Elder, Michigan State University; Richard Ganzel, Sierra Nevada College; Alan Kessler, The University of Texas at Austin; Douglas Lemke, Pennsylvania State University; Andrew Long, University of Mississippi; Michael Mastanduno, Dartmouth College; Sean M. McDonald, Bentley College; Philip Meeks, Creighton University; Jeffrey S. Morton, Florida Atlantic University; Layna Mosley, University of North Carolina, Chapel Hill; Gene Mumy, The Ohio State University; Jim Pletcher, Denison University; Herman Schwartz, University of Virginia; Cliff Staten, Indiana University Southeast; and Christianne Hardy Wohlforth, Dartmouth College. Frank Boyd read an early version of Chapter 4 and pointed me to literature that greatly strengthened it. Zia Cromer, who patiently read two versions of the complete manuscript, also helped improve the text in important ways. Milada Vachudova was a seemingly tireless reader who greatly improved the book.

Finally, I owe a large debt of gratitude to all of those scholars whose research made this book possible. You have taught me much, and I only hope that in writing the book I have treated your work accurately and fairly. Of course, in spite of all of this support, I alone am responsible for any errors of fact or interpretation.

Thomas Oatley

Chapter 1

International Political Economy

We live in a global economy. How many times have you heard or read that short sentence in the last month? If you watch the cable news networks or read the major newspapers, probably more than a couple of times. What does it mean? To paraphrase the famous British economist John Maynard Keynes, I think it means in part that, from my home in North Carolina, I can order an iPod designed by an American company, but manufactured by an East Asian company, some polo shirts produced in Bangladesh, and buy and sell stocks in British and French companies all before I have finished my morning coffee (which, by the way, was grown in Sumatra). In part, therefore, living in a global economy means the products I regularly consume are as likely to come from a distant country as from the United States.

Living in a global economy also means that global economic forces play a large role in determining many of our career opportunities. Forty years ago, for example, people in my home state could find reasonably well-paying jobs in local textile mills. Today, most of these mills and the jobs they once provided are gone, and few young North Carolinians seek, much less find, employment in this industry. During the same period, however, high-technology firms moved to North Carolina. IBM, Lockheed, GlaxoSmithKline, and many other high-technology firms all operate within a few miles of my home. Charlotte, the state's largest city, has emerged as one of the country's largest financial centers, home to one of the nation's largest banks, Bank of America. High-technology companies and financial institutions today provide thousands of jobs for North Carolinians. Thus, the opportunities available to the typical North Carolinian are far different today than they were only 30 years ago. I'm sure that the state you live in has seen similar changes. The global economy has played a central role in bringing about these changes. Living in a global economy means, therefore, that a large component of your economic life is shaped by global, rather than national (much less local), economic forces.

International political economy (IPE) studies life in the global economy. It focuses most heavily on the enduring political battle between the winners and losers

1

from global economic exchange. While all societies benefit from participation in the global economy, these gains are not distributed evenly among individuals. Global economic exchange raises the income of some people and lowers the income of others. The distributive consequences of global economic exchange generate political competition in national and international arenas. The winners seek deeper links with the global economy in order to extend and consolidate their gains, while the losers try to erect barriers between the global and national economies in order to minimize or even reverse their losses. International political economy studies how the enduring political battle between the winners and losers from global economic exchange shapes the evolution of the global economy.

This chapter introduces IPE as a field of study. It begins by providing a broad overview of the substantive issues that IPE examines and the kinds of questions scholars ask when studying these issues. The chapter then briefly surveys a few of the theoretical frameworks that scholars have developed in order to answer the questions they pose. The chapter concludes by providing a roadmap to the material we cover in the rest of this book.

What Is International Political Economy?

International political economy studies the political battle between the winners and losers from global economic exchange. Consider, for example, the decision by the Bush administration to raise tariffs on imported steel in the spring of 2002. The decision to raise the steel tariff was prompted by lobbying by the owners of American steel firms and the United Steel Workers of America. The steel industry lobbied for higher tariffs because they were losing from trade. Imported steel was capturing a large share of the American market, resulting in a large number of plant closings and layoffs. Thirty-four American steel mills filed for bankruptcy between 1997 and 2002, forcing about 18,000 workers from their jobs. Steel producers and steel workers recognized that higher tariffs would protect them from this competition, thereby reducing the number of American steel mills in distress and slowing the rate at which steel workers were losing their jobs.

The higher steel tariff had negative consequences for other groups in society, however. The tariff hurt American industries that use steel to produce goods, such as auto manufacturers, because these firms had to pay more for steel. The tariff also harmed foreign steel producers, who could sell less steel in the American market than before the tariff was raised. Groups that suffered from the tariff turned to the political system to try to reverse the Bush administration's decision. In the United States, the Consuming Industries Trade Action Coalition (or CITAC), a business association that represents firms that use steel (and other imported inputs) to produce other goods, pressured the Bush Administration and Congress to lower the steel tariff. Foreign steel producers lobbied their governments to pressure the United States to reverse the decision. In response, the European Union and Japan threatened to retaliate by raising tariffs on goods that the United States exports to their markets and initiated an investigation within the World Trade Organization (WTO)—the international organization that has responsibility for such disputes. The story of the steel tariff thus nicely illustrates the central focus of international political economy as a field of study: how the political battle between the winners and losers from global economic exchange shapes the economic policies that governments adopt.

The steel tariff also highlights the many distinct elements that international political economy must incorporate to make sense of the global economy. To fully understand the steel tariff, we need to know something about the economic interests of the businesses and workers who produce and consume steel. Understanding these interests requires us to know economic theory. Moreover, we need to know something about how political processes in the United States transform these economic interests into trade policy. This requires knowledge of the American political system and the American trade policy process. In addition, we need to know something about how a policy decision made by the United States affects businesses and workers based in other countries (more economic theory for this), and we need to know how the governments in those countries are likely to respond to these consequences (which requires knowledge about the political systems in the various countries). Finally, we need to know something about the role that international economic organizations like the WTO play in regulating the foreign economic policies that governments adopt. Thus, understanding developments in the global economy requires us to draw on economic theory, explore domestic politics, examine the dynamics of political interactions between governments, and familiarize ourselves with international economic organizations. While such an undertaking may seem daunting, this book introduces you to each of these elements and teaches you how to use them to deepen your understanding of the global economy.

One way scholars simplify the study of the global economy is to divide the substantive aspects of global economic activity into distinct issue areas. Typically, the global economy is broken into four such issue areas: the international trade system, the international monetary system, multinational corporations (or MNCs), and economic development. Rather than studying the global economy as a whole, scholars will focus on one issue area in relative isolation from the others. Of course, it is somewhat misleading to study each issue area independently. MNCs, for example, are important actors in the international trade system. The international monetary system exists solely to enable people living in different countries to engage in economic transactions with each other. It has no purpose, therefore, outside consideration of international trade and investment. Moreover, problems arising in the international monetary system are intrinsically connected to developments in international trade and investment. Trade, MNCs, and the international monetary system in turn all play an important role in economic development. Thus, each issue area is deeply connected to the others. In spite of these deep connections, the central characteristics of each area are sufficiently distinctive that one can study each in relative isolation from the others, as long as one remains sensitive to the connections among them when necessary. We will adopt the same approach here.

The international trade system is centered upon WTO, to which some 147 countries belong and through which they have created a nondiscriminatory international trade system. This means that in the international trade system, each country gains access to all other WTO members' markets on equal terms. In addition, the WTO and its predecessor, the General Agreements on Tariffs and Trade (GATT), have enabled governments to progressively eliminate tariffs and other barriers to the cross-border flow of goods and services. As these barriers have been dismantled, world trade has grown steadily. Today, goods and services worth about $7.6 trillion flow across national borders each year. During the last 10 years, however, regional trading arrangements have arisen to pose a potential challenge to the WTO-centered trade system. These regional trade arrangements, such as the North American Free Trade Agreement (NAFTA), are trading blocs composed of a small number of countries who offer each other preferential access to their markets. Scholars who study the international trade system investigate how the political battle between the winners and losers from global economic exchange shapes the creation, operation, and consequences of the WTO-centered system and the emerging regional trading frameworks.

The international monetary system enables people living in different countries to engage in economic transactions with each other. People living in the United States who want to buy goods produced in Japan must be able to price these Japanese goods in dollars. In addition, while Americans earn dollars, Japanese spend yen, so somehow dollars must be converted into yen for such purchases to occur. The international monetary system facilitates international exchange by performing these functions. When it performs these functions well, international economic exchange flourishes. When it doesn't, the global economy can slow or even collapse. Scholars who study the international monetary system focus on how political battles between the winners and losers of global economic exchange shape the creation, operation, and consequences of this system.

Multinational corporations occupy a prominent and often controversial role in the global economy. A multinational corporation is a firm that controls production facilities in at least two countries. The largest of these firms are familiar names such as Ford Motor Company, General Electric, and General Motors. The United Nations estimates that there are more than 60,000 MNCs operating in the contemporary global economy. These firms collectively control more than 900,000 production plants and employ about 86 million people across the globe. Together, they account for about one-quarter of the world's economic production and about one-third of the world's trade. MNCs have been controversial in part because of their size, but more importantly, because they extend managerial control across national borders. Corporate managers based in the United States, for example, make decisions that affect economic conditions in Mexico and other Latin American countries, in Western Europe, and in Asia. Scholars who study MNCs focus on a variety of economic issues, such as why these large firms exist and what economic impact they have on the countries that host their operations. Scholars also study how the political battle between the winners and losers from MNC activity shapes government efforts to regulate the activities of MNCs.

Finally, a large body of literature studies economic development. Throughout the postwar period, developing country governments have adopted explicit development strategies that they believed would raise incomes by promoting industrialization. The success of these strategies has varied. Some countries, such as the Newly Industrializing Countries (NICs) of East Asia (Taiwan, South Korea, Singapore, and Hong Kong) have been so successful in promoting industrialization and raising per capita incomes that they can no longer be considered developing countries. Other countries, particularly in sub-Saharan Africa and in parts of Latin America, have been less successful. Governments in these countries adopted different development strategies than the NICs throughout much of the postwar period and realized much smaller increases in per capita incomes. Students of the politics of economic development focus on the specific strategies that developing countries' governments adopt and attempt to explain why different governments adopt different strategies. In addition, these students are concerned about which development strategies have been relatively more successful than others (and why) and about whether participation in the international economy facilitates or frustrates development. In trying to make sense of these aspects of development, IPE scholars emphasize how the political battle generated by the distributive consequences of the global economy shapes the development strategies that governments adopt.

Those who study the global economy through the lens of international political economy are typically interested in doing more than simply describing government policies and contemporary developments in these four issue areas. Most scholars aspire to make more general statements about how politics shape the policies that governments adopt in each of these issue areas. Moreover, most scholars want to draw more general conclusions about the consequences of these policies. As a consequence, two abstract and considerably broader questions typically shape the study of trade, money, MNCs, and development. First, how exactly does politics shape the decisions that societies make about how to use the resources that are available to them? Second, what are the consequences of these decisions? Because these two over-arching questions are central to what we cover in this book, it is worth taking a closer look at each of them now.

How do politics shape societal decisions about how to allocate available resources? For example, how does a society decide whether the labor and capital it has available will be used to produce semiconductors or clothing? While this question might appear quite remote from the issue areas just discussed, the connections are actually quite close. The foreign economic policies that a government adopts—its trade policies, its exchange rate policies, and its policies toward MNCs—affect how that society's resources are used. A decision to raise tariffs, for example, will encourage business owners to invest and workers to seek employment in the industry that is protected by the tariff. A decision to lower tariffs will encourage business owners and workers currently employed in the newly liberalized industry to seek employment in other industries. A change in tariff policy, therefore, will affect how society's resources are used. Foreign economic policies are in turn a product of politics, the process through which societies make collective decisions. Thus, the study of international political economy is in many respects the study of how the political battle between the winners and losers from global economic exchange shapes the decisions that societies make about how to allocate the resources they have available to them.

These decisions are complicated by two considerations. On the one hand, all resources are finite. As a result, choices about how to allocate resources will always be made against a backdrop of scarcity. Any choice in favor of one use of a resource therefore necessarily implies a choice to forgo another possible use. On the other hand, in every society groups will disagree about how available resources should be used. Some groups will want to use the available resources to produce cars and semiconductors, for example, while others will prefer to use these resources to produce clothing and agricultural products. Societies consequently will always confront competing demands for their finite resources. One of the important goals of IPE as a field of study is to investigate how such competing demands are aggregated, reconciled, and transformed into foreign economic policies.

The second abstract question asks what are the *consequences* of the choices that societies make about resource allocation? These decisions have two very different consequences. Decisions about resource allocation have **welfare consequences**—that is, they determine the level of societal well-being. Some choices will maximize social welfare—that is, they will make society as a whole as well off as is possible given existing resources. Other choices will cause social welfare to fall below its potential, in which case different choices about how to use resources would make society better off. Decisions about resource allocation also have **distributional consequences**—that is, they influence how income is distributed between groups within countries and between nations in the international system.

Welfare and distributional consequences are both evident in the American steel tariff. Because the tariff makes it more profitable to produce steel in the United States than it would be otherwise, some investment capital and workers who might otherwise be employed in highly efficient American industries such as information technology or biotechnology will be used in the less efficient American steel industry. The tariff thus causes the United States to use too many of its resources in economic activities that it does less well and too few resources in activities that it does better. As a consequence, the United States is poorer with a high tariff on steel than it would be without it.

The steel tariff also redistributes income. Because the tariff raises the price of steel in the United States, it redistributes income from the consumers of steel, such as American firms that use steel in the products they manufacture and the American consumers who purchase goods made out of steel, to the steel producers. In addition, because the tariff makes it more difficult for foreign steel firms to sell in the American market, it redistributes income from foreign steel producers to American steel producers. The steel tariff, like many economic policies, affects both the level and the distribution of income within a society.

These two abstract questions give rise to two very different research traditions within IPE. One tradition focuses on explanation, while a second focuses on evaluation. **Explanatory studies,** which relate most closely to our first abstract question, are oriented toward explaining the foreign economic policy choices that governments make. Such studies most often attempt to answer "why questions." For example, why does one government choose to lower tariffs and open its economy to trade, while another government continues to protect the domestic market from imports? Why did governments create the World Trade Organization? Why do some governments maintain fixed exchange rates while others allow their currencies to float? Why do some governments allow MNCs to operate in their economies with few restrictions, while other governments attempt to regulate MNC activity? Each of these questions asks us to explain a specific economic policy choice made by a government or to explain a pattern of choices within a group of governments. In answering such questions, we are most concerned with explaining the policy choices that governments make and pay less attention to the welfare consequences of these policy choices.

Evaluative studies, which are related most closely to our second abstract question, are oriented toward assessing policy outcomes, making judgments about them, and proposing alternatives when the judgment made about a particular policy is a negative one. A **welfare evaluation** is primarily interested in whether a particular policy choice raises or lowers social welfare. For example, does a decision to liberalize trade raise or lower national economic welfare? Does a decision to turn to the International Monetary Fund and accept a package of economic reforms promote or retard economic growth? More broadly, do current policies encourage society to use its available resources in ways that maximize economic welfare, or would alternative policies that encouraged a different allocation result in higher economic welfare? Because such evaluations are concerned with the economic welfare consequences of policy outcomes, they are typically based on economic criteria and rely heavily upon economic theories.

Scholars also sometimes evaluate outcomes in terms that extend beyond narrow considerations of economic welfare. In some instances, scholars evaluate outcomes in terms of their distributional consequences. For example, many of the groups that are members of the contemporary backlash against globalization are highly critical of international trade because they believe that workers lose and business gains from trade liberalization. Implicit in this criticism is an evaluation of how global trade distributes income across groups within countries and across countries within the international system. Evaluations may also extend the frame of reference within which outcomes are evaluated beyond purely economic efficiency. For example, even those who agree that international trade raises world economic welfare might remain critical of globalization because they believe that it degrades the environment, disrupts traditional methods of production, or has other negative social consequences that outweigh the economic gains. Explanation and evaluation both play an important role in international political economy. This book, however, focuses primarily upon explanation and secondarily upon evaluating the welfare consequences of government policies.

Studying International Political Economy

Scholars working within the field of international political economy have developed a large number of theories to answer the two questions posed earlier. Three traditional schools of political economy—the mercantilist school, the liberal school, and the Marxist school—have shaped the development of these theories over the last 100 years. Each of these three traditional schools offers distinctive answers to the two questions, and these differences have structured much of the scholarly and public debate about international political economy.

While the three traditional schools remain influential, more and more often students of international political economy are developing theories to answer our two questions from outside the explicit confines of these traditional schools. One prominent approach, and the approach that is developed throughout this book, suggests that the foreign economic policies that governments adopt emerge from the interaction between societal actors' interests and political institutions. We begin our examination of how people study international political economy with a broad overview of these alternative approaches. We look first at the three traditional schools, highlighting the answers they provide to our two questions and pointing to some of the weaknesses of these schools that have led students to move away from them. We then examine the logic of an approach based on interests and institutions in order to provide the background necessary for the more detailed theories that we develop throughout the book.

Traditional Schools of International Political Economy

Historically, theories of international political economy have been developed in three broad schools of thought: mercantilism (or nationalism), liberalism, and Marxism. **Mercantilism** is rooted in 17th- and 18th-century theories about the relationship between economic activity and state power. The mercantilist literature is large and varied, yet mercantilists do generally adhere to three central propositions. (See, e.g., Viner 1960; Hecksher 1935.) First, the classical mercantilists argued that national power and wealth were tightly connected. National power in the international state system is derived in large part from wealth. Wealth, in turn, is required to accumulate power. Second, the classical mercantilists argued that trade provided one way for countries to acquire wealth from abroad. Wealth could be acquired through trade, however, only if the country ran a positive balance of trade, that is, if the country sold more goods to foreigners than it purchased from foreigners. Third, the classical mercantilists argued that some types of economic activity are more valuable than others. In particular, mercantilists argued that manufacturing activities should be promoted while agriculture and other nonmanufacturing activities should be discouraged.

"Modern" mercantilism applies these three propositions to contemporary international economic policy:

1. Economic strength is a critical component of national power.
2. Trade is to be valued for exports, but governments should discourage imports whenever possible.
3. Some forms of economic activity are more valuable than others.

Manufacturing is preferred to the production of agricultural and other primary commodities, and high-technology manufacturing industries such as computers and telecommunications are preferable to mature manufacturing industries such as steel or textiles and apparel.

The emphasis on wealth as a critical component of national power, the insistence on maintaining a positive balance of trade, and the conviction that some types of economic activity are more valuable than others leads mercantilists to argue that the state should play a large role in determining how society's resources are allocated. Economic activity is too important to allow decisions about resource allocation to be made through an uncoordinated process such as the market. Uncoordinated decisions can result in an "inappropriate" economic structure. Industries and technologies that may be desirable from the perspective of national power might be neglected, while industries that do little to strengthen the nation in the international state system may flourish. In addition, the country could develop an unfavorable balance of trade and become dependent upon foreign countries for critical technologies. The only way to ensure that society's resources are appropriately used is to have the state play a large role in the economy. Economic policy can be used to channel resources to those economic activities that promote and protect the national interest and away from those that fail to do so.

Liberalism, the second traditional school, emerged in Britain during the 18th century to challenge the dominance of mercantilism in government circles. Adam Smith and other liberal writers, such as David Ricardo (who first stated the modern concept of comparative advantage), were scholars that were attempting to alter government economic policy. The theory they developed to do so, liberalism, challenged all three central propositions of mercantilism. First, liberalism attempted to draw a strong line between politics and economics. In doing so, liberalism argued that the purpose of economic activity was to enrich individuals, not to enhance the state's power. Second, liberalism argued that countries do not enrich themselves by running trade surpluses. Instead, countries gain from trade regardless of whether the balance of trade is positive or negative. Finally, countries are not necessarily made wealthier by producing manufactured goods rather than primary commodities. Instead, liberalism argued, countries are made wealthier by making products that they can produce at a relatively low cost at home and trading them for goods that can be produced at home only at a relatively high cost. Thus, according to liberalism, governments should make little effort to influence the country's trade balance or to shape the types of goods the country produces. Government efforts to allocate resources will only reduce national welfare.

In addition to arguing against substantial state intervention as advocated by the mercantilists, liberalism argued in favor of a market-based system of resource allocation. Giving priority to the welfare of individuals, liberalism argues that social welfare will be highest when people are free to make their own decisions about how to use the resources they possess. Thus, rather than accepting the mercantilist argument that the state should guide the allocation of resources, liberals argue that resources should be allocated through voluntary market-based transactions between individuals. Such exchange is mutually beneficial—as long as it is voluntary, then both parties to any transaction will benefit. Moreover, in a perfectly functioning market, individuals will continue to buy and sell resources until the resulting allocation offers no further opportunities for mutually beneficial exchange. The state plays an important, though limited, role in this process. The state must establish clear rights concerning ownership of property and resources. The judicial system must enforce these rights and the contracts that transfer ownership from one individual to another. Most liberals also recognize that governments can, and should, resolve **market failures,** which are instances in which voluntary market-based transactions between individuals fail to allocate resources to socially desirable activities.

Marxism, the third traditional school, originated in the work of Karl Marx as a critique of capitalism. It is impossible to characterize briefly the huge literature that has expanded on or been influenced by Marx's ideas. According to Marx, capitalism is characterized by two central conditions: the private ownership of the means of production (or capital) and wage labor. Marx argued that the value of manufactured goods was determined by the amount of labor used to produce them. However, capitalists did not pay labor the full amount of the value they imparted to the goods they produced. Instead, the capitalists who owned the factories paid workers only a subsistence wage and retained the rest as profits with which to finance additional investment. Marx predicted that the dynamics of capitalism would lead eventually to a revolution that would do away with private property and with the capitalist system that private property supported.

Three dynamics would interact to drive this revolution. First, Marx argued that there is a natural tendency toward the concentration of capital. Economic competition would force capitalists to increase their efficiency and increase their capital stock. As a consequence, capital would become increasingly concentrated in the hands of a small, wealthy elite. Second, Marx argued that capitalism is associated with a falling rate of profit. Investment leads to a growing abundance of productive capital, which in turn reduces the return to capital. As profits shrink, capitalists are forced to further reduce wages, worsening the plight of the already impoverished masses. Finally, capitalism is plagued by an imbalance between the ability to produce goods and the ability to purchase goods. Large capital investments continually augment the economy's ability to produce goods, while falling wages continually reduce the ability of consumers to purchase the goods being produced. As the three dynamics interact over time, society becomes increasingly characterized by growing inequality between a small wealthy capitalist elite and a growing number of impoverished workers. These social conditions eventually cause workers (the proletariat, in Marxist terminology) to rise up, overthrow the capitalist system, and replace it with socialism.

In contrast to liberalism's emphasis on the market as the principle mechanism of resource allocation, Marxists argue that capitalists make decisions about how society's resources are used. Moreover, because capitalist systems promote the concentration of capital, investment decisions are not typically driven by market-based competition, at least not in the classical liberal sense of this term. Instead, decisions about what to produce are made by the few firms that control the necessary investment capital. The state plays no autonomous role in the capitalist system. Instead, Marxists argue that the state operates as an agent of the capitalist class. The state enacts policies that reinforce capitalism and thus the capitalists' control of resource allocation. Thus, in contrast to the mercantilists who focus on the state and the liberals who focus on the market, Marxists focus on large corporations as the key actor determining how resources are to be used.

In the international economy, the concentration of capital and capitalists' control of the state is transformed into the systematic exploitation of the developing world by the large capitalist nations. In some instances, this exploitation takes the form of explicit colonial structures, as it did prior to World War II. In other instances, especially since World War II, exploitation is achieved through less intrusive structures of dominance and control. In all instances, however, exploitation is carried out by large firms based in the capitalist countries that operate, in part, in the developing world. This systematic exploitation of the poor by the rich implies that the global economy does not provide benefits to all countries; all gains accrue to the capitalist countries at the top of the international hierarchy.

The three traditional schools of political economy thus offer three distinctive answers to our question of how politics shape the allocation of society's resources. Mercantilists argue that the state guides resource allocation in line with objectives shaped by the quest for national power. Liberals argue that politics ought to play little role in the process, extolling instead the role of market-based transactions among autonomous individuals. Marxists argue that the most important decisions are made by large capitalist enterprises supported by a political system controlled by the capitalist class.

Each traditional school also offers a distinctive framework to evaluate the consequences of resource allocation. Mercantilists focus on the consequences of resource allocation for national power. The central question a mercantilist will ask is, "Is there some alternative allocation of resources that would enhance the nation's power in the international system?" Liberals rely heavily upon economic theory to focus principally upon the welfare consequences of resource allocation. The central question a liberal will ask is, "Is there some alternative allocation of resources that would enable the society to improve its standard of living?" Marxists rely heavily upon theories of class conflict to focus on the distributional consequences of resource allocation. The central question a Marxist will ask is, "Is there an alternative political and economic system that will promote a more equitable distribution of income?" Thus, liberalism emphasizes the welfare consequences of resource allocation, while mercantilism and Marxism each emphasize a different aspect of the distributional consequences of these decisions.

These very different allocation mechanisms and unique evaluative frameworks generate three very different images of the central dynamic of IPE. (See Table 1.1.) Mercantilists argue that the international political economy is characterized by distributional conflict as governments compete to attract and maintain desired industries. Liberals argue that international economic interactions are essentially harmonious. Because all countries benefit from international trade, power has little impact on national welfare, and international economic conflicts are rare. The central problem, from a liberal perspective, is creating the international institutional framework that will enable governments to enter into agreements through which they can create an international system of free trade. Marxists argue that the international political economy is characterized by the distributional conflict between labor and capital within countries and by the distributional conflict between the advanced industrialized countries and developing countries within the international arena.

These three traditional schools have structured studies of, and debate about the international political economy for a very long time. And while the presence of all three will be felt in many ways throughout the pages of this book, we will spend little more time examining them directly. In their place, we will emphasize an analytical framework that has been developed during the last 15 years or so and that focuses on how the interaction between societal interests and political institutions determine the foreign economic policies governments adopt.

Interests and Institutions in International Political Economy

To explain the policy choices made by governments, this book concentrates on the interaction between societal interests and political institutions. Such an approach suggests that to understand the foreign economic policy choices that governments make, we need to understand two aspects of politics. First, we need to understand where the interests, or economic policy preferences, of groups in society come from. Second, we need to examine how political institutions aggregate, reconcile, and ultimately transform competing interests into foreign economic policies and a particular international economic system.

Table 1.1
Three Traditional Schools of International Political Economy

	Mercantilism	Liberalism	Marxism
Most Important Actor	The State	Individuals	Classes, Particularly the Capitalist Class
Role of the State	Intervene in the economy to allocate resources	Establish and enforce property rights to facilitate market-based exchange	Instrument of the capitalist class uses state power to sustain capitalist system
Image of the International Economic System	*Conflictual:* Countries compete for desirable industries and engage in trade conflicts as a result of this competition.	*Harmonious:* The international economy offers benefits to all countries. The challenge is to create a political framework that enables countries to realize these benefits	*Exploitative:* Capitalists exploit labor within countries; rich countries exploit poor countries in the international economy
Proper Objective of Economic Policy	Enhance power of the nation–state in international state system	Enhance aggregate social welfare	Promote an equitable distribution of wealth and income

Interests are the goals or policy objectives that the central actors in the political system and in the economy—individuals, firms, labor unions, other interest groups, and governments—want to use foreign economic policy to achieve. In focusing on interests, we will assume that individuals and the interest groups that represent them always prefer foreign economic policies that raise their incomes to policies that reduce their incomes. Thus, whenever a group confronts a choice between one policy that raises its income and another that lowers its income, it will always prefer the policy that raises its income. We focus on two mechanisms to explain the formation of these policy interests.

First, people have **material interests** that arise from their position in the global economy. The essence of this approach can be summarized in a simple statement: Tell me where you work and what you do, and I'll tell you what your foreign economic policy preferences are. Consider once again the American steel tariff. Whether a particular individual supports or opposes this tariff depends upon where he or she works. If you are an American steelworker, you favor the tariff because it reduces the likelihood that you will lose your job. If you own an American steel mill, you will also favor the tariff, because it helps ensure a market and a relatively high price for the steel you produce. Suppose instead, however, that you are an American autoworker or that you own a substantial share of General Motors (GM). In this case, you will oppose the steel tariff. Higher steel prices mean that it costs more to produce cars. As cars become more expensive, fewer are sold and consequently fewer are produced. The tariff thus increases the chances that autoworkers will be laid off and it causes GM to earn smaller profits. These are compelling reasons for autoworkers and their employers to oppose the higher steel tariff. In short, one's position in the economy powerfully shapes one's preferences about foreign economic policy. As we shall see, economic theory enables us to make some powerful statements about the foreign economic policy preferences of different groups in the economy.

Second, interests are often based on ideas. **Ideas** are mental models that provide a coherent set of beliefs about cause-and-effect relationships. In the context of economic policy, these mental models typically focus on the relationship between government policies and economic outcomes. Not surprisingly, therefore, economic theory is a very important source of ideas that influence how actors perceive and formulate their interests. By providing clear statements about cause-and-effect economic relationships, economic theories can create an interest in a particular economic policy. The theory of comparative advantage, for example, claims that reducing tariffs raises aggregate social welfare. A government that believes this theory might be inclined to lower tariffs in order to realize these welfare gains. Alternatively, a government might adopt high tariffs because a different economic theory (the infant industry argument, for example) suggests that tariffs can promote economic production in ways that raise national income. What matters, therefore, is not whether a particular idea is true or not, but whether people in power, or people with influence over people with power, believe the idea to be true. Thus, ideas about how the economy operates can be a source of the preferences that groups have for particular economic policies.

Understanding where interests come from will enable us to specify with some precision the competing demands that politicians will confront when making foreign economic policy decisions. It does not tell us anything about how these competing interests are reconciled and transformed into foreign economic policies. To understand how interests are transformed into policies, we need to examine political institutions. **Political institutions** establish the rules governing the political process. By establishing rules, they enable groups within countries, and groups of countries in the international state system, to reach and enforce collective decisions.

Political institutions determine which groups are empowered to make choices and establish the rules these "choosers" will use when doing so. In domestic political systems, for example, democratic institutions promote mass participation in collective choices, while authoritarian systems restrict participation to a narrow set of individuals. In international economic affairs, governments from the advanced industrialized countries often make decisions with little participation by developing countries.

Political institutions also provide the rules that these groups use to make decisions. In democratic systems, the usual choice rule is majority rule, and policies are supposed to reflect the preferences of a majority of voters or legislators. In international economic organizations, the choice rule is often relative bargaining power, and decisions typically reflect the preferences of the more powerful nations. Political institutions thus allow groups to make collective decisions and, in doing so, determine who gets to make these decisions and how they are to be made.

Political institutions also help enforce these collective decisions. In many instances, individuals, groups, and governments have little incentive to comply with the decisions that are produced by the political process. This is particularly the case for those groups whose preferences diverge from those embodied in the collective choice. And even in cases where a group or a country as a whole does benefit from a particular decision, it may believe it could do even better if it cheated a little bit. If such instances of noncompliance are widespread, then the political process is substantially weakened.

This problem is particularly acute in the international state system. In domestic political systems, the police and the judicial system are charged with enforcing individual compliance with collective decisions. The international system has neither a police force nor a judicial system through which to enforce compliance, however. Consequently, it can be very tempting for governments to attempt to "cheat" on the international economic agreements they conclude with other governments. International institutions like the WTO and the International Monetary Fund (IMF) can help governments enforce the international agreements that they conclude.

A focus on interests and institutions will allow us to develop a set of reasonably comprehensive answers to our first question: How do politics shape societal decisions about how to allocate resources? The explanations we construct will almost always begin by investigating the source of competing societal demands for income and then explore how political institutions aggregate, reconcile, and ultimately transform these competing demands into foreign economic policies and a particular international economic system. This approach may not always provide a full explanation of the interactions we observe in the international political economy, but it does provide a solid point of departure.

The Organization of the Book

We apply this framework to the international political economy by using three additional devices to help us organize our investigation. First, we divide the field of international political economy into the traditional four issue areas. The first half of the book is devoted to trade and production. We look at the creation and evolution of the multilateral trade system. We examine why this system was created, how governments have used the system to liberalize trade, and what challenges it currently confronts. We also examine the role of multinational corporations in the global economy. The second half of the book focuses on creation and evolution of international monetary and financial systems.

Each issue area is further subdivided by level of analysis. Some chapters focus on the international politics of the global economy, while others focus on the domestic politics of foreign economic policy. In examining the interaction between interests and institutions in the international system, we examine how the distribution of power in the international state system shapes international economic institutions such as the WTO and the IMF, as well as political and economic interactions within these institutions. In addition, we examine how international economic transactions, including international trade, the activities of multinational corporations, and international capital flows, as well as changes in the distribution of power, transform the global economy and the national economies upon which it is based.

Each issue area is further subdivided between politics in the advanced industrialized countries—the United States, Western Europe, Japan—and politics in the developing world. This division has little to do with the need to develop distinct theoretical frameworks for each group. Instead, it reflects the fact that the two groups differ on a number of important dimensions, and these differences give rise to different relationships with and policies toward the international economic system. The two groups have different economic structures. The advanced industrialized countries produce and export capital-intensive and technology-intensive goods and services while most developing countries are heavily dependent upon labor-intensive goods and primary commodities. In the international financial system, advanced industrialized countries are lenders while developing countries are borrowers. The two groups are not equally powerful. The advanced industrialized countries have more power and can use this power to shape the rules governing international trade and finance. The developing countries have less power and typically have had to accept the rules of the system as given. As a result of these differences in economic structure and international power, the two groups have had very different experiences with the international economic system. For this reason, one chapter in each issue area focuses more heavily upon the advanced industrialized countries while another focuses more heavily upon the developing countries.

Finally, each issue is subdivided by level of analysis. Some chapters focus on the international politics of the global economy, while others focus on the domestic politics of foreign economic policy. In examining international politics, we focus on the interaction between power and competing interests shapes the creation and evolution of the global economy. In examining domestic politics, we examine how the interaction between interests and institutions within societies shapes foreign economic policy choices. Of course, the international and the domestic politics of the global economy do not function in isolation from each other. Thus, even as we separate them for the purpose of discussion, we continually make connections between international and domestic political economy.

Conclusion

International political economy studies the political battle between the winners and losers from global economic exchange. It examines how this political competition shapes the evolution of the international trade and monetary systems, affects the ability of MNCs to conduct their operations, and influences the development strategies governments adopt. Thus, international political economy suggests that it is hard to understand anything about the global economy without understanding how political competition unfolds.

International political economy scholars traditionally have studied the global economy through the lens of three schools of thought. Each school offers a distinctive window on the global economy, and each emphasizes one aspect of global economic exchange—cooperation, competition between governments, and competition between labor and capital—as the central defining element of politics in the global economy.

This book relies on an approach that emphasizes the interaction between societal interests and political institutions. Such an approach will enable us to develop models that provide insights into how the global economy generates winners and losers, into how these groups compete to influence the policies that governments adopt, and into how the policies that governments adopt affect the evolution of the global economy.

Key Terms

Distributional Consequences

Explanatory Studies

Evaluative Studies

Ideas

Interests

Liberalism

Market Failures

Material Interests

Marxism

Mercantilism

Political Institutions

Welfare Consequences

Welfare Evaluation

Suggestions for Further Reading

The two best treatments of mercantilism can be found in Jacob Viner's *Studies in the Theory of International Trade* (London: Allen & Unwin, 1960) and Eli Heckscher's *Mercantilism* (London: Allen & Unwin, 1935). Adam Smith's *The Wealth of Nations* (New York: Bantam Classics, 2003) remains the most authoritative statement of liberalism. Vladimir Il'ich Lenin's *Imperialism: the Highest Stage of Capitalism* (New York: International Publishers, 1933) provides the seminal Marxist approach to international political economy. For a more general treatment of the three traditional schools, see Robert Gilpin's *The Political Economy of International Relations* (Princeton: Princeton University Press, 1987).

CHAPTER 2

The World Trade Organization and the World Trade System

National economies are becoming deeply connected. You probably notice these connections most as a consumer, since many of the goods you buy are produced, either in whole or in part, in a foreign country. This is certainly the case for me. Most of my clothes are manufactured in Bangladesh and other developing countries. My car was assembled in Mexico from parts produced in Germany. My computer was assembled in the Philippines from components that were designed and manufactured in at least five other countries. Thus, my consumption (and yours) has become internationalized. And what is true about our consumption is obviously also true about production. While we once thought in terms of national firms, it makes less and less sense to do so. Is Ford, for example, still an American company? It produces many of its cars in Mexico from parts that are manufactured throughout the world. The cars are in turn sold in markets throughout the world. Production, too, has become internationalized.

Internationalization has been brought about by the rapid growth of world trade. Global trade has grown during the last 60 years at an average rate of about 6 percent per year. As a result, total world trade has risen from about $84 billion in 1953 to approximately $7.6 trillion in 2000 (World Trade Organization 2001, p. 9). Never before in history has international trade grown so rapidly for such a long period. Even more importantly, trade has consistently grown more rapidly than world economic output. Consequently, each year a greater proportion of the goods and services produced in the world are created in one country and consumed in another. It is the fact that trade has grown more rapidly than the world output, rather than the growth of trade itself, which is causing the internationalization of consumption and production.

None of this has occurred spontaneously. While one could argue that the growth of trade reflects the operation of global markets, all markets rest on political structures. This is certainly the case with global markets. World trade has grown so rapidly over the last 60 years because an international political structure, the World Trade Organization and its predecessor, the General Agreement on Tariffs and Trade, has supported and encouraged such growth. Most political scientists who study the global economy believe that, had governments never created this institutional framework after World War II, or had they created a different one, world trade would not have grown so rapidly. Internationalization, therefore, has been brought about by the decisions governments have made about the rules and institutions that govern world trade.

Because trade plays so important a role in our lives, and because trade is made possible by the political institution that structures trade relationships, it is vital for us to understand the political dynamics of the world trade system. This chapter begins developing that knowledge. It starts by providing a broad overview of the WTO's three core components. We then examine how the global distribution of power shapes the creation and evolution of international trade systems. We then explore some contemporary issues in the WTO, focusing on its expanding scope and growing decision making problems. The chapter concludes by examining regional trade arrangements, considered by many the greatest current challenge to the WTO.

What Is the WTO?

The World Trade Organization (located on the shore of the beautiful Lac Leman in Geneva, Switzerland) is the hub of an international political system under which governments agree to accept commonly negotiated and enforced rules to govern world trade. Throughout most of the postwar period, the General Agreement on Tariffs and Trade fulfilled the role now played by the WTO. In 1995, GATT was folded into the newly established WTO, but it has not disappeared. It continues to provide many of the rules governing international trade relations. The creation of the WTO, therefore, did not produce a wholly new set of international trade rules. The rules at the center of the world trade system are those that were initially established in 1947 and that have been gradually revised, amended, and extended ever since.

The WTO is relatively small compared with other international organizations. Although 147 countries belong to the WTO, it has a staff of only about 600 people and a budget of roughly $130 million. The World Bank, by contrast, has a staff of about 9,300 people and an operating budget of close to $1 billion. As the center of the world trade system, WTO provides a forum for trade negotiations, administers the trade agreements that governments conclude, and provides a mechanism through which governments can resolve trade disputes. As a political system, the WTO can be broken down into three distinct components: a set of principles and rules, an intergovernmental bargaining process, and a dispute settlement mechanism.

The WTO is based on two core principles: market liberalism and nondiscrimination. **Market liberalism** provides the economic rationale for the trade system. Market liberalism asserts that an open, or liberal, international trade system raises the world's standard of living. Every country—no matter how poor or how rich—enjoys a higher standard of living with trade than it can achieve without trade. Moreover, the gains from trade are greatest—for each country and for the world as a whole—when goods can flow freely across national borders unimpeded by government-imposed barriers. The claim that trade provides such gains to all countries is based on economic theory we examine in detail in Chapter 3. For our purposes here, it is sufficient to recognize that this claim provides the economic logic upon which the WTO is based.

Nondiscrimination is the second core principle of the multilateral trade system. Nondiscrimination ensures that each WTO member faces identical opportunities to trade with other WTO members. The principle takes two specific forms within the WTO. The first form, called **Most Favored Nation** (MFN), prohibits governments from using trade policies to provide special advantages to some countries and not to others. MFN is found in Article I of GATT and states, "any advantage, favour, privilege, or immunity granted by any contracting party to any product originating in or destined for any other country shall be accorded immediately and unconditionally to the like product originating in or destined for the territories of all other contracting parties." Stripped of this legal terminology, MFN simply requires each WTO member to treat all WTO members the same way as they treat their favorite trading partner. For example, the United States cannot apply lower tariffs to goods imported from Brazil (a WTO member) than it applies to goods imported from other WTO member countries. If the United States reduces tariffs on goods imported from Brazil, it must extend these same tariff rates to all other WTO members. MFN thus assures that all countries have access to foreign markets on equal terms.

WTO rules do allow some exceptions to MFN. The most important exception concerns regional trade arrangements. Governments are allowed to depart from MFN if they join a free trade area or customs union. In the North American Free Trade Agreement (NAFTA), for example, goods produced in Mexico enter the United States duty free, while the United States imposes tariffs on the same goods imported from other countries. In the European Union, goods produced in France enter Germany with a lower tariff than goods produced in the United States. A second exception is provided by the **Generalized System of Preferences** (GSP), enacted in the late 1960s. The GSP allows the advanced industrialized countries to apply lower tariffs to imports from developing countries than they apply to the same goods coming from other advanced industrialized countries. These exceptions aside, MFN ensures that all countries trade on equal terms.

National treatment is the second form of nondiscrimination found in the WTO. **National treatment** prohibits governments from using taxes, regulations, and other domestic policies to provide an advantage to domestic firms at the expense of foreign firms. National treatment is found in Article III of GATT, which states that "the products of the territory of any contracting party imported into the territory of any other contracting party shall be accorded treatment no less favourable than that accorded to like products of national origin in respect of all laws, regulations and requirements affecting their internal sale, offering for sale, purchase, transportation, distribution or use."

In plainer English, national treatment requires governments to treat domestic and foreign versions of the same product ("like products" in GATT terminology) similarly once they enter the domestic market. For example, the U.S. government cannot establish one fuel efficiency standard for foreign cars and another for domestic cars. If the U.S. government wants to advance this environmental goal, it must apply the same requirement to domestic and foreign auto producers. Together, MFN and national treatment ensure that firms in every country face the same market opportunities and barriers in the global economy.

These two core principles are accompanied by hundreds of other rules. Since 1947, governments have concluded about 60 distinct agreements that together fill about 30,000 pages. These rules jointly provide the central legal structure for international trade. As a group, these rules constrain the policies that governments can use to control the flow of goods, services, and technology into and out of their national economies. Some of these rules are proscriptive, such as governments cannot discriminate. Others are prescriptive, such as governments must protect intellectual property. All rules entail obligations to other WTO members that impose constraints on the ability of governments to regulate the interaction between the national and the global economies.

All WTO rules are created by governments through the WTO's second component, intergovernmental bargaining. **Intergovernmental bargaining** is the WTO's primary decision-making process and it focuses on negotiating agreements that directly liberalize trade and indirectly support that goal. To liberalize trade, governments must alter policies that restrict the cross-border flow of goods and services. Such policies include **tariffs,** which are taxes that governments impose on foreign goods entering the country. They also include a wide range of **nontariff barriers** such as health and safety regulations, government purchasing practices, and many other government regulations. Intergovernmental bargaining focuses on negotiating agreements that reduce and eliminate these government-imposed barriers to market access.

Rather than bargain continuously, governments organize their negotiations in bargaining rounds, each with a definite starting date and a target date for conclusion. At the beginning of each round, governments meet as the WTO **Ministerial Conference,** the highest level of WTO decision making. Meeting for three or four days, governments establish an agenda detailing the issues that will be the focus of negotiation and set a target date for the conclusion of the round. Once the Ministerial Conference has ended, lower level national officials based at WTO headquarters in Geneva conduct detailed negotiations on the topics embodied in the agenda. Periodic stock takings are held to reach interim agreements. Once negotiations have produced the outlines of a complete agreement, a final Ministerial Conference is held to conclude the round. The resulting agreement is then ratified by WTO members and implemented according to an agreed timetable.

To date, eight of these bargaining rounds have been concluded, and a ninth, the Doha Round, began in 2001. (See Table 2.1.) These bargaining rounds are usually extended affairs. While the earlier rounds were typically concluded relatively quickly, the trend over the last 30 years has been for multiyear rounds. The Uruguay Round, for example, was officially launched in 1986 (though it had been discussed since 1982) and was not concluded until December 1993. The Doha Round, launched in 2001, is unlikely to be concluded before the end of 2005 and may not conclude until well into 2006. The growing length of bargaining rounds reflects the growing complexity of the issues at the center of negotiations and the growing diversity of interests among WTO member governments. We will return to these issues later in this chapter.

The rules established by intergovernmental bargaining provide a framework of law for international trade relations. Participation in the WTO, therefore, requires governments to accept common rules that constrain their actions. By accepting these constraints, governments shift international trade relations out of an anarchic international environment in which "might makes right" into a rule-based system in which all

A CLOSER LOOK

The Doha Round

We can gain a better understanding of the WTO bargaining process by examining the evolution of negotiations in the current round. The Doha Round was launched at the WTO's Fourth Ministerial Conference held in Doha, Qatar in November 2001. In Doha, bargaining over what should be the subject of negotiations yielded an ambitious agenda. As in previous rounds, governments agreed (1) to negotiate additional tariff reductions (though, in Doha, they agreed to focus specifically on products exported by developing countries), (2) to incorporate existing negotiations in services into the Doha Round, and (3) to pursue meaningful liberalization of trade in agricultural products. To the latter end, they agreed to reduce barriers to market access, to eliminate agricultural export subsidies, and to substantially reduce domestic production subsidies. The agenda also called for negotiations on aspects of trade-related intellectual property rights, for negotiations to change existing WTO rules regarding antidumping and subsidies investigations, to clarify the rules pertaining to regional trade agreements, and to review the operation of the dispute settlement mechanism. Moreover, governments agreed to negotiations through which they would explore various aspects of the relationship between trade and the environment. Finally, members agreed to consider launching negotiations on trade and investment, competition policy, government procurement, and trade facilitation (four issues that are collectively referred to as "the Singapore Issues") at the next Ministerial Conference in 2003. Negotiations on all of these issues would be treated as a "single undertaking," meaning that everything must be agreed or nothing is agreed. Negotiations were to be concluded by January 1, 2005.

The Doha Agenda was just that—an agenda for negotiations. It contained no details about the form that any eventual final agreement would take. The elaboration of these details was the goal for additional negotiations between the member governments. These negotiations began at WTO headquarters in Geneva in early 2002 and continued through the summer of 2003. These initial negotiations (conducted for the most part by national delegations staffed by career civil servants or foreign service officers) were not designed to reach a final agreement, but instead explored areas of agreement and disagreement. In doing so, they would set the stage for a stocktaking exercise scheduled for the WTO's Fifth Ministerial Conference in Cancún, Mexico, in September of 2003. While much of the work proceeded smoothly, it quickly became evident that two issues presented the largest obstacles to a successful conclusion of the round. First, developing countries were demanding deeper liberalization of trade in agriculture than the United States and the European Union were willing to accept. Second, the EU was insisting that negotiations on the Singapore issues be initiated in 2004, but developing countries were unwilling to negotiate on new issues until they had achieved substantial gains in the talks on agriculture. In the late summer of 2003, negotiations in Geneva paused as governments prepared for the Cancún Ministerial Conference.

As trade ministers gathered in Cancún in September 2003, they hoped to achieve two broad goals that would push the Doha Round into the home stretch. The

Continued

first was to bridge the gap between the United States and the European Union, on the one hand, and the developing countries, on the other, concerning agriculture and the Singapore issues. This would be possible in Cancún because trade ministers had political authority to make the substantial concessions that were necessary to bridge this gap; the lower level officials who had been negotiating in Geneva lacked such authority. A simple compromise appeared possible: The United States and the European Union would agree to substantial liberalization in agriculture, and the developing countries would allow negotiations to begin on at least some of the Singapore issues. Second, once these major obstacles had been removed, governments would agree on a broad framework for the final agreement. The national delegations based in Geneva would then be asked to work out the precise details during the next year. Remaining disagreements, if there were any, would be resolved through bargaining by national trade ministers at the Sixth Ministerial Conference scheduled for 2005. Neither goal was achieved. The European Union and United States were unwilling to meet the developing countries demands regarding agriculture, and the developing countries refused to allow negotiations on the Singapore issues. Unable to resolve these two disagreements, governments couldn't elaborate a broad framework to guide subsequent negotiations in Geneva. The Cancún Ministerial adjourned, therefore, with the negotiations in complete disarray.

It took almost a year for governments to get the negotiations back on track. On August 1, 2004, after a grueling two-week negotiating session that was itself concluded by a 24-hour session that drew in high-level national officials, governments reached the agreement that had eluded them in Cancún. The European Union and the United States finally accepted the outlines of an agreement liberalizing trade in agriculture that was acceptable to developing countries, although the precise details of the deal must still be worked out through additional negotiations. In exchange, developing countries agreed to begin negotiations on one of the four Singapore issues: trade facilitation. It was also agreed that the other three Singapore issues would not be negotiated during the Doha Round. The current goal is to conclude the round at the Sixth Ministerial Conference to be held in Hong Kong, China, in December 2005. If the past is a useful guide to how these negotiations will evolve, then an agricultural agreement that is acceptable to all the major players will prove difficult to reach, and a final resolution will be found only (if at all) at the last possible moment.

countries have common rights and responsibilities. In this way, the multilateral trade system brings the rule of law into international trade relations.

The World Trade Organization's third major component, the **dispute settlement mechanism,** ensures that governments comply with the rules they establish. As in all political systems, individual compliance with established rules is not guaranteed. While most governments comply with most of their WTO obligations most of the time, there are times when they don't. Moreover, if all governments believed they could disregard WTO rules with impunity, they would comply less often. The dispute settlement mechanism ensures compliance by helping governments resolve disputes and by authorizing punishment in the event of non-compliance.

The dispute settlement mechanism ensures compliance by providing an independent quasi-judicial tribunal. This tribunal investigates the facts and the relevant WTO rules whenever a dispute is initiated and then reaches a finding. A government found

Table 2.1
Trade Negotiations within GATT/WTO, 1947–2005

Name and Year of Round	Subjects Covered	Participating Countries
1947 Geneva	Tariffs	23
1949 Annecy	Tariffs	13
1951 Torquay	Tariffs	38
1956 Geneva	Tariffs	26
1960–61 Dillon Round	Tariffs	26
1964–67 Kennedy Round	Tariffs and Antidumping	62
1973–79 Tokyo Round	Tariffs	
	Nontariff Measures	102
	Framework Agreements	
1986–1993 Uruguay Round	Tariffs	123
	Nontariff Measures	
	Rules	
	Services	
	Intellectual Property Rights	
	Textiles and Clothing	
	Agriculture	
	Dispute Settlement	
	Establishment of WTO	
2002– The Doha Round	Tariffs	147
	Agriculture	
	Services	
	Intellectual Property Rights	
	Government Procurement	
	Rules	
	Dispute Settlement	
	Trade and the Environment	
	Competition Policy	
	Electronic Commerce	
	Other Issues	

Source: World Trade Organization 1995, 9 and WTO website.

to be in violation is required to alter the offending policy or compensate the country or countries that are harmed. We will examine the dispute settlement mechanism in greater detail in Chapter 3.

The World Trade Organization, therefore, is an international political system that regulates national trade policies. It is based on a set of rules that constrain what governments can do to restrict the flow of goods into their countries and to encourage the export of domestic goods to foreign markets. All of these rules have been created (and can be amended) through a process of consensus-based intergovernmental bargaining. And because compliance with the rules cannot be taken for granted, governments have established a dispute settlement mechanism to help ensure that members comply. By creating rules, establishing a decision making process to extend and revise them, and enforcing compliance, governments have brought the rule of law into international trade relations.

Power and Interests in the World Trade System

Why does the WTO exist? How long will it last? Answering these questions requires us to think a little bit about how the interaction between power and interests shapes the evolution of the world trade system and it requires us to think a little bit about the role that international institutions like the WTO play in this system. Here, we focus on the role of power and interests. Chapter 3 focuses in detail on the role of international institutions.

Political economists who study the world trade system have argued that its evolution is powerfully driven by changes in the distribution of power in the international state system. The world trade system has alternately shifted between periods in which it is open and liberal to periods in which it is closed and discriminatory. Political economists have developed **hegemonic stability theory** to explain these shifts. Political systems such as the WTO reflect the interests of those who create them. Most often, these systems are established by society's most powerful actors and persist as long as the powerful are willing and able to maintain them.

Hegemonic stability theory applies this logic to world trade. It argues that a **hegemon**—defined as a country that produces a disproportionately large share of the world's total output and leads in the development of new technologies—has an economic interest in creating an open and liberal international trade system. As the hegemon's dominance declines, it becomes less supportive of liberal trade and the system shifts toward greater protectionism. World trade thus moves from openness to protectionism in synchrony with changes in the global distribution of economic power.

Hegemonic Power and the Creation of the Postwar Trade System

The logic of hegemonic stability theory has been used to understand changes in the world trade system during the last 150 years. Great Britain emerged as hegemon during the 19th century and used its power to establish and maintain a stable and open world economy. The industrial revolution originated in Great Britain and consequently British industry quickly achieved global predominance. By the mid-19th century, Great Britain produced 20 percent of the world's manufacturing output (Kennedy 1988, 190).

Global economic exchange flourished under British hegemony. Trade within Europe and between Europe and the rest of the world grew at what were then unprecedented rates. Financial capital flowed across borders in volumes that we have not seen since, and millions of people moved from Europe to North America, Latin America, and Australia in search of new economic opportunities. British hegemony, therefore, created and sustained an open, liberal, and highly stable global economy in which goods, capital, and labor flowed freely across borders.

British hegemony began to erode in the late 19th century as other countries industrialized. By the turn of the century, the United States had emerged as Great Britain's chief economic rival. America's ascent was steep. In 1820, the American economy was only one-third the size of Great Britain's. By 1870, the British and American economies were roughly the same size. On the eve of the First World War, the American economy was more than twice as large as Great Britain's (Maddison 2001, 261). By the end of World War II, the United States alone was producing almost half of the world's manufactured goods. (See Table 2.2.) Still, the transition from British to American hegemony was rough. Great Britain became increasingly unable to maintain an open world economy, and the United States was not yet ready to do so. Consequently, the world trade system slid into discriminatory and protectionist trade blocs.

The low point in this hegemonic transition came in the wake of World War I. World War I devastated the global economy. Trade slowed, capital stopped flowing, and governments began to tightly restrict the movement of people across borders as well. Although the British tried to reconstruct the world economy in the 1920s, they lacked the resources to do so. The United States could have used its power and resources to re-establish a liberal world economy, but it was not willing to do so, preferring instead to retreat back into a protectionist isolationism. Consequently, the world economy was never restored to sound foundations.

When the Great Depression struck in 1929, world trade collapsed into discriminatory and highly protectionist trade blocs. The United States raised tariffs sharply in 1930. Other governments transformed their colonies into discriminatory trade blocs. Britain created the Imperial Preference System in the summer of 1932, a trading bloc based on the principle of "home producers first, empire producers second, and foreign producers last" (Richardson 1936, 138). France limited imports and discriminated in favor of imports from its colonies (Jones 1934). Germany created a system of discriminatory trading arrangements in Eastern and Central Europe, and Japan followed suit in Asia. As protectionism rose, world trade fell sharply. (See Table 2.3.) Thus, in this period of hegemonic transition, the declining hegemon lacked the ability to establish

Table 2.2
Shares of World Manufacturing Production

	1880	1900	1913	1928
United States	14.7	23.6	32.0	39.3
Great Britain	22.9	18.5	13.6	9.9
Germany	8.5	13.2	14.8	11.6
France	7.8	6.8	6.1	6.0

Source: Kennedy 1988, 259.

Table 2.3
Collapse of World Trade

(Average Monthly World Trade, $US millions)	
1929	2,858
1930	2,327
1931	1,668
1932	1,122

Source: Kindleberger 1974, 140.

an open trade system, while the rising hegemon was unwilling to do so (Kindleberger 1974). Without a hegemon willing and able to create and maintain a liberal trade system, world trade collapsed into discriminatory and protectionist blocs.

American trade policy gradually shifted in line with its hegemonic status. American protectionism in the 19th century was based on a simple calculation. American industry refused to open the American market to imports, because it could not compete against British imports. At the same time, American industry had little interest in exporting, since it could not compete against British firms in foreign markets. Consequently, American industry viewed protectionism as the best policy. These calculations changed as American industry rose to international preeminence. Imports became less threatening because American industry could compete against even the strongest foreign producers. Exports became more attractive because American industry could outsell most competitors in foreign markets. This produced a new attitude toward protectionism; American industry became increasingly willing to accept lower tariffs at home in exchange for lower tariffs abroad.

These changing calculations became embodied in American trade policy during the 1930s. The principle turning point came in 1934, when President Franklin Delano Roosevelt requested congressional authorization to negotiate bilateral tariff agreements. Under the resulting **Reciprocal Trade Agreements Act** (RTAA), Congress authorized Roosevelt to reduce U.S. tariffs by as much as 50 percent in exchange for equivalent concessions from other countries. The United States negotiated 19 such bilateral treaties between 1934 and 1938 (Butler 1998, 183). Although these treaties did little to liberalize world trade, they clearly reflected the growing American willingness to exchange access to the American market for expanded export opportunities. By 1940, therefore, the United States was increasingly willing to reduce American tariffs in exchange for equivalent access to foreign markets.

This change in American policy began to shape the world trade system during the 1940s as the United States and Great Britain began discussing postwar international economic arrangements. Bilateral talks between the United States and Great Britain were extended into multilateral negotiations in 1945, and by 1947 negotiations had produced an agreement on the postwar trade system. The resulting trade system, GATT, embodied American economic interests. Its core logic mirrored the logic of RTAA: "I'll open my market to your goods if you open your market to mine." Nondiscrimination reflected the American determination to prevent Great Britain and France from organizing their colonial trade in ways that disadvantaged American industry.

During the 1950s, the United States used its hegemonic power to strengthen GATT. Motivated in part by the emerging Cold War, the United States assisted economic reconstruction in Western Europe. Through the Marshall Plan, the United States provided funds that allowed Europe to import critical goods from the United States. Moreover, between 1948 and 1958, the United States engaged in asymmetric trade liberalization. Economic weakness caused by the war rendered European governments unwilling to open their markets to U. S. goods. As a result, the benefits from GATT rounds held in this period accrued largely to the Europeans. The United States opened its market to European exports while Europe continued to discriminate against American goods. By assisting postwar reconstruction and allowing Europeans to export to the American market, the United States fostered rapid economic recovery.

By the early 1960s, European governments were ready to engage in far-reaching, and more equitable, trade liberalization.

Hegemonic Decline and the World Trade System

Hegemonic stability theory suggests that the world trade system should weaken, and perhaps even crumble, as American hegemony declines. And between 1950 and 1970, the global balance of economic power did indeed shift against the United States as a consequence of economic and political developments in Japan and Western Europe.

During the 1960s, the Japanese economy grew at average annual rates of more than 10 percent, compared with average growth rates of less than 4 percent for the United States. And while Japanese growth slowed during the 1970s and 1980s, Japan continued to grow more rapidly than the United States. Faster growth allowed Japan to catch up to the United States. In the early 1960s, the United States produced 40 percent of the world's manufactured goods while Japan produced only 5.5 percent. By 1987, the United States' share of world manufacturing production had fallen to 24 percent while Japan's share had increased to 19.4 percent (Dicken 1999, 28). In less than 30 years, therefore, Japan had transformed itself from a vanquished nation into a powerful force in the world economy.

Western Europe also emerged as a powerful force in the world economy during this period. Unlike Japan, however, no single European country has emerged as a global economic power. Germany maintained a stable share of world manufacturing output, France and Great Britain saw their shares fall (Dicken 1998, 28, 30). What Western European countries have been unable to do individually, however, they have done collectively through the European Union (EU). Together, the 4 largest EU members (Germany, France, Great Britain, and Italy) produce about 22 percent of world output (Dicken 1998, 28), and, along with the other 21 members of the EU, they act as a single unit in the international trade system. There is a single EU market (the world's largest single market) and a single EU tariff applied to all goods entering the EU market. In addition, EU countries negotiate as a single actor in the WTO. By pooling their economic potential, Western European countries emerged as a powerful force in the international trade system.

During the 1980s and 1990s, it seemed that the erosion of American hegemony was causing the United States to embrace protectionism. The United States began running trade deficits in the 1970s, importing more than it exported, and these deficits continued to grow during the 1980s. American policymakers interpreted these deficits as evidence of declining competitiveness, particularly in high-technology industries. Measures of the United States' comparative advantage in high-technology industries suggested that it was losing ground in critical sectors such as mechanical equipment, electronics, scientific instruments, and commercial aircraft. And what the United States appeared to be losing, Japan, and to a lesser extent, the EU, appeared to be gaining. Statistics suggested that as the American share of global high-technology markets fell (from 30 percent to 21 percent between 1970 and 1989), Japan's share of this market rose (from 7 percent to 16 percent in the same period) (Tyson 1995, 19). Thus, the trade deficit and the apparent decline in American high-technology industries seemed to point to identical conclusions: The United States was losing ground to Japan.

The United States responded by adopting a more aggressive trade policy—a shift that was interpreted by many as signaling a decline in American support for multilateralism. The United States increasingly relied on bilateral initiatives and regularly threatened to deny access to the American market to force changes in other countries' trade policies (Krueger 1995). Japan was the principal (though not the sole) target of this new assertiveness. The United States pressured Japan to engage in a series of negotiations during the 1980s and 1990s aimed at opening the Japanese market to American exports. This more assertive American policy caused many analysts to worry that the multilateral trade system was in jeopardy.

Many analysts argued that American assertiveness reflected "the syndrome of hegemonic decline." As American hegemony eroded, the United States was becoming more protectionist and less supportive of the multilateral trade system. World trade would slow as other governments responded with higher trade barriers of their own. Some argued that the destructive tendencies arising from hegemonic decline would be given additional impetus by the end of the Cold War, which deprived the United States, Japan, and the EU of the common purpose provided by the alliance against the Soviet threat. Robert Gilpin, a political economist at Princeton University summarized this pessimistic outlook, arguing that "at the opening of the 21st century, all the elements that have supported an open global economy have weakened" (Gilpin 2000, 347). By this logic, hegemonic decline has indeed led to a weakening of the multilateral trade system.

Hegemonic stability theory may lead us astray here, however, for many other developments indicate that the multilateral trade system remains robust. Rather than abandoning the multilateral trade system, governments strengthened and extended it. In fact, the list of accomplishments is impressive. Governments have completed two bargaining rounds since 1970 and are now engaged in a third. Governments have further reduced tariffs, created multilateral rules in new trade-related areas—thereby extending the WTO's scope—and established a new institution, the World Trade Organization. Moreover, the WTO enjoys greater support from developing countries and from the former Soviet Bloc than it did at the height of American hegemony. Indeed, more than 50 countries have joined the WTO since the mid-1980s. All of these factors suggest that the WTO has not been weakened by America's hegemonic decline. As one analyst concludes, "the institutions that took hold after World War II continue to provide governance now, and the economic interests and political consensus that lie behind them are more, not less, supportive of an open world economy today than during the Cold War" (Ikenberry 2000, 151).

Why does hegemonic stability seem to lead us astray? One possibility is that it doesn't. The WTO may be weakening gradually and therefore somewhat imperceptibly. Maybe in 10 years we will see this weakening much more clearly than we can today. Another possibility, however, is that hegemonic stability theory misleads us because it neglects the role of international institutions such as the WTO. Maybe the importance of American hegemony lay in its ability to create an international institution that, in turn, facilitated trade liberalization. Once such an institution has been established, hegemony is not necessary to sustain it. The WTO will remain strong as long as governments believe that they benefit from liberal trade and as long as the WTO helps them achieve that goal. This idea suggests that hegemonic stability theory's focus on power needs to be complemented by a greater appreciation of how WTO helps governments achieve and sustain trade liberalization. We take up that topic in Chapter 3.

This does not mean that hegemonic stability theory does not help us understand the trajectory of the WTO. For, even though many analysts may have misjudged how the world trade system would evolve at the end of the 20th century, the underlying logic of their analysis was on target. The WTO will weaken when the world's largest trading nations decide that it no longer meets their interests.

The Evolving WTO: New Directions, New Challenges

While the core elements of the world trade system have been broadly constant for almost 60 years, other aspects have been changing substantially. These trends will play a large role in shaping the evolution of the WTO during the next 10 years. Two such trends, the extension of the scope of WTO rules and the growing difficulty of reaching agreement within the WTO, are particularly significant. Together they have profoundly transformed the WTO and raise fundamental questions about the ability of governments to continue to achieve their goals through this system.

During the last 20 years, WTO rules have extended in scope far beyond the initial concern with tariffs. Early bargaining rounds focused exclusively on tariff reductions. The rationale for doing so was simple. In 1947, the average tariff applied to manufactured goods was 40 percent. High tariffs were a major obstacle to international trade, as they meant that a foreign product cost 40 percent more than the equivalent domestic product. Such large price differences posed a large obstacle to trade. The surest way to liberalize trade, therefore, was to reduce tariffs. Today, average tariffs stand at only 4 percent and have ceased to pose a substantial obstacle to international trade (Jackson 1997). Governments have thus begun to focus on other trade barriers.

As attention has shifted to nontariff barriers, WTO rules have extended in scope to cover a wider range of government policies. In doing so, WTO rules have begun to regulate areas that have traditionally been the exclusive preserve of national governments. Four such areas—intellectual property, trade in services, trade-related investment measures, and standards—each the subject of an agreement concluded under the Uruguay Round, illustrate the expanding scope of WTO rules.

Governments negotiated the Agreement on Trade Related Aspects of Intellectual Property (TRIPs), to protect **intellectual property.** (See Ryan 1998, Sell 1998, and Harrison 2004.) According to the World Intellectual Property Organization, intellectual property can be defined as "creations of the mind: inventions, literary, and artistic works, as well as symbols, names, images, and designs used in commerce". This definition, then, includes such things as the Nike "swoosh," the distinctive design of an iPod, a Hollywood movie, computer software, and the chemical formulas embodied in modern pharmaceutical products. Intellectual property is protected through patents, copyrights, and trademarks that give the creator the exclusive right to profit from his or her invention or artistic work.

It became apparent during the 1980s that many developing countries were doing little to protect intellectual property created by foreign firms. Firms and individuals were making counterfeit versions of Microsoft software, American movies, Nike and Adidas sneakers, Calvin Klein and Guess jeans, pharmaceutical products, and other items. The ease with which anyone could purchase counterfeit or pirated products at much reduced prices throughout the developing world indicated that Western firms were losing billions of dollars. Moreover, such piracy, many argued, reduced the incentive to invent new products. In negotiating TRIPs, governments created multilateral rules that require all WTO members to protect intellectual property and prevent such piracy. Intellectual property rights have thus become subject to binding international rules.

Governments also created new rules to govern international trade in services. A **service** is an economic activity that does not involve manufacturing, farming, or resource extraction. Incorporated in services is a wide range of economic activities, including financial services such as banking and insurance, transportation services such as shipping and tourism, business services such as consulting and accounting, and telecommunications. The service sector accounts for about 60 percent of economic activity in the advanced industrialized countries and for about 22 percent of world trade. Moreover, since the early 1980s, international trade in services has grown more rapidly than trade in manufactured goods (Hoekman and Kostecki 1995, 127). Yet, in spite of the importance of the service sector, there were no international rules governing international trade in services until the conclusion of the Uruguay Round.

Liberalizing trade in services often requires substantial changes to national policies. The major obstacle to trade in services usually lies in national regulations that prevent foreign service firms from operating in the local market. Such regulations prevent American telephone companies from providing telephone service in West European countries, for example, and limit the ability of American and European and insurance companies to operate in many developing countries. Liberalizing trade in services, therefore, often requires substantial changes to national regulations. The General Agreement on Trade in Services, concluded in the Uruguay Round, removed a small number of these barriers and created a framework for negotiations aimed at additional liberalization (Hoekman and Kostecki 1995, 141). Such negotiations have been ongoing in telecommunications, maritime transport, and financial services since 1995, and continue in the Doha Round.

Governments also negotiated rules on government policies toward multinational corporations (MNCs). These **Trade-Related Investment Measures** (TRIMs) limited the ability of governments to regulate certain aspects of MNC activities. In particular, TRIMs restricted the ability of governments to impose performance requirements on MNCs. Many governments have traditionally used such regulations to require foreign firms to purchase a certain percentage of their inputs from domestic producers or to export a certain percentage of their production. Preventing the use of such performance requirements represents an extension of international trade rules into a policy domain that was previously the exclusive preserve of national governments.

Finally, governments negotiated agreements that constrain the use of standards to regulate national product markets. Two such agreements have been concluded, an

POLICY ANALYSIS AND DEBATE

Regulating Risk in the World Trade Organization

Question
How should governments manage the risk associated with genetically modified organisms (GMOs)?

Overview
Technology has allowed humans to manipulate nature. We can now genetically modify seed corn to make it resistant to certain herbicides and insects. We can also genetically modify rice to enhance its vitamin A content. In addition, we can genetically modify cotton, adding color in order to reduce the need to rely on chemical dies. And while GMOs entered commercial use only in 1996, they have been widely adopted. The biotechnology revolution in agriculture offers substantial benefits in the form of higher crop yields at a lower cost. This gain is not trivial in a world that must produce food to feed more than 8 billion people by 2050.

However, GMOs might also damage human health or the environment. Currently, the scientific community has no evidence that GMOs damage either. Yet, we have a very short history with these products, and any negative consequences may become evident only after many years. Thus, GMOs pose uncertain risks: They might be harmful, or they might not be. Some societies are more willing to accept these unknown risks than others. Genetically modified organisms are widely used in commercial agriculture in the United States. In contrast, the European Union prohibited the commercialization of products containing GMOs until quite recently and continues to regulate them quite tightly.

These different approaches to risk spill over into the WTO. Products containing GMOs enter into international trade. Consequently, when a government tightly regulates the local sale of GMOs, it is erecting a de facto trade barrier. Governments have been trying to develop a common approach to the risks connected with GMOs. How should governments approach the risks involved with these products?

Policy Options
- **Certain Harm Principle:** Scientific evidence must demonstrate that a product causes harm before a government can prohibit imports of that product.
- **Precautionary Principle:** Governments can prohibit imports of a product with unknown health consequences until scientific evidence proves that it is safe.

Policy Analysis
- How much risk do you consider acceptable?
- Does the precautionary principle ever expose society to risk?
- Does one approach reduce risk substantially more than the other?

Take a Position
- Which option do you prefer? Justify your choice.
- What criticisms of your position should you anticipate? How would you defend your recommendation against this critique?

Resources
Online: Search for the "precautionary principle" and the EU report "Communication from the Commission on the Precautionary Principle." There are also some useful

Continued

links at Duke University's Center for Environmental Solutions "Precaution Project Page." Look also at the WTO's webpage on the Sanitary and Phytosanitary Agreement.

In Print: J.B. Wiener and M.D. Rogers. 2002. "Comparing Precaution in the United States and Europe," *Journal of Risk Research,* 5 (4):317–349; J.D. Graham and J.B. Weiner, eds. 1995. *Risk vs. Risk: Tradeoffs in Protecting Health and the Environment* (Cambridge: Harvard University Press).

agreement on Technical Barriers to Trade, and the Agreement on Sanitary and Phytosanitary Measures (SPS) that focuses on food safety and animal and plant health. Both agreements pose similar issues, so we will focus on the more controversial of the two, the SPS. All governments adopt regulations to protect consumers from unsafe foods. For example, when the United States recently discovered that a couple American cows had mad cow disease, other countries banned the import of American beef. Nothing in the WTO prohibits discrimination against American beef in this or other similar situations.

Potential problems arise when a government uses such regulations to shelter domestic producers from foreign competition. Suppose the United States wants to protect American avocado growers from competition against cheaper Mexican avocados. They assert that Mexican avocados contain pests that harm American plants (even though they don't) and ban Mexican avocados from the American market. This is disguised protectionism—an effort to protect a local producer against foreign competition hidden as an attempt to protect plant health in the United States.

The SPS attempts to strike a balance between allowing governments to protect against legitimate health risks and preventing them from using health and safety regulations to protect domestic producers. This is a difficult balance to strike. It is not easy to determine the real underlying motives behind a government's decision to ban the import of a particular product. Has the EU banned the import of hormone-treated beef because of a sincere concern about potential health consequences or because it wants to protect European beef producers from American competition? As a consequence, these rules require governments to accept the current scientific conclusions about the risks generated by such products. Almost necessarily, therefore, such rules clearly extend deeply into a critical element of national authority; the ability to determine what risks society should be exposed to and protected from.

Thus, as the focus of negotiations has shifted toward nontariff barriers, WTO rules have begun to intrude more deeply into aspects of national policies that have not traditionally been subject to international negotiation and agreement. This trend continues in the Doha Round, in which governments not only are negotiating agreements on agriculture that will limit government subsidies to farmers, but also are continuing to negotiate on service sector liberalization. Indeed, as governments move beyond the Doha Round, it is likely that negotiations will increasingly focus on national regulatory barriers to trade.

The second major challenge facing the WTO arises from the growing difficulty of reaching agreements. This reflects three developments. First, WTO membership has increased sharply since 1985. (See Table 2.4.) More than 50 countries have joined the

Table 2.4
New Members of GATT/WTO, 1985–2004

Armenia	2003	Latvia	1999
Albania	2000	Lesotho	1998
Angola	1994	Liechtenstein	1994
Antigua and Barbados	1987	Lithuania	2001
Bahrain	1993	Macao	1991
Botswana	1987	Mali	1993
Brunei Darussalam	1993	Mexico	1986
Bulgaria	1996	Moldova	2001
China	2001	Mongolia	1997
Costa Rica	1990	Morocco	1987
Croatia	2000	Mozambique	1992
Djibouti	1994	Namibia	1992
Dominica	1993	Nepal	2004
Ecuador	1996	Oman	2000
El Salvador	1991	Panama	1997
Estonia	1999	Papua New Guinea	1994
Fiji	1993	Paraguay	1994
Former Yugoslavia Republic of		Qatar	1994
Macedonia	2003	Saint Kitts and Nevis	1994
Georgia	2000	Saint Lucia	1993
Grenada	1994	Saint Vincent and the Grenadines	1993
Guatemala	1991	Slovak Republic	1993
Guinea	1994	Slovenia	1994
Guinea Bissau	1994	Solomon Islands	1994
Honduras	1994	Swaziland	1993
Hong Kong	1986	United Arab Emirates	1994
Jordan	2000	Venezuela	1990
Kyrgyz Republic	1998		

Source: World Trade Organization

multilateral trade organization since 1985, increasing total membership to 147 countries. An additional 26 countries have applied for membership and are currently engaged in accession negotiations. Assuming all of these negotiations are successfully completed, WTO membership will reach 173 countries during the next few years. Even if all governments have similar interests, more members would make the decision making harder—it is just hard to gain consensus among 147 countries.

Yet, not all members have similar interests. Instead, growing membership has brought more diverse interests into the WTO. Indeed, the organization brings together wealthy advanced industrialized countries, middle-income developing countries, and extremely poor developing countries. The vastly different economic structures in these three groups generate very different interests. Consider intellectual property rights. Low-income countries don't produce many new technologies, but do use a lot of foreign technology. Consequently, low-income countries have little interest in protecting intellectual property and may actually prefer rules that allow them to use new technologies at low cost. Advanced industrialized countries produce lots of technology and have a great interest in strong rules to protect this technology. Given these different interests, it is difficult to reach agreement on intellectual property rules. What is true for intellectual property is true for most issues: As interests grow diverse, reaching agreement becomes more difficult.

The complications arising from the greater diversity of interests within the WTO is compounded by a growing array of interested groups outside it. Few interest groups (other than businesses) paid much attention to GATT when negotiations focused solely on tariffs. Over the last 10 years, however, hundreds of groups have mobilized in opposition to what they view as the unwelcome constraints imposed by new WTO rules. Domestic environmental groups fear that WTO rules will undermine existing environmental regulations. Human rights organizations fear that WTO rules threaten indigenous communities and subject workers to sweatshop conditions. Public health groups fear WTO rules make it more difficult for governments to acquire medicines vital to treating public health emergencies. This mobilization makes it increasingly difficult for governments to build domestic support for the international compromises that WTO agreements require. In short, the range of international and domestic interests that must be taken into account to reach agreement within the WTO has grown increasingly diverse, making it much harder to reach agreement.

The combination of an expanding scope and growing diversity of interests has generated questions about whether current WTO decision-making procedures remain appropriate or whether they should be changed. Some such questions focus on the effectiveness of WTO decision making: Can 147 governments at different stages of economic development reach agreements that provide meaningful trade liberalization? Other questions focus on the legitimacy of WTO decision making: Should rules that constrain national regulations be negotiated without the full participation of civil society?

Both questions are important, but they point to contradictory conclusions about the types of reforms required. Concerns about the effectiveness of WTO negotiations point to decision-making reforms aimed at limiting the number of governments actively participating in negotiations. One such proposal advocates the creation of a steering committee, a WTO equivalent of the United Nations Security Council, with authority to develop consensus on trade issues. (See Schott and Watal 2000.) Such reform would make it easier to reach agreement, but would do so by making negotiations less inclusive.

Concerns about the legitimacy of WTO decision making point to reforms aimed at allowing nongovernmental organizations (NGOs) to participate in WTO bargaining. Opening the WTO to such participation, NGOs argue, would ensure that trade interests are balanced against other social concerns. While such reforms might make WTO decision making more inclusive, they would also make it even more difficult to reach agreement within the agency. Thus, while there is dissatisfaction with current decision-making procedures, there is a lack of consensus about whether and, if so, how these procedures should be changed. We will return to this issue in Chapter 16. The most important potential consequence of such a development is that governments will find that the WTO is an increasingly less useful forum within which to pursue their trade objectives. If they come to that conclusion, they will begin to seek alternatives.

The Greatest Challenge?
Regional Trade Arrangements and WTO

One alternative that may gain particular appeal are regional trade arrangements. Indeed, many observers believe that regional trade arrangements pose the single greatest challenge to the multilateral trade system. Regional trade arrangements pose a challenge to the WTO because they offer an alternative, and more discriminatory, way to organize world trade.

A **regional trade arrangement** (RTA) is a trade agreement between two or more countries, usually located in the same region of the world, in which each country offers preferential market access to the other. RTAs come in two basic forms: free trade areas and customs unions. In a **free trade area,** like the North American Free Trade Agreement, governments eliminate tariffs on other members' goods, but each member retains independent tariffs on goods entering their market from nonmembers. In a **customs union,** like the EU, member governments eliminate all tariffs on trade between customs union members and impose a common tariff on goods entering the union from nonmembers.

Because RTAs provide tariff-free market access to some countries, but not to others, they are inherently discriminatory. Though such discrimination is inconsistent with GATT's core principle, GATT's Article XXIV allows countries to form RTAs as long as the level of protection imposed against nonmembers is no higher than the level of protection applied by the countries prior to forming the arrangement. Nevertheless, the discriminatory aspect of RTAs makes many worry about the impact they will have on the nondiscriminatory trade encouraged by the WTO.

Such worries arise because of the rapid proliferation of RTAs. According to the WTO, there are currently between 190 and 250 RTAs in operation. If all RTAs now planned are created, there may be as many as 300 RTAs in effect by the end of 2005. The vast majority of these RTAs are free-trade agreements, which account for about 86 percent of existing RTAs and for 99 percent of arrangements currently being negotiated. (See Figure 2.1.) More than half of these arrangements are bilateral agreements. The others are "plurilateral" agreements that include at least three countries. RTAs are densely concentrated in Europe and the Mediterranean region. (See Figure 2.2.) Agreements between countries in Western, Eastern, and Central Europe, and in the Mediterranean account for almost 70 percent of RTAs in operation. North and South America take second place, accounting for about 12 percent. The rest of the world seems less enthusiastic about RTAs, as countries in sub-Saharan Africa and Asia-Pacific participate in very few.

The rapid growth of RTAs during the last 15 years reflects a number of distinct factors. The collapse of the Soviet bloc and the subsequent disintegration of the Soviet Union resulted in the rapid proliferation of RTAs. These countries sought new ways to organize their trade, and they sought access to west European markets. Consequently, a large number of agreements were reached between countries within the region and between these countries and the EU (WTO 2000 b). Moldova, for example, entered RTAs with eight other newly independent countries formed from the former Soviet Union between 1992 and 1996. Russia entered at least nine RTAs with this same set of

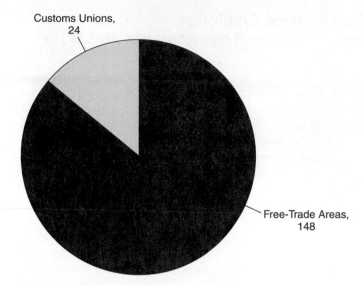

Figure 2.1   Regional Trade Arrangements, 2000.
Source: The World Trade Organization 2000.

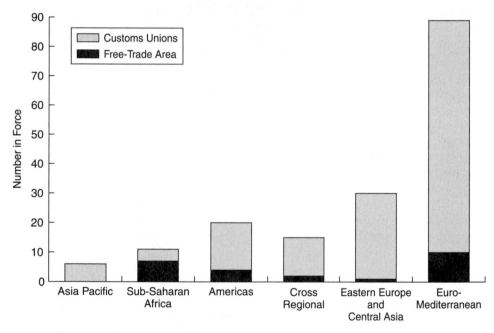

Figure 2.2   Geographic Location of Regional Trade Arrangements.
Source: The World Trade Organization 2000.

countries. Ten Eastern and Central European countries reached bilateral RTAs with the European Union between 1991 and 1997. There were also substantial changes in developing country trade policies in the late 1980s and early 1990s, and this led to a greater willingness to enter RTAs (WTO 2000b). Mexico, for example, negotiated RTAs not only with the United States and Canada (NAFTA), but also with Chile, Costa Rica, and Nicaragua. Chile negotiated RTAs with Colombia, Ecuador, and Peru, in addition to completing the agreement it reached with Mexico.

While these changes help us understand why a larger number of states were willing to undertake trade liberalization, it does not fully explain why so many of these countries chose to liberalize trade through RTAs rather than through the WTO. Idiosyncratic factors played an important role. Countries created out of the disintegrating Soviet Union had to find new ways to regulate their trade relatively quickly. An RTA probably offered the quickest solution. Therefore, many of these RTAs replaced structures previously provided by the Soviet Union. Central and Eastern European countries sought RTAs with the EU in part because they wanted better access to the EU market and in part because each planned to seek full EU membership. The EU responded by establishing free-trade agreements as the first step in the accession process. In all of these cases, RTAs emerged as expedient solutions to pressing trade problems in a rapidly changing economic environment.

Scholars have also advanced more general ideas to account for the proliferation of RTAs. Some place primary emphasis on a country's desire to gain more secure access to the market of a particularly important trading partner. In the U.S.–Canada free-trade agreement concluded in the late 1980s, for example, Canada sought secure access to the U.S. market—the most important destination for Canada's exports. During much of the 1980s, the United States had been regularly using antidumping and countervailing duty investigations to protect American producers from Canadian imports. Such measures clearly interfered with the ability of Canadian producers to export to the American market. The Canadian government hoped that the U.S.–Canada Free Trade Agreement would give Canada "some degree of exemption" from these measures (Whalley 1998, 72–73).

Other scholars place primary emphasis on a government's need to signal a strong commitment to economic reform. Governments use RTAs to convince foreign partners that they will maintain open markets and investor-friendly policies. This argument has been most commonly applied to Mexico's decision to seek a free-trade agreement with the United States. Mexico shifted from a highly protectionist to a more liberal trade policy in the mid-1980s. The success of that strategy hinged in part on Mexico's ability to attract foreign investment from the United States. The Mexican government feared, however, that American investors would not believe that the Mexican government was committed to its new strategy. What would prevent Mexico from shifting back to protectionism and nationalizing foreign investments? If American businesses didn't believe the Mexican government was committed to this liberal strategy, they would be reluctant to invest in Mexico. Absent American investment, Mexico would be deprived of foreign capital that was critical to the success of its strategy.

A free-trade agreement with the United States allowed Mexico to signal to American investors the depth of its commitment to market liberalization. It did so in part because NAFTA contained very clear and enforceable rules concerning the treatment of foreign investment located in Mexico. A similar type of argument might be used to understand at least part of the interest that Eastern and Central European governments had in signing free-trade agreements with the EU. These governments were also reorienting their economic policies and trying to attract foreign investment. Like Mexico, they might have needed an external institution, such as an agreement with the EU, to signal to foreign investors their commitment to market reforms. Arguments of this type actually place less emphasis on the trade benefits that might result from an RTA and focus more on the need to attract foreign investment.

Other scholars argue that countries enter RTAs to increase their bargaining power in multilateral trade negotiations. A small country bargaining individually in the WTO lacks power because it does not have a large market to offer. By pooling a group of small countries, the market that can be offered to trade partners in WTO negotiations increases substantially. Consequently, each member might gain larger tariff concessions in WTO negotiations. Current American enthusiasm for RTAs might also be seen as an attempt to gain bargaining power in the WTO. As it has become more difficult to reach decisions within the WTO, the United States has explicitly threatened to rely more on free-trade agreements. By doing so, the United States denies its market to countries unwilling to make concessions in the WTO. The fear of losing access to the U.S. market could cause governments to make concessions in the WTO that they would not otherwise make. The threat to rely more on RTAs and less on the WTO, therefore, enhances American power in the organization.

Regardless of the specific motivation behind the creation of RTAs, their rapid growth raises questions about whether they challenge or complement the WTO. This is not an easy question to answer. For, on the one hand, RTAs do liberalize trade, a mission they share with the WTO. In this regard, RTAs complement the WTO. On the other hand, RTAs do institutionalize discrimination within world trade. In this regard, RTAs challenge the WTO.

Economists conceptualize these competing consequences of RTAs as **trade creation** and **trade diversion.** Consider an RTA between France and Germany. Because the RTA eliminates tariffs on trade between France and Germany, more Franco–German trade takes place. This is trade creation. Because the RTA does not eliminate tariffs on trade between France and Germany, on the one hand, and the United States, on the other, some trade between the United States and Germany is replaced by trade between France and Germany. This is trade diversion. An RTA's net impact on trade is the difference between the trade it creates and the trade it diverts. If more trade is created than diverted, the RTA has liberalized trade. If more trade is diverted than created, the RTA has pushed the world toward protectionism.

Which of these effects predominates in existing RTAs? Nobody really knows, in large part because it is difficult to evaluate trade creation and trade diversion empirically. It is especially difficult once we begin to think about how RTAs evolve once created. An RTA that originally diverts more trade than it creates might over time create more trade than it diverts. Or an RTA could evolve in the opposite direction. Consider the first case. Some scholars have argued that RTAs exert a kind of gravitational force on countries that are not currently members. Countries that do not belong to the EU, but engage in lots of trade with it, have a strong incentive to join. So it is no surprise, therefore, that over the last 40 years the EU has expanded from 6 to 25 member countries. Some see a similar dynamic at work in the Western Hemisphere. Mexico's decision to seek a free-trade agreement with the United States was at least partially motivated by concerns about the cost of being outside a U.S.–Canada Free Trade

Area that had been negotiated in the late 1980s (Gruber 2000). The interest of many Latin American countries in a Free Trade Area of the Americas (FTAA) is at least partially a consequence of Mexico's entry into NAFTA (Baldwin 1995). Over time, this gravitational pull attracts so many additional members, that a regional RTA evolves into a global free-trade area. In this optimistic scenario, RTAs lead eventually to global free trade in which trade creation outweighs trade diversion and RTAs complement the WTO.

By contrast, the creation of a large RTA in one region could encourage the formation of rival and more protectionist RTAs in other regions. In this scenario, NAFTA as well as FTAA could be seen as an American response to the EU. An emerging free-trade area in Pacific Asia could be seen as a response to regionalism in Europe and the Western Hemisphere. In this view, world trade is becoming increasingly organized into three regional and rival trade blocs. Once regional trading blocs have formed, each bloc might raise tariffs to restrict trade with other regions. A tariff increase by one RTA could provoke retaliation by the others, leading to a rising spiral of protection that undermines global trade liberalization (Frankel 1997, 210). In this case, trade diversion outweighs trade creation and RTAs poses an obvious challenge to the WTO.

It is impossible to predict which of these two scenarios is the more likely. The world does seem to be moving toward three RTAs: one in Europe, one in the Western Hemisphere, and one in Asia. At the same time, governments appear to be aware of the challenges RTAs pose to the WTO, as they have created a WTO committee on RTAs that is exploring the relationship between these arrangements and the multilateral system. Only time will tell, however, whether RTAs will develop into discriminatory trade blocs that engage in tariff wars or if instead they will pave the way for global free trade.

Conclusion

The multilateral trade system is an international political system. It provides rules that regulate how governments can use policies to influence the cross-border flow of goods and services. It provides a decision-making process through which governments revise existing rules and create new ones. And it provides a dispute settlement mechanism that allows governments to enforce common rules. By promoting nondiscriminatory international trade, by establishing a formal process for making and revising rules, and by allowing governments to enforce the rules they create, the WTO reduces impact of raw power on international trade relationships. In short, the WTO brings the rule of law to bear in international trade relations.

The scope of WTO rules has expanded substantially during the last 15 years and will likely expand further in the future. Consequently, WTO rules are increasingly extending into aspects of policy that have previously been the exclusive domain of national governments. Growing membership and the mobilization of domestic interest groups have made it more difficult to reach decisions within the WTO. At present, the full consequences of this challenge are unclear. Can governments reform decision making in the system in a way that simultaneously enhances the legitimacy and the efficiency? The spread of regional trade arrangements offer an alternative way of organizing world trade relations. Whether these arrangements will evolve in a manner that complements the WTO or whether they will instead provide an increasingly attractive alternative to the WTO remains open to debate.

Like all political systems, the WTO reflects the interests of the powerful. Its creation reflected the interests of a hegemonic United States; its strengthening during the Cold War era reflected the growing interest of European and Japanese governments that trade liberalization promised real gains. And while one can argue that the WTO reflects only the interests of the advanced industrialized countries, the trends over the last 20 years suggest otherwise. The rapid growth in the number of countries joining the WTO during that period suggests that most of the world's governments believe that they are better off with the WTO than without it. This doesn't mean that the system is perfect. It does suggest, however, that in the contemporary global economy, the majority of the world's governments believe that they do better when world trade is organized by a system based on nondiscrimination and market liberalism than they do in a discriminatory, protectionist, and rule-free environment. The WTO will weaken, and perhaps even crumble, when governments no longer believe this is true.

Key Terms

Customs Union

Dispute Settlement Mechanism

The Doha Round

Free Trade Area

Generalized System of Preferences

Hegemon

Hegemonic Stability Theory

Intellectual Property

Intergovernmental Bargaining

International Trade Organization (ITO)

Market Liberalism

Ministerial Conference

Most Favored Nation

National Treatment

New Protectionism

Nondiscrimination

Nontariff Barriers

Reciprocal Trade Agreements Act

Regional Trade Arrangement (RTAs)

Tariffs

Trade Creation

Trade Diversion

Trade-Related Investment Measures

World Trade Organization (WTO)

Web Links

You can visit the World Trade Organization at *http://www.WTO.org*.

The EU maintains a website dedicated to its trade policy at *http://europa.eu.int/comm/trade/*.

Japan maintains websites dedicated to international trade at The Ministry of Foreign Affairs: *http://www.mofa.go.jp/policy/economy/wto/index.html*.

Ministry of Economy, Trade, and Industry (METI): *http://www.meti.go.jp/english/index.html*.

The United States Trade Representative maintains websites dedicated to the WTO and other multilateral trade at *http://www.ustr.gov/wto/index.shtml*.

Government information on NAFTA can be found at the following sites:

Canada—*http://www.dfait-maeci.gc.ca/nafta-alena/menu-e.asp*.

Mexico—*http://www.naftaworks.org/*. (This site is maintained by the Mexican embassy in Washington, DC)

The United States—*http://www.ustr.gov/regions/whemisphere/nafta.shtml*.

Suggestions for Further Reading

For a detailed discussion of the origins and development of the rules governing international trade, see John H. Jackson, *The World Trading System: Law and Policy of International Economic Relations* (Cambridge: MIT Press, 1997).

Unfortunately, there is no single book that provides a good overview of the GATT bargaining rounds. Detailed treatments of the political dynamics of the last three rounds of negotiations can be found in Ernest H. Preeg, *Traders and Diplomats: An Analysis of the Kennedy Round of Negotiations under the General Agreement on Tariffs and Trade* (Washington, DC: the Brookings Institution, 1995); Gilbert R. Winham, *International Trade and the Tokyo Round Negotiation* (Princeton: Princeton University Press, 1986); and Ernest H. Preeg, *Traders in a Brave New World: The Uruguay Round and the Future of the International Trading System* (Chicago: University of Chicago Press, 1995). See Bernard Hoekman and Michel M. Kostecki, *The Political Economy of the World Trading System: the WTO and Beyond*, 2nd ed. (New York: Oxford University Press, 2001) for an extended analytical account of the politics of the world trade system.

CHAPTER 3

The Political Economy of International Trade Cooperation

Why does the World Trade Organization exist? There are two ways to answer this question. One approach emphasizes the particular historical process that led to its creation. As we saw in Chapter 2, the United States had an economic interest in creating the GATT after World War II, and it had the power required to do so. The world trade system was thus shaped by the specific configuration of power and interests in place following the Second World War. An alternative approach emphasizes a more abstract logic wherein the WTO exists because it helps governments work together in pursuit of mutual gain. According to this approach, the world trade system is treated as a specific instance of the more general problem of cooperation.

Cooperation is not always easily achieved, even when everybody recognizes that they all could gain from it. Cooperation is often difficult because people often have strong incentives to not cooperate. These incentives are driven in part by a desire to take advantage of others and in part by a desire to avoid being taken advantage of. But regardless of whether people are trying to gain advantage, or whether they are simply trying to avoid being exploited, the behavior yields the same result: cooperation is stymied and people are worse off than they could be. Applied to world trade, this logic suggests that countries can gain substantially from cooperation aimed at liberalizing world trade. Yet, because some governments want to take advantage of others, while all governments want to avoid being exploited in this fashion, no government is willing to liberalize trade. Consequently, societies are deprived of the benefits that trade confers. In order for cooperation to emerge in any society, therefore, people must be assured that cooperation on their part will be met by cooperation from others.

Individuals cannot easily provide these assurances to each other. If you think that someone wants to take advantage of you, you will probably disregard the person's request that you "trust him" (or her). The necessary trust can emerge gradually over time. But if you can't cooperate with each other without trust, and if building trust requires cooperation, then you are stuck. Societies often solve this problem by creating institutions, which provide the necessary assurances by punishing people who try to take advantage of others. For example, every time you enter into a contract with someone, the power of the state stands behind you to ensure that you and the party you contract with comply with the agreement. Applied to world trade, this logic suggests that trade liberalization is possible only if an international institution such as the WTO can ensure that all governments comply with the agreements they make. The WTO does this by creating conditions that enable governments to enforce the agreements they conclude. The WTO exists, therefore, because it enables societies to cooperate and capture the welfare gains that trade offers.

This chapter develops the foregoing abstract logic of cooperation in three essential steps. First, we examine trade theory to gain a firm understanding of why trade offers welfare gains to all countries. This examination is important in its own right, but it also highlights the gains available from international cooperation aimed at liberalizing trade. Second, using a standard model of cooperation called the **prisoners' dilemma,** we examine why cooperation to capture the welfare gains available from trade is difficult. Third, we examine how the WTO helps governments cooperate in order to liberalize trade and capture these welfare gains.

The Economic Case for Trade

Why should countries trade? The standard answer is that countries should trade because trade makes them better off. The reason trade makes societies better off, however, can be tricky to grasp. The prominent economist Paul Krugman has argued that even many scholars and journalists who spend their lives writing about the global economy have a less than full understanding of why trade makes societies better off (Krugman 1997, 117–125). Because understanding the rationale for trade is central to understanding the global economy, and because understanding that rationale can be difficult to grasp, we examine it in detail.

In thinking about why countries trade, we must answer two different questions. First, what precisely do we mean when we say that trade makes societies better off? That is, what are "**gains from trade,**" how do economists conceptualize them, where do they come from, and who gets them? Second, we need to ask, Why does trade necessarily generate these gains? Answering this question requires us to explore the logic of **comparative advantage.**

We explore these two questions with the use of two different theoretical frameworks. The first framework is called a "**partial equilibrium**" model. This approach focuses on the market for a single commodity rather than on the entire economy (hence the name partial). It highlights how production and consumption of this single commodity change in response to trade. By doing so, it allows us to see exactly what is meant by gains from trade. The second framework is called a "**general equilibrium**" model. This approach focuses on the entire economy (hence the name general). It highlights how the production and consumption of *all* goods in an economy change in response to trade. Thus, the approach not only highlights the gains from trade, but also illustrates the concept of comparative advantage, which is the underlying reason these gains exist. Together, the two frameworks help us understand what the gains from trade are and why trade necessarily creates them.

The Gains from Trade in Partial Equilibrium

The simplest way to illustrate the gains from trade is to examine what happens in the market for a single commodity when a country shifts from autarky to trade. We start with an autarkic country—that is, a country that does not engage in any trade. The domestic market for a single commodity—say, shirts—is represented in Panel A of Figure 3.1. The horizontal axis represents quantity—that is, the number of shirts demanded by domestic consumers and supplied by domestic manufacturers. The vertical axis represents the price of shirts. The figure also shows demand and supply curves. The demand curve—the downward-sloping line labeled d—tells us the total number of shirts that domestic consumers will buy at every price. This curve slopes downward because consumers will buy more shirts as their price falls. The supply curve—the upward sloping line labeled s—tells us the total number of shirts that domestic producers will supply at every price. The supply curve slopes upward because domestic producers will supply more shirts as the price rises. The number of shirts that will be produced and consumed at equilibrium, as well as the price for which they will sell, will be determined by the intersection of the supply and demand curves. Therefore, the quantity of shirts produced is Q, and these shirts will sell at price p.

We now need to introduce two concepts: **consumer surplus** and **producer surplus.** Producer and consumer surplus are aggregate measures of welfare. Consider consumer surplus first. If you look at the demand curve, you will notice that a few people (those represented by the top left portion of the demand curve) are willing to pay a high price to buy shirts. Yet, these people are able to purchase shirts at the much lower market price. The difference between what these people are willing to pay and the market price that they do pay provides them a surplus. Consumer surplus aggregates all of these individual consumer gains. Total consumer surplus is equal to the area below the demand curve and above the price line.

Producer surplus is the analogous concept on the supply side. Some producers (those represented by the lower left portion of the supply curve) are willing to supply shirts at a relatively low price. Yet, when these producers sell their shirts, they receive the much higher market price. The difference between how much each producer is willing to receive to produce shirts and what each does receive represents that producer's surplus. Producer surplus aggregates all of these individual producer gains. Total producer surplus is equal to the area above the supply curve and below the price line. Together, consumer and producer surpluses depict the amount and the distribution of social welfare generated in this market.

We can now examine what happens to equilibrium shirt production and consumption when the United States shifts from autarky to trade (Panel B). When trade occurs, the price of shirts is determined by the interaction between world supply and demand. Because most national economies are small in relation to the world economy, each country's individual demand for and supply of goods will not affect total world demand or total world supply. Therefore, domestic shirt producers and consumers have no influence on the price of the shirts sold in the domestic market. This logic is

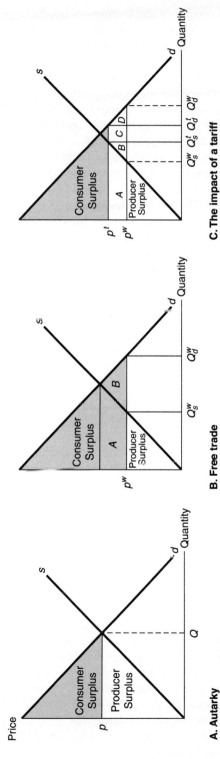

A. Autarky

B. Free trade

C. The impact of a tariff

Figure 3.1   Trade in Partial Equilibrium.

identical to that of individual producers and consumers operating in a perfectly competitive market, where each individual is a "price taker." Rather than focus on an individual in the domestic market, here we focus on a national economy in the global economy. And just as no individual in a perfectly competitive market is large enough to alter prices in that market, no single country is a large enough producer or consumer of shirts to affect the world price. Thus, domestic producers and consumers of shirts are "world price takers." This world price is depicted as p^w in Panel B of Figure 3.1.

How many shirts will domestic producers supply and domestic consumers buy at the world price? Domestic producers supply shirts up to the amount Q_s^w, the point at which the world price intersects the domestic supply curve. Domestic consumers buy shirts up to the amount Q_d^w, the point at which the world price intersects the domestic demand curve. At the world price, therefore, domestic consumers buy more shirts than domestic producers supply. Demand for shirts in excess of domestic shirt production, an amount equal to $(Q_d^w - Q_s^w)$, is satisfied by imports. Trade has thus changed equilibrium shirt production and consumption. Domestic shirt production falls, domestic shirt consumption rises, and imports fill the difference between them.

Aggregate social welfare is higher under this new equilibrium than it is under autarky. The improvement in aggregate welfare is the gain from trade. We can see this improvement by looking at how trade has changed consumer and producer surplus. Consumer surplus expands by the areas labeled A and B, while producer surplus shrinks by the area labeled A. Since we know that consumer surplus measures consumer welfare, we know that trade has made consumers better off. And because we know that producer surplus measures producer welfare, we know that trade has made producers worse off.

Gains from trade arise because the amount by which consumers gain is greater than the amount that producers lose. This difference is the triangle labeled B, and it represents the gain from trade. Less abstractly, society gains from trade because consumers have more money in their pockets with trade than without. And even though producers lose money from trade, the amount of money that consumers gain is so large that they could fully compensate shirt producers for their losses and still have more money in their pockets. This is what is meant by the claim that trade raises social welfare.

Rarely do countries move from autarky to free trade. Instead, governments typically influence trade by raising or lowering tariffs. This partial equilibrium approach allows us to see how such changes in tariffs alter equilibrium production and consumption and social welfare. Suppose that those American shirt producers who lose from trade convince the government to impose a tariff on imported shirts. This tariff is a tax that the government imposes on imported shirts. The tariff thus raises the domestic price of shirts. In panel C, this effect is illustrated by the shift from the world price p^w to the higher price p^t. The change in price produces a new equilibrium. Domestic producers supply more shirts at the higher price, and domestic production therefore expands from Q_s^w to Q_s^t (the point where the new domestic price p^t intersects the supply curve). Consumers buy fewer shirts at the higher price, so consumption falls from Q_d^w to Q_d^t (the point where the new domestic price (p^t) intersects the demand curve). Finally, because domestic production increases while domestic consumption falls, imports fall (from $[Q_d^w - Q_s^w]$ to $[Q_d^t - Q_s^t]$. Thus, the tariff has increased domestic production and reduced domestic consumption and imports compared with the level of those variables in the free-trade world.

What are the welfare consequences of shifting from free trade to this tariff-based equilibrium? Consumer surplus shrinks compared with the free-trade case by the areas labeled A, B, C, and D. Producer surplus expands by the amount equal to the area labeled A. The tariff thus transfers welfare from consumers to producers. The area labeled C is transferred from consumers to the government as revenue from the tariff. This revenue may be spent on government services that benefit consumers, so it does not necessarily reflect a consumer loss. What is left are regions B and D, which represent efficiency losses: losses of consumer surplus that are not offset by an increase in producer surplus or by government tariff revenue.

Efficiency losses take two forms. The triangle labeled D is a consumption distortion loss. It arises because the tariff causes domestic consumers to buy too few shirts, given their preferences and the world price of shirts. The triangle labeled B is a production distortion loss. It arises because the tariff causes domestic producers to manufacture too many shirts, given domestic production costs and the world price (Krugman and Obstfeld 1994). Together, the two types of efficiency loss represent the welfare losses that give protectionism a bad name.

How large are the costs of protection, and how much would the United States gain if existing protection was dismantled? We can put real dollar figures on these abstract concepts using a study conducted in the early 1990s. (Table 3.1.) Total consumer losses in the 11 sectors of the American economy most heavily protected by tariffs amounted to almost $2.3 billion per year. While the magnitude of this loss varied across sectors, from $376 million in women's footwear to $64 million in the ball-bearing industry, consumers were made worse off by the imposition of a tariff in every instance. **Voluntary export restraints** (VERs) in apparels alone cost consumers more than $21 billion. Altogether, all VERs reduced consumer surplus by almost $25 billion. In total, therefore, American protection costs American consumers more than $27 billion. Producers captured a large share of these consumer losses. Tariff protection yielded about $718 million of extra income for producers, and the VERs provided an additional $12 billion. Producer gains varied across industries, from $162 million for glassware producers to $13 million for ball-bearing producers, but they always gained from protection.

A portion of consumer losses is transferred to the U.S. government and to foreign producers. Tariff protection furnishes the U.S. government with about $1.4 billion per year in revenue. VERs provide quota rents to foreign producers. **Quota rents** are above-market returns created by the associated quota. Rents arise because quotas restrict the number of foreign goods that can be sold in the domestic market below the level that domestic consumers want to buy. With supply held below demand, foreign producers can charge a higher price for each good they sell. Suppose, for example, that during the 1980s American consumers wanted to buy 4 million Japanese cars at the market price. The VER that the United States negotiated with Japan, however, allowed Japan to export only 2.3 million cars to the United States. Because the VER kept the number of Japanese cars supplied to the American market substantially below the number Americans wanted to buy, each Japanese car sold at a higher price than it would have without the VER. The quota rent is the difference between the high price Japanese auto producers received for each car with the VER and the lower price they would have received in the absence of the VER. In the apparel industry, which has been heavily protected with quotas, rents

Table 3.1
The Costs of Protection in the United States (Millions of Dollars)

Product Category	Loss of Consumer Surplus (A+B+C+D)	Gain in Producer Surplus (A)	Tariff Revenue or Quota Rents (C)	Deadweight Loss (B+D)
Tariffs				
Ball Bearings	64	13	50	1
Canned Tuna	309	127	172	10
Ceramic Articles	102	18	81	2
Ceramic Tiles	139	45	92	2
Frozen Concentrated Orange Juice	281	101	145	35
Glassware	266	162	95	9
Luggage	211	16	169	26
Polyethylene Resins	176	95	60	20
Rubber Footwear	208	55	141	12
Women's Footwear, except athletic	376	70	295	11
Women's Handbags	148	16	119	13
Total	2,280	718	1,419	141
Voluntary Export Restraints				
Apparel	21,158	9,901	8,956	2,301
Textiles	3,274	1,749	1,345	181
Machine Tools	542	157	350	35
Total	24,974	11,807	10,651	2,517

Source: Hufbauer and Elliot 1994.

equal almost $9 billion per year. Total transfers from American consumers to the U.S. government as tariff revenue and to foreign producers as quota rents amount to about $12 billion.

The efficiency losses are moderate, but still significant. Overall, American society loses more than $2.5 billion per year as a direct result of protection in the 14 sectors listed in Table 3.1. Whether we consider these losses to be substantial depends in part upon the context we use to evaluate them. They are small as a percentage of total U.S. income, amounting to less than 1 percent of GNP per year. This amount may seem even smaller if we apportion it equally across all the people that participate in the U.S. economy—only about $13 per person, per year. Paying such a low price to protect American workers' jobs in these industries may seem reasonable. We get a different picture, however, if we consider how much it costs to save a single job. Every job that protection saves costs American consumers $170,000 per year, an amount that is about six times the average annual income of the typical manufacturing worker. The cost falls substantially to $54,000 per job if we consider only the efficiency losses rather than the total loss of consumer surplus. But even this lower figure is considerably higher than the average annual income of manufacturing workers (Hufbauer and Elliott 1994, 11). Seen in this context, the costs of protection are rather high.

The partial equilibrium framework we have set forth thus provides concrete meaning to the idea of gains from trade. In particular, it highlights two important aspects of these gains. First, the gain from trade is a welfare gain: society enjoys greater welfare with trade than it does without trade. Second, individuals, in their role as consumers, capture these gains. That is, trade allows individuals to consume more products for the same amount of money than they can without trade. This means that every dollar a consumer earns goes further in the marketplace. Trade thus raises consumer income.

The Gains from Trade in General Equilibrium

The partial equilibrium framework helps us understand the gains from trade, but it doesn't help us understand why these gains exist or, more profoundly, why these gains must exist for every country. Nor does it help us think about the broader economic consequences of international trade. To grasp these issues, we need to examine a general equilibrium model of trade. A general equilibrium model examines how trade alters equilibrium production and consumption in the economy as a whole. Thus, whereas in the partial equilibrium model we saw shirt production fall as imports rose, in the general equilibrium model we can see that while shirt production falls, the production of other goods rises. The standard general equilibrium model of trade, which we develop here, is called the $2 \times 2 \times 2$ model, as it is based on two countries, each of which produces two goods using two factors of production.

Before we develop this general equilibrium model, we must establish a few core concepts. The first is the **production possibility frontier (PPF).** Countries are endowed with factors of production in finite amounts. Consequently, any decision to use factors to produce one good means that these factors are not available to produce other goods. A decision to allocate capital and labor to the production of computers, for example, requires the country to forgo the production of some number of shirts. These forgone shirts are what economists call opportunity costs, and the production possibility frontier allows us to measure these opportunity costs quite precisely.

Consider an illustrative PPF for the United States. Let's assume that the country has a fixed stock of labor and capital that it can use in combination to produce two goods: shirts and computers. Suppose that, if the United States allocates all of its labor and capital to computer production, it can produce 100 million computers (point A in Figure 3.2), and if it allocates all labor and capital to shirts, it can produce 300 million shirts (point B in the figure). If we now connect A and B with a line, we have defined a production possibility frontier for the United States. Along this line lie all combinations of shirts and computers that the United States can produce using all of its factors of production. As we move from A to B, capital and labor are reallocated away from computer production to shirt production. The slope of the line, called the **marginal rate of transformation,** tells us exactly how many shirts the nation forgoes for each computer it produces. In this example, every computer the United States produces costs three shirts. Because an autarkic country cannot consume more than it produces, the PPF also defines the limits of consumption.

We can draw the PPF either as a straight line, as in our example, or as a curved line. Which we select depends upon the assumption we make about the nature of the opportunity costs that the United States faces. A straight PPF embodies the assumption that the country faces constant opportunity costs. Every additional computer

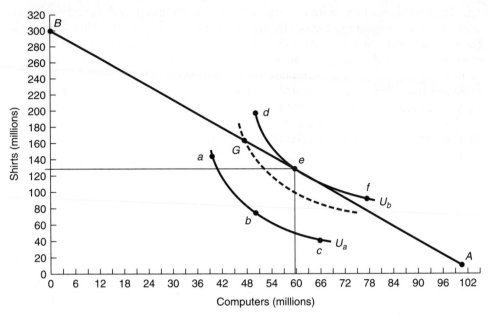

Figure 3.2   U.S. Production Possibility Frontier.

always costs three shirts. If we assume constant opportunity costs, we also implicitly assume that the United States enjoys constant returns to scale in production. This means that whenever the factors employed in shirt production are increased by some factor, we will increase the amount of shirts produced by the same factor; for example, if we double the amount of labor and capital employed in shirt production, we double the number of shirts produced. Alternatively, we could assume that the United States faces *increasing* opportunity costs and connect points A and B with a curved line that bends out from the origin. Under this assumption, the shift from producing 49,999,999 computers to 50 million computers still costs three shirts, but when the United States moves from producing 89,999,999 to 90 million computers, it costs seven shirts. Thus, the opportunity cost of producing each good rises as the nation dedicates a larger share of its factors to the production of a single good. If we assume that the United States faces increasing opportunity costs, we are also implicitly assuming that factors yield diminishing marginal returns. This means that the number of additional computers the United States can produce for each additional worker employed in computer produc- tion will fall as the number of workers employed in computer production rises. Most contemporary models assume that factors yield diminishing marginal returns. To keep things simple, we will assume constant marginal returns.

Our second core concept, **consumption indifference curves,** helps us under- stand what specific combination of computers and shirts American consumers will purchase. Consumers will acquire shirts and computers in the combination that maxi- mizes the consumers' collective utility. Economists conceptualize consumer utility by means of indifference curves. We assume that consumers prefer more to less; there- fore, consumer utility increases as we move away from the origin. Some combinations of shirts and computers, such as those at points a, b, and c in Figure 3.2, yield the same amount of utility. If asked to choose between these three, our consumer will say, "I like them all the same." If we connect every combination of shirts and computers that provides our consumer with the same amount of utility with a curved line such as U_a, we have drawn an **indifference curve.** Our consumer enjoys identical utility from every combination of shirts and computers that falls on U_a. We can also draw a second indifference curve U_b that links the combinations d, e, and f. Each of these combinations yields more utility than a, b, or c and are thus said to lie on an indifference curve that is higher than U_a. Our consumer is thus indifferent among d, e, and f. Were we to repeat this exercise for every possible combination of shirts and consumers within the two-dimensional space of Figure 3.2, we would have a complete indifference map.

Three additional characteristics of indifferences curve are important. First, indifference curves typically slope downwards. Their slope, called the **marginal rate of substitution,** tells us how much of one good the consumer is willing to give up to acquire an additional unit of the second good. Second, indifference curves typically bend inward toward the origin. This bending reflects the assumption of diminishing marginal utility. Thus, the first computer provides a large improvement in utility, but each successive computer provides a smaller increase in utility. Consequently, although the consumer might be willing to give up a large number of shirts to acquire her first computer, she will be willing to give up fewer shirts to acquire her sixth computer. Finally, when we focus on production and consumption for an entire society, we construct *community* indifference curves rather than individual indifference curves. Community indifference curves aggregate utility for all consumers in that society. In this example, then, our community indifference curves embody the aggregated preferences of all American consumers.

Together, the production possibility frontier and indifference curves allow us to define equilibrium production and consumption of shirts and computers in our hypothetical autarkic American economy. Production and consumption will occur at the point where the marginal rate of transformation (the slope of the PPF) is equal to the marginal rate of substitution (the slope of the indifference curve). Stated differently, production and consumption will occur where the PPF and the indifference curve are tangent—point e in Figure 3.2.

Why must production and consumption occur only at this point? Suppose the United States initially produced and consumed at point G. Society can gain greater utility than that derived at G (consumers can shift to a higher indifference curve) by consuming fewer shirts and more computers. We would therefore expect consumers to demand fewer shirts and more computers, and we would expect production to shift in response, producing more computers and fewer shirts. Beyond e, however, consuming additional computers and fewer shirts *decreases* consumer utility. Consequently, consumers will begin to demand more shirts and fewer computers. Only at e is it impossible to achieve higher utility from a different combination of shirts and computers. Consumer utility is thus maximized by producing and consuming at e. Under autarky, therefore, equilibrium production and consumption in the United States in our hypothetical model equals 60 million computers and 120 million shirts.

To see how trade changes this equilibrium, we must introduce a country for the United States to trade with. We will assume that the only other country in the world is

China. We construct China's production possibility frontier just as we did for the United States. (See Figure 3.3.) Let's suppose that if China dedicates all of its labor and capital to computers, it can produce 20 million computers. If it dedicates all of its labor and capital to shirt production, it can produce 400 million shirts. Connecting these two points yields China's production possibility frontier. Given our assumptions, China's marginal rate of transformation is 20: every computer China produces carries opportunity costs of 20 shirts. We then find the point of tangency between China's consumer indifference curves and the production possibility frontier to identify equilibrium production and consumption in an autarkic China. On the basis of our assumptions, equilibrium production and consumption in autarkic China yields 13 million computers and 140 million shirts.

We can now see how trade between the United States and China affects equilibrium production and consumption in both countries. (See Figure 3.4.) Trade changes equilibrium production by causing each country to specialize in the production of one good. The United States specializes in computer production and stops producing shirts. China specializes in shirt production and stops producing computers. Specialization arises from the conclusions each draws from a simple price comparison. The United States acquires more shirts per computer when it buys the shirts from China than when it produces them at home. A computer buys 20 shirts from China, whereas at home a computer buys only 3 shirts. Why should the United States produce shirts at home when it can acquire them for substantially less in China? The United States thus stops producing shirts, produces only computers, and acquires the shirts it wants from China.

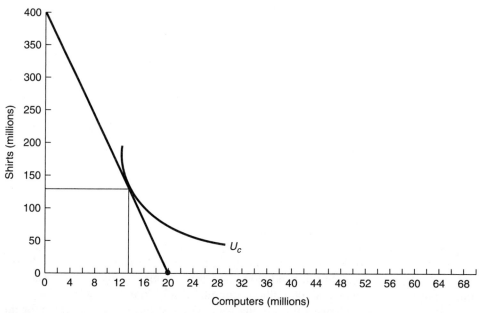

Figure 3.3   China's Production Possibility Frontier.

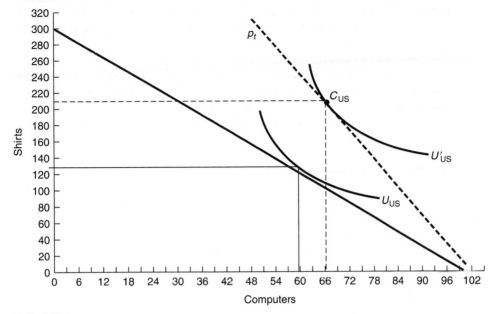

United States

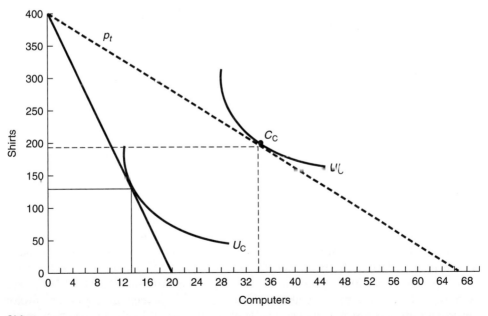

China

Figure 3.4   Equilibrium with Free Trade and Complete Specialization.

Similarly, China acquires more shirts per computer when it buys them from the United States than when it produces them at home. China can acquire a computer from the United States for only 3 shirts, whereas if it produces computers at home each computer costs 20 shirts. Why should China produce computers when it can acquire them much less expensively from the United States? China therefore stops producing computers, specializes in shirts, and acquires the computers it wants through trade with the United States. Trade thus changes equilibrium production in both countries: the U.S. specializes in computer production and China specializes in shirt production.

To see how trade affects equilibrium consumption in both countries, we need to know the price at which the United States and China will exchange shirts for computers. We know that this price must fall somewhere between 3 and 20 shirts per computer. We could solve for the exact price that will arise, but we'll simply assume that the two agree to trade at 6 shirts per computer. This new price is depicted in Figure 3.4 as the dashed line labeled p_t. Now we must find the combination of shirts and computers that maximizes consumer welfare in each country at this new price. To do so, we find the point of tangency between the new price line and our consumer indifference curves. These points are labeled C_{US} and C_C respectively.

Equilibrium consumption in both countries has thus expanded beyond what was possible under autarky. American consumption expands from 60 million computers and 120 million shirts under autarky to 75 million computers and 150 million shirts under free trade. Chinese consumption expands from 13 million computers and 140 million shirts under autarky to 25 million computers and 250 million shirts under free trade. At this new equilibrium, both countries consume more shirts and computers than they could under autarky. Consequently, consumers achieve greater utility, which is reflected in the move to higher indifference curves (U'_{US} and U'_C respectively). This additional consumer utility is the gain from trade.

Trade between the United States and China is thus beneficial for both countries. This specific example is an illustration of the broader claim that *every* country gains by specializing in goods it produces relatively well and trading them for the goods it produces relatively less well. This is the principle of comparative advantage. Note that these gains are not dependent upon having an absolute cost advantage in a particular industry. The United States does not gain because it produces computers more cheaply than China; rather, it gains because it can acquire more shirts per computer in China than it can at home. And these gains exist even if shirts cost more to produce in China than in the United States. Thus, even countries that produce every good at a higher cost than all other countries wind up gaining from trade by specializing in the goods they produce best. This is the logic of comparative advantage.

What determines which goods a particular country will produce relatively well and which it will produce relatively less well? The **Heckscher-Ohlin (or H-O) model,** which is named after the two Swedish economists Eli Heckscher and Bertil Ohlin, who first developed this approach, provides the standard answer. The H-O model argues that comparative advantage arises from differences in countries' **factor endowments.** Factors are the basic tools of production. When firms produce goods, they employ labor and capital in order to transform raw materials into finished goods. "Labor," obviously, refers to workers. Capital encompasses the entire physical plant that is used in production, including the buildings that house factories and the machines on the assembly lines inside these factories.

Countries possess these factors of production in different amounts. Some countries, such as the United States, have a lot of capital, but relatively little labor. Other countries, such as India, have a lot of labor, but relatively little capital. These different factor endowments in turn shape the cost of production. A country's abundant factor will be cheaper to employ than its scarce factor. In the United States and other advanced industrialized countries, capital is relatively cheap and labor is relatively expensive. In India and other developing countries, labor is relatively cheap and capital is relatively expensive.

Because countries have different factor endowments and face different factor prices, countries will hold a comparative advantage in different goods. A country will have a comparative advantage in goods produced using a lot of their abundant factor and a comparative disadvantage in goods produced using a lot of their scarce factor. In the U.S. auto industry, for example, payments to labor account for between 25 and 30 percent of the total cost of production. A much larger share of the costs of production arises from capital expenditures—that is, expenditures on the machines, assembly lines, and buildings required to build cars (Dicken 1998). In contrast, in the U.S. apparel industry, wages paid to workers account for the largest share of production costs, while capital expenditures account for a much smaller share. It follows that countries like the United States and Japan, which have a lot of capital and relatively little labor, will have a comparative advantage in producing cars and a comparative disadvantage in producing clothing. By the same logic, developing countries such as India and Bangladesh, which have a lot of labor and relatively little capital, will have a comparative advantage in producing clothing and a comparative disadvantage in producing cars.

Thus, in our example, the United States has a comparative advantage in computers and not in shirts because the U.S. is abundantly endowed with physical and human capital and poorly endowed with low-skilled labor. China, by contrast, has a comparative advantage in shirts and not in computers because China is abundantly endowed with labor and poorly endowed with human and physical capital. Comparative advantage tells us, therefore, that all countries gain from trade by specializing in the goods that rely heavily on the factors of production that they hold in abundance and exchanging them for goods that rely heavily on the factors of production that are scarce in their economies.

The Politics of Trade Cooperation

If trade liberalization raises the standard of living, then why don't governments simply liberalize trade? Governments don't liberalize trade because politics intervenes in two important ways. First, politics causes governments to invert the logic of trade theory. Trade theory suggests that imports are good because they allow societies to consume things more cheaply. Exports are the unfortunate price that societies must pay to import. From the perspective of trade theory, therefore, societies should seek to import as much as possible in exchange for as few exports as possible. Given this logic, **unilateral trade**

liberalization—that is, eliminating tariffs and other barriers to imports without receiving **reciprocal tariff** reductions from other countries—is perfectly sensible.

Governments adopt the opposite logic, however. Governments believe that exports are good and should be expanded as much as possible, while imports are bad and should be limited. From this standpoint, unilateral trade liberalization makes no sense. To fully understand why politics causes governments to invert the logic of trade theory, we must delve deeply into the domestic politics of trade policy, a task we take up in the next chapter. Here, we note only that the interests of domestic firms are heavily represented in domestic trade politics, while the interests of consumers are often overlooked. As a result, governments care little about consumer gains and care a lot about trade's impact on domestic industries.

Moreover, not all domestic industries gain from trade liberalization. Firms in comparatively advantaged industries do gain, but those in comparatively disadvantaged industries lose. As a general rule, therefore, governments (1) strive to open foreign markets so that domestic competitive industries can increase exports and (2) continue to protect the less competitive domestic industries from imports. Consequently, in this political world, trade liberalization becomes possible only through international agreements that provide reciprocal tariff reductions.

As a direct consequence of the latter fact, reciprocal agreements have become the standard approach to trade liberalization. The ability of governments to conclude trade agreements is frustrated, however, by the second intervention of politics: the **enforcement problem,** which refers to the fact that governments cannot be certain that other governments will comply with the trade agreements that they conclude (Keohane 1984; Conybeare 1984; Oye 1986). As a result, governments will be reluctant to enter into trade agreements, even when they recognize that they would benefit from doing so. While this might seem counter-intuitive, we can use a simple game-theory model, called the prisoners' dilemma, to see how the enforcement problem can frustrate the efforts of governments to conclude mutually beneficial trade agreements.

Suppose that China and the United States protect their comparatively disadvantaged industries with high tariffs, thereby blocking all trade between them in shirts and computers. Suppose also that the Chinese and American governments both know that each would benefit from a reciprocal agreement which eliminated these tariffs. Would they be able to conclude the agreement? The prisoners' dilemma tells us that they will be unable to do so.

In the prisoners' dilemma, China and the United States each have two strategy choices: each can open its market to the other's exports, which we will call *liberalize*, or each can use tariffs to keep the other's products out of its domestic market, which we will call *protect*. The situation of two governments with two strategy choices each generates the two-by-two matrix depicted in Figure 3.5.

Each cell in this matrix corresponds to a strategy combination, and these strategy combinations produce outcomes. We can describe all the outcomes by starting in the top left cell and moving clockwise. One word about the notation we use before we proceed: It is conventional to list the strategy choice of the row player (the player who selects its strategy from the rows of the matrix) first and the strategy choice of the column player (the player who selects its strategy from the columns of the matrix) second. Thus, the strategy combination referred to as *"Liberalize/Protect"* means that the row

United States

	Liberalize	Protect
Liberalize	L,L *I*	L,P *II*
Protect	P,L *IV*	P,P *III*

(with **China** labeling the rows)

Preference Orders:
China: ***P,L*** > ***L,L*** > ***P,P*** > ***L,P***
United States: ***L,P*** > ***L,L*** > ***P,P*** > ***P,L***

Figure 3.5   The Prisoner's Dilemma and Trade Liberalization.

player, which in this case is China, has played the strategy *Liberalize*, while the column player, which is the United States, has played the strategy *Protect*.

We can now describe the four outcomes:

- *Liberalize/Liberalize*: Both countries eliminate tariffs. China exports shirts to the United States, and the United States exports computers to China.
- *Liberalize/Protect*: China eliminates tariffs while the United States does not. The United States exports computers to China, but China cannot export shirts to the United States.
- *Protect/Protect*: Both retain their tariffs. No trade takes place.
- *Protect/Liberalize*: The United States eliminates tariffs while China does not. China exports shirts to the United States, but the United States cannot export computers to China.

Now we must determine how each government ranks these four outcomes. How much utility do they realize from each outcome? China ranks them in the following order:

protect/liberalize > liberalize/liberalize > protect/protect > liberalize/protect,
where the "greater than" sign means "is preferred to." It is not hard to justify this ranking:

- China gains the most utility from *protect/liberalize*, wherein China exports shirts to the United States and protects its computer producers from American competition.
- China gains less utility from *liberalize/liberalize* than from *protect/liberalize*. With *liberalize/liberalize*, China can export to the United States, but must open its market to American imports.
- China gains less utility from *protect/protect* than from *liberalize/liberalize*. With *protect/protect*, China protects its domestic market, but cannot export to the United States.
- China gains less utility from *liberalize/protect* than from *protect/protect*. With *liberalize/protect*, China opens its market to the United States, but does not get access to the American market.

In words, China's most preferred outcome is unreciprocated access to the U.S. market. Its second-best outcome is reciprocal tariff reductions, which is in turn better than reciprocal protection. China's worst outcome is a unilateral tariff reduction.

The prisoners' dilemma is a symmetric game. This means that the United States faces the exact same situation as China. Consequently, the United States' payoff order is identical to China's payoff order. The only difference arises from the notation we use. Like China's most preferred outcome, that of the United States is unreciprocated access to the other's market, but for the United States this is the outcome *liberalize/protect*. Also, like China's least preferred outcome, that of the United States is granting the other unreciprocated access to its market, which for the United States is the outcome *protect/liberalize*. Thus, the payoff order of the United States is identical to the Chinese payoff order, but the position of the most and least preferred outcomes are reversed: *liberalize/protect > liberalize/liberalize > protect/protect > protect/liberalize*.

We can now see how China and the United States will play this game and what outcome will result. Each country has a dominant strategy—a single strategy that always returns a higher payoff than all other strategies. *Protect* is this dominant strategy. *Protect* dominates *liberalize* as a strategy because each government will always realize higher utility by playing *protect* than by playing *liberalize*.

We can see why *protect* is a dominant strategy by working through China's best responses to the various U.S. strategies. Suppose the United States plays the strategy *liberalize*. If China plays *liberalize* in response, China receives its second most preferred outcome (*liberalize/liberalize*). If China plays *protect* in response, China receives its most preferred outcome (*protect/liberalize*). Thus, if the United States plays *liberalize*, China's best response—the strategy that returns the highest utility—is *protect*.

Now suppose the United States plays *protect*. If China responds with *liberalize*, it receives its least preferred outcome (*liberalize/protect*). If China responds with *protect*, however, it receives its second least preferred outcome (*protect/protect*). Thus, if the United States plays *protect*, China's best response is to play *protect*.

Protect, therefore, "dominates" *liberalize* as a strategy; that is, *protect* yields more utility for China than *liberalize* does, regardless of the strategy that the United States plays. Because the prisoners' dilemma is symmetric, *protect* is also the dominant strategy of the United States. Since both governments have dominant strategies to play *protect*, the game always yields the same outcome: China and the United States each play *protect*, and the game ends with the *protect/protect* outcome. Both countries retain tariffs.

This outcome has two important characteristics. First, it is **Pareto suboptimal.** Pareto optimality is a way to conceptualize social welfare. An outcome is Pareto optimal when no single actor can be made better off without at the same time making another actor worse off. Pareto suboptimal refers to outcomes in which it is possible for at least one actor to improve its position without any other actor being made worse off. In the prisoners' dilemma, the *protect/protect* outcome is Pareto suboptimal because both governments realize higher payoffs at *liberalize/liberalize* than at *protect/protect*. Thus, rational behavior on the part of each individual government, playing its dominant strategy *protect*, produces a suboptimal collective outcome. China and the United States are both poorer than they would be if they liberalized trade.

POLICY ANALYSIS AND DEBATE

Fisheries Subsidies and the WTO

Question
Should the WTO regulate commercial fishing subsidies?

Overview
Many governments subsidize commercial fishing. Worldwide, such subsidies amount to $10–15 billion each year. This may not seem like a lot of money, but it is significant when you consider that the first-sale value of all fish caught in the world is only about $81 billion. Japan provides by far the largest amount of subsidies. The European Union, the United States, Canada, and Russia also subsidize their commercial fishing fleets, but substantially less than the Japanese do theirs. Subsidies raise the return to commercial fishing and thus encourage more people to engage in this activity than would in the absence of government support.

As a result of government subsidies, the world's fisheries are being depleted. According to the World Wildlife Fund, the global fishing fleet is 250 percent larger than it should be to balance the number of fish caught with the ability of the world's major fisheries to sustain themselves. Consequently, a quarter of the world's major fisheries are overexploited (stocks reduced to the point where they are unable to recover to their original population levels) and half are fully exploited (annual catch rate reaching sustainable replacement levels). If catch rates increase further in these latter fisheries, they, too, will see declining fish populations.

The United Nations, the World Bank, the Organization for Economic Cooperation and Development, and even the WTO have all decried the impact of such subsidies on the world's fisheries. Yet, governments continue to subsidize commercial fishing. How can this damaging practice be limited?

Policy Options
- Work primarily through national political systems. Use education, lobbying, and public-interest groups to persuade governments to reduce subsidies.
- Create enforceable international rules that limit government subsidies to their commercial fishing fleets.

Policy Analysis
- Use the prisoners' dilemma to model the strategic situation that governments face.
- Rather than "protect" and "liberalize," assume that each government can "subsidize" or "not subsidize" its fleet.
- Work through the precise meaning of each of the four possible outcomes in this subsidies game, focusing not only on whether governments offer subsidies in each outcome, but also on the consequences each outcome would have for the world's fisheries. For example, when all governments subsidize, fishing fleets expand and fish stocks decline.
- Solve this version of the prisoners' dilemma.

Take a Position
- Given your analysis, which option do you think is more likely to succeed?
- Do you think the prisoners' dilemma captures the central political problem posed by these subsidies?

Continued

Resources

Online: Current WTO negotiations on fishing subsidies. You might also search for the World Wildlife Fund's study "Turning the Tide of Fishing Subsidies." See also Gareth Porter, "Fisheries Subsidies, Overfishing, and Trade," *http://www.sdnbd.org/sdi/issues/environment/article/1.pdf*

In Print: J. Samuel Barkin and George E. Shambaugh, eds. *Anarchy and the Environment: the International Relations of Common Pool Resources* (Albany: SUNY Press, 1999).

Second, the *protect/protect* outcome is a **Nash equilibrium**—an outcome at which neither player has an incentive to change strategies unilaterally. If China changes its strategy from *protect* to *liberalize,* the outcome shifts to *liberalize/protect,* China's least preferred outcome. Thus, China has no incentive to change its strategy unilaterally. If the United States changes its strategy from *protect* to *liberalize,* the outcome moves to *protect/liberalize,* the least preferred outcome of the United States. Thus, the United States has no incentive to change its strategy unilaterally either. Putting these two points together reveals the prisoners' dilemma's central conclusion: even though China and the United States would both gain from reciprocal tariff reductions, neither has an incentive to reduce tariffs. More broadly, the prisoners' dilemma suggests that even when *all* countries would clearly benefit from trade liberalization, political dynamics trap governments in a protectionist world.

Governments are unable to conclude agreements that make them all better off because each fears getting the "sucker payoff." If China and the United States agree to liberalize trade, and then China complies with this agreement, but the United States does not, the United States has exploited China. China suffers the "costs" of rising imports without getting the "benefit" of increased exports. The gains from trade liberalization could be achieved, of course, if governments could enforce international trade agreements. Governments could agree in advance to play *liberalize* strategies if they were confident that cheating would be caught and punished. Moreover, because cheating would be punished, each country would comply with the agreement. The international system provides no enforcement mechanism, however. Whereas domestic political systems rely upon the police and the judicial system to enforce laws, the international system does not have an authoritative and effective judicial system. Instead, the international system is anarchic; that is, it is a political system without an overarching political authority capable of enforcing the rules of the game.

The WTO and Trade Cooperation

We can now consider the role the WTO plays in the world trade system. Trade theory tells us that trade is mutually beneficial. The logic of the prisoners' dilemma suggests, however, that, governments cannot capture these gains because they are unable to enforce the required agreements. To capture gains, governments must devise some mechanism that provides assurances that cooperation by one country will be met with cooperation by others. The WTO helps provide these assurances and, in doing so, enables governments to liberalize trade and capture the available welfare gains. To understand how the WTO fulfills this role, we must first examine the conditions under which cooperation can emerge in a prisoners' dilemma. Then we can examine how the WTO helps create those conditions.

While the prisoners' dilemma is pessimistic about the prospect for international trade cooperation, such cooperation is not impossible within the context of the game. Cooperation can emerge if three specific conditions are met. First, cooperation can emerge in an **iterated prisoners' dilemma**—that is, in a game played repeatedly by the same governments. (See Taylor 1976; Axelrod 1984; Keohane 1984; Oye 1986.) Iteration changes the nature of the reward structure that governments face. In a one-shot play of the prisoners' dilemma, countries make a one-time choice and receive a one-time payoff. In an iterated game, however, governments make repeated choices and receive a stream of payoffs over time. Assuming that the other two necessary conditions are met, governments will prefer the stream of payments they receive from cooperating over time to the payoff they receive from cheating on an agreement. Iterating the game can therefore make it rational for a government to play the *liberalize* strategy.

Second, governments must use reciprocity strategies to enforce the *liberalize/liberalize* outcome. While many reciprocity strategies exist, the most well known is called **tit for tat** (Axelrod 1984). In tit for tat, each government plays the strategy that its partner played in the previous round of the game. Trade liberalization by one government in one round of play is met by trade liberalization from the other government in the next round. Should one government play *protect* in one round (i.e., cheat on an existing trade agreement) the other government must play *protect* in the next round of play. Playing such tit-for-tat strategies allows governments to reward each other for cooperation and punish each other for cheating.

Finally, governments must care about the payoffs they will receive in future rounds of the game. If governments fully discount future payoffs, the iterated game essentially reverts back to a single play of the prisoners' dilemma; when it does, the threat of punishment in the next round of play can hardly be expected to promote cooperation in this round. But if governments care about the future, and if they use a reciprocity strategy such as tit for tat, then cooperation in an iterated prisoners' dilemma becomes rational: each government can realize a larger stream of payoffs by cooperating than it can realize by defecting.

The WTO provides the first two of these three necessary conditions. The WTO helps iterate the game by creating expectations of repeated interaction. Membership in the WTO has been relatively stable. While the number of countries that belong to the WTO has increased over time, very few countries have left the organization after joining. As a consequence, WTO members know that the governments with which they negotiate today will be the governments with which they negotiate tomorrow, next year, and on into the future. In addition, WTO members interact regularly within the organization. Governments have already concluded eight formal bargaining rounds and are now engaged in the ninth such round. In addition to holding these formal rounds of negotiations, the WTO draws governments together for annual and semiannual reviews of national trade policies. By bringing the same set of governments together in a regularized pattern of interaction, the World Trade Organization iterates intergovernmental trade interactions.

The WTO also provides the information that governments need in order to use reciprocity strategies. To use a tit-for-tat strategy effectively, governments must know when their partners are complying with trade agreements and when they are cheating. The WTO makes this knowledge easier to obtain by collecting and disseminating information on its members' trade policies. Moreover, WTO rules provide clear standards against which governments' trade policies can be evaluated. The WTO's most-favored-nation clause, for example, prohibits discriminatory practices except under a set of well-defined circumstances. Further, the WTO's rules governing domestic safeguards define the conditions that must be met in order for governments to temporarily opt out of commitments. These detailed rules increase transparency, meaning that it is easier for governments to determine whether a specific trade measure adopted by a particular government is or is not consistent with WTO rules. The high-quality information and the transparency provided by the WTO allow governments to monitor the behavior of other WTO members. Monitoring in turn makes it easier for governments to use reciprocity strategies to enforce trade agreements.

The ability of governments to use the WTO to enforce trade agreements is most clearly evident in the organization's dispute settlement mechanism which follows a standard procedure agreed upon by all members of the WTO during the Uruguay Round. (See Figure 3.6.) A dispute is initiated when a government brings an alleged violation of WTO rules to the organization's Dispute Settlement Body (DSB) (consisting of all WTO members). The DSB initially encourages the governments involved in the dispute to try to resolve the conflict through direct consultations. If such consultations are unsuccessful, the DSB creates a formal panel to investigate the complaint.

The panel is typically composed of three experts in trade law who are selected by the DSB in consultation with the governments that are involved in the dispute. The panel reviews the evidence in the case, meets with the parties to the dispute and with outside experts if necessary, and prepares a final report that it submits to the DSB. The DSB must accept the panel's final report, unless all WTO members, including the government that initially brought the complaint, vote against its adoption.

Both governments can appeal the panel's decision. If an appeal is requested, the DSB creates an Appellate Body composed of three to five people drawn from a list of seven permanent members. The Appellate Body can uphold, reverse, or modify the panel's findings, conclusions, and recommendations. The appellate report is given to the DSB for approval, and, as with the panel report, the DSB can reject the report only with the consent of all member governments. If, at the end of this process, it is determined that the disputed trade measure is inconsistent with WTO rules, the government must alter its policy to conform to the rule in question or compensate the injured parties. The entire dispute settlement process, from initiation to appellate report, is supposed to take no longer than 15 months.

A recent case involving the European Union's banana import regime illustrates this dispute settlement mechanism in operation and highlights how governments use the system to enforce trade agreements. The banana case began in 1993 when the European Union removed all tariffs on bananas imported from former French and British colonies in Africa, the Pacific, and the Caribbean while continuing to impose

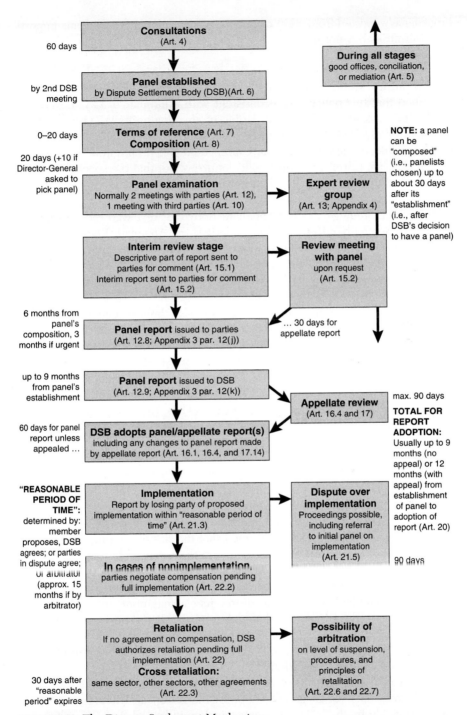

Figure 3.6   The Dispute Settlement Mechanism.
Source: The World Trade Organization, *http://www.wto.org/english/thewto_e/whatis_e/tif_e/disp2_e.htm.* Reproduced with the permission of the World Trade Organization.

tariffs on bananas imported from other countries. By waiving tariffs on banana imports from some countries but not others, the EU began to discriminate against bananas produced in other countries.

In the mid-1990s, Ecuador, Guatemala, Honduras, Mexico, and the United States—all countries whose export interests were harmed by the new EU banana policy—claimed that this policy was inconsistent with a number of GATT rules. In other words, they accused the European Union of cheating on its WTO obligations. Consultations in early 1996 failed to resolve the dispute, so the DSB established a panel which concluded that the European Union could give preferential treatment to bananas from African, Caribbean, and Pacific countries, but that the specific arrangements it had used discriminated illegally against Latin American producers and the American firms Chiquita and Dole (*Europe*, May 1999, 24B). The European Union appealed the panel's findings, but the Appellate Body that reviewed the case largely upheld them. In September 1997, the DSB adopted the Appellate Body report and demanded that the European Union implement WTO-consistent policies by January 1, 1999. Thus, the European Union was found to be "cheating" on a trade agreement it had entered and was required to bring the offending policies in line with those obligations.

The changes the European Union made to its banana import regime in response raised further concerns in the countries that had brought the original complaint. In August 1998, these countries requested further consultations with the European Union to determine whether the new measures were consistent with WTO rules. Consultations were again unproductive, and in December 1998, Ecuador requested the original WTO panel to examine the new EU measures. The panel found that the new measures were not fully consistent with WTO rules. Thus, the European Union had "cheated" in the first place by implementing a banana import regime inconsistent with its WTO obligations and had "cheated" again when altering these policies in response to the ruling of the DSB.

Recognizing that the European Union was unlikely to comply with its WTO obligations unless it was costly not to do so, the United States asked the WTO for permission to suspend $520 million in tariff concessions it had previously granted to the European Union. In essence, the United States was asking for permission to retaliate against the European Union, which then argued that the size of the proposed retaliation was disproportionate to the injury to American trade caused by the EU banana policy. WTO arbitration, initiated at the request of the European Union, agreed with it and authorized the United States to suspend only $191.4 million of previous tariff concessions. The European Union once again altered its banana import regime, this time shifting 100,000 tons of the EU market that had previously been reserved for African, Caribbean, and Pacific producers to Latin American banana producers. In response, the United States suspended its sanctions and the banana dispute was brought to a close (*The Financial Times* 12 April 2001, 14).

The banana case illustrates how governments can use tit-for-tat strategies to enforce trade agreements. An alleged defection by the European Union prompted an impartial investigation by the WTO. This investigation indicated that EU policy violated WTO rules, and when the European Union failed to bring its policies into line with its obligations, the United States retaliated by withdrawing concessions it had previously made to the European Union. In the language of the iterated prisoners' dilemma, the European Union defected and the United States, playing a tit-for-tat strategy, defected in response. Moreover, American retaliation came only after the WTO had determined that it was justified and that the scale of the retaliation was proportionate to the injury suffered. While the WTO's dispute resolution mechanism focuses our attention on a legalistic version of tit-for-tat, it allows us to see in a very detailed way how the organization can promote trade cooperation by helping governments enforce trade agreements.

The WTO thus helps governments gain the assurances they need in order to conclude the trade agreements required to capture the gains from trade. The WTO provides this assurance by allowing governments to monitor the behavior of their trade partners and enforce the trade agreements they reach. By doing so, the WTO enables societies to capture the welfare gains that trade provides. In the absence of the WTO or an institution that performed similar functions, it is unlikely that governments would be able to reach the agreements required to liberalize trade. Each society, and thus the world as a whole, would be poorer as a result.

Conclusion

The WTO exists because it facilitates international cooperation, thereby enabling societies to capture the welfare gains made available from trade. Trade raises social welfare by enabling consumers to enjoy a higher level of utility than they would if they consumed only goods produced at home. The principle of comparative advantage tells us that these welfare gains do not require a country to have an absolute advantage in anything. As long as a country is better at doing some things than others, it gains by specializing in what it does relatively well and trading for everything else.

Politics, however, makes it difficult for societies to realize the gains from trade. For reasons we examine in greater detail in the next chapter, governments often neglect consumer interests in favor of producer interests. Consequently, governments can capture the gains from trade only if they can negotiate international trade agreements. Yet, cooperation is often very difficult. Governments must believe that cooperation on their part will be reciprocated by cooperation from their partners. Furthermore, they must believe that their partners will not try to take advantage of them. Finally, as the prisoners' dilemma highlights, unless such assurances are provided, governments have little incentive to cooperate. The international system, however, lacks the equivalent of a state to enforce agreements; thus, governments face a pervasive enforcement problem when they try to cooperate for mutual gain. Consequently, it is difficult for governments to conclude mutually beneficial agreements, and as a result, societies have lower standards of living.

The WTO helps raise standards of living by assisting governments in solving this enforcement problem. By enabling governments to feel reasonably secure that their partners will comply with the agreements they enter into, the WTO provides the assurances necessary to achieve cooperation. Strictly speaking, the WTO is not an international equivalent of a state, for it does not have the authority or the capacity to punish governments that fail to comply with trade agreements. Instead, the WTO facilitates international cooperation by providing an infrastructure that allows governments to enforce agreements themselves. By establishing a set of mutually agreed-upon rules, by helping governments monitor the extent to which their partners comply with those rules, and by providing a dispute settlement mechanism that helps governments resolve those issues of compliance which do arise, the WTO enables governments to enforce the trade agreements that they reach. The WTO thus gives countries enough assurance that all governments will live up to the agreements they enter into and that no government will be able to take advantage of the others. By providing this infrastructure, the WTO enables governments to conclude the trade agreements necessary to capture the welfare gains from trade.

Key Terms

Comparative Advantage

Consumer Surplus

Consumption Indifference Curves

Dispute Settlement Mechanism

Enforcement Problem

Factor Endowments

Gains from Trade

General Equilibrium

Heckscher-Ohlin Model

Indifference Curves

Iterated Prisoners' Dilemma

Marginal Rate of Substitution

Marginal Rate of Transformation

Nash Equilibrium

Nontariff Barriers

Pareto Suboptimal

Partial Equilibrium

Prisoners' Dilemma

Producer Surplus

Production Possibility Frontier

Quota Rent

Reciprocal Tariff

Tit for Tat

Unilateral Trade Liberalization

Voluntary Export Restraints

Web Links

If you want more help understanding comparative advantage and gains from trade, visit the website maintained by Douglas Ruby. The site provides an in-depth discussion of trade theory and an interactive module that allows you to see how different parameters alter the gains from trade. Visit this site at *http://www.digitaleconomist.com/ca_4010.html.*

The WTO website, *http://www.WTO.org,* remains the best source for detailed information about how the organization operates. Particularly useful might be the information on the system's dispute settlement mechanism, available at *http://www.wto.org/english/tratop_e/ dispu_e/dispu_e.htm.*

Suggestions for Further Reading

For an approach that emphasizes the intuitive aspects of the theory of comparative advantage and downplays explicit theory, see Russell D. Roberts, *The Choice: A Fable of Free Trade and Protectionism* (Englewood Cliffs, NJ: Prentice Hall, 1994). For an excellent account of the historical development of the theory of comparative advantage and of those theories that have challenged the central claim of this theory, see Douglas Irwin, *Against the Tide: An Intellectual History of Free Trade* (Princeton: Princeton University Press, 1996).

To delve more deeply into the logic of international cooperation and the role international institutions play in facilitating such cooperation, see Robert O. Keohane, *After Hegemony: Cooperation and Discord in the Global Economy* (Princeton: Princeton University Press, 1984), and Robert Axelrod, *The Evolution of Cooperation* (New York: Basic Books, 1984).

CHAPTER 4

A Society-Centered Approach to the Politics of Trade

Our focus on the international politics of trade in the last two chapters ignored an important question: What determines the specific trade objectives that governments pursue when bargaining within the WTO, when negotiating regional trade arrangements, or when making unilateral trade policy decisions? We take up this question in this chapter and the next by examining two approaches to the politics of trade (or, simply, trade politics) that are rooted in domestic politics. In this chapter, we examine a society-centered approach to the subject—an approach which argues that a government's trade policy objectives are shaped by politicians' responses to interest groups' demands. On this view, the European Union's reluctance to liberalize European agriculture reflects EU policymakers' responses to the demands of European farmers. Similarly, the Japanese government's commitment to high tariffs on imported rice reflects that government's need to respond to the demands of Japanese rice growers, and the American effort to open foreign markets to U.S. high technology and service exports, while continuing to protect the American textile, apparel, and steel industries, reflect the influence that industry-based interest groups exert on U.S. trade policy.

To understand the political dynamics of this competition among industries, the society-centered approach emphasizes the interplay between organized societal interests and political institutions. The approach is based on the recognition that trade has distributional consequences. In North Carolina, people employed in the textile and apparel industry—traditionally a large employer in the state—have been hit hard by trade liberalization. Between 2000 and 2004, 207 textile and apparel factories closed, and about 44,000 people lost their jobs. In contrast, North Carolinians employed in the pharmaceutical industry or in finance have benefited from trade liberalization: The average wage earned by people employed in these industries rose in the first half of this decade, as did the total number of jobs available in the two industries. In North Carolina, therefore, some people have gained from trade, while others have lost.

These distributional consequences generate political competition, as the winners and losers from trade turn to the political arena to advance and defend their economic interests. The American Textile Manufacturers Institute and the National Council of Textile Organizations, business associations representing textile and apparel firms, pressure U.S. politicians for more stringent controls on textile and apparel imports. They are joined by other associations representing businesses harmed by trade liberalization. Soon, a protectionist coalition gradually begins to form. The Coalition of Service Industries, a business association that represents American financial-service firms (and many other service industry firms) pressures the U.S. government to conclude WTO negotiations aimed at liberalizing world trade in services. As other groups that benefit from expanded trade join them, a pro-liberalization coalition begins to form. Exactly how this competition unfolds—which groups organize to lobby, what coalitions arise, how politicians respond to interest-group demands, which group's interests are reflected in trade policy, and which groups' interests are not—is shaped by the political institutions within which the competition takes place.

This chapter develops the analytical tools that are at the core of a society-centered approach. We focus first on interest-group preferences: which groups prefer protectionism, which prefer liberalization, and why. We use trade theory to develop some systematic expectations about trade policy preferences and we use collective action theory to understand which groups will organize to pursue their interests. Next, we turn our attention to political institutions, looking at how different institutional frameworks create different kinds of interest representation. We then use these tools to examine American trade politics in the postwar era. The chapter concludes by discussing some of the weaknesses of the society-centered approach.

Trade Policy Preferences

Because a society-centered approach argues that trade policy reflects interest-group demands, it devotes considerable attention to the source, content, and organization of those demands. In doing so, it strives to be systematic. To be systematic, this approach derives trade policy preferences from trade's impact on individual incomes. For reasons we explore shortly, trade raises some incomes and lowers others, and it does so in predictable ways. These income consequences in turn determine individuals' trade policy preferences. Once we know what kinds of trade policies people want, we can begin to think about what factors determine whether groups of people with similar trade policy preferences will organize in order to lobby the government to adopt their preferred policy.

Here, we examine two standard models of trade policy preferences: the factor model and the sector model. The two models agree that raising and lowering tariffs redistributes income, and they agree that these income consequences are the source of trade policy preferences. Each model offers a distinctive conception of how trade's income consequences divide society. We examine each model and then turn our attention to the collective action problem that shapes the ability of groups with common interests to organize in order to lobby the government on behalf of their desired policy.

Factor Incomes and Class Conflict

The factor model argues that trade politics is driven by competition between factors of production: competition between labor and capital—between workers and capitalists. Labor and capital have distinct trade policy preference because trade's income effects divide society along factor lines. Whenever tariffs are lowered and trade expanded (or raised and trade restricted), one factor will experience rising income while the other will see its income fall. Trade, therefore, places labor and capital in eternal competition with each other over the distribution of national income. To fully understand the reason for this competition, we need to look at how trade affects factor incomes.

In pursuit of this aim, we are going to make some assumptions. First, we will assume that there are only two countries in the world: the United States and China. Second, we will assume that both countries produce two goods: shirts and computers. Third, we will assume that each country uses two factors of production—labor and capital—to produce both goods. Fourth, we will assume that the production of shirts relies heavily on labor and less heavily on capital, while computer production requires a lot of capital and little labor. Finally, we will assume that the United States is endowed with a lot of capital and little labor, while China is endowed with a lot of labor and little capital. These assumptions merely restate the standard trade model that we discussed in Chapter 3.

The preceding assumptions also allow us to state a few things. First, capital will be relatively cheap and labor will be relatively expensive in the United States, while the opposite will be the case in China. Consequently, the United States will export the capital-intensive good (computers) and import the labor-intensive good (shirts). By contrast, China will export the labor-intensive good and import the capital-intensive good. We can now see what happens to factor incomes in the United States and China as they engage in trade.

We look first at what happens in the United States. As demand for American shirts falls, American firms manufacture fewer of them. As shirt production falls, apparel firms liquidate the capital they had invested in shirt factories and lay off their employees. At the same time, American computer firms are expanding production in response to the growing Chinese demand for U.S. computers. As American computer production expands, computer firms demand more capital and labor, and they begin to employ the capital and labor released by the shirt industry.

There is an imbalance, however, between the amount of labor and capital being released by the shirt industry and the amount being absorbed into the computer industry. The imbalance arises because the two industries use labor and capital in different proportions. The labor-intensive shirt industry uses a lot of labor and little capital, so, as it shrinks, it releases a lot of labor and less capital. The capital-intensive computer industry employs lots of capital and less labor, so, as it expands, it demands more capital and less labor than the shirt industry is releasing.

Consequently, the price of capital and labor will change. More capital is being demanded than is being released, causing the price of capital to rise. People who own capital, therefore, now earn a higher return than they did prior to trade with China. Less labor is being demanded than is being released, causing the price of labor to fall. Workers, therefore, now earn less than they did prior to trade with China. For the United States, then, trade with China causes the return to capital to rise and wages to fall.

The same dynamic is taking place in China, but in the opposite direction. As demand for Chinese computers falls, Chinese firms manufacture fewer computers. As computer production falls, Chinese computer manufacturers liquidate the capital they have invested in computer factories and lay off their employees. Chinese shirt firms are expanding in response to the growing demand in the United States, and they demand more capital and labor. The Chinese shirt industry thus absorbs capital and labor released from the computer industry.

Again, however, there is an imbalance between the factors being released and those being demanded. The computer industry uses lots of capital and little labor, so, as it shrinks, it releases lots of capital and only a little labor. Yet, the shirt industry employs a lot of labor and relatively little capital. So, as it expands, it demands more labor and less capital than the computer industry releases.

Consequently, the relative prices of capital and labor change. More labor is being demanded than is being released, causing the price of labor to rise. Less capital is demanded than is being released, causing the price of capital to fall. Trade with the United States has caused the wages earned by Chinese workers to rise and the return to Chinese capital to fall.

Trade between the United States and China has thus caused changes in the incomes earned by workers and capitalists in both countries. We can be very precise about which factor incomes rise and which factor incomes fall as a result of trade. In both the United States and China, the income of the scarce factor falls while the income of the abundant factor rises. Thus, abundant American capital and abundant Chinese labor both gain from trade; scarce American labor and scarce Chinese capital both lose.

We can state this relationship more generally. Trade raises the income of society's abundant factor and reduces the income of society's scarce factor. If we allow this trade to continue uninterrupted, then, over time, factor incomes in the United States and China will equalize. That is, wages for American workers will fall and wages for Chinese workers will rise, until wages in the two countries are the same. The return to capital in the two countries will also equalize. The return to Chinese capital will fall and the return to American capital will rise, until the return to capital in the two countries is the same. The tendency for trade to cause factor prices to converge is known as **factor-price equalization** (or the **Stolper-Samuelson theorem,** in honor of the two economists—Paul Samuelson and Wolfgang Stolper—who first recognized this consequence of trade in the mid-1940s). Factor price equalization is a powerful statement about the distributional consequences of trade.

Trade policy preferences follow directly from these income effects. Because trade causes the scarce factor's income to fall, scarce factors want to minimize trade. Scarce factors thus demand high tariffs in order to protect the domestic market from imports. Because trade causes the abundant factor's income to rise, abundant factors want to maximize trade. Abundant factors thus prefer low tariffs in order to capture the gains from trade. In the United States and other advanced industrialized countries, the factor model predicts that owners of capital (the abundant factor) will prefer liberal trade

POLICY ANALYSIS AND DEBATE

Trade Adjustment

Question

How should governments respond to the economic dislocation caused by trade?

Overview

Most economists believe that trade does not change the *number* of jobs in the local economy. Instead, trade changes the *kinds* of jobs that are available. Jobs in import-competing industries disappear as firms shut down or move offshore. In the meantime, jobs are created in export-oriented industries. The jobs created offset the jobs lost. The jobs being created are quite different from the ones that are eliminated. In North Carolina, for example, trade has eliminated low-skilled jobs in the apparel industry while creating high-skilled jobs in high-technology industries. Society as a whole is much better off over the long run with these high-paying jobs than it is with low-paying jobs.

In the short run, however, the inevitable adjustment creates some real policy dilemmas. It is difficult for workers to move from low-skilled to high-skilled jobs. Typically, low-skilled workers have a high school education at best and in many instances are 40 years old or older. This segment of the population finds it very difficult to become employed in high-technology industries. Moreover, even if it weren't so difficult, many would find it necessary to abandon the communities in which they were born and raised in order to take a job in a new town. What policies should governments use to manage this trade adjustment problem?

Policy Options

*   **Protectionism:** Governments should raise tariffs or use other means to protect industries threatened by import competition. By protecting industries from import competition, this policy would protect the most vulnerable from the forces of economic dislocation.
*   **Adjustment Assistance:** Governments should establish programs to retrain workers. By offering such programs, this policy would help workers move from declining to expanding industries with less difficulty.

Policy Analysis

*   What are the costs and the benefits of each policy?
*   Who pays the costs for each policy?
*   Is one policy more feasible politically than the other? If so, why?

What Do You Think?

*   Which policy do you advocate? Justify your choice.
*   What criticisms of your position would you anticipate? How would you defend your recommendation against those criticisms?

Resources

Online: Do an online search for U.S. government trade adjustment policy. Compare the U.S. approach with that of another country. (Sweden provides a strong contrast). Search for the terms "trade adjustment assistance Sweden" and "labor market policy Sweden".

Continued

In Print: Alan V. Deardorff and Robert Stern. 2000. *The Social Dimensions of U.S. Trade Policy* (Ann Arbor, MI: University of Michigan Press); Susan M. Collins, ed. 1998. *Imports, Exports, and the American Worker.* (Washington, DC: The Brookings Institution).

policies while workers (the scarce factor) will prefer protectionist trade policies. In developing countries, the factor model predicts that labor will prefer liberal trade policies while owners of capital will prefer protection. Because trade's income effects divide society along factor lines, trade politics will be driven by unending conflict between labor and business (or capital). Since this competition pits workers against capitalists, the factor model is often called a class-based model of trade politics.

The factor model highlights the economic interests driving the political debate over globalization. The factor model suggests that the debate over globalization is a conflict over the distribution of national income between American labor and American business. Because trade reduces the income of American workers, these workers and the organizations that represent them have an incentive to oppose further liberalization and to advocate more protectionist policies. And indeed, American labor unions have been highly critical of globalization. The AFL-CIO, a federation of 64 labor unions representing 13 million American workers, has been among the most prominent critics of globalization. While the AFL-CIO does not consider itself protectionist, it played a leading role in organizing the protest against the WTO in Seattle in December 1999. In addition, it has fought consistently to prevent the passage of fast-track authority. It is also highly critical of NAFTA and the proposed Free Trade Area of the Americas (FTAA).

Conversely, because trade raises the return to American capital, American businesses should be strong supporters of globalization. And American business has been highly supportive of globalization. The Business Roundtable, a business association composed of the chief executives of the largest American corporations, strongly supports globalization. It has been an active lobbyist for fast-track authority, it supports NAFTA and the FTAA, and it strongly supported China's entry into the WTO. The National Association of Manufacturers, which represents about 14,000 American manufacturing firms, also supports the WTO and regional trade arrangements.

Thus, American labor and capital demands reflect the income consequences that the factor model highlights. The scarce factor, American labor, opposes trade liberalization, while the abundant factor, American capital, supports it. At a broad level, American trade politics is driven by competition over national income between workers and capitalists.

Having depicted trade politics as class conflict, we conclude this section with an important qualification. The emergence of eternal conflict between workers and capitalists is based on the assumption, embodied in our simple two-factor model, that American labor is homogenous: All workers are identical. Workers are not homogeneous, however, and at a minimum, we must divide labor into distinct skill categories, such as low- and high-skilled workers, and treat each category as a distinct factor of production. A model that allows for different skill categories among workers yields different conclusions about trade's impact on the incomes of American workers. In such a model, trade still reduces the income of low-skilled U.S. workers; high-skilled workers, however, which are an abundant factor in the United States, would see their incomes rise.

Sector Incomes and Industry Conflict

The **sector model** argues that trade politics is driven by competition among industries. Industries have distinct preferences, because trade's income effects divide society along industry lines. Whenever tariffs are raised or lowered, wages and the return to capital employed in some industries both rise, while wages and the return to capital employed in other industries both fall. Trade, therefore, pits the workers and capitalists employed in one industry against the workers and capitalists employed in another industry in the conflict over the distribution of national income.

The sector model argues that trade divides society across industry, rather than factor, lines because the assumptions it makes about factor mobility are quite different from the assumptions embodied in the factor model. **Factor mobility** refers to the ease with which labor and capital can move from one industry to another. The **factor model** assumes that factors are highly mobile—that labor and capital can move easily from one industry to another. Thus, capital currently employed in the apparel industry can quickly be shifted to the computer industry. Similarly, workers currently engaged in apparel production can easily shift to computer production. When factors are mobile, peoples' economic interests are determined by their factor ownership. Workers care about what happens to labor, while capitalists care about the return to capital.

The sector model, by contrast, assumes that factors are not easily moved from one industry to another. Instead, factors are tied, or **specific** to, the sector in which they are currently employed. Thus, capital currently employed in apparel production is stuck in that industry and cannot easily move to the computer industry—for, of what use is a loom or a spinning machine in the computer industry? Workers also often have industry-specific skills that do not transfer easily from one sector to another. For example, a worker who has spent 15 years maintaining sophisticated automated looms and spinning machines in an apparel plant cannot easily transfer these skills to computer production. In addition, the geography of industry location often means that quitting a job in one industry to take a job in another requires workers to physically relocate. Shifting from apparel production to automobile production might require a worker to move from North Carolina to Michigan. Logistical obstacles to physical relocation can be insurmountable. A worker may not be able to sell his house because the decline of the local industry has contributed to a more general economic decline in his community. Complex social and psychological factors also intervene, as it is difficult to abandon the network of social relations that one has developed over many years. The combination of specific skills, logistical problems, and attachments to an established community means that labor cannot always move from one industry to another.

When factors are immobile, trade affects the incomes of all factors employed in a given industry in the same way. We can see why by returning to our U.S.–China example. Consider the apparel industry first. Shirt imports from China lead to less shirt production in the United States. Factories are closed and workers are laid off. As in the factor model, apparel workers see their incomes fall. In contrast to the factor model, however, the owners of capital employed in apparel production also see their incomes fall. Why? Because capital is immobile; therefore, capital employed in apparel production cannot move into the computer industry. As demand for American shirts falls, demand for capital employed in the American shirt industry must also fall. As it does, the return to this capital must fall as well. Thus, workers and business owners in the apparel sector both suffer from trade.

The same dynamics are evident in the computer industry. Trade's impact on the return to capital employed in that industry is similar to its impact in the factor model. As computer production expands, increasing demand for capital raises the return to capital employed in the computer industry. Trade's impact on the incomes of workers employed in the computer industry, however, is quite different from the factor model's prediction. The factor model tells us that computer workers see their incomes fall as they compete against the workers released by the apparel industry. With more people chasing fewer jobs, all workers' incomes fall. The sector model argues, to the contrary, that computer workers' incomes rise. Because labor is immobile, the workers released by the apparel industry cannot move into the computer industry. Greater demand for labor in the computer industry increases the wages paid to workers already employed in the industry. Thus, capital and labor employed in the American computer industry both gain from trade. When factors are immobile, therefore, the incomes of labor and capital employed in a particular sector rise and fall together.

When factors are immobile, it makes little sense to speak of a unified labor interest or of a unified capital interest. Workers don't have common trade policy interests. The apparel worker loses from trade; the computer worker gains. Nor do capitalists have common policy interests. Roger Milliken, owner of the world's largest privately owned textile firm, Milliken & Company, and Michael Dell, founder of Dell Computers, have very different trade interests. Milliken loses from trade while Dell gains. Instead, interests are defined in terms of the industry in which people work or have invested their capital. Apparel workers and Roger Milliken will have a common interest in trade policy. Computer workers and Michael Dell will have a common interest in trade policy. Trade politics is then driven by competition between, on the one hand, the workers and capitalists who gain from trade, and on the other, the workers and capitalists who lose. The result is not class conflict, but conflict between industries.

We can be very precise about which industries gain and which lose from trade. Labor and capital employed in industries that rely intensively on society's abundant factor (i.e., the country's comparatively advantaged industries) both gain from trade. In the advanced industrialized countries, this means that labor and capital employed in capital-intensive and high-technology industries, such as computers, pharmaceuticals, and biotechnology, gain from trade. As a group, these industries are referred to as the **export-oriented sector.** Conversely, labor and capital employed in industries that rely intensively on society's scarce factor (i.e., the country's comparatively disadvantaged industries) lose from trade. In the advanced industrialized countries, this means that the incomes of owners of capital and workers employed in labor-intensive sectors, such as apparel and footwear, will fall as a result of trade. As a group, these industries are commonly referred to as the **import-competing sector.** Thus, the sector model argues that trade politics is driven by competition between the import-competing and export-oriented sectors.

The sector model adds a nuance to our understanding of the political debate over globalization. Whereas the factor model suggests that the debate over globalization pits labor against capital, the sector model suggests that this political debate often pits capital and labor in import-competing industries against capital and labor in export-oriented industries. We might expect, therefore, that UNITE (the Union of Needle-trades, Industrial and Textile Employees), the principal union in the American apparel industry, and the American Textile Manufacturers Institute, a business association representing U.S. textile firms, would both oppose globalization. Indeed, that is what we find. UNITE has been a vocal opponent of NAFTA, of the FTAA, and of fast-track authority. For its part, the American Textile Manufacturers Institute (ATMI) has not been critical of all trade agreements, but it has opposed free-trade agreements with South Korea and Singapore, has been highly critical of the American decision to grant China permanent normal trade status, and does not support further opening of the U.S. market to foreign textiles through multilateral trade negotiations (ATMI 2001). In general, labor and capital employed in textile and apparel are both skeptical of globalization.

By contrast, the sector model predicts that capital and labor employed in export-oriented industries will both support globalization. It is relatively easy to document such support among American export-oriented firms. A coalition of business associations representing U.S. high-technology firms—including the Consumer Electronics Association, Electronic Industries Alliance, Information Technology Industry Council, MultiMedia Telecommunications Association, and Semiconductor Industry Association—has supported fast-track authority, the approval of normal trade relations with China, NAFTA, and the FTAA. It is more difficult to document attitudes of workers employed in these industries, in large part because those workers are not organized to the same extent as low- and medium-skilled workers in manufacturing industries. However, workers in high-technology industries are predominantly high skilled, and, on average, high-skilled workers are more supportive of trade liberalization than are low-skilled workers (Scheve and Slaughter 2001). While this is indirect evidence, it is consistent with the prediction that both labor and capital employed in American high-technology industries will support globalization.

The factor and sector models thus both argue that trade policy preferences are determined by the income consequences of trade. Trade raises the incomes of some groups and lowers the incomes of others. Those who gain from trade prefer trade liberalization, while those who lose prefer protectionism. Each model, however, offers a distinct pattern of trade policy preferences, based on distinct conceptions of how the income effects of trade divide society. (See Table 4.1.) The factor model states that trade divides society across factor lines; consequently, trade politics is driven by conflict between labor and capital. The sector model states that trade divides society along sector lines; consequently, trade politics is driven by conflict between import-competing and export-oriented industries. These distinct patterns are based on the assumptions each model makes about factor mobility. The factor model assumes that factors are highly mobile; therefore, people define their interests in terms of factor ownership.

Table 4.1
Two Models of Interest-Group Competition over Trade Policy

	The Factor Model	The Sector Model
The principal actors	Factors of production or classes	Industries or sectors
How mobile are factors of production?	Perfectly mobile across sectors of the economy	Immobile across sectors of the economy
Who wins and who loses from international trade?	*Winner:* Abundant factor—capital in the advanced industrialized countries	*Winner:* Labor and capital employed in export-oriented industries
	Loser: Scarce factor—labor in the advanced industrialized countries	*Loser:* Labor and capital employed in import-competing sectors
Central dimension of competition over trade policy	Protectionist labor *versus* Liberalizing capital	Protectionist import-competing industries *versus* Liberalizing export-oriented industries

The sector model assumes that factors are immobile; thus, people define their interests in terms of the industry in which they earn their living.

Organizing Interests: The Collective Action Problem and Trade Policy Demands

Individuals' preferences are not transformed automatically into political pressure for specific trade policies. Transforming individual preferences into political demands requires that the individuals who share a common preference organize in order to exert influence on the policy-making process. Organizing can be difficult, however—so difficult, in fact, that groups with common interests may not organize at all. This idea might seem counterintuitive; if trade affects incomes in predictable ways, and if people are rational, then why wouldn't people with common interests join forces to lobby for their desired policy? The answer is that groups often can't organize because they confront a **collective action problem** (Olson 1965).

Collective action problems arise from a phenomenon called **free riding**—situations in which an individual relies on others to bear the costs of a program from which the individual derives benefits (Sandler 1992, 17). My experience with public radio offers an excellent example. My local public radio station uses voluntary contributions from its listeners and businesses to finance 87 percent of its budget. Without these voluntary contributions, the station would go off the air. As a regular listener, I benefit immensely from the station's existence, and my life would be greatly diminished were the station shut down. Yet I have never contributed to the station. Instead, I rely upon others to pay for the station's operations. In other words, I free ride on other listeners' contributions. My behavior is not unique; 80 percent of listeners never contribute.

Free riding occurs because, in any large group with a common objective, all group members will realize benefits once the common objective has been achieved. Yet the contribution each individual makes toward this goal is too small to affect the final outcome. In my case, I recognize that whether I do or do not contribute $100 to the radio station is unlikely to determine whether the station continues to operate or is shut down.

Now consider the more meaningful example of consumers and trade policy. As a group, the 200 million or so consumers that live in the United States would all gain from free trade. These 200 million people thus have a common interest in unilateral trade liberalization. To achieve this goal, however, consumers will have to lobby the government. Such lobbying is costly: money is required to create an organization, to pay for a lobbyist, and to contribute to politicians' campaigns, and time must be dedicated to fund-raising and organizing. No individual consumer has an incentive to pay these costs.

Instead, most consumers will perform the following very simple calculation: My contribution to this campaign will make no perceptible difference to the group's ability to achieve free trade. Moreover, I will benefit from free trade if the group is successful, regardless of whether I have or have not contributed. Therefore, I will let other consumers spend their money and time; that is, I will ride for free.

Because all consumers have an incentive to free ride, no one contributes time and money, no one lobbies, and consumer interests fail to influence trade policy. Thus, even though consumers share a common goal, the collective action problem prevents them from exerting pressure on politicians to achieve that goal. And what is true for consumers is true for all groups with a common interest. The incentive to free ride makes collective action in pursuit of a common goal very difficult.

The severity of the collective action problem depends in part upon the size of the group. In large groups, each individual contribution is very small relative to the total contribution, and as a result, each individual has only a small impact on the ability of the group to achieve its objective. Consequently, each individual can conclude that the group can succeed without his or her contribution. In large groups, therefore, the incentive to free ride faced by each individual is very strong, and large groups face severe collective action problems. In small groups, each individual contribution is large relative to the total contribution; therefore, each contribution has a greater impact on the group's ability to achieve its common goal. It then becomes more difficult for any individual to conclude that the group can succeed without his or her contribution. As a result, the incentive to free ride is weaker in (though not altogether absent from) small groups. Thus, we would expect organization to be easier as the size of the group with a common interest shrinks.

The logic of collective action helps us understand three important characteristics of trade politics. First, it helps us understand why producers, rather than consumers, dominate trade politics. Consumers are a large and homogenous group, and each individual consumer faces a strong incentive to free ride. Consequently, contributions to a "Consumers for Free Trade" interest group are substantially less than the underlying common interest in free trade would seem to dictate. In contrast, most industries are made up of a relatively small number of firms. Producer groups can thus more readily organize to lobby the government in pursuit of their desired trade policies. The logic of collective action helps us understand why producers' interests dominate trade politics while consumer interests are often neglected.

Second, the logic of collective action suggests that trade politics will exhibit a bias toward protectionism. A tariff provides large benefits to the few firms producing in the protected industry. The costs of a tariff, however, are distributed across a large number of individuals and firms. A higher tariff on steel, for example, provides large benefits to the relatively small number of American steel producers and their workers. By contrast, the costs of a steel tariff fall on everyone who consumes steel—a group that includes most American consumers, as well as all firms that use steel as an input in their production processes. The small group of steel producers that benefit from the higher tariff can fairly easily overcome the collective action problem to lobby for protection. The large and heterogeneous group that bears the costs of the tariff finds it much more difficult to organize for collective action. Given these differing abilities to organize, trade politics is dominated by import-competing industries demanding protection.

Finally, the logic of collective action helps us understand why governments rarely liberalize trade unilaterally, but have been willing to do so through negotiated agreements. Reciprocal trade agreements make it easier for export-oriented industries to overcome the collective action problem. (See Bailey et al. 1997; Gilligan 1997; Milner 1988.) Reciprocal trade agreements provide large benefits in the form of access to foreign markets to small groups of export-oriented firms. Reducing foreign tariffs on microprocessors for personal computers, for example, provides substantial gains to the three American firms that dominate this industry: Intel, Advanced Micro Devices (AMD), and Motorola. These three firms will solve the collective action problem they face and lobby for trade liberalization at home in exchange for the removal of foreign barriers to their exports.

Reciprocal trade agreements thus transform the large and heterogeneous pro-liberalization interests into smaller groups of export-oriented industries that can more easily organize to pursue common goals. This transformation in turn alters the balance of interest-group pressure that politicians face. Whereas only protectionist interests lobby when the government sets trade policy unilaterally, both protectionists and liberalizers mobilize when the government negotiates international agreements. More balanced political pressures make politicians more willing to liberalize trade.

In a society-centered approach, therefore, trade politics is driven by competition among organized interest groups. And while this competition sometimes revolves around class conflict that pits workers against business owners, and at other times revolves around industry conflict that pits import-competing industries against export-oriented industries, the core conflict in, and the ultimate stakes of, the competition are always and everywhere the same: in competing over trade policy, interest groups are fighting to distribute national income. The stakes of this competition are high for all involved. The winners are rewarded with rising incomes. The losers become poorer.

Political Institutions and Interests in American Trade Politics

Political institutions shape how competition among organized interests unfolds. They do so by establishing rules that influence the way people behave. These rules influence how people organize and thus determine whether interests organize around factor or industry lines. Rules influence how organized interests exert pressure on the political process and determine whether interest groups lobby the legislature or whether they exert influence through political parties. Rules influence which interests politicians must respond to and thus determine which interests gain representation and which do not. Because political institutions shape the way people behave, they have an important impact on who ultimately wins the battle over national income.

Understanding how political institutions shape this competition requires us to examine the interaction between trade policy interests and political institutions in a particular case. We adopt that approach here, examining the interplay between interests and institutions in American trade politics. The American case provides a fascinating example of how a coalition of export-oriented interests that were determined to pursue a liberal trade policy in the context of political institutions biased toward protectionism created new political institutions that made trade liberalization possible.

A coalition of export-oriented interests has provided the political support for post-war trade liberalization in the United States. This coalition emerged in 1932 under the banner of the Democratic party. The New Deal realignment of the early 1930s brought capital-intensive manufacturing, export-oriented agriculture, and organized labor (most of which was based in capital-intensive manufacturing) together in support of Franklin D. Roosevelt's bid for the presidency. (See Ferguson 1984; Frieden 1988.) In the 1932 elections, the Democrats captured the White House and gained majorities in the House and Senate.

While this coalition of export-oriented interests had a clear interest in trade liberalization, there was little chance that they could rely upon congressional legislation to achieve their objective. Indeed, at the onset of the Great Depression in 1930, Congress had passed the protectionist **Smoot-Hawley Act,** which raised the average tariff to a historic high of almost 60 percent (Pastor 1980, 77–78).

The problem the pro-liberalizing coalition faced extended well beyond Smoot-Hawley and in fact lay deep within the institutional foundations of American politics. To fully understand the problem, we need to look at these institutions in some detail. First, the rules governing American elections play a large role in shaping how groups organize and how interests are brought into the political system. The American electoral system is based on single-member districts: the nation is divided into mutually exclusive electoral districts, and one person is elected to represent each district. To win elections in this system, politicians must satisfy the demands of their districts' residents, who typically are employed in only a small number of industries. The wages paid in these industries will in turn play a large role in supporting the rest of the district economy—the retail and service-sector businesses that provide jobs for many other people in the community.

Such electoral systems create incentives for groups to organize around narrow industry lines, and they create incentives for elected officials to represent the narrow interests of the industries in their districts. Moreover, if the logic of collective action is right, then legislators will face unbalanced pressures within their districts: industries needing protection will be most likely to organize, while groups that benefit from trade liberalization are least likely to do so. Consequently, American electoral institutions create strong incentives for elected officials to bring the narrow industry-specific interests of import-competing industries into Congress.

In Congress, legislative dynamics practically guarantee that any effort to protect a single industry will be transformed into legislation that protects lots of industries. To see why this is so, suppose that a representative from Pennsylvania introduces legislation to raise tariffs on steel. A higher steel tariff would benefit a few steel producers in a few congressional districts, but it would also impose costs on all of the districts that do not produce, but do consume, steel. In order to get representatives from Michigan (where the auto industry is very important and is a large steel consumer) to vote for a higher steel tariff, the representative from Pennsylvania will have to support a high tariff on automobiles. The initial legislation is thus transformed into a bill that raises tariffs on steel *and* cars. Other legislators will now ask for higher tariffs for industries in their districts as the price for their support for this bill. Accordingly, the legislation is again amended to add higher tariffs for still more goods. This dynamic, a process that has been called **logrolling,** produces a final tariff bill that raises tariffs on a much larger number of items than any individual legislator desires.

That is precisely what happened under the Smoot-Hawley Act. Initial legislation proposed only a moderate increase in tariffs on farm products. Once that legislation entered Congress, however, legislators from farm districts dominated by small farmers facing competition from imported potatoes, cream, butter, and eggs joined forces with legislators from districts dominated by labor-intensive manufacturers of such items as shoes, watches, apparel, gloves, and some luxury goods. As a result of this coalition, the bill was amended more than a thousand times in the Senate and wound up raising tariffs on almost 20,000 items in the American tariff schedule (Pastor 1980, 78; Eichengreen 1989b).

Legislators cannot easily escape this logrolling dynamic. While all may want to limit the amount of protection granted to industries outside their own districts, each recognizes that a refusal to support protection for industries in other districts will cause other legislators to refuse to support protection for industries in his or her own district. As one senator stated in the debate over the Smoot-Hawley Act, "I will not vote for a tariff upon the products of another State if the Senators from that State vote against protecting the industries of any State" (quoted in Pastor 1980, 80).

Cordell Hull, a staunch proponent of free trade who had represented Tennessee in the House and then the Senate before becoming Roosevelt's secretary of state, recognized that congressional dynamics limited the prospects for durable trade liberalization: "It would have been folly to go to Congress and ask that Smoot-Hawley be repealed or its rates reduced. . . . This [approach had] . . . always resulted in higher tariffs because the special interests enriched by the tariffs went to their respective congressmen and insisted on higher rates" (quoted in Destler 1986, 13). As the export-oriented coalition thus contemplated how to achieve trade liberalization in the early 1930s, it recognized that durable trade liberalization could be achieved only by institutional change that removed the tariff-setting authority from Congress.

In particular, tariff-setting authority had to be shifted from Congress to the executive, which was more likely than Congress to pursue a liberal trade policy because the executive operates within a different institutional context. First, the president represents a national constituency rather than a single district. Because legislators represent

A CLOSER LOOK

Trade Politics in the European Union

National governments do not fully control trade policy in the European Union. Instead, the union's founding document, the Treaty of Rome, gives the European Commission the authority to determine European Union trade policy toward non-members. Because it is a customs union, the European Union imposes a common external tariff on imports entering the union from outside. In WTO negotiations, therefore, the European Union negotiates as a single actor, and it is the European Commission that conducts these negotiations on behalf of all of the member governments.

The ability of the commission to exercise its authority over trade policy is limited, however, by the political and institutional relationships within which it operates. (See Hayes 1993, 15; Schuknecht 1992, 37; Johnson 1998; Meunier and Nikolaidis 1999; Nugent 1994.) Of particular importance in this regard is the Council of Ministers, the European Union's principal decision-making body. In the context of trade policy, the Council of Ministers is composed of the trade ministers of each of the European Union member governments, and these trade ministers set the parameters within which the commission must operate as it negotiates in the WTO or in other international arenas.

The process works in the following manner: The Commission develops a general set of recommendations for a proposed round of multilateral negotiations. In developing these recommendations, it works closely with the "Article 113 Committee," which is an EU committee composed of national civil servants, usually the national trade ministers' top aides (Gray 1985). The commission's recommendations are then submitted to the Council of Ministers for approval. Often, such approval is accompanied by strict limits on the ability of the Commission to make concessions that extend beyond the agreed recommendation. As a consequence, when the commission is faced with the need to make a large concession to achieve one of its objectives in the WTO, it will usually have to go back to the Council of Ministers to gain the approval of national governments. Thus, even though the EU Commission has legal authority over trade policy, it exercises this authority under the close scrutiny of the union's member governments.

The trade policy objectives that EU member governments instruct the Commission to pursue reflect the demands placed upon these national governments by domestic interest groups. While it is impossible to trace such demands in each of the 25-member countries, we can sketch out the basic pattern of demands that is present in the European Union. As in the United States and Japan, export-oriented industries in capital-intensive manufacturing and services have lobbied for multilateral trade liberalization. But there have been important exceptions, as mature capital-intensive manufacturing industries such as steel and automobiles have grown increasingly protectionist in the face of international competition. As in the United States and Japan, internationally traded services—particularly financial services based in London and Frankfurt—have lobbied for liberalization of trade in services since the early 1980s. Again in parallel with the United States and Japan, politically influential import-competing manufacturers have lobbied for protection and against multilateral liberalization. European-based textile and apparel industries have been

Continued

the most important opponents of liberalization, as they have been in the United States and, increasingly, in Japan. European firms in high-technology sectors have also been at a disadvantage internationally and have therefore been ambivalent about liberalization. Finally, European agriculture is not competitive internationally, and EU farmers have lobbied consistently for protection. As a consequence, European agriculture is heavily protected from foreign competition. Overall, EU trade policies reflect a pattern of societal group interests quite similar to what we see in Japan: capital-intensive manufacturing and service industries promote liberalization, while labor-intensive manufacturing industries, high-technology sectors, and agriculture promote protection.

single districts, they can gain the benefits of a higher tariff for producers based in their districts and impose the costs of that tariff on people and businesses living outside their districts. By contrast, the president has nowhere to push the costs of protection, because his constituency extends into every district. Consequently, the president must weigh the benefits that a tariff provides to one district against the cost it imposes on other districts. Because the president must incorporate the costs of a tariff into his calculation, he will prefer less protectionism than the typical legislator will.

In addition, the executive can reduce tariffs by negotiating reciprocal agreements with foreign governments. As we have seen, such reciprocal agreements create an incentive for export-oriented interests to organize and lobby for trade liberalization. The entry of pro-liberalizing groups alters the balance of interest-group pressure and makes legislators more willing to support liberalization. The executive is thus more likely than Congress to pursue a liberal trade policy and, by doing so through negotiated agreements, can generate the political support that liberalization requires.

The Roosevelt administration proposed such institutional change in 1933, and Congress responded by passing the **Reciprocal Trade Agreements Act** (RTAA) of 1934. Under this legislation, Congress delegated to the executive the authority to reduce tariffs by as much as 50 percent, in exchange for equivalent concessions from foreign governments. Why would a Congress so intent on raising tariffs in 1930 pass legislation only four years later that authorized the executive to lower tariffs?

Students of American trade policy have suggested a number of explanations for this reversal. Some have argued that Congress passed the RTAA because it recognized that it was producing bad trade policy (Destler 1995; Lohman and O'Halloran 1994). As foreign governments raised tariffs on American exports in retaliation for the Smoot-Hawley Act, and as the American and world economies fell deeper into depression, it became clear that high tariffs were contributing to the economic crisis. Aware that they could not escape the political logic that led to protectionism, legislators delegated authority to the executive "to protect themselves from the direct one-sided pressure from producer interests that had led them to make bad law" (Destler 1995, 14).

Others argue that the liberal emphasis of the RTAA resulted from shifting congressional majorities (Pastor 1980). The Republican party, which was the party of protection throughout the nineteenth and early twentieth centuries, held a majority of seats in Congress in 1930 and used it to pass the protectionist Smoot-Hawley Act. The

Republicans lost the majority to the Democrats in both the House and Senate in the 1932 elections, however. Democrats used their majority to pass trade-liberalizing legislation. The Smoot-Hawley Act and the RTAA simply represented a continuation of a longer historical pattern in which Republican majorities raised protection and Democrat majorities lowered it.

Still others highlight the importance of the RTAA itself (Bailey, Goldstein, and Weingast 1997), arguing that, even though the Democrats enjoyed a congressional majority after 1932, they did not have enough votes to reduce American tariffs unilaterally. Many Democrats at the time believed that unilateral tariff reductions would generate a flood of imports and, consequently, that support for legislation which proposed unilateral reductions would be "politically dangerous" (Bailey, Goldstein, and Weingast 1997, 317). Yet, by linking reductions in American tariffs to the opening of foreign markets to American exporters, the RTAA created a large congressional coalition in support of trade liberalization: "It [was] easier to build majority support for reductions (and harder to form a coalition to negate an agreement) when tariffs [were] coupled with changes in access to foreign markets" (Bailey, Goldstein, and Weingast 1997, 318). In short, reciprocal agreements created an incentive for export-oriented firms to lobby their representatives. This incentive in turn balanced the interest-group pressures that legislators faced.

While each of these explanations highlights a different reason for the passage of the RTAA, all agree that the act represented an important change in the institutional framework governing American trade politics. By delegating authority for trade policy to the executive, Congress removed tariffs from a legislative process that made sustained liberalization difficult. This institutional change has had a lasting impact on American trade politics, as the basic approach initiated in 1934 remains at the center of such politics. (See Table 4.2.) As a result, Congress has not voted on a comprehensive tariff act since 1930. Instead, U.S. tariffs have been changed through GATT/WTO negotiations and through administrative procedures. In short, postwar trade liberalization was made possible through the interaction between the interests of export-oriented producers and institutional change that reduced congressional influence over tariffs.

Congress did not give the executive a completely free hand in trade policy. Instead, Congress has continued to influence trade policy by setting the parameters within which the executive operates. (See O'Halloran 1994.) This has been achieved in part by writing explicit constraints on executive action into the legislation delegating authority and in part by delegating authority only for short periods of time. The 1934 RTAA, for example, authorized the president to reduce American tariffs only by 50 percent, and even this authority expired after three years. Subsequent extensions adopted essentially the same approach.

In addition, in a practice that began with the 1974 Trade Act, Congress began to require all agreements negotiated under this delegated authority to be ratified by Congress under the **fast-track** procedure. Congress instituted fast track because the GATT's Tokyo Round focused on a number of issues that required changes to American trade law. Of particular concern were negotiations on antidumping and countervailing-duty investigations. Congress was unwilling to give prior consent to any changes to American laws that might emerge from the Tokyo Round. At the same time, it could not easily establish parameters within which the executive would have to negotiate.

Table 4.2
Important American Trade Legislation, 1934–2002

Legislation	President
1934 Reciprocal Trade Agreements Act (RTAA)	Roosevelt
1937 RTAA Extension	Roosevelt
1940 RTAA Extension	Roosevelt
1943 RTAA Extension	Roosevelt
1945 RTAA Extension	Roosevelt
1948 RTAA Extension	Truman
1949 RTAA Extension	Truman
1951 RTAA Extension	Truman
1953 RTAA Extension	Eisenhower
1954 RTAA Extension	Eisenhower
1955 RTAA Extension	Eisenhower
1958 RTAA Extension	Eisenhower
1962 Trade Expansion Act	Kennedy
1974 Trade Act	Nixon
1979 Trade Agreements Act	Carter
1984 Trade and Tariff Act	Reagan
1988 Omnibus Trade Act	Reagan
2001 Trade Policy Authority Act	Bush

The solution was to allow the executive to negotiate, but to require Senate approval of the resulting agreement. In setting these broad parameters on executive action in conjunction with the delegated authority, Congress ensures that its concerns are taken into account during negotiations.

Congress also created a new agency inside the Executive Office of the President, called the **United States Trade Representative** (USTR), to lead and coordinate American trade policy. During the early postwar period, the State Department took the lead in GATT negotiations. By the late 1950s, however, Congress was becoming concerned that the State Department was not the best representative of American commercial interests. Too often, the congressional leadership argued, State Department officials viewed trade negotiations through the lens of America's broader foreign policy objectives. As a consequence, the State Department was frequently willing to achieve these broader foreign policy goals by sacrificing the interests of American industries, in essence opening American markets without gaining equivalent access to foreign markets.

To ensure that American commercial interests were well served in GATT negotiations, Congress created a new agency called the Special Trade Representative (STR) as part of the 1962 Trade Expansion Act. The STR was to be the "chief representative of the United States during trade negotiations" and was to coordinate the positions of various executive branch agencies for these negotiations. In addition, Congress required the STR to seek advice from industry, agriculture, and labor during trade negotiations. In 1974, Congress made the USTR a statutory unit of the Executive Office and gave it its current name. Today, the USTR sets and administers U.S. trade policy, is the nation's chief trade negotiator, and represents the United States in the WTO and other international trade organizations. Through all of these mechanisms, Congress has maintained a considerable degree of influence over how the executive uses the trade policy authority that Congress delegates.

Congress has also continued to influence trade policy by responding to demands from import-competing industries. Rather than responding to these demands by directly raising tariffs, however, Congress established a rule-based system of **administered protection** to consider the demands of individual industries. (See Goldstein 1986.) Industries can seek protection through two different administrative channels.

First, an industry can pursue protection through the "escape clause" included in American trade legislation (Sections 201 and 204 of the 1974 Trade Act) and embodied in Article XIX of GATT. Article XIX states that governments can provide protection if "any product is being imported . . . in such increased quantities and under such conditions as to cause or threaten serious injury to domestic producers." To gain import protection via this remedy, the industry must file a case with the U.S. International Trade Commission (ITC), an independent and nonpartisan quasi-judicial federal agency that provides trade expertise to Congress and the executive. The ITC then conducts an investigation to determine whether imports are causing substantial damage to the industry in question. If the ITC determines that imports are causing substantial harm to the industry, it recommends to the executive that relief be granted. The executive then decides whether to provide such relief. When President George W. Bush raised tariffs on imported steel in the spring of 2002, for example, he did so on the basis of an ITC investigation undertaken during 2001 under Section 201 of the 1974 Trade Act.

Second, a firm can apply for protection in cases of "unfair trade"—cases in which a foreign firm is dumping goods in the American market or a foreign government is subsidizing the production or export of a good. Petitions for relief from unfair trade go through a two-stage administrative process. In the first stage, the Commerce Department determines whether foreign firms are dumping or a foreign government is providing subsidies. If the department finds evidence of such practices, the case then goes to the ITC, which determines whether dumping or subsidies are a cause of substantial injury to the domestic industry. If the ITC and the Commerce Department both reach positive findings, then the tariff is raised to offset the margin of dumping or the subsidy. This system of administered protection allows industry demands for protection to be handled on a case-by-case basis within a system guided by legal rules and administrative procedures.

In short, desiring liberalization, but facing a legislative process that made liberalization difficult, politicians representing export-oriented interests created political institutions that reduced the role played by Congress in making American trade policy. The interaction between societal interests and these institutional arrangements then created a political system within which trade liberalization could be lastingly achieved. This institutional framework allowed the United States to participate in GATT, and through the GATT process, the United States progressively reduced barriers to trade. It is unlikely that the United States would have been able to pursue a trade policy that was as durably liberal in the absence of that institutional change.

Thus, the creation of institutions that limited the role played by Congress in trade policy has been a critically important aspect of postwar trade liberalization. Equally important was the process established for handling industry demands for protection. Individual demands could not simply be ignored, because the affected industries might then build a legislative coalition that reversed the liberal emphasis of American trade policy. The system of administered protection allowed demands for protection to be handled on a case-by-case basis. This in turn allowed protectionist pressure to be diverted away from the legislature, where congressional dynamics could generate broader protectionist legislation, and on to administrative agencies immune to such dynamics.

The preceding historical context makes it clear that the contemporary political debate over fast-track authority has implications that extend beyond the terms under which the United States participates in the current round of WTO negotiations. This debate suggests that congressional support for the institutions that have made postwar liberalization possible may be weakening.

At the base of this weakening support lie some important changes in the interests of many American industries. As postwar reconstruction was completed in Europe and Japan, as American tariffs have been reduced, and as competitive manufacturing industries emerged in East Asia and Latin America, American industry began to confront a much more competitive economic environment. For many industries, tougher competition implied costly adjustment. As a consequence, some groups that had supported trade liberalization in the early postwar period increasingly became advocates of protectionism.

Perhaps chief among these groups is organized labor. Since the early 1970s, the AFL CIO has grown more critical of the pro-liberalization stance of American trade policy and has in many instances advocated a more protectionist policy. Mature capital-intensive manufacturing industries, such as the auto and steel industries, also have become less supportive of trade liberalization. These industries have repeatedly sought protection from foreign competition during the last 25 years. It is not surprising that the two groups of industries would become wary of liberalization. Most labor unions represent workers employed in mature capital-intensive manufacturing industries like the auto and steel industries, which have seen the comparative advantage they enjoyed in the years immediately following World War II gradually erode. Their change from export-oriented industries to import-competing industries has been accompanied by a change in their trade policy preferences.

Congress has been responsive to growing demands for protection. During the 1970s, Congress loosened the guidelines governing administered protection (Destler 1995, Chapter 6). These changes reduced the threshold for determining whether an industry was injured from imports. The previous standard required imports to be the major cause of injury; the new, much less stringent standard required imports to be a "substantial cause of injury or threat thereof" (Destler 1995, 143). Congress also granted the ITC more independence, greatly reduced the time frame within which petitions for relief had to be decided, and transferred the authority for investigating antidumping and countervailing-duty petitions from the Treasury Department to the Commerce Department, which it was believed would be more receptive to demands for protection (Destler 1995, 150). These changes made it easier for industries to get a positive finding and, therefore, made it more likely that firms facing import competition would petition for relief. As a result, petitions for relief, and the amount of relief provided, both rose sharply in the wake of the newly legislated reforms. (See Destler 1995, Chapter 6.)

The last 25 years have thus brought a trend of growing protectionist sentiment into Congress and growing congressional assertiveness in American trade policy. These changes in turn reflect changes in the balance of power among the industry groups that legislators represent: groups in import-competing industries appear to be growing in influence, and export-oriented industries seem to be experiencing a weakening of influence. The outcome of this political competition will in turn shape the future direction of American trade policy, in part by shaping the institutions through which that policy is made.

As the American case illustrates, using a society-centered approach to study trade politics requires us to examine the interplay between individual interests and political institutions. And when we apply this framework to particular countries, we need to be sensitive to how the specific political institutions in place give form to the competition among organized interests. If we were to study trade politics in a Western European country, for example, we might explore whether proportional representation electoral systems create incentives for groups to organize along factor rather than sector lines. We might explore whether competition among groups in the parliamentary systems common in Western Europe differs in predictable ways from competition within the American presidential system. We might explore whether there are other instances in which organized interests altered political institutions in order to achieve their trade policy objectives. And while such studies would produce different conclusions about how trade politics unfolds, all would share an identical underlying dynamic: trade politics is driven by competition among organized interests over the distribution of national income.

Conclusion

While a society-centered approach helps us understand how the interaction between societal interests and political institutions shapes trade politics, it does have weaknesses. We conclude our discussion of this approach by looking at the three most significant weaknesses. First, a society-centered approach does not explain trade policy outcomes. It tells us that trade politics will be characterized by conflict between the winners and losers from international trade, and it does a fine job telling us who the winners and losers will be. It does not help us, however, explain which of these groups will win the *political* battle. Presumably, a country's trade policy will embody the preferences of society's most powerful interests. To explain trade policy outcomes, therefore, we need to be able to evaluate the relative power of the competing groups. The society-centered approach provides little guidance about how to measure this balance of power. The temptation is to look at trade policy outcomes and infer that the most powerful groups are those whose preferences are reflected in that policy. Yet, looking at outcomes renders the approach tautological: we assume that the preferences of powerful groups are embodied in trade policy and then infer the power of individual groups from the content of trade policy. Thus, the society-centered approach is better at explaining why trade politics is characterized by competition among organized interests than at telling us why one group outperforms another in this competition for influence.

Second, the society-centered approach implicitly assumes that politicians have no independent trade policy objectives and play no autonomous role in trade politics. This assumption is probably misleading. Politicians are not simply passive recorders of interest-group pressures. As Ikenberry et al. (1988, 8) note, politicians and political institutions "can play a critical role in shaping the manner and the extent to which social forces can exert influence" on trade policy. Politicians do have independent trade policy objectives, and the constellation of interest groups that politicians confront is not fixed. Indeed, politicians can actively attempt to shape the configuration of interest-group pressures that they face. They can, for example, mobilize latent interest groups that have a preference for liberalization or protection by helping them overcome their collective action problem. By doing so, politicians can create coalitions of interest groups that support their own trade policy objectives. Political institutions also affect the extent to which societal groups can influence policy. In some countries, political institutions insulate politicians from interest-group pressures, thereby allowing the politicians to pursue their trade policy objectives independently of interest-group demands. We will examine this relationship in greater detail when we look at the state-centered approach in the next chapter.

Finally, the society-centered approach does not address the motivations of noneconomic actors in trade politics. Societal interest groups other than firms, business associations, and labor unions do attempt to influence trade policy. In the United States, for example, environmental groups have played a prominent role, shaping the specific content of the North American Free Trade Agreement and attempting to shape the negotiating agenda of the Doha Round. Human-rights groups have also become active participants in American trade politics, particularly with regard to America's relationship with China. Human-rights groups have consistently sought to deny Chinese producers access to the U.S. market in order to encourage the Chinese government to show greater respect for human rights. The assumption that trade politics is driven by the reactions of interest groups to the impact of international trade on their incomes provides little insight into the motivations of noneconomic groups. The society-centered approach tells us nothing about why groups that focus on the environment or on human rights spend resources attempting to influence trade policy. Nor does it provide any basis with which to make sense of such groups' trade policy preferences. In the past, such a weakness could perhaps be neglected, because noneconomic groups played only a small role in trade politics. The contemporary backlash against globalization suggests, however, that these groups must increasingly be incorporated into society-centered models of trade politics.

While we recognize that these weaknesses of the society-centered approach are important, they are not reasons to reject the approach. The appropriate measure of any theory or approach is not whether it incorporates everything that matters, or even whether it explains every outcome that we observe. All theories abstract from reality in order to focus more sharply on a number of key aspects. Consequently, the appropriate measure of any theory or approach is whether it is useful; that is, does it provide us with a deeper understanding of the enduring features of the phenomenon of interest?

On this measure, the society-centered approach scores high. By focusing on how trade shapes the fortunes of different groups in society, it forces us to recognize that the enduring features of trade politics revolve around a continual struggle for income between the winners and losers from international trade.

Key Terms

Administered Protection	Import-competing Sector
Collective Action Problem	Logrolling
Export-oriented Sector	Reciprocal Trade Agreements Act
Factor Mobility	Sector Model
Factor Model	Smoot-Hawley Act
Factor-Price Equalization	Specific (Factors)
Fast Track	Stolper-Samuelson Theorem
Free Riding	United States Trade Representative

Web Links

You can visit the United States Trade Representative at *http://www.ustr.gov.*
For the positions of American businesses on international trade, visit:
   The U.S. Trade Alliance at *http://www.us-trade.org/other/about_ustrade.htm.*
   The Business Round Table at *http://www.brtable.org/issue.cfm/9.*
For the positions of American unions on international trade, visit:
   The AFL-CIO at *www.afl-cio.org.*
   UNITE at *http://www.uniteunion.org/index.htm.*
The United Steelworkers of America maintain a number of trade-related websites that can be reached through *http://www.uswa.org/tradesites.html.*

Suggestions for Further Reading

For an excellent introduction and an interesting attempt to resolve the debate over the factor and sector models of trade policy preferences, see Michael Hiscox, *International Trade and Political Conflict: Commerce, Coalitions, and Mobility* (Princeton: Princeton University Press, 2002). For a deeper understanding of the collective action problem, it is hard to do better than the classic by Mancur Olson, *The Logic of Collective Action: Public Goods and the Theory of Groups* (Cambridge: Harvard University Press, 1965).

The literature on U.S. trade politics is enormous. The best available introduction is probably I. M. Destler, *American Trade Politics*, 3rd ed. (Washington, DC: Institute for International Economics, 1992). Unfortunately, there has been much less written in English on the trade policy process in the European Union and Japan. For the European Union, see John P. Hayes, *Making Trade Policy in the European Community* (London: The MacMillan Press, 1993). For Japan, see Chikara Higashi, *Japanese Trade Policy Formulation* (New York: Praeger, 1983).

CHAPTER 5

A State-Centered Approach to Trade Politics

In October of 2004, the United States lodged a complaint with the World Trade Organization's dispute settlement mechanism in which it alleged that France, Britain, Germany, and Spain were illegally subsidizing the European commercial aircraft manufacturer Airbus SAS. The U.S. move punctuated a decade during which Airbus successfully challenged the American firm Boeing for dominance in the global market for commercial aircraft. Only 20 years ago, Airbus appeared to pose little threat to Boeing; Boeing jets commanded almost two-thirds of global commercial aircraft sales, while Airbus airliners captured only slightly more than 15 percent. As each year passed, however, Airbus drew closer until, early in the current decade, it finally caught up with Boeing, with each firm capturing roughly half of the global market. Within this changing market context, U.S. Trade Representative Robert Zoellick argued that, while subsidies to Airbus may once have been justified, that time had long since passed. The European Union quickly responded to the American complaint. Asserting that the American move was "obviously an attempt to divert attention from Boeing's self-inflicted decline," the union initiated a counterdispute with the WTO in which it alleged that Boeing was receiving "massive subsidies" of its own from the U.S. government (Pae 2004).

How do we make sense of this trade conflict? A society-centered approach suggests that we should look at the political influence of the industries concerned—and indeed, there is little doubt that Boeing has substantial influence in American politics. President George W. Bush explicitly acknowledged this influence during the 2004 campaign when he promised Boeing workers that he would end EU subsidies to Airbus even if he had to initiate a WTO dispute to do so. Yet, the conflict also raises issues that are not readily incorporated into the society-centered approach. In particular, this dispute isn't an instance of conflict between an American import-competing industry and a foreign export-oriented industry. Instead, the conflict is between two export-oriented firms battling over global market share. Moreover, the conflict does not revolve around one government's use of tariffs to protect domestic producers from foreign competition, but instead focuses on the use of government subsidies to support the domestic firm as it competes for global market share.

There is also a difference hinted at by Zoellick's statement: while there once may have been a justification for EU subsidies to Airbus, that time has now long passed. This statement suggests that there may be instances in which government intervention can raise social welfare and may thus be justified. Yet, the standard model of trade that provides the basis for the society-centered approach pretty much rules out such welfare-improving intervention. To fully understand the U.S.-EU trade conflict in the commercial aircraft industry, therefore, we have to broaden our understanding of the economics, and perhaps also the politics, of international trade.

We gain such a broader understanding in this chapter, by developing a state-centered approach to trade politics. A state-centered approach argues that national policymakers intervene in the economy in pursuit of objectives that are determined independently of domestic interest groups' narrow, self-interested concerns. Moreover, this approach suggests that intervention may (but need not) raise aggregate social welfare. We examine the state-centered approach with a particular focus on government intervention designed to promote the development of specific national industries. We look first at the broader economic justification for protectionism that is aimed at creating internationally competitive industries; then we narrow our focus to the use of such measures by the advanced industrialized countries in high-technology industries; finally, we apply the logic of this approach to the current U.S.–EU conflict in the commercial aircraft industry. We conclude the chapter by looking briefly at some of the weaknesses of the state-centered approach.

States and Industrial Policy

A state-centered approach is based on two central assumptions, both of which contrast sharply with the assumptions embodied in the society-centered approach. The first assumption concerns the impact of protectionism on aggregate social welfare. Whereas the society-centered approach argues that protectionism reduces social welfare by depriving society of the gains from trade and employing society's resources in comparatively disadvantaged industries, the state-centered approach argues that, under certain circumstances, trade protection can raise social welfare.

The second assumption concerns whether governments can operate independently of interest-group pressures. Whereas the society-centered approach argues that national policy reflects the balance of power among competing interest groups, the state-centered approach argues that, under specific circumstances, governments are relatively unconstrained by interest-group demands. As a consequence, a government's trade and economic policies embody the goals of national policymakers rather than the demands of domestic interest groups. The state-centered approach combines these two assumptions to suggest that, under a specific set of circumstances, governments will intervene in the domestic economy with tariffs, production subsidies, and other policy instruments in ways that raise aggregate social welfare.

To fully understand this approach, we need to understand the conditions under which such intervention may raise social welfare. We can then examine the institutional characteristics that enable national policymakers to act autonomously from interest groups in order to capture these welfare gains.

The Infant-Industry Case for Protection

The economic justification for the state-centered approach rests on the claim that targeted government intervention can increase aggregate social welfare. This claim stands in stark contrast to the conclusions drawn from the standard model of trade that we examined in Chapter 3 and extended in our discussion of the domestic adjustments to trade in Chapter 4. By assumption, the standard model rules out such welfare-increasing government intervention. In the standard model, society does best by removing all forms of trade protection and specializing in its comparatively advantaged industry. Maintaining protection merely deprives society of the welfare gains from trade.

Moreover, in the standard model, nothing makes it difficult for factors currently employed in comparatively disadvantaged industries to move into the comparatively advantaged sector. Factors of production will move into comparatively advantaged industries because it is profitable to do so: the returns in these industries are higher than the returns in the comparatively disadvantaged industries. The movement will take time, there will be adjustment costs, and there is a case to be made for government policies that help individuals manage these costs, but such policies are oriented toward shifting workers and resources into sectors where they would go anyway. In this model, tariffs and other forms of protection can only make society worse off by preventing factors from moving out of low-return and into high-return industries. In the world depicted by the standard trade models, therefore, government intervention cannot raise social welfare.

Accordingly, in order to claim that a tariff and other forms of government intervention raise social welfare, one must be able to demonstrate that something prevents factors from entering into industries that yield higher returns than are available in other sectors of the economy. Historically, this justification has been provided by the infant-industry case for protection. The **infant-industry case for protection** argues that there are cases in which newly created firms (infants, so to speak) will not *initially* be efficient, but could be efficient in the long run if they are given time to mature. Consequently, a short period of tariff protection will enable these industries to become efficient and begin to export. Once this point has been reached, the tariff can be removed. The long-run welfare gains created by the now-established industry will be greater than the short-run losses of social welfare imposed by the tariff.

There are two reasons an industry may not be efficient in the short run, but could be efficient in the long run: economies of scale and economies of experience (Kenen 1994, 279–281). **Economies of scale** arise when the cost of production varies with the size of the output—that is, when the unit cost of producing falls as the number of units produced rises. For example, it is quite costly to develop a new commercial aircraft. Estimates put the cost of developing Boeing's new 7E7 at around $3 billion. The unit cost of production will be very high if Boeing produces only a few of these planes, as we must divide this fixed cost by a small number of final goods. The unit cost falls substantially, however, if Boeing produces a thousand of the new planes. What we see, then, is that not only the unit cost, but also the average cost, of each unit falls as the number of units produced rises. Firms in industries with such economies of scale face a dilemma, however: They can produce efficiently and begin to export once they pro-duce enough output to achieve the available economies of scale, but in an open econ-omy, they must compete immediately against established foreign producers that have already achieved economies of scale. Consequently, a new firm will have a hard time selling its higher average cost output in the face of competition from lower cost firms. As a result, the new firm will never reach the level of output necessary to achieve economies of scale. In such cases, a tariff might improve welfare. By imposing a tariff, the government could effectively deliver the domestic market to the infant domestic firm. With a guaranteed market, the domestic firm could sell its early high-cost output to domestic consumers and eventually produce enough to achieve economies of scale. Once it had done so, it could compete against foreign producers without the need for tariff protection. The tariff would then be removed.

Economies of experience arise when efficient production requires specific skills that can be acquired only through production in the industry. In many industries, efficient production requires "seasoned managers, skilled workers, and reliable suppli-ers of equipment and materials" (Kenen 1994, 280). Because, by definition, these skills are lacking in an infant industry, it will be costly to produce the early units of out-put. Over time, however, management skills improve, workers learn how to do their tasks efficiently, and reliable suppliers are found and supported. Costs of production fall as experience is gained. For example, when Airbus built its first jet, it took 340,000 person-hours to assemble the fuselage. As Airbus gained experience, however, the time required to assemble the jets fell rapidly. By the time Airbus had produced 75 aircraft, only 85,000 person-hours were required to assemble the fuselage, and eventually this number fell to 43,000 person-hours (McIntyre 1992, 36). The efficiency gains realized as a result of these dynamics are often called "moving down the learning curve." Again, however, the new firm faces a dilemma: In an unprotected market, it won't be cost competitive in the face of established foreign producers; consequently, it will never be able to produce enough output to realize economies of experience. As with economies of scale, a tariff can allow the infant industry to realize the cost savings available from economies of experience and achieve greater efficiency. Once it has done so, it can begin to export and the tariff can be removed.

Tariffs and other forms of government intervention sometimes improve social welfare, then, because a disjuncture between the social and private returns from a particular industry may prevent the shift of factors out of relatively low-return indus-tries and into relatively high-return industries (Balassa and Associates 1971, 93). In other worlds, certain industries may offer high social returns over the long run (i.e., they will provide large benefits to society as a whole), but the short-run private returns (i.e., the profits realized by the person or firm making the investment) are likely to be negative. Consequently, factors don't move automatically into the potentially high return industry. In that case, a tariff or another form of government intervention may encourage factors to move into the industry by raising the short-run return above what it would be without the tariff. By doing so, such policies improve social welfare in the long run.

A CLOSER LOOK

Criticism of the Infant-Industry Case for Protection

Many economists are skeptical about the claim that government intervention is the best response to the problems highlighted by the infant-industry argument. (See Kenen 1994, 281.) First of all, a tariff is rarely the best policy response to the central problem the infant industry confronts. Economists argue that a subsidy is a much better approach because it is more efficient, and the reason is that subsidies target the same policy goal—helping the domestic industry cover the gap between its production costs and established foreign producers' costs—but they don't reduce consumer welfare, as tariffs do (Kenen 1994, 281).

However, a government subsidy may not improve social welfare either. The case against a subsidy arises from the fact that a firm which will be profitable in the long run, but must operate at a loss in the short run, should be able to borrow from private capital markets to cover its short-run losses. Such borrowing obviates the need for a subsidy because it enables the firm to sell its goods at the world price and cover its short-term losses with the borrowed funds. Thus, as long as capital markets are efficient and not "strongly averse to risk," infant industries should be able to borrow at an interest rate that reflects the social rate of return on capital. If a firm can't borrow at such an interest rate, then the market is essentially saying that this industry is not the best place to invest society's scarce resources. Consequently, the firm shouldn't be supported with *either* subsidies or tariffs (Kenen 1994, 281). In other words, when capital markets are efficient, the firm should borrow rather than rely on the government; if it can't borrow, the government shouldn't help it either.

This critique of government intervention fails to hold in two circumstances. First, a firm may be reluctant to borrow from private markets when the problem it faces arises from economies of experience. In such instances, borrowed funds yield long-run efficiency by allowing workers employed at a particular firm to gain the skills required to operate efficiently. Yet, once workers have acquired these skills, they may go to work for other firms. If they do, the firm that has paid for their training will be unable to achieve economies of experience and, as a result, will not be able to repay the loan. In this instance, government support for the industry might be helpful, but economists argue that government assistance in such cases should take the form of broad government-funded training programs rather than narrow subsidies to a specific firm.

The criticism of subsidies also fails to hold if the private capital market is inefficient and therefore won't lend to a firm entering an infant industry. If this is the case, the firm will have little capacity to gain the financial resources it needs to cover its short-term losses. Even here, however, economists argue that a subsidy or a tariff may not be the right response. If the government is determined to support the development of a specific industry, then it should do what the private capital market won't and extend loans to firms in that industry rather than provide a subsidy. If, however, the government is interested primarily in raising social welfare, economists argue, then the best thing it can do in this circumstance is strengthen the private capital

Continued

market so that it does operate efficiently (Baldwin 1969). Thus, even though most economists agree that there will be instances in which firms that are not efficient in the short run can become efficient in the long run, there is considerable skepticism about the extent to which government intervention is the only, much less the best, solution to this dilemma.

The logic of the infant-industry case for protection has been adopted by governments in many late-industrializing countries. A **late-industrializing country** is a country that is trying to develop manufacturing industries in competition with established manufacturing industries in other countries. The term obviously describes most developing countries in the contemporary international economic system, but it once described many of today's advanced industrialized countries, including the United States, as they attempted to develop manufacturing industries in the face of dominant British manufacturing power in the 19th century. Indeed, the infant-industry argument was first developed by an American, Alexander Hamilton, in 1791, as an explicit policy for the development of the manufacturing industry in the United States. Hamilton's argument was further elaborated by the German political economist Frederick List in the mid-19th century. Like Hamilton, List was interested primarily in thinking about how the German government could encourage the growth of manufacturing industries in the face of established British dominance. The infant-industry argument continued to have an important impact on government trade policies throughout the 20th century. Many argue that Japan's postwar trade policies reflect the logic of the infant-industry argument, because the Japanese government used a variety of policy instruments to encourage the development of advanced manufacturing industries to oppose American competitive advantages. Many developing-country governments also embraced the logic of the infant-industry argument throughout the early postwar periods, as we will see in greater detail in Chapter 6.

The policies that governments have adopted to promote the development of infant industries are known collectively as **industrial policy.** The term can be defined as the use of a broad assortment of instruments, such as tax policy, subsidies (including the provision of state credit and finance), traditional protectionism, and government procurement practices, in order to channel resources away from some industries and direct them toward those industries the state wishes to promote. The use of such policies is typically based on long-term economic development objectives defined in terms of boosting economic growth, improving productivity, and enhancing international competitiveness. The specific goals that governments pursue often are determined by explicit comparisons with other countries' economic achievements (Wade 1990, 25–26). In postwar Japan, for example, the explicit goal of Japanese industrial policy was to catch up with the United States in many high-technology industries. In much of the developing world, industrial policy was oriented toward creating economic structures that paralleled those of the advanced industrialized countries. In using state power in this way, governments can influence decisions about the utilization of scarce societal resources in ways that improve social welfare.

State Strength: The Political Foundation of Industrial Policy

The ability of any government to design and implement an effective industrial policy is dependent upon the political institutions within which it operates. The various institutional characteristics that make some states more and others less able to design and implement coherent industrial policies are summarized by the concept of **state strength,** defined as the degree to which national policymakers (a category that includes elected and appointed officials) are insulated from domestic interest-group pressures.

Strong states are states in which policymakers are highly insulated from such pressures, while **weak states** are states in which policymakers are fully exposed to those pressures. Strong states are characterized by a high degree of centralization of authority, a high degree of coordination among state agencies, and a limited number of channels through which societal actors can attempt to influence policy. In contrast, weak states are characterized by decentralized authority, a lack of coordination among agencies, and a large number of channels through which domestic interest groups can influence economic policy.

These characteristics of political institutions make it easier for strong states to formulate long-term plans embodying the national interest. In weak states, policymakers must respond to the particularistic and often short-run demands of interest groups. Strong states may also be more able than weak states to remove protection once an infant industry has matured. In addition, strong states may be more able to implement industrial policies that redistribute societal resources, because policymakers need worry less that policies which redistribute resources from one domestic group to another will have a negative impact on their position in power.

Japan is often depicted as the preeminent example of a strong state that has been able and willing to use industrial policy to promote economic development. (See, e.g., Johnson 1982.) The Japanese state centralizes power and provides limited channels of access to domestic interest groups. Because it is such a highly centralized state, Japan has been able to pursue a coherent industrial policy throughout the postwar period. The Ministry of International Trade and Industry (MITI; now called the **Ministry of Economy, Trade, and Industry,** or METI) and the Ministry of Finance (MoF) were the principal agencies involved in developing and implementing industrial policy. In the immediate postwar period, these agencies gave priority to economic reconstruction and to improving the prewar industrial economy. Since the 1960s, greater emphasis has been placed on promoting rapid economic growth and developing internationally competitive high-technology industries (Pempel 1977, 732).

With this goal firmly in mind, the Japanese state pursued an active industrial policy (called "administrative guidance") through which it channeled resources to those industries it determined were critical to Japanese success. Together, MITI and MoF targeted specific industries for development, starting with heavy industries (steel, shipbuilding, automobiles) in the early postwar period and then shifting to high-technology industries during the 1970s. The state pressured firms to invest in the industries targeted for development, and those which made such investments benefited from tariff and nontariff forms of protection, tax credits, low-cost financing, and other government subsidies. Some scholars suggest that Japan's remarkable postwar economic performance was a direct result of this state-centered approach to economic development (Johnson 1982).

France also relied heavily upon industrial policies throughout much of the postwar period (Wilkinson 1984; Hart 1992). The French state is highly centralized, and French bureaucracies are tightly insulated from societal group pressures, as in Japan. This structure allowed the French government to pursue an industrial policy aimed at developing key industries, with little direct influence from domestic interest groups. A former director of the Ministry of Industry described the policymaking process: "First, we make out a report or draw up a text, then we pass it around discreetly within the administration. Once everyone concerned within the administration is agreed on the final version, then we pass this version around outside the administration. Of course, by then it is a *fait accompli* and [interest-group] pressure cannot have any effect" (quoted in Katzenstein 1977, 18).

In the early postwar period, the French state formulated development plans to "establish a competitive economy as an essential base for political independence, economic growth, and social progress" (Katzenstein 1977, 22). French industrial policy in this period was based on a strategy of "National Champions," under which specific firms in industries deemed by France to be critical to French economic development received support. In the 1950s and 1960s, for example, two steel companies and a small number of auto producers (Renault, Simca, Peugeot) received state support. During the 1960s and 1970s, France attempted to develop a domestic computer industry by channeling resources to specific French computer companies, such as Machines Bull. Most regard this strategy as having been relatively unsuccessful, because French national champions failed to become competitive in international markets (Hart 1992). However, the current French government seems poised to revive this approach: in early 2005, it announced the creation of a new industrial policy oriented toward promoting National Champions in high-technology industries.

In contrast to Japan and France, the United States is characterized as a weak state (Katzenstein 1977; Ikenberry et al. 1988). Political power in the United States is decentralized through federalism, through the division of powers within the federal government, and through independent bureaucratic agencies. This decentralization of power in turn provides multiple channels through which domestic interest groups can attempt to influence policy. Consequently, "American state officials find it difficult to act purposefully and coherently, to realize their preferences in the face of significant opposition, and to manipulate or restructure their domestic environment" (Ikenberry et al. 1988, 11). American trade and economic policy therefore more often reflect the interests of societal pressure groups than the "national interest" defined by state policymakers.

This does not mean that the United States has been unable to support critical industries. American national security and defense policies have channeled substantial resources to maintaining technological leadership over potential rivals. To maintain this lead, the U.S. government has financed the basic research that underlies many high-technology products, including computers, telecommunications equipment, lasers, advanced materials, and even the Internet. In addition, Department of

Defense contracts have supported firms that produce both military and civilian items. Thus, even though the United States is a weak state, we do see a form of industrial policy in the U.S. government's support for basic research and in its defense-related procurement practices designed to meet national security objectives.

The state-centered approach therefore argues that state policymakers can use industrial policy to improve social welfare. In contrast to the standard model of trade, this approach holds that factors might not move automatically from relatively low return industries into relatively high return industries. In such instances, targeted government intervention, in the form of a tariff or a production subsidy can encourage movement into these industries. Over the long run, the welfare gains generated by high-return industries are substantially larger than the welfare losses incurred during the period of protection. The ability of policymakers to pursue such policies effectively, however, is strongly influenced by the institutional structure of the state in which they operate. In strong states, such as Japan and France, policymakers are insulated from domestic interest groups and are therefore able to use industrial policy to promote economic development. In weak states, such as the United States, policymakers cannot easily escape interest-group pressures. As a consequence, trade and economic policy are more likely to reflect the particularistic demands of these groups than any broader conceptions of social welfare.

Industrial Policy in High-Technology Industries

High-technology industries are one area in which governments in many of the advanced industrialized countries have relied heavily upon industrial policies. Boosting the international competitiveness of such industries has been the principal goal of such policies. High-technology industries are highly valued for the contribution they make to national income. These industries tend to earn **rents;** that is, they earn a higher-than-normal return on an investment, and they pay higher wages to workers than do standard manufacturing industries. In addition, relatively recent developments in economic theory that build on the basic insight of the infant-industry case for protection suggest that governments can use industrial policy to create internationally competitive domestic high-technology industries. We examine these issues here, focusing first on the economic theories that justify the use of industrial policy in high technology industries and then examining two cases in which industrial policy appears to have enabled high-technology firms based in Japan and the European Union to become internationally competitive at the apparent expense of high-technology firms based in the United States. We conclude by returning to the current U.S.-EU dispute in commercial aircraft.

Strategic-Trade Theory

Strategic-trade theory provides the theoretical justification for industrial policy in high-technology industries. **Strategic-trade theory** expands on the basic insight of the infant-industry case for protection. Like the infant-industry case, strategic-trade theory asserts that government intervention can help domestic firms achieve economies of scale and experience in order to become efficient and competitive in global markets. In contrast, however, to the classical infant-industry argument, which assumes that markets are perfectly competitive, strategic-trade theory asserts that many high-tech industries are characterized by oligopolistic competition—that is, they feature competition between only a few firms. The combination of economies of scale and experience, on the one hand, and oligopolistic competition, on the other, creates a theoretical rationale for government intervention to raise national income.

An **oligopoly** is an industry dominated by a small number of firms. The world auto industry, for example, is dominated by only about eight firms. The world market for long-distance commercial aircraft is dominated by only two firms. Such industries are clearly different from, say, agriculture, in which thousands of farms produce for the world market. Economic dynamics in oligopolistic market structures are quite unlike the dynamics we see in perfectly competitive markets. The economic analysis of oligopolistic competition can be complex, however, and a detailed analysis of such competition would take us far from our primary concern. Consequently, we will leave that analysis aside and simply state that firms operating in oligopolistic markets earn **excess returns**—profits greater than could be earned in equally risky investments in other sectors of the economy (Krugman and Obstfeld 1994, 282).

Suppose an American firm dominates the world market for commercial aircraft. Then the United States captures the excess returns available in this industry. As a result, American workers employed in the industry, as well as the people who have invested their savings in it, earn higher incomes than they would earn in the next-best use of their labor or savings. American national income is higher than it would be otherwise. If, by contrast, a European firm dominates the world market for commercial aircraft, then Europe captures the excess returns and enjoys the higher "national" income. And because an oligopolistic industry is an industry in which only a limited number of firms can operate, only a small number of countries can capture the available excess returns. It is certainly reasonable to suppose, therefore, that societies would compete over these industries. Strategic-trade theory thus suggests that, in some industries, global economic interaction gives rise to zero-sum competition over the excess returns available in oligopolistic high-tech industries.

Who is likely to win this competition? In the absence of intervention by any government, the firm that is the first to enter a particular industry will win and, in doing so, effectively deter subsequent entry by potential rivals. Thus, such industries offer a **first-mover advantage**—an advantage that arises from economies of scale and experience. Suppose an American high-tech firm is the first to produce and market a product such as a certain kind of commercial jet aircraft. Because achieving economies of scale and experience is central to the ability to produce commercial jets efficiently, the United States, by virtue of being first into the market, has a production cost advantage over any rivals that might want to enter the market at a later time. As a consequence, a European firm that could be competitive once it achieved economies of scale and experience is deterred from entering the industry because the cost advantage enjoyed by the established American firm makes it very difficult to sell enough aircraft to achieve these economies. After all, who will buy the new entrant's higher cost output? Absent such sales, the new firm will never realize the economies of scale and experience that are essential to long-term success. The U.S. firm, therefore, has an advantage in the industry only because it is the first into the market. Consequently, the United States will enjoy the higher national income yielded by the excess returns in the commercial aircraft industry. Other countries are denied these excess returns, even though, were they able to achieve the necessary economies of scale and experience, they would be every bit as successful as the American first mover.

Government intervention may have a powerful effect on the willingness of a latecomer to enter an industry. That is, targeted government intervention may enable late entrants to successfully challenge first movers. Government intervention shifts the excess returns that are available in a particular industry from a foreign country to the national economy. The reasoning behind this statement can be illustrated with some fairly simple game theory (Krugman 1987). Let's assume that there are two firms, one American and one European, interacting in a high-tech industry—say, commercial aircraft—that will support only one producer. Each firm has two strategies: to produce commercial aircraft or not to produce the aircraft. The payoffs that each firm gains from the four possible outcomes are depicted in Figure 5.1a. There are two possible equilibrium outcomes in this game, one in which the American firm produces and the European firm does not, and one in which the European firm produces and the American firm does not. Thus, this particular high-tech industry will be based in the United States or in Europe, but never in both countries. Whichever country hosts the firm earns 100 units in income.

Which country captures the industry depends upon which firm is first to enter the market. Let's suppose, on the one hand, that the American firm is first to enter the industry and has realized economies of scale and experience. In this case, the European firm has no incentive to enter the industry, because, by doing so, it would earn a profit of –5 units. If we assume, on the other hand, that the European firm is first to enter the market, then it realizes economies of scale and experience. In this case, the

		European Firm	
		Produce	Not Produce
American Firm	Produce	−5, −5	100, 0
	Not Produce	0, 100	0, 0

5.1a Payoff Matrix with No Subsidy

		European Firm	
		Produce	Not Produce
American Firm	Produce	−5, 5	100, 0
	Not Produce	0, 110	0, 0

5.1b Payoff Matrix with European Subsidy

Figure 5.1   The Impact of Industrial Policy in High-Technology Industries.

American firm has no incentive to enter the market. Thus, even though both firms could produce the product equally well, the firm that enters first dominates the industry. According to strategic-trade theory, therefore, the firm that is first to enter a particular high-technology industry will hold a competitive advantage, and the country which is home to that firm will capture the rents available in the industry.

Against this backdrop, we can examine how governments can use industrial policy to assist domestic high-technology firms. Government intervention can help new firms enter an established high-technology industry to challenge, and eventually compete with, established firms. Government assistance to these new firms can come in many forms. Governments may provide financial assistance to help their new firms pay for the costs of research and development. Such subsidies lessen the costs that private firms must bear in the early stages of product development, thereby reducing the up-front investment a firm must make to enter the industry. In this manner, European governments participating in the Airbus consortium have subsidized the development of Airbus aircraft. Governments may also guarantee a market for the early and more expensive versions of the firm's products. Tariffs and quotas can be used to keep foreign goods out, and government purchasing decisions can favor domestic producers over imports. The Japanese government, for example, purchased most of its supercomputers from Japanese suppliers in the 1980s, even though the supercomputers produced by Cray Industries, an American firm, were cheaper and performed better. The guaranteed market allows domestic firms to sell their high-cost output from the early stages of production at high prices. The combination of financial support and guaranteed markets allows domestic firms to enter the market and move down the learning curve. Once the new firms have realized economies of scale, they can compete against established firms in international markets.

We can see the impact of such policies on firms' production decisions by returning to our simple game. (See Figure 5.1b.) Again, suppose that the American firm is the first to enter the market and dominates the industry. Suppose, however, that this time European governments provide a subsidy of 10 units to the European firm. The subsidy changes the payoffs the European firm receives if it produces. In contrast to the no-subsidy case, the European firm now makes a profit of 5 units when it produces, even if the American firm stays in the market. The subsidy therefore makes it rational for the European firm to start producing. Even more, government support for domestic high-technology firms has a second consequence that stems from the oligopolistic nature of high-tech industries. Because such industries support only a small number of firms at profitable levels of output, the entry of new firms into the sector must eventually cause other firms to exit. Thus, government policies that promote the creation of a successful industry in one country undermine the established industry in other countries.

This outcome is also clear in our simple game. Once the European firm begins producing, the American firm earns a profit of –5 units if it continues to produce and a profit of 0 units if it exits the industry. Exit, therefore, is the American firm's rational response to the entry of the European firm. Thus, the small 10-unit subsidy provided by European governments enables the European firm not only to eliminate the first-mover advantage enjoyed by the American firm, but ultimately to drive the American firm out of the industry. As a consequence, Europe's national income rises by 100 units (the 110-unit profit realized by the European firm, minus the 10-unit subsidy from

European governments), while America's national income falls by 100 units. Thus, a small government subsidy has allowed Europe to increase its national income at the expense of the United States.

Strategic-trade theory suggests, therefore, that the location of high-technology industries has little to do with cross-national differences in factor endowments and a lot to do with market structure and the assumptions we make about how production costs vary with the quantity of output. This is a world in which the classical model of comparative advantage doesn't hold. Rather, international competitiveness and the pattern of international specialization in high-technology industries are attributed as much to the timing of market entry as to underlying factor endowments.

Strategic Rivalry in Semiconductors and Commercial Aircraft

The semiconductor industry and the commercial aircraft industry illustrate these kinds of strategic trade rivalries between the United States, Japan, and the European Union in the contemporary global economy. In the semiconductor industry, American producers enjoyed first-mover advantages and dominated the world market until the early 1980s. The semiconductor industry prospered in the United States in part due to government support in the form of funding for research and development (R&D) and for defense-related purchases. The U.S. government financed a large portion of the basic research in electronics—as much as 85 percent of all R&D prior to 1958, and as much as 50 percent during the 1960s. At the same time, the U.S. defense industry provided a critical market for semiconductors. Defense-related purchases by the United States government absorbed as much as 100 percent of total production in the early years. Even in the late 1960s, the government continued to purchase as much as 40 percent of production. These policies allowed American semiconductor firms to move down the learning curve and realize economies of scale. This first mover-advantage was transformed into a dominant position in the global market: in the early 1970s, U.S. semiconductor producers controlled 98 percent of the American market and 78 percent of the European market.

Beginning in the 1970s, the Japanese government targeted semiconductors as a sector for priority development and used two policy measures to foster a Japanese semiconductor industry. First and most important, the Japanese government employed a variety of measures to protect Japanese semiconductor producers from American competition. Tariffs and quotas kept American chips out of the Japanese market. The Japanese government also approved very few applications for investment by foreign semiconductor firms and restricted the ability of American semiconductor firms to purchase Japanese firms. As a direct result, American semiconductor firms were unable to jump over trade barriers by building semiconductor production plants in Japan. The Japanese industrial structure—a structure in which producers develop long-term relationships with input suppliers—helped ensure that Japanese firms which used semiconductors as inputs purchased from Japanese rather than American suppliers. Finally, government purchases of computer equipment discriminated against products that used American chips in favor of computers that used Japanese semiconductors. Second, the Japanese government provided financial assistance to more than 60 projects connected to the semiconductor and computer industry. Such financial assistance helped cover many of the R&D costs Japanese producers faced.

The extent of Japanese protectionism can be appreciated by comparing U.S. market shares in the U.S., EU, and Japanese markets. Whereas American semiconductor firms controlled 98 percent of the American market and 78 percent of the EU market in the mid-1970s, they held only 20 percent of the Japanese market (Tyson 1995, 93). By 1976, Japanese firms were producing highly sophisticated chips and had displaced American products from all but the most advanced applications in the Japanese market. Success in the Japanese market was followed by success in the global market: In 1979, for the first time, Japan exported more semiconductors than it imported. By 1986, Japanese firms had captured about 46 percent of global semiconductor revenues, while the American firms' share had fallen to 40 percent (Tyson 1995, 104–105). Thus, by protecting domestic producers and subsidizing R&D costs, the Japanese government helped Japanese firms successfully challenge American dominance of the semiconductor industry.

A similar dynamic is evident in U.S.–European competition in the commercial aircraft sector. Two American firms—Boeing and Douglas (later, McDonnell Douglas)—dominated the global market for commercial aircraft throughout the postwar period, in part because of U.S. government support of the industry, provided through the procurement of military aircraft (Newhouse 1982; U.S. Congress Office of Technology Assessment 1991, 345). Work on military contracts enabled the two major American producers to achieve economies of scale in their commercial aircraft operations. Boeing, for example, developed one of its most successful commercial airliners, the 707, as a modified version of a military tanker craft, the KC-135. Producing the military aircraft allowed Boeing to reduce the cost of developing the commercial airliner. As a matter of fact, jets benefited from the experience Boeing had gained in developing the B-47 and the B-52 bombers (U.S. Congress 1991, 345). As Joseph Sutter, a Boeing executive vice president, noted, "We are good . . . partly because we build so many airplanes. We learn from our mistakes, and each of our airplanes embodies everything we have learned from our other airplanes" (quoted in Newhouse 1982, 7). The accumulated knowledge from military and commercial production gave the two American producers a first-mover advantage in the global market for commercial airliners sufficient to deter new entrants.

In 1967, the French, German, and British governments launched Airbus Industries to challenge the global dominance of Boeing and McDonnell Douglas. From 1970 to 1991, these three European governments provided between $10 billion and $18 billion of financial support to Airbus Industries, an amount equal to about 75 percent of the cost of developing Airbus airliners (U.S. Congress 1991, 354). As a consequence, by the early 1990s Airbus Industries had developed a family of commercial aircraft capable of serving the long-range, medium-range, large passenger, and smaller passenger routes. Airbus's entry into the commercial aircraft industry had a dramatic impact on global market share. As Table 5.1 makes clear, in the mid-1970s Boeing and McDonnell Douglas dominated the market for large commercial airliners. Airbus began to capture market share in the 1980s, however, and by 1990 it had gained control

POLICY ANALYSIS AND DEBATE

Government Support of High-Technology Industries

Question

Should the U.S. government adopt policies that promote the development of high technologies?

Overview

Craig Barnett, the chief executive officer of Intel, the American microprocessor producer, recently wrote that the new East Asian players in the global marketplace "pose a threat to the United States' economic and technological leadership" (Barnett 2004, 76). Barnett asserts that governments in these countries are playing an important role in building a technological infrastructure (such as broadband communications systems), offering tax incentives to induce research and development, and "deploying a more educated and motivated work force than the United States."

Similar forces are at work in the European Union. We have seen how EU governments used Airbus to challenge Boeing's dominance. More recently, France has announced the creation of an industrial innovation agency that will fund basic research in high-technology industries. In contrast, the percentage of national income that the U.S. government uses to fund basic R&D has declined by a little more than one-third during the last 15 years. Consequently, Barnett argues, the United States must "rethink the government's role in research and development" in order to "prioritize investment in the industries of the future." Without a substantially increased government commitment, "the U.S. innovation pipeline will dry up." How should the U.S. respond to the use of technology policies in the rest of the world?

Policy Options

- **Prohibit the Use of Such Policies:** Use the WTO to negotiate rules that limit direct and indirect government support of industry. Then use the WTO's dispute settlement mechanism to enforce compliance with these rules.
- **Expand U.S. High-Technology Policies:** Expand existing programs and establish new ones to promote the development and commercialization of new technologies by American firms.

Policy Analysis

- Are governments better able to identify promising new technologies than the private sector is? Why or why not?
- How do you measure the social welfare gains from an emerging idea? Can a welfare-improving subsidy be provided without such measurement?
- What are the potential consequences for the United States of not adopting a high-technology policy?

What Do You Think?

- Which policy do you advocate? Justify your choice.
- What criticisms of your position would you anticipate? How would you defend your recommendation against those criticisms?

Resources

Online: Search for "high technology policy China" (or Japan, or Taiwan, or South Korea). Compare differences in the approach to high technology adopted by the

Continued

Clinton and Bush administrations. Search for "high technology policy Clinton" and "high technology policy Bush."

In Print: See "Suggestions for Further Reading" in this chapter.

of 30 percent of the market for large commercial airliners. In 1994, Airbus sold more airliners than Boeing for the first time, and sales in the ensuing ten years indicate that 1994 was no fluke, as Airbus has firmly established itself as a dominant force in the global market for long-range commercial jets. As a consequence of Airbus's success, a substantial portion of the rents available from the production and sale of commercial airliners has been transferred from the United States to Europe. Thus, by subsidizing the initial costs of aircraft development, European governments have been able to capture a significant share of the global market for commercial aircraft—and the income generated in that sector—at the expense of the United States.

Strategic trade rivalries of this kind have been a source of conflict in the international trade system. Countries losing high-technology industries as a consequence of the industrial policies pursued by other countries can respond by supporting their own firms to offset the advantages enjoyed by foreign firms or by attempting to prevent foreign governments from using industrial policy. In the United States, which considered itself a victim of the industrial policies adopted by Japan and the European Union, the national debate has focused on responses to the two countries. Considerable pressure emerged during the 1980s and early 1990s for a national technology policy. Proposals were advanced for the creation of a government agency charged with reviewing global technology and "evaluating the likely course of key American industries; comparing these baseline projections with visions of industry paths that would be compatible with a prosperous and competitive economy; and monitoring the activities of foreign governments and firms in these industries to provide an early warning of potential competitive problems in the future" (Tyson 1995, 289). Many recommended that the U.S. government reduce its R&D support for military and dual-use projects (projects with

Table 5.1
Market Share in Global Commercial Aircraft

	Boeing	McDonnell Douglas°	Airbus
1975	67%	33%	0
1985	63%	20%	17%
1990	54%	16%	30%
2004	49%	n.a.†	51%

°Merged with Boeing in 1997; its commercial aircraft fleet is no longer produced.
†n.a.=not available.
Source: Data for 1975–1990 are calculated from Tyson 1995, 158–159. Data for 2004 reflect orders received by each company in 2004 through December. For Airbus, see *http://www.airbus.com/doc/media/ordersndeliveries/orders_n_deliveries.xls*. For Boeing, see *http://active.boeing.com/commercial/orders/index.cfm*.

both military and commercial applications) and increase the amount of support provided to strictly commercial applications. Proponents of a national technology strategy also encouraged greater cooperation between the public and private sectors on pre-competitive research over a wide range of advanced technologies. Such proposals played an important role in the first Clinton administration's thinking about international trade—a role reflected in Clinton's selection of Laura D'Andrea Tyson, an economist and one of the most prominent proponents of such policies, to be the chair of his Council of Economic Advisors.

The United States also put considerable pressure on other governments to stop their support of high-technology industries. A series of negotiations with Japan conducted during the 1980s and early 1990s was designed to pry open the Japanese market to internationally competitive American high-technology industries. Such negotiations took place on semiconductors, computers, telecommunications, and other sectors. The rationale for these negotiations is evident from the previous discussion about first-mover advantages. If Japanese firms could be denied a protected market for their early production runs, they would never realize the economies of scale required to compete in international markets. Opening the Japanese market to American high-technology producers would prevent the emergence of competitive Japanese high-technology firms and thereby help maintain American high-technology leadership. During the 1980s and early 1990s, therefore, the United States responded strategically to the use of industrial policies by Japan and, to a lesser extent, the European Union and adopted policies designed to counter them.

It is within this context that we can understand the current U.S.–EU conflict in the commercial aircraft industry. Boeing has long been concerned about the gains Airbus has made in the global market and has often pressured the U.S. government to try to limit the subsidies that European governments offer. In 1992, the United States and the European Union reached an agreement which specified that neither would provide subsidies greater than one-third of the total cost of developing a new airliner or greater than 3 percent of the firm's annual revenue. In early summer of 2004, the Bush administration, facing considerable pressure from Boeing, informed the European Union that it was time to renegotiate this agreement. The time for such a move looked right, at least to Boeing, for both companies were beginning to develop new aircraft, and Boeing argued that each should do so without government support. As Boeing CEO Henry Stonecipher said, the 1992 agreement "no longer reflected market realities" and had "outlived its usefulness" (King 2004). Given Airbus's current market position, it should stop expecting European governments to give it "truckloads" of money to cover a portion of new-aircraft development. "We're saying enough is enough. You're very successful, you're delivering and selling more airplanes than Boeing. . . . Why don't you go to the bank and borrow money?" It was, Boeing argued, "time for Airbus to accept the financial and marketplace risks that true commercial companies experience" (Becker 2004; Casert 2004).

Efforts to renegotiate the 1992 agreement proved unsuccessful. While EU officials seemed willing to accept the American claim that Airbus had received government support (though they denied that such support amounted to more than a token), they asserted that Boeing had itself been the beneficiary of $23 billion of government subsidies since 1992. These subsidies had come, the EU argued, from U.S. government

R&D contracts and from $3.2 billion in tax reductions, tax exemptions, and infrastructure improvements provided by the state of Washington. Consequently, the EU was willing to discuss a reduction in European assistance to Airbus only in conjunction with an American willingness to accept a reduction in such assistance for Boeing. When the United States proved unwilling to either accept the EU claim or provide information that would dispute the claim, the negotiations broke down. Days later, the United States announced that it was withdrawing from the 1992 agreement and filed a dispute with the WTO alleging that the EU was in violation of its WTO obligations concerning the use of subsidies that cause harm to foreign competitors. The European Union responded immediately by initiating its own WTO dispute in which it alleged the same thing of the United States. The stakes are high, as estimates suggest that sales of large commercial aircraft over the next 20 years will generate $2 trillion (Blustein 2004b). It remains to be seen whether American or European producers will capture this income.

Conclusion

While a state-centered approach directs our attention to the important role that states play in shaping the structure of their domestic economies, it does have at least three important weaknesses. First, the state-centered approach lacks explicit microfoundations. The approach asserts that states act in ways that enhance national welfare. A discerning student must respond to this assertion by asking one simple question: what incentive does the state have to act in ways that do in fact enhance national welfare? Anyone who has visited the Palace of Versailles in France or spent any time reading about the experience of other autonomous rulers knows that autonomous states have as much (if not more) incentive to act in the private interests of state officials as they have to act in the interest of society as a whole. Why, then, would autonomous state actors enrich society when they might just as easily enrich themselves? Answering this question requires us to think about how state actors are rewarded for promoting policies that enhance national welfare and punished for failing to do so. In answering the question, we develop microfoundations—explanations that set out the incentive structure which encourages state officials to adopt policies that promote national welfare. But the state-centered approach currently does not offer a good answer to the question. The reward structure that state policymakers face cannot be elections, for that pushes us back toward a society-centered approach. The reward structure might be security related; one could reasonably argue that states intervene to enhance the power and position of the nation in the international system. We must still explain, however, how these broad concerns about national security create incentives for individual policymakers to make specific decisions about allocating resources. The point is not that such microfoundations could not be developed, but rather no one appears yet to have done so. As a result, the state-centered approach provides little justification for its central assertion that states regularly act in ways that enhance national welfare.

Second, the assumption that states make policy independently of domestic interest-group pressure is misleading. Even highly autonomous states do not stand above *all* societal interests. While interest groups need not dictate policy, as the society-centered approach claims, they do establish the parameters in which policy must be made. Even in Japan, which probably comes closest to the ideal autonomous state, the Liberal Democrat Party's (LDP) position in government was based in part on the support of big business. Is it merely a coincidence that Japanese industrial policy channeled resources to big business, or did the Japanese state adopt such policies because they were in the interest of one of the LDP's principal supporters? Thus, whereas the society-centered approach assumes too little room for autonomous state action, the state-centered approach assumes too much state autonomy. We may learn more by fitting the two approaches together. Such a combination would lead us to expect that governments will intervene in the economy to promote specific economic outcomes, but also that often such policies are consistent with, and shaped by, the interests of the coalition of societal groups upon which the government's power rests.

Finally, strategic-trade theory itself, which provides the intellectual justification for government intervention in high-technology industries, has a considerable number of weaknesses. Strategic-trade theory is as much a prescriptive account—an account used to derive policy proposals—as it is an explanatory mechanism. As such, it has some important limitations. For example, the claim that government intervention can improve national welfare is not particularly robust. The conclusions inferred from any theory are sensitive to the assumptions underlying the theory. If the conclusions change greatly when some of the underlying assumptions are altered, then the confidence one has in the accuracy of the theory must be greatly diminished. Strategic-trade theory has been criticized for producing strong conclusions only under a relatively restrictive set of assumptions. While the specific criticisms are too detailed to consider here, the bottom line is that altering the assumptions about how one country's established firms respond to a foreign government's subsidy of its firms, about how many firms are in the sector in question, and about where firms sell their products can either weaken the central claim considerably or introduce so much complexity into the model that the policy implications become opaque.

Thus, strategic-trade theory does not provide unambiguous support for the claim that government intervention in high-technology industries can raise national income. In addition, even if we assume that strategic-trade theory is correct, it is not easy for governments to identify sectors in which intervention will raise national income. It is difficult to identify sectors that offer such gains and then to calculate the correct subsidy that will shift the activity in question to domestic producers at a net gain to social welfare. If governments choose the wrong sectors or provide too little or too much support, intervention can reduce, rather than raise, national welfare. Thus, the precise policy implications of strategic-trade theory are unclear, in part because the theory itself is weak and in part because it is not easy to translate its simpler conclusions into effective policies.

In spite of these weaknesses, the state-centered approach provides a useful check on the tendency of the society-centered approach to focus exclusively on the interests of societal interest groups. The state-centered approach points our attention to the interests of government officials and underscores the need to think about the ability of these officials to act independently from, and even against, the interests of domestic interest groups. By focusing our attention in that direction, the state-centered approach suggests that trade policy may not always reflect the balance of power between interest groups and tells us that we might need to take into account how state interests intervene in this competition in ways that produce outcomes that no interest groups desire. Yet, in spite of these useful insights, the absence of clearly specified microfoundations appears to represent a fatal flaw in this approach. Without such foundations, the approach can tell us that autonomous state officials will act, but it cannot tell us *how* they will act. Adding the requisite microfoundations, perhaps by combining the dynamics highlighted by the society-centered approach with the rich institutional environment emphasized by the state-centered approach, would enable us to begin thinking about the conditions under which state officials have the capacity for autonomous action and about the ends to which such autonomous officials would direct their energies.

Key Terms

Economies of Experience	Ministry of Economy, Trade, and Industry
Economies of Scale	Oligopoly
Excess Returns	Rents
First-Mover Advantage	State Strength
Industrial Policy	Strategic Trade Theory
Infant-Industry Case for Protection	Strong States
Late Industrializing Country	Weak States

Web Links

Roger McCain, an economics professor at Drexel University, maintains a good online economics textbook that explores, among other topics, the economics of imperfect competition. Visit *http://william-king.www.drexel.edu,* and follow the links to *Essential Principles of Economics*.

Suggestions for Further Reading

Douglas Irwin provides an excellent discussion of the historical development of the infant-industry case for protection in his *Against the Tide: an Intellectual History of Free Trade* (Princeton: Princeton University Press, 1996). The original formulation can be found in Alexander Hamilton, Secretary of the Treasury, *Report on Manufactures*, communicated to the House of Representatives, December 5, 1791, in S. McKee, Jr. (ed.), *Papers on Public Credit, Commerce and Finance* (New York, Columbia University Press, 1934).

On the issues posed by industrial policy toward high-technology industries, see Laura D'Andrea Tyson, *Who's Bashing Whom? Trade Conflict in High Technology Industry* (Washington, DC: Institute for International Economics, 1995). For a more polemical discussion written by a former trade negotiator in the Reagan administration, see Clyde V. Prestowitz, *Trading Places: How We Are Giving Our Future to Japan and How to Reclaim It* (New York: Basic Books, 1988). A more technical treatment is given in Paul R. Krugman, ed., *Strategic Trade Policy and the New International Economics* (Cambridge: Cambridge University Press, 1986).

CHAPTER 6

Trade and Development I: Import Substitution Industrialization

Mexico has experienced an economic revolution during the last 20 years. Until the mid-1980s, Mexico was one of the most heavily protected and highly directed non-socialist economies in the world. Importing anything into the country required formal government approval. Even with such approval, tariffs were very high, averaging over 25 percent and rising as high as 100 percent for many goods. Moreover, Mexico did not belong to GATT, and it was hard to imagine any conditions under which Mexico would seek a free-trade agreement with the United States. Behind these high tariff walls, the Mexican government intervened deeply in the domestic economy. Government-owned financial institutions channeled investment capital to favored private industries and projects. The government created state-owned enterprises in many sectors of the economy (about 1,200 of them by 1982) that together attracted more than one-third of all industrial investment (La Porta and López-de-Silanes 1997). Today, by contrast, Mexico is one of the most open developing countries in the world. Mexico entered GATT in 1987 and NAFTA in the early 1990s. The Mexican government has retreated sharply from involvement in the domestic economy. It has sold state-owned enterprises, liberalized a wide variety of market-restricting regulations, and begun to integrate Mexico deeply into the global economy. In less than ten years, the Mexican government opened Mexico to foreign competition and drastically scaled back its role in managing Mexican economic activity.

Mexico's experience is hardly unique. Few developing countries participated actively in the world trade system until the mid-1980s. Most governments erected very high trade barriers, and to the extent that they participated at all in GATT, they sought to alter the rules governing international trade. Convinced that GATT was biased against their interests, developing countries worked through the United Nations to create international trade rules that they believed would be more favorable toward industrialization in the developing world. Like the Mexican government, most governments intervened extensively in their countries' domestic economies in an attempt to promote rapid industrialization. Drawing on, extending, and modifying the logic of the infant-industry case for protection, governments used the power of the state to try to push resources out of agriculture and into manufacturing. And, as is the case with Mexico, these policy orientations have changed fundamentally since the late 1980s. Most developing countries have dismantled the protectionist systems they created and maintained in the first 30 years of the postwar period, have become active participants in the WTO, and have abandoned the quest to institute far-reaching changes to international trade rules. Most have greatly reduced the degree of government intervention in the domestic economy, selling state-owned enterprises and deregulating domestic markets.

This chapter and the next examine how political and economic forces have shaped the adoption and evolution of these new trade and development policies. The current chapter examines why so many developing countries' governments intervened deeply in their domestic economies, insulated themselves from international trade, and sought changes in international trade rules. The next chapter focuses on why so many governments have dismantled these policies during the last 20 years. We look first at how economic and political change throughout the developing world brought to power governments supported by import-competing interests. We then examine the economic theory that guided policy during those times. As we shall see, this theory provided governments in the developing world with a compelling justification for transforming the protectionism sought by the import-competing producers that supported them into policies which emphasized industrialization through state leadership. Having built this base, we turn our attention to the specific policies that governments pursued during that period, looking first at their domestic strategy for industrialization and then examining their efforts to reform the international trade system.

Domestic Interests, International Pressures, and Protectionist Coalitions

Developing countries' trade policies underwent a sea change in the first half of the twentieth century. Up until the First World War, those developing countries which were independent, as well as those regions of the world held in colonial empires, adopted liberal trade policies. They produced and exported agricultural goods and other primary commodities to the advanced industrialized countries and imported most of the manufactured goods they consumed. Governments and colonial rulers made little effort to restrict this trade. But by the late 1950s, these liberal trade policies had been replaced by a protectionist approach that dominated the developing countries' trade policies until the late 1980s and whose remnants remain important in many countries today. We begin our investigation of developing countries' trade and development policies by looking at this initial shift to protectionism.

Trade and development policies in developing countries have been strongly shaped by political competition between the country and the city, or, in slightly different terms, between rural-based agriculture and urban-based manufacturing. Political competition between these two groups reflects, in turn, the pattern of comparative advantage generated by the factor endowments common to most developing coun-

Table 6.1
Economic Structure in Developing Countries (Sector as a Percent of GDP)

	Agriculture			Manufacturing			Other Industry*			Services		
	1960	1980	1995	1960	1980	1995	1960	1980	1995	1960	1980	1995
Sub-Saharan Africa	36	24	20	12	12	15	18	24	15	40	38	48
East Asia and the Pacific	46	27	18	16	27	32	7	12	12	31	32	38
South Asia	49	39	30	13	15	17	6	9	10	33	35	41
Latin America	16	10	10	21	25	21	10	12	12	53	51	55

Figures may not sum to 100 because of rounding.
*Includes mining, construction, gas, and water.
Sources: Data for 1960 from World Bank, *World Tables,* 3d ed. (Washington, DC: The World Bank, 1983). Data for 1980 and 1995 from World Bank, *World Development Indicators* (Washington, DC.: The World Bank, 1997).

tries. In general, developing countries are abundantly endowed with land and poorly endowed with capital (Lal and Myint 1996, 104–110).

The relative importance of land and capital in developing countries' economies can be appreciated by examining the structure of those economies, together with exports, as presented in Tables 6.1 and 6.2. For the time being, we will focus on 1960, as this will allow us to put to the side the consequences of the development policies that governments adopted during the postwar period. With a few exceptions (particularly in Latin America), between one-third and one-half of all economic activity in developing countries in 1960 was based in the agricultural sector, while less than 15 percent was based in manufacturing. By contrast, agriculture accounted for only 5 percent of GDP in the advanced industrial economies. If we include the "other industry" category, which incorporates mining, then, in 1960, in all regions of the developing world other than Latin America, agriculture and nonmanufacturing industries accounted for more than half of all economic activity.

A similar pattern is evident in the commodity composition of developing countries' exports (Table 6.2). The **commodity composition of exports** measures the types of goods that a country exports. In 1962, developing countries' exports were heavily concentrated in primary commodities: agricultural products, minerals, and other raw materials. Roughly speaking, in each developing country, primary commodities accounted for more than 50 percent of exports, and in more than half of the countries listed in Table 6.2, primary commodities accounted for more than 80 percent of exports. In addition, the range of primary commodities each developing country exported was generally quite small. Some countries were **monoexporters;** that is, their exports were almost fully accounted for by one product. In the mid-1980s, for example, more than 80 percent of Burundi's export earnings came from coffee, while cocoa accounted for 75 percent of Ghana's export earnings (Cypher and Dietz 1997, 339). Similar patterns were evident in Latin America: in 1950, coffee and cocoa made up about 69 percent of Brazil's exports, and copper and nitrates constituted about 74 percent of Chile's exports (Thorp 1999, 346). The structure of their economies and

Table 6.2
Developing Countries' Export Composition (Sector as a Percent of Total Exports)

	Fuels, Minerals, and Metals			Other Primary Commodities			Manufactures		
	1962	1980	1993	1962	1980	1993	1962	1980	1993
Sub-Saharan Africa									
Cameroon	21	33	51	75	64	35	4	4	14
Ghana	73	17	25	31	82	52	1	1	23
Kenya	2	36	16	89	52	66	9	13	19
Nigeria	11	97	94	81	2	4	8	0	2
South Africa	23	33	16	47	28	11	26	40	74
Zaire	16	56	69	75	14	13	10	31	18
East Asia and the Pacific									
Hong Kong	2	2	2	3	5	3	93	93	96
Indonesia	37	76	32	63	22	15	0	3	53
Malaysia	n.a.	35	14	n.a.	46	21	n.a.	20	65
Singapore	52	31	14	18	18	6	30	51	80
South Korea	24	1	3	57	9	4	20	90	94
Taiwan	n.a.	2	2	n.a.	10	5	n.a.	88	93
South Asia									
India	9	8	7	47	33	18	44	59	75
Pakistan	0	8	1	75	44	14	25	48	85
Latin America									
Argentina	2	6	11	95	71	57	3	23	32
Bolivia	91	86	56	4	11	25	5	3	19
Brazil	9	11	12	88	50	28	3	39	60
Chile	87	65	43	8	25	38	4	10	19
Mexico	24	73	17	60	15	9	16	12	75

n.a = not available.
Sources: Data for 1962 from World Bank, *World Tables,* 3d ed. (Washington, DC: The World Bank, 1983). Data for 1980 and 1993 from World Bank, *World Development Indicators* (Washington, DC: The World Bank, 1997).

the composition of their exports thus underline the central point: developing countries are abundantly endowed with land and have little capital.

The specific-factors model allows us to examine how these factor endowments have shaped developing countries' trade politics during the last 100 years. As we learned in Chapter 4, a specific factor is a factor of production that cannot be shifted from one economic sector to another. In the context of developing countries, the specific-factors model leads us to focus on two sectors dealing in traded goods: agriculture and manufacturing. In keeping with the supposition of limited factor mobility, we assume that land is specific to agriculture while capital is specific to manufacturing. We also assume that our third factor—labor—is mobile across sectors. Most labor in developing countries is low skilled and can readily be employed either in low-skilled manufacturing or in agriculture. Such labor is highly mobile among sectors and will move to whichever sector is paying the higher wage. Finally, because land is abundant while capital is scarce, agriculture is the export-oriented sector and manufacturing is the import-competing sector. The export-oriented sector, landowners in this case, realize rising incomes from open trade and see their incomes fall under protection. The import-competing sector, the manufacturing industry in this case, realizes income gains from protection and incurs losses from trade liberalization.

This simple model allows us to generate some basic expectations about the underlying dynamics of trade politics in developing countries. When agricultural interests dominate politics, trade policy will be open and liberal. Because the returns are higher in agriculture than in manufacturing, most labor will be employed in agriculture. When manufacturing interests dominate politics, trade policy will be protectionist, and because protection raises the return to labor and capital employed in manufacturing relative to agriculture, labor will move out of agriculture and into manufacturing. The specific-factors model suggests, therefore, that trade politics in developing countries will be characterized by competition between agricultural and manufacturing interests.

While this two-sector model highlights political competition between rural agriculture and urban manufacturing, it omits one important element of urban interests: Many urban residents in developing countries are not employed in manufacturing. Instead, they work for the government, in the retail sector, or in other nonmanufacturing activities. We can capture this group's trade policy interests by adding a third sector, called the nontraded-goods sector, to manufacturing and agriculture. The **nontraded-goods sector** encompasses all economic activities that do not enter into international trade, either because the good is too costly to transport, as are houses and concrete, or because, in some cases, the good or service must be performed locally, as are the railway system, many public utilities, health care, auto repair, and the retail sector in general. In addition, government employees, such as civil servants, teachers, and military personnel, work in the nontraded-goods sector. Because nontraded goods do not face international competition, international trade affects incomes in the nontraded good sector primarily through its impact on the prices of the traded goods that people employed in the nontraded-goods sector purchase. People employed in the nontraded-goods sector realize income gains from policies that reduce the prices of traded goods and losses from policies that raise these prices.

Developing countries pursued liberal trade policies prior to World War I because export-oriented agricultural interests dominated those countries' political systems. The precise political form of this domination differed considerably across regions. In Latin America, an indigenous landowning elite dominated domestic politics. In Argentina and Chile, for example, the landowners controlled government, often in an alliance with the military. While these political systems were constitutionally democratic, participation was restricted to the elite, a group that amounted to about 5 percent of the population, in a system that has been characterized as "oligarchic democracy" (Skidmore and Smith 1989, 47). In other Latin American countries such as Mexico, Venezuela, and Peru, dictatorial and often military governments ruled, but they pursued policies that protected the interests of the landowners (Skidmore and Smith 1989, 47). With landowners dominating domestic politics, Latin American governments pursued liberal trade policies that favored agricultural production and export at the expense of manufactured goods (Rogowski 1989, 47). As a result, most Latin American countries were highly open to international trade, producing and exporting agricultural goods and other primary commodities and importing manufactured goods from Great Britain, Europe, and the United States.

In Asia and in Africa, export-oriented agricultural interests dominated local politics through colonial structures. In Taiwan and Korea, for example, Japanese colonization led to the development of **enclave agriculture**—that is, export-oriented agricultural sectors that had few linkages to other parts of the local economy (Haggard 1990). Agricultural producers bought little from local suppliers and exported most of their production. In both countries, agricultural production centered on the production and export of rice; in Taiwan, sugarcane was a staple crop as well. In Africa, colonial powers—Britain and France in particular—encouraged the production of cash crops and raw materials that could be exported to the mother country (Hopkins 1979; Ake 1981, 1996). In the Gold Coast (now Ghana), the cocoa industry was a small part of the economy in 1870. British colonists then promoted the development of cocoa production, so that, by 1910, the country had become the world's largest cocoa producer and cocoa accounted for 80 percent of the Gold Coast's exports. In Senegal, France promoted the production of groundnuts, so that production rose from 200,000 tons to 600,000 tons between 1914 and 1937, and close to half of the land cultivated in Senegal was dedicated to groundnut production (Ka and Van de Walle 1994, 296). Similar patterns with other commodities were evident in other African colonies (Hopkins 1979).

These political arrangements began to change in the early twentieth century. As they did, the dominance of export-oriented interests gave way to the interests of import-competing manufacturers. In many instances, the most important triggers for this change originated outside of developing societies. In Latin America, international economic shocks beginning with the First World War and extending into the Second World War played a central role (Thorp 1999, Chapter 4). Government-mandated rationing of goods and primary commodities in the United States and Europe during the two World Wars made it difficult for Latin American countries to import many of the consumer goods they had previously purchased from the industrialized countries. In addition, falling commodity prices associated with the Great Depression and the disruption of normal trade patterns arising from the Second World War reduced the amount of foreign exchange that Latin American countries earned from their primary commodity exports. The interruption of "normal" Latin American trade patterns led governments in many countries to introduce trade barriers and to begin producing many of the manufactured goods that they had previously imported. The rise of domestic manufacturing in turn produced a growing urban middle class as workers and industrialists began to move out of agricultural production and into manufacturing industries.

The emergence of manufacturing industries gave rise to interest groups, industry-based associations, and labor unions to promote economic policies favorable to people working in the import-competing sector. The creation of organized groups to represent the interests of import-competing manufacturing generated its own political logic. On the one hand, the groups that saw their incomes rise from protection had a strong incentive to see protectionist policies continued in the postwar period. (See Rogowski 1989; Haggard 1990.) On the other hand, the emergence of new organized interests and a growing urban middle class created an opportunity for politicians to construct new political coalitions based on the support of the urban sectors. In Argentina, for example, Juan Peron rose to power in the late 1940s with the support of labor, industrialists, and the military. A similar pattern was evident in Brazil, where Getulio Vargas was elected to the presidency in 1950 with the support of industrialists, government civil servants, and urban labor. Nor were Argentina and Brazil unique: Throughout Latin America, postwar governments were much less tightly linked to landed interests than governments had been before World War I. Instead, governments rose to power on the basis of political support from interest groups whose incomes were derived from import-competing manufacturing (Cardoso and Faletto 1979). Such governments had a clear incentive to maintain trade policies that protected those incomes.

In Asia and Africa, the declining political influence of export-oriented agricultural interests and the growing influence of import-competing manufacturing occurred as a result of decolonization. In Asia—particularly in Korea and Taiwan—political change resulted from the defeat of Imperial Japan in World War II. (See Haggard 1990.) In South Korea, the defeat of Japan transferred power from a foreign colonizer to indigenous groups, and while the South Korean landowning class initially dominated postwar politics, the Korean War of the early 1950s and a series of land reforms implemented during that same decade greatly reduced the power of rural landowners and increased the relative power of the emerging urban sector. On Mainland China, the Japanese defeat was followed by the defeat of the nationalist Chinese government and the migration of the Chinese nationalists to the island of Taiwan. Once installed in Taiwan, the Chinese nationalists instituted land reforms to assert their authority over indigenous landowners and to prevent a repeat of their experience on the mainland, where the rural sectors had supported the Communists. As in South Korea, these land reforms reduced the power of landowners and increased the power of urban–industrial sectors.

Africa's transition came later, as the decolonization of Sub-Saharan Africa occurred only in the 1950s and early 1960s, and it took a slightly different form. The push toward decolonization was led by a coalition of indigenous professional elites who had been educated by the colonial powers and had then acquired positions in the administration of colonial economic and political rule. One factor motivating Africa's push for independence was dissatisfaction with the discriminatory practices of colonial administration. Colonial rulers had tightly restricted the ability of the local population to share in the wealth generated by domestic economic activity. Colonies were run for the profit of the colonists, with colonial economic enterprises staffed and managed by men from the colonial power. The local population had limited opportunities to participate in these economic arrangements other than as workers. The nationalist struggles for independence that emerged in the 1950s and succeeded over the next 15 years sought to transfer control over existing economic practices from the colonial governments to indigenous elites. As a consequence, import-competing manufacturing in Africa played a much smaller role in early postindependence politics than did the nontraded-goods sector. The indigenous elites as Claude Ake (1981, 142) has argued, "wanted to inherit a system rather than to revolutionise it."

The period demarcated by the start of the First World War and the end of decolonization in Sub-Saharan Africa thus brought a fundamental change to patterns of political influence in developing countries. Political structures once dominated by export-oriented agricultural interests were now largely under the control of import-competing manufacturing interests. Consequently, governments beholden to the import-competing sector had a clear incentive to abandon liberal trade policies and continue the protectionist arrangements that had been put in place during the 1930s. As we will see, the political interest in protectionism was reinforced by an elaborate theoretical structure which argued that protectionism was the only path to the establishment of industrialized economies.

The Structuralist Critique: Markets, Trade, and Economic Development

The adoption of protectionism in most developing countries reflected the interests of the politically influential import-competing manufacturing sector, but it did not represent a coherent strategy for economic development. And most governments were committed, at least rhetorically, to the adoption of policies that would promote economic development. Most governments wanted to shift resources out of agricultural production and into manufacturing industries because they believed that poverty resulted from too heavy a concentration on agricultural production. Higher standards of living could be achieved only through industrialization, and according to what was then the dominant branch of development economics, called **structralism,** the shift of resources from agriculture to manufacturing would not occur unless the state adopted policies to bring it about. (See Lal 1983; Little 1982.)

The belief that the market would not promote industrialization provided the intellectual and theoretical justification for the two central aspects of the development strategies adopted by most governments throughout much of the postwar era. Because structuralism played such an important role in shaping developing countries' trade and development policies, understanding the policies governments adopted requires us to understand the structuralist critique of the market. We first look at the structuralist critique of the domestic market in developing countries and then turn our attention to the structuralist critique of the international market and the international trade system.

Market Imperfections in Developing Countries

Structuralists argued that imperfections within developing countries' markets posed serious obstacles to industrialization, which would require a substantial reallocation of resources from agricultural production to manufacturing industries. The critical question for industrialization, therefore, was how best to achieve this reallocation. Structuralists argued that the domestic market could not be expected to bring about the necessary shift of resources. They were skeptical about the market because they believed that developing world economies were inflexible: "[Economic] change is inhibited by obstacles, bottlenecks, and constraints. People find it hard to move or adapt, and resources tend to be stuck" in the sectors in which they are currently employed (Little 1982, 20).

Most important, according to the structuralists, was the belief that the market would not promote investment in manufacturing industries. As economist Tibor Scitovsky wrote at the time,

> In an economy in which economic decisions are decentralized [that is, in a market economy], a system of communication is needed to enable each person who makes economic decisions to learn about the economic decisions of others and coordinate his decision with theirs. In the market economy, prices are the signaling device that informs each person of other people's economic decisions; and the merit of perfect competition is that it would cause prices to transmit information reliably and people to respond to this information properly. Market prices, however, reflect the economic situation as it is and not as it will be. For this reason, they are more useful for co-ordinating current production decisions, which are immediately effective and guided by short-run considerations, than they are for co-ordinating investment decisions, which have a delayed effect and—looking ahead to a long future period—should be governed not by what the present economic situation is but by what the future economic situation is expected to be. The proper co-ordination of investment decisions, therefore, would require a signaling device to transmit information about present plans and future conditions as they are determined by present plans; and the pricing system fails to provide this (1954, 150).

The structuralists pointed to two coordination problems that would limit investment in manufacturing industries. The first problem, called **complementary demand,** arose in the initial transformation from an economy based largely on subsistence agriculture (agricultural production in which people consume their farm production rather than sell it for cash) to a manufacturing economy (Rosenstein-Rodan 1943). In an economy in which few people earned a money wage, no single manufacturing firm would be able to sell its products, unless a large number of other manufacturing industries were started simultaneously. Suppose, for example, that 100 people are taken out of subsistence agriculture and paid a wage to manufacture shoes, while the rest of the population remains in nonwage agriculture. To whom will the new shoe factory sell its shoes? The only workers earning money are those producing shoes, and it is unlikely that these 100 workers will purchase all of the shoes that they make. In order for this shoe factory to succeed, other factories employing other people must be created at the same time.

Suppose instead, then, that 500,000 workers are taken out of subsistence agriculture and simultaneously employed in a large number of factories producing a variety of different manufactured goods; some make shoes, others make clothing, and still others produce refrigerators or processed foods. With this larger number of wage earners, manufacturing enterprises can easily sell their goods. Shoe workers can buy refrigerators and clothes, workers in the clothing factory can purchase shoes, and so on. Thus, a manufacturing enterprise will be successful only if a large number of other manufacturing firms are started at the same time.

This coordination problem arises because no single entrepreneur has an incentive to create a manufacturing enterprise, unless he or she is certain that others will invest as well. Thus, no one will invest in a manufacturing industry unless the potential investors can somehow coordinate their behavior to ensure that all will invest in manufacturing industries at the same time. Structuralists argued that the market, which encouraged autonomous investment decisions by independent economic actors, would not promote the necessary coordination. The problem of complementary demand thus meant that if investment were left to the market, there would be little investment in manufacturing industries.

The second coordination problem, called **pecuniary external economies,** arose from interdependencies among market processes (Scitovsky 1954). Think about the economic relationship between a steel plant and an automobile factory. Suppose that the owners of a steel factory invest to increase the amount of steel they can produce. As steel production increases, steel prices begin to fall. The automobile factory, which uses a lot of steel in producing cars, begins to realize rising profits as the price of one of its most important inputs falls. These increasing profits in the automobile industry could induce the owners of the car plant to invest to expand their own production capacity. Such a simultaneous expansion of the steel and auto industries would raise national income.

The two firms face a coordination problem, however. On the one hand, the owners of the steel plant will not increase steel production unless they are sure that the auto industry will increase car production. On the other hand, the owners of the auto plant will not increase auto production unless they are certain that the steel producer will make the investments needed to expand steel output. Thus, unless investment decisions in the steel and auto industry are coordinated and taken together, neither firm will invest to increase the amount it can produce. Once again, structuralists argued, the market could not be expected to solve this coordination problem.

The market's inability to coordinate investment decisions was a serious problem for governments intent on transforming the structure of their economies. If the market would not coordinate investment decisions, then investments in manufacturing industries necessary to drive the process of industrialization would not be made. Structuralists argued that the way to overcome these coordination problems and initiate industrialization was with a state-led **big push.** The state would engage in economic planning and either make necessary investments itself or help coordinate the investments of private economic actors. Thus, what the market could not bring about, the state could achieve through intervening in the economy. The structuralist critique of the market therefore provided a compelling theoretical justification for state-led strategies of industrialization.

Market Imperfections in the International Economy

Structuralists also argued that international trade provided few benefits to developing countries. This argument was formulated during the 1950s, principally by Raul Prebisch, an Argentinean economist who worked for the United Nations Economic Commission for Latin America (ECLA), and Hans Singer, an academic development economist. According to the **Singer–Prebisch theory,** participation in the GATT-based trade system would actually make it harder for developing countries to industrialize by depriving them of critical resources.

The Singer–Prebisch theory divides the world into two distinct blocks—the advanced-industrialized **core** and the developing-world **periphery**—and then focuses on the terms of trade between them. The **terms of trade** relate the price of a country's exports to the price of its imports. An improvement in a country's terms of trade means that the price of the goods it exports is rising relative to the price of the goods it imports, while a decline in a country's terms of trade means that the price of the goods it exports is falling relative to the price of the goods it imports. As a country's terms of trade decline, it must exchange a larger volume of domestic production (it must export more) for a given amount of foreign production (imports). As a country's terms of trade improve, it can acquire a given amount of imports for a smaller quantity of exports. Thus, an improvement in its terms of trade makes a country richer, while a decline in its terms of trade makes it poorer.

Because the typical developing country exports primary commodities and imports manufactured goods, income in developing countries is sensitive to the terms of trade between primary commodities and manufactured goods. A fall in the price of primary commodities relative to that of manufactured goods lowers developing countries' incomes. A rise in the price of primary commodities relative to that of manufactured goods raises their incomes.

The Singer–Prebisch theory argues that developing countries' terms of trade deteriorate steadily over time. Two mechanisms are seen as the cause of this secular decline. First, the periphery's terms of trade deteriorate due to the different consequences of productivity improvements in the core and periphery. (See Lewis 1954; United Nations 1964; Gilpin 1987, 275–276.) An improvement in productivity reduces the cost of producing a single good, and such a cost reduction allows the firm to either reduce the price of the good or pay higher wages. Core-country economies are characterized by full employment and strong labor unions. Labor in those countries is thus in a strong position when bargaining with firms; consequently productivity improvements are transformed into rising wages and stable prices.

Developing countries, by contrast, have large amounts of underemployed labor and weak labor unions. Labor in developing countries is thus in a weak position when bargaining with firms; consequently productivity improvements are transformed into stable wages and falling prices (United Nations 1964, 15). Because productivity gains yielded stable prices for core-country manufactured goods and falling prices for periphery-country commodities, the amount that developing countries must export to acquire a given volume of imports rises continuously over time.

Structuralists also emphasized differences in the income elasticity of demand for primary commodities versus industrial goods. The **income elasticity of demand** is the degree to which a change in income affects demand for a particular good. Low income elasticity of demand means that a large increase in per capita income produces little change in demand for a particular good. High income elasticity of demand means that a small increase in income produces a large change in demand for a particular good. Structuralists argued that the income elasticity of demand for primary commodities was quite low. **Engel's law,** which informed the structuralists, holds that people spend smaller percentages of their total income on food and other primary commodities as their incomes rise.

Thus, as incomes rise in the core countries, a smaller and smaller percentage of those countries' income will be spent on imports of primary commodities. But as income rises in the periphery countries, a larger percentage of *those* countries' income will be spent on manufactured imports from the core. Falling demand for primary commodities will cause the periphery countries' export prices to fall, while rising demand for manufactured goods will cause the periphery countries' import prices to rise. Rising import prices relative to export prices yields deteriorating terms of trade.

Stripped of all the economic terminology, the structuralists' point was remarkably simple: in contrast to classical trade theory's claim that free trade provides clear benefits to all countries, the structuralists argued that developing countries did not necessarily benefit from international trade. In a world in which developing countries exchange primary commodities for manufactured goods, core countries capture most, if not all, of the gains from trade. According to the structuralists, therefore, the GATT-based multilateral trade system was highly disadvantageous for developing countries.

Moreover, the income losses caused by the secular decline in their terms of trade constrained the ability of developing countries to industrialize. In order to industrialize, developing countries had to import **capital goods**—that is, machines used to produce other goods, as well as many intermediate inputs. The ability of developing countries to import capital and intermediate goods, however, was determined in large part by their export earnings. Yet, the purchasing power obtained from their export earnings was falling over time. Thus, the secular decline in the terms of trade made it harder for developing countries to import things that were critical for industrialization.

The validity of the Singer–Prebisch theory has been questioned. Most controversial has been the claim that developing countries face a continuous decline in their terms of trade. Measuring the long-term trend in a country's terms of trade is complicated by the fact that developing countries experience frequent terms-of-trade shocks. A **term-of-trade shock** is a sudden and unanticipated, but usually temporary, change in a country's terms of trade caused by factors outside the country's direct control. In the mid-1970s, for example, a severe frost in Brazil, one of the world's largest coffee producers, destroyed a significant portion of the Brazilian coffee crop and coffee trees. As a result, the world price of coffee rose steeply. By April 1977, the world price of coffee had risen to more than six times the price that had prevailed in June 1975 (Deaton 1999, 28). Thus, the terms of trade for other coffee-exporting nations, such as Colombia, Kenya, and Tanzania, improved suddenly and dramatically for reasons fully exogenous to their economies. Other shocks are negative. The decline in world economic activity during the late 1990s and early 2000s, for example, reduced the global demand for petroleum, and lower demand was associated with falling oil prices in world markets.

When terms-of-trade shocks are frequent, a country will experience a decline in its terms of trade in some years and a rise in others. The conclusion we reach about the general trend over a longer period of time will be sensitive to when we begin and end our measurement. If, for example, you compare a country's terms of trade following a positive shock in 1960 with its terms of trade 40 years later immediately following a large negative shock, you are likely to conclude that the country's terms of trade have declined over the entire period. Conversely, if you compare a country's terms of trade following a negative shock in 1960 and a positive shock in 2000, you may conclude that the country's terms of trade have generally improved over the intervening 40 years. Still, even taking into account the measurement problems, recent research does lend some support to the structuralists' claim (Borensztein et al. 1994; see also Bloch and Sapsford 2000). Between 1957 and 1987, prices of primary commodities other than oil fell by about three-quarters of 1 percent per year relative to prices of manufactured goods, while between 1968 and 1987, the deterioration increased to 1.57 percent per year. (See Cypher and Dietz 1997, 180.)

While structuralism's critique of markets within developing countries and of the international trade system has been severely criticized, the objective validity of structuralism is not our central concern. What matters for our purposes is that developing countries *believed* that the structuralist critique was correct. Governments of developing countries were convinced that industrialization would not occur if left to markets at home or if those countries participated in the GATT-based international trade system. This conviction played an important role in shaping the trade and development policies that developing countries adopted.

Domestic and International Elements of Trade and Development Strategies

Structuralism enabled governments to transform the protectionist trade policies that benefited their principal political supporters into comprehensive state-led development strategies. The trade and development policies that most governments adopted following World War II had both a domestic and an international dimension. At home, the desire to promote rapid industrialization led governments to adopt state-led development strategies that were sheltered by high protectionist barriers. In the international arena, concern about the distributional implications of international trade led developing countries to seek far-reaching changes to the GATT-based trade system. This reform effort was characterized by a concerted attempt to shift the international trade system away from the market-based liberalism embodied in GATT and toward an alternative set of rules and institutions that the developing countries believed would better enable them to industrialize. We examine each dimension in turn.

Import Substitution Industrialization

Industrialization required a shift of resources out of agriculture and into manufacturing. Skepticism about the ability of the market to promote this necessary reallocation of resources implied that industrialization would occur only if the state played a leading role. States played this leading role by adopting a development strategy called **import substitution industrialization,** or ISI. The strategy of ISI was based on a simple logic: countries would industrialize by substituting domestically produced goods for manufactured items they had previously imported.

The approach was conceptualized as a two-stage strategy. (See Table 6.3.) Its initial stage was "wholly a matter of imitation and importation of tried and tested procedures" (Hirschman 1968, 7). **Easy ISI,** as this first stage was often called, focused on developing domestic manufacturing industries that would be capable of producing relatively simple consumer goods, such as soda, beer, apparel, shoes, and furniture. The rationale behind the focus on simple consumer goods was threefold. First, there was a large domestic demand for them that was currently satisfied by imports. Second,

Table 6.3
Stages of Industrialization in Mexico and Brazil, 1880–1970

	Commodity Exports, 1880–1930	Primary ISI, 1930–1955	Secondary ISI, 1955–1968
Main Industries	Mexico: Precious metals, minerals, oil Brazil: Coffee, rubber, cocoa, cotton	Mexico and Brazil: Textiles, food, cement, iron and steel, paper, chemicals, machinery	Mexico and Brazil: Automobiles, electrical and nonelectrical machinery, petrochemicals, pharmaceuticals
Major Economic Actors	Mexico: Foreign investors Brazil: National private firms	Mexico and Brazil: National private firms	Mexico and Brazil: State-owned enterprises, transnational corporations, and national private firms
Orientation of the Economy	World market	Domestic market	Domestic market

Source: Gereffi 1990, 19.

because these items were mature products, the technology and machines necessary to produce them could be easily acquired from the advanced industrialized countries. Third, the production of relatively simple consumer goods relies heavily on low-skilled labor, allowing developing societies to draw their populations into manufacturing activities without making large investments to upgrade their skills.

Governments expected to realize two broad benefits from this first stage. Initially, the expansion of manufacturing activities, particularly if a portion of the resulting profits was reinvested, would increase wage-based employment as underutilized labor was drawn out of agriculture and into manufacturing. In addition, the experience gained in these manufacturing industries would allow domestic workers to develop skills, collectively referred to as **general human capital,** that could be subsequently applied to other manufacturing businesses. Of particular importance were the management and entrepreneurial skills that would be gained by the people who worked in and managed the manufacturing enterprises established in this stage. Success in the easy stage would therefore create many of the ingredients necessary to make the transition to the second, harder stage of ISI.

Easy ISI would eventually cease to bear fruit. The domestic market's capacity to absorb the kinds of simple consumer goods produced at this stage would quickly be exhausted, and the range of such goods that could be produced would be limited. At some point, therefore, developing countries would need to shift from easy ISI to a second-stage strategy that pushed them into more complex manufacturing activities. One possibility would be to shift to what some have called an **export substitution strategy,** in which the labor-intensive manufactured industries developed in easy ISI begin to export rather than continue to produce exclusively for the domestic market. This strategy is called export substitution because manufactured goods begin to substitute for primary commodities in the country's exports.

The second alternative, and the one actually adopted by many governments in Latin America and Africa, was called **secondary ISI.** In this approach, emphasis shifts from the manufacture of simple consumer goods to the production of consumer durable goods, intermediate inputs, and the capital goods needed to produce consumer durables. In Argentina, Brazil, and Chile, for example, governments decided to promote domestic automobile production as a central component of secondary ISI. Each country imported cars in pieces, called "complete knockdowns," and assembled the pieces into a car for sale in the domestic market. Domestic auto firms were required to gradually increase the percentage of locally produced parts used in the cars they assembled. In Chile, for example, 27 percent of a locally produced car's components had to be manufactured domestically in 1964. The percentage rose to 32 percent in 1965 and then to 45 percent in 1966 (Johnson 1967).

By increasing the percentage of local components of cars and other goods in this manner, governments hoped to promote the development of backward linkages throughout the economy (Hirschman 1958). **Backward linkages** arise when the production of one good, such as a car, increases demand in industries that supply components for that good. Thus, increasing the percentage of locally produced components of cars, by in turn increasing the demand for individual car parts, would increase domestic part production. The latter would in turn increase demand for inputs into part production: steel, glass, and rubber, for example. Industrialization, therefore, would spread backwards from final goods, to intermediate inputs, to capital goods as backward linkages multiplied.

Governments promoted secondary ISI by relying heavily on three policy instruments: trade barriers, government planning, and investment policy. The justification for trade barriers was provided by the infant-industry argument and by recurrent shortages of foreign exchange. Because export earnings were limited, while many elements critical to industrialization—many of the intermediate inputs, as well as almost all of the capital goods (at least at first)—had to be imported, governments controlled foreign trade tightly. Governments managed trade to ensure that expenditures of scarce foreign exchange were consistent with overall development objectives (Bhagwati 1978, 20–33). Protection also allowed infant industries to gain experience needed to compete against established producers. In Brazil and India, for instance, the state prohibited imports of any good for which there was a domestic substitute, regardless of price differences and, to a large extent, of quality differences as well.

The scale and the structure of protection that governments used to promote industrialization are illustrated in Table 6.4, which focuses on Latin America in 1960. In all but two of the countries listed in the table, nominal protection on nondurable consumer goods was well over 100 percent, and for all but three countries, the nominal tariffs on consumer durables were also over 100 percent. While Mexico and Uruguay stand out as clear exceptions to this pattern, this has more to do with those countries' extensive use of import quotas in place of tariffs than with an unwillingness to protect domestic producers (Bulmer-Thomas 1994, 279). It is also clear that tariffs were lower for semi-manufactured goods, industrial raw materials, and capital goods (all of which were items that developing countries needed to import in connection with industrialization) than they were for consumer goods. This pattern of tariff escalation was common in much of the developing world (Balassa and Associates 1971).

Most governments also relied heavily on explicit five-year plans. Developed by government agencies, these plans were designed to "serve as guidelines for public expenditures and for economic policies" (Little 1982, 35). Planning was used to determine which industries would be targeted for development and which would not, to fig-

Table 6.4
Nominal Protection in Latin America, circa 1960 (percent)

	Nondurable Consumer Goods	Durable Consumer Goods	Semi-manufactured Goods	Industrial Raw Materials	Capital Goods
Argentina	176	266	95	55	98
Brazil	260	328	80	106	84
Chile	328	90	98	111	45
Colombia	247	108	28	57	18
Mexico	114	147	28	38	14
Uruguay	23	24	23	14	27
European Economic Community	17	19	7	1	13

Source: Bulmer-Thomas, 1994, Table 9.1, p. 280.

ure out how much should be invested in a particular industry, and to evaluate how investment in one industry would influence the rest of the economy. The plan thus served as the coordination device that governments believed was necessary, given the belief that the market could not itself coordinate investment decisions.

With a plan in place, governments used investment policies to promote targeted industries. Most governments either nationalized or heavily controlled the financial sector. While we will look at this in greater detail in Chapter 14, here it is important to note that state control of the financial system enabled the government to direct financial resources to targeted industries. Governments also invested directly in those economic activities in which they thought the private sector would not invest. Much of the infrastructure necessary for industrialization—things such as roads and other transportation networks, electricity, and telecommunications systems—it was argued, would not be created by the private sector. In addition, the private sector lacked access to the large sums of financial support needed to make huge investments in a steel or auto plant. Moreover, it was claimed that private sector actors lacked the technical sophistication required for the large-scale industrial activity involved in secondary ISI.

Governments invested in these areas by creating **state-owned enterprises**—firms that were fully owned by the state—or by creating mixed-ownership enterprises that combined state and private-sector participation. In Brazil, for example, state-owned enterprises controlled more than 50 percent of total productive assets in the chemical, telecommunications, electricity, and railways industries and slightly more than one-third of all productive assets in metal fabrication (Trebat 1983). In Africa, governments in Ghana, Mozambique, Nigeria, and Tanzania each created more than 300 state-owned enterprises, and in many African countries, state-owned enterprises accounted for 20 percent of total wage-based employment (World Bank 1994b, 101). In India, state-owned enterprises made up for 27 percent of total employment and 62 percent of all productive capital (Krueger 1993a, 24–5).

While the import-competing manufacturing industry benefited from ISI policies, export-oriented agriculture bore many of the costs. (See Krueger 1992; Krueger, Schiff, and Valdes 1991; Binswanger and Deininger 1997.) Governments taxed agricultural exports (Krueger 1992, 16), frequently through government-owned marketing boards that controlled the purchase and export of agricultural commodities. Often established as the sole entity with the legal right to purchase, transport, and export agricultural products, marketing boards set the price that farmers received for their crops. In the typical arrangement, the marketing board would purchase crops from domestic farmers at prices well below the world price and then sell the commodities in the world market at the world price. The difference between the price paid to domestic farmers and the world price represented a tax on agricultural incomes that the state could use to finance government-favored projects in industry (Amsden 1979; Bates 1988; Krueger 1992). The trade barriers used to protect domestic manufacturing firms from foreign competition also represented a tax on the incomes of people working in agriculture. Tariffs and quantitative restrictions raised the domestic price of manufactured goods well above the world price. People employed in the agricultural sector, who were consumers rather than producers of these manufactured goods, therefore paid a much higher price for them than they would have in the absence of tariffs and quantitative restrictions (Krueger 1992, 9).

A CLOSER LOOK

Import Substitution Industrialization in Brazil

In the late 19th and early 20th century, Brazil was the classic case of a country that exported primary commodities. Its principal crop, coffee, accounted for a large share of its production and the overwhelming majority of its export earnings. This economic structure was supported by a political system dominated by the interests of coffee producers and other agricultural exporters (Bates 1997). Political authority in Brazil was decentralized, and the states used their power in the country's federal system to influence government policy. As a result, Brazil pursued a liberal trade policy throughout the late 19th and early 20th centuries. The First World War and the Great Depression disrupted these arrangements. The world price for coffee fell sharply in the late 1920s and early 1930s, generating declining terms of trade and rising trade deficits. The government responded to this crisis by adopting protectionist measures to limit imports. The initial turn to protectionism was accompanied by political change. A military coup in 1930 handed power to Getulio Vargas, who centralized power by shifting political authority from the states to the federal government. While Vargas did not adopt an import substitution industrialization strategy, this period represented in many respects the easy stage of ISI (Haggard 1990,165–166). Protectionism promoted the growth of light manufacturing industries, at a rate of 6 percent per year between 1929 and 1945 (Thorp 1999, 322). Concurrently, the centralization of power created a state that could intervene effectively in the Brazilian economy. While the export-oriented interests did not lose all political influence in this new political climate, the balance of power had clearly shifted toward new groups emerging in urban centers: the professionals, managers, and bureaucrats that constituted the emerging middle class and the nascent manufacturing interests. As Brazil moved into the post-World War II period, therefore, the stage was set for the transition to secondary ISI.

A full-blown import substitution industrialization strategy emerged in the 1950s. The government restricted imports tightly with the so-called law of similars, which effectively prohibited the import of goods similar to those produced in Brazil. In 1952, the Brazilian government created the National Economic Development Bank (BNDE), an important instrument for industrial policy through which the Brazilian state could finance industrial projects. In the late 1950s, the government created a new agency, the National Development Council, to coordinate and plan its industrialization strategy. In taking up its task, the Council was heavily influenced by structuralist ideas (Haggard 1990, 174). Studies conducted within these agencies—and, in some instances, in collaboration with international agencies such as the UN Economic Commission on Latin America—focused on how best to promote industrialization (Leff 1969, 46). Most of these studies came to similar conclusions: industrialization in Brazil would quickly run into constraints caused by inadequate transportation networks (road, rail, and sea), shortages of electric power, and the underdevelopment of basic heavy industries such as steel, petroleum, chemicals, and nonferrous metals. Building up those industries thus became the focus of the government's development policies. The Brazilian government had little faith that the private sector would create and expand these critically important industries. Instead, policymakers determined that the state would have to play a leading role. In the early

Continued

1950s, the state nationalized the oil and electricity industries and began investing heavily in the expansion of capacity in both. A similar approach was adopted in the transportation sector (in which the government owned the railways and other infrastructure), in the steel industry, and in telecommunications. By the end of the 1950s, the state accounted for 37 percent of all investment made in the Brazilian economy. As a result, the number of state-owned enterprises grew rapidly, from fewer than 35 in 1950 to more than 600 by 1980.

Beyond creating these basic industries, the Brazilian government also sought to create domestic capacity to produce complex consumer goods. To achieve this objective, Brazil, in contrast to many other developing countries, drew heavily upon foreign investment to promote the development of certain industries. The auto industry is an excellent example. In 1956, the Brazilian government prohibited all imports of cars. Any foreign producer that wanted to sell cars in the Brazilian market would have to set up production facilities in the country. To ensure that such foreign investments were not simple assembly operations in which the foreign company imported all parts from its suppliers at home, the Brazilian government instituted local rules that required the foreign automakers operating in the country to purchase 90 percent of their parts from Brazilian firms. In order to induce foreign automakers to invest in Brazil under these conditions, the government offered subsidies; by one account, the subsidies offset about 87 percent of the total investment between 1956 and 1969. Relying on this strategy, Brazilian auto production rose from close to zero in 1950 to almost 200,000 cars in 1962.

Brazil's import substitution industrialization strategy helped transform the country's economy in a remarkably short time. Imported consumer nondurable goods (the products targeted during easy ISI) had been almost completely replaced with domestic production by the early 1950s (Bergsman and Candal 1969, 37). Imported consumer durables, the final goods targeted in secondary ISI, fell from 60 percent of total consumption to less than 10 percent of total consumption by 1959. Imports of capital goods also fell, from 60 percent of total domestic consumption in 1949, to about 35 percent of consumption in 1959, and then to only 10 percent by 1964. Finally, imports of intermediate goods, the inputs used in producing final goods, also fell continually throughout the decade, to less than 10 percent of total consumption by 1964. Thus, as imports were barred and domestic industries created, Brazilian consumers and producers purchased a much larger percentage of the goods they used from domestic producers and a much smaller percentage from foreign producers. As a consequence, the importance of manufacturing in the Brazilian economy increased sharply: whereas manufacturing accounted for only 26 percent of total Brazilian production in 1949, by 1964 it accounted for 34 percent.

Such government policies transferred income from rural agriculture to the urban manufacturing and nontraded-goods sectors. The size of the income transfers was substantial. As summarized in a recent World Bank study,

> the total impact of interventions . . . on relative prices [between agriculture and manufacturing] was in some countries very large. In Ghana . . . farmers received only about 40 percent of what they would have received under free trade. Stated in another way, the real incomes of farmers would have increased by 2.5 times had farmers been able to buy and sell under free trade prices given the commodities they in fact produced. While Ghanaian total discrimination against agriculture was huge, Argentina, Cote

d'Ivoire, the Dominican Republic, Egypt, Pakistan, Sri Lanka, Thailand, and Zambia also had total discrimination against agriculture in excess of 33 percent, implying that in all those cases, farm incomes in real terms could have been increased by more than 50 percent by removal of these interventions (Krueger 1992, 63).

Thus, ISI redistributed income. Groups in the export-oriented sector that enjoyed little political influence saw their incomes fall. Groups in the import-competing sector that enjoyed considerable influence with ruling elites saw their incomes rise.

The strategy of import substitution industrialization promoted rapid economic growth in the 1960s and 1970s: developing countries' economies grew at annual average rates of between 6 percent and 7.6 percent during this period. In many countries, it was the manufacturing sector that drove economic growth. Argentina, Brazil, Chile, Mexico, Mozambique, Nigeria, Pakistan, and India, to select only a few examples, all enjoyed average annual rates of manufacturing growth between 5 and 10 percent during the 1960s. A glimpse back at Table 6.1 indicates that, in Latin America, manufacturing's share of the total economy increased substantially between 1960 and 1980, and a quite similar pattern is evident in Africa as well. Thus, while the policies that governments adopted had important effects on the distribution of income, they also appeared to be transforming developing societies from producers of primary commodities into modern industrialized economies.

Reforming the International Trade System

Developing countries also tried to alter the rules governing international trade. One of their principal objectives in pursuing such reforms was to create mechanisms that would transfer income from core countries to the periphery as compensation for the losses resulting from their deteriorating terms of trade.

As early as 1947, India, Brazil, Chile, and Australia expressed concerns that the rules the United States and Great Britain were writing for the GATT and the ITO failed to address the economic problems that developing countries faced (Kock 1969, 38–42). Advancing the infant-industry justification for protection, many developing countries argued that their firms could not compete with established producers in the United States and Europe. Yet, GATT rules not only made no provision for the infant-industry justification, but, indeed, explicitly prohibited the use of quantitative restrictions and tightly restricted the use of tariffs. Developing countries insisted that they be given a relatively free hand in the use of trade restrictions to promote economic development, because GATT failed to do so.

Developing countries continued to press for GATT reforms throughout the 1950s (Kock 1969, 238; Finger 1991). While few concrete reforms resulted from these early efforts, they did produce a study, called the **Haberler Report,** that was conducted under the guidance of the GATT and published in 1958. The study was conducted in an attempt to understand why developing countries' trade performance was so poor. It focused particularly on the impact of primary-commodity price fluctuations and agricultural protection in the advanced industrialized countries on developing countries. (See Campos et al. 1958.) The report represented a "turning point in the GATT's relations with less-developed countries" (Dam 1970, 228), providing intellectual support for the structuralists' main arguments by suggesting that the GATT was "relatively unfavorable to primary producing countries" and concluding "that developing countries were losing ground under the GATT" (Finger 1991, 212). By supporting the developing countries' principal claims, the Haberler Report altered political dynamics in the international trade system. Henceforth, not only would the demands for reform made by the developing countries be more far reaching, but the ability of the advanced industrialized countries to dismiss those demands out of hand would be greatly weakened.

By the early 1960s, a coalition of developing countries dedicated to the pursuit of far-reaching reform of the international trade system had emerged. This coalition would engage in a 20-year campaign to fundamentally alter the rules governing international trade. Its first important success was achieved with the formation of the **United Nations Conference on Trade and Development (UNCTAD)** in March of 1964. UNCTAD was established as a body dedicated to promoting the developing countries' interests in the world trade system. At the conclusion of this first UNCTAD conference, 77 developing-country governments signed a joint declaration that called for reform of the international trade system. Thus was born the **Group of 77** (G77), which led the campaign for systemic reform. During the next 20 years, trade relations between the developing world and the advanced industrialized countries revolved almost wholly around competing conceptions of how to organize international trade embodied in GATT and UNCTAD. While the advanced industrialized nations defended the market-based GATT, the Group of 77 used UNCTAD, and the United Nations more broadly, to try to reduce GATT's role in international trade and redistribute global income from the core to the periphery.

During the 1960s, developing countries used UNCTAD to pursue three international mechanisms that would provide them a larger share of the gains from trade (Kock 1969; UNCTAD 1964; Williams 1991). Developing countries pressed for the creation of **commodity price stabilization** schemes. Commodity price stabilization was to be achieved by setting a floor below which commodity prices would not be allowed to fall and by creating a finance mechanism, funded largely by the advanced industrialized countries, to purchase commodities when prices threatened to fall below the established floor. If commodity prices could be effectively stabilized at relatively high levels, the deterioration of developing countries' terms of trade could be slowed, if not ended altogether. Recognizing that commodity price stabilization schemes could not "offer a complete solution for all commodities or for all situations," developing countries also sought direct financial transfers from the advanced industrialized countries. Such transfers would compensate developing countries for the purchasing power they were losing from their declining terms of trade (UNCTAD 1964, 80). Developing countries also sought greater access to core-country markets, pressuring the advanced industrialized countries to eliminate trade barriers on primary commodities and to provide manufactured exports from developing countries with preferential access to the core countries' markets.

These reform efforts yielded few concrete results. Core countries did modify the GATT charter, however: In 1964, three articles focusing on developing countries' trade problems were included in **GATT Part IV.** These three articles called upon core countries to improve market access for commodity exporters, to refrain from raising barriers to the import of products of special interest to the developing world, and to

POLICY ANALYSIS AND DEBATE

Intellectual Property and the WTO

Question
How should the world balance the equity and efficiency aspects of intellectual property?

Overview
NIEO demands for low-cost technology transfers find their contemporary manifestation in the debate over the developing world's access to patented drugs used to treat HIV/AIDS. The world's highest HIV infection rates are in the world's poorest societies, and while Western drug companies have developed antiretroviral therapies to treat the disease, a month of treatment with these drugs costs substantially more than average annual incomes in those countries. Many have argued that HIV/AIDS therapies should be made available at low cost to the developing world.

This debate is a very stark form of a broader debate surrounding the equity and efficiency issues generated by intellectual property. Equity issues arise because, once knowledge exists, it can be transmitted from one society to another at practically no cost. A drug, after all, is knowledge about how specific chemical compounds affect the human body—and it is easy for an Indian drug company to use knowledge created by Western firms to produce HIV drug therapies that are substantially less expensive than the Western versions. Yet, the TRIPS agreement prevents the Indian firm from selling its lower cost therapies to African countries. Access to intellectual property is thus restricted to those who can afford to pay.

Efficiency issues arise because society would have less innovation if intellectual property rights were not protected. Intellectual property is costly to develop. Estimates suggest that it costs about $850 million to develop a single new drug. If firms cannot recoup these costs, few will invest in creating knowledge, and we would not have anti-retroviral therapies. Consequently, society would be worse off, for it could not treat serious diseases. To promote innovation, therefore, governments have to protect intellectual property. What is the appropriate balance between equity and efficiency?

Policy Options
- Place all intellectual property in the public domain. This allows all to benefit from intellectual property, regardless of their income.
- Protect intellectual property for a limited time in order to allow innovators to recoup their investment.

Policy Analysis
- To what extent does the specific issue (HIV/AIDS) shape your approach to the question? That is, would you have the same view if the preceding discussion focused on computer software? Why or why not?
- Can governments make decisions on a case-by-case basis after knowledge exists? Why or why not?

Take a Position
- Which option do you prefer? Justify your choice.
- What criticisms of your position should you anticipate? How would you defend your recommendation against these criticisms?

Continued

Resources
Online: Visit the WTO webpage on the TRIPs agreement. The World Intellectual Property Organization (WIPO) also maintains a useful website (www.wipo.int), and Oxfam (*www.oxfam.org.uk*) has useful information.
In Print: Susan Sell, *Private Power, Public Law: The Globalization of Intellectual Property Rights* (Cambridge: Cambridge University Press, 2003). Peter Drahos and Ruth Mayne, eds., *Global Intellectual Property Rights: Knowledge, Access and Development* (London: MacMillan Press, 2002).

engage in "joint action to promote trade and development" (Kock 1969, 242). In the absence of meaningful changes in the trade policies pursued by the advanced industrialized countries, however, Part IV offered few concrete gains to developing countries. The advanced industrialized countries also allowed the developing countries to opt out of strict reciprocity during GATT tariff negotiations. The developing countries that belonged to the GATT were therefore able to benefit from the tariff reductions made by the advanced industrialized countries without having to make tariff reductions in return. Benefits from this concession were more apparent than real, however: GATT negotiations focused primarily on manufactured goods produced by the advanced industrialized countries and excluded agriculture, textiles, and many other labor-intensive goods. Developing countries were therefore exporting few of the goods on which the advanced industrialized countries were actually reducing tariffs. In the late 1960s, the advanced industrialized countries agreed to the **Generalized System of Preferences** (GSP), under which manufactured exports from developing countries gained preferential access to advanced industrialized countries' markets. This concession, too, was of limited importance, because advanced industrialized countries often limited the quantity of goods that could enter under preferential tariff rates and excluded some manufacturing sectors from the arrangement entirely.

Even though their efforts during the 1960s had achieved few concrete gains, the Group of 77 escalated its demands for systemic reform in the early 1970s. The limited success realized during the 1960s heightened the Group of 77's dissatisfaction with the structure of the international trade system. Then, in 1973, the world's major oil-producing countries, working together in the Organization of Petroleum Exporting Countries (OPEC), used their control of oil to improve their terms of trade. OPEC's ability to use commodity power to improve its terms of trade with the advanced industrialized countries and, in so doing, extract income from the core strengthened the belief within the Group of 77 that commodity power could be exploited to force fundamental systemic change.

Growing dissatisfaction and greater confidence combined to produce a set of more radical demands known collectively as the **New International Economic Order** (NIEO); (see Krasner 1985), an attempt by the Group of 77 to create an international trade system whose operation was to be made "subordinate to the perceived development needs" of developing countries (Gilpin 1987, 299). The NIEO, which the UN General Assembly adopted in December 1974, embodied a set of reforms that, if implemented, would have radically altered the operation of the international economy. In addition to encompassing the three mechanisms that developing countries had demanded during the 1960s, the NIEO included rules that would give governments in developing countries greater control over multinational corporations operating in their countries, easier and cheaper access to northern technology, a reduction in foreign debt, increased foreign aid flows, and a larger role in the decision-making processes of the World Bank and International Monetary Fund.

Governments in the advanced industrialized countries again proved unwilling to make significant concessions, and by the mid-1980s the NIEO had fallen from the agenda of the world trade system. The failure of the NIEO has been attributed to a number of factors. First, developing countries were unable to establish and maintain a cohesive coalition. The heterogeneity of developing countries' interests made it relatively easy for the advanced industrialized countries to divide the Group of 77 by offering limited concessions to a small number of governments in exchange for defection from the broader group. In addition, the Group of 77 had hoped that OPEC would assist it by linking access to oil to acceptance of the NIEO. But OPEC governments were unwilling to use their oil power to help other developing countries achieve broader trade and development objectives. Finally, by the late 1970s, many developing countries were facing serious balance-of-payments problems and were forced to turn to the International Monetary Fund (IMF) and the World Bank for financial support. The need to obtain IMF and World Bank assistance gave the advanced industrialized countries considerable influence over economic and trade policies in the developing world.

Conclusion

Throughout much of the postwar period, developing countries insulated themselves from the world trade system. The interaction between domestic politics, on the one hand, and economic shocks and decolonization, on the other, gave rise to governments throughout the developing world that were highly responsive to the interests of import-competing manufacturing industries and a growing class of urban workers. Influenced greatly by structuralism, most governments transformed the then-existing political incentive to protect these domestic manufacturing industries into ambitious state-led development strategies. Structuralism's critique of the ability of domestic and international markets to promote industrialization led governments to intervene in domestic markets to overcome imperfections that reduced private incentives to invest.

To the extent that developing countries participated in the global trade system at all, their participation was aimed at bringing about far-reaching reform of the rules governing the system. Again, the structuralist critique served an important role in this effort, arguing that developing countries could not expect to gain from trade with the advanced industrialized countries until they themselves had industrialized and that trade based on the rules embodied in GATT would only make such industrialization harder to achieve. Rather than accept participation in the global economy on what they viewed as vastly unequal terms, developing countries battled to change the rules governing international trade in order to capture a larger share of the gains from North–South trade. Thus, an international struggle over the distribution of the gains from trade was an almost necessary counterpart of the domestic strategy of redistributing resources from agriculture to industry embodied in import substitution industrialization.

Was the strategy of state-led industrialization successful? As we will see in the next chapter, the answer to this question remains in dispute. What there seems be less disagreement about, however, is that the specific import substitution industrialization strategies adopted by many governments in Latin America, South Asia, the Middle East, and parts of Sub-Saharan Africa failed to deliver on their promises. (See Todaro 2000, 507–509.) While we will look at the key weaknesses in detail in the next chapter, here we will note only the following: In many countries, ISI did promote the fairly rapid development of a "modern" industrial sector. However, the costs of doing so were frequently very high, and more often than not, the industries that were established failed to operate efficiently. High costs arose in large part from the loss of export earnings in the internationally competitive primary sectors. This in itself would not have been bad if the resources being shifted to the newly created industries had been used efficiently. Too often, however, they were not. By reducing competition, high tariffs reduced the incentive for these infant firms to become more efficient. The preference for large capital-intensive industries failed to make the best use of the factors that were readily available in the local economy. Many governments were unwilling to close down inefficient firms and opted instead to continue to subsidize their operation.

As a consequence, much of the resources that were extracted from agriculture were wasted in the pursuit of rapid industrialization. Eventually, the accumulation of these inefficiencies forced developing countries to embark on radical reforms. How they did so, the details of the specific reforms that governments adopted, and the impact of these reforms are issues we take up in the next chapter.

Key Terms

Backward Linkages	Import Substitution Industrialization
Big Push	Income Elasticity of Demand
Capital Goods	Monoexporters
Commodity Composition of Exports	New International Economic Order
Commodity Price Stabilization	Nontraded-Goods Sector
Complementary Demand	Pecuniary External Economies
Core	Periphery
Easy ISI	Secondary ISI
Enclave Agriculture	Singer–Prebisch Theory
Engel's Law	State-owned Enterprises
Export Substitution Strategy	Structuralism
GATT Part IV	Terms of Trade
General Human Capital	Terms-of-Trade Shock
Generalized System of Preferences	United Nations Conference on Trade and
Group of 77	Development
Haberler Report	

Web Links

The United Nations Conference on Trade and Development can be found at
http://www.unctad.org and the Group of 77 website at *http://www.g77.org*.

Visit the World Bank at *http://www.worldbank.org*.

You can also visit the regional development banks:

The African Development Bank: *http://www.afdb.org*.

The Inter-American Development Bank: *http://www.iadb.org*.

The Asian Development Bank: *http://www.adb.org*.

The WTO devotes a section of its site to developing countries and the international trade system:
http://www.wto.org/english/tratop_e/devel_e/devel_e.htm.

The Electronic Development and Environment Information System (ELDIS), based at the Institute of Development Studies in Sussex, England, maintains a website with good links to information about development issues. This page can be found at *http://nt1.ids.ac.uk/eldis/eldis.htm*.

Suggestions for Further Reading

For a readable introduction to structuralism and development strategies more generally, see Ian Little, *Economic Development* (New York: Basic Books, 1982). For an in-depth look at Latin America, see Jeffry Frieden, Manuel Pastor, Jr., and Michael Tomz, eds., *Modern Political Economy and Latin America: Theory and Policy* (Boulder: Westview Press, 2000), and Victor Bulmer-Thomas, *The Economic History of Latin American since Independence* (Cambridge, Cambridge University Press, 2003).

For a detailed examination of the New International Economic Order, see Stephen Krasner, *Structural Conflict: the Third World against Global Liberalism* (Berkeley: University of California Press, 1985).

CHAPTER 7

Trade and Development II: Economic Reform

Whereas structuralism and import substitution industrialization shaped development strategies during the first 35 years of the postwar period, the last 20 years have been dominated by neoliberalism and export-oriented industrialization. In contrast to structuralism, with its skepticism of the market and faith in the state, **neoliberalism** is highly skeptical of the state's ability to allocate resources efficiently and places great faith in the market's ability to do so. And in contrast to structuralism's advocacy of protectionism and state intervention is neoliberalism's advocacy of the withdrawal of the state from the economy, the reduction (ideally, elimination) of trade barriers, and reliance on the market to generate industries that produce for the world market.

Like structuralism, neoliberalism has dramatically affected policy. Across the developing world, governments have reduced tariffs and removed other trade barriers, thereby opening their economies to imports. They have sold state-owned enterprises to private groups. They have deregulated domestic markets and allowed prices to reflect the underlying scarcity of resources. They have shifted their emphasis from producing for the domestic market to producing for the global market. Countries that had never joined the GATT sought membership in the WTO. Thus, the last 20 years have brought a complete reversal of the development strategies that most governments had adopted. Belief in the power of states has been replaced by belief in the efficacy of the market; skepticism about trade has been replaced by concerted efforts to integrate deeply into the world trade system. Neoliberalism has replaced structuralism as the guiding philosophy of economic development.

The shift from structuralism to neoliberalism emerged from the interplay between three developments in the global economy. First, by the early 1970s, import substitution industrialization was generating some serious economic imbalances. The emergence of these imbalances suggested that economic reform of some type was required, although it did not point to a specific solution. Second, at about the same time, it was becoming apparent that a small group of East Asian countries were outperforming all other developing countries. In only 30 years, these East Asian countries transformed themselves from traditional agricultural societies into powerful industrialized economies capable of producing sophisticated products that were sold in Western markets. East Asian societies achieved this success through what many viewed as a neoliberal strategy: rather than insulate themselves from the global economy, they integrated deeply into world markets. The contrast between economic performance in East Asia and that in the rest of the developing world suggested, therefore, that a neoliberal strategy might deliver better results than import substitution could. Consequently, neoliberalism offered a compelling model upon which to base reforms. Third, a severe economic crisis in the early 1980s forced governments to finally embark on reform, and as they did, the International Monetary Fund and World Bank strongly encouraged them to base reform on the neoliberal model.

We examine each of these three developments. We look first at the factors that caused import substitution industrialization to generate economic imbalances. This examination allows us to understand the problems ISI created and the reasons that reform of some type was necessary. We then turn our attention to the East Asian countries. We briefly compare their performance with that of the rest of the developing world. We next examine two contrasting explanations for this remarkable performance, one that emphasizes the neoliberal elements of those countries' strategies, and one that emphasizes the role East Asian states played in the development process. We then turn to economic crisis and reform. We look at how the crisis pushed developing countries to the World Bank and IMF and at how these two institutions shaped the content of the reforms governments adopted. The chapter concludes by examining the challenges that developing countries now confront as active participants in the WTO.

Emerging Problems with Import Substitution Industrialization

By the late 1960s, import substitution industrialization was generating important economic imbalances, indicating that the approach might be nearing its limit as a useful development strategy. Two such imbalances were particularly important. The first lay in government budgets, in which ISI tended to generate persistent deficits because it prescribed heavy government involvement in the economy. Since governments believed that the private sector would not invest in industries that were important for the success of secondary ISI, governments themselves often made the investments, either in partnership with private-sector groups or alone by creating state-owned enterprises.

Yet, many of these state-owned enterprises never became profitable. By the late 1970s, state-owned enterprises in developing countries were running combined operating deficits that averaged 4 percent of GDP (Waterbury 1992, 190). Governments kept these enterprises afloat by using funds from the state budget. The combination of government investment and the subsequent need to cover the losses of state-owned enterprises contributed to large budget deficits throughout the developing world.

Domestic politics aggravated the budget deficits generated by ISI. For many governments, the urban residents employed in the nontraded-goods sector provided critical political support. Governments maintained this support by raising the standard of living of urban residents through subsidies for essential items. Electricity, water and sewer, transportation, telephone service, and food were all made available to urban residents at prices well below the market price. This was possible only by using government revenues to cover the difference between the true cost and the price charged. In addition, many governments used state-owned enterprises and the civil service to provide jobs to urban dwellers. In Benin, for example, the civil service tripled in size between 1960 and 1980, not because the government needed so many civil servants, but because the government needed to find some way to employ urban residents. Governments used state-owned enterprises for similar purposes. However, such practices simply added to government expenditures while doing little to increase government revenues, thereby worsening the budget deficit.

Import substitution industrialization also generated a second important imbalance: persistent current-account deficits. The **current account** registers a country's imports and exports of both goods and services. A current-account deficit means that a country is importing more than it is exporting. Import substitution gave rise to current-account deficits because it generated a considerable demand for imports while simultaneously reducing the economy's ability to export. On the import side, ISI generated a steady demand for imported capital goods and inputs. Industrialization required countries to import the necessary machines, and once these machines were in place, production required the continued import of critical intermediate inputs that were not produced in the domestic economy. Somewhat ironically, therefore, import substitution industrialization became heavily dependent upon imports.

Exports declined for two reasons. First, the manufacturing industries created through import substitution were not competitive in international markets. Production in many of the heavy industries that governments targeted in secondary ISI is characterized by economies of scale. The domestic market in most developing countries, however, was too small to allow domestic producers to realize economies of scale. These inefficiencies were compounded by excess capacity—the creation of more production capacity than the domestic market could absorb. (See Little, Scitovsky, and Scott 1970, 98.) Consequently, the newly created manufacturing industries could not export to the world market.

Second, the policies that governments used to promote industrialization weakened export-oriented agriculture, thereby causing agricultural exports to fall. The decline in agricultural production was most severe in Sub-Saharan Africa, which, as a region, taxed farmers more heavily than did other developing countries (Schiff and Valdes 1992). Heavy tax burdens reduced farmers' incentives to produce, and as a result, the rate of growth of agriculture declined. In Ghana, for example, the real value of the payments that cocoa farmers received from the government marketing board fell by about two-thirds between 1960 and 1965. Falling prices gave cocoa farmers little incentive to invest in order to maintain, let alone increase, cocoa output (Killick 1978, 119). In addition, cocoa farmers smuggled much of what they did produce into the Ivory Coast, where they could sell cocoa at world prices (Herbst 1993, 40).

These microeconomic inefficiencies were reinforced by the tendency of most governments to maintain overvalued exchange rates. The exchange rate is the domestic currency price of foreign currencies. Ideally, a government should maintain an exchange rate that equalizes the prices of goods in the domestic and foreign markets.

However, under import substitution industrialization, many governments intentionally set the exchange rate higher than that, and as a result, foreign goods were cheaper in the home market than they should have been and domestic goods were more expensive in foreign markets than they should have been. Because foreign goods were underpriced in the domestic market, capital goods and intermediate inputs could be acquired from abroad at a lower cost than they could be produced at home. This difference in price created a strong incentive to import, rather than creating the capacity to produce the goods locally. The result was rising imports. Because domestic goods were overpriced in foreign markets, domestic producers, even when efficient, found it difficult to sell their products in those markets. The result was falling exports.

The emergence of the twin imbalances of budget deficits and current-account deficits indicated that ISI was creating an economic structure that couldn't pay for itself. Many of the manufacturing industries created during secondary ISI could not sell their products at prices that covered their costs of production. Many developing countries could not export enough to pay for the imports demanded by the manufacturing industries they were creating. The system was therefore unsustainable. That is, the imbalances could not persist forever; some reform was clearly necessary.

Yet, the domestic political dynamics that had given rise to import substitution also made it exceedingly difficult for governments to implement the far-reaching reforms that were needed to remove the imbalances. On the one hand, most governments remained committed to rapid industrialization based on the logic of ISI. Far-reaching reforms would require them to reevaluate both this goal and the underlying strategy they were using to achieve it. And the only available alternative to ISI was a market-oriented development strategy (one we look at in detail in the next section). In the 1960s and 1970s, however, it was precisely this market-oriented strategy that the Group of 77 was fighting against in the UNCTAD and with the NIEO. Even moderate reforms held little appeal. Most governments were unwilling to scale back their industrialization strategies. Instead, they looked for a way to cover the twin deficits without having to scale back their ambitious plans.

Even if governments had been more willing to implement reforms, they would have faced considerable obstacles to doing so, because the political dynamics of ISI had created a vested interest in the continuation of the system. On the one hand, government intervention had established an environment conducive to **rent seeking** (Krueger 1974; Bhagwati 1982)—efforts by private actors to use the political system to achieve a higher-than-market return on an economic activity. Consider, for example, the consequences of government controls on imports. Governments controlled imports by requiring all residents who wanted to import something to first gain the permission of government authorities. Such import-licensing systems created an incentive for rent seeking. The restrictions themselves meant that imported goods were scarce. As a consequence, imports purchased at the world price could be sold at a much higher price in the domestic market. The difference between the world price and the domestic price provided a rent to the person who imported the good. A government license to import, therefore, was potentially very valuable. Consequently, people had incentives to pay government civil servants to acquire licenses, and government civil servants had incentives to sell them.

Such behavior was extraordinarily costly as people invested considerable time and energy pursuing licenses rather than engaging in productive behavior. It has been estimated, for example, that these forms of rent seeking cost India about 7 percent and Turkey about 15 percent of their national incomes during the 1960s (Krueger 1974, 294). Because so many people inside the government and in the economy were benefiting from the opportunities for rent seeking, they had a very strong incentive to resist any efforts by the government to dismantle the system.

The balance of power among domestic interest groups also greatly limited the ability of governments to embark on meaningful reform. Because governments depended so heavily upon urban residents for political support, they could not easily reduce benefits provided to that group (Waterbury 1992, 192). In 1971, for example, the Ghanaian prime minister devalued the exchange rate in an attempt to correct Ghana's current-account deficit. Concern that devaluation would raise the prices of many imported goods consumed by urban residents contributed to a coup against the government a few days later. Once in power, the new regime quickly restored the exchange rate to its previous overvalued level (Herbst 1993, 22–23). What message did that send to politicians who might be contemplating measures to address the economic imbalances they were facing?

More broadly, over time the "political support of special interests for import substitution grew. . . . Rather than changing policies when the consequences of further restrictiveness of the trade and payments regime became obvious, the political process in the short run resulted in increased support for it" (Krueger 1993b, 353). At the same time, those groups one might have expected to oppose the system—particularly the export-oriented producers—grew weaker as the incentives created by ISI caused them to exit export-oriented activities in favor of economic activities that were promoted and protected.

By the early 1970s, therefore, many developing countries faced growing budget and current-account deficits. Reform was constrained by governments' adherence to ISI and by resistance from the domestic groups that benefited greatly from that strategy. Facing economic imbalances, and unwilling and unable to adopt reforms, many developing-country governments kept the system running by relying heavily on foreign loans, which provided both the funds that governments needed to finance their current-account deficits and the funds required to finance investment in industry.

Yet, reliance on foreign loans could provide only a temporary solution; foreign lenders would eventually begin to question whether money they had lent could be repaid. When they concluded that it couldn't, they would be unwilling to advance additional loans, and governments would be forced to address the imbalances that ISI had created. That point was reached in the early 1980s and ushered in a period of crisis and reform. Before we can examine this period, however, we must look at economic developments in East Asia, as these developments played a critical role in shaping the content of the reforms adopted throughout the developing world after 1985.

The East Asian Model

While import substitution industrialization was generating imbalances in Latin America and Sub-Saharan Africa, a small number of East Asian countries were realizing dramatic gains on the basis of a very different development strategy. Four of these East

Table 7.1
Comparative Economic Performance, Selected Developing Countries
(Average Annual Rates of Change)

	1965–1990	1985–1995
Growth of per Capita GNP		
East Asia and the Pacific	5.3	7.2
Sub-Saharan Africa	0.2	−1.1
South Asia	1.9	2.9
Latin America and the Caribbean	1.8	0.3
Growth of Manufacturing		
East Asia and the Pacific	10.3	15.0
Sub-Saharan Africa	n.a.°	0.2
South Asia	4.5	5.3
Latin America and the Caribbean	8.3	2.5
Growth of Exports		
East Asia and the Pacific	8.5	9.3
Sub-Saharan Africa	6.1	0.9
South Asia	1.8	6.6
Latin America and the Caribbean	−1.0	5.2

°n.a. = not available.
Source: World Bank, *World Development Report,* various issues.

Asian economies—Hong Kong, Singapore, South Korea, and Taiwan—consistently outperformed all other developing countries throughout the entire postwar period. This superior economic performance is evident in three simple economic indicators. (See Table 7.1.)

First, between 1965 and 1990, the rate of per capita income growth in these four East Asian economies was, on average, more than twice as high as the rate of income growth in Latin America and South Asia and more than 26 times the rate of per capita income growth in Sub-Saharan Africa.

Second, East Asian manufacturing output grew at a very rapid rate, averaging 10.3 percent per year between 1965 and 1990. While Latin America fared relatively well in comparison to East Asia for the early part of the postwar period, Latin American rates of growth were not sustained.

Third, East Asian exports grew rapidly, while exports from other developing countries grew hardly at all. The contrast with Latin America is perhaps most striking: whereas East Asian exports grew at an annual average rate of 8.5 percent between 1965 and 1990, Latin American exports in the same period shrank by an average of 1 percent per year. The contrast with Africa was also stark: while exports from Sub-Saharan Africa grew relatively rapidly between 1965 and 1980, by the mid-1980s this rate of growth had dropped sharply.

The consequences of these faster growth rates are illustrated in Tables 6.1, 6.2, and 7.2. The importance of manufacturing industries in the East Asian economies grew while the importance of agriculture diminished. Similarly, while agriculture's share of GNP shrank in both Africa and Latin America, but, in contrast to the situation

Table 7.2
GNP per Capita, Selected Developing Countries (1985 US Dollars)

	1960	1990	Percent Change
Hong Kong	2,247	14,849	561
Singapore	1,658	11,710	606
Taiwan	1,256	8,063	542
South Korea	904	6,673	638
Mexico	2,836	5,827	105
Malaysia	1,420	5,124	261
Argentina	4,462	4,706	5
Chile	2,885	4,338	50
Brazil	1,784	4,042	127
Thailand	943	3,580	280
Zaire/Congo	489	2,211	352
Indonesia	638	1,974	211
Pakistan	638	1,394	118
India	766	1,264	65
Nigeria	567	995	75
Kenya	659	911	38
Zambia	965	689	−29
Tanzania	319	534°	67

°Data for 1988.
Source: Penn World Tables.

in East Asia, manufacturing's share failed to grow. The increased importance of manufacturing in East Asia was translated into significant changes in the commodity composition of East Asia's exports. (See Table 6.2.) By the mid-1990s, manufactured goods accounted for more than 80 percent of East Asian exports. By contrast, only in Brazil, Mexico, India, and Pakistan did manufactured goods account for more than 50 percent of total exports by the 1990s, and most of these gains were realized after 1980. Finally, incomes (i.e., gross national product per capita) in East Asia soared above those in other developing countries (Table 7.2). In 1960, per capita incomes in East Asia were lower than per capita incomes in Latin America; by 1990, East Asian incomes were higher than—in some cases twice as large as—per capita incomes in Latin America.

Why did East Asian countries outperform other developing countries by such a large margin? Most who study East Asian development agree that the countries in the region distinguished themselves from other developing countries by pursuing an export-oriented strategy of development. In an **export-oriented strategy,** emphasis is placed on producing manufactured goods that can be sold in international markets. Such an approach contrasts sharply with the emphasis on producing for the domestic market, a central tenet of ISI. Where scholars disagree is on the relative importance of the market versus the state in creating these export-oriented industries. One position, the neoliberal interpretation, is articulated most forcefully by the International Monetary Fund and the World Bank. This thesis argues that East Asia's success was a product of market-friendly development strategies. Another position, the state-oriented interpretation, is advanced by many scholars specializing in East Asian political economy. This viewpoint argues that East Asia's success is due in large part to state-led industrial policies.

The IMF and the World Bank contend that East Asia's economic success derived from their adoption of a neoliberal approach to development. In particular, this interpretation places primary emphasis on East Asia's embrace of international markets and ability to maintain a stable macroeconomic environment. (See World Bank 1989, 1991, 1993; Little 1982; Lal 1983; for critiques, see Toye 1994 and Rodrik 1999.) Most East Asian governments adopted ISI strategies in the immediate postwar period. Unlike governments in Latin America and Africa, however, East Asian governments shifted to export-oriented strategies once they had exhausted the gains from easy ISI. Thus, whereas Latin American and African governments followed easy ISI with secondary ISI, both of which emphasized production for the domestic market, the East Asian governments followed easy ISI by encouraging the manufacturing industries they had created under easy ISI to export to the advanced industrialized countries.

In Taiwan, for example, the government shifted in 1958 from production for the domestic market to a strategy that emphasized production for export markets. South Korea adopted similar reforms in the early 1960s. A second wave of newly industrializing countries (NICs)—a group that includes Indonesia, Malaysia, and Thailand—adopted similar reforms beginning in the late 1960s (World Bank 1993). The emphasis on exports forced Asian manufacturing firms to worry about international competitiveness. This approach stood in great contrast to that of Latin American firms, which produced for domestic markets sheltered from foreign competition. As a result, the World Bank and IMF argue, Asian societies invested their resources in domestic industries that were profitable in world markets, while Latin American and African governments did not.

The shift to export-oriented strategies was followed by selective import liberalization. Asian governments did not engage in wholesale import liberalization. The Taiwanese and South Korean governments continued to rely heavily on tariff and nontariff barriers to protect domestic markets. In Taiwan, for example, approximately two-thirds of imports were subject to some form of tariff or nontariff barrier greater than 30 percent, and as late as 1980 more than 40 percent of imports faced protection greater than 30 percent (World Bank 1993, 297). A similar pattern appeared in South Korea, where, as late as 1983, "most sectors were still protected by some combination of tariffs and nontariff barriers" (World Bank 1993, 297). However, selective liberalization helped promote exports by reducing the cost of critical inputs. By reducing tariffs on key intermediate goods, such as looms and yarn in the textile industry, domestic producers were able to acquire inputs at world prices. This kept exports competitive in international markets. The export orientation thus promoted investments in sectors that exploited an underlying comparative advantage, while import liberalization helped ensure that these sectors' advantages were not eliminated by high input prices.

East Asian governments also maintained stable macroeconomic environments. Three elements of the macroeconomic environment were particularly important. First, inflation was much lower in East Asia than in other developing countries. Between 1961 and 1991, East Asian economies experienced an average rate of inflation of only 7.5 percent over the period. By contrast, annual inflation rates in the rest of the developing world averaged 62 percent over the same period (World Bank 1993, 110). Second, because inflation was kept under control, East Asian governments were able to maintain appropriately valued exchange rates. In many developing countries, high inflation caused the domestic currency to rise in value against foreign currencies, making things difficult for exporters. In the East Asian countries, by contrast, governments were able to maintain exchange rates that allowed domestic firms to remain competitive in foreign markets. (We will explore exchange-rate issues in greater detail in Chapter 14.) Third, East Asian governments pursued relatively conservative fiscal policies. They borrowed little, and when they did borrow, they tapped domestic savings rather than turning to international financial markets. This approach was in stark contrast to that of Latin American governments, which accumulated large public-sector deficits financed with foreign capital. More conservative fiscal policies allowed East Asian governments to minimize the growth of foreign debt.

This stable macroeconomic environment had beneficial consequences for Asian economic performance. Low inflation promoted high rates of saving and investment (World Bank 1993, 12). Savings rates in the Asian NICs averaged more than 20 percent of GDP per year, almost twice the level attained in other developing countries, while investment rates were 7 percentage points of GDP higher, on average, than in other developing countries (World Bank 1993, 16, 221). A stable macroeconomic environment also made it easier to open the economy to international trade. Because inflation was low and exchange rates were maintained at appropriate levels, trade liberalization did not generate large current-account deficits that forced the government to reimpose trade barriers. Finally, the ability to maintain relatively stable and appropriately valued **real exchange rates** encouraged private actors to invest in export-oriented industries.

The interaction among the export orientation, the relatively liberal import policy, and the stable macroeconomic environment promoted economic development. As Doner and Hawes (1995, 150) put it, the

> pattern of limited government intervention in the market, coupled with cheap labor and an open economy, [has] guaranteed the private sector stability and predictability, the means to achieve competitiveness on a global scale, and access to the international market so that entrepreneurs could actually discover areas where they have comparative advantage. In shorthand, the model is often reduced to "getting the prices right" and letting market-based prices determine resource allocation. Doing so results in export growth that is in turn positively correlated with broader economic growth.

According to the World Bank and IMF, East Asia succeeded because markets played a large role, and states played a small role, in allocating resources.

Other scholars have argued that East Asia's successful pursuit of an export-oriented development strategy had less to do with allowing markets to work and much more to do with well-designed government industrial policies. (See Wade 1990; Amsden 1989; Haggard 1990). In what has come to be called the **East Asian model of development,** economic development is conceptualized as a series of distinct stages of industrialization. Government intervention at each stage is aimed at identifying and promoting specific industries that are likely to be profitable in the face of international competition. In the first stage, industrial policy promotes labor-intensive light industry, such as textiles and

other consumer durables. In the second stage, industrial policy emphasizes heavy industries such as steel, shipbuilding, petrochemicals, and synthetic fibers. In the third stage,
governments target skill- and research-and-development-intensive consumer durables
and industrial machinery, such as machine tools, semiconductors, computers, telecommunications equipment, robotics, and biotechnology. Governments design policies and organizations to promote the transition from one stage to the other (Wade 1994, 70).

These three stages of industrialization are evident in Taiwan and South Korea.
(See Table 7.3.) In Taiwan, industrialization focused initially on light manufacturing,
textiles in particular. By the mid-1950s, textiles were Taiwan's most important export.
The government also encouraged the domestic production of simple consumer
durable goods such as television sets. In the late 1950s, the Taiwanese government
began to emphasize the heavy industries characteristic of the second stage of ISI. A
joint venture between several Taiwanese firms and an American firm was formed in
1954 to produce synthetic fibers (Wade 1990, 80). In 1957, a plant to produce
polyvinyl chloride was constructed under government supervision and then handed to
a private entrepreneur, Y.C. Wang (Wade 1990, 79). The government created state-
owned enterprises in the steel, shipbuilding, and petrochemical industries. During the
1970s, government emphasis shifted to skill- and R&D-intensive industries, with particular emphasis on machine tools, semiconductors, computers, telecommunications,
robotics, and biotechnology (Wade 1990, 94). By the mid-1980s, electrical and electronic goods had replaced textiles as Taiwan's largest export (Wade 1990, 93).

The South Korean government adopted similar policies (Amsden 1989). In the
1950s, the government emphasized textile production, and textiles became South
Korea's first important manufacturing export. During the late 1960s, emphasis shifted to
the second stage of ISI, as the South Korean state initiated the development of the chemical and heavy-machinery industries. In 1968, the government created the Pohang Iron
and Steel Company, known as POSCO, which subsequently became one of the world's
leading steel producers. The government also provided extensive support to Hyundai
Heavy Industry, a shipbuilder formed in the early 1970s and that subsequently became a
world leader in this industry. During the late 1970s, the South Korean government began
to give priority to skill- and R&D-intensive sectors, and it is during this period that the
South Korean electronics and automobile industries began to emerge (Amsden 1989).

In the East Asian model, therefore, government policy drives industrialization
from initial low-skilled, labor-intensive production to capital-intensive forms of production and from there to industries that rely on high-skilled labor and research and
development. Each stage is associated with particular types of government policies,
and as each stage reaches the limits of rapid growth, emphasis shifts to the next stage
in the sequence (Wade 1994, 71). Moreover, at each stage, governments stress the
need to develop internationally competitive industries.

East Asian governments implemented industrial policies in pursuit of four broad
objectives: reducing the cost of investment funds in the selected industries, creating
incentives to export, protecting infant industries, and promoting the acquisition and
application of skills. Taiwan and South Korea created incentives to invest in industries that state officials identified as critical to development. To do so, governments in
both countries provided firms investing in these industries with preferential access to
low-cost credit. In South Korea, the government nationalized the banks in the early

Table 7.3
Stages of Industrialization in Taiwan and South Korea, 1880–1970

	Commodity Exports 1880–1930	Primary ISI 1930–1955	Primary Export-oriented Industries 1955–1968
Main Industries	Taiwan: Sugar, rice South Korea: Rice, beans	Taiwan and South Korea: Food, beverages, tobacco, textiles, clothing, cement, light manufactures (wood, leather, rubber, and paper products)	Taiwan and South Korea: Textiles and apparel, electronics, plywood, plastics (Taiwan), wigs (South Korea), intermediate goods (chemicals, petroleum, paper, and steel products)
Major Economic Actors	Taiwan and Korea: Local producers (colonial Japan)	Taiwan and South Korea: Private national firms	National private firms, multinational corporations, state-owned enterprises
Orientation of the Economy	External markets	Internal market	External markets

Source: Gereffi 1990, 19.

1960s and in the ensuing years fully controlled investment capital. Control of the banks allowed the government to provide targeted sectors with access to long-term invest-ment capital at below market rates of interest (Haggard 1990, 132). While the banking sector was not nationalized in Taiwan, the government did influence banks' lending decisions. During the 1960s, banks were provided with government-formulated lists of industries that were to receive preferential access to bank loans. During the 1970s, the banks themselves were required to select five or six industries to target in the coming year. As a result, about 75 percent of investment capital was channeled to the govern-ment's targeted industries (Wade 1990, 166).

Asian governments also implemented policies that encouraged exports. One method was to link preferential access to investment capital to export performance. In Taiwan, for example, firms that exported paid interest rates of only 6–12 percent, while other borrowers paid 20–22 percent (Haggard 1990, 94). In South Korea, short-term loans were extended "without limit" to firms with confirmed export orders (Haggard 1990, 65). Credit was also made available to exporters' input suppliers and to these suppliers' suppliers (Haggard 1990, 65–66). In addition, "deliberately undervalued exchange rates" improved the competitiveness of exports in international markets (World Bank 1993, 125). Finally, a variety of measures were used to ensure that domes-tic firms could purchase their intermediate inputs at world prices. These measures often entailed the creation of free-trade zones and export-processing zones—areas of the country into which intermediate goods could be imported duty free as long as the finished goods were exported. Export-processing zones allowed domestic producers to avoid paying tariff duties that would raise the final cost of the goods they produced.

The Taiwanese and South Korean governments also protected infant industries at each stage. In some instances, the measures they used were straightforward forms of protection. The South Korean government, for example, enacted legislation in 1983 that "prohibited the import of most microcomputers, some minicomputers, and selected models of disk drives," in order to protect domestic producers in the com-puter industry (Amsden 1989, 82). POSCO initially produced steel behind high import barriers. In other instances, protection was less transparent. Hyundai Heavy Industry, for instance, was protected in part through a government policy that required Korean crude-oil imports to be carried in ships operated by a merchant marine that Hyundai Heavy Industry had itself created (Amsden 1989, 273). Similar policies were adopted in Taiwan, where, for example, the China Steel Corporation, a state-owned enterprise, has been able to exclude imports of the types of steel it produces (Wade 1990, 131). In these ways, new firms were protected against imports (Wade 1990, 132).

Finally, the Taiwanese and South Korean governments put in place policies that raised skill levels. These policies were of particular importance in the transition from second-stage heavy industry to third-stage skill- and research-intensive industries. Investments in education were made to improve labor skills. In Taiwan, enrollment in secondary schools had reached 75 percent of the eligible age group by 1980. Enroll-ment increases were accompanied by rising expenditures on education; per pupil expenditures increased eightfold in primary schools, threefold in secondary schools, and twofold at the university level between the early 1960s and 1980s (Liu 1992, 369). Similar patterns are evident in South Korea, where enrollment in secondary schools increased from 35 percent in 1965 to 88 percent in 1987 and "real expenditures per pupil at the primary level rose by 355 percent" (World Bank 1993, 43, 45).

Governments also invested in their countries' scientific infrastructure, to facilitate the application of skills to research-and-development activities. In Taiwan, the Industrial Technology Research Institute was formed in 1973, and nonprofit organizations were created during the 1970s to perform research and disseminate the results to firms in the private sector. A science-based industrial park designed to realize agglomeration effects was created in 1980 (Haggard 1990, 142). In South Korea, tax incentives were used to induce *chaebols,* the large South Korean firms, to create laboratories for research-and-development purposes. An industrial estate for computer and semiconductor production was created, and the Electronics and Telecommunications Research Institute, a government-funded institute oriented toward product development was formed in the industrial estate (Amsden 1989, 82). These policies raised skill levels and created an infrastructure that allowed the more highly skilled labor force to work to its full potential. This skill upgrading was critical to the transition to the third stage of the industrialization process.

The two explanations discussed thus present different arguments for East Asia's success. One suggests that East Asia succeeded because governments allowed markets to work. The other suggests that East Asia succeeded because governments used industrial policy to promote economic outcomes that the market could not produce. Which argument is correct? While we lack definitive answers, we may conclude that both explanations have value. By "getting prices right," the export orientation and the stable macroeconomic environment encouraged investments in industries in which East Asian countries had or could develop comparative advantage. By targeting sectors where comparative advantage could be created, by reducing the costs of firms operating in those sectors, by encouraging firms to export, and by upgrading skills, industrial policy encouraged investments in areas that could yield high returns. As Stephan Haggard (1990, 67) has summarized, macroeconomic "and trade policies established a permissive framework for the realization of comparative advantage, and more targeted policies pushed firms to exploit it."

While the relative importance of the state and the market in accounting for East Asia's success remains in dispute, what is clear is that the experience of the East Asian NICs was vastly different from the experience of Latin America and Sub-Saharan Africa. East Asian governments adopted development strategies that emphasized exports rather than the domestic market, and they realized substantial improvements in per capita income. The development strategies adopted by Latin American and sub-Saharan African governments emphasized the domestic market over exports and led to large economic imbalances and only modest improvements in per capita incomes. Consequently, when economic crises forced governments to adopt reforms, the East Asian example provided a powerful guide for the kind of reforms that would be implemented.

Structural Adjustment and the Politics of Reform

While the imbalances generated by ISI created the need for reform, and while East Asia's success based on a different approach provided an attractive alternative model, governments began to implement reforms only under the pressure created by a severe economic crisis. We will examine this crisis in detail in Chapter 14; here, we need to say a few words about it in order to understand how it contributed to the adoption of neoliberal reforms throughout the developing world.

Economic crises emerged in the early 1980s in large part as a consequence of governments' decision to cover their budget and current-account deficits with foreign loans. Using foreign loans to finance budget and current-account deficits is not an inherently poor choice. But two factors made this decision a particularly bad one for developing countries in the 1970s. First, many of the funds that governments borrowed were used to pay for large infrastructure projects or domestic consumption, neither of which generated the export revenues needed to repay the loans. As a result, the amount that developing countries owed to foreign lenders rose, but their ability to repay the debt did not.

Second, between 1973 and 1982, developing countries were buffeted by three international shocks: an increase in the price of oil, a reduction in the terms of trade between primary commodities and manufactured goods, and higher interest rates on the foreign debt those countries had accumulated. These shocks increased the amount of foreign debt that developing countries owed to foreign banks, raised the cost of paying that debt, and greatly reduced export earnings. By the early 1980s, a number of developing countries were unable to make the scheduled payments on their foreign debt.

Many turned to the International Monetary Fund (IMF) and the World Bank for financial assistance. These agencies offered financial assistance, but it was explicitly linked to the implementation of a package of neoliberal reforms. The World Bank and IMF encouraged governments to adopt such reforms under the banner of **structural adjustment programs**—policy reforms designed and promoted by the World Bank and IMF that strive to reduce the role of the state and increase the role of the market in the economy. The specific content of the reforms that the IMF and World Bank advocated were shaped by their belief that East Asia's economic success had resulted from export-oriented and market-based development strategies. (See World Bank 1991, 1993.) In the World Bank's own words, "the approach to development that seems to have worked most reliably, and which seems to offer most promise, suggests a reappraisal of the respective roles for the market and the state. Put simply, governments need to do less in those areas where markets work, or can be made to work, reasonably well" (1991, 9).

To this end, structural adjustment emphasized changing those aspects of developing economies which were most unlike conditions in Asia. Governments were encouraged to create a stable macroeconomic environment, to liberalize trade, and to privatize state-owned enterprises (Williamson 1990; 1994). Macroeconomic stability was to be achieved by transforming government budget deficits into budget surpluses. This change would reduce the demand for imports, thereby reducing developing countries' current-account deficits. Governments also were encouraged to liberalize imports, by dismantling import-licensing systems, shifting from quota-based forms of protection to tariffs, simplifying complex tariff structures, and reducing tariffs and opening their economies to imports.

The IMF and the World Bank also encouraged the **privatization** of state-owned enterprises—that is, selling such enterprises to private individuals and groups. The IMF and World Bank argued that reducing government involvement in the economy

Table 7.4
Countries Adopting Trade and Domestic Policy Reforms, 1980–1996

Africa		Latin America	
Benin	Malawi	Argentina	Honduras
Burkina Faso	Mali	Barbados	Mexico
Burundi	Mauritania	Bahamas	Nicaragua
Cameroon	Mauritius	Belize	Panama
Central African Republic	Mozambique	Bolivia	Paraguay
Chad	Niger	Brazil	Peru
Congo	Nigeria	Chile	Suriname
Cote d'Ivoire	Rwanda	Colombia	Trinidad and Tobago
Ethiopia	Senegal	Costa Rica	Uruguay
Gabon	Sierra Leone	Dominican Republic	Venezuela
The Gambia	Tanzania	Ecuador	
Ghana	Togo	El Salvador	
Guinea	Uganda	Guatemala	
Guinea-Bissau	Zambia	Guyana	
Kenya	Zimbabwe	Haiti	
Madagascar			

Source: World Bank 1994a; Thorp 1999.

would foster competition and that greater competition would in turn help create a more efficient private sector that could drive economic development. Through structural adjustment, therefore, governments were encouraged to scale back the role of the state in economic development and enhance the role played by the market.

Many governments undertook structural adjustment between 1983 and 1995. (See Table 7.4.) Tariffs throughout the developing world fell substantially beginning in the mid-1980s. (See Figure 7.1.) While average tariffs still remain higher in developing countries than in the advanced industrialized countries, they have been cut in half, on average, since the early 1980s. Many governments have also substantially reduced their reliance upon nontariff barriers to trade. In Latin America, average tariffs fell from 41.6 percent prior to the crisis to 13.7 percent by 1990 (Inter-American Development Bank 1997, 12). While it is hard to get accurate measures of the coverage of nontariff barriers, Table 7.5 provides some evidence on the scope of such measures in a number of developing countries. A general trend toward the elimination of these obstacles to trade is evident.

Privatization became a priority objective in the late 1980s. In Latin America, "more than 2,000 publicly owned firms, including public utilities, banks, and insurance companies, highways, ports, airlines, and retail shops, were privatized" between 1985 and 1992 (Edwards 1995, 170; see also Corbo 2000). In general, African governments have moved less rapidly than Latin American governments to carry out structural adjustment reforms. (See World Bank 1994a, 1994b.) Many African governments have in fact begun to liberalize trade, shifting away from quotas and lowering tariffs, but progress has been slow. Privatization has moved even more slowly, with less than one-fifth of state-owned enterprises having been privatized by the mid-1990s. As governments

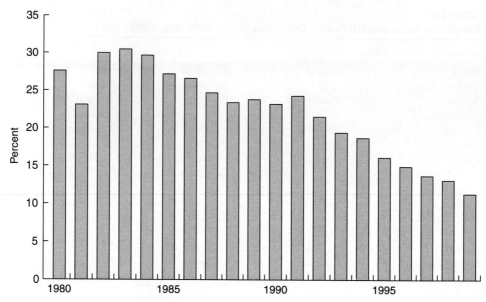

Figure 7.1   Average Tariffs, Developing Countries.
Source: World Bank.

Table 7.5
Nontariff Barriers in Developing Countries (as a Percent of All Industry Categories)

	1989–1994	1995–1998
Hong Kong, China	2.1	2.1
Indonesia	53.6	31.3
Korea	50.0	25.0
Malaysia	56.3	19.6
Singapore	1.0	2.1
Thailand	36.5	17.5
India	99.0	93.8
Nigeria	14.4	11.5
South Africa	36.5	8.3
Morocco	58.3	13.4
Turkey	5.2	19.8
Argentina	3.1	2.1
Brazil	16.5	21.6
Chile	5.2	5.2
Colombia	55.2	10.3
Mexico	27.8	13.4
Uruguay	32.3	0.0

Source: World Bank.

liberalized their economies, they gradually became more deeply integrated into the world trade system.

The structural adjustment programs were expected to reduce average incomes and redistribute income across groups in the short run and generate faster growth and higher average incomes in the long run. Most developing countries did experience a sharp fall in per capita income as they began to implement reforms. In Latin American countries, national incomes fell by about 8 percent between 1981 and 1984, while in African countries, incomes fell, on average, by about 1.2 percent per year throughout the 1980s (Thorp 1999, 220; World Bank 1993).

Structural adjustment also redistributed income from industry and the urban non-traded goods sector to agriculture and other export-oriented industries. In Guinea, for example, reform yielded a threefold increase in the price coffee producers received for their crops (Arulpragasam and Sahn 1994, 73–76). In The Gambia, producer prices on groundnuts tripled as a consequence of structural adjustment policies (Jabara 1994, 309). These policies hurt producers based in the import-competing sector, as well as those employed in the nontraded-goods sector. In The Gambia, for example, the government raised the price of petroleum products, public transportation, water, electricity, and telecommunications in connection with structural adjustment (Jabara 1994, 309). In Guinea, the elimination of government rice subsidies doubled the price that households paid for rice, an important staple in their diets (Arulpragasam and Sahn 1994, 79).

Privatization usually resulted in large job losses in these import-competing manufacturing industries, while scaling back the size of the civil service eliminated jobs in the nontraded-goods sector. In Guinea, the civil service was reduced in size from 104,000 in 1985 to 71,000 in 1989 (Arulpragasam and Sahn 1994, 91). In The Gambia, government employees were reduced by 25 percent in 1985–1986, and wages and salaries of those retained in the government sector were frozen (Jabara 1994, 312, 318). In pursuing structural adjustment, therefore, governments redistributed income: export-oriented producers benefited from the successful implementation of these policies, while people employed in the import competing and nontraded goods sectors saw their incomes fall.

These short-run economic consequences of structural adjustment drove the domestic politics of reform. (See Nelson 1990; Remmer 1986; Haggard and Kaufman, 1992, Oatley 2004). Groups that would lose from structural adjustment attempted to block the reforms, while those who stood to gain attempted to promote reform. Governments were forced to mediate between them, and in many countries governments were heavily dependent upon political support from the import-competing and nontraded-goods sectors. Thus, reforms were hard to implement.

Over time, however, the economic crisis triggered a realignment of interests, discrediting those groups associated with the old regime and the old policies and giving greater influence to groups that proposed an alternative approach (Krueger 1993a). The economic crisis thus forged a new political consensus asserting that the old order had failed and that a new strategy was required. By weakening key interest groups and by forcing many to redefine their interests, the crisis gradually eroded many of the political obstacles to far-reaching reform. Yet, this process took time, as reforms could

A CLOSER LOOK

Structural Adjustment in Mexico

The Mexican government embarked on structural adjustment in the mid-1980s. Between 1985 and 1990, the policies adopted in connection with structural adjustment radically shifted the direction of Mexico's economy. (See Lustig 1998; Córdoba 1994.) In part, the changes reflected pressures exerted by the World Bank, from which Mexico borrowed $2.3 billion in 1986 and 1987. The scope of the reforms, however, suggested that the Mexican government was doing more than responding reluctantly to external pressure. Trade liberalization, one of the centerpieces of reform, began in earnest in 1985, and its initiation was heralded by the announcement that Mexico had applied to join GATT. At that time, Mexico was one of the most heavily protected economies in the world. More than 90 percent of the domestic economy was protected by import licenses, in some industries tariffs were as high as 100 percent, and the average tariff stood at 23.5 percent. Trade liberalization occurred in three stages between 1985 and 1993. First, the government reduced the coverage of the import-licensing system, so that, by 1990, only 20 percent of imports were subject to explicit government approval, and the accompanying requirements were restricted to a limited number of sensitive sectors, including natural gas, petroleum refining, automobiles, and agriculture. Next, the government simplified the tariff structure, shifting from a system with ten tariff rates to a system with only five rates and capping the highest rate at 20 percent. From this base, the government then gradually reduced tariffs, which fell from an average of 23.5 in 1985 to an average of only 12.5 by 1990. Finally, in 1990, the Mexican government initiated negotiations with the United States and Canada that culminated in the creation of NAFTA.

Trade liberalization was accompanied by the liberalization of foreign direct investment. Until the mid-1980s, the operation of foreign firms in the Mexican economy was tightly restricted. Foreigners were completely excluded from many sectors of the Mexican economy, and they could hold only a minority share of firms in all other sectors. In February 1984, the government relaxed some of these restrictions by allowing majority ownership by foreign firms in 33 selected industries. The restrictions were further relaxed in 1989 by an expansion of the sectors in which foreign firms could control as much as 100 percent of a Mexican firm. Thus, in addition to opening the Mexican economy to imports, the government opened the economy to investments by multinational corporations.

The government also dismantled its industrial policy, which had been a central component of Mexico's ISI strategy. Mexican industrial policy used financial incentives and import controls to promote specific industries. More than 700 programs had been put in place between 1965 and 1970, and 1,200 more had been established during the 1970s. The government began to dismantle these programs in the early 1980s as the crisis first hit. The programs were reduced in number and oriented toward critical industries, particularly automobiles, pharmaceuticals, capital goods, and petrochemicals. But even these last remnants of ISI were dismantled in the late 1980s. The government eliminated many of the financial incentives it had previously used to encourage investment, eliminated rules governing domestic content for for-

Continued

eign firms operating in these industries, and relaxed the rules restricting foreign direct investment.

The government also began reducing its role in the Mexican economy in other ways. In 1983, privatization was undertaken with a change to the Mexican constitution that limited the sectors in which the government could maintain state-run monopolies. Then, between 1985 and 1990, the government either sold to private investors or liquidated 875 of the 1,155 state-owned enterprises that had been in existence in 1982. Also greatly reduced was the degree to which the government directly controlled prices. Between 1950 and 1980, the government had used price controls to ensure that domestic industry could acquire its most important inputs at relatively low and stable prices. In the early 1990s, Mexico began to dismantle this system. It shortened the list of items subject to price controls, reduced the difference between the controlled price and the international price, and attempted to inject greater flexibility into the price-setting mechanism. The government liberalized many primary-commodity sectors, eliminating regulations governing the production and marketing of cacao beans and cacao products, coffee, and sugar, among others. It relaxed restrictions on fishing, allowing private individuals, corporations, and foreigners to fish in Mexican waters. These and other deregulations created greater competition within the industries concerned and allowed market-based processes, rather than state actors, to play the more important role in determining the outcome of the competition.

All of the reforms just described had a dramatic impact on Mexican incomes. Overall, economic growth between 1982 and 1987 averaged −0.4 percent, and per capita income fell from $3,500 in 1981 to $3,024 in 1988. As a result, the percentage of the population living in poverty increased from about 42 percent in the early 1980s to about 48 percent in 1989. The sharp drop in incomes stabilized in the late 1980s, however, when positive growth resumed. The Mexican economy has grown at an average rate of 3.5 percent per year since 1989, and per capita incomes have risen to $3,600 by 1999. Reform also affected the relative positions of groups in the Mexican economy (Lustig 1998; Damian 2000). Hardest hit were those who had benefited most from ISI. Government employees saw their incomes fall by an average of 12 percent per year during the second half of the 1980s. Manufacturing workers were also hit hard, experiencing average income losses of 6.2 percent per year in the same period. People employed in agriculture and in export-oriented manufacturing industries fared better. Incomes in these sectors fell, too, but much less than incomes in other sectors. Agricultural wages fell an average of only 3.8 percent per year. Workers employed in the export-oriented maquiladora industries fared substantially better than other manufacturing workers, as they saw wages fall by only 0.2 percent in 1986–1987.

be implemented only after new governments responsive to new interests had replaced the governments that presided over import substitution industrialization.

Because the political battle over reforms involved an intense distributive struggle, governments implemented reforms unevenly, in fits and starts, and, in many instances, only partially. As a result, it is difficult to evaluate the extent to which the wrenching short-run consequences have been offset by stronger economic growth and higher average per capita incomes over the long run. As Table 7.6 indicates, some countries pushed through the low growth that characterized the period of crisis and reform during the 1980s and

Table 7.6
Trade Openness and Growth, 1980–2002

	Trade as a Percent of GDP		Average Annual Growth of GDP (%)	
	1990	2002	1980–1990	1990–2002
Argentina	11.6	33.7	−0.7	2.7
Bolivia	33.1	39.5	−0.2	3.6
Brazil	11.7	24.3	2.7	2.7
Chile	53.1	55.2	4.2	5.9
Costa Rica	60.2	73.8	3.0	4.9
Mexico	32.1	52.4	1.1	3.0
Peru	22.3	26.9	−0.1	4.1
Latin America	23.1	41.2	1.7	2.9
Benin	30.0	37.8	2.5	4.9
Cameroon	30.5	38.6	3.4	2.4
The Gambia	69.1	67.3	3.6	3.3
Ghana	35.7	75.3	3.0	4.3
Kenya	38.1	43.6	4.2	1.9
Uganda	10.2	36.2	2.9	6.9
Sub-Saharan Africa	40.8	55.3	1.6	2.6

Source: World Bank 2004. World Development Indicators Online,
http://www.worldbank.org/data/wdi2004/index.htm.

resumed more rapid growth beginning in the 1990s. In the crisis-and reform-decade, most Latin American countries grew sluggishly, if at all. Average growth rates have been substantially higher since the early 1990s, however, and in 2004 Latin American growth rose to 5.5 percent. The picture in Africa is a bit more mixed, as African governments have struggled with structural adjustment. Moreover, efforts to implement economic reform have been overtaken by civil and international conflict. Even so, average economic growth during the last 12 years has been higher than the average during the 1980s.

Comparing average growth rates across decades is misleading, however, because such comparisons fail to recognize that some governments have reformed much more than others. Thus, to get a better appreciation of the impact of reforms on long-run growth, we need to control for the variation in reform across countries. Figure 7.2 depicts the relationship between progress on reform and the gain in economic growth between the 1980s and the 1990s. Progress on reform is measured as the change in an index of structural adjustment developed by researchers at the Inter-American Development Bank. This index summarizes the extent to which national economies are characterized by stable macroeconomic conditions, liberal trade, privatized industries, and flexible labor markets. The higher the score on the index (which ranges from 0 to 1), the closer the country approximates the "neoliberal ideal." I calculated the change in this index between 1985 and 1995 for each country, to measure the extent to which each has moved from ISI toward a neoliberal framework. I then plotted this measure of structural change against the difference between average growth in the 1990s and average growth in the 1980s. Neoliberalism leads us to expect a strong positive rela-

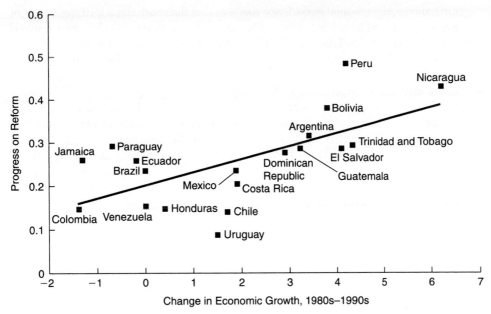

Figure 7.2 Reform and Growth in Latin America.
Source: Reform Index from IADB 1997, 96; Growth Rates from World Bank World Development Indicators.

tionship between progress on reform and change in growth: countries that have reformed the most should see large improvements in growth, while countries that have reformed less should see small growth gains. That expectation finds some support in this simple graph. The overall relationship is positive, indicating that countries which have progressed furthest along the trajectory of reforms have experienced larger gains in growth. Countries that have reformed less have realized smaller, and in some cases, negative, changes in growth.

Even this more nuanced evaluation is misleading, however, because it compares the wrong growth rates. To fully understand reform's impact on long-run growth, we really need to compare growth rates after reform with growth rates that would have occurred had governments never implemented reform. That is, suppose Latin American governments continued along the path they were on in the early 1970s. What rate of economic growth would they then have realized during the 1980s and 1990s? We can compare these growth rates with growth rates following reform to see reform's impact on long-run growth. This comparison is obviously difficult to make, because we can't replay history to see what would have happened if governments had not adopted reforms. The best we can do is estimate what growth rates would have been for Latin American countries had they not adopted reforms. A number of such analyses have been conducted, and they suggest that Latin American growth in the postreform period has been between 1.9 and 2.2 percentage points higher than it would have been had governments not implemented reforms. (See Easterly, Loayza, and Montiel 1997; Montiel Fernández-Arias 2002; Lora and Barrera 1997; and the useful summary in IADB 1997, 54.)

On balance, then, available evidence suggests that the short-run adjustment costs of structural adjustment have been followed by stronger growth than would have occurred in the absence of reform. This is not to suggest that the resumption of growth has eliminated poverty in Latin America or sub-Saharan Africa. It hasn't. In fact, during much of the last 20 years, poverty rates have remained stubbornly high and national income has remained very unevenly distributed. Even the staunchest supporters of neoliberalism don't claim that this approach guarantees that poverty will be eliminated. Instead, they argue that neoliberalism offers the surest path to that goal. As David Dollar and Aart Kraay, two researchers at the World Bank, argue, growth through trade is good for the poor. (See Dollar and Kraay 2004, 2002.) Over time, the short-run pains brought about by structural adjustment should be rewarded with falling poverty and a narrowing of the income gap between the advanced industrialized countries and the developing world. It remains to be seen whether this optimistic perspective will be realized.

Developing Countries and the WTO

Developments in the WTO will play an important role in determining whether the neoliberal optimism mentioned in the previous section is warranted. For, as developing countries have embraced neoliberalism, economic progress has come to depend heavily upon gaining access to world markets. In part, gaining such access involves maintaining a domestic economic climate that encourages the creation of competitive industries. Equally important, however, is the willingness of the advanced industrialized nations to open their markets to the competitive products being produced in the developing world. Success on this dimension hinges critically upon developments within the WTO. In particular, can developing countries use the WTO to begin to dismantle the barriers that the advanced industrialized countries maintain against their imports?

The central challenge that developing countries face in the WTO arises from the political economy of trade in the advanced industrialized countries. Trade politics in those countries generates barriers to imports in many of the industries in which developing countries hold a comparative advantage. Agriculture, on the one hand, and textiles and apparel, on the other, are the two sectors in which the bias against developing countries' exports is perhaps greatest. Many developing countries have a comparative advantage in agriculture. Yet, three aspects of advanced industrialized country policies make it difficult for developing countries to capitalize on this advantage.

Tariffs pose the most obvious obstacle to the ability of developing countries to export agricultural products to the United States, Western Europe, and Japan. In addition to tariffs, however, governments in the advanced industrialized countries subsidize agricultural production heavily. In the year 2000 alone, the advanced industrialized countries provided a total of $327 billion of financial assistance to domestic farmers. These subsidies increase agricultural production in the advanced industrialized countries, reducing the demand for imports from developing countries. In addition, governments in the advanced industrialized countries subsidize exports, thereby displacing other countries' farm products from world markets and driving down the world price of these commodities. EU price supports, for example, caused EU wheat production to increase by 2.5 percent per year between 1970 and 1998. As a consequence, whereas the EU was a net importer of wheat in the early 1960s, by the early 1970s it had become a net exporter of wheat.

Finally, **tariff escalation**—the practice of imposing higher tariffs on goods whose production involves relatively more processing—makes it difficult for developing countries to export processed food to the industrialized countries. Unprocessed agricultural commodities face the lowest tariffs, semiprocessed goods face higher tariffs, and fully processed goods face still higher tariffs. Such a structure of protection in the advanced industrialized countries makes it difficult for developing countries to move into the higher value-added segments of the food industry.

Developing countries also have a comparative advantage in labor-intensive manufactures. Yet, many domestic labor-intensive manufacturing industries remain heavily protected by the advanced industrialized countries. Protection has been particularly prominent in the textile and apparel industries. As part of the Uruguay Round, the advanced industrialized countries agreed to dismantle the quota-based regime governing world trade in textiles and apparel, called the **multifiber arrangement.** Quotas limiting imports are to be replaced by tariff-based protection, and these tariffs are to then be liberalized. The advanced industrialized countries were allowed to defer most liberalization until the end of the ten-year phase-in, however, and most have taken advantage of this opportunity. As a result, the liberalization that has occurred thus far has done little to expand export opportunities for developing countries' producers. And even when quotas have finally been eliminated, this sector will remain heavily protected: about half of the advanced industrialized country textile imports face tariffs above 10 percent. Moreover, in the fall of 2004, the United States began threatening to raise tariffs on Chinese apparel imports under the WTO safeguards clause. This episode suggests that governments in the advanced industrialized countries may find innovative ways to protect domestic producers once the quota regime is fully dismantled.

Protection of textiles and apparel producers highlights the broader pattern of protection of manufacturing industries in the advanced industrialized countries. Manufactured goods exported from the developing world face tariffs that are four times higher than the tariffs applied to exports from other advanced industrialized countries. The discrepancy arises solely from the commodity composition of exports in the two regions. Developing countries produce and export goods that compete with import-competing sectors in the advanced industrialized world, and industries in these sectors have been successful at maintaining protection. Advanced industrialized countries export goods that compete with the export-oriented sector in other advanced industrialized markets, and while the average tariff that the advanced industrialized countries apply to manufactured goods is quite low (only 3.4 percent), labor-intensive goods often confront **tariff peaks,** which are tariff rates above 15 percent. And it isn't only the advanced industrialized countries that are the culprits: developing countries face higher tariffs when they export manufactured goods to developing countries (an average of 12.8 percent) than when they export to the advanced industrialized world. (See Hertel and Martin 2000.) Thus, the ability of developing countries to export manufactured goods into world markets will require them to engage in meaningful reciprocal trade liberalization.

The gains that developing countries could realize from the elimination of trade barriers are substantial. A number of studies have estimated the impact that trade liberalization would have on incomes in the developing world. The size of the income gain obviously depends in part on the extent of liberalization. The most widely reported estimate was based on an analysis performed by the World Bank in the period leading up to the launch of the Doha Round (World Bank 2001b). According to this analysis, eliminating existing barriers to developing countries' exports could yield as much as $500 billion in additional income to developing countries over a ten-year period. This amount represents a full 5 percent increase in national incomes for developing countries (World Bank 2001b, 168), a figure that is substantially more than total foreign aid flows to the developing world.

Developing countries also face a new challenge from more recent efforts by the United States to bring core labor standards into the WTO. Developing countries have strenuously resisted this initiative. India, Egypt, Indonesia, China, and Pakistan have been vocal opponents of these linkages, as has the Third World Network (TWN), a group of intellectuals based in research institutes in developing countries. The problem is not that all developing countries are unwilling to protect workers' rights (although some of them are). Instead, developing countries oppose the linkage between trade and labor standards for two reasons. First, many governments from developing countries believe that the push to include labor standards into the WTO is driven by import-competing interests as a new form of protectionism. As Murasoli Maran, India's minister of commerce and industry, told the Indian parliament shortly after the 1999 Seattle WTO Summit, the attempt to bring labor standards into the WTO represents a "pernicious way of robbing our comparative advantage. Many developing countries consider it as a maneuver by wealthy nations to force our wages up, to undermine our competitiveness" (*New York Times* December 17, 1999, C4). Second, developing countries face a power imbalance in the WTO. The TWN argues that, because the advanced industrialized countries dominate the WTO, any labor standards incorporated in that organization "would only be used as a weapon by developed countries against developing countries" (O'Brien et al. 2000, 87). For these reasons, many governments from the developing world argue that it would be better to keep labor standards separate from trade considerations.

Will developing countries be able to use the WTO to remove the obstacles they face? Some signs are encouraging. The Doha Round agenda emphasizes the need to address the concerns of developing countries and highlights the positive contribution that trade can make to economic development. In addition, developing countries have thus far been able to keep labor standards out of the WTO. Other signs are less encouraging. The European Union remains reluctant to implement far-reaching reforms of the Common Agriculture Policy, and liberalization of world trade in agriculture will make little progress as long as the union maintains this position. Moreover, labor-intensive industries in the advanced industrialized countries are turning to administered forms of protection—antidumping and countervailing-duty investigations, as well as safeguard actions—with growing frequency. Current American pressure on China regarding trade in textiles and apparel is only one example of this dynamic. Thus, even if tariff peaks in these industries are eliminated, the threat of new trade barriers remains. Only time will tell whether developing countries can gain the expanded access to markets in the advanced industrialized countries upon which the success of the new export-oriented development strategies so many of them have adopted depends.

POLICY ANALYSIS AND DEBATE

Core Labor Standards and the WTO

Question
Should the WTO require developing countries to strengthen their labor standards?

Overview
Working conditions in many developing countries are very poor. A number of objectionable practices have been documented: long hours, very low wages, physical and psychological harassment, exposure to toxic chemicals, and dangerous machinery without safety equipment. Such practices appear to be most prevalent in locally owned firms producing apparel, footwear, toys, and sporting goods under contract for Western firms.

Growing awareness of such practices led the United States to try to use WTO negotiations to establish rules that linked market access to the implementation of specific labor standards. These "Core Labor Standards," developed by the International Labor Organization during the 1990s, include freedom of association and collective bargaining, the elimination of forced and compulsory labor, the abolition of child labor, and the elimination of discrimination in the workplace. Some have suggested that two further standards—pay and workplace conditions—be added. By bringing labor standards into the WTO, governments could use the dispute settlement mechanism to enforce compliance. Governments that refused to adopt higher standards would face higher trade barriers.

Developing countries have resisted the linkage between trade and labor standards, because they see it as a new form of protectionism. Martin Khor, the director of the Third World Network (and a prominent critic of many other aspects of globalization), argued, "developing countries fear that . . . they want to protect jobs in the North by reducing the low-cost incentive that attracts global corporations to the developing countries" (Khor 1999). Many economists have also questioned the link, arguing that developing countries' comparative advantage lies in low-cost labor. Higher standards would diminish this advantage. Should developing countries be forced to strengthen their labor standards?

Policy Options
- Negotiate enforceable WTO rules that require developing countries to adopt labor standards equivalent to those in the West.
- Allow developing countries to regulate their national labor markets as they see fit

Policy Analysis
- Why are labor standards low in developing countries?
- Will bringing core labor standards into the WTO necessarily raise the cost of labor in developing countries? Could this linkage hurt developing countries' exports in other ways?
- In the absence of the linkage, will developing countries' labor standards ever improve?

Take a Position
- Which option do you prefer? Justify your choice.
- What criticisms of your position should you anticipate? How would you defend your recommendation against these criticisms?

Continued

Resources
Online: Search for the National Labor Committee report on conditions in Central America. Other reports are also available online. Search also for the Scholars against Sweatshop Labor (SASL) and for the "Third World Intellectuals and NGOs Statement against Linkage." You might also visit the ILO and read the core labor standards.
In Print: John Miller, "Why Economists are Wrong about the Antisweatshop Movement," *Challenge* 46 (January–February 2003): 93–122. Kimberly Ann Elliott, *Can Labor Standards Improve under Globalization?* (Washington, DC: Institute for International Economics, 2003).

Conclusion

Neoliberalism supplanted structuralism as the guiding philosophy of economic development as a result of the interplay among three factors in the global economy. Import substitution generated severe economic imbalances that created pressure for reform of some type. The success of East Asian countries that adopted an export-oriented development strategy provided an alternative model for development. Finally, the emergence of a severe economic crisis in the early 1980s, a crisis that resulted in part from the imbalances generated by ISI and in part from developments in the global economy, pushed governments to launch reforms under the supervision of the IMF and World Bank. By the mid-1980s, most governments were implementing reforms that reduced the role of the state and increased the role of the market in economic development.

The implementation of these reforms has been neither quick nor painless. The depth of the reforms brought substantial short-run costs as average incomes fell and as this smaller income was redistributed among groups. The proponents of neoliberal reforms argue that the short-run costs are worth paying, however, for they establish the framework for strong and sustainable growth far into the future. Achieving that outcome will require developing societies to consolidate and build upon the reforms already implemented. In addition, it will require the advanced industrialized countries to accept short-run adjustment costs of their own in order to meet the legitimate demands that developing countries now make about market access.

The adoption of neoliberal reforms in the developing world is also transforming the global economy. For the first time since the early 20th century, the developing world has integrated itself into that economy. In doing so, developing countries have altered the dynamics of global economic exchange. Standard trade theory tells us to expect trade between capital-abundant and labor-abundant societies. Yet, trade barriers have greatly limited such trade for most of the postwar era. As these barriers have fallen during the last 20 years, trade between countries with different factor endowments has become increasingly important. Businesses are increasingly locating their activities in those parts of the world where they can be performed most efficiently. Labor-intensive aspects of production are being shifted to developing societies, while the capital-intensive aspects of production remain in the advanced industrialized countries. The expansion of North–South trade is thus creating a new global division of labor.

Key Terms

Current Account

East Asian Model of Development

Export-oriented Industrialization

Export-oriented Strategy

Multifiber Arrangement

Neoliberalism

Privatization

Real Exchange Rates

Rent Seeking

Structural Adjustment

Tariff Escalation

Tariff Peaks

Web Links

The United Nations Conference on Trade and Development website can be found at *http://www.unctad.org* and the Group of 77 website at *http://www.g77.org*.

Visit the World Bank at *http://www.worldbank.org*.

You can also visit the regional development banks:

The African Development Bank: *http://www.afdb.org*.

The Inter-American Development Bank: *http://www.iadb.org*.

The Asian Development Bank: *http://www.adb.org*.

The WTO devotes a section of its site to developing countries and the international trade system: *http://www.wto.org/english/tratop_e/devel_e/devel_e.htm*.

The Electronic Development and Environment Information System (ELDIS), based at the Institute of Development Studies in Sussex, England, maintains a website with good links to information about development issues. The site is found at *http://nt1.ids.ac.uk/eldis/eldis.htm*.

Suggestions for Further Reading

On the Asian Model, see Robert Wade, *Governing the Market: Economic Theory and the Role of Government in East Asian Industrialization* (Princeton: Princeton University Press, 1990), and Stephan Haggard, *Pathways from the Periphery: The Politics of Growth in the Newly Industrializing Countries* (Ithaca, NY: Cornell University Press, 1990). For a concise summary of the World Bank view, see World Bank, *The East Asian Miracle: Economic Growth and Public Policy* (Washington, DC: World Bank, 1994).

On structural adjustment, see Tony Killick, *Aid and the Political Economy of Policy Change* (London: Routledge, 1998), and World Bank, *Adjustment in Africa: Lessons from Country Case Studies* (Washington, DC: World Bank, 1998). On the politics of reform, a useful place to start is Stephan Haggard and Robert Kaufman, eds., *The Politics of Economic Adjustment: International Constraints, Distributive Conflicts, and the State* (Princeton: Princeton University Press, 1992), and John Williamson, ed., *The Political Economy of Policy Reform* (Washington, DC: Institute for International Economics, 1994). For a more recent work, see Anne O. Krueger, *Economic Policy Reform* (Chicago: University of Chicago Press, 2000).

CHAPTER 8

Multinational Corporations in the Global Economy

Multinational corporations occupy a prominent and often controversial role in the global economy. When a corporation based in one country creates a new production facility in a foreign country or buys an existing one, it extends managerial control across national borders. This managerial control enables the firm to make decisions about how and where to employ resources that have consequences for the country in which it is based and for the country in which it invests. Jobs, income, and technology might be acquired or lost, and the economic agendas of national governments might be promoted or stymied as a result of the decisions made by such multinational corporations. In many instances, the decisions that firms make are based on global strategies for corporate success, rather than on the basis of conditions within any of the countries in which the firm conducts its business. As a result, multinational corporations, perhaps more than any other element of the international economic system, highlight the tensions inherent in an economy which is increasingly organized along global lines and political systems that continue to reflect exclusive national territories.

Because multinational corporations operate simultaneously in national political systems and global markets, they have been the subject of considerable controversy among governments and among observers of the international political economy. Some consider multinational corporations to be productive instruments of a liberal economic order: multinational corporations ship capital to where it is scarce, transfer technology and management expertise from one country to another, and promote the efficient allocation of resources in the global economy. Others consider multinational corporations to be instruments of capitalist domination: multinational corporations control critical sectors of their hosts' economies, make decisions about the use of resources with little regard for host country needs, and weaken labor and environmental standards. About all that these two divergent perspectives agree upon is that multinational corporations are both primary drivers of, and beneficiaries of, the dynamics of globalization.

This chapter and the next examine the economics and the politics of multinational corporations (MNCs). This chapter focuses on a few of the core economic issues concerning these geographically far-reaching organizations. The first section provides a broad overview of MNCs in the global economy. We define what MNCs are, briefly examine their origins and development, and then examine some statistics that depict the rapid growth of MNCs over the last 20 years and the industries in which MNC activities are most heavily concentrated. The second section examines the standard economic theory that has been developed to explain the existence of MNCs. This theory will both deepen our understanding of the differences between MNCs and other firms and help us to understand when we are likely to see MNCs operating and when we are likely to see national firms. The final section examines the impact of MNCs on the countries that host their foreign investments. We look first at the potential benefits that MNCs can bring to host countries and then examine how MNC activities sometimes limit the extent to which host countries are able to realize those benefits.

MNCs in the Global Economy

For many people, a multinational corporation and a firm that engages heavily in international activities are one and the same thing. Yet, an MNC is more than just a firm that engages in international activities, and many firms that engage heavily in international activities are not, strictly speaking, multinational corporations. MNCs are only a subset of internationally active firms. The standard definition of a multinational corporation is a firm that "controls and manages production establishments—plants—in at least two countries" (Caves 1996, 1). This definition is a useful starting point, highlighting two critical aspects of MNCs. First, MNCs place multiple production facilities under the control of a single corporate structure. Thus, ownership of multiple facilities is a centrally important component of an MNC. Many firms are engaged in international activities, but do not own factories outside of their country of residence. Such firms are not MNCs. Second, MNCs are firms that have internationalized their activities: the production facilities that each multinational firm owns are located in different countries across the globe. Many firms may own multiple facilities, but in some cases all of these facilities are located within one country. Such firms are not MNCs. Putting these two characteristics together allows us to suggest that multinational corporations are distinguished from other firms by their extension of corporate ownership and corporate decision-making power across national borders.

The preceding definition does not capture the full range of MNC activities, however. Multinational corporations are simultaneously engaged in economic production, international trade, and cross-border investment. Consider, for example, the U.S.-based company General Electric (GE), which is regularly ranked among the world's largest MNCs. GE controls some 250 plants located in 26 countries in North and South America, Europe, and Asia. While production in these facilities is obviously important, the ability to engage in international trade is equally critical to GE's success. Many of the goods GE produces cross national borders, either as finished consumer goods or as components for other finished products. Washers, dryers, and microwave ovens that GE produces in Asia and Latin America, for example, are sold in the United States and Europe. Some of the jet engines GE produces in the United

States are sold to Airbus. Finally, to create this global production and trade network, GE has had to make many cross-border investments. Each time that GE establishes a new production facility, or upgrades an existing facility, in a foreign country, it invests in that country. MNCs are thus also an important source of foreign capital for the countries that host their affiliates. Thus, while GE certainly controls and manages factories in at least two countries, this does not describe the full range of GE's international activities. Like all MNCs, GE engages simultaneously in production, trade, and cross-border investment.

Multinational corporations are not recent inventions. They first emerged as significant and enduring components of the international economy during the late nineteenth century. This first wave of multinational business was dominated by Great Britain, the world's largest capital-exporting country in that century. British firms invested in natural resources and in manufacturing within the British Empire, the United States, Latin America, and Asia. In 1914, British investors controlled almost half of the world's total stock of foreign direct investment, and multinational manufacturing was taking place in a large number of industries, including chemicals, pharmaceuticals, the electrical industry, machinery, automobiles, tires, and processed food (Jones 1996, 29–30). American firms began investing abroad in the late nineteenth century. Singer Sewing Machines became the first American firm to create a permanent manufacturing facility abroad when it built a plant in Glasgow, Scotland, in 1867 (Wilkins 1970, 41–42). By the 1920s, the United States was overtaking Britain as the world's largest source of foreign direct investment. (See Jones 1996.)

American firms dominated foreign direct investment following the Second World War. Concerned with postwar reconstruction and unwilling to risk the balance-of-payments consequences of capital outflows, European and Japanese governments discouraged outward foreign direct investment. As a consequence, American firms accounted for two-thirds of all new MNC affiliates created between 1945 and 1960 (Dunning 1996). The largest share of American investment went to Europe, for manufacturing. The push by American firms to invest in Europe was given additional impetus by the formation of the European Economic Community in the late 1950s. Much U.S. investment was oriented toward gaining access to the newly integrating European market. Other American firms invested in developing countries, in Canada, and in Australia, and much of this investment was oriented toward extracting natural resources.

The dominance of American multinational corporations has diminished since 1960 as first European and then Japanese firms began to invest overseas. More recently, the increased role of MNCs based in other advanced industrialized countries has been accompanied by the emergence of foreign direct investment by MNCs based in Asia and Latin America. Thus, while American firms continue to play a large role in the international economy, they are not nearly as dominant today as they were in the early postwar period.

While MNCs are not a recent innovation, what is novel is the rate at which firms have been transforming themselves into MNCs. We can see the unprecedented growth of MNCs in two different sets of statistics. The first tracks the number of MNCs operating in the global economy. (See Figure 8.1.) In 1969, just at the tail end of the period of American dominance, there were only about 7,300 MNC parent firms operating in the global economy. By 1988, 18,500 firms had entered the ranks of multi-

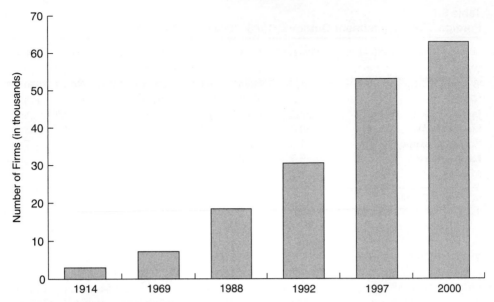

Figure 8.1 The Growth of MNC Parent Firms.
Source: Gable and Bruner 2003, 3.

national corporations, an impressive growth in 20 years. During the next 12 years, however, the number of MNCs operating in the global economy more than tripled, rising to an estimated 61,582 parent firms in 2000. Together, these parents control a total of 926,948 foreign affiliates. Thus, in just over 30 years, the number of firms engaged in international production has increased about ninefold.

The second set of statistics tracks the growth of foreign direct investment over the same period. **Foreign direct investment** (FDI) occurs when a firm based in one country builds a new plant or a factory, or purchases an existing one, in a second country. A national corporation thus becomes a multinational corporation by making a foreign direct investment. As Table 8.1 illustrates, the total volume of foreign direct investment has grown dramatically during the last 17 years. During the late 1980s, cross-border FDI flows equaled about $180 billion per year. The figure almost doubled by the mid-1990s and then continued to increase throughout the second half of the 1990s. Foreign direct investment peaked at more than $1 trillion per year in 1999 and 2000, before falling back during the last five years. As a consequence, the world's stock of FDI, the total amount of foreign investment in operation, has grown from $692.7 billion in 1980 to $8.2 trillion in 2003, close to a twelvefold increase in a 23-year period (UNCTAD 2004, 376). Both sets of statistics highlight the same pattern: the last 23 years has brought a dramatic acceleration of the number of firms that are internationalizing their activities.

As the number of MNCs has increased, the role that they play in the global economy has likewise gained in importance. The United Nations estimates that multinational corporations currently produce about 10 percent of the world's total gross domestic product and employ some 54.2 million people worldwide (UNCTAD 2004,

Table 8.1
Foreign Direct Investment Outflows, 1986–2003 ($US Billions)

	1986–1991	1992–1997	1998	1999	2000	2001	2002	2003
World	180.5	328.2	687.2	1,092.3	1,186.8	721.5	596.5	612.2
Western Europe	100.4	161.7	436.5	763.9	859.4	447.0	364.5	350.3
North America	31.3	88.6	165.4	226.6	187.3	161.0	141.8	173.4
Japan	33.1	20.2	24.2	22.7	31.6	38.3	32.3	28.8
Southeast Asia	8.3	39.0	32.5	39.2	80.0	45.1	34.7	23.5
Eastern Europe	n.a.°	1.2	2.3	2.5	4.0	3.5	4.9	7.0
Latin America	n.a.°	9.5	19.9	31.3	13.7	12.0	6.0	10.7
Africa	n.a.°	2.2	2.0	2.6	1.3	−2.5	.1	1.3

°n.a. = not available.
Source: UNCTAD 2004, 372–375.

8–9). Much of this activity is concentrated in a relatively small number of firms. The one hundred largest MNCs (half of which are listed in Table 8.2 on page 170) account for more than 12 percent of the total foreign assets controlled by all MNCs, for 14 percent of all MNC's sales, and for 13 percent of all MNC's employment (UNCTAD 2004, 9). MNCs also conduct about one-third of the world's trade (UNCTAD 2004, 9). Much of this is **intrafirm trade**—that is, trade that takes place between an MNC parent and its foreign affiliates. In the United States, for example, one-third of all exports are intrafirm exports, and as much as 40 percent of imports are intrafirm imports (Grimwade 2000, 134). It has been estimated that intrafirm trade accounts for 30 to 40 percent of world trade (Dunning 1996, 77). MNCs thus play an important role in the contemporary global economy, and this role has been growing at a rapid pace during the last 25 years.

While MNCs, of course, have a global reach, MNC activities are overwhelmingly concentrated in the advanced industrialized countries. We can see just how concentrated MNC operations are by looking at some statistics on the nationality of parent firms and on the global distribution of FDI flows. It is hardly surprising that the advanced industrialized countries are home to the world's largest MNCs and provide the largest share of the world's foreign direct investment. Ninety-seven of the 100 largest MNCs are headquartered in the United States, Western Europe, or Japan, and about 75 percent of all MNC parent corporations are based in advanced industrial countries. (See Table 8.3.) The advanced industrialized countries have historically been the largest suppliers of FDI as well. During most of the 1980s, the United States, Western Europe, and Japan together supplied about 90 percent of FDI. (See Table 8.1.) Their share fell to about 82 percent during the early 1990s with the emergence of new East Asian MNCs as important foreign investors. Over the last five years, however, the distribution reverted to the earlier pattern, with the advanced industrialized countries providing 92 percent of all foreign direct investment between 1998 and 2003 (UNCTAD 2004, 372).

The advanced industrialized countries have also been the most important recipients of the world's foreign direct investment. Throughout most of the postwar period and up until the late 1980s, Western Europe and the United States regularly attracted

a little more than three-quarters of the world's total FDI inflows each year. (See Table 8.4.) This share fell during the 1990s, and by 1997 the share of FDI flowing into Europe and the U.S. had dropped to about half the total. (See Figure 8.2.) As with FDI outflows, however, this trend has reversed itself during the last five years: between 1998 and 2003, Western Europe and North American attracted about 70 percent of all FDI. While the future evolution of the precise distribution of new investments between the advanced industrialized and developing worlds bears watching, this should not disguise the fact that whether we look at parent firms or FDI flows, we see quite clearly that the vast majority of MNC activities are concentrated in the advanced industrialized world. That is, most such activities involve American and Japanese firms investing in Europe, European and Japanese firms investing in the United States, and American and European firms investing in Japan.

While MNC activities are concentrated in the advanced industrialized world, MNC activities in the developing world have increased substantially during the last 20 years. They have done so in two ways. Historically, developing countries have hosted MNC investments, but the amount of FDI they have attracted has been relatively small. Since the late 1980s, however, MNCs have been investing more heavily in developing countries. As a group, the developing world saw its share of FDI inflows rise from one-quarter to almost one-half of total world investment between 1980 and 1997. (See Table 8.4 and Figure 8.2.) These greater investments were not evenly distributed across the developing world, however, but have been heavily concentrated in a small number of Asian and Latin American countries. Asia's share of FDI inflows doubled, rising from one-tenth to one-fifth of the total, between 1986 and 1997, with China alone attracting more than half of all FDI inflows into East Asia between 1993 and 1997. Latin America's share of world FDI inflows also more than doubled over the same period, increasing from 6 percent of total world FDI in the late 1980s to 14 percent in 1997. Yet, only four countries—Brazil, Argentina, Chile, and Mexico—captured 53 percent of these inflows. Thus, MNC investment in the developing world has increased during the last 20 years, but the majority of this investment has been concentrated in a very small number of developing countries. Much of the developing world, and particularly sub-Saharan Africa, saw little increase in FDI during the period.

The last 20 years has also seen some developing countries emerge as home bases for MNC parent firms. According to the United Nations, one-quarter of the world's MNC parent firms in 2002 were based in developing countries. Again, however, this development is limited to a small number of countries, such as Hong Kong, China, South Korea, Singapore, Taiwan, Venezuela, Mexico, and Brazil. Moreover, these developing-world MNCs are considerably smaller than MNCs based in the advanced industrialized world. Only three developing country MNCs (Cemex, a Mexican construction materials company; Samsung, the South Korean electronics giant; and Hutchison Whampoa, a Hong Kong–based diversified company) ranked among the world's 100 largest MNCs in 2002. As a group, the 50 largest MNCs from developing countries control only a combined $195 billion of foreign assets, less than 10 percent of the foreign assets controlled by the 50 largest MNCs based in the advanced industrialized countries (UNCTAD 2004, 21–23). While MNCs based in developing countries are small, the emergence of these MNCs is nonetheless a significant change in the global economy. It indicates that, for the first time in history, some developing countries

Table 8.2
The Fifty Largest MNCs, Ranked by Foreign Assets (2002)

Firm	Country	Industry	Assets (Millions of U.S. Dollars)		Foreign Employment
			Foreign	Total	
General Electric	United States	Electronics	229,001	575,244	315,000
Vodafone Group, PLC	United Kingdom	Telecommunications	207,622	232,870	56,667
Ford Motor Company	United States	Automotive	165,024	295,222	188,453
British Petroleum	United Kingdom	Petroleum	126,109	159,125	97,400
General Motors	United States	Automotive	107,926	370,782	101,000
Royal Dutch Shell	Netherlands/U.K.	Petroleum	94,402	145,392	65,000
Toyota	Japan	Automotive	79,433	167,270	85,057
Total Fina Elf	France	Petroleum	79,032	89,450	68,554
France Telecom	France	Telecommunications	73,454	111,735	102,016
Exxon/Mobil Corporation	United States	Petroleum	60,802	94,940	56,000
Volkswagen Group	Germany	Automotive	57,133	114,156	157,887
E. On	Germany	Electricity, Gas, and Water	52,294	118,526	42,063
RWE Group	Germany	Electricity, Gas, and Water	50,699	105,116	55,563
Vivendi Universal	France	Media	49,667	72,682	45,772
Chevron/Texaco	United States	Petroleum	48,489	77,359	37,038
Hutchison Whampoa Limited	Hong Kong	Diversified	48,014	63,284	124,942
Siemens, AG	Germany	Electronics	47,511	76,474	251,340
Electricité de France	France	Electricity, Gas, and Water	47,385	151,835	50,437
Honda Motor	Japan	Automotive	43,641	63,755	42,885
News Corporation	Australia	Media	40,331	45,214	31,220
Roche Group	Switzerland	Pharmaceuticals	40,152	46,160	61,090
Suez	France	Electricity, Gas, and Water	38,379	44,805	138,200
BMW, AG	Germany	Automotive	37,604	58,192	20,120
ENI Group	Italy	Petroleum	36,991	68,987	36,973
Nestlé, SA	Switzerland	Food and Beverages	36,145	63,007	150,232

continued

Table 8.2
The Fifty Largest MNCs, Ranked by Foreign Assets (2002)

Firm	Country	Industry	Foreign	Total	Foreign Employment
			Assets (Millions of U.S. Dollars)		
Daimler/Chrysler	Germany/United States	Automotive	35,778	196,375	72,560
Telefónica, SA	Spain	Telecommunications	35,720	71,327	88,401
IBM	United States	Electronics	34,951	96,484	178,602
Conoco/Phillips	United States	Petroleum	32,094	76,836	23,934
Wal-Mart Stores	United States	Retail	30,709	94,685	300,000
Sony Corp	Japan	Electronics	29,821	69,476	94,000
Carrefour, SA	France	Retail	28,594	40,804	271,031
Hewlett-Packard	United States	Electronics	28,247	70,710	56,326
Asea Brown Boveri (ABB)	Switzerland	Electrical Equipment	28,155	29,533	131,321
Unilever	Netherlands/U.K.	Diversified	27,937	46,752	193,000
Philips Electronics	Netherlands	Electronics	27,880	33,849	140,827
Novartis	Switzerland	Pharmaceuticals	25,874	45,588	40,282
Aventis	France	Pharmaceuticals	23,753	32,574	37,802
AOL Time Warner, Inc.	United States	Media	23,476	115,450	18,555
Repsol YPF, SA	Spain	Petroleum	23,121	39,902	14,072
AES Corporation	United States	Electricity, Gas, and Water	22,784	33,776	24,284
Deutsche Post World Net	Germany	Transport and Storage	22,782	170,503	108,609
BASF, AG	Germany	Chemicals	22,694	36,781	39,078
Endesa	Spain	Electricity, Gas, and Water	22,460	50,503	12,334
Anglo American	United Kingdom	Mining and Quarrying	22,450	33,581	147,000
Compagnie De Saint-Gobain, SA	France	Construction Materials	22,361	31,604	122,373
Phillip Morris	United States	Diversified	21,513	87,540	40,795
Pfizer, Inc.	United States	Pharmaceuticals	21,161	46,356	72,000
Mitsui & Co, Ltd.	Japan	Wholesale Trade	21,020	54,286	14,611

Source: UNCTAD 2004, 276–278.

Table 8.3
Parent Corporations and Affiliates, by Region, 2002

	Parent Corporations Based in Economy	Foreign Affiliates Located in Economy
Developed Economies	45,077	102,560
Western Europe	36,133	75,664
United States	3,235	15,712
Japan	3,371	3,870
Other Developed Economies	4,270	7,459
Developing Economies	14,192	580,638
Africa	1,163	6,849
Latin America and Caribbean	2,475	46,117
Asia	10,535	527,119
Central and Eastern Europe	2,313	243,750

Source: UNCTAD 2004, 273–274.

Table 8.4
Foreign Direct Investment Inflows, 1986–2003 ($US Billions)

	1986–1991	1992–1997	1998	1999	2000	2001	2002	2003
World	180.5	310.9	240.9	1,086.8	1,388.0	817.6	678.8	559.6
Western Europe	100.4	100.8	263.0	500.0	697.4	368.8	380.2	310.2
North America	31.3	68.3	197.2	308.1	380.8	186.9	83.9	36.5
Japan	3.1	1.2	3.2	12.7	8.3	6.2	9.2	6.3
Southeast Asia	8.3	69.6	92.1	109.1	142.7	102.2	86.3	96.9
Eastern Europe	n.a.°	11.5	24.3	26.5	27.5	26.4	31.2	21.0
Latin America	n.a.°	38.2	82.5	107.4	97.5	88.1	51.4	49.7
Africa	n.a.°	5.9	9.1	11.6	8.7	19.6	11.8	15.0

°n.a. = not available.
Source: UNCTAD 2004, 367–371.

really are shifting from a position in which they are only the host to foreign MNCs to a position in which they are both host of foreign firms and home to domestic MNCs.

The rapid growth of multinational corporations during the last 25 years has pushed these firms into the center of the debate about globalization. Indeed, practically every aspect of globalization has been linked to the activities of MNCs. Ross Perot, for example, claimed during his unsuccessful bid for the presidency in 1992 that NAFTA would produce a "giant sucking sound" as American MNCs shifted jobs from the United States to their affiliates located in Mexico. Other critics of globalization claim that MNC affiliates based in developing countries are sweatshops engaged in the systematic exploitation of workers in those countries. Still others argue that the ability of MNCs to move production wherever they want is gradually eroding a broad range of government regulations designed to protect workers, consumers, and the environment. We will examine these arguments in greater detail in Chapter 16. For our purposes here, it is sufficient to note that criticism of MNC activities has emerged from

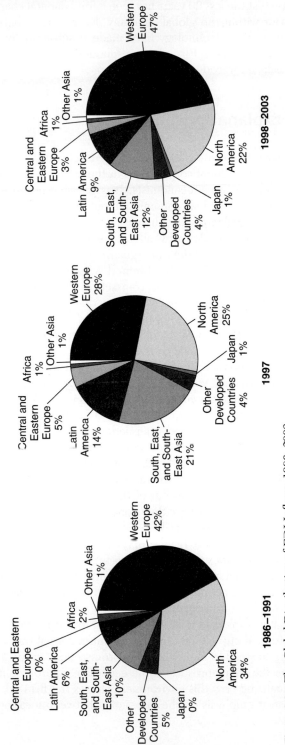

1986–1991

1997

1998–2003

Figure 8.2 The Global Distribution of FDI Inflows, 1986–2003.

Source: UNCTAD 2004.

the growing sense that the last 20 years has seen a fundamental change in the nature of corporate behavior within the global economy. Falling trade barriers and improvements in communications technology have made it substantially easier for firms to internationalize their activities. Firms have responded to these changes by internationalizing at historically unprecedented rates.

Economic Explanations for MNCs

Although firms have been internationalizing their activities at unprecedented rates, the prevalence of multinational corporations in the contemporary international economy is puzzling to neoclassical economists. It is puzzling because firms choose how they will participate in the global economy, and opting to make a large investment in a far-off country is not the obvious first choice.

In fact, one might wonder why all of the economic transactions that occur between MNC parent firms and their foreign affiliates are not simply handled through the market. When the GAP or the Limited acquire clothes from producers in Bangladesh, they handle most of these transactions through the market. They sign contracts with locally owned Bangladeshi firms that produce clothes and then sell them to the retailer. The GAP and the Limited do not own the firms that produce their clothes. In other instances, however, almost identical transactions are taken out of the market. When Volkswagen decided to assemble some of its cars in Mexico, it could have signed contracts with locally owned Mexican firms, which then could have produced components that met Volkswagen's specifications, assembled them into Jettas, Beetles, and Golfs, and sold the finished cars to Volkswagen. Volkswagen didn't opt for this market-based approach, however, but instead built an assembly plant in Mexico. Volkswagen thus took the economic transactions that would otherwise have taken place between suppliers of components, assemblers, and corporate headquarters out of the market and placed them under the sole control of Volkswagen headquarters. The rapid growth of MNCs implies that an increasing number of firms have opted to take their international transactions out of the market and internalize them within a single corporate structure. Why have they done so?

In finding an answer to this puzzle, we deepen our understanding of how MNCs are something more distinctive than simply "large firms." While many MNCs *are* large, what truly distinguishes them from other firms is the fact that they organize and manage their international activities very differently than other firms do. A traditional firm relies on markets; it acquires its inputs from independently owned firms and it sells its outputs to other individually owned firms. An MNC, by contrast, buys inputs from factories that it owns, and it sells a portion of its output to factories that it owns. And a firm's decision about whether to conduct international transactions through the market or whether instead to internalize these transactions inside a single corporation reflects some specific characteristics of the economic environment in which it operates. In conceptualizing how this environment shapes the firm's decision, economists have placed greatest emphasis on the interaction between locational advantages and market imperfections.

Locational Advantages

As a first step, we need to understand the factors that encourage a firm to internationalize its activities. That is, what factors determine when a firm will stop sourcing all of its inputs and selling all of its output at home and begin acquiring its inputs or selling a portion of its output in foreign markets? At a very broad level, it is obvious that a firm will internationalize its activities when it believes that it can profit by doing so. **Locational advantages** derive from specific country characteristics that provide such opportunities. Historically, locational advantages have been based on one of three specific country characteristics: a large reserve of natural resources, a large local market, and opportunities to enhance the efficiency of the firm's operations. A firm based in one country will internationalize its activities in an attempt to profit from one of these characteristics in a foreign country.

Locational advantages in **natural-resource investments** arise from the presence of large deposits of a particular natural resource in a foreign country. The desire to profit from the extraction of these natural resources was perhaps the earliest motivation for international activities. The American copper firms Anaconda and Kennecott, for example, made large direct investments in mining operations in Chile in order to secure copper supplies for production in the United States. American and European oil companies have invested heavily in the Middle East because the countries of that region hold so large a proportion of the world's petroleum reserves. Many European companies invested heavily in mining and other natural-resource-intensive industries in sub-Saharan Africa and Latin America during the late 19th century. And the desire to gain access to natural resources remains important today. Indeed, as Table 8.5 illustrates, petroleum and mining together account for about 10 percent of the 100 largest MNCs currently in operation. Complementary assets—that is, the infrastructure necessary to support drilling, mining, or farming—are also important for natural-resource-oriented direct investments. Complementary assets include (1) the state of the host country's infrastructure, such as the rail system and seaports, which allows firms to transport raw materials from the source to the final market, and (2) the availability and cost of utilities, such as water and electricity.

Locational advantages for **market-oriented investments** arise from large consumer markets that are expected to grow rapidly over time. This type of advantage is typically created by tariff and nontariff barriers that make it difficult for foreign firms to export to the market. By investing inside the country, firms essentially jump over such barriers, to produce and sell in the local market. Firms looking to sell their products in foreign markets clearly prefer countries with large and growing demand to those with small and stagnant demand. In addition, the degree of industry competition within the host country is important. The less indigenous competition there is in a particular foreign market, the easier it will be for the MNC to sell its products in that market. Finally, the existence of tariff and nontariff barriers to imports is another important consideration for this type of investment. Countries that have large and fast-growing markets, with a relatively small number of indigenous firms in the particular industry, and that are sheltered from international competition represent attractive opportunities for market-oriented MNC investment. By this logic, the European Union, the United States, China, and India may offer attractive locations for firms

Table 8.5
Industry Composition of the Top 100 MNCs

	1990	1998	2002
Electronics/electrical equipment/computers	14	17	8
Motor vehicle and parts	13	14	10
Petroleum (exploration, refining, distribution) and mining	13	11	10
Food, beverages, tobacco	9	10	6
Chemicals	12	8	3
Pharmaceuticals	6	8	10
Diversified	2	6	4
Telecommunications	2	6	7
Trading	7	4	2
Retailing	0	3	6
Utilities	0	3	9
Metals	6	2	3
Media	2	2	5
Construction	4	1	4
Machinery/engineering	3	-	5
Other	7	5	8

Source: UNCTAD 2000, 78; UNCTAD 2004, 279–280.

contemplating a market-oriented investment, whereas Costa Rica, Madagascar, and Burma would be much less attractive.

Much of the cross-border investment in auto production within the advanced industrialized world fits into this category. During the 1960s, many American automotive MNCs made direct investments in the European Union to gain access to the emerging common market. During the 1980s and early 1990s, Japanese and German automotive MNCs such as Toyota, Nissan, Honda, BMW, and Mercedes built production facilities in the United States in response to the emergence of voluntary export restraints (VERs) that limited auto imports. As Table 8.5 indicates, like petroleum and mining, the auto industry is heavily represented among the largest MNCs, accounting for another 10 percent of the 100 largest. Of course, the desire to gain access to foreign markets has not been limited to the auto industry, but has been an important motivation for much foreign direct investment in manufacturing as well.

Finally, locational advantages in **efficiency-oriented investments** arise from the availability at a lower cost of the factors of production that are used intensively in the production of a specific product. In these efficiency-oriented investments, parent firms allocate different stages of the production process to different parts of the world, matching the factor intensity of a production stage to the factor abundance of particular countries. In computers, electronics, and electrical equipment, for example, the human and physical capital-intensive stages of production, such as design and chip fabrication, are performed in the capital-abundant advanced industrialized countries, while the more labor-intensive assembly stages of production are performed in labor-abundant developing countries. In the auto industry in contrast, the capital-intensive design and production of individual parts such as body panels, engines, and transmissions is performed in advanced industrialized countries, and the more labor-intensive assembly of the individual components into automobiles is performed in developing countries. Locational advantages thus arise from factor endowments. When the contemplated investment is in low-skilled, labor-intensive production, labor-abundant countries have obvious advantages over labor-scarce countries. When the contemplated investment draws heavily upon advanced technology, the availability of a pool of highly trained scientists is important. American firms in the computer industry, for example, have opted to base many of their overseas activities in East Asian countries, where the average skill level is very high, rather than in Latin America, where, on average, skill levels are lower.

Locational advantages thus provide the economic rationale for a firm's decision to internationalize its activities. These advantages can arise from a country's underlying comparative advantage, as in mineral deposits or abundant labor. They can also be a product of government policies, as in the existence of high tariffs or the creation of a reliable economic infrastructure. Whatever the underlying source, locational advantages create a compelling motivation for a firm based in one country to engage in economic transactions with a foreign country. Locational advantages thus help us understand why some firms opt to internationalize their activities and some do not, for some firms can profit from internationalizing their activities while others cannot. The concept also helps us understand why a firm elects to engage in economic transactions with one country rather than another, for some countries offer potential benefits from cross-border exchange, while others do not.

Market Imperfections

While locational advantages help us understand why some firms opt to internationalize their activities, they do not help us understand why firms sometimes choose to take the resulting transactions out of the market and place them within a single corporate structure. Why didn't American firms simply buy copper from Chilean firms, rather than establish their own mining operations in Chile? Why didn't American computer firms simply buy semiconductors and other components from indigenous East Asian firms, rather than create their own chip fabrication factories in East Asia? Why didn't American auto firms simply export to the European Union and Brazil, rather than build assembly plants in those countries?

To understand why firms sometimes take their transactions out of the market and place them under the control of a single corporate structure, we need to examine the impact of market imperfections. A **market imperfection** arises when the price mechanism fails to promote a welfare-improving transaction. In the global economy, this means that, under certain conditions, firms will be unable to profit from an existing locational advantage unless they internalize the international transaction. Two different market imperfections have been used to understand two different types of internalization: horizontal integration and vertical integration.

Horizontal integration occurs when a firm creates multiple production facilities, each of which produces the same good or goods. In the international economy, horizontally integrated MNCs produce the same product in multiple national markets. Auto producers are a good example. Ford, General Motors, Volkswagen, and the major

Japanese auto producers each produce essentially the same line of cars in factories located in the United States, in Western Europe, and in Japan. Firms integrate horizontally when a cost advantage is gained by placing a number of plants under common administrative control (Caves 1996, 2). Such cost advantages most often arise when intangible assets are the most important source of a firm's revenue.

An **intangible asset** is something whose value is derived from knowledge or from "a set of skills or repertory routines possessed by the firm's team of human (and other) inputs" (Caves 1996, 3). An intangible asset can be based on a patented process or design, or it can arise from "know-how shared among employees of the firm" (*Ibid.*, 3). Coca-Cola, for example, transformed a single piece of knowledge—the formula for Coke—into a global soft-drink empire. The income of most pharmaceutical firms is also based on knowledge, in the form of the chemical composition of the drugs they produce. Microsoft is able to dominate the global software industry in part because its programmers have a deep understanding of the operating system used on most PCs. Microsoft programmers can use this knowledge to develop software that performs better on Windows-based computers than the software produced by its competitors. In all of these examples, firms are deriving income from an intangible asset—that is, from knowledge in some form.

Intangible assets often give rise to horizontally integrated firms because those assets are difficult to sell or license to other firms at a price that accurately reflects their true value. In other words, markets will fail to promote exchanges between a willing seller of an intangible asset and a willing buyer. The market failure arises because owners of knowledge-based assets confront what has been called the "fundamental paradox of information": "[The] value [of the information] for the purchaser is not known until he has the information, but then he has in effect acquired it without cost" (Teece 1993, 172). In other words, in order to convey the full value of an intangible asset, the owner must reveal so much of the information upon which the asset's value is based that the potential purchaser no longer needs to pay to acquire the asset. If the owner is unwilling to reveal that information, potential buyers will be unsure of the asset's true value and will therefore be reluctant to pay for the asset.

Suppose, for example, that I have developed a production process which reduces by one-half the cost of manufacturing cars. This innovation is purely a matter of how the production process is organized and managed, and has nothing to do with the machines and technology actually used to produce cars. I try to sell this knowledge to Ford Motor Company, but, in our negotiations, Ford's board of directors is skeptical of my claim that I can cut the firm's costs by 50 percent. The board members insist that I disclose fully how I will accomplish this before they will even consider purchasing my knowledge, and they want specifics. Once I disclose all of the details, however, they will know exactly what changes they need to make in order to realize the cost reductions. As soon as they have this knowledge, they have no reason to pay me to acquire it. Like all other owners of intangible assets, I will receive less than my asset's true worth when I sell it to another firm.

Such market failures create incentives for horizontal integration. Suppose an individual owns an intangible asset that can generate more revenue than is currently being earned, because demand for the goods produced with the use of this asset will be greater than can be met from the existing production facility. How can the owner earn the additional revenue that the asset will generate? The only way he or she can do so is to create additional production sites—that is, to integrate horizontally and allow each of these facilities to make use of the intangible asset. Because the same firm owns all of the production sites, it can realize the full value of its intangible asset without having to try to sell it in an open market. Horizontal integration, therefore, internalizes economic transactions for intangible assets.

Vertical integration refers to instances in which firms internalize their transactions for intermediate goods. An intermediate good is an output of one production process that serves as an input into another production process. Standard Oil, which dominated the American oil industry in the late nineteenth century, is a classic example of a vertically integrated firm. Standard Oil owned oil wells, the network through which crude oil was transported from the well to the refinery, the refineries, and the retail outlets at which the final product was sold. Thus, each stage of the production process was contained within a single corporate structure. Why would a single firm incorporate the various stages of the production process under a single administrative control, rather than purchase its inputs from independent producers and sell outputs to other independent firms, either as inputs into additional production or as final goods to independent retailers?

To explain the internalization of transactions within a single vertically integrated firm, economists have focused on problems caused by specific assets. A **specific asset** is an investment that is dedicated to a particular long-term economic relationship. Consider a hypothetical case of a shipowner and a railroad. The shipowner would like to transport the goods he delivers to his dock to market by rail. He contacts the railroad and asks that a rail spur be built from the main line down to the dock so that he can offload goods directly onto railcars. If the railroad agrees to build the spur, then this spur will be dedicated to the transport of that particular shipowner's goods to the main rail line. Moreover, once the rail spur down to the dock is built, the resources used to build it can be reallocated at some cost to the railroad. In other words, this rail spur is an asset—an investment that will yield a return—that is dedicated to, or specific to, the ongoing relationship between the shipowner and the railroad owner. That is to say, the rail spur is a specific asset.

Specific assets create incentives for vertical integration because it is difficult to write and enforce long-term contracts. Returning to our example of the shipowner and the railroad, suppose that, under the terms of the initial agreement, the shipowner agreed to pay the railroad a certain fee per ton to carry goods to market once the spur was built. This initial fee made it profitable for the railroad to build the spur. Once the spur has been built, however, the shipowner has an incentive to renegotiate the initial contract to achieve a more favorable shipping rate. The shipowner recognizes that, because the railroad must incur costs if it decides to reallocate the resources it used to build the spur, the railroad owner will be better off accepting renegotiated terms than refusing to carry the goods. Thus, the existence of a specific asset creates possibilities for opportunistic behavior once the investment has been made: one party in the long-term relationship can take advantage of the specific nature of the asset to extract a larger share of the value from the transaction (Teece 1993, 166–169; Williamson 1985).

This problem would disappear if it were costless to enforce the initial contract. But even when the judicial system will enforce contracts, the legal fees associated with the dispute, along with the income lost by the railroad as the dispute works its way through civil litigation, can be substantial. The railroad owner might be better off accepting a renegotiated contract at slightly lower rates than paying the costs arising from enforcing the initial contract.

The recognition that asset specificity creates incentives for opportunistic behavior after the investment has been made can cause economic actors to refuse to make investments. In our example, the railroad owner will recognize that the shipowner has an incentive to behave opportunistically after the spur is built; therefore, quite rationally, the railroad owner will refuse to build the spur. As a result, a mutually beneficial transaction between the shipper and the railroad—the creation of a rail spur in exchange for payments for transporting goods from the dock to market—will go unrealized.

By incorporating the two parties to the transaction within the same ownership structure, vertical integration eliminates the problems arising from specific assets. If the shipowner also owned the railroad (or vice versa), there would be little incentive for opportunistic behavior once the rail spur had been built. The shipping division of this now vertically integrated firm could pay the firm's railroad division a smaller fee for transporting its goods, but this would simply shift revenues and expenditures between units of the same firm; the firm's overall bottom line would remain constant. By internalizing transactions involving specific assets, therefore, vertical integration enables welfare-improving investments that would not otherwise be made.

Firms thus internalize their transactions—take them out of the market and place them under the control of a single corporate structure—in response to market imperfections. When firms earn a substantial share of their revenues from intangible assets, they face strong incentives to integrate horizontally—that is, to create multiple production facilities, all controlled by a single corporate headquarters. When firms earn a substantial share of their revenues from specific assets, they face strong incentives to integrate vertically—that is, to place all of the various stages of production under the control of a single corporate structure. In both cases, the incentive to take transactions out of the market and place them within a single corporate structure arises from the inability of the market to accurately price the value of the asset that generates the firm's income.

Locational Advantages, Market Imperfections, and MNCs

While locational advantages and market imperfections often occur independently of each other, we expect to see multinational corporations—firms that internalize economic transactions across national borders—when both factors are present. Locational advantages tell us that cross-border activity will be profitable, while market imperfections tell us that the firm can take advantage of these opportunities only by internalizing the transactions within a single corporate structure.

Table 8.6 illustrates how the interaction between locational advantages and market imperfections shapes the kinds of firms we expect to see in the global economy. When locational advantages and intangible assets are both present, we expect to find horizontally integrated MNCs that have undertaken foreign investment to gain market access. Horizontally integrated MNCs are therefore often present in manufacturing sectors. Foreign direct investments by auto producers in other advanced industrial countries' markets are perhaps the prototypical example of this type of MNC. In the auto industry, intangible assets arising from knowledge about the production process are of great value to individual firms, but are hard to price accurately in the market.

Table 8.6
Market Imperfections, Locational Advantages, and MNCs

		Market Imperfection	
		Intangible Assets	**Specific Assets**
Locational Advantages	**Yes**	Horizontally integrated MNC Market-based	Vertically integrated MNC Natural-resource based Cost based
	No	Horizontally integrated firm	Vertically integrated firm

Together with important locational advantages—especially the availability of large local markets—intangible assets induce foreign investment. Western Europe and the United States offer large markets for automobiles, and governments in the European Union and in the United States have used VERs to restrict imports from foreign auto producers. The combination of market imperfections and locational advantages in the auto industry has therefore led to considerable foreign direct investment by all of the major auto producers in the European and American markets.

When locational advantages combine with specific assets, we expect to find vertically integrated MNCs that have invested in a foreign country either to gain secure access to natural resources or to reduce their costs of production. The best example of firms investing to secure access to natural resources is found in the oil industry. An oil refinery must have repeated transactions with the firms that are drilling for oil. The refinery is highly vulnerable to threats to shut off the flow of oil, because an inconsistent supply would be highly disruptive to its oil refineries and distribution networks. Thus, we would expect a high degree of vertical integration in the oil industry. This knowledge helps us understand why petroleum companies are so heavily represented in the world's 100 largest MNCs.

The best example of firms investing abroad to reduce the cost of production may be found in the factories built by auto producers in developing countries. The individual components involved in auto production are complex and specific to the final good: one cannot produce a Ford with parts designed for a Nissan. Thus, auto producers must have long-term relationships with their parts suppliers, and these relationships create incentives for vertical integration across borders. It is no surprise, therefore, that the auto industry is also heavily represented in the 100 largest MNCs.

The matrix presented in Table 8.6 also points to those industries in which we would not expect to find a significant amount of MNC activity. When locational advantages exist, but there are neither intangible nor specific assets, we do not expect to find a significant amount of MNC activity. Instead, firms will prefer to purchase their inputs from independent suppliers and sell their products through international trade, or they will prefer to enter into sub-contracting arrangements with firms located in the foreign country and owned by foreign residents. Apparel production fits nicely into this category. Apparel production is a labor-intensive activity and is increasingly done in labor-abundant developing countries. The major retailers in the advanced industrialized world, such as GAP and Limited, rely heavily upon producers located in developing countries, but they rarely own the firms that produce the apparel they sell. Instead, they enter into contracting relationships with independent firms.

Nor would we expect to find significant amounts of MNC activity in those industries in which market imperfections exist, but locational advantages are absent. In such instances, firms do have an incentive to integrate horizontally and vertically, but integrated firms cannot easily expand sales into foreign markets, are not heavily dependent upon foreign sources of raw materials, and cannot easily reduce their costs by exploiting cost differentials between their home country and foreign countries. As a result, firms in these industries have little incentive to extend their activities across national borders. Such firms are most typically found in the nontraded-goods sector of the economy.

In sum, MNCs are more than just large firms. MNCs are firms that have responded in predictable ways to the specific characteristics of the economic environment in which they operate. The creation of an MNC is most often the result of a corporate response to a locational advantage and a market imperfection. Locational advantages create incentives to extend operations across borders in order to extract natural resources, sell in foreign markets, or achieve cost reductions. Intangible and specific assets create incentives for firms to shift their economic transactions out of the market and into a single corporate structure. When locational advantages and market imperfections coexist, we expect to find MNCs—firms that have internalized transactions across national borders.

MNCs and Host Countries

Up to this point, we have focused exclusively on what MNCs are, where they operate, and why they are established. In doing so, we have neglected the impact of MNCs on the countries that host their affiliates. We conclude the chapter by looking at this important dimension of MNC activity. Foreign direct investment creates a dilemma for host countries. On the one hand, FDI has the potential to make a positive contribution to the host country's economic welfare by providing resources that are not readily available elsewhere. On the other hand, because MNC affiliates are managed by decision makers based in foreign countries, there is no guarantee that FDI will in fact make such a contribution. The politics of host country–MNC relations, a topic that we explore in depth in the next chapter, revolves largely around governments' efforts to manage this dilemma. Here, we look at the benefits that FDI confers on host countries in theory, as well as at a few MNC practices that can erode these benefits.

MNCs can bring to host countries important resources that are not easily acquired otherwise. Access to these resources thus offers the potential for substantial economic gains for host countries. Three such resources are perhaps the most important. First, foreign direct investment can transfer savings from one country to another. Economic growth is dependent upon investment—in physical capital (buildings and machines) as well as in human capital. To invest, however, a society needs to save, and in the absence of some form of foreign investment, a society can invest only as much as it is able to save. Foreign investment allows a society to draw on the savings of the rest of the world. By doing so, the country can enjoy faster growth than would be possible if it were forced to rely solely on its domestic savings. Moreover, because MNCs create fixed investments—they build factories that are not easily removed from the country—this type of cross-border capital flow is not subject to many of the problems posed by other kinds of capital flows. In particular, fixed investments are substantially more stable than financial capital flows and thus do not generate the boom and bust cycles we will examine in Chapters 14 and 15. In addition, because MNCs invest by creating domestic affiliates, direct investment does not raise host countries' external indebtedness. Of the many possible ways that savings can be transferred across borders, direct investment might be the most stable and least burdensome for the host countries.

MNCs can also bring technology and managerial expertise to host countries. Because MNCs control intangible assets based on specialized knowledge, the investments they make in host countries can often lead to this knowledge being transferred to indigenous firms. In Malaysia, for example, Motorola Malaysia transferred the technology required to produce a particular type of printed circuit board to a Malaysian firm, which then developed the capacity to produce these circuit boards on its own (Moran 1999, 77–78). In the absence of the technology transfer, the indigenous firm would not have been able to produce the products.

Such technology transfers can generate significant positive externalities with wider implications for development. (See Graham 1996, 123–130.) **Positive externalities** arise when economic actors in the host country that are not directly involved in the transfer of technology from an MNC to a local affiliate also benefit from this transaction. If, for example, the Malaysian Motorola affiliate were able to use the technology it acquired from Motorola to produce inputs for other Malaysian firms at a lower cost than these inputs were available elsewhere, then the technology transfer would have a positive externality on the Malaysian economy.

MNCs can also transfer managerial expertise to host countries. Greater experience at managing large firms allows MNC personnel to organize production and coordinate the activities of multiple enterprises more efficiently than host country managers can. This knowledge is applied to the host country affiliates, allowing them to operate more efficiently as well. Indigenous managers in these affiliates learn these management practices and can then apply them to indigenous firms. In this way, managerial expertise is transferred from the MNC to the host country.

Finally, MNCs can enable host country producers to gain access to marketing networks. When direct investments are made as part of a global production strategy, the local affiliates of the MNC and the domestic firms that supply these affiliates become integrated into a global marketing chain. Such integration creates export opportunities that would otherwise be unavailable to indigenous producers. The Malaysian firm to which Motorola transferred the printed circuit board technology, for example, not only wound up supplying Motorola Malaysia, but also began to supply components to 11 Motorola plants worldwide. These opportunities would not have arisen had the firm not been able to link up with Motorola Malaysia.

MNCs thus offer substantial benefits to the countries that host their affiliates. They bring foreign savings to the host country, thereby enabling the host to enjoy a higher rate of investment. They transfer technology and managerial expertise to the host country, thereby enabling the host to experience substantial productivity gains.

They provide the host country with access to global marketing networks, thereby enabling the host to expand production beyond what would be possible otherwise.

MNCs provide these benefits at a price, however. To capture the benefits that MNCs offer, a country must be willing to allow foreign corporate decision makers to make decisions about how resources will be used in the host country. As long as foreign managers make decisions about how much capital and technology are transferred to the host country, about how the resources MNCs bring to the host country will be combined with local inputs, and about how the revenues generated by the local affiliate will be used, there will be some chance that a particular investment will not enhance, and may even detract from, the welfare of the host country.

MNCs can reduce, rather than increase, the amount of funds available for investment in the host country, as a result of a number of different practices. MNCs sometimes borrow on the host country capital market instead of bringing capital from their home country. This practice crowds out domestic investment; that is, by using scarce domestic savings, the MNC prevents domestic firms from making investments. MNCs also often earn rents on their products and repatriate most of these earnings. Consequently, the excess profits wind up in the MNC's home country rather than remaining in the host country, where they could be used for additional investment.

In addition, MNCs typically charge their host country affiliates licensing fees or royalties for any technology that is transferred. When the affiliates pay these fees, additional funds are transferred out of the host country to the MNC's home base. Finally, MNCs often require the local affiliate to purchase inputs from other subsidiaries of the same corporation. These internal transactions take place at prices that are determined by the MNC parent, a practice called transfer pricing. Because such transactions are internal to the MNC, the parent can set the prices at whatever level best suits its global strategy. When the parent overcharges an affiliate for the goods it imports from affiliates based in other countries and underprices the same affiliate's exports, revenues are transferred from the local affiliate to the MNC parent. Sometimes such transfers can be very large: an investigation revealed that Colombia paid $3 billion more for pharmaceutical imports through MNCs than it would have paid in market-based transactions. All of these practices reduce the amount of funds that are available to finance new projects in the host country. In extreme cases, MNCs might *reduce* the total amount of funds available for investment, rather than increase them.

An MNC might also drive established host country firms out of business. Suppose an MNC enters an industry already populated by local firms. Suppose also that the MNC controls technology or management skills that enable it to produce at a lower cost than the local firms. As the MNC affiliate's local production expands, the established local firms will begin to lose sales to this new low-cost competitor. Some of these businesses will eventually fail. The failure of the local final-good producers may have a secondary impact on local input suppliers. Local firms often acquire their inputs from local firms. In contrast, most MNCs source their inputs from global networks of suppliers. If the new MNC affiliate drives local firms out of business, then the demand for the inputs provided by local firms will fall. The local input suppliers will thus face serious pressure, and many of them will probably go out of business as well. While such instances may be an example of a more efficient firm replacing less efficient competitors, the dynamic is one in which local firms are gradually replaced by foreign firms and local managers by foreign managers. And if the transfer of skills and technology from foreign to local producers is one of the purported benefits of foreign direct investment, then a dynamic in which foreign firms drive local firms out of business suggests that very little technology transfer is occurring.

Technology transfers can be further limited by the incentive that MNCs have to maintain fairly tight control over technology and managerial positions. As we have seen, one of the principal reasons for MNC investment arises from the desire to maintain control over intangible assets. Given this desire, it is hard to understand why an MNC would make a large fixed investment in order to retain control over its technology, but then transfer that technology to host country firms. The transfer of managerial expertise may be limited also, because MNCs are often reluctant to hire host-country residents into top-level managerial positions. Thus, the second purported benefit of MNCs—the transfer of technology and managerial expertise—can be stymied by the very logic that causes MNCs to undertake FDI. If this happens, MNC affiliates will function like enclaves, failing to be tightly integrated into the rest of the host country economy and never realizing any spillover effects.

Finally, MNCs' decisions about how to use the revenues generated by their affiliates may bear no relationship to the host country government's economic objectives. In a world in which governments cared little about the type of economic activity that was conducted within their borders, this would be of little consequence. But when governments use a wide variety of policy instruments to try to promote certain types of economic activity, whether it be manufacturing in a developing country or high-technology industries in an advanced industrialized country, foreign control of these revenues can pose serious obstacles to government policy. If, for example, a country's export earnings derive entirely from copper exports, but a multinational corporation controls the country's copper-mining operations, then decisions about how to use the country's foreign exchange earnings will be made by the MNC rather than by the government. Or if the revenues generated by the local affiliate are sufficient to finance additional investment, decisions about whether this investment will be made in the host country or somewhere else and, if in the host country, then in which sector, are made by the MNC rather than by the government. In short, MNCs' control over the revenues generated by their affiliates makes it difficult for governments to channel resources toward the economic activities they are trying to encourage.

Host countries therefore face a dilemma in their relationship with MNCs. On the one hand, MNCs can provide resources to host countries, including access to new sources of capital, innovative technologies, managerial expertise, and market linkages that are not available elsewhere. These resources have the potential to make important contributions to the host country economy, and they are not readily acquired without accepting foreign direct investment. On the other hand, because foreign direct investment extends foreign managerial control into the host country's economy, there is no guarantee that a particular investment will in fact yield the aforesaid benefits. An MNC might consume scarce local savings, replace local firms, refuse to transfer technology, and repatriate all of its earnings. This dilemma has led many to suggest that governments may need to play an active role in structuring the conditions under which MNCs operate within their economies. As we will see in the next chapter, much of the

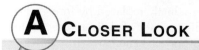

CLOSER LOOK

Singer Sewing Machines in Taiwan

The experience of Singer Sewing Machines in Taiwan highlights how governments can manage foreign direct investment to ensure that such investments provide substantial benefits for the host country (UNCTAD 1999, 211). Singer first invested in Taiwan in 1964. At the time, there were a large number of Taiwanese firms manufacturing sewing machines. Most of these firms relied on old technology, and the industry as a whole lacked standardization. As a result, Taiwanese producers found it difficult to compete in international markets. The Taiwanese government intended to use Singer to upgrade the capacity of this local industry, rather than to substitute for domestic firms.

To promote this transformation, the Taiwanese government imposed some strict conditions on Singer's investment. Domestic content requirements required Singer to purchase 83 percent of the parts it used in the sewing machines it produced in Taiwan from Taiwanese producers within one year. To achieve this goal, the government demanded that Singer provide local parts-producing firms with standardized blueprints for the necessary parts. In addition, Singer was required to provide technical experts that could assist the local firms as they began to produce the needed parts. The government also forced Singer to allow the Taiwanese firms that were manufacturing complete sewing machines to purchase parts from the local parts producers that Singer was assisting. Finally, the government imposed an export requirement on Singer under which exports of Singer machines produced in Taiwan would increase rapidly.

Singer complied with all of these requirements. Forced to purchase such a large share of its inputs from local suppliers, Singer quickly provided blueprints and part specifications to all local parts producers, thereby allowing them to work to common specifications and standards. Singer held classes for local parts producers in the technical and managerial aspects of the business. Technical and management experts were dispatched to train workers in local parts firms and to reorganize the entire system of production in Taiwan. Singer also provided technical assistance to Taiwanese sewing machine manufacturing firms—the firms that represented competition for Singer—at no cost to those firms. As a direct result of these measures, substantial technology was transferred from Singer to local sewing machine firms. In addition, the domestic content requirement created backward linkages between the final sewing machine producers and the parts suppliers. By the late 1960s, Singer was purchasing all of the parts (except needles) it used to produce sewing machines in Taiwan from Taiwanese firms. Moreover, 86 percent of Singer's local production was exported. Taiwanese sewing machine manufacturers also became more competitive internationally and began capturing export markets. Thus, by regulating the terms under which Singer Sewing Machines invested in Taiwan, the Taiwanese government was able to use a foreign MNC to promote the development of an internationally competitive domestic sewing machine industry.

politics of MNCs revolves around government efforts to shape these conditions in order to extract as many benefits from MNCs that they can and to minimize the costs of ceding managerial control to foreign decision makers.

Conclusion

The last 20 years has seen rapid growth in the number of multinational corporations operating in the global economy. As we enter the 21st century, the number of such corporations is nine times the number in operation in the early 1980s. As that number has increased, the role these firms play in global production, trade, and cross-border investment has also increased. The activities of contemporary MNCs are heavily concentrated in the advanced industrialized countries. Most foreign direct investment in the global economy involves a firm based in one advanced industrialized country establishing a facility in another advanced industrialized country. And while MNCs have recently begun to shift more of their activities in to the developing world, only a small number of developing countries have received substantial amounts of investment. It will take many more years of investment before the developing world's share of MNC activities approaches the share of the advanced industrialized countries.

MNCs are more than just large firms. They are firms that organize and manage their activities quite differently than traditional firms do. In particular, they have opted to remove many of their international transactions from the market and place them within a single corporate structure. Thus, while many firms engage in international activities, only a subset of these firms—those which own productive establishments in at least two countries—can be classified as MNCs. MNCs have opted for this distinctive organization structure because they face opportunities to profit from international exchange; but because they earn a substantial share of their income from intangible and specific assets, they can capture these profits only by internalizing the associated transactions. Thus, the modern multinational corporation has emerged as an organizational response to a specific economic problem in the global economy.

Most analysts of MNC activities believe that foreign direct investment can benefit the host country as well as the investing firm. Such investments can transfer savings, technology, and managerial expertise to host countries and can allow local producers to link into global marketing networks. None of these resources are readily available to host countries—especially developing host countries—unless they are willing to open themselves to MNC activity. Yet, opening a country to MNC activity does not guarantee that the benefits will be realized. MNCs are profit-making enterprises, and their activities are oriented toward that end, and not toward raising the welfare of their host countries. Consequently, societies that host MNCs face a dilemma: they need to attract MNCs to capture the benefits that foreign direct investment can offer, but they need to ensure that MNCs' activities actually deliver those benefits. As we shall see in the next chapter, most of the politics of MNCs revolve around government efforts to manage this dilemma.

Key Terms

Efficiency-oriented Investment

Foreign Direct Investment

Horizontal Integration

Intangible Asset

Intrafirm Trade

Locational Advantages

Market Imperfection

Market-oriented Investment

Multinational Corporation

Natural-Resource Investment

Positive Externalities

Specific Asset

Vertical Integration

Web Links

General information about MNCs: The United Nations Conference on Trade and Development publishes an annual volume, called *World Investment Report*, that surveys trends in foreign direct investment. The full text of this publication, as well as that of other UNCTAD publications related to MNCs can be found at
http://www.unctad.org/wir/contents/wir01content.en.htm.

The monthly periodical *Multinational Monitor* maintains a website from which you can access many of their articles. Visit *http://www.essential.org/monitor/.*

The Electronic Development and Environment Information System (ELDIS), based at the Institute of Development Studies in Sussex, England, maintains a website with good links to information about MNCs. This page can be found at *http://www.ids.ac.uk/eldis/transnat/tnc_lele.htm.*

Suggestions for Further Reading

For a good introduction to the economics of multinational corporations, see Richard E. Caves, *Multinational Enterprise and Economic Analysis* (Cambridge: Cambridge University Press, 1996). Another excellent source is John H. Dunning, *Multinational Enterprises and the Global Economy* (Reading: Addison Wesley, 1993).

The best single source on the history of multinational corporations is Geoffrey Jones, *The Evolution of International Business: An Introduction* (London: Routledge, 1996). The most comprehensive treatment of American MNCs is Myra Wilkins, *The Emergence of Multinational Enterprise: American Business Abroad from the Colonial Era to 1914* (Cambridge: Harvard University Press, 1970). Current challenges confronted by MNCs are examined in Raymond Vernon, *In the Hurricane's Eye: The Troubled Prospects of Multinational Enterprises* (Cambridge: Harvard University Press, 1998).

CHAPTER 9

The Politics of Multinational Corporations

Tip O'Neill, a former Speaker of the U.S. House of Representatives, once said, "All politics is local." He might have said the same thing about economic production. For no matter how "globalized" the world economy becomes, economic production will always be based in local communities and will always employ resources drawn from those communities. MNCs do not alter this basic reality. MNCs do alter the nature of economic decision making, however. Historically, decisions about production have been made by local business owners with reference to local conditions. When MNCs are involved, however, foreign managers make production decisions with reference to global conditions. Yet, while the frame of reference for much economic decision making has shifted, the frame of reference for *political* decision making has not. Governments continue to address local concerns in response to the demands of local interest groups. As one prominent scholar of MNCs has written, "the regime of nation states is built on the principle that the people in any national jurisdiction have a right to try to maximize their well being, as they define it, within that jurisdiction. The MNC, on the other hand, is bent on maximizing the well being of its stakeholders from global operations, without accepting any responsibility for the consequences of its actions in individual national jurisdictions" (Vernon 1998, 28).

The tension inherent in these overlapping decision-making frameworks shapes the domestic and the international politics of multinational corporations. In the domestic arena, most governments have been unwilling to forgo the potential benefits of foreign investment, yet few have been willing to allow foreign firms to operate without restriction. Consequently, most governments have used national regulations and bargained with individual MNCs to ensure that the operations of foreign firms are consistent with national objectives. Governments' efforts to regulate MNCs' activities carries over into international politics. Host countries, especially in the developing world, pursue international rules that codify their right to control the activities of foreign firms operating within their borders. Countries that serve as home bases for MNCs—essentially, the advanced industrialized countries—pursue international rules that protect their overseas investments by limiting the ability of host countries to regulate MNCs' activity.

We examine these dynamics here. We look first at how governments have attempted to restrict the activities of MNCs operating in their home markets. As we will see, governments in the developing and developed world both used a variety of instruments to extract as many of the benefits from FDI as they could, while at the same time minimizing the perceived costs arising from allowing foreign firms to control local industries. We then focus on efforts, unsuccessful to date, to negotiate international rules defining the respective rights and obligations of host countries and MNCs.

Regulating MNCs

Rather than forgo the potential benefits available from hosting MNC affiliates, most governments have used national regulations to define the terms under which MNCs operate within their borders. Governments have used such regulations proscriptively and prescriptively. That is, they have prohibited foreign firms from engaging in certain activities, and they have required them to engage in others. All of these regulations have been oriented toward the same goal: extracting as many of the benefits from FDI as possible, while simultaneously minimizing the cost associated with ceding decision-making authority over a portion of the local economy to foreign firms. We look first at how developing countries attempted to regulate MNC activity and then turn our attention to the practices that are common in the advanced industrialized world. As we will see, even though both developed and developing countries regulated MNC activities, developing countries have relied far more heavily on such practices. Thus, we conclude this section by examining why the two groups of countries adopted such different approaches toward MNCs.

Regulating MNCs in the Developing World

In the early postwar period, most developing-country governments viewed MNCs with considerable unease. "The association of foreign companies with former colonial powers, their employment of expatriates in senior positions, their past history (real or imagined) of discrimination against local workers, and their embodiment of alien cultural values all contributed to the suspicion with which foreign [multinational corporations] were regarded" in developing countries (Jones 1996, 291). Governments in newly independent developing countries wanted to establish their political and economic autonomy from former colonial powers, and often this entailed taking control of existing foreign investments and managing the terms under which new investments were made.

Concerns about foreign dominance reflected the continuation of historical practice. Most developing countries entered the postwar period as primary-commodity producers and exporters. Yet, MNCs often controlled these sectors and the export revenues they generated. In the aluminum industry, for example, six MNCs controlled 77 percent of the nonsocialist world's bauxite output, 87 percent of its alumina output, and 83 percent of its production of aluminum. In agricultural products, the 15 largest agricultural MNCs controlled approximately 80 percent of developing countries' exports (United Nations Commission on Transnational Corporations 1983). And while foreign direct investment shifted toward manufacturing activity during the 1960s, MNC affiliates also played an important role in these sectors. In Singapore, MNC affiliates currently account for 52 percent of all manufacturing employment, 75 percent of all sales, and approximately 61 percent of all exports. In Malaysia, the figures are comparable: 44 percent of manufacturing employment, 53 percent of sales, and 51 percent of exports (UNCTAD 2001). While Singapore and Malaysia sit at the high end of the spectrum, MNCs also control large segments of manufacturing activity in other developing countries. In Brazil and Mexico, for example, MNCs account for 13 percent and 18 percent of employment, respectively, and in Mexico they account for 21 percent of exports.

Allowing foreign corporations to control critical sectors raised political and economic concerns. The central political concern was that foreign ownership of critical natural-resource industries compromised the hard-won national autonomy achieved by the developing countries' struggle for independence. It seemed incongruent to achieve political independence from colonial powers and yet continue to struggle under the economic dominance of the colonial power's multinational firms. Economic concerns arose as governments adopted import substitution industrialization strategies. If MNCs were allowed to control export earnings, governments would be unable to use these resources to promote their development objectives. Moreover, if MNCs were allowed to enter the local economy freely, there would be no necessary relationship between the investments they made and the government's development goals. Foreign direct investments might remain in the extractive industries, and manufacturing investments might be accompanied by little transfer of technology or might be labor, rather than capital, intensive. As a result, economic development would continue to be shaped by foreign agents instead of the government's development objectives.

In general, developing countries responded to these concerns by regulating, and not blocking, foreign direct investment. Rather than shut themselves off completely from the potential benefits FDI promised, governments sought to control access to their economies in order to ensure that the benefits were in fact delivered. Governments did block foreign investment in some sectors of the economy. For example, MNCs were excluded from ownership of public utilities, iron and steel, retailing, insurance and banking, and extractive industries (Jenkins 1987, 172). When foreign firms already owned enterprises in these sectors, governments nationalized the industries. Through **nationalization,** the host country government took control of an affiliate created by an MNC.

In most instances, nationalization was accompanied by compensation to the MNC. As Figure 9.1 illustrates, the number of nationalizations grew rapidly during the late 1960s and remained high throughout the first half of the 1970s. Nationalizations occurred most often in the extractive industries and in public utilities such as power generation and telecommunications. Nationalization served both political and economic objectives. Politically, governments could rally domestic support and silence domestic critics "by taking over the most obvious symbols of 'foreign exploitation'" (Shafer 1983, 94). Nationalization also made "rational economic planning possible for

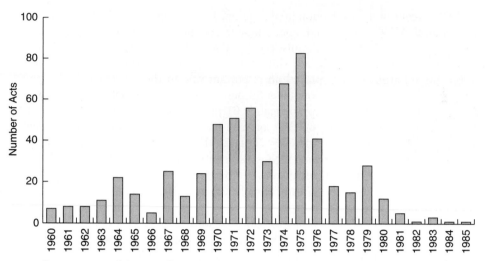

Government policies usually applied to a type of economic activity rather than to a specific firm. Thus, the number of firms affected is much higher than the number of acts of expropriation.

Figure 9.1   Expropriation Acts in Developing Countries.
Source: Vernon, 1998, 6.

the economy as a whole and enhance[d] the government's financial position suffi-ciently to make economic diversification and . . . balanced economic growth attain-able" (Shafer 1983, 93–94).

Most governments created regulatory regimes to influence the activities of the MNCs that did invest. Many developing countries required local affiliates to be major-ity owned by local shareholders, instead of allowing MNCs to own 100 percent of the affiliate. Local ownership, governments believed, would translate into local control of the affiliate's decisions. Governments also limited the amount of profits that MNC affiliates could repatriate, as well as how much affiliates were allowed to pay parent firms for technology transfers. Such measures, governments believed, would help ensure that the revenues generated by MNC activity within the country remained in the country, where they would be available for local use.

Governments also imposed **performance requirements** on local affiliates in order to promote a specific economic objective. If a government was trying to promote backward linkages, for example, it required the affiliate to purchase a certain percent-age of its inputs from domestic suppliers. If the government was promoting export industries, it required the affiliate to export a specific percentage of its output. Some governments also required MNCs to conduct research and development inside the host country. Finally, many governments limited MNCs' access to the local capital market. All of these restrictions were aimed at avoiding the downside of MNC involve-ment, while simultaneously trying to capture the benefits that MNCs could offer.

Of course, not all developing countries adopted identical regimes. Governments that pursued import substitution industrialization strategies imposed the most restric-tive regimes. India, for example, hosted a large stock of foreign investment upon achieving independence. The Indian government was determined, however, to limit the role of MNCs in the Indian economy (Jones 1996, 299). To achieve this goal, the government enacted highly restrictive policies toward new foreign investments and began to "dislodge" existing investments (Encarnation 1989). It dislodged existing enterprises that owned more than 40 percent of the local subsidiary by forcing them to choose between selling equity to Indian firms or leaving India altogether. Exceptions were made only for firms operating in high-priority areas or using sophisticated technologies. As a result of its policies, India experienced a net capital outflow during the 1970s as some MNCs, such as Coca-Cola and IBM, left and few new investments arrived.

Other developing countries actively sought foreign direct investment in connection with the shift to secondary import substitution, but regulated the terms under which MNCs could invest. Brazil, for example, sought foreign direct investment, but tried to ensure that all investment contributed to the government's development objectives. In developing an indigenous auto industry, for example, the government effectively banned all imports of cars in 1956. By doing so, it forced foreign auto manufacturers to produce in Brazil in order to gain access to the Brazilian market.

Because the Brazilian market was quite large, the Brazilian government was able to encourage foreign investment on terms that promoted domestic auto production. It did so in part by using performance requirements. The Brazilian government imposed high domestic content requirements on MNCs; 35 to 50 percent of the car's content had to be locally produced in 1956, and the figure was increased to 90-95 percent by the mid-1960s. As a consequence, by the mid-1960s, eight foreign-controlled firms were producing cars in Brazil for sale in the local market, and by 1980 over 1 million cars were being produced annually. Thus, even those developing countries which welcomed MNCs sought to ensure that their activities corresponded with the government's development goals.

Governments that adopted export-oriented development strategies, such as the East Asian NICs, were relatively more open to foreign direct investment. Singapore and Hong Kong imposed almost no restrictions on inward foreign investment; to the contrary, Singapore based its entire development strategy on attracting foreign investment. South Korea and Taiwan were less open to investment than Singapore and Hong Kong: In both countries, the government developed a list of industries that were open to foreign companies, but proposals to invest in these industries were not automatically approved. Each project had to meet requirements concerning local content, the transfer of technologies, the payment of royalties in connection with technology transfers, and the impact on imports (Haggard 1990, 199).

Still, Taiwan and South Korea did more to attract foreign investment than did most governments in Latin America or Africa. Beginning in the mid-1960s and early 1970s, both the Taiwanese and the South Korean government created export processing zones (EPZs) to attract investment. **Export-processing zones** are industrial areas in which the government provides land, utilities, a transportation infrastructure, and, in some cases, buildings to the investing firms, usually at subsidized rates (Haggard 1990, 201). Foreign firms based in EPZs are allowed to import components free of duty, as long as all of their output is exported. Taiwan created the first EPZ in East Asia in 1965, and South Korea created its first in 1970. These assembly and export platforms attracted a lot of investment from American, European, and Japanese MNCs and helped fuel the takeoff of East Asian exports during the 1970s. Finally, both countries further liberalized foreign investment during the mid-1970s in an attempt to attract high-technology firms into the local economies (Haggard and Cheng 1987).

Most developing countries have greatly liberalized foreign direct investment since the 1980s. Of the 1,035 investment policy changes that governments reported making between 1991 and 1999, 94 percent made foreign direct investment easier (UNCTAD 2004). Sectors previously closed to foreign investment, such as telecommunications and natural resources, have been opened. Restrictions on 100 percent foreign ownership have been lifted in most countries. Restrictions on the repatriation of profit have been eased.

Two factors have encouraged developing countries to ease their restrictions on MNC activities. First, the restrictive investment regimes yielded disappointing results (Jones 1996). Foreign direct investment fell during the 1970s as the wave of nationalizations and tight restrictions led MNCs to seek opportunities in less risky and less constraining markets. MNCs that did operate in developing countries were reluctant to bring in new technologies, and the sectors that governments had nationalized performed well below expectations (Shafer 1983). In short, efforts to foster industrialization by managing MNC activity yielded disappointing results. Second, the decision to liberalize FDI came as part of the broader shift in development strategies. Under ISI, governments intervened heavily in the economy, and intervention in FDI was part of the overall effort to guide industrialization. Governments intervened less in all segments of the economy as they adopted market-based strategies.

Developing countries' governments have not abandoned efforts to control MNC activity. While they have become more open to foreign direct investment, they "continue to look on multinational enterprises from the vantage point of their past experiences. Much as they welcome the contribution of foreign-owned enterprises . . . these countries will have grave doubts from time to time about the long-term contribution of such enterprises, especially as they observe that the grand strategy of the enterprise is built on the pursuit of global sources and global markets" (Vernon 1998, 108).

Regulating MNCs in the Advanced Industrialized Countries

The typical advanced industrialized country has been more open to foreign direct investment and less inclined to regulate the activities of MNCs than the typical developing country has been. Only Japan and France enacted regulations that required explicit government approval for a manufacturing investment by a foreign firm (Safarian 1993). Most governments of industrialized countries have excluded foreign firms from owning industries deemed "critical," but they have not drawn the lists of sectors from which foreign firms are excluded so broadly as to discourage MNC investment (Safarian 1993). In the United States, for example, foreign firms cannot own radio and television broadcasting stations, cannot own a domestic airline, and are prohibited from participating in defense-related industries. Nor are American restrictions unique, as most advanced industrialized countries prohibit foreign ownership in many of these same sectors.

Japan was the clearest exception to this tendency throughout much of the postwar period. Until 1970, Japan tightly regulated inward foreign direct investment. (See Safarian 1993; Mason 1992.) Japanese government ministries reviewed each proposed foreign investment and approved very few. Proposals that were approved usually limited foreign ownership to less than 50 percent of the local subsidiary. Such restrictions were motivated by the Japanese government's economic development objectives. Government officials feared that Japanese firms would be unable to compete with MNCs if foreign direct investment was fully liberalized. In particular, the Japanese government feared that unrestricted foreign direct investment would prevent the development of domestic industries capable of producing the technologies deemed critical to the country's economic success (Mason 1992, 152–153). Regulations on inward investment, in other words, formed an important component of Japan's industrial policy.

Japanese restrictions on inward direct investment were designed to discourage foreign direct investments and to encourage the inflow of foreign technology (Mason 1992, 151). Japanese officials first pressured foreign firms to license their technologies to Japanese firms. If this strategy proved unsuccessful, the Japanese government would consider a direct investment, but it often attempted to force the foreign firm to create a joint venture with a Japanese firm in order to transfer technology to Japanese firms working in the same industry. Only if a firm was unwilling to license its technology or to form a joint venture—and then, only if that firm controlled technologies that were not available elsewhere—did the Japanese government permit the creation of a wholly owned foreign subsidiary in Japan, and even then, the government often attached conditions to the investment. IBM, for example, was forced to license critical technologies to seven Japanese competitors in exchange for being allowed to produce computers in Japan.

Japanese investment restrictions have been greatly liberalized since the late 1960s. In 1967, Japan increased the number of industries open to foreign investment and began to allow 100 percent ownership in some sectors. Additional measures taken in the 1970s and early 1980s further liberalized inward foreign direct investment, so that Japan now has no formal barriers to such investments. Many scholars argue, however, that structural impediments continue to pose obstacles to foreign investment in Japan. For example, the cross-holding ownership that characterizes Keiretsu groups makes it difficult for foreign firms to purchase existing Japanese enterprises. Also, the Japanese distribution system, based on a large number of small retailers, makes it difficult for foreign firms to market their products in Japan. Thus, even though government restrictions on FDI have been eliminated, Japan continues to attract only a small share of the world's foreign investment. (See Figure 8.2.)

Despite the general tendency toward greater openness, governments in the advanced industrialized countries have been sensitive to foreign control of critical sectors. Two instances illustrate such concerns. During the 1960s, the French government became concerned about losing national economic autonomy as a result of the large foreign direct investments made by American MNCs following the formation of the European Union. (See Servan-Schreiber 1968.) What concerned the French government most was foreign ownership in industries subject to rapid technological change—particularly electronics and computers. The French government believed that these industries, along with defense, aerospace, and the nuclear industry, were too important to be controlled by foreign corporations (Jones 1996, 277–278). When the American MNC General Electric attempted to acquire Machines Bull, France's largest computer company, the move sparked a policy response. The French government instituted a more restrictive policy, governing all inward direct investment. Proposed foreign investments were carefully screened, and many were rejected. In cases where a foreign MNC was attempting to purchase an existing French firm, the government would actively seek a French buyer. These more restrictive measures were greatly eased beginning in the 1980s, and today France actively seeks MNC investments.

A similar reaction was evident in the United States during the late 1980s in response to a large increase in inward foreign investment. During the 1980s, Japan became a major direct investor in the United States, as did European multinationals. Between 1985 and 1993, the stock of foreign direct investment in the United States more than doubled, increasing from $184 billion to $445 billion (Graham 1996, 16). The rapid rise of foreign direct investment, especially by Japanese MNCs, sparked concerns about foreign ownership of critical sectors of the American economy, particularly in computers and semiconductors. Such concerns were most prominent in a proposed sale of Fairchild Semiconductor to the Japanese firm Fujitsu. Although Fujitsu ultimately withdrew its bid for Fairchild, this proposed transaction sparked concern that foreign firms were gaining too much control over the American defense industry. Congress responded by passing legislation (the **Exon–Florio Amendment** to the 1988 Omnibus Trade Act) that allowed the executive to block foreign acquisitions of American firms for reasons of national security. These concerns diminished greatly during the 1990s as Japanese investment in the United States dwindled (Graham 1996, 20).

Thus, even though the advanced industrialized countries have been more open to foreign direct investment than developing countries have been, governments in the former have attempted to manage the terms under which MNCs invest in their countries. Governments that used industrial policies have attempted to protect national firms from competition by restricting foreign investment. Even governments that refrained from promoting active industrial policies restricted foreign ownership of sensitive industries, such as those at the forefront of high-technology sectors as well as industries closely connected to national security.

Bargaining with MNCs

While many host countries try to restrict MNC activities, few can dictate the terms under which MNCs invest. Instead, host countries and MNCs often bargain over the terms under which investment takes place. We can think of this bargaining as oriented toward reaching agreement on how the income generated by an investment will be distributed between the MNC parent and the host country. The precise distribution will be determined by each side's relative bargaining power.

Bargaining power arises from the extent to which each side exerts monopolistic control over things valued by the other. On the one hand, to what extent does the host country have monopolistic control over things vitally important to the MNC? Does the host country control natural resources that are not available in other parts of the world? Does the host country control access to a large domestic market? Does the host country control access to factors of production that yield efficiency gains that cannot be achieved in other countries? The more the host country has exclusive control over things of value to the MNC, the more bargaining power it has. Equally critical is the extent to which the MNC exerts monopolistic control over things of value to the host country. Does the MNC control technology that cannot be acquired elsewhere? More broadly, are there other MNCs capable of making, and willing to make, the contemplated investment? The more the MNC has exclusive control over things the host country values, the more bargaining power the MNC has. Bargaining power, therefore, is a function of monopolistic control.

Host countries have the greatest bargaining power when they enjoy a monopoly and the MNC does not. In such cases, the host country should capture most of the gains from investment. In contrast, an MNC has its greatest advantage when it enjoys a monopoly and the host country does not. In these cases, the MNC should capture the largest share of the gains from investment. Bargaining power is approximately equal when both sides have a monopoly. In such cases, each should capture an equal share of the gains from the investment. The gains should also be evenly distributed when neither side has a monopoly on things the other values. In these cases, neither side has much bargaining power, and they should divide the gains relatively equally. The distribution of the gains from any investment, therefore, will be determined by the relative bargaining power of the host country and the MNC.

We can apply the logic of this kind of bargaining analysis to investments in natural-resource industries and in low-skilled labor-intensive manufacturing industries. In natural-resource investments, bargaining power often initially favors the MNC. Few countries enjoy a monopoly over any natural resource; thus, MNCs can choose where to invest. Also, because an MNC often does have a monopoly over the capital, the techniques, and the technology required to extract and refine the natural resources, and because the return on the investment is initially uncertain, the MNC bears all of the risk. Thus, the MNC can exploit this power asymmetry to initially capture the larger share of the gains from the investment.

Over time, however, bargaining power begins to shift to the host country in a dynamic that has been called the **obsolescing bargain** (Moran 1974). The MNC cannot easily remove its fixed investment from the country, so the investment becomes a hostage. In addition, the MNC's monopoly over technology diminishes as the technology is gradually transferred to the host country and indigenous workers are trained. If the investment proves successful, uncertainty about the return on the investment diminishes. Unable to threaten to leave the country without suffering substantial costs, and no longer controlling technology needed by the host country, the MNC sees its earlier bargaining power weaken while the host country's power strengthens. The host country can exploit this power shift to renegotiate the initial agreement and extract a larger share of the gains from the project. Indeed, one might suggest that the widespread nationalizations during the 1960s and 1970s reflected precisely this shift of bargaining power to host countries.

MNCs enjoy more bargaining power than host countries in low-skilled labor-intensive manufacturing investments. On the one hand, no host country enjoys a monopoly on low-skilled labor; thus, MNCs can pick and choose between many potential host countries. Nor are such investments very susceptible to the obsolescent bargain. Often, investments in low-skilled manufacturing entail a relatively small amount of fixed capital that can be readily moved out of a particular country. In addition, technology in many manufacturing industries changes rapidly and is therefore not easily transferred to the host country. Consequently, unlike natural-resource investments, manufacturing investments do not become hostages, and host countries do not gain power once the investment has been made (Kobrin 1987).

Evidence that MNCs enjoy greater bargaining power than do host countries when it comes to manufacturing investment can be seen in the growing competition between host countries to attract such investment. This competition has emerged in the form of **locational incentives**—packages host countries offer to MNCs that either increase the return of a particular investment or reduce the cost or risk of that investment (UNCTAD 1995, 288–289). Host countries offer two types of incentives to MNCs. Most offer tax incentives. In one such incentive, MNCs are granted a reduced corporate income tax rate. Many governments also provide "tax holidays," usually a period of five years during which the firm pays no tax. MNCs are also exempted from import duties, are permitted to depreciate their investment at an accelerated rate, and are allowed substantial deductions from their gross income. Many advanced industrialized countries also offer MNCs direct financial incentives. In some instances these are provided as a grant from the government to the MNC, in some as a subsidized loan (Moran 1999, 95).

The willingness of governments to offer locational incentives and the size of the typical package have both increased rapidly during the last 20 years. Across the entire Organization for Economic Cooperation and Development (OECD), 285 incentive programs offering a total of $11 billion were provided to MNCs in 1989. By 1993—the last year for which comprehensive data are available—362 programs offering incentives totaling $18 billion were provided. Within the United States, the typical package averaged between $50 and 70 million, but the value of that package has been increasing (Moran 1999).

Some evidence of the broader growth of incentives is provided in Table 9.1. Note the rapid growth in the per job cost of government incentives. In the early 1980s, the largest per job cost of incentives was just below $50,000 and the average was about $30,000. By the early 1990s, the average per job cost was well over $100,000 for similar types of investment. "All this suggests that competition for FDI with incentives is pervasive, and is even more so now than it was ten years ago. Many countries have increased their incentives in order to divert investment away from competing host countries. . . . This has been so regardless of whether the countries involved were large or small, rich or poor, developed or developing" (UNCTAD 1995, 298). The growing use of locational incentives suggests that host countries are at a disadvantage when bargaining with MNCs over manufacturing investments.

In sum, few governments have allowed foreign firms to operate without any restrictions, and many have actively managed the terms of their activities, in part by using national regulations and in part by bargaining with MNCs. As we have seen, the typical advanced industrialized country has been less inclined to try to restrict the activities of foreign firms than has the typical developing country. We conclude this section, therefore, by considering a few factors that account for this difference.

Three such factors are probably most important. First of all, developing countries have been more vulnerable to foreign domination than advanced industrialized countries have been. The advanced industrialized countries have larger and more diversified economies than the developing countries; consequently, a foreign affiliate is more likely to face competition from domestic firms in an advanced industrialized country

Table 9.1
Host Country Incentive Packages, 1983–1995

Location	Year	Firm	Other Locations Considered	Government Support ($US Millions)	Company's Investment ($US Millions)	Employees	Support per Job
Smyrna, Tennessee	1983	Nissan	Georgia	33.0	745–848	1,300	25,384
Flat Rock, Michigan	1984	Mazda	Alabama, Iowa, Kansas, Missouri, Nebraska, North Carolina, Oklahoma, South Carolina, Tennessee	48.5	745–750	3,500	13,857
Georgetown, Kentucky	1985	Toyota	Georgia, Indiana, Kansas, Missouri, Tennessee	149.7	823.9	3,000	49,900
Lafayette, Indiana	1986	Fuji-Isuzu	Illinois, Kentucky	86.0	480–500	1,700	50,588
Setubal, Portugal	1991	Auto Europa Ford Volkswagen	United Kingdom, Spain	483.5	2,603	1,900	254,451
Tuscaloosa, Alabama	1993	Mercedes-Benz	Georgia, Nebraska, North Carolina, South Carolina, Tennessee	250.0	300	1,500	166,667
North-East England	1994–95	Samsung	France, Germany, Portugal, Spain	89.0	690.3	3,000	29,675
Spartanburg, South Carolina	1994	BMW	Oklahoma, Nebraska	130.0	450	1,200	108,333
Castle Bromwich, Birmingham, Whitley, United Kingdom	1995	Jaguar	Detroit, Michigan	128.72	767	1,000	128,720
Hambach, Lorraine, France	1995	Mercedes-Benz Swatch	Belgium, Germany	111.0	370	1,950	56,923

Source: UNCTAD 1995, 296–297.

A CLOSER LOOK

Luring the German Luxury Car Producers to the U.S. South

In the early 1990s, the German automaker BMW decided to create a new assembly plant outside Germany. Such a move represented a real shift for BMW, which had never previously assembled cars outside of Bavaria. The firm's decision to begin assembling cars outside Germany was motivated by a determination to reduce its costs. German automakers were earning about $28 an hour, far greater than the average of $16 an hour that unionized autoworkers make in the United States. In addition, the persistent strengthening of the German mark against the dollar during the late 1980s had further eroded the ability of BMW to compete in the American market. BMW spent three years and looked at 250 different sites in 10 countries before deciding in 1992 to build the plant in Spartanburg, South Carolina (Faith 1993). In late September 1992, BMW began construction of the $400 million assembly plant that would employ some 2,000 people and produce as many as 90,000 cars a year. In 1998, BMW expanded this production facility from 1.2 million square feet to 2.1 million square feet. The facility remains BMW's only American production site (*www.BMW.com*).

Why did BMW choose Spartanburg over other potential sites? A range of considerations, including financial incentives offered by the state of South Carolina, shaped BMW's decision to base production in Spartanburg. First, the city had some advantages arising from its location; it is close to Charleston, South Carolina, a deepwater seaport, and is connected to this port by a good interstate highway. This transportation network would allow BMW to transport the cars destined for overseas markets easily. In addition, labor in South Carolina was relatively cheap—averaging about $10 to $15 an hour—and nonunionized. In addition, the state and local government in South Carolina put together a financial package that offset a substantial share of BMW's investment. Officials advanced about $40 million to purchase the 900 acres of land upon which the plant would be built, and they agreed to lease the site to BMW for only $1 per year. In addition, about $23 million was spent preparing the site and improving the infrastructure, including such things as water, sewer, and roads. Another $71 million of tax breaks were offered over a 20-year period. Finally, state, local, and federal money was provided to improve the airport in nearby Greenville (Harrison 1992). Altogether, the incentives offered by South Carolina to BMW totaled about $135 million, an amount equal to $67,500 for each job BMW would create.

The use of financial incentives to attract an investment from a German automaker reached new heights in Alabama's courtship of Mercedes–Benz in the mid-1990s. For reasons identical to those that motivated BMW, Mercedes–Benz decided to build an assembly plant outside of Germany (Myerson 1996). The firm eventually constructed a $300 million plant in Vance, Alabama, employing about 1,200 workers to produce 65,000 sport utility vehicles each year. In its initial search for suitable sites, Mercedes focused on 62 possibilities, none of which were in Alabama. As Andreas Renschler, who led the search for the site, remarked, "Alabama was totally unknown" (quoted in Myerson 1996). Government officials in

Continued

Alabama were determined to attract Mercedes to their state, however. The governor, James E. Folsom, Jr., flew to Mercedes headquarters in Stuttgart three times and, working with other state politicians, put together a financial package to attract the German firm to Alabama. The package included $92.2 million to purchase and pre-pare the site for construction, $75.5 million in infrastructure improvements for water, sewage, and other utilities, $5 million each year to pay for employee training, and tax breaks. In addition, at a cost of about $75 million, the state of Alabama agreed to pur-chase 2,500 of the sport utility vehicles that Mercedes intended to build in the factory. The total package was estimated at between $253 and $300 million, an amount equal to $200,000 to $250,000 for each job Mercedes intended to create (Waters 1996).

While BMW and Mercedes officials publicly deny that the incentive packages they received played an important role in their decisions to invest in Spartanburg and Vance, respectively, it is hard to escape the conclusion that these packages did mat-ter. In BMW's case, the incentive probably mattered at the margin. Spartanburg was one of at least two suitable sites in the United States. (Omaha, Nebraska, was the other site that BMW considered.) The willingness of South Carolina to offer a more generous package of incentives than Nebraska did probably tipped the balance in its favor. In the case of Mercedes, it seems clear that Vance, Alabama, held few of the natural advantages enjoyed by sites in North Carolina and South Carolina, the other two finalists in the competition. In fact, the site Mercedes considered in North Car-olina enjoyed many of the same characteristics that had attracted BMW to Spartan-burg. The willingness of Alabama to offer an incentive package more than twice as large as that offered by North Carolina—which is reported to have offered Mercedes about $109 million in incentives—probably enabled Alabama to overcome its initial disadvantage (Burritt 1994).

Because incentive packages do shape the investment decisions that firms make, governments cannot easily opt out of the incentive game. As Harlan Boyles, former treasurer of North Carolina, commented following the Mercedes–Alabama deal, "All the competition [for investment] has been forced upon the states" by the MNCs. "Until there is meaningful reform and an agreement between states not to participate, very little will change" (quoted in McEntee 1995). Of course, while Boyles's comment was directed at competition for investment among states within the United States, its logic applies equally well to competition among national governments in the international economy.

than in a developing country. The lack of diversification is compounded by the fact, in the early postwar period, most FDI in the developing world was concentrated in polit-ically sensitive natural-resource industries. In contrast, most FDI in the advanced industrialized countries flowed into manufacturing industries. As a result, foreign firms were much more likely to dominate a developing country than an advanced industrial-ized country, and the advanced industrialized countries have felt less compelled to reg-ulate MNC activity.

There also appears to be a strong correlation between a country's role as a home for MNCs and its policies toward inward FDI. The two largest foreign investors during the last 140 years—the United States and the United Kingdom—have also been the most open to inward foreign investment. Japan began to open itself to inward investment as Japanese firms started to invest heavily in other countries. When countries both host foreign firms and are home base to MNC parents, they are unlikely to adopt policies that reflect purely host country concerns. Attempts by the United States or Great Britain to regulate inward foreign direct investment would invite retaliation that would make it harder for their own firms to invest abroad. Because developing countries have historically hosted foreign investment, but have rarely been home bases for MNCs, their concerns are more narrowly based on host country issues untempered by the fear of retaliation.

Finally, there have been fundamental differences in how governments approach state intervention in the national economy. Whereas many developing countries pursued import substitution industrialization strategies that required state intervention, most advanced industrialized countries have been more willing to allow the market to drive economic activity. Different attitudes about the government's role in the national economy translated into different approaches to foreign direct investment. Even the exceptions to the nonintervention tendency in the advanced industrialized countries are consistent with this factor: the two governments that were most restrictive toward foreign direct investment, Japan and France, were also the two governments that relied most heavily on industrial policies to promote domestic economic activity. Thus, attempts to regulate MNC activity was most likely in countries where governments played a large role in the economy.

All of these factors suggest that we are unlikely to see an abrupt shift away from the more liberal attitude toward FDI that has prevailed in the developing world since the late 1990s back to the more restrictive practices that characterized much of the postwar period. Developing countries have become more diversified and are now attracting more foreign investment in manufacturing than in natural resources. As a consequence, some, though certainly not all, of these countries are less vulnerable to foreign domination today than they were in the mid-twentieth century. In addition, some developing countries are gradually moving away from only hosting foreign investment to being a home base for MNC parents as well. This trend, while involving only a small number of East Asian and Latin American countries, will gradually make these governments increasingly reluctant to restrict the activities of foreign firms they host. Finally, there is no evidence of an impending shift back toward interventionist strategies. As long as developing countries continue to pursue liberal strategies, they will continue to make it easier, rather than harder, for foreign firms to participate in the local economy.

The International Regulation of MNCs

There are no comprehensive international rules governing the activities of MNCs. This is not because governments have never tried to create multilateral rules. In fact, governments have repeatedly tried to create such rules during the last 50 years. But to date, these efforts have yielded little. There are partial rules set out within the WTO, as well as less binding rules within the OECD. There are also some well-established international rules, such as the investment chapter of the North American Free Trade Agreement, that apply to a few countries. The reason there are no comprehensive international investment rules is that conflict between the capital-exporting advanced industrialized countries and the capital-importing developing countries has prevented agreement on such rules. Developing countries have advocated international rules that codify their right to control foreign firms operating within their borders. Advanced industrialized countries have pursued rules that protect foreign investment by limiting the ability of host countries to regulate the MNCs operating in their economies. Given these divergent goals, agreement on comprehensive rules has proved impossible. We next examine the efforts to negotiate international investment rules, tracing them from the late 19th century.

Historically, international rules governing foreign direct investment have been based on four legal principles. First, foreign investments are private property to be treated at least as favorably as domestic private property. Second, governments have a right to expropriate foreign investments, but only for a public purpose. Third, when a government does expropriate a foreign investment, it must compensate the owner for the full value of the expropriated property, or, in legal terminology, compensation must be "adequate, effective, and prompt" (Akehurst 1984, 91–92). Finally, foreign investors have the right to appeal to their home country in the event of a dispute with the host country. Although such principles are designed to protect the property of foreign investors and therefore clearly reflect the interests of the capital-exporting countries, capital-exporting and capital-importing countries alike accepted them throughout the 19th century (Lipson 1985). The one exception came from Latin American governments' challenge to the right of foreign governments to intervene in host countries in support of their firms. By the late 19th century, Latin American governments were invoking the **Calvo doctrine** (named after the Argentinean legal scholar Carlos Calvo, who first stated it in 1868), which argues that no government has the right to intervene in another country to enforce its citizens' private claims (Lipson 1985, 19).

The capital-importing countries began to challenge these legal principles more intensively following World War I (Lipson 1985). The first challenge came in the Soviet Union, where the 1917 revolution brought to power a Marxist–Leninist government that rejected the idea of private property. The comprehensive nationalization of industry that followed "constituted the most significant attack ever waged on foreign capital" and radically redefined the role of the government in the economy (Lipson 1985, 67). Some Latin American governments also began to expropriate foreign investments during this period, particularly in the extractive industries and public utilities. These acts broadened the notion of "public purpose" that stood behind the internationally recognized right of expropriation, extending it from its traditional association with eminent domain to a much wider association with the state's role in the process of economic development. In addition, such widespread nationalizations posed a challenge to the principle of compensation. The Soviet government linked compensation of foreign investors, for example, to claims on Western governments for damages caused by their militaries during the civil war that followed the revolution (Lipson 1985, 67).

The United States attempted to reestablish the traditional legal basis for invest-ment protection following the Second World War. As the largest and, in the immediate postwar period, only capital-exporting country, the United States had a clear interest in establishing multilateral rules that secured American overseas investments. But U.S. efforts to achieve this goal by incorporating the historical legal principles into the International Trade Organization ran into opposition from the capital-importing coun-tries. Governments from Latin America, India, and Australia were able to create a final set of articles that elaborated the right of host countries to regulate foreign invest-ments within their borders more than they provided the security that American busi-ness was seeking (Brown 1950; Lipson 1985, 87). Consequently, American business strongly opposed the ITO's investment components. As the U.S. National Foreign Trade Council commented, "[The investment] article not only affords no protection for foreign investments of the United States but it would leave them with less protec-tion than they now enjoy" (Diebold 1952, 18). Opposition to the investment articles from American business proved a major reason for the ITO's failure to gain congres-sional support.

The ITO experience is important for two reasons. First, the failure of the ITO meant that there would be no international rules governing foreign direct investment. Instead, GATT became the center of the trade system, and that treaty had little to say about foreign investment. Second, and more broadly, the failure of the ITO reflected a basic conflict that has dominated international discussions about rules regulating for-eign direct investment to this day. Led by the United States, the advanced industrial-ized countries, in their role as capital exporters, have placed greatest emphasis on creating international rules that regulate host country behavior in order to protect the interests of their MNCs. Developing countries, by contrast, in their role as capital importers, have placed greatest emphasis on creating international rules that regulate the behavior of MNCs in order that those countries maintain control over their national economies. This basic conflict has prevailed for more than 50 years of discus-sions about international investment rules and has thus far prevented agreement on any comprehensive rules.

During the 1960s and 1970s, developing countries largely set the agenda for inter-national discussions about foreign direct investment. Working through the United Nations, the developing countries sought to create international investment rules that reflected their interests as capital importers. The effort to regulate MNCs became a central element of the New International Economic Order, under which developing countries sought two broad objectives that were designed to "maximize the contribu-tions of MNCs to the economic and social development of the countries in which they operate" (Sauvant and Aranda 1994, 99).

Developing countries sought international recognition of their right to exert full control over all economic activity within their territories. To this end, those countries secured the passage of the **United Nations Resolution on Permanent Sover-eignty over Natural Resources** in 1962. This resolution recognized the right of host countries to exercise full control over their natural resources and over the foreign firms operating within their borders extracting those resources. The resolution affirmed the right of host country governments to expropriate foreign investments and to determine the appropriate compensation in the event of expropriation (de Rivero

1980, 92–93; Akehurst 1984, 93). The intent of the resolution, and of the others that followed during the 1960s and 1970s, was to shift the legal basis for compensation away from payment for the full value of the expropriated property to payment that would be in line with what the expropriating government determined to be appropriate. As Akehurst (1984, 93) points out, this approach implied that compensation was likely to be quite low.

Developing countries also sought to write a code of conduct that would regulate MNC behavior. Such a code aimed to regulate MNC activity in five broad areas (Asante 1980, 124; de Rivero 1980, 95–96). First, the code would prevent MNCs from interfering in the internal affairs of their host countries. Second, the code would regulate MNCs' economic activities within host countries to ensure that these activities conformed to governments' stated development objectives. Third, the code would ensure that technology and management skills were transferred to host countries on favorable terms. Fourth, the code would regulate the repatriation of MNC profits. Finally, the code would encourage MNCs to reinvest profits in the host countries. In short, the various components of the code were designed to ensure that MNCs would make as large a contribution as possible to the countries in which they operated. Those components would do so by ensuring that MNC activities "were compatible with the medium and long-term needs which the governments in the capital importing countries had identified in their development plans" (de Rivero 1980, 96).

The developing countries' efforts to write a code of conduct for MNCs, like the broader NIEO, of which that code formed one part, met opposition from the advanced industrialized countries. Whereas the developing countries wanted the code to be binding, the advanced industrialized countries pushed for a voluntary code; and whereas the developing countries wanted to regulate only MNCs, the capital-exporting governments insisted that any code that regulated MNC behavior be accompanied by a code that regulated the behavior of host countries (Sauvant and Aranda 1994, 99). Governments worked on both codes throughout the late 1970s and early 1980s, completing drafts of both by 1982. The resulting codes were never implemented, however, but they were never formally rejected either. Instead, the codes remained in limbo for ten years until, in 1992, a U.N. committee recommended that governments seek an alternative approach (Graham 1996, 78–79).

By the early 1980s, bargaining power in international negotiations was shifting back toward the advanced industrialized countries. These capital-exporting countries used this advantage to shift the agenda back toward regulating host country behavior. Some initial steps were taken during the Uruguay Round. Under pressure from the United States, trade-related investment measures (TRIMs) were placed on the agenda. A **Trade-related investment measure** is a government policy toward foreign direct investment or MNCs that has an impact on the country's imports or exports. For example, domestic-content or trade-balancing requirements force firms to import fewer inputs or export more output than they would without such government-imposed requirements. Consequently, such requirements distort international trade. In placing TRIMs on the GATT agenda, the United States sought to limit the ability of host countries to use such measures. The United States sought an expansive agreement that addressed 13 different government policies, including domestic sales requirements, exchange restrictions, export requirements, investment incentives, licensing requirements, remittance restrictions, technology transfer requirements, and trade-balancing requirements, affecting foreign investments (Croome 1995). Such rules would restrict virtually all aspects of host country efforts to manage foreign firms. Many of the other advanced industrialized countries supported the U.S. effort, although not all shared the American desire for such a far-reaching agreement. Japan supported the U.S. objectives most strongly. The EU proposed a shorter list of policy restrictions, and the Scandinavian countries wanted to restrict the agreement to domestic-content and export performance requirements.

Developing countries strongly opposed the scope of American objectives. Most were reluctant to see TRIMs incorporated into the GATT at all. Opposition was strongest among a group of large countries led by Argentina, Brazil, China, Egypt, India, and Nigeria. This group argued that "development considerations outweighed whatever adverse trade effects TRIMs might have, and that no new GATT provisions to regulate them were needed" (Croome 1995, 258). In contrast to the broad objectives sought by the advanced industrialized countries, the developing-country group wanted to restrict any final agreement to measures that addressed "the direct and significant adverse trade effects" of investment policies (Croome 1995, 259). Even then, the group wanted to limit the effect of such measures, putting forward a list of 13 development objectives that its members claimed justified the use of investment measures. The only international restriction the group proposed was a nonbinding approach that would encourage governments to "seek to avoid" using TRIMs in a way that distorted trade or caused injury to another GATT member.

A limited agreement was eventually reached. Two changes made the final agreement possible. On the one hand, the advanced industrialized countries scaled back the scope of their demands, agreeing to focus on four investment measures: domestic-content rules, trade-balancing measures that required a firm's imports to be offset by its exports, restrictive foreign exchange practices, and constraints on the ability to link investment incentives to export performance requirements. On the other hand, developing countries' attitudes toward foreign direct investment had also changed since the early 1980s: As we saw earlier, the late 1980s brought the progressive liberalization of those countries' policies toward foreign direct investment, as well as a decrease in the nationalist, passionate, and anti-MNC feelings that had prevailed throughout the 1970s. This reduction in developing countries' perceived need to regulate MNC activity extensively translated into a greater willingness to accept some international rules that constrained their behavior as host countries.

The failure to achieve a more extensive agreement in the Uruguay Round led the advanced industrialized countries to begin negotiation on a **Multilateral Agreement on Investment** (MAI) in the OECD in May 1995. The OECD appeared to offer at least three advantages over the WTO as a forum for an investment agreement. Because OECD membership is restricted to the advanced industrialized countries, all of which shared a commitment in principle to liberal rules, negotiations in the OECD seemed less likely to be blocked by conflicts among the participants than would negotiations in the WTO. Moreover, because about 65 percent of all FDI takes place within the advanced industrialized world, an agreement among OECD members would govern the majority of international investment. Finally, an OECD-based agreement would not preclude participation by developing countries. The agreement was envisaged as an instrument to which non-OECD governments could accede if they desired.

The MAI was intended to promote further liberalization of foreign direct investment and to provide greater security to foreign investors. Liberalization was to be achieved by basing the agreement on two central principles. The first was national treatment, which requires governments to treat foreign-owned firms operating in their economy no differently than domestic firms. The second principle was most favored nation, which required governments to treat the foreign firms from each party to the agreement on the same terms it accorded to firms from all other parties to the agreement. The two principles implied that governments could not discriminate against firms from any country in favor of domestic firms or foreign firms from other countries. To provide greater security to foreign investors, the agreement incorporated the historical standard governing expropriation, thereby codifying the right to prompt, effective, and adequate compensation. In addition, the draft agreement restricted the ability of governments to limit the ability of firms to remit profits, dividends, and proceeds from the sale of assets. The agreement was also to provide for a dispute settlement mechanism patterned on that of NAFTA, which would allow for both state-to-state claims and firm-to-state claims.

Negotiations proved fruitless, however, due to conflict among OECD governments and to strong and vocal opposition from groups outside the process. Conflict among OECD governments slowed the negotiating process greatly, as governments first established the guidelines and then busied themselves writing exceptions to the general rules. The treaty's preamble contained 17 footnotes registering the concerns and qualifications of the various governments (Kobrin 1998). By 1997, OECD governments had attached several hundred pages of exceptions covering the sale of farmland, cultural industries—film and television in particular—and government-sponsored investment promotion agencies (*The Economist* March 14, 1998, 81). The U.S. pressed for the inclusion of labor and environmental standards, despite opposition from other OECD governments. Developing countries also began to express opposition to the emerging agreement, arguing that it regulated host country behavior, but did nothing to regulate MNC activities. Moreover, developing countries were concerned that the MAI would subsequently be used as a template for a wider investment agreement negotiated within the WTO. They would then be forced to accept investment rules that they had played no role in negotiating.

Perhaps the strongest opposition to the MAI came from an unexpected source: a large and vocal coalition of interest groups from across the world. Public opposition was sparked by the posting of the draft of the MAI on a website belonging to Public Citizen in February 1997. (Public Citizen is a nonprofit public-interest group founded by Ralph Nader.) The posting of the treaty was followed by the rapid emergence of a transnational coalition of interest groups opposed to the MAI. As Stephen Kobrin notes, "[A] coalition of strange bedfellows arose in opposition to the treaty, including the AFL–CIO, Amnesty International, Australian Conservation Foundation, Friends of the Earth, Public Citizen, Sierra Club, Third World Network, United Steelworkers of America, Western Governors' Association, and World Development Movement" (Kobrin 1998, 98). It has been estimated that, in all, some 600 organizations in almost 70 countries spoke out against the proposed treaty (Kobrin 1998, 97). Interest-group opposition focused on specific components of the proposed treaty and on broader concerns about globalization (Kobrin 1998). The specific concerns about the treaty included claims that, while the MAI provided considerable rights to MNCs and

(A) CLOSER LOOK

Protecting Investment in NAFTA

The North American Free Trade Agreement contains the most fully developed rules of any international investment agreement. These rules are embodied in Chapter 11 of the agreement and are based on five central principles (Graham 1996, 82–83). The principle of national treatment requires all political authorities—federal, state, provincial, and local—to treat all investors from other NAFTA countries no less favorably than they treat domestic investors. The principle of most favored nation ensures that no NAFTA government treats an investor from another NAFTA country less favorably than it treats investors from outside NAFTA. In addition, Chapter 11 prohibits new performance requirements and requires governments to phase out existing performance requirements. Governments are also prohibited from restricting the ability of a domestic affiliate of a foreign firm from converting its profits and other revenues into any currency it desires at the prevailing market rate of exchange. Finally, the agreement allows member governments to expropriate foreign investments only for a public purpose, and in the event of such expropriation, the investor must be compensated at fair market value.

Chapter 11 also establishes a mechanism for settling investment disputes. What is most distinctive about the settlement of investment disputes under NAFTA is that private investors can seek arbitration of a dispute with a NAFTA nation's government. In most international economic agreements, disputes must be initiated and pursued by governments; private investors have no standing. In NAFTA, a corporation has the right to pursue a claim against a member government if a government policy that violates the rules embodied in Chapter 11 harms the investor's interests. In advancing a claim against a member government, an investor must first attempt to resolve the dispute through consultations. It may then pursue relief through the country's domestic courts or use binding arbitration under the United Nations Commission on International Trade Law (UNCITRAL) or the World Bank's International Centre for the Settlement of Investment Disputes (ICSID). Arbitration panels can award monetary compensation to the corporation or require the government to restore any property that has been expropriated. In no instance, however, can an arbitration panel require a government to rescind a policy measure.

Critics have pointed to substantive and procedural problems with NAFTA's Chapter 11. (See Public Citizen 2001; Bottari 2001.) Considerable criticism has been directed at Article 1110, which requires governments to compensate investors for acts of expropriation. Controversy arises because the broad language of Article 1110 requires governments to compensate investors for policies that are "tantamount to" expropriation. "Corporations have used this provision to challenge or seek compensation for what are called 'regulatory takings'" (Bottari 2001, 4). A regulatory taking is a case in which a government regulation designed to protect the environment or promote some other public goal also substantially reduces the value of a property. Suppose, for example, that a landowner is prohibited from developing her property because it provides a habitat for a species protected by the Endangered Species Act. She might then claim that the Endangered Species Act is "tantamount to expropria-

Continued

tion" because it greatly reduces the market value of her land and restricts her ability to use her property. Article 1110 allows corporations to seek monetary compensation from governments in such cases.

An American firm called the Ethyl Corporation initiated the first such case under NAFTA in 1996. The Ethyl Corporation produces a chemical called methylcyclopenta-dienyl manganese tricarbonyl, or MMT, that is added to gasoline to improve engine performance. The firm exports MMT to Canada, where Canadian refineries add it to gasoline sold in the Canadian market. In 1996, the Canadian parliament began debating legislation that would ban the import and interprovincial transportation of MMT. If passed, this legislation would end Ethyl Corporation's exports to Canada. In September of 1996, the firm notified the Canadian government that it was suing for $251 million compensation under Chapter 11. Ethyl Corporation claimed that the pro-posed ban violated Chapter 11 in many ways. Most important, Ethyl argued that, by preventing it from continuing to profit from its exports to Canada, the law would be tantamount to an expropriation of Ethyl's assets. An arbitration panel was created in UNCITRAL, but before the panel could issue a ruling, the Canadian government set-tled the dispute. It opted not to ban MMT and paid Ethyl Corporation $16 million in legal fees and damages (Public Citizen 2001). Critics argue that this case shows how private corporations can use the "tantamount to" expropriation clause to reverse gov-ernment regulations that promote public health and protect the environment.

Chapter 11 has also been criticized for the lack of accountability and trans-parency in its arbitration panels. The typical arbitration panel is composed of only three people, selected in part by the parties to the dispute. In the ICSID, for example, the investor bringing the claim and the national government each select an arbitrator, and the two arbitrators then select a third. The arbitration process is closed to public participation, and little detail about the case is provided. Moreover, there is no regu-larized process of appeal. Consequently, say critics, "The almost complete lack of transparency and public participation . . . combined with the vast power of tribunals to grant an infinite amount of taxpayer dollars to corporations that successfully bring NAFTA suits, raise questions as to whether it is an appropriate venue for the arbitra-tion of such significant issues of public concern" (Public Citizen 2001, 7).

imposed obligations on host countries, it provided no rights to host countries and imposed no obligations on MNCs concerning workers, consumers, or the environ-ment. In addition, opponents argued that the treaty imposed too many constraints on the ability of national and local governments to regulate economic activity. Finally, opponents claimed that the dispute settlement mechanisms that were to be created as part of the agreement shifted power away from democratically elected national politi-cians to international bureaucrats with little accountability to the public. More broadly, opponents argued that the MAI was yet another development in the larger phenome-non of globalization that gave too much power to large corporations at the expense of labor and national sovereignty.

The combination of conflict among OECD governments about the specific con-tent of the treaty, opposition from developing countries outside the negotiations, and public opposition proved fatal. As opposition grew, progress in the negotiations slowed. In April 1997, the OECD announced that there would be a six-month pause. When negotiations resumed in October, the deadline for completion was pushed forward to

POLICY ANALYSIS AND DEBATE

The Race to the Bottom

Question

How should governments respond to the threat of a "race to the bottom" dynamic that weakens public interest regulation?

Overview

Some scholars have argued that the growth of MNC activity has given rise to a "race to the bottom" dynamic in government regulation. The world's governments maintain different regulatory standards. Some enact stringent regulations concerning how firms can treat workers, how they must handle their toxic waste and other pollutants, and how they must conduct their other business activities. Others maintain less stringent regulatory environments, allowing firms to engage in activities that are illegal in other countries.

Many of these regulations affect production costs. It is more expensive, for example, for a firm to treat chemical waste before it is disposed than simply to dump the raw waste in a landfill. Hence, national regulations that require firms to treat their chemical waste raise production costs. Consequently, even if all other production costs in two countries are the same, different regulatory standards can make it less costly to produce in the country with the lower standard.

MNCs might therefore engage in regulatory arbitrage. That is, they might shift their activities out of countries with stringent regulatory standards and into countries with lax regulatory standards. Governments in high-standard countries will then feel pressure to relax their standards in order to encourage firms to keep production at home. As a consequence, national regulation will increasingly converge on the regulatory practices of the least restrictive country. Governments that refuse to engage in this competition for investment will be left behind, enjoying the benefits of strict regulations, but suffering the cost of substantially less investment. How should governments respond to the threat of this race to the bottom?

Policy Options

- Negotiate international rules that harmonize regulations throughout the world. Creating common regulations will prevent regulatory arbitrage and the race to the bottom.
- Restrict foreign direct investment and the activities of multinational corporations. Such restrictions would limit corporations' mobility, thus enabling governments to maintain distinct national regulations.

Policy Analysis

- Is regulatory arbitrage necessarily a bad thing from the perspective of economic efficiency? Why or why not?
- How easy or difficult will it be for governments to reach agreement about common regulatory standards? How should we weigh these costs?

Take a Position

- Which option do you prefer? Justify your choice.
- What criticisms of your position should you anticipate? How would you defend your recommendation against these criticisms?

Continued

Resources
Online: Search for "Race to the Bottom" MNCs. This search will yield more information than you can possibly digest, much of it highly critical of globalization. Miles Kahler's paper, "Modeling Races to the Bottom," surveys many of the issues concerned.
In Print: David Vogel and Robert Kagan, eds., *The Dynamics of Regulatory Change: How Globalization Affects National Regulatory Policies* (Berkeley: University of California Press, 2004); Daniel Drezner, "Bottom Feeders," *Foreign Policy* 121 (November/December 2000): 64–70; Debora Spar and David Yoffie, "Multinational Enterprises and the Prospects for Justice," *Journal of International Affairs* 52 (Spring 1999): 557–581.

May 1998. When this deadline passed without a completed treaty, the deadline was pushed forward again to May 1999. Meanwhile, opposition began to affect the governments that were negotiating. The New Zealand government stated that it would refuse to sign the treaty, and governments in France and the United Kingdom either withdrew their support completely or began to reconsider their position (Warkentin and Mingst 2000). Negotiations ceased in December 1998 without a final treaty.

Thus, although governments have spent almost 30 years negotiating rules to govern MNCs and host country activities—within the UN, within the GATT, and within the OECD—they have yet to conclude an extensive set of regulations. Conflict between the capital-exporting countries and the capital-importing countries over the basic purpose of such a regime is the primary reason for this lack of success. Governments have been unable to agree whether such rules should regulate host countries or MNCs. The obvious compromise—that international rules might usefully regulate both—has yet to materialize in a meaningful way. The more recent emergence of the antiglobalization campaign has added another obstacle on the already crowded path to the successful negotiation of a set of international rules through which to regulate foreign direct investment.

Conclusion

The politics of multinational corporations emerge from the competing interests of host countries, MNCs' home countries, and MNCs themselves. Each group has distinctive interests regarding foreign direct investment. MNCs want to operate freely across the globe, with few government-imposed restrictions on their activities. Host countries want to ensure that the MNCs operating within their borders provide benefits to the local economy that offset the loss of decision-making authority that is inherent in foreign ownership. MNCs' home countries want to ensure that their firms' overseas investments are secure. The politics of MNCs emerges when these distinct interests come into conflict with each other.

As we have seen, almost all governments impose some restrictions on the activities of foreign firms that operate inside their countries. Many governments, especially in the developing world, have tried to harness multinationals to their development objectives, but even the advanced industrialized countries have been unwilling to allow foreign firms to control critical sectors of the national economy. Similarities arise from the common concern about the local impact of foreign decision making. Differences arise from the fact that most developing countries are only hosts to MNC activities, while the advanced industrialized countries are both hosts and home bases. Consequently, developing countries' concerns about foreign domination are not tempered by the need to ensure that foreign governments respect the investments of the developing countries' own MNCs.

The basic conflict between capital-importing and capital-exporting countries is evident also in the international politics of MNCs. In the international arena, politics have revolved around efforts to negotiate comprehensive rules for international investment. Yet, conflict between the capital-exporting and the capital-importing countries has so far prevented agreement on comprehensive investment rules. As we have seen, this conflict reflects a basic disagreement about what the rules should regulate. Should international rules regulate the ability of host countries to control the MNCs that invest in their countries, or should international rules regulate the range of activities that MNCs are allowed to engage in? The inability of the advanced industrialized countries and the developing countries to agree upon an answer to this question, as well as the apparent unwillingness of both groups to compromise, has prevented the creation of comprehensive rules to regulate international investment.

Key Terms

Calvo Doctrine

Exon–Florio Amendment

Export-processing Zones

Locational Incentives

Multilateral Agreement on Investment

Nationalization

Obsolescing Bargain

Performance Requirement

Trade-related Investment Measures

United Nations Resolution on Permanent Sovereignty over Natural Resources

Web Links

Information about the aborted Multilateral Agreement on Investment can still be found on the web at a few sites. Try the following ones:

Put together by students for a course at University of California, Irvine, is *http://darwin.bio.uci.edu/~sustain/issueguides/MAI/index.html*.

The Council of Canadians maintains a site with old press releases from the group's anti-MAI campaign in 1998–1999, as well as with links and some publications, at *http://www.canadians.org/campaigns/campaigns-mai.html*.

Public Citizen maintains a website dedicated to NAFTA's Chapter 11 and its possible extension to the Free Trade Area of the Americas at *http://www.citizen.org/trade/nafta/CH__11/*.

A large amount of information about Chapter 11 cases, as well as links to recent papers analyzing investment protection under NAFTA, can be found at *http://www.naftaclaims.com*.

Suggestions for Further Reading

For a detailed discussion of the obsolescing bargain model and an application of this model to Chile, see Theodore H. Moran, *Multinational Corporations and the Politics of Dependence: Copper in Chile* (Princeton: Princeton University Press, 1974).

For a detailed description of the policies governments have used to regulate MNCs and foreign direct investment in the postwar period, see A.E. Safarian, *Multinational Enterprises and Public Policy: A Study of Industrial Countries* (Brookfield, VT: Edward Elgar, 1993).

For an overview of international negotiations over investment rules prior to the MAI, see Samuel K.B. Asante, "United Nations Efforts at International Regulation of Transnational Corporations," in Kamal Hossain, ed., *Legal Aspects of the New International Economic Order,* (London: Frances Pinter, 1980).

For a sophisticated response to many of the criticisms of MNC activities, see Edward M. Graham, *Fighting the Wrong Enemy: Antiglobal Activities and Multinational Enterprises* (Washington, DC: Institute for International Economics, 2000).

CHAPTER 10

The International Monetary System

The sole purpose of the international monetary system is to facilitate international economic exchange. Most countries have national currencies that are not generally accepted as legal payment outside their borders. You wouldn't get very far, for example, if you tried to use dollars to purchase a pint of ale in a London pub. If you want this pint, you have to first exchange your dollars for British pounds. If you are an American car dealer trying to import Volkswagens for your dealership, you will need to find some way to exchange your dollars for euros. If you are an American trying to purchase shares in a Japanese company, you will have to find some way to acquire Japanese yen. Distinct national currencies thus may pose an important obstacle to international trade and financial transactions. International transactions are possible only with an inexpensive means of exchanging one national currency for another. The international monetary system's primary function is to provide this mechanism. When the system functions smoothly, international trade and investment can flourish; when the system functions poorly, or when it collapses completely (as it did in the early 1930s), international trade and investment grind to a halt.

While the purpose of the international monetary system is simple, the factors that determine how it works are more complex. For example, how many dollars it costs an American tourist to buy a British pound, a euro, or 100 Japanese yen (or any other foreign currency) is determined by the sum total of the millions of international transactions that Americans conduct with the rest of the world. Moreover, for these currency prices to remain stable from one month to the next, the United States must somehow ensure that the value of the goods, services, and financial assets that it buys from the rest of the world equals the value of the products it sells to the rest of the world. Any imbalance will cause the dollar to gain or lose value in terms of foreign currencies. While these issues may seem remote, they matter substantially to your well-being. For every time the dollar loses value against foreign currencies, you become poorer; conversely, you become richer whenever the dollar gains value. This is true whether you travel outside the United States or not.

This chapter and the next develop a basic understanding of the international monetary system. This chapter presents a few central economic concepts and examines a bit of postwar exchange-rate history. Chapter 11 builds on this base while examining contemporary international monetary arrangements. In the current chapter, we explore one basic question: why do we live in a world in which currency values fluctuate substantially from week to week, rather than in a world of more stable currencies? The answer we propose is that the international monetary system requires governments to choose between currency stability and national economic autonomy. Given the need to choose, the advanced industrialized countries have elected to allow their currencies to fluctuate in order to retain national autonomy.

The Economics of the International Monetary System

We begin by examining three economic concepts that are central to understanding the international monetary system. We look first at exchange rates and exchange-rate systems. We then examine the balance of payments and conclude by looking closely at the dynamics of balance-of-payments adjustment.

Exchange-Rate Systems

An exchange rate is the price of one currency in terms of another. As I write this sentence, for example, the dollar–yen exchange rate is 109, which means that 1 dollar will purchase 109 Japanese yen. A currency's exchange rate is determined by the interaction between the supply of and the demand for currencies in the **foreign exchange market**—the market in which the world's currencies are traded. When an American business needs yen to pay for goods imported from Japan, for example, it goes to the foreign exchange market and buys them. Thousands of such transactions undertaken by individuals, businesses, and governments each day—some looking to buy yen and sell dollars and others looking to sell yen and buy dollars—determine the price of the dollar in terms of yen and the prices of all of the world's currencies. Imbalances between the supply of and the demand for currencies in the foreign exchange market cause exchange rates to change. If more people want to buy than sell yen, for example, the yen will gain value, or appreciate. Conversely, if more people want to sell than buy yen, the yen will lose value, or depreciate.

An **exchange-rate system** is a set of rules governing how much national currencies can appreciate and depreciate in the foreign exchange market. There are two prototypical systems: fixed exchange-rate systems and floating exchange-rate systems. In a **fixed exchange-rate system,** governments can allow only very small changes in their currency's exchange rate. In such systems, governments establish a fixed price for their currencies in terms of some external standard, such as gold or another country's currency. (Under post-World War II arrangements, for example, the United States fixed the dollar to gold at $35 per ounce.) The government then maintains this fixed price by buying and selling currencies in the foreign exchange market. In order to conduct these transactions, governments hold a stock of other countries' currencies as **foreign exchange reserves.** Thus, if the dollar is selling below its fixed price against the yen in the foreign exchange market, the U.S. government will sell yen that it is holding in its foreign exchange reserves and will purchase dollars. These transactions will reduce the supply of dollars in the foreign exchange market, causing the dollar's value to rise. If the dollar is selling above its fixed price against the yen, the U.S. government will sell dollars and purchase yen. These transactions increase the supply of dollars in the foreign exchange market, causing the dollar's value to fall. The yen the United States acquires then become part of its foreign exchange reserves. Such government purchases and sales of currencies in the foreign exchange market are called **foreign exchange market intervention.** In a fixed exchange-rate system, the government must prevent its currency from changing value, and it does so by buying and selling currencies in the foreign exchange market.

In a **floating exchange-rate system,** there are no limits on how much an exchange rate can move in the foreign exchange market. In such systems, governments do not maintain a fixed price for their currencies against gold or any other standard. Nor do governments engage in foreign exchange market intervention to influence the value of their currency. Instead, the value of one currency in terms of another is determined entirely by the activities of private actors—firms, financial institutions, and individuals—as they purchase and sell currencies in the foreign exchange market. If private demand for a particular currency in the market falls, that currency depreciates. Conversely, if private demand for a particular currency in the market increases, that currency appreciates. In contrast to a fixed exchange-rate system, therefore, a pure floating exchange-rate system calls for no government involvement in determining the value of one currency in terms of another.

Fixed and floating exchange-rate systems represent the two ends of a continuum. Other exchange-rate systems lie between these two extremes. Some are essentially fixed exchange-rate systems that provide a bit of flexibility. In a **fixed-but-adjustable exchange-rate system**—the system that lay at the center of the post-World War II monetary system and the European Union's regional exchange-rate system between 1979 and 1999—currencies are given a fixed exchange rate against some standard and governments are required to maintain this exchange rate. However, governments can change the fixed price occasionally, usually under a set of well-defined circumstances. Other systems lie closer to the floating-exchange-rate end of the continuum, but provide a bit more stability to exchange rates than a pure float. In a **managed float,** which perhaps most accurately characterizes the current international monetary system, governments do not allow their currencies to float freely. Instead, they intervene in the foreign exchange market to influence their currency's value against other currencies. However, there are usually no rules governing when such intervention will occur, and governments do not commit themselves to maintaining a specific fixed price against other currencies or an external standard. Because all exchange-rate systems fall somewhere between the two extremes, one can usefully distinguish between such systems on the basis of how much exchange-rate flexibility or rigidity they entail.

In the contemporary international monetary system, governments maintain a variety of exchange-rate arrangements. Some governments allow their currencies to float. Others, such as most governments in the European Union, have opted for rigidly fixed exchange rates. Still others, particularly in the developing world, maintain fixed-but-adjustable exchange rates. However, the world's most important currencies—the dollar, the yen, and the euro—are allowed to float against each other, and the monetary authorities in these countries engage only in periodic intervention to influence their values. Consequently, the contemporary international monetary system is most often described as a system of floating exchange rates. We will examine the operation of this system in detail in Chapter 11.

Is one exchange-rate system inherently better than another? Not necessarily. Rather than rank systems as better or worse, it is more useful to recognize that all exchange-rate systems embody an important trade-off between exchange-rate stability, on the one hand, and domestic economic autonomy, on the other. Fixed exchange rates provide exchange-rate stability, but they also prevent governments from using monetary policy to manage domestic economic activity. Floating exchange rates allow governments to use monetary policy to manage the domestic economy, but do not provide much exchange-rate stability. (We explore the reasons for this trade-off when we look at balance-of-payments adjustment.) Whether a fixed or a floating exchange rate is better, therefore, depends a lot on how governments view each side of this trade-off. Fixed exchange rates are better for governments that value exchange-rate stability and that are less concerned with domestic autonomy. Floating exchange rates are better for governments that value domestic autonomy more than exchange-rate stability.

The Balance of Payments

The **balance of payments** is an accounting device that records all international transactions between a particular country and the rest of the world for a given period (typically a calendar year). For instance, any time an American business exports or imports a product, the value of that transaction is recorded in the U.S balance of payments. Any time an American resident, business, or government loans funds to a foreigner or borrows funds from a foreign financial institution, the value of the transaction is recorded. All of the government's international transactions are also recorded. When the U.S. government spends money in Iraq supporting the military, or provides foreign aid to Egypt, these payments are recorded in the balance of payments. By recording all such transactions, the balance of payments provides an aggregate picture of the international transactions the United States conducts in a given year.

Table 10.1 presents the U.S. balance of payments for 2003, the latest year for which complete data are currently available. The transactions are divided into two broad categories: the current account and the capital account. The **current account** records all current (nonfinancial) transactions between American residents and the rest of the world. These current transactions are divided into four subcategories. The *trade account* registers imports and exports of goods, including manufactured items and agricultural products. The *service account* registers imports and exports of service sector activities, such as banking services, insurance, consulting, transportation, tourism, and construction. The *income account* registers all payments into and out of the United States in connection with royalties, licensing fees, interest payments, and profits. Finally, the *unilateral transfers account* registers all unilateral transfers from the United States to other countries and vice versa. Among such transfers are the

Table 10.1
U.S. Balance of Payments, 2003 (Millions of U.S. Dollars)

Current Account	
Trade in Goods	
Imports	−1,260,674
Exports	713,122
Trade in Services	
Net Military Transactions	−12,626
Net Travel and Transportation Receipts	−10,303
Other Services, Net	73,973
Balance on Goods and Services	**−496,508**
Income Receipts	294,385
Income Payments	−261,106
Balance on Income	**−33,279**
Unilateral Transfers, Net	**−67,439**
Balance on Current Account	**−530,668**

Capital Account	
Total U.S. Owned Assets Abroad	**−283,414**
U.S. Official Reserve Assets	−1,523
Other U.S. Government Assets	−537
U.S. Private Assets	−285,474
Foreign Owned Assets in the United States	**829,173**
Foreign Official Assets	248,573
Other Foreign Assets	580,759
Balance on Capital Account	**545,759**
Overall Balance (Statistical Discrepancy)	**15,091**

Source: U.S. Government Economic Report of the President, 2005, Table B-103.

wages that immigrants working in the United States send back to their home countries, gifts, and foreign-aid expenditures by the U.S. government. In all four categories, payments by the United States to other countries are recorded as debits, while payments from other countries to the United States are recorded as credits. Debits are balanced against credits to produce an overall *current-account balance*. In 2003, the United States ran a current-account deficit of about $531 billion. In other words, total payments by American residents to foreigners were $531 billion greater than foreigners' total payments to American residents.

The **capital account** registers financial flows between the United States and the rest of the world. Any time an American resident purchases a financial asset—a foreign stock, a bond, or even a factory—in another country, this expenditure is registered as a capital outflow. Each time a foreigner purchases an American financial asset, the expenditure is registered as a capital inflow. Capital outflows are registered as negative items, while capital inflows are registered as positive items, in the capital account. In 2003, American residents other than the U.S. government purchased about $285 billion worth of foreign financial assets, while foreigners purchased about $829 billion of

American financial assets. Capital outflows are set against capital inflows to produce a capital-account balance. In 2003, the U.S. capital-account balance was just less than $546 billion. To calculate the overall balance-of-payments position, simply add the current account and the capital account together. In 2003, the United States ran an overall balance of payments surplus of $15 billion.

The current and capital accounts must be mirror images of each other. That is, if a country has a current account deficit, it must have a capital-account surplus. Conversely, if a country has a current-account surplus, it must have a capital-account deficit. Grasping why this relationship must exist is easiest in the case of a country with a current-account deficit. Having a current-account deficit means that the country's total expenditures in a given year—all of the money spent on goods and services and on investments in factories and houses—are larger than its total income in that year. The U.S. case is instructive. American consumers spent a combined total of $7.8 trillion in 2003 (United States Government, 2005, Table B-1). The U.S. government spent an additional $2.1 trillion. American firms and households invested yet an additional $1.7 trillion. Altogether, these expenditures totaled $11.5 trillion. American residents earned only $11.0 trillion in total income in 2003. The difference between what American residents earned and what they spent is thus roughly $500 billion. Now look back at the "Balance on Goods and Services" in Table 10.1. It, too, is approximately $500 billion. (The two would match exactly if we used exact, rather than rounded, numbers.) Hence, the American current-account deficit equals the difference between American income and American expenditures.

The United States was able to spend more than it earned in income because the rest of the world was willing to lend to American residents. The U.S. capital-account surplus thus reflects the willingness of residents of other countries to finance American expenditures in excess of American income. If the rest of the world were unwilling to lend to American borrowers, the United States could not spend more than it earned in income. Thus, a country can have a current-account deficit only if it has a capital-account surplus.

The same logic applies to a country with a current-account surplus. Suppose we divide the world into two countries: the United States and the rest of the world. We know that the United States has a current-account deficit with the rest of the world and thus the rest of the world has a current account surplus with the United States. If the United States can have a current-account deficit only if the rest of the world lends money to the United States, then the rest of the world can have a current-account surplus with the United States only if it lends money to American residents. If it doesn't, Americans can't buy as many of the rest of the world's goods. The rest of the world's current-account surplus (as well as the American current-account deficit) will then disappear. Thus, a country that has a current-account surplus must have a capital-account deficit. In terms of our income and expenditure framework, a current-account surplus means that the country is spending less than it earns in income. The balance—the country's savings—is lent to countries with current-account deficits.

Balance-of-Payments Adjustment

While the current and capital accounts must balance each other, there is no assurance that the millions of international transactions that individuals, businesses, and governments conduct every year will necessarily produce this balance. When they don't, the country faces an imbalance of payments. A country might have a current-account deficit that it cannot fully finance through capital imports, for example, or it might have a current-account surplus that is not fully offset by capital outflows. When an imbalance arises, the country must bring its payments back into balance. The process by which a country does so is called **balance-of-payments adjustment.** Fixed and floating exchange-rate systems adjust imbalances in different ways.

In a fixed exchange-rate system, balance-of-payments adjustment occurs through price changes in those countries with deficits and those with surpluses. We can most readily understand this adjustment process through a simple example. Suppose there are only two countries in the world—the United States and Japan—and suppose further that they maintain a fixed exchange rate according to which $1 equals 100 yen. The United States has purchased 800 billion yen worth of goods, services, and financial assets from Japan, while Japan has purchased $4 billion of items from the United States. Thus, the United States has a deficit, and Japan a surplus, of $4 billion.

This payments imbalance creates an imbalance between the supply of and the demand for the dollar and yen in the foreign exchange market. American residents need 800 billion yen to pay for their imports from Japan. They can acquire this 800 billion yen by selling $8 billion. Japanese residents need only $4 billion to pay for their imports from the United States. They can acquire the $4 billion by selling 400 billion yen. Thus, American residents are selling $4 billion more than Japanese residents want to buy, and the dollar begins to depreciate against the yen.

Because the exchange rate is fixed, the United States and Japan must prevent this depreciation. Thus, both countries intervene in the foreign exchange market, buying dollars in exchange for yen. Intervention has two consequences. First, it eliminates the imbalance in the foreign exchange market as the governments provide the 400 billion yen that American residents need in exchange for the $4 billion that Japanese residents do not want. With the supply of each currency equal to the demand in the foreign exchange market, the fixed exchange rate is sustained. Second, intervention changes each country's money supply. The American money supply falls by $4 billion, while Japan's money supply increases by 400 billion yen. Thus, by intervening in the foreign exchange market and altering their money supplies, the two governments have successfully defended the fixed exchange rate.

A change in the money supplies in Japan and the United States in turn alters prices in the two countries. The reduction of the U.S. money supply causes American prices to fall. The expansion of the money supply in Japan causes Japanese prices to rise. As American prices fall and Japanese prices rise, American goods become relatively less expensive than Japanese goods. Consequently, American and Japanese residents shift their purchases away from Japanese products and toward American goods. American imports (and hence Japanese exports) fall, while American exports (and hence Japanese imports) rise. As American imports (and Japanese exports) fall and American exports (and Japanese imports) rise, the payments imbalance is eliminated. Adjustment under fixed exchange rates thus occurs through changes in the relative price of American and Japanese goods brought about by the changes in money supplies caused by intervention in the foreign exchange market.

Here, then, is the basic trade-off inherent in exchange-rate systems that I mentioned earlier. When a system maintains a fixed exchange rate, the government adjusts the balance of payments by using monetary policy to prevent the exchange rate from moving in response to the foreign exchange market imbalance. Because the government must use monetary policy to maintain the fixed exchange rate, the government cannot use monetary policy to manage domestic economic activity. Thus, while a fixed exchange rate provides considerable exchange-rate stability, it also requires the government to give up substantial domestic economic autonomy.

In floating exchange-rate systems, balance-of-payments adjustment occurs through exchange-rate movements. Let's go back to our U.S.–Japan scenario, keeping everything the same, except this time allowing the currencies to float rather than requiring the governments to maintain a fixed exchange rate. Again, the $4 billion payments imbalance generates an imbalance in the foreign exchange market: Americans are selling more dollars than Japanese residents want to buy. Consequently, the dollar begins to depreciate against the yen. Because the currencies are floating, however, neither government intervenes in the foreign exchange market. Instead, the dollar depreciates until the market clears. In essence, as Americans seek the yen they need, they are forced to accept fewer yen for each dollar. Eventually, however, they will acquire all of the yen they need, but will have paid more than $4 billion for them.

The dollar's depreciation lowers the price in yen of American goods and services in the Japanese market and raises the price in dollars of Japanese goods and services in the American market. A 10 percent **devaluation** of the dollar against the yen, for example, reduces the price that Japanese residents pay for American goods by 10 percent and raises the price that Americans pay for Japanese goods by 10 percent. By making American products cheaper and Japanese goods more expensive, depreciation causes American imports from Japan to fall and American exports to Japan to rise. As American exports expand and imports fall, the payments imbalance is corrected.

Once again, the basic trade-off inherent in exchange-rate systems is apparent. With a floating exchange rate, the government adjusts the balance of payments by allowing the exchange rate to change in response to the foreign exchange market imbalance. Because the government need not use monetary policy to prevent this movement of currency, the government can use monetary policy to manage the domestic economy. Thus, while a floating exchange rate provides less exchange-rate stability than a fixed exchange rate, it allows governments to retain substantial domestic economic autonomy.

In both systems, therefore, balance-of-payments adjustment occurs as prices fall in the country with the deficit and rise in the country with the surplus. Consumers in both countries respond to these price changes by purchasing fewer of the now-more-expensive goods in the country with the surplus and more of the now-cheaper goods in the country with the deficit. These shifts in consumption alter imports and exports in both countries, moving each of their payments back into balance. The mechanism that causes these price changes is different in each system, however. In fixed exchange-rate systems, the exchange rate remains stable and price changes are achieved by changing the money supply in order to alter prices inside the country. In floating exchange-rate systems, internal prices remain stable, while the change in relative prices is brought about through exchange-rate movements.

Before we conclude this discussion, we must add one critically important wrinkle to our understanding of adjustment under fixed exchange rates. As we have seen, this kind of adjustment requires domestic price changes, and while domestic prices are flexible in the long run, some prices will be quite inflexible in the short run, especially when prices must fall to eliminate a deficit. One of the least flexible prices in the short run is the price of labor, or wages. Imagine how you would react if your employer appeared one day and said, "The money supply has fallen by 10 percent this year due to ongoing balance-of-payments adjustment, so I am going to have to reduce your pay by 10 percent." Yet, this is exactly what is implied by the assertion that all prices must fall in a country with a deficit. The price of labor must fall just as much as the price of goods and services. Yet, labor unions and national employment laws often prevent wages from falling, at least in the short run.

When wages are inflexible, adjustment under fixed exchange rates occurs first through reductions in output and employment and only later through price changes. Because wages respond more slowly than other prices to a monetary contraction, employers find that the price of their products is falling, while their costs of production are not. They respond by slowing production, thereby causing output to fall, and by releasing workers, thereby causing employment to fall. Over time, rising unemployment will reduce the economywide wage, and output and employment will eventually recover to their original levels (but at a lower price level). However, the country must first traverse a painful economic recession. Thus, when prices are inflexible, adjustment under a fixed exchange rate occurs through an initial reduction in domestic output and an initial increase in unemployment.

The output and employment consequences of balance-of-payments adjustment are the principal reason we live in a world of floating exchange rates. In essence, governments face a trade-off: they can maintain a fixed exchange rate, or they can enjoy domestic economic autonomy. If a government wants to maintain a fixed exchange rate, it must accept the occasional recession caused by balance-of-payments adjustment. If a government is unwilling to accept these domestic adjustment costs, it cannot maintain a fixed exchange rate. The trade-off between exchange-rate stability and domestic economic autonomy has been the central factor driving the international monetary system toward floating exchange rates during the last 100 years. We turn now to examine how this trade-off first led governments to create innovative international monetary arrangements following World War II and then caused the system to collapse into a floating exchange rate system in the early 1970s.

The Rise and Fall of the Bretton Woods System

The **Bretton Woods system** represents both a first and a last in the history of the international monetary system. On the one hand, Bretton Woods represented the first time that governments explicitly and systematically made exchange rates a matter of international cooperation and regulation. Drawing lessons from their experiences during the interwar period, governments attempted to create an innovative system that would enable them to enjoy exchange-rate stability and domestic economic autonomy. On the other hand, the Bretton Woods system represents the final effort, at least to date, to base the international monetary system on some form of fixed exchange rates. The effort was relatively short lived. The system was not fully implemented until 1959, and by the early 1960s it was beginning to experience the stresses and strains that brought about its collapse into a system of floating exchange rates in the early 1970s.

Creating the Bretton Woods System

American and British policymakers began planning for postwar monetary arrangements in the early 1940s. Harry Dexter White, an economist working at the U.S. Treasury, developed an American plan, while John M. Keynes, an economist who was advising the British Treasury, developed a British plan. Bilateral consultations yielded a joint U.S.–British plan that was published in 1943. This "Joint Statement," as the plan was called, served as the basis for the Articles of Agreement that emerged from a multilateral conference attended by 44 countries in Bretton Woods, New Hampshire, in 1944. The resulting international monetary system, the Bretton Woods system, was based on an explicit code of conduct for international monetary relations and an institutional structure centered on the International Monetary Fund (IMF).

The resulting Bretton Woods system attempted to establish a system of fixed exchange rates in a world in which governments would no longer be unwilling to accept the loss of domestic economic autonomy that such a system required. Governments had become increasingly reluctant to accept the domestic adjustments imposed by fixed exchange rates as a result of a shift in the balance of political power within European political systems following World War I. We will explore these developments in greater detail in Chapter 12 when we focus on the domestic politics of exchange-rate policy. For now, we note only that the growing strength of labor unions ensured that deficit adjustment would occur through falling output and rising unemployment, while the emergence of mass-based democracies made governments reluctant to accept these costs.

The emergence of political constraints on domestic adjustment ruled out a return to rigidly fixed exchange rates following World War II. Yet, floating exchange rates were viewed as no more acceptable. It was widely agreed that the experiment with floating exchange rates in the 1930s had been disastrous. As an influential study published by the League of Nations in 1944 summarized, "If there is anything that the interwar experience has demonstrated, it is that [currencies] cannot be left free to fluctuate from day to day under the influence of market supply and demand" (quoted in Dam 1982, 61). In creating the Bretton Woods system, therefore, governments sought a system that would provide stable exchange rates *and* simultaneously afford domestic economic autonomy. To achieve these goals, the Bretton Woods system introduced four innovations: greater exchange-rate flexibility, capital controls, a stabilization fund, and the International Monetary Fund.

First, Bretton Woods explicitly incorporated exchange-rate flexibility. The system was based on fixed-but-adjustable exchange rates. Each government established a central parity for its currency against gold, but could change this price of gold when facing a **fundamental disequilibrium.** The term was applied to cases of large payments imbalances. While governments were never able to define this term precisely, it was generally accepted that it referred to payments imbalances large enough to require inordinately painful domestic adjustment. In such cases, governments could devalue their currency. Exchange rates would thus be fixed on a day-to-day basis, but governments could change the exchange rate when they needed to correct a large imbalance. It was hoped that this element of flexibility would reduce the need for domestic adjustment while still providing stable exchange rates.

Governments were also allowed to limit international capital flows. An important component of the international economy, capital flows allow countries to finance current-account imbalances and to use foreign funds to finance productive investment. Many governments believed, however, that capital flows had destabilized exchange rates during the interwar period. Large volumes of capital had crossed borders, only to be brought back to the home country at the first sign of economic difficulty in the host country. This system resulted in "disequilibrating" capital flows in which countries with current-account deficits shipped capital to countries with current-account surpluses, rather than "equilibrating" flows in which countries with surpluses exported capital to countries with deficits in order to finance current-account deficits. The resulting payments deficits required substantial domestic adjustments that governments were unwilling to accept.

In the early 1930s, most governments began to limit capital flows with **exchange restrictions**—government regulations on the use of foreign exchange. In the most restrictive regimes, the central bank establishes a monopoly on foreign exchange. Any private actor wanting foreign currency or wanting to exchange foreign currency into the domestic currency must petition the central bank, which can then restrict the types of transactions for which it exchanges currencies. It might, for example, refuse to supply foreign currency to a domestic resident who wants to buy financial assets in a foreign country. Alternatively, it might refuse to supply domestic currency to a foreign resident who wants to buy domestic financial assets. By controlling purchases and sales of foreign exchange in this manner, governments can limit financial capital flows into and out of their domestic economies.

Following World War II, the question was whether governments could retain these exchange restrictions. American policymakers wanted all restrictions eliminated in order to restore liberal international capital markets. Other governments wanted to retain the restrictions. Keynes, for example, believed that it was "vital" to "have a means . . . of controlling short-term speculative movements of flights of currency" (cited in Dam 1982, 98). In the absence of such controls, Keynes argued, exchange rates would be vulnerable to speculative attacks that would force governments to float their currencies. Keynes's position carried the day. The IMF's Articles of Agreement required governments to allow residents to convert the domestic currency into foreign currencies to settle current-account transactions, but they allowed (but did not require) governments to restrict the convertibility of their currency for capital-account transactions. Most governments took advantage of this right, and as a consequence, international capital flows were tightly restricted until the late 1970s.

The Bretton Woods system also created a **stabilization fund**—a credit mechanism consisting of a pool of currencies contributed by member countries. Each country that participated in the Bretton Woods system was assigned a share of the total fund (called a quota), the size of which corresponded to its relative size in the global economy. Each country then contributed to the fund in the amount of its quota, paying 25 percent in gold and the remaining 75 percent in its national currency. As the world's largest economy, the United States had the largest quota, a contribution of

$2.75 billion. Britain had the second-largest quota, a contribution of $1.3 billion. Other governments had much smaller quotas; France, for example, had a quota of only $450 million, while Panama's was only $0.5 million. In 1944, the stabilization fund held a total of $8.8 billion. A government could draw on the fund when it faced a balance-of-payments deficit. Doing so would obviate the need to respond to a small payments deficit by devaluing currency or by imposing barriers to imports (De Vries and Horsefield 1969, 23–24).

Finally, the Bretton Woods system created an international organization, the International Monetary Fund (IMF), to monitor member countries' macroeconomic policies and balance-of-payments positions, to decide when devaluation was warranted, and to manage the stabilization fund. The IMF was intended to limit two kinds of opportunistic behavior. First, the exchange-rate system created the potential for competitive devaluations. Governments could devalue to enhance the competitiveness of their exports. If one government devalued in an attempt to boost exports, other governments would be likely to devalue in response, setting off a tit-for-tat dynamic that would destroy the exchange-rate system (Dam 1982, 63–64). Second, governments might abuse the stabilization fund. Easy access to this fund might encourage governments to run large balance-of-payments deficits. Countries could import more than they exported and then draw on the stabilization fund to finance the resulting deficit. If all governments pursued such policies, the stabilization fund would be quickly exhausted and countries would face large deficits that they could not finance. Countries would then float their currencies and perhaps restrict imports as well.

The IMF limited such opportunistic behavior by having authority over exchange-rate changes and over access to the stabilization fund. For exchange-rate changes, the Articles of Agreement specified that governments could devalue or revalue only after consulting the IMF, which would then evaluate the country's payments position and either agree or disagree with the government's claim that it faced a fundamental disequilibrium. If the IMF opposed the devaluation, the government could still devalue, but it would not be allowed to draw from the stabilization fund (Dam 1982, 90). The IMF also controlled access to the fund. IMF rules limited the total amount that a government could borrow to 25 percent of its quota per year, up to a maximum of 200 percent of its quota at any one time. It was agreed, however, that governments would not have automatic access to these funds. Each member government's quota was divided into four *credit tranches* of equal size, and drawings from each tranche required approval by the IMF's **Executive Board.** Approval for drawings on the first tranche was automatic, as these withdrawals represented borrowings against the gold that each member had paid into the stabilization fund. Drawing on the higher credit tranches, however, was conditional. **Conditionality** required a member government to reach agreement with the IMF on the measures it would take to correct its balance of payments deficit before it could draw on its higher credit tranches. Conditionality agreements typically require governments to reduce the growth of the money supply and to reduce government spending. Conditionality thus forces governments to correct the domestic economic imbalances that cause their balance-of-payments problems. The practice of IMF conditionality is controversial, and we will return to it in greater detail in Chapter 14.

The Bretton Woods system represented an attempt to create an international monetary system that would reconcile fixed exchange rates and domestic economic autonomy through four innovations. (1) The stabilization fund enabled governments to maintain fixed exchange rates in the face of small imbalances of payments. (2) Limiting capital flows ensured that imbalances remained small and developed slowly from trade flows, rather than suddenly from large capital flows. (3) Exchange-rate flexibility shielded governments from costly domestic adjustment. Finally, (4) The IMF would ensure that governments did not abuse the system.

Implementing Bretton Woods: From Dollar Shortage to Dollar Glut

Governments had intended to implement the Bretton Woods system immediately following the Second World War. This proved impossible, however, because European governments held such small foreign exchange reserves (dollars and gold) that they were unwilling to make their domestic currencies freely convertible into foreign currencies. Governments needed to conserve what little foreign exchange they had to import food, capital goods, inputs, and many of the other critical components essential to economic reconstruction. Allowing residents to convert the domestic currency freely into dollars or gold, as the rules of Bretton Woods required, would produce a run on a country's limited foreign exchange reserves. Governments would then have to reduce imports and slow the pace of economic reconstruction.

An aborted British attempt to restore the convertibility of the pound in 1947 starkly illustrated the threat (Eichengreen 1996, 103). Under pressure from the United States, and with the support of a $3.75 billion American loan, the British government allowed holders of the British pound to purchase gold and dollars for current-account transactions. Those who held pounds rushed to exchange them for dollars and, in doing so, consumed the American loan and a large share of Britain's other foreign exchange reserves in only six weeks. As its reserves dwindled, the British government suspended the convertibility of the pound. Convertibility—and indeed the implementation of the Bretton Woods system—would have to wait until European governments had accumulated sufficient foreign exchange reserves.

In order for European governments to accumulate foreign exchange reserves, however, dollars had to be transferred from the United States to European governments. The U.S. balance-of-payments deficit provided the mechanism through which this transfer was achieved. (See Figure 10.1.) Initially, the United States exported dollars to Europe and other parts of the world through foreign aid and military expenditures. The Marshall Plan, initiated in 1947 and implemented between 1948 and 1952, is the most prominent example of this American policy. By the late 1950s, however, private capital was also flowing from the United States to Europe (Block 1977). American deficits meant that more dollars flowed out from the United States each year than flowed in. These dollars were accumulated by European governments, which held them as foreign exchange reserves and used them to pay for imports from the United States and other countries. Governments could exchange whatever dollars they held into gold at the official price of $35 an ounce. By 1959, this mechanism had enabled European governments to accumulate sufficient dollar and gold reserves to accept fully convertible currencies. In 1959, therefore, the Bretton Woods system was finally implemented, almost 15 years after it had been created.

American policy during the 1950s also had an unintended consequence: the dollar became the system's **primary reserve asset.** In this role, the dollar became the cur-

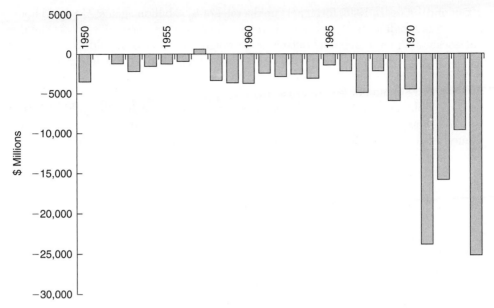

Figure 10.1   U.S. Balance of Payments, 1950–1974.
Source: Block 1977.

rency that other governments held as foreign exchange reserves and used to make their international payments and to intervene in foreign exchange markets. This was reasonable: the United States was the largest economy in the world, and at the end of the Second World War the United States held between 60 and 70 percent of the world's gold supply. The dollar was fixed to gold at $35 per ounce, and other governments were willing to hold dollars because dollars were "as good as gold." As a consequence, however, the stability of the Bretton Woods system came to depend upon the ability of the U.S. government to exchange dollars for gold at $35 an ounce.

The American ability to fulfill this commitment began to diminish as the postwar dollar shortage was transformed into an overabundance of dollars, or a **dollar glut,** during the 1960s. The dollar glut was the natural consequence of continued American balance of payments deficits. Between 1958 and 1970, the United States ran average annual payments deficits of $3.3 billion. These deficits remained fairly stable during the first half of the 1960s, but then began to grow after 1965. Deficits were caused by U.S. military expenditures in connection with the Vietnam War and expanded welfare programs at home, as well as by the unwillingness of the Johnson and Nixon administrations to finance these expenditures with higher taxes. The result was an expansionary macroeconomic policy in the United States that sucked in imports and encouraged American investors to send capital abroad. The dollars accumulated by governments in the rest of the world as the inevitable result of these American deficits represented foreign claims on the American government's gold holdings.

The rising volume of foreign claims on American gold led to **dollar overhang:** foreign claims on American gold grew larger than the amount of gold that the U.S. government held. The emergence and subsequent worsening of dollar overhang can be seen in the evolution of foreign dollar holdings and the U.S. gold stock during the

1950s and 1960s. In 1948, foreigners held a total of $7.3 billion against U.S. gold holdings of $24.8 billion. In this period, therefore, there was no uncertainty regarding the American ability to redeem all outstanding foreign claims on U.S. gold. By 1959, foreign dollar holdings had increased to $19.4 billion, while U.S. gold holdings had fallen to $19.5 billion, of which $12 billion had to be reserved as backing for domestic claims and therefore could not be used to satisfy foreign demands for gold. By 1970, American gold holdings stood at $11 billion, while foreign claims against this gold had risen to $47 billion. Thus, persistent balance-of-payments deficits reduced the ability of the United States to meet foreign claims on American gold reserves at the official price of $35 an ounce.

Dollar overhang threatened the stability of the Bretton Woods system. (See Triffin 1960.) As long as the dollar remained the system's primary reserve asset, the growth of dollars circulating in the global economy would have to keep pace with the expansion of world trade. This meant that dollar overhang would worsen. Yet, as that happened, people would lose confidence in the ability of the American government to exchange dollars for gold at $35 an ounce. Once this confidence evaporated, anyone who held dollars would rush to sell them before the dollar was devalued or American gold reserves were exhausted. Declining confidence in the dollar, in other words, would encourage foreign dollar holders to bet against the dollar's fixed exchange rate with gold. Eventually, this dynamic would generate crises that would undermine the system.

Preventing these crises was complicated by the dollar's central role in the system. The United States would have to reverse its balance-of-payments position to eliminate dollar overhang. Rather than run deficits that pumped dollars into the international economy, the United States would have to run surpluses that pulled dollars back in. Yet, because the dollar served as the system's primary reserve asset, reducing the number of dollars circulating in the global economy would reduce the liquidity that financed world trade. As governments defended their fixed exchange rates in the face of this contraction of liquidity, the world economy could be pushed into a deflationary spiral (Eichengreen 1996, 116). The Bretton Woods system therefore faced a dilemma: dollar overhang would eventually trigger crises that undermined the system of fixed exchange rates, but measures to strengthen the dollar could trigger global deflation that might also destroy the system.

This liquidity problem, as it came to be called, was not simply an obscure technical matter. It was also a source of political conflict, particularly between France and the United States. The French argued that the United States gained considerable advantages from the dollar's role as the system's primary reserve asset. No other country could run persistent balance-of-payments deficits, because it would eventually run out of foreign exchange reserves and be forced to eliminate the deficit. But the United States did not face this reserve constraint: it could run deficits as long as other governments were willing to accumulate dollars. The French claimed that this asymmetry enabled the United States to pursue an "imperialistic" policy. In the economic arena, the United States could buy French companies, and in the geostrategic arena, the United States could expand its activities with few constraints, as it was doing in Vietnam (Dam 1982, 144). The French government decried this "exorbitant privilege" and advocated the creation of an alternative reserve asset to provide international liquidity. The French even advocated a return to the gold standard to eliminate the benefits the

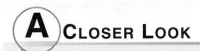

A CLOSER LOOK

Dollar Overhang and the Confidence Problem

In early May of 1962, James Tobin wrote a memo to President John F. Kennedy in which he explained the reasons for, and the consequences of, dollar overhang. The memo, extracts of which are reproduced here, not only provides an excellent explanation of the central problem the United States faced, but also highlights how dollar overhang generated political problems for the Kennedy administration.

MEMORANDUM FOR THE PRESIDENT, 5 MAY, 1962

The United States Operates a Bank for the World

This "Bank" is not a formal institution. It has no legal existence, no physical address, no clearly defined balance sheet. Nevertheless it is this Banking function which dominates our gold problem and magnifies our balance of payments difficulties. Some "deposits" in this Bank are the dollar bank deposits and short-term securities owned by foreign *central banks and governments.* We permit these depositors to exchange their dollars for gold whenever they please. At present these "deposits" amount to $10.3 billion, compared to $4.6 billion ten years ago.

In addition, there are $10.8 billion of dollar deposits (compared to $4.3 billion in 1952) and liquid securities owned by foreign *private* banks, business firms, and individuals, and by international lending institutions. These foreign owners cannot exchange their dollars for our gold. But they can sell them to their central banks, and thereby increase the official "deposits" in the Bank, which can be cashed for gold.

The reserves of the Bank are the U.S. gold stock. At the end of January these amounted to $16.8 billion, of which $11.4 billion are legally committed as backing for the U.S. domestic money supply. (Ten years ago, this Bank had gold reserves of $23.1 billion, of which $11.4 billion were needed to cover the domestic money supply.)

The Deposits of the Bank are Uninsured

A foreign central bank which holds dollars instead of converting them into gold runs the risk that we will choose to, or be forced to, lower the gold value of the dollar or stop paying out gold for dollars on demand. This is why our official depositors do not want to have too big a part of their own reserves in the form of uninsured deposits. That is why they from time to time cash dollars into gold. If any large part of the $10.8 billion private (and international) foreign dollar holdings were sold to foreign central banks, the central banks would almost surely turn most of them into gold.

Before the days of deposit insurance in the U.S., an ordinary commercial bank was in this same situation. Its depositors could ask for cold cash—coins and currency, including gold. No bank had enough reserves to pay its depositors if all of them wished to withdraw their deposits at the same time. A depositor was always running the risk that the bank would "fail." And whenever enough depositors thought this risk was too great, they made the bank fail. The only way we got out of this was to institute

Continued

government deposit insurance, which guaranteed to the depositors that $1 of bank deposit will always be worth a dollar bill.

The same danger—a run on the Bank—is what we are now up against in the international sphere. But so far we haven't advanced to the obvious solution, a way of guaranteeing the Bank's depositors against loss.

The U.S. Balance of Payments and the Bank

A U.S. balance of payments deficit adds to the dollars in foreign hands, private and official. If foreign banks and individuals get more dollars than they want, they sell them to their own central banks for their local currencies. If the central banks thus acquire more dollars than they want, they use them to buy gold from us. In 1961

The deficit was	$2.5 billion
But private foreign holders only wished to hang on to	$1.3 billion
Hence they sold	$1.2 billion to foreign central banks.
But central banks only wished to hang on to	$0.5 billion
Hence they cashed	$0.7 billion in for gold,
The rest of the deficit	$1.8 billion remains outstanding

Adding to the dollar claims (or claims but one step removed) on our gold stock.

The Overhang of Dollar Liabilities, and "Confidence"

Ending the payments deficit will stop the growth of our Bank's liabilities. But even when we have no balance of payments deficit, the $21.1 billion of dollar liabilities resulting from the past will still be hanging over our heads—claims or potential claims against our gold which could be exercised at any moment. Even without payments deficits, we can lose gold as these claims move between depositors. Dollars may move from private stocks to official holders who by tradition prefer gold, or from a central bank that willingly holds dollars to one that likes gold.

Furthermore, it is this overhang which places us at the mercy of the "confidence" which foreign central bankers, private bankers, and financial pundits have in the dollar. The state of "confidence" is a funny thing—fragile, irrational, contagious, political, unpredictable . . . So long as we have to worry about "confidence," we are not masters in our own house. Domestic policy is perpetually inhibited by what this or that measure may do—or by what someone thinks it may do—to confidence in the dollar. In particular, measures to stimulate employment and growth are inhibited—even though in the long run unemployment and economic stagnation also weaken confidence. Worse yet, foreign confidence is heavily dependent upon the views of our natural political opponents at home—the financial community and the conservative press. Their views of the dollar are colored by their political and ideological opposition to any and all active government policy for economic expansion. These vocal financial conservatives weaken foreign confidence in the dollar. Then they can use the

Continued

issue of confidence as a weapon to oppose domestic policies they have always opposed anyway.

Source: James Tobin, "Memorandum for the President," 5 May, 1962. Record Group 56. Records of the Under Secretary of State for International Affairs, Box 117. National Archives and Records Administration, Archives II, College Park, Maryland.

United States realized from the dollar's role in the system. Efforts to solve the liquidity problem, therefore, became inextricably linked to American power in the international monetary system and in the wider global arena.

Governments did respond to the liquidity problem, by creating a new reserve asset to supplement the dollar. Working in conjunction with the IMF, governments created the Special Drawing Right (SDR), a reserve asset managed by the International Monetary Fund and allocated to member governments in proportion to the size of their quotas. The SDR is not backed by gold or any other standard, cannot be used by private individuals, and is not traded in private financial markets. Its sole purpose is to provide a source of liquidity that governments can use to settle debts with each other arising from balance-of-payments deficits. The intention was that SDRs would supplement dollars as a source of liquidity in the international monetary system. The first allocation of SDRs occurred in 1970. By this time, however, the Bretton Woods system was moving toward its ultimate demise, and the SDR never played an important role.

The End of Bretton Woods: Crises and Collapse

The continued viability of the Bretton Woods system depended upon restoring confidence in the dollar, and this in turn required eliminating the underlying payments imbalances. Adjustment could be achieved through one of three paths: devalue the dollar against gold, restrain economic activity in the United States in order to reduce American imports, or expand economic activity in the rest of the world in order to increase American exports. Governments proved unwilling to adopt any of these measures. Instead, they were paralyzed by political conflict over who should bear the costs of the adjustments necessary to eliminate the imbalances that were weakening the system.

The simplest solution would have been to devalue the dollar against gold. Devaluation was not easily achieved, however. American policy makers believed that they could not change the dollar's exchange rate unilaterally. If they devalued against gold, Europe and Japan would simply devalue in response. As a consequence, the only way to devalue the dollar was to convince European and Japanese governments to revalue their currencies. Europe and Japan were unwilling to revalue their currencies against the dollar, however, because doing so would remove any pressure on the United States to undertake adjustment measures of its own (Solomon 1977, 170). **Revaluation,** in other words, would let the United States off the hook.

With currency realignment off the table, only two other solutions were left: adjustment through economic contraction in the United States or adjustment through economic expansion in other countries. In the United States, neither the Johnson nor the Nixon administration was willing to adopt the policies required to eliminate the U.S. balance-of-payments deficit. U.S. Secretary of the Treasury Henry Fowler spelled out the two American options in a memo to President Johnson in mid-1966. The United States could either "reduce the deficit by cutting back U.S. commitments overseas," a choice that would entail "major changes in [U.S.] foreign policy," or "reduce the deficit by introducing new economic and balance of payments measures at home" (United States Department of State). Neither option was attractive. The Johnson administration was not willing to allow the balance of payments to constrain its foreign-policy goals, and restricting domestic economic activity to correct the deficit was politically inconvenient.

Richard M. Nixon, who assumed the presidency in 1969, was no more willing to adopt policies to eliminate the American deficit. Instead, the Nixon administration blamed other governments for the strains emerging in the international monetary system (Dam 1982, 186). The dollar's weakness was not a result of the American balance-of-payments deficit, the administration claimed, but was instead caused by surpluses in Germany and Japan. Because other governments were at fault, the administration began to push these other governments to change policies, acting "like a bull in a china shop," threatening to wreck the international trade and financial system unless other governments supported the dollar in the foreign exchange market and took measures to stimulate imports from the United States (Eichengreen 1996, 130).

Governments in Western Europe and Japan initially supported the dollar, in large part "because [the dollar] was the linchpin of the Bretton Woods system and because there was no consensus on how that system might be reformed or replaced" (Eichengreen 1996, 130). But there were clear limits to their willingness to continue to do so. The case of Germany illustrates both sides. Germany had done more to support the dollar than any other European government. The German government had agreed not to exchange the dollars it was accumulating for American gold, in stark contrast to the French, who regularly demanded gold from the United States for the dollars they acquired. In addition, Germany had negotiated a series of "offset payments" through which a portion of American military expenditures in Germany were offset by German expenditures on American military equipment. Such payments reduced the extent to which American military expenditures in Europe contributed to the U.S. balance-of-payments deficit.

Germany's willingness to support the dollar, however, was limited by that country's aversion to inflation. Germany had experienced hyperinflation during the 1920s, with prices rising at the rate of 1,000 percent per month in 1923. This experience had caused German officials and the German public to place great value on price stability. (See Emminger 1977; Henning 1994.) Supporting the dollar threatened to increase German inflation. As confidence in the dollar began to erode, dollar holders began to sell dollars and buy German marks. Intervention in the foreign exchange market to prevent the mark from appreciating expanded the German money supply and created inflation in the country, which then made Germany reluctant to support the dollar indefinitely. Continued German support would be based on clear evidence that the United States was adopting domestic policies that were reducing its payments deficit.

Governments, then, were therefore unwilling to accept the domestic economic costs arising from the adjustments needed to correct the fundamental source of weakness in the system. As a consequence, the United States continued to export dollars into the system, dollar overhang worsened further, and confidence in the dollar's fixed exchange rate with gold began to erode. As confidence eroded, **speculative attacks**— large currency sales sparked by the anticipation of an impending devaluation—began to occur with increasing frequency and mounting ferocity. In the first six months of 1971, private holdings of dollars fell by $3 billion, a sign that people were expecting the dollar to be devalued (Dam 1982, 187). European governments purchased more than $5 billion defending the dollar's fixed exchange rate. The speculative attacks reached a new high in May as Germany purchased $2 billion in only two days, a record amount at that time (Kenen 1994, 500). The need for such massive intervention breached the limits of German willingness to support the dollar, and the German government floated the mark.

Speculative attacks resumed in the summer of 1971, and in August the Nixon administration suspended the convertibility of the dollar into gold and imposed a 10 percent surcharge on imports. (See Gowa 1983.) The United States had abandoned the central component of the Bretton Woods system; it would no longer redeem foreign governments' dollar reserves for gold.

Governments made one final attempt to rescue the Bretton Woods system. During the fall of 1971, they negotiated a currency realignment that they hoped would reduce the U.S. payments deficit and stabilize the system. The realignment was finalized in a December meeting held at the Smithsonian Institution in Washington, DC. The dollar was devalued by 8 percent against gold, its value falling from $35 per ounce to $38 per ounce. European currencies were revalued by about 2 percent, thus producing a total devaluation of the dollar of 10 percent. In addition, the margins of fluctuation in the exchange-rate system were widened from 1 percent to 2.25 percent, to give the system a bit more exchange-rate flexibility.

While Nixon hailed the Smithsonian realignment as "the greatest monetary agreement in the history of the world," it solved neither the economic imbalances nor the political conflicts that were the cause of the system's weakening. The United States refused to adopt measures to reduce its payments deficit. Rather than tighten monetary policy to support the new exchange rate, the Nixon administration loosened monetary policy, "triggering the greatest monetary expansion in the postwar era" (Emminger 1977, 33). German officials remained unwilling to accept the inflation that was the necessary consequence of intervention to support the mark against the dollar. With neither government willing to adjust to support the new exchange rates, speculative attacks quickly reemerged. A massive crisis in the first months of 1973 brought the system down, as most advanced industrialized countries abandoned their fixed exchange rates and floated their currencies.

Thus, the postwar attempt to create an international monetary system that provided exchange-rate stability and domestic economic autonomy was ultimately unsuccessful. The reasons for its failure are not hard to find. Some argue that the system was undermined by dollar overhang. Others suggest that it was destroyed by the speculative attacks that ultimately forced governments to abandon fixed exchange rates. While these factors were important, the fundamental cause of the system's collapse lay in the adjustment problem. To sustain fixed exchange rates, governments had to accept the domestic costs of balance of payments adjustment. No government was willing to do

POLICY ANALYSIS AND DEBATE

Who Should Adjust?

Question
Who should adjust in order to eliminate payments imbalances?

Overview
The payments imbalances at the center of the Bretton Woods system generated a distributive conflict about who should bear the cost of adjustment. The United States ran a large deficit, while Europe and Japan ran large surpluses. The elimination of either of these imbalances would necessarily eliminate the other. The situation gave rise to the dispute concerning who should alter its policies in order to adjust. Should the United States restrict its monetary and fiscal policies to shrink its deficit, or should Europe and Japan expand their monetary and fiscal policies to reduce their surpluses? The inability of governments to agree on how to distribute these adjustment costs eventually brought the Bretton Woods System down.

Distributive conflict over the costs of adjusting the balance of payments is of more than historical interest. The contemporary global economy has large current-account imbalances quite similar to those at the center of the Bretton Woods system. The United States runs large current-account deficits. Asian countries, most of which peg their currencies to the dollar, run large current-account surpluses. Asian surpluses finance American deficits. Rather than accumulating claims to American gold, however, as European governments did under Bretton Woods, Asia accumulates U.S. Treasury bills, which represent a claim on future American income.

Distributive conflict over the costs of adjustment has arisen during the last few years as current-account imbalances have expanded. Since 2000 or so, the United States has been pressuring China (one of the largest countries with a surplus) to devalue its currency. China has resisted such pressure thus far. Given the current size of the American deficit, one can imagine that the United States will pressure other Asian countries to adjust as well. Thus, the conflict over who adjusts shapes contemporary international monetary relations, just as it shaped monetary politics in the Bretton Woods system. Who should alter policies to eliminate large payments imbalances?

Policy Options
- The United States should implement the domestic policy changes required to reduce the size of its current-account deficit.
- The United States should pressure Asia to implement the domestic policies required to reduce the size of their current-account surpluses.

Policy Analysis
- What policies would the United States need to implement to eliminate its deficit? What would Asia have to do to eliminate its surplus?
- Is one of the two policy options less painful for the world economy than the other? If so, which one and why?

Take a Position
- Which option do you prefer? Justify your choice.
- What criticisms of your position should you anticipate? How would you defend your recommendation against these criticisms?

Continued

Resources
Online: Search for "Are We Back to a Bretton Woods Regime?" and "The Dollar and the New Bretton Woods System".
In Print: To examine past instances of distributive conflict, see Barry J. Eichengreen, *Golden Fetters: the Gold Standard and the Great Depression* (New York: Oxford University Press, 1992), and Barry J. Eichengreen and Marc Flandreau, eds., *The Gold Standard in Theory and History,* 2d ed. (New York: Routledge, 1997).

so. The United States was unwilling to accept the unemployment that would have arisen from eliminating its deficit, and Germany was unwilling to accept the higher inflation required to eliminate its surplus. This unwillingness to adjust aggravated the dollar overhang, which then created an incentive to launch speculative attacks against the dollar.

Conclusion

The creation and collapse of the Bretton Woods system highlights two central conclusions about the workings of the international monetary system. First, even though governments would like to maintain stable exchange rates and simultaneously preserve their domestic economic autonomy, no one has yet found a way to do so. Governments confront this trade-off because each country's balance-of-payments position has a direct impact on its exchange rate. When a country has a payments deficit, the resulting imbalance in the foreign exchange market causes the currency to depreciate. When a country has a payments surplus, the foreign exchange market imbalance causes the currency to appreciate. If the government is pledged to maintain a fixed exchange rate, it must intervene in the foreign exchange market to prevent such currency changes. As governments do so, they alter the money supply, thereby sparking the changes in the domestic economy needed to correct the payments imbalance. If a government is unwilling to accept these domestic adjustments, it will be unable to maintain a fixed exchange rate. The Bretton Woods system collapsed because neither Germany nor the United States was willing to accept the domestic adjustments needed to sustain it.

Second, when forced to choose between a fixed exchange rate and domestic economic autonomy, governments have opted for domestic economic autonomy. They have done so because domestic adjustment is costly. In the short run, the country with the deficit must accept falling output, rising unemployment, and recession in order to maintain its fixed exchange rate. As American behavior in the Bretton Woods system illustrates, governments are rarely willing to do so. The country with the surplus must accept higher inflation, and as Germany's behavior in the Bretton Woods system indicates, governments are no more willing to accept these costs. Governments in the advanced industrialized countries have been unwilling to pay the domestic economic costs in order to maintain fixed exchange rates against each other. Consequently, the world's largest countries have allowed their currencies to float against each other since the early 1970s.

The shift to floating exchange rates did not reflect agreement among governments that the international monetary system would perform better under floating rates than under fixed rates (although many economists did argue that it would). Instead, the shift to floating exchange rates reflected the political conclusion that fixed exchange rates were too costly. Thus, the answer to the question posed in this chapter's introduction is that we live in a world of floating exchange rates because politics makes governments unwilling to accept the domestic costs imposed by fixed exchange rates.

Key Terms

Balance of Payments

Balance-of-Payments Adjustment

Bretton Woods System

Capital Account

Conditionality

Current Account

Devaluation

Dollar Glut

Dollar Overhang

Executive Board

Exchange-Rate System

Exchange Restrictions

Fixed Exchange-Rate System

Fixed-but-adjustable Exchange-Rate System

Floating Exchange-Rate System

Foreign Exchange Market

Foreign Exchange Market Intervention

Foreign Exchange Reserves

Fundamental Disequilibrium

Managed Float

Primary Reserve Asset

Revaluation

Speculative Attacks

Stabilization Fund

Web Links

Visit the International Monetary Fund at *www.IMF.org.*

Suggestions for Further Reading

Perhaps the most readable account of the evolution of the international monetary system during the last 100 years is Barry J. Eichengreen, *Globalizing Capital: A History of the International Monetary System* (Princeton: Princeton University Press, 1996). For a detailed account of the interwar period, see Barry J. Eichengreen, *Golden Fetters* (Oxford: Oxford University Press, 1994).

For further exploration of the Bretton Woods System, see Robert Solomon, *The International Monetary System, 1945–1976: An Insider's View* (New York: Harper & Row Publishers, 1977); Joanne Gowa, *Closing the Gold Window: Domestic Politics and the End of Bretton Woods* (Ithaca: Cornell University Press, 1983), and Francis J. Gavin, *Gold, Dollars, and Power: the Politics of International Monetary Relations, 1958–1971* (Chapel Hill: University of North Carolina Press, 2004).

CHAPTER 11

Contemporary International Monetary Arrangements

Governments abandoned the Bretton Woods system because they wanted more domestic economic autonomy. The exchange-rate system they have lived with ever since has delivered this autonomy. Over the last 30 years, the advanced industrialized countries have been able to manage their domestic economies with much greater independence than they ever had under Bretton Woods. The price of this enhanced autonomy, however, has been large exchange-rate movements. Exchange-rate changes of 25 percent per year have been common since 1973, and these large currency movements have been somewhat disruptive to national economies. Governments have responded to the changes by engaging in cooperation, to varying degrees and with varying duration, in order to try to limit exchange-rate movements. The story of the contemporary international monetary system, therefore, is in many respects a story about the search for the elusive ideal balance between domestic economic autonomy and exchange-rate stability.

This search has been conducted under the watchful eyes of ever more deeply integrated international financial markets. Whereas most advanced industrialized countries used a variety of measures to prohibit capital flows under the Bretton Woods system, they all eliminated such controls beginning in the late 1970s. As they did, the amount of capital that crossed international borders grew sharply. As international capital flows increased, governments discovered that the trade-off between exchange-rate stability and domestic economic autonomy sharpened. Whereas variants of fixed-but-adjustable exchange-rate systems might once have offered the possibility of reconciling stable exchange rates with domestic autonomy, it appears that such systems are no longer a viable policy option. Consequently, while governments search for a balance between autonomy and stability, international financial markets increasingly force them to choose one or the other exclusively.

This chapter examines the contemporary system in detail. We look first at the causes and consequences of international financial integration. We then turn our attention to how the system of floating exchange rates has operated, with a particular

146–68; Cohen 1996). Governments that were determined to reduce the state's involvement in the economy came to power in many advanced industrialized countries in the early 1980s. Many liberalized domestic financial markets and dismantled capital controls. One of the first to do so was Great Britain. The British Conservative Party, led by Margaret Thatcher, gained a parliamentary majority in the spring of 1979. In October, Thatcher eliminated Britain's capital controls. It has even been reported that she instructed the British Treasury to destroy all documents pertaining to capital controls, to make it difficult for a future government to reimpose them. Overnight, therefore, Britain abandoned its 40-year effort to insulate its national financial system from international financial flows. Other EU governments dismantled capital controls in the late 1980s as part of the single-market project. (See Story and Walter 1997, 254–257.) By the early 1990s, few governments in the advanced industrialized world placed any restrictions on cross-border capital flows.

Liberalization has not been limited to the advanced industrialized countries. Many developing countries have also become more deeply integrated into the international financial system since the late 1980s. The World Bank (1997) estimates that only 2 developing countries were "highly integrated" into the international financial system in the late 1980s. But by 1994, 13 developing countries were highly integrated into the international financial system, and 24 more had reached a moderate level of integration. As a consequence, financial capital began to flow to developing countries. In 1996, $240 billion of foreign capital flowed into developing countries, more than three times the amount that had flowed into them in the late 1970s. By the end of the decade, developing countries were receiving about 30 percent of total global equity capital flows, compared with only about 2 percent in the late 1980s. As with foreign direct investment, the flows of financial capital to the developing world have been concentrated in a small number of countries. Twelve developing countries account for about 80 percent of all private capital flows to the developing world. These countries should look familiar by now; they include the East Asian economies and China, as well as a few Latin America countries, notably Brazil, Mexico, and Argentina. We will examine capital flows to developing countries in greater detail in Chapters 14 and 15.

International financial flows have risen dramatically since the mid-1970s. New international bank loans and bond issues grew from $100 billion in 1975 to almost $900 billion in 1998. Between 1986 and 1998, the average *daily* turnover in foreign exchange markets grew from $850 billion to $1.5 trillion. By 2004, daily turnover had reached a new peak at $1.9 trillion (Bank for International Settlements 2005). The most important consequence of international financial integration for our purposes is that it has greatly complicated management of the exchange rate. On the one hand, capital flows and the underlying current-account imbalances they finance have contributed to large and often disruptive exchange-rate movements. Governments have responded by trying to limit those movements. Yet, large capital flows have substantially raised the cost of doing so. In essence, in the current system, governments can stabilize exchange rates only if they fully surrender domestic economic autonomy by entering permanently fixed exchange-rate systems. International financial integration, therefore, has led to dissatisfaction with floating exchange rates and made it more difficult to move toward a system that provides more stability.

A CLOSER LOOK

The Unholy Trinity

We can deepen our understanding of the trade-off between domestic economic autonomy and exchange-rate stability with the use of a concept called "the Unholy Trinity." The concept starts from the recognition that governments have three policy goals, each of which is desirable in its own right: (1) a fixed exchange rate, (2) autonomy of monetary policy (using monetary policy to manage the domestic economy), and (3) capital mobility (allowing financial capital to flow freely into and out of the domestic financial system). It then tells us that a government can achieve only two of these three goals simultaneously. If a government wants monetary policy autonomy, it must choose between capital mobility and a fixed exchange rate. If a government wants a fixed exchange rate, it must choose between monetary policy autonomy and capital mobility.

An example illustrates this trade-off in practice. In early 1981, France was maintaining a fixed exchange rate within the European monetary system. In spite of this commitment, it adopted an expansionary monetary policy and cut French interest rates. France was relatively open to capital flows, so financial markets responded to the lower interest rates by selling francs and purchasing foreign currencies. These capital outflows produced an imbalance in the foreign exchange market. Demand for the franc fell, and it began to depreciate within the European monetary system.

If France wanted to maintain the fixed exchange rate, it had to intervene in the foreign exchange market. Intervention would reduce the supply of francs, thereby causing French interest rates to rise and tightening monetary policy. The franc would stabilize once French interest rates again equaled interest rates in foreign countries. Thus, to defend the exchange rate, France would have to reverse its initial monetary expansion. Because France was unwilling to raise interest rates, it was forced to devalue the franc. Given capital mobility, therefore, France was forced to choose between using monetary policy to stimulate the French economy and using monetary policy to maintain a fixed exchange rate.

The French government could have maintained the fixed exchange rate *and* used monetary policy to manage the domestic economy (at least for a while) if it had prevented capital flows. Suppose France implemented capital controls and then cut interest rates and expanded the money supply. The fall in French interest rates would then have created an incentive for capital to move out of France, but the capital controls would have prevented it from actually doing so. Without capital outflows, no large imbalance would develop in the foreign exchange market, and the franc would not depreciate. Thus, a government that prohibits capital flows can maintain a fixed exchange rate and retain monetary policy autonomy.

Restricting capital mobility, however, does not provide complete autonomy; it merely relaxes the trade-off between exchange-rate stability and autonomy. Even if France had prohibited capital flows before embarking on its monetary expansion, it would have been forced eventually to choose between the fixed exchange rate and the monetary expansion. It would have been forced to do so because the monetary expansion would have generated a current-account deficit as greater demand led to

Continued

rising imports. The current-account deficit would in turn generate an imbalance in the foreign exchange market, causing the franc to depreciate. France would then have to intervene to prevent this depreciation. Continued intervention would eventually exhaust France's foreign exchange reserves. France would then have to either allow the franc to depreciate or tighten monetary policy. Thus, even if capital flows are restricted, France still faces a trade-off between exchange-rate stability and monetary autonomy.

The trade-off is stricter in a world with capital flows, however, than it is in a world without capital flows, for two reasons. First, when capital is mobile, imbalances arise rapidly following a change in monetary policy. In a world without capital flows, imbalances arise slowly as the current account moves into deficit. Second, in a world with capital flows, imbalances can be very, very large. The imbalance equals the difference between large capital outflows and much smaller capital inflows. This difference can be as much as billions of dollars per day. In a such a without capital flows, imbalances remain pretty small. In such a world, imbalances equal the gap between imports and exports, and while this gap might be large over the course of the year, on any given day it will be relatively small and will never approach the multibillion-dollar gaps that characterize a world with capital flows.

Because imbalances are smaller and emerge more slowly in a world without capital flows, a government's foreign exchange reserves last longer than they do when capital is mobile. The large imbalances generated by capital outflows can rapidly exhaust a government's foreign exchange reserves; indeed, a government can run through its reserves in a day or two. France spent $32 billion in a single week defending the franc against a speculative attack in 1992. In a similar vein, Great Britain spent half of its foreign exchange reserves in two days. In a world without capital flows, the smaller imbalances generated by current-account deficits do not exhaust a government's foreign exchange reserves nearly so quickly. A government can pursue monetary expansion and spend its reserves defending the exchange rate over the course of the year. Still, reserves will eventually run out, and when they do, the government will be forced to tighten monetary policy or float the currency. Prohibiting capital flows, therefore, doesn't eliminate the trade-off between monetary policy autonomy and exchange-rate stability, but it does relax it substantially.

Life Under Floating Exchange Rates

Governments abandoned the Bretton Woods system because they wanted greater domestic economic autonomy. They were willing to accept less exchange-rate stability as the necessary price for attaining this autonomy. How much autonomy have they enjoyed, and how much exchange-rate instability have they had to accept as the price for their domestic economic autonomy? We look at each side of this "balance sheet."

Governments hoped to gain domestic autonomy in two ways. First, they hoped to gain the ability to conduct independent national monetary policies. Practically speaking, this means that one government could pursue an expansionary monetary policy while another could pursue a restrictive monetary policy. With monetary policies on distinct trajectories, the exchange rate would move. Consequently, macroeconomic developments in one country could evolve independently from macroeconomic developments in other countries. Second, governments hoped that adjustment in response to exogenous economic shocks would occur through exchange-rate movements rather than through changes in domestic output. No longer would governments be forced to contract their money supplies and push their economies into recession in order to eliminate an imbalance of payments. Most observers believe that floating exchange rates have delivered both forms of autonomy.

Data on the evolution of national inflation rates provide some basic evidence on the ability of governments to pursue independent monetary policies (Krugman and Obstfeld 2003, 590–591). In a fixed exchange-rate system in which governments enjoy little autonomy, inflation rates in all countries should remain close together. Conversely, if governments enjoy considerable autonomy, we would expect to see greater variation in national inflation rates. Figure 11.1 presents data on inflation rates in the United States, Western Europe, and Japan between 1967 and 1989. The data clearly show that national inflation rates remained close together throughout the late 1960s even as average inflation rose. This relationship suggests that governments enjoyed little domestic economic autonomy under the Bretton Woods system—and eventually, as we saw in Chapter 10, it was Germany's unwillingness to accept the higher inflation caused by intervening to support the dollar that led to the system's collapse.

The gap between the lowest and the highest inflation rates widened substantially following the shift to floating exchange rates in 1973. No longer bound to use monetary policies to support the fixed exchange rate, governments could direct those policies toward achieving their domestic economic objectives. The widening gap in national inflation rates so evident in Figure 11.1 suggests two things. First, governments

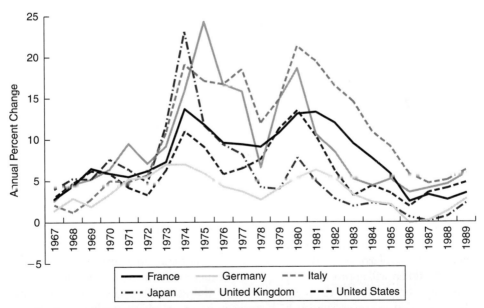

Figure 11.1　Annual Inflation Rates in the Advanced Industrialized Countries.
Sources: 1970–1989 from the IMF, *http://www.imf.org/external/pubs/ft/weo/2002/01/data/pcpi_b.csv.*
1967–1969: France, Germany, and Italy from Krugman and Obstfeld p. 562; United States from *Economic Report of the President, http://www.gpoaccess.gov/eop/tables04.html#erp4;* Japan from Keizai Koho Center, *http://www.kkc-usa.org/index.cfm/1825.*

wanted to pursue distinct goals, with some more concerned about stemming inflation and others more concerned with preventing recession. Second, each government was able to pursue its own domestic economic objective with few external constraints. As a consequence, the gap between national inflation rates widened substantially during the 1970s, and governments were much more able to pursue independent domestic economic goals under the system of floating rates than they were under Bretton Woods.

Governments also hoped that floating exchange rates would reduce the domestic economic cost of adjustment to exogenous economic shocks. Suppose that world demand for American exports fell or the world price of American imports rose for some reason. Both events would generate a balance-of-payments deficit. With a fixed exchange rate, the United States would have to respond to this deficit by tightening monetary policy in order to maintain the dollar peg. Monetary contraction, however, would depress domestic output and raise unemployment. By contrast, with a floating exchange rate, the government could allow the dollar to depreciate and could avoid having to push the economy into a substantial recession that would reduce output and raise unemployment.

The consensus among international economists is that floating exchange rates provided such autonomy, at least in response to major international shocks. The most significant such shock came in the 1970s in the form of sharp rises in oil prices in 1974 and again in 1979. Higher oil prices produced large payments deficits for oil-importing countries: the price of an important import rose, while exports did not increase enough to cover this new expense. Few governments would have been willing to accept the severe domestic economic costs required to adjust to these higher oil prices under fixed exchange rates. The advanced industrialized countries did experience very slow economic growth and rising unemployment throughout the seventies, in large part due to domestic adjustment to higher energy prices. Thus, countries did not fully escape such adjustment. Yet, most economists believe that the fall in output and the rise in unemployment would both have been much greater had governments tried to maintain fixed exchange rates rather than allow their currencies to float (Krugman and Obstfeld 2003, 579).

Floating exchange rates, therefore, have provided considerably more domestic economic autonomy than governments enjoyed under Bretton Woods. Governments knew that this gain would come at the price of less exchange-rate stability, but they have been surprised by how much exchange rates actually move and have been concerned about the impact of these movements on domestic and international economic activity. Exchange rates have become substantially less stable in two distinct ways. On the one hand, they have become considerably more volatile since 1973. **Exchange-rate volatility** refers to short-run movements in which a currency appreciates by one or two percentage points in one month and then depreciates by the same amount the next. Volatility is caused by short-term imbalances between the supply of and demand for individual currencies in international financial markets. If people purchasing American financial assets, for example, are seeking more dollars than others are willing to sell, the dollar will appreciate. If people are selling more dollars than others are willing to buy, the dollar will depreciate. Volatility, therefore, emerges from short-term imbalances that necessarily arise in foreign exchange markets conducting between $1 trillion and $1.5 trillion worth of business per day.

Exchange rates have also been subject to longer term misalignments. **Exchange-rate misalignments** are large exchange-rate changes over a relatively long period of time. Figure 11.2 illustrates the exchange rates of the dollar, the yen, the German mark, and the euro between 1979 and 2003. The currency movements depicted represent changes in the value of the dollar, yen, mark, and now the euro, by as much as 50 percent in only one or two years. Such misalignments also arise from capital flows, but rather than being caused by short-term imbalances, they are caused by financial flows that finance large current-account imbalances. The appreciation of the dollar in the first half of the 1980s, for example, was caused by American macroeconomic and current-account imbalances. In the early 1980s, the Reagan administration cut taxes and increased spending, causing the budget deficit and the current-account deficit to widen sharply. The widening-current account deficit required larger capital inflows, and U.S. interest rates rose sharply to attract those inflows. As capital responded to the high American interest rates, the demand for the dollar rose substantially and caused the dollar to appreciate against the yen and the mark. The sharp appreciation of the dollar was therefore a consequence of the inflows of capital required to finance the widening U.S. current-account deficit. More broadly, exchange rate misalignments are driven by the international financial flows that result from underlying macroeconomic and current-account imbalances.

These exchange-rate movements disrupt international economic exchange. Short-term volatility makes it difficult for businesses to predict the profitability of international trade. Suppose you are an American producer who exports to the European Union and is paid by the importer in euros. You sign a contract establishing the euro price you will receive for your goods, send the goods, and expect payment in 60 days. Say that the dollar is trading for 1 euro on the day you ship your goods, but falls to 1.05 euros on the day you receive payment. Then the dollar amount of your sale, and therefore your profit, has fallen by 5 percent between the time the contract is signed and payment

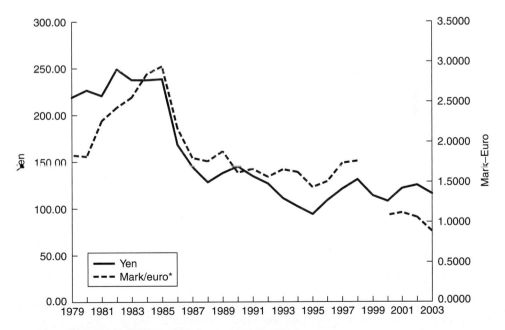

*From 2000, data are for the dollar–euro exchange rate.

Figure 11.2 Dollar's Value Against the Yen, the Mark, and the Euro.
Source: Economic Report of the President, 2004.

is made. Because exchange-rate volatility makes it difficult to predict the profitability of trade, businesses may become less willing to engage in trade. After all, most businesses operate on a pretty small profit margin—5 to 9 percent. Thus, small exchange-rate movements can make a big impact on profitability. Volatility may be more of a problem in theory, however, than in practice. Financial markets have responded to greater exchange-rate volatility by creating instruments that allow businesses to protect themselves against currency risk. Businesses can purchase options to buy a foreign currency 30, 60, or 90 days in the future at today's exchange rate, thereby protecting themselves against short-term exchange-rate movements. Consequently, economists disagree about the extent to which volatility actually does depress international trade.

Misalignments also complicate the planning of international transactions. Businesses cannot insure themselves against misalignments because financial markets do not provide insurance against currency movements more than one year in the future. As a result, businesses that engage in international trade and investment are fully exposed to large and persistent exchange-rate movements. Such exposure can discourage investment. Imagine, for example, that you are contemplating building a factory in the United States. Exchange-rate movements will influence the amount that you will be able to export and the amount of import competition that you will face. If the dollar is weak, then the investment will be profitable: you will be able to export your goods, and you will face little competition from imports in the domestic market. If the dollar is strong, however, the investment may not be profitable: your goods will be uncompetitive on international markets, and imports will crowd your goods out of the domestic market. The profitability of your contemplated investment, therefore, depends in part on what happens to the dollar's exchange rate during the productive life of your factory. Given the changes in the dollar's value over the past 20 years, can you confidently predict what will happen to the dollar over the next 10? If not, will you make the investment, or is it too risky? Thus, a reduction in investment is one possible consequence of the uncertainty generated by currency misalignments.

Misalignments can also spark political demands for trade protection. The strong dollar of the early 1980s, for example, harmed American producers. Manufacturing industries began to confront intense import competition. Caterpillar, for example, the American producer of earthmoving machines, saw its exports fall from $3.5 billion in 1981 to $1.6 billion in 1983 (Funabashi 1988, 71). American agricultural producers also suffered, losing $8.5 billion worth of exports between 1981 and 1985 (Funabashi 1988, 69). Manufacturing industries and agricultural producers turned to the political system for relief, pressuring Congress to protect them from imports. Congress was responsive to these pressures. In April of 1985, the U.S. Senate unanimously passed an anti-Japan resolution that accused the Japanese of being closed to American exports, and other protectionist legislation began making its way through the House of Representatives (Funabashi 1988, 73). The appreciation of the dollar therefore spilled over into trade politics, where it sparked demands for "fair trade" and strengthened congressional support for protectionist legislation.

While governments have enjoyed greater domestic economic autonomy than they had under Bretton Woods, they have accepted less stable exchange rates as the price for doing so. Do the gains outweigh the costs? There is no single answer to this question. Economists disagree about how much autonomy governments actually enjoy under floating exchange rates, and they disagree about the economic costs imposed by exchange-rate movements. Some believe that the benefits are small and the costs are substantial; thus, they advocate moving back toward a system of more heavily managed exchange rates. Others argue that the benefits are substantial, while exchange-rate movements impose few costs. For this group, the current system is the best choice.

Managing Exchange Rates in a World of Mobile Capital

What matters most for our purpose is what governments think. The way governments have responded to exchange-rate movements suggests that they believe that the costs imposed by these movements are too high. No government has been willing to accept a pure float, and most have attempted to manage their exchange rate to some degree. Governments disagree, however, about how costly the movements are and about how much domestic autonomy they are willing to give up in order to limit them. Consequently, some groups of countries have been more willing to manage their exchange rates than others. Cooperation has been deepest within the European Union, in which member governments have engaged in regularized and institutionalized cooperation to minimize currency movements. Cooperation has been more sporadic and less formalized among the broader group of advanced industrialized countries. These governments have periodically worked together to limit movements of the dollar, the yen, and the mark (and now the euro) and have occasionally discussed deeper forms of cooperation. Still, while there have been sporadic calls for more sustained efforts to cooperatively manage exchange rates among the advanced industrialized countries, the rising volume of deepening international financial markets has made such cooperation increasingly costly.

Exchange-Rate Cooperation in the European Union

Governments in the European Union have pursued formal and institutionalized exchange-rate cooperation since the late 1970s. European governments have desired more stable intra-European exchange rates for two reasons. First, exchange rate instability is costly for the typical EU country, which is highly open to trade and which trades most with other EU countries. As a result, exchange-rate movements within the European Union are much more disruptive to individual EU countries than they are in the broader international monetary system. (See Frieden 1996.) In other words, the cost of floating in the European Union is so high that European governments are more willing to sacrifice domestic autonomy to stabilize their exchange rates.

Second, most European governments do not consider the loss of domestic economic autonomy to be very costly. While European governments that participated in EU exchange-rate systems lost the ability to pursue independent monetary policies, by the early 1980s few governments thought this sacrifice to be costly. Meaningful costs arise when governments want to pursue different monetary policies but cannot. In such cases, one government must accept a policy it does not want. During the 1970s, for example, EU governments moved on divergent paths. Some, such as the French and the Italians, pursued expansionary macroeconomic policies that boosted their inflation rates. Others, such as Germany and the Netherlands, were more conservative and emphasized the maintenance of low inflation. In this environment, each government guarded its economic independence jealously, and participating in a common exchange-rate system would have been quite costly.

Giving up domestic autonomy is not costly when all governments are pursuing the same domestic objective. When all governments use monetary policy to achieve the same objective, no one will be forced to follow a policy that it does not like. Consequently, giving up domestic autonomy is not particularly costly. By the late 1970s, most EU governments believed that reducing inflation had to be their chief objective, and as a consequence, almost all governments began to use monetary policy to restrict inflation. Because all governments were pursuing low inflation, all could participate in a common exchange-rate system without any having to sacrifice its ability to achieve its domestic economic objective. Thus, the cost of participating in a fixed exchange-rate system was quite low. Accordingly, facing potentially large gains from stabilizing exchange rates and low costs from sacrificing domestic economic autonomy, the European Union moved to establish a regional exchange-rate system in the late 1970s.

The resulting exchange-rate system, called the **European monetary system** (EMS), began operation in 1979. The EMS was a fixed-but-adjustable system in which governments established a central parity against a basket of EU currencies called the European Currency Unit (ECU). Central parities against the ECU were then used to create bilateral exchange rates between all EU currencies. EU governments were required to maintain their currency's bilateral exchange rate within 2.25 percent of its central bilateral rate. In practice, however, the EMS quickly evolved into an exchange rate system centered upon Germany.

It made sense to center the system on Germany. The German mark was the strongest EU currency, and German inflation was the lowest in the union. Moreover, the German central bank, the *Bundesbank*, was the most reluctant participant in the EMS. The *Bundesbank* was concerned that it would be forced to continually intervene in the foreign exchange market to support the weaker European currencies. Continued intervention to defend these weaker currencies would raise German inflation, just as intervention to defend the dollar had done under Bretton Woods. The *Bundesbank* was thus quite reluctant to engage in foreign exchange market intervention to fix the mark against other EU currencies. Instead, the *Bundesbank* used German monetary policy to maintain low inflation in Germany, and the other EU governments engaged in foreign exchange market intervention to fix their currencies to the mark. The burden of maintaining fixed exchange rates therefore fell principally upon the countries with high inflation.

Few observers initially gave the EMS much chance of success. Inflation rates averaged just above 10 percent in EU countries, while German inflation stood below 5 percent. Such divergent rates of inflation, reflecting substantially different monetary policies, could easily pull the system apart. Indeed, the EMS got off to a rocky start. Currency realignments were frequent in the system's first years of operation, and a conflict between France and Germany almost destroyed the system in 1981–1983. Conflict arose when newly elected French president François Mitterrand adopted an expansionary macroeconomic policy in 1981. This expansion caused French inflation to rise, the French balance of payments to deteriorate, and the franc to weaken in the EMS. Mitterrand blamed the franc's weakness on the restrictive macroeconomic policies pursued in Germany (and the other EU countries), refused to alter French policy, and demanded that Germany loosen its policy in line with France. After 18 months of uncertainty about whether Mitterrand would remove the franc from the system or accept the system's constraints, he reversed course and adopted restrictive macroeconomic policies. The EMS stabilized in the following years. During the next five years, inflation rates in EU countries converged and currency realignments became infrequent. The EMS had defied its critics' expectations. The EMS worked, however, primarily because its member governments placed high value on stable exchange rates and because they all pursued the same domestic economic objective: keeping inflation low. Consequently, participation in the system did not require any government to give up the pursuit of its domestic objectives.

The EU began to plan for monetary union in 1988. In a **monetary union,** governments permanently fix their exchange rates and introduce a single currency. The European Union's push for monetary union emerged from two factors. First, European governments began to reinvigorate the process of economic integration during the late 1980s. New projects had been rare during the 1970s, as the oil shock, the collapse of the Bretton Woods system, and the ensuing economic stagnation made few governments willing to open their economies any further. In the mid-1980s, EU governments relaunched integration by agreeing to eliminate the remaining barriers to intra-EU trade and capital flows. The Single European Act, as this agreement was called, was directly linked to monetary union because many EU officials believed that the gains from a single market could be realized only with a single currency. (See Emerson 1992.) In particular, and for reasons we explore in greater detail shortly, governments believed that the EMS would be vulnerable to speculative attacks once they had eliminated all restrictions on intra-European capital flows. The completion of the single market, therefore, created strong pressures to shift from the EMS to monetary union.

At the same time, many EU governments were becoming dissatisfied with the asymmetry at the center of the EMS. When they were striving to reduce inflation, most governments were content to place Germany at the center of the EMS and to relieve the *Bundesbank* of the need to engage in foreign exchange intervention. They were less content with this asymmetry once inflation had fallen. Many European governments began to question why the *Bundesbank* should continue to set monetary policy for the system as a whole. They argued that the *Bundesbank* should be required to conduct a share of the foreign exchange market intervention necessary to fix the mark in the EMU. In addition, because German monetary policy was transmitted by the EMS throughout the European Union, the other EU governments argued that they should have some influence over that policy. By 1987, France and Italy, along with some officials in the European Commission, were suggesting that it was time to reform the EMS in order to reduce Germany's privileged role in the system (Oatley 1997). Monetary union thus emerged from the broader project of completing the single market and from narrower concerns about the asymmetry of the way the burden was shared within the EMS.

European governments spent most of the 1990s preparing to enter monetary union. The Maastricht Treaty establishing monetary union was completed in December 1991. Over the next eight years, EU governments completed the task of economic convergence, giving particular attention to maintaining low inflation, reducing government budget deficits, and trying to reduce government debt. In addition, governments created the infrastructure for monetary union. A new European Central Bank (ECB) was created, the accounting systems in the private and public sectors were altered, and the new currency unit was designed and produced. On January 1, 1999, governments took the penultimate step toward monetary union by permanently fixing their exchange rates, transferring authority over monetary policy to the ECB, and introducing the electronic euro. Governments took the final step in January 2002, introducing euro bills and coins and removing national currencies from circulation. At present, Economic and monetary union (EMU) does not incorporate all EU member countries: Great Britain, Denmark, and Sweden have opted out of the project. Each retains the right to adopt the single currency at a later date, but to date none have indicated when, or even if, they will do so.

The EU, therefore, has shifted away from floating exchange rates for intra-European transactions. It has done so in a series of steps, first creating the EMS, then negotiating and preparing for EMU, and finally establishing the single currency. EU governments have been willing to embrace such rigid exchange rates because exchange rate movements disrupted intra-EU trade, and with all governments giving priority to achieving and maintaining low inflation, the required sacrifice of domestic economic autonomy was not considered costly.

Exchange-Rate Cooperation in the Group of 5

There has been much less cooperation with regard to managing exchange rates among the United States, Germany, Japan, Great Britain, and France. Known collectively as the **Group of 5,** or G5, these countries have periodically cooperated to manage exchange rates during the last 20 years. The most recent high point of such cooperation occurred in the late 1980s. Cooperation emerged in 1985 following an extended period during which the United States pursued a policy of **benign neglect** toward the dollar's exchange rate. Under this policy, the first Reagan administration did nothing as the U.S. budget and current-account deficits widened and capital inflows caused the dollar to appreciate sharply. Rather than viewing the dollar's appreciation with alarm, the Reagan administration initially proclaimed that it was a symbol of American economic strength. But the harm that the strong dollar caused American manufacturing soon became apparent as protectionist forces gained strength in the U.S. Congress. This shift propelled the Reagan administration to reevaluate its dollar policy. In the first year of Reagan's second term in office, the administration considered what steps it could take to stop the dollar's climb and engineer a gradual depreciation. Of particular importance was the decision to appoint James A. Baker, III, as secretary of the treasury, and one of Baker's first objectives in that capacity was to reduce the dollar's value.

The moment looked favorable. The dollar's appreciation appeared to have peaked, and in the spring of 1985 the dollar actually began to depreciate. Baker initiated discussions with the German, Japanese, British, and French governments to see whether they would be willing to cooperate in order to achieve a substantial realignment of the dollar, yen, and mark (Funabashi 1988). Initial discussions led to a meeting of the G5 finance ministers at the Plaza Hotel in New York City on September 22, 1985. In a compact known as the **Plaza Accord,** the five governments agreed to reduce the value of the dollar against the Japanese yen and the German mark by 10 to 12 percent. To achieve this realignment,

POLICY ANALYSIS AND DEBATE

The Dollar versus the Euro?

Question
Should the United States take measures to ensure that the dollar retains its dominant role in international finance?

Overview
The creation of the euro brings forth a potential rival to the U.S. dollar's dominance of the international monetary system. Since World War II, the dollar has been the preeminent international currency and the currency most often held as foreign exchange reserves. It is also the currency most often used in foreign exchange market transactions and is the favored currency for settling international claims. Finally, it is the currency most often held by individuals in countries with chronically unstable currencies. The euro, backed by the economic power of the European Union and supported by an independent European Central Bank, now offers a potentially appealing alternative to the dollar.

Some observers have suggested that, with the advent of the euro, we should witness a shift in currency use across the globe. Governments that had held only dollars in their foreign reserves should accumulate and hold euros in order to diversify their holdings. Trade that has traditionally been priced in dollars, such as world trade in oil, may be increasingly priced in euros. People who once looked to the dollar as the best guarantor of their purchasing power might turn instead to the euro, which might then replace the dollar as the world's most important currency. What, if anything, should the United States do in response to the potential challenge posed by the euro?

Policy Options
- Take steps to ensure that the dollar remains the dominant currency in global markets.
- Allow market forces to determine whether the dollar or the euro plays the dominant role during the 21st century.

Policy Analysis
- What benefits does the United States gain from the dollar's dominance of global finance?
- If the euro does threaten to assume the dollar's current role, what would the United States have to do to secure the dollar's position?

Take a Position
- Which option do you prefer? Justify your choice.
- What criticisms of your position should you anticipate? How would you defend your recommendation against these criticisms?

Resources
Online: Search for Ben S. Bernanke, "The Euro at 5—Ready for a Global Role?" Also interesting is C. Fred Bergsten's evaluation; search for "The Euro and the Dollar: Toward a Finance G2?" The European Central Bank considers the euro's international role in the online pamphlet "Review of the International Role of the Euro."

Continued

In Print: Patricia Pollard, "The Creation of the Euro and the Role of the Dollar in International Markets," *Federal Reserve Bank of St. Louis Review* 83 (September 2001): 17–36; C. Fred Bergsten, 1997. "The Dollar and the Euro," *Foreign Affairs* 76 (July–August 1997): 83–95. Special issue of the *Journal of Policy Modeling* (July 2002). For an examination of the shift from a system dominated by the pound to one dominated by the dollar, see Susan Strange, *Sterling and British Policy: A Political Study of an International Currency in Decline* (New York: Oxford University Press, 1971).

governments consented to intervene in the foreign exchange markets whenever it appeared that the market was pushing the dollar up. In other words, rather than pushing the dollar down, the G5 would try to prevent the market from pushing it up. They agreed to allocate $18 billion to these interventions, with the United States, Germany, and Japan each bearing 25 percent of the total costs, and Britain and France sharing the other 25 percent. Over the next 15 months, governments intervened in the foreign exchange market whenever the dollar's depreciation appeared to be slowing or threatening to reverse. By early 1987, the dollar had fallen almost 40 percent from its peak.

The Plaza Accord was followed by discussion among the G5 governments about deeper exchange-rate cooperation. The G5 governments discussed the creation of a variant of fixed-but-adjustable exchange rates called a **target zone,** in which all currencies would have a central parity surrounded by wide margins—one prominent proposal advocated margins of plus or minus 10 percent—within which the exchange rate would be allowed to fluctuate (Williamson 1983; Solomon 1999). When a currency moved outside the margins, governments would be obligated to intervene in the foreign exchange market or alter domestic interest rates in order to bring it back inside.

The G5 governments also discussed coordinating macroeconomic policy to promote current account adjustment in the United States, Germany, and Japan. The United States pressured Germany and Japan to adopt more expansionary fiscal policies, largely by reducing taxes, in order to spur domestic demand and increase imports. For its part, the United States would adopt a more restrictive fiscal policy to reduce the size of its budget deficit, thereby decreasing domestic demand and U.S. imports. In conjunction with the dollar's depreciation, the coordination of fiscal policies would promote current-account adjustment. These discussions failed to achieve concrete results. Both proposals required governments to use macroeconomic policy to manage the exchange rate, and governments were no more willing to accept such constraints on their domestic economic autonomy in the late 1980s than they had been in the early 1970s.

Interest in exchange-rate cooperation among the G5 has declined substantially since the late 1980s. In large part, this reflects a belief that foreign exchange market intervention has little influence on exchange rates. With a daily turnover of about $1 trillion in the foreign exchange market, governments simply lack the resources required to make more than a small dent in the supply of or demand for individual currencies. Moreover, most governments sterilize their foreign exchange market interventions. In **sterilized intervention,** a government first intervenes in the foreign exchange market and then reverses its operations in the domestic securities market. For example, if the United States purchased $4 billion in the foreign exchange market, it would turn around and buy $4 billion worth of Treasury securities in the securities market, thus injecting $4 billion back into the

American money supply. The net effect of the two operations on the U.S. money supply is zero. There is little belief that such practices can move currencies by substantial amounts.

Some governments are more skeptical about the utility of intervention than others. American officials are quite skeptical, and their skepticism is reflected in the fact that the United States has intervened only twice between September 1995 and October 2003 (Federal Reserve Bank of New York 2003). The European Central Bank also has been reluctant to engage in intervention; its annual reports indicate that it did not intervene at all between January 2001 and December 2003 and did so only four times in 2000. Japan is much more willing to intervene and did so 36 times between January 2000 and March 2003. Consequently, only a few episodes of coordinated foreign exchange market intervention have occurred since 1990. These interventions have been much less ambitious than the Plaza Accord, however, and generally have been undertaken in response to market instabilities. The rapid depreciation of the dollar in late 1994 and early 1995, for example, prompted coordinated intervention by 13 central banks. Only two episodes of coordinated intervention have occurred since 1995, the most recent coming in 2000 to slow the depreciation of the euro (Schwartz 1996, 2000).

The G5 today faces issues quite similar to those posed by American deficits during the 1980s. While the United States has run current-account deficits for 30 years, these deficits have recently reached historic levels, growing to almost 5 percent of GDP in 2003 and 2004. (See Figure 11.3.) American deficits are offset by large current-account surpluses in other parts of the world. Japan enjoys the largest surplus, which has averaged about 3 percent of its GDP since 2001. The East Asian newly industrializing countries also have large current-account surpluses, equal to more than 7 percent of their combined GDP in 2003. The Euro area (the countries that participate in

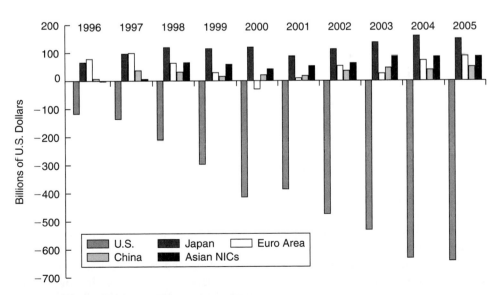

Note: Data for 2004 and 2005 are IMF estimates.

Figure 11.3   Current-Account Balances, 1996–2005.
Source: IMF *World Economic Outlook,* September 2004, pp. 236, 239. *http://imf.org/external/pubs/ft/weo/2004/02/pdf/statappx.pdf.*

the European Union's economic and monetary union), has also run a surplus, though only of about 1 percent of GDP. China runs large current-account surpluses as well. These surpluses finance the American deficit, which, overall, absorbs about 6 percent of the world's total savings (IMF 2002, 66).

As a result, the United States' foreign debt has risen rapidly. At the end of 2004, total U.S. foreign debt equaled about $8 trillion, roughly equal to 70 percent of U.S. GDP. About a quarter of this amount was owed by the U.S. government to foreign lenders. The remaining three-quarters has been borrowed by private individuals and businesses. Focusing solely on U.S. foreign liabilities (what the nation owes foreigners) overstates American foreign indebtedness. We gain a more accurate account if we subtract the foreign financial assets owned by American residents from the American financial assets owned by foreigners. This figure, called the **international investment position,** provides the net indebtedness. At the end of 2003, total foreign claims on the United States stood at $8 trillion, while American claims on foreign countries stood at $5.1 trillion, producing an international investment position for the United States of approximately −$2.9 trillion, an amount equal to about 25 percent of U.S. gross domestic product (Abaroa 2004, 37). The IMF has estimated that if the United States continues to run large current-account deficits, its international investment position could rise as high as 40 percent of U.S. GDP within the next five years (Mühleisen and Towe 2004).

There is a growing belief that the U.S. current-account deficit is unsustainable and that adjustment will come in the near future. (See e.g., Mann 2002.) The dollar's depreciation during the last two years may be a sign that this adjustment has already begun. Such adjustment, if it occurs, could follow two paths, one somewhat catastrophic and one that is a bit less costly. The more catastrophic scenario involves adjustment imposed by financial markets. If no adjustments are made, the United States is likely to continue to accumulate foreign debt. At some point, foreigners will decide that it is too risky to continue lending to the United States. If foreign lending dries up, the United States will be forced to eliminate its current-account deficit quickly. Such rapid adjustment would have severe consequences for the American economy, causing output to fall, unemployment to rise, and the American standard of living to drop sharply. Nor would the economic consequences be restricted to the United States. A sudden collapse of economic growth in the United States would reverberate around the world. Asian and European economies would suffer as their exports to the United States collapsed. A crisis involving the dollar and the American financial system could damage the international financial system.

Avoiding this path and adjusting in a more orderly fashion will require cooperation among the Group of 5. Such cooperation would be very much along the lines of the proposals advanced during the late 1980s in connection with the Plaza Accord. The United States would reduce its budget deficit, while the countries with surpluses expand demand in their countries. Macroeconomic policy coordination along these lines would reduce American imports and expand consumption in the countries with surpluses. Governments could also cooperate to ensure that the dollar's depreciation occurs gradually rather than quickly. Only time will tell whether in fact the U.S. current-account deficit is unsustainable, and if so, whether adjustment will occur smoothly through cooperation or will instead come through a crisis that imposes substantial costs on the American and global economies.

Speculative Attacks and the Prospect for Exchange-Rate Reform

Currently, there is little prospect that the Group of 5 will move toward more extensive exchange-rate cooperation in the near future. In fact, international financial integration is probably making such cooperation less, rather than more, likely. Many prominent observers of the international monetary system, such as Stanley Fischer, former first deputy managing director of the IMF, and Lawrence Summers, former secretary of the treasury in the Clinton administration, have argued that fixed-but-adjustable exchange rate systems are increasingly unworkable in a world of mobile international capital (Fischer 2001; Summers 2000).

Fixed-but-adjustable exchange-rate systems are increasingly unworkable because they are vulnerable to speculative attacks. A speculative attack can be defined as the sudden emergence of very large sales of a currency sparked by the anticipation of devaluation. In the Bretton Woods system, for example, market participants sold large volumes of dollars in anticipation of devaluation of the dollar against gold. In the early 1990s, market participants sold large volumes of British pounds, Italian lira, French francs, and other currencies in anticipation of devaluations within the EMS. Speculative attacks create large imbalances between the supply of and the demand for a particular currency in the foreign exchange market, and large balance-of-payments deficits for the country being attacked. These imbalances force the government facing an attack to intervene in the foreign exchange market to defend the exchange rate. The government will rarely hold sufficient foreign exchange reserves to correct the imbalance, however. In most instances, therefore, the government will have to raise domestic interest rates and impose domestic economic adjustments in order to support its exchange rate.

Fixed-but-adjustable exchange rates are particularly vulnerable to speculative attacks because they are based on the premise that governments can and will periodically realign exchange rates. The recognition that governments can alter exchange rates creates a perverse dynamic in financial markets. Participants in such markets will try to anticipate devaluations in order to sell the currency likely to be devalued before devaluation actually occurs. The belief that devaluation is impending can in fact be sufficient to spark a speculative attack. The attack prompts currency sales on such a scale that governments are unable (because they lack sufficient foreign exchange reserves) or unwilling (because they refuse to raise interest rates high enough) to defend the exchange rate. Devaluation thus takes place whether planned by the government or not. Thus, the central premise of fixed-but-adjustable exchange rate systems—that governments should periodically realign exchange rates—appears to be sufficient to generate speculative attacks that make it impossible to maintain such systems for extended periods.

A crisis in the EMS in 1992–1993 illustrates the dynamics of speculative attacks. The crisis developed in the wake of German economic unification in 1990. Unification accelerated German inflation, and the *Bundesbank* responded by raising interest rates.

To maintain their fixed exchange rates against the mark, other EU governments had to match German interest-rate increases. As European interest rates rose, European economies were pushed into recession. Financial markets began to question whether EU governments would be willing to endure protracted recessions simply to maintain a fixed exchange rate with Germany.

As doubts grew among market participants, they began selling the currencies they believed were the most likely candidates for devaluation. They attacked the British pound and the Italian lira first and then moved on to attack the Swedish krona, the French franc, and other currencies as well. The volume of currency sales and the amount of foreign exchange market intervention was unprecedented. The British government spent $20 billion—about half of its foreign exchange reserves—in a single day in an unsuccessful attempt to defend the pound (Eichengreen and Wyplosz 1993). The Swedish central bank spent $26 billion—an amount roughly equal to 10 percent of Sweden's GNP, or about $3,500 per Swede—in its unsuccessful defense of the krona's peg. The French government spent $32 billion in a single week to defend the franc (Eichengreen 1996, 173–174). Speculative attacks continued periodically into 1993. They ended only after governments widened the margins within which currencies were allowed to fluctuate from 2.5 percent to 15 percent. Nor is the EMS crisis unique: similar crises have occurred in developing countries. We will examine these in Chapter 15.

Such speculative attacks appear to be eliminating fixed-but-adjustable exchange rates as a viable policy option. Between 1991 and 2003, the number of countries maintaining fixed-but-adjustable exchange rates fell by almost one-half, from 98 to 51, while the number of countries with floating or permanently fixed exchange rates increased greatly. (See Figure 11.4.) In percentage terms, 62 percent of the world's countries maintained a fixed-but-adjustable exchange rate in 1991, while only 28 percent did in 2003. There has thus been a clear shift away from this exchange-rate system and toward the two extremes of floating and permanently fixed exchange rates. Many observers attribute this change to the growing difficulty of maintaining fixed-but-adjustable exchange rates in a world of internationally mobile capital. If the Group of 5 wants to stabilize exchange rates, therefore, it will probably not be able to do so by moving back toward a Bretton Woods type of system. Instead, the group will have to adopt some type of permanently fixed exchange rates, as achieved by the European Union through monetary union. There are no signs, however, that the Group of 5 is willing to consider a single currency for the international monetary system.

The alternative, of course, is to combine exchange-rate reform with renewed efforts to limit international capital flows. Recent proposals have called for the introduction of a Tobin tax on international currency transactions in order to stem speculative attacks. Named after Nobel prizewinning economist James Tobin, who first proposed the idea in 1972, a **Tobin tax** is a small tax on foreign exchange market transactions. In Tobin's proposal, this tax would be high enough to discourage short-term capital flows, but not high enough to discourage long-term capital flows or international trade. Such a tax, in Tobin's own words, would "put sand in the wheels of international finance" by slowing cross-border capital flows rather than ending them altogether. The revenues generated by this tax, some groups suggest, could be used to fund antipoverty programs in developing countries.

Few advanced industrialized countries have expressed support for the Tobin tax or for any other form of capital control. The EU created a working group in the fall of

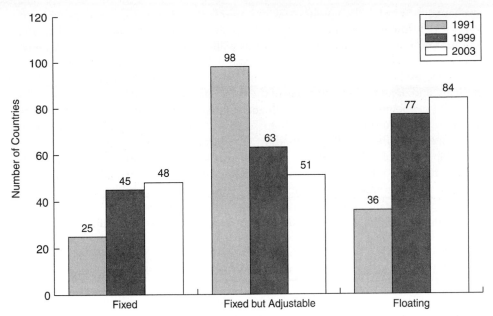

Figure 11.4 Change in Exchange-Rate Arrangements, 1991–2003.
Source: Fischer 2001; IMF 2003a.

2001 to examine the Tobin tax, as well as speculative activity in financial markets more generally. Given skepticism about such measures in many of the large EU countries, however, nothing has come from this initiative. In the wider international community, the United States has expressed no interest, and the IMF's Managing Director Horst Koehler has questioned the feasibility of implementing a Tobin tax. There is little indication, therefore, that the advanced industrialized countries are willing to reintroduce capital controls. Consequently, they will be unlikely to embark on any far-reaching effort to provide greater exchange-rate stability in the international monetary system.

Conclusion

Floating exchange rates have enabled governments to enjoy domestic monetary autonomy, but at the cost of greater exchange-rate instability. A good portion of this instability has been produced by the interaction between underlying payments imbalances and the dynamics unleashed by international financial integration. The churning of the world's foreign exchange markets has made exchange rates more volatile, with potentially harmful effects on international trade and investment, while the large capital flows needed to finance current-account imbalances have contributed to large exchange-rate misalignments that can discourage investment and spark political processes that lead to higher protectionism.

Governments in the advanced industrialized countries have responded to these developments by searching for the appropriate balance between exchange-rate stability and domestic economic autonomy. In the European Union, the high costs of exchange-rate instability combined with a perception that giving up domestic auton-omy was a low-cost sacrifice to promote exchange-rate cooperation and monetary union. The Group of 5 has been much less willing to sacrifice domestic autonomy in order to maintain stable exchange rates between the dollar, euro, and yen. Increasingly, stabilizing exchange rates requires governments to coordinate their monetary and fiscal policies, and none are willing to accept the compromises that such coordination entails.

The deepening of international financial integration has further complicated this dynamic by requiring governments to sacrifice more autonomy to maintain stable exchange rates. Because fixed-but-adjustable systems are no longer viable, exchange-rate stability among the dollar, yen, and euro may well require governments to create a monetary union of the United States, Japan, and the European Union. The contempo-rary international monetary system, therefore, poses some real dilemmas. While gov-ernments are not entirely happy with the costs imposed by exchange-rate movements, they remain unwilling to sacrifice domestic autonomy to prevent them.

Key Terms

Benign Neglect

Eurodollars

European Monetary System

Exchange-Rate Misalignments

Exchange-Rate Volatility

Group of 5

International Investment Position

Monetary Union

Plaza Accord

Sterilized Intervention

Target Zone

Tobin Tax

Web Links

Visit the International Monetary Fund at *www.IMF.org*.

The Bank for International Settlements publishes an annual report in which it surveys develop-ments in international financial markets. This report can be found at *www.BIS.org*.

You can learn more about the EU's economic and monetary union at the website maintained by the European Central Bank: *http://www.ecb.int/*.

Suggestions for Further Reading

For the evolution of the international financial system since the Second World War, see Eric Helleiner, *States and the Re-emergence of Global Finance: From Bretton Woods to the 1990s* (Ithaca: Cornell University Press, 1994), and Robert Solomon, *Money on the Move: The Revolution in International Finance since 1980* (Princeton: Princeton University Press, 1999).

For those interested in the European monetary system, see Peter Kenen, *Economic and Monetary Union in Europe: Moving beyond Maastricht* (Cambridge: Cambridge University Press, 1995), Kathleen MacNamara, *The Currency of Ideas* (Ithaca: Cornell University Press, 1997), and Thomas Oatley, *Monetary Politics: Exchange Rate Cooperation in the European Union* (Ann Arbor: University of Michigan Press, 1997).

CHAPTER 12

A Society-Centered Approach to Monetary and Exchange-Rate Politics

Our focus on the international monetary system in the last two chapters hinted at, but did not deeply explore, an important question: what determines the specific exchange-rate policies that governments adopt? More specifically, why do some governments fix their exchange rates while others float? Why do some governments prefer strong and maybe even over-valued currencies, while others prefer weak and under-valued currencies? We take up all these questions in this chapter and the next by examining two approaches to monetary and exchange-rate politics rooted in domestic politics. This chapter develops a society-centered approach—an approach which argues that governments' monetary and exchange-rate policies are shaped by politicians' responses to interest-group demands. Thus, the European Union's willingness to fix exchange rates reflects EU governments' responses to the demands of domestic interest groups. Similarly, the American reluctance to fix the dollar, or even to do much to stabilize it, reflects American policymakers' responses to the demands of American interest groups.

To understand the political dynamics of this competition, the society-centered approach emphasizes the interplay between organized interests and political institutions. This approach is based on the recognition that monetary policy and exchange-rate movements have distributional consequences. For example, when the dollar rose in value by about 30 percent against America's largest trading partners between 1995 and 2001, some groups benefited and some suffered. American businesses and consumers could import goods at lower prices. This translated into higher real incomes for consumers and lower production costs for businesses. But the strong dollar hurt others, as American exporters found it increasingly difficult to sell in foreign markets. Gaylord Container Corporation, for example, lost sales in Germany because the strong dollar made it difficult to compete against Scandinavian and Canadian producers (Hilsenrath 2001). Import-competing businesses also faced tougher foreign competition in the U.S. market. Automatic Feed Company, based outside Toledo, Ohio, makes machines that unroll 75,000-pound coils of steel for automakers. As the dollar strengthened, the firm retreated from exporting to focus on the American market, only to discover that American carmakers were buying less expensive machines from Germany (Hilsenrath 2001). For these exporters, the strong dollar yielded falling incomes.

These distributional consequences generate political competition as the winners and losers turn to the political arena to advance and defend their economic interests. Businesses that benefit from a weak dollar pressure the government for policies that will keep the dollar undervalued against foreign currencies. Thus, as the dollar rose in 2001, the National Association of Manufacturers and the Business Roundtable pressured the Bush administration to abandon its strong-dollar policy (Phillips and Sesit 2001). Businesses that benefited from a strong dollar, such as the Wall Street firms that gained from importing foreign capital, lobbied to keep the dollar strong. Exactly how this competition unfolds—which groups organize to lobby, what coalitions arise, how politicians respond to interest-group demands, which groups' interests are reflected in monetary and exchange rate policy and which groups' interests are not— are shaped by specific characteristics of the political institutions within which the competition unfolds.

The sections that follow develop this society-centered approach to monetary and exchange-rate policy. We focus first on the trade-off between domestic economic autonomy and exchange-rate stability. We examine how changes in political institutions and innovations in economic theory combined to create incentives for governments to value domestic autonomy more than exchange-rate stability. We then explore three society-centered models of monetary and exchange-rate policy. The chapter concludes by considering some weaknesses of this approach.

Electoral Politics, the Keynesian Revolution, and the Trade-off Between Domestic Autonomy and Exchange-Rate Stability

In the previous two chapters, we learned that governments confront a trade-off between exchange-rate stability and domestic economic autonomy. To maintain a fixed exchange rate, a government must surrender its ability to manage the domestic economy. To manage the domestic economy, a government must accept a floating exchange rate. While this trade-off has always been present, it is only since the 1920s that governments have chosen domestic economic autonomy over exchange-rate stability. Prior to World War I, most governments sacrificed domestic economic autonomy in order to maintain fixed exchange rates in the gold standard. Our first goal is to understand how changes in domestic politics and economic theory that occurred during the interwar period led governments to place greater value on domestic economic autonomy and attach less importance to exchange-rate stability.

The transformation of electoral systems—the rules governing who has the right to vote—throughout Western Europe following the First World War fundamentally changed the balance of power in domestic political systems. The new balance of power had tremendous repercussions on government attitudes toward economic management. Prior to the First World War, electoral systems in most West European coun-

tries were extremely restrictive. The right to vote was generally limited to males, usually 25 years or older, who met explicit property or income conditions. In European
countries with parliamentary governments, less than one-quarter of the total male
population in the relevant age group met these conditions. In Great Britain, for example, only 3.3 percent of the population could vote until 1884; reforms enacted that year
extended the right to vote to about 15 percent of the population. Even in Denmark,
where the right to vote was much broader, mass participation was restricted to elections for the lower house (the *Folketing*), and the monarch did not have to respect
lower house majorities in forming governments (Miller 1996).

European electoral systems were substantially reformed after the First World War.
By 1921, restrictive property-based electoral rules had been eliminated and universal
male suffrage had been adopted in all Western European countries. Changes in electoral laws had a profound impact on the constellation of political parties in Western
European parliaments. To illustrate this political transformation, Table 12.1 displays
the share of parliamentary seats held by each of the major political parties in a few
Western European countries before and after the First World War. Prior to World War I,
political parties of the right—Conservatives, Liberals, and Catholics—dominated
European parliaments. Although parties of the left were not totally absent from parliaments, only in one country, Belgium, did a leftist party capture a significant share of
parliament. Even there, however, the Belgian Catholic Party's parliamentary majority
meant that the political left had little influence on policy in this period.

After World War I, leftist parties—Socialists, Social Democrats, and Labour—
became large—and in some instances, the largest—parliamentary parties in the

Table 12.1
Percentages of Seats Held by Parties in Parliament, Pre- and Post-World War I

	1870–1900	1920–1930
Belgium	Catholic (46–93%)	Catholic (40%)
	Liberals (4–53%)	Liberal (12–15%)
		Workers Party (35–40%)
Denmark	Liberals (60–75%)	Social Democrats (32–40%)
	Conservatives (25–30%)	Liberals (30–35%)
		Conservative (16–20%)
France	Republicans (60–80%)	Republican Union (30–35%)
		Socialists (16–25%)
		Radical Socialists (17–25%)
Germany	Center (20%)	Social Democrats (20–30%)
	National Liberals (12–30%)	National People's Party (20%)
	Conservatives (10–20%)	Center (13%)
		People's Party (10%)
Netherlands	Liberal Union (35–53%)	Catholics (28%)
	Catholics (25%)	Social Democrats (20%)
	Anti-Revolutionary (15–25%)	Anti-Revolutionary (12%)
Britain	Conservatives (37–50%)	Conservative (40–67%)
	Liberals (26–48%)	Labour (30–47%)

Source: Mackie and Rose 1991.

Western European countries. This shift in the balance of political power within European parliaments altered the pattern of societal interests that were represented in the political process. Before World War I, the propertied interests represented by the political parties of the right had a virtual monopoly on political power, while the interests of workers were all but excluded from the political process. Following World War I, working-class interests gained an authoritative voice in national parliaments. As a consequence, in order to maintain their hold on political power, governments were forced to respond for the first time to the demands of workers.

The change in the balance of political power between the right and the left in turn had consequences for economic policy. In political systems monopolized by the right, governments had many incentives to protect the assets of the propertied classes and few incentives to adopt policies that favored workers. In practice, this meant that governments pursued policies that kept inflation to a minimum, because high inflation erodes the real value of wealth. A fixed exchange rate under the gold standard, which effectively limited a government's ability to generate inflation, was fully consistent with this policy objective.

Once the political power of workers strengthened, however, governments no longer had any incentives to give priority only to low inflation. Instead, politicians now had a competing incentive to deliver economic conditions that were more in line with workers' interests. And workers, who, on average, hold little wealth and whose standard of living thus depends heavily upon their weekly pay, have less concern about inflation. What workers care about are the employment opportunities available to them and the wages they earn in those jobs. The rise of worker power therefore created political incentives for governments to adopt economic policies that would raise employment and keep wages relatively high. Such policies were not always consistent with a continued commitment to the gold standard. The shift in political power produced by electoral reform, therefore, created political incentives to move away from the rigid constraints of a fixed exchange-rate system in order to avoid the domestic costs of adjusting the balance of payments.

The second important change during the interwar period arose from revolutionary ideas in economic theory that emerged during the 1930s. These ideas provided a compelling theoretical rationale for governments to use monetary policy to manage the domestic economy. John Maynard Keynes spurred this revolution in his role as academic economist. Keynes's most influential work was shaped by his observations of the British economy during the 1920s and 1930s. What Keynes focused on in particular was unemployment. British unemployment rose to about 20 percent in the early 1920s and never fell below 10 percent during the remainder of the decade (Skidelsky 1994, 130; Temin 1996). Such persistently high rates of unemployment defied the expectations of neoclassical economics, the standard economic theory at the time.

Neoclassical economics argued that such persistent high unemployment was impossible because markets have equilibrating mechanisms that keep the economy at full employment. High unemployment meant that the demand for labor was lower than the supply of labor at the prevailing wage rate. Because labor markets are no different from any other market, an imbalance between supply and demand should give rise to an adjustment process that eliminates the imbalance. In this case, the excess supply of labor represented by high unemployment should cause the price of labor—wages—to fall. Then, as the price of labor falls, the demand for labor will increase. Eventually, such adjustments will guide the economy back to full employment. In neo-classical theory, therefore, unemployment was expected to give rise to an automatic adjustment process that would lead the economy back to full employment.

The persistence of high unemployment in interwar Britain caused Keynes to reevaluate the neoclassical explanation of unemployment (Lekachman 1966; Skidelsky 1994). Keynes's thinking culminated in a book he wrote in the early 1930s (and published in 1936) called *The General Theory of Employment, Interest, and Money*, which challenged neoclassical economics in two connected ways (Keynes 1980). First, Keynes suggested that neoclassical economists were wrong to think that an economy would always return to full employment automatically. For reasons that we shall explore in a moment, Keynes argued that an economy could get stuck at an equilibrium characterized by underutilized production capacity and high unemployment. Second, Keynes argued that governments need not accept persistent high unemployment. Instead, governments could use macroeconomic policy—monetary policy and fiscal policy—to restore the economy to full employment.

According to Keynes, economies can get stuck at high levels of unemployment because of the fragility of investment decisions. Investment expenditures typically account for about 20 percent of total national expenditures. Variation in investment expenditures, therefore, can have an important influence on the overall level of economic activity: when investment rises, the economy grows, and when investment falls, the economy stagnates. Investment decisions, in turn, are strongly influenced by firms' expectations about the future demand for their products. When firms expect future demand to be strong, they will invest and the economy will experience robust growth. When firms expect future demand to be weak, however, they will make few new investments and economic growth will slow. If an economy is hit by some sort of shock that causes domestic demand to collapse and unemployment to rise, firms will develop very pessimistic forecasts of the demand for their products in the future. New investments will not be made and the economy will remain stuck at a high level of unemployment. This, according to Keynes, is what had happened to Britain during the 1920s.

Because Keynes believed that the cause of persistent high unemployment ultimately lay in inadequate demand for goods, he proposed that governments use fiscal and monetary policy to manage **aggregate demand**—the sum of all consumption and investment expenditures made by the government, by domestic and foreign consumers, and by producers. When we talk about managing aggregate demand, we are therefore talking about policies that increase or decrease these expenditures. Governments manage aggregate demand with fiscal and monetary policies, each of which affects aggregate demand in a different way. Fiscal policy affects aggregate demand directly. When the government cuts taxes without reducing expenditures, aggregate demand increases because private individuals' consumption expenditures increase by some proportion of the tax reduction. When the government increases its expenditures without raising taxes, total government expenditures rise. The additional demand for goods and services that results from these increased expenditures causes firms to hire more workers to produce the additional goods being demanded.

Monetary policy affects aggregate demand indirectly, by changing domestic interest rates. An increase in the money supply will cause the domestic interest rate to fall. Lower interest rates make it cheaper to borrow. As the cost of borrowing falls, the demand for investment-related expenditures, such as new homes, and high-price consumer items, such as cars, rises because these are usually purchased with credit and are therefore sensitive to the interest rate. Firms will then hire more workers in order to produce the higher level of output being demanded. A monetary expansion, therefore, will lead to falling interest rates, lower interest rates will increase aggregate demand, and increased aggregate demand will cause output and employment to rise.

In short, Keynes argued that by spending when others would not or by increasing the money supply to induce others to spend, the government could increase demand in the economy. By increasing total demand in the economy, investment would rise and unemployment would fall. Thus, by using macroeconomic policy to manage aggregate demand, governments could keep the economy running at full employment. Keynes's *General Theory* therefore represented a substantial challenge to the prevailing wisdom about the role governments could and should play in managing the domestic economy. Neoclassical economists saw the market economy as an inherently stable system that would return automatically to full employment following a shock that raised unemployment. There was therefore no need for active government management of the economy. In contrast, Keynes saw the market economy as potentially unstable and susceptible to large and sustained departures from full employment. Such an unstable economic system needed a stabilizer, and in Keynes's vision governments could perform this stabilizing function by using macroeconomic policy to manage aggregate demand. In one remarkable book, Keynes "rewrote the content of economics and transformed its vocabulary. . . . [He] informed the world that fatalism toward economic depression, mass unemployment, and idle factories was wrong" (Lekachman 1966, 59).

The ascent of the political left in national parliaments and of Keynesian theories combined to generate a revolution in macroeconomic policy making. This revolution began prior to the Second World War and gathered strength during and after the War. The Great Depression that began with the 1929 American stock market crash played an important role in spreading the Keynesian revolution beyond Britain. The Depression brought persistent high unemployment to much of Western Europe and to the United States, and this helped convince governments of the shortcomings of neoclassical theory. Experience with government economic management during the Second World War, when governments intervened extensively to mobilize resources for the War, gave governments a degree of confidence in the policy measures Keynes offered as solutions to the problem of persistent high unemployment (Hall 1989).

By the War's end, most governments had reevaluated the role they could and should play in the domestic economy. Legislation enacted in the United States and Great Britain illustrates the impact that this reevaluation had on government policy. In 1945, the U.S. Congress considered the "Full Employment Act," which assigned to the federal government the responsibility for maintaining full employment. While Congress did not pass the 1945 act, in 1946 the bill was renamed and passed as the Employment Act. And while the Employment Act replaced the term "full employment" with "maximum employment," the bill nevertheless symbolized a fundamental change: no longer would the U.S. government leave the operation of the American economy fully to market forces (Stein 1994, 76–77). In Britain, the government published a "White Paper on Employment Policy" in 1944, which stated in its very first line, "the government accepts as one of [its] primary aims and responsibilities the maintenance of a high and stable level of employment after the war" (cited in Hall 1986, 71). This commitment provided the foundation for the macroeconomic policies of successive British governments until the late 1970s.

In most countries, governments relied more heavily upon monetary policy than fiscal policy to manage aggregate demand. While fiscal policy was useful in theory, it proved cumbersome in practice. Government budgets are planned on the basis of an annual spending cycle and cannot easily be changed in response to changing economic conditions. Moreover, government budgets must be passed by national legislatures; thus, even if governments could make incremental adjustments to overall spending on a quarterly or monthly basis, securing legislative approval each time is a difficult task. Monetary policy, by contrast, is much easier to manipulate. Interest rates can be easily reduced or raised without elaborate planning. Even more importantly, in most countries governments retained authority over monetary policy and could therefore make interest-rate decisions without legislative approval. Thus, for both practical and political reasons, governments relied more heavily on monetary policy than on fiscal policy to manage domestic economic activity.

Together, electoral reform and the Keynesian revolution had a profound effect on exchange-rate policies. Electoral reform altered the balance of political power, shifting the center of gravity away from the propertied classes and toward the workers. This shift created political incentives to use monetary policy to manage the domestic economy. The Keynesian revolution made governments and publics more aware of the policy measures that could be used to promote employment and at the same time broke the neoclassical strictures on their use. As a consequence, voters have come to expect governments to manage the economy, and governments have responded by becoming more willing to use monetary policy to meet these expectations (Hall 1989, 4).

In this world, exchange-rate politics revolves around competition between groups with very different interests. In some cases, this competition involves factor- or class-based groups pressing the government to adopt their preferred monetary policy. In other cases, it involves sector-based groups pressuring the government to adopt their preferred exchange rate policy. In all instances, monetary and exchange-rate politics is driven by competition between groups pressuring the government to use these policies in ways that advance or defend their economic interests. We turn now to look at three models of this competition.

Society-Based Models of Monetary and Exchange-Rate Politics

Scholars have developed three society-based models of monetary and exchange-rate politics: an electoral model, a partisan model, and a sectoral model. The electoral and the partisan models assume that a government's exchange rate policy reflects its monetary policy decisions. Both models assume that *all* governments want to retain monetary policy autonomy in order to manage the domestic economy. Sometimes the monetary policy that a government adopts is consistent with a fixed exchange rate, and sometimes it is not. In order to understand the government's exchange-rate policies, the models presented examine how politics shapes monetary policy.

The sectoral model assumes that a government's exchange-rate policy is determined by competition between sector-based interest groups. This model does not assume that all governments value monetary policy autonomy more than exchange-rate stability. Instead, it assumes that the various interest groups value each side of this trade-off differently. Some groups attach considerable value to exchange-rate stability and little value to monetary autonomy; others attach little value to exchange-rate stability and considerable value to monetary autonomy. Whether a government fixes the exchange rate or whether it retains monetary autonomy is determined by the balance of power among these competing groups. While the models each provide a distinct perspective, they all agree that exchange-rate policies emerge from political competition.

The Electoral Model of Monetary and Exchange-Rate Politics

The electoral model argues that exchange-rate policy reflects decisions that governments make concerning monetary policy. It assumes that governments care most about monetary policy autonomy and will maintain a fixed exchange rate only when the monetary policy required to do so corresponds with their domestic economic objectives, which are in turn shaped by the need to win elections.

In democratic political systems, governments must periodically stand for reelection. In most advanced industrialized societies, domestic economic conditions have an important influence on how voters evaluate incumbent governments. Economic conditions can influence how people vote in two different ways. At the simplest level, we might expect people to be **pocketbook voters**—individuals who vote for or against a government depending upon how they personally have fared under that government. A voter whose income rose under a particular government will vote for the incumbent, while a voter who lost her job or saw her income fall under a particular government will vote against it in the next election.

Alternatively, we might expect people to evaluate a government less on the basis of their personal experience and more on the basis of aggregate economic performance. In this approach, called the **sociotropic model,** people support a government that has delivered strong economic growth, low levels of unemployment, and moderate inflation. People will vote against a government that has reigned over recession, rising unemployment, and high inflation. (See Lewis-Beck 1988.) Whether we assume that people are pocketbook voters or instead that they evaluate governments on the basis of the broader economic environment, the central point remains the same: voters reward a government that has delivered good economic conditions and punish a government that has delivered a poor economic environment.

Because voters hold politicians accountable for prevailing economic conditions, governments have an incentive to establish their macroeconomic policy objectives with at least one eye on the electoral calendar. (See Kramer 1971; Nordhaus 1989;

A CLOSER LOOK

Exchange-Rate Arrangements in the OECD

Monetary Union	Fixed but Adjustable	Managed Floating	Floating
Austria	Denmark	Czech Rep.	Australia
Belgium	Hungary	Slovak Rep.	Canada
Finland			Great Britain
France			Iceland
Germany			Japan
Greece			Korea
Ireland			Mexico
Italy			New Zealand
Luxembourg			Norway
Netherlands			Poland
Portugal			Sweden
Spain			Switzerland
			Turkey
			United States

Source: IMF, "Classification of Exchange Rate Arrangements and Monetary Policy Frameworks," http://www.imf.org/external/np/mfd/er/2004/eng/0604.htm, 2004 (accessed February 1, 2005).

The preceding table nicely illustrates the variety of exchange-rate arrangements currently maintained by the advanced industrialized countries. Notice how sharply the pattern reflects the "bipolar" view that we first encountered in Chapter 11. Most, though not all, of the EU countries maintain permanently fixed exchange rates within an economic and monetary union (EMU). The vast majority of the other OECD countries float their currencies. Only a few countries maintain intermediate arrangements, and the traditional fixed-but-adjustable exchange rate is clearly an unpopular choice. We also see variation within the EU: while most EU countries are in the EMU, Denmark, Sweden, and the United Kingdom, as well as the new EU members (Hungary, the Czech Republic, the Slovak Republic, and Poland) are not.

We could add to the variation evident in the table by tracking changes in these currency arrangements over time. For example, most EU countries allowed their exchange rates to float during the 1970s, before stabilizing them within the European monetary system (EMS) in the 1980s and moving to EMU in the 1990s. At the same time, Great Britain and Sweden both maintained fixed-but-adjustable exchange rates within the EMS in the early 1990s, but then both countries withdrew from the system and floated in 1992. Japan offers another example. While listed as a country that floats its currency, Japan concerns itself greatly with the yen's value against the dollar and moves through periods when it intervenes heavily to affect the yen's value against the dollar and periods when it intervenes little.

Continued

The current variation in exchange-rate arrangements presented in the table, as well as changes in these exchange-rate arrangements over time, cries out for explanation. Why have some EU governments permanently fixed their exchange rates while others have continued to float? Why do some countries that haven't yet joined the EMU float their currencies while others maintain more stable exchange rates? Why do some of those who are outside of the EMU, but want exchange-rate stability, peg their exchange rate while others pursue a managed float? More broadly, why have so many EU governments embraced rigidly fixed exchange rates while much of the rest of the advanced industrialized countries maintain floating exchange rates? These are the questions that theories of monetary and exchange-rate policies based on domestic politics attempt to answer.

Tufte 1978; Drazen 2000.) In particular, politicians may be more likely to adopt expansionary macroeconomic policies in the 18 months prior to an election in order to create strong economic growth and falling unemployment at the time of the election (Tufte 1978, 9). Even if politicians are not inclined to engineer preelectoral economic booms (and existing research does not provide compelling evidence that there is a systematic electoral cycle in macroeconomic policy), they still may believe that voters will punish them for poor economic conditions. As an election approaches, politicians might therefore be reluctant to adopt macroeconomic policies that reduce growth and raise unemployment, such as raising interest rates or reducing a budget deficit. The important point is that, because economic performance shapes how people vote, politicians will be less inclined to adopt economic policies that slow economic growth and raise unemployment and more inclined to adopt policies that boost economic growth and lower unemployment.

The influence of electoral politics on macroeconomic policy can in turn affect a government's willingness to maintain a fixed exchange rate. Because governments must stand for reelection, and because macroeconomic conditions shape their electoral fortunes, governments may be less willing to accept the constraints on monetary policy that are imposed by a fixed exchange rate as the next election approaches. Given a choice between maintaining a fixed exchange rate and engineering a preelection jump in economic growth, governments will choose the latter. Alternatively, governments may be less willing to tighten monetary policy to maintain a fixed exchange rate in the months preceding an election. That is, given a choice between raising interest rates in order to support a fixed exchange rate and allowing the currency to float, the government will choose the latter. In short, as an election approaches, a government that is otherwise committed to a fixed exchange rate may be much less willing to adopt the policies required to maintain that exchange rate.

One of the most widely publicized instances of a government sacrificing a fixed exchange rate to electoral politics occurred in the United States in the early 1970s. The nation ended the convertibility of the dollar into gold in August 1971 and devalued the dollar by 10 percent in the ensuing months. According to one scholar, the decision by President Richard M. Nixon to break the link with gold and devalue was viewed "through a lens that focused on the 1972 presidential election, then 15 months away" (Gowa 1983, 163). American economic conditions in 1971 were not enhancing the prospects of Nixon's reelection. Early in his first term Nixon had allowed his economic team to reduce inflation, which was at a then-high level of about 5 percent, and by 1970 the American economy had slipped into a recession, with unemployment beginning to rise (Stein 1994, Chapter 5).

The rise in unemployment evoked painful memories for Nixon. In 1960, as the vice president, he had run for president against John F. Kennedy. The 1960 campaign took place in the context of a recession, and in October unemployment increased by almost half a million. Nixon was convinced that the rise in unemployment just prior to the November election caused him to lose to Kennedy. "All the speeches, television broadcasts, and precinct work in the world could not counteract that one hard fact" of higher unemployment, he later wrote (Nixon 1962, 309). Nixon was determined to avoid again falling victim to an economic slump in the 1972 election.

With economic forecasts predicting that unemployment would rise to 6 percent in 1972, the Nixon administration decided to make the reduction of unemployment the number-one objective of macroeconomic policy (Tufte 1978, 48). As one senior administration official later recounted, "[In 1971] the word went out that 1972, by God, was going to be a good year" (cited in Tufte 1978, 48). Action was taken on both monetary and fiscal policy. The administration made it known that it wanted the Federal Reserve Bank (the Fed) to increase the rate of growth of the money supply, and the Fed obliged (although it remains unclear whether the Fed's expansion was coincidental or a direct response to White House pressure). In addition, government spending was increased through a range of measures. By the middle of 1971, the Nixon administration was using monetary and fiscal policies to reduce unemployment in the run-up to the 1972 presidential election.

The consequences for the dollar's fixed exchange rate against gold were clear and dramatic. The boost to domestic demand caused by the expansionary policy widened the U.S. trade deficit. Interest-rate cuts led to capital outflows. The combination of a widening current account balance and capital outflows worsened the overall U.S. balance-of-payments position and provoked gold outflows. It quickly became apparent that the Nixon administration would have to choose between its domestic economic expansion and the dollar's fixed exchange rate (Gowa 1983, 170). In an August 1971 meeting at Camp David, therefore, the Nixon administration made two decisions that were inextricably linked: to push forward with macroeconomic expansion in the hope that this would reduce unemployment in the period before the election, and to end the convertibility of the dollar into gold, in effect devaluing the dollar. One might suggest, therefore, that the Bretton Woods system collapsed so that Nixon might win the 1972 presidential election.

The end of dollar convertibility thus nicely illustrates the logic of the electoral approach to exchange-rate policy. President Nixon's concern that high unemployment would reduce his chances for reelection led him to adopt expansionary macroeconomic policies. When it became apparent that those policies were inconsistent with a fixed exchange rate, the Nixon administration devalued the dollar.

While the electoral approach highlights an important dynamic driving macroeconomic and exchange-rate policy, it suffers from two important weaknesses. First, it offers only a limited explanation of exchange-rate policy. It tells us that a government might abandon a fixed exchange rate prior to an election, but it tells us little about exchange-rate policy at other times. If the government wins the election, for example, will it return to a fixed exchange rate? Second, the electoral approach does not provide deterministic predictions. The approach does not claim that all governments will abandon a fixed exchange rate prior to an election. Rather, it suggests only that governments sometimes have an incentive to do so. Thus, the electoral approach offers a quite limited explanation of exchange-rate policy.

The Partisan Model of Exchange-Rate Politics

The partisan approach also links exchange-rate policy to the government's monetary policy decisions. Like the electoral model, the partisan model assumes that every government values monetary autonomy more than exchange-rate stability. All governments will thus maintain a fixed exchange rate only when the monetary policy required to do so is consistent with its domestic economic objectives. In the partisan model, however, different political parties pursue distinct macroeconomic objectives. Some parties use monetary policy to reduce unemployment and are forced to float their currency. Other parties use monetary policy to limit inflation and can more readily maintain a fixed exchange rate.

The partisan model is based on a trade-off between unemployment and inflation called the **Phillips curve,** named after British economist A.W. Phillips, who was the first to posit such a relationship in 1958. The model suggests that a government can reduce unemployment only by raising the rate of inflation and can reduce inflation only by causing higher unemployment. One can clearly see the trade-off between inflation and unemployment that American policymakers faced between 1961 and 1970. (See Figure 12.1.) Each data point in the figure represents the rate of inflation and of unemployment for a single year. Notice how, in the years when inflation was low, unemployment was high, while in years when unemployment was low, inflation was high. This relationship produces the negative-sloping line on the figure, characteristic of the Phillips curve trade-off.

Political economists have cited the apparent trade-off between inflation and unemployment to suggest that different political parties use macroeconomic policy to move the domestic economy to different portions of the Phillips curve. Parties from the political left, such as Socialist parties, Social Democratic parties, Communist parties in Western Europe, the Labour party in Britain, and the Democratic party in the United States, have traditionally given priority to achieving a low level of unemployment, even though this entails higher inflation. Such parties will try to shift the economy to the upper left portion of the Phillips curve. Parties from the political right, such as the Conservative party in Britain, the Republican party in the United States, Liberal parties, and Christian Democratic parties in Europe, have traditionally given priority to low inflation, even though this entails higher unemployment. These parties will use macroeconomic policy to move the economy to the lower right portion of the Phillips curve.

These distinct partisan macroeconomic policies reflect the interests of the different social groups represented by parties of the left and parties of the right. Leftist parties traditionally have had strong ties to organized labor. In Western Europe, for example, the emergence and development of the labor movement was intimately con-

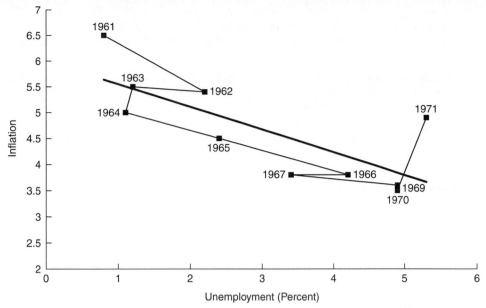

Figure 12.1   The Phillips Curve in the United States, 1961–1971.
Source: Economic Report of the President, 2002.

nected to the emergence and development of leftist political parties. Each of the large union confederations in European countries developed close ties to the political left. In Great Britain, labor union leaders composed about half of the delegates present at the conference that founded the modern Labour Party in 1900. Labor unions support leftist political parties because, once in office, these parties can help them achieve their objectives. Since employment is a central concern of labor unions, the tight link between organized labor and leftist parties creates an incentive for leftist governments to use macroeconomic policy to maintain high levels of employment.

Parties of the right have traditionally had closer links to business interests, the financial sector, and the middle class. These social groups tend to hold more accumulated wealth than workers. Moreover, because they are typically employed in high-skilled and management-related positions rather than in low-skilled manufacturing positions, they tend to be more insulated from changes in the unemployment rate than are most unionized employees. As a result, these groups are typically less concerned about unemployment and more concerned about protecting the value of their accumulated wealth. Because, in modern economies, people maintain large portions of their wealth in financial instruments, the desire to protect the value of wealth is transformed into a desire to protect the real value of financial assets. And since inflation erodes the real value of financial wealth, wealth holders and the parties of the right that represent them have an interest in, and thus an incentive to adopt, macroeconomic policies that maintain stable prices and therefore the interests of people with accumulated wealth.

A large body of research suggests that leftist and rightist governments in the advanced industrialized countries have in fact pursued distinct macroeconomic policies throughout the postwar period. Research on Western European democracies has found that leftist governments have been more willing to tolerate inflation and more inclined to pursue expansionary fiscal and monetary policies than rightist governments have been (Oatley 1997, 1999; Garrett 1998). Studies of macroeconomic policy and its outcomes in the United States have identified similar patterns. Eight of the ten recessions that have occurred in the United States between 1946 and 2002, for example, came under Republican administrations, and only two occurred under Democratic administrations (Keech 1995, 72–73). Moreover, historically, unemployment rates have been 2 percentage points higher, on average, under Republican than under Democratic administrations, while the growth of incomes has been 6 percentage points lower under Republican leadership than under Democrats (Hibbs 1987). Republican administrations appear, therefore, to be more willing to tolerate rising unemployment in order to restrain inflation than are Democratic administrations. While there have certainly been exceptions to this general pattern, research suggests that political parties from the left and right have in fact pursued distinct macroeconomic policies when in office.

Distinct partisan macroeconomic policies can give rise to distinct partisan exchange-rate policies. According to the partisan approach, leftist parties are less likely to maintain a fixed exchange rate. Expansionary policies will reduce domestic interest rates and raise domestic demand. These factors will in turn cause capital outflows and increasing imports. Capital outflows and a widening current-account deficit will, in their turn, lead to foreign exchange market imbalances and a weakening currency. Committed to domestic expansion, leftist governments are likely to resist the policy changes required to support a fixed exchange rate against these pressures. Conservative parties, by contrast, are more likely to maintain a fixed exchange rate. Restrictive monetary policies are less likely to generate capital outflows or to increase domestic demand. As a result, conservative governments are unlikely to confront persistent imbalances in the foreign exchange market and therefore will not be forced to change their monetary policies to sustain a fixed exchange rate. Conservative governments are therefore more likely to establish and maintain a fixed exchange rate. In sum, the partisan approach suggests that leftist governments are less likely than rightist governments to maintain a fixed exchange rate.

The politics of macroeconomic policy in France between 1978 and 1982 nicely illustrates how changes in the partisan composition of a government can affect macroeconomic and exchange-rate policies. A center-right government, led by President Valéry Giscard d'Éstaing and Prime Minister Raymond Barre, held office in France during much of the 1970s. Giscard and Barre gave priority to reducing inflation (Oatley 1997). This choice was by no means dictated by economic conditions. French inflation was high during the 1970s, rising to 13 percent in 1975 and hovering around 10 percent for the rest of the decade. But French unemployment had also risen steadily throughout the 1970s, from a low of 2.7 percent in 1971 to 6 percent by the end of the decade. The government's decision to give priority to reducing inflation thus reflected a partisan preference.

The emphasis on reducing inflation was accompanied by a willingness to establish and maintain a fixed exchange rate for the French franc. Both Giscard and Barre saw a fixed exchange rate as a useful constraint. Fixing the franc would constrain

French monetary policy by forcing the government to dedicate that policy to maintaining the exchange rate. Because the franc was pegged to the German mark, fixing it would require a restrictive monetary policy. In addition, a binding exchange rate would force French industry and labor to slow the growth of wages that was fuelling inflation. Operating under this logic, Giscard d'Éstaing worked with the German government and other members of the European Union to create the European monetary system.

This emphasis on reducing inflation, along with the associated policy of a fixed exchange rate, was abandoned in the early 1980s, when the Socialist Party, led by François Mitterrand, defeated Giscard d'Éstaing in presidential elections in May of 1981. Mitterrand quickly abandoned the anti-inflation stance in an attempt to reduce French unemployment. Again, this decision was not dictated by economic conditions. Inflation had remained strong, rising to about 13 percent in 1981, despite the previous government's efforts to reduce it. Unemployment had also continued to rise in the late 1970s and early 1980s, reaching what was then a postwar high of 7 percent in 1981. Mitterrand's decision to focus on unemployment and pay less attention to inflation was thus a reflection of his government's close ties to the French working class.

Mitterrand's government implemented expansionary macroeconomic policies. The budget deficit was increased, pumping more government spending into the economy, and the Bank of France reduced domestic interest rates. This expansion was inconsistent with the franc's fixed exchange rate inside the EMS. Financial capital began flowing out of France in response to the falling interest rates. The French current-account deficit widened as strong domestic demand limited the goods available for export and pulled in imports. The deteriorating balance-of-payments position weakened the franc in the foreign exchange market, generating a series of speculative attacks against the franc's parity in the EMS. Rather than abandon its effort to reduce unemployment, the Socialist government devalued the franc three times between May 1981 and March 1983. Thus, a leftist government implemented an expansionary policy that was inconsistent with a fixed exchange rate and, when forced to choose between the two objectives, abandoned the fixed exchange rate.

The French case therefore highlights how partisan politics can shape macroeconomic and exchange-rate policies. A rightist government committed to low inflation tightened monetary policy and embraced a fixed exchange rate. The leftist government that followed gave priority to reducing unemployment, adopted expansionary macroeconomic policies in pursuit of that objective, and repeatedly devalued the currency. While the partisan approach tells us more about how politics shapes monetary and exchange-rate politics than the electoral approach does, it, too, has weaknesses. Its chief weakness is that partisan macroeconomic policies are differentiated too sharply. Not all leftist governments pursue expansionary macroeconomic policies and adopt floating exchange rates. The French Socialists, for example, embraced a fixed exchange rate inside the EMS in mid-1983 and then maintained that rate for the remainder of the decade. Nor do all rightist governments adopt fixed exchange rates. The Conservative Party government led by Margaret Thatcher that governed Britain throughout the 1980s, for example, steadfastly refused to adopt a fixed exchange rate for the pound. And even once the pound was placed in the EMS after John Major replaced Thatcher in 1990, it was a Conservative party government that took the pound out of the system and returned to a floating exchange rate in 1992. Thus, while the partisan approach highlights the historical tendency for distinct partisan macroeconomic and exchange-rate policies, it is important to remain sensitive to the specific context in applying that approach to a particular case.

The Sectoral Model of Exchange-Rate Politics

The sectoral model links exchange-rate policy choices to competition between sector-based interest groups. Unlike the electoral and partisan models, the sectoral model does not assume that all governments value monetary autonomy more than exchange-rate stability. Instead, government preferences reflect interest-group preferences—and interest groups hold different preferences over the trade-off between domestic economic autonomy and exchange-rate stability. Some interest groups prefer floating, others fixed, exchange rates. Some interest groups prefer a strong currency, others a weak currency. Each group lobbies the government on behalf of its preferred exchange-rate policy, and the overall policy is determined by the group that has the greatest influence.

The sectoral model splits domestic actors into four domestic interest groups or sectors: import-competing producers, export-oriented producers, nontraded-goods producers, and the financial services industry. (See Frieden 1997a, 1991.) We have encountered each of these groups previously, so we will not describe their characteristics again here. Each group has preferences over the two dimensions of exchange-rate policy described in the previous paragraph: fixed or floating rates and a strong or weak currency.

Preferences over exchange-rate stability reflect the importance each sector attaches to that stability and to monetary policy autonomy. On the one hand, are the sector's economic interests damaged by excessive exchange-rate volatility or by large exchange-rate misalignments? Sectors whose economic interests are damaged by exchange-rate movements place considerable value on exchange-rate stability. Sectors whose interests are not damaged by such movements place less value on exchange-rate stability. On the other hand, does surrendering monetary policy autonomy damage the sector's economic interests? Sectors that conduct most of their business in the domestic economy want to ensure that domestic economic conditions provide adequate demand. They will therefore place considerable value on monetary policy autonomy. Sectors that conduct most of their business in international markets are less concerned about domestic economic conditions. They therefore place very little value on monetary policy autonomy. Thus, sectors that are harmed by exchange-rate movements and that lose little from surrendering monetary autonomy prefer fixed exchange rates. Sectors that are not harmed by exchange-rate movements and that lose from the loss of monetary policy autonomy prefer floating exchange rates.

This framework generates clear preferences for three of the four sectors. The export-oriented sector prefers a fixed exchange rate. Export-oriented producers are heavily engaged in international trade, and exchange-rate movements damage their economic interests. They therefore place great value on exchange-rate stability. Because export-oriented producers are heavily engaged in foreign trade, they lose very little if the government cannot use monetary policy to manage the domestic economy. They therefore attach little value to monetary policy autonomy. The export-oriented sector is thus willing to give up monetary policy autonomy in order to maintain a fixed exchange rate.

The nontraded-goods and the import-competing sectors prefer a floating exchange rate. Neither of these sectors is deeply integrated into the global economy; both generate their revenues from sales in the domestic market. As a consequence, neither sector is not greatly affected by exchange-rate movements, and both attach little value to exchange-rate stability. Moreover, because producers in these sectors conduct their business in the domestic economy, they have a keen interest in retaining the government's ability to use monetary policy to manage that economy. They therefore assign great value to monetary policy autonomy. The nontraded-goods and the import-competing sectors thus want to retain monetary policy autonomy, and they accept flexible exchange rates in order to do so.

The financial services sector's preferences are less clear. Financial services are highly internationalized and exchange-rate movements can damage their interests. This international exposure creates some interest in exchange-rate stability. At the same time, however, financial institutions profit from exchange-rate volatility. Currency trading has become an important source of profits for the financial services industry. In addition, banks offer services that help businesses engaged in international trade manage their exchange-rate risk (Destler and Henning 1989, 133). Thus, it is not clear how much value the financial service sector attaches to exchange-rate stability. Financial institutions do, however, value monetary policy autonomy. They depend upon the central bank to maintain the stability of the domestic banking system and to keep domestic inflation in check. Both objectives require monetary policy autonomy. In addition, financial institutions are damaged by excessive fluctuations in domestic interest rates, and using monetary policy to maintain a fixed exchange rate can produce more volatile domestic interest rates. These crosscutting interests have led many to conclude that, on balance, the financial sector prefers monetary policy autonomy and is willing to accept exchange-rate flexibility (Destler and Henning 1989, 133–134; see Frieden 1991 for an alternative view).

Sectors also have preferences regarding the level of the exchange rate. These preferences arise from the impact that currency values have on incomes in each sector. The export-oriented and import-competing sectors both prefer a weak or undervalued currency. A weak domestic currency reduces the foreign currency cost of domestic traded goods and raises the domestic currency cost of foreign traded goods. These price levels enhance the competitiveness of export-oriented producers in global markets, thereby allowing them to expand their exports. They also reduce the competitiveness of foreign producers in the domestic market, making it easier for import-competing producers to dominate the home market. Thus, firms in the traded-goods sector prefer an undervalued or weak currency.

The nontraded-goods sector prefers a strong or overvalued currency. People employed in the nontraded-goods sector consume a lot of traded goods. A strong domestic currency reduces the domestic currency price of traded goods, both those imported from abroad and those produced at home. When the dollar appreciates, for example, foreign goods become cheaper in the American market and domestic producers must match these falling prices to remain competitive. A strong or overvalued exchange rate, therefore, raises the incomes of people employed in the nontraded-goods sector. For that reason, this sector prefers a strong currency.

The financial services sector again has crosscutting interests. Financial institutions benefit from a strong currency because it allows them to purchase foreign assets at a lower price. But other factors create an interest in a weak currency. Most financial institutions, including those deeply involved in international business, continue to lend heavily to domestic firms. Because an overvalued exchange rate harms firms in the traded-goods sector, a strong currency can weaken financial institutions that have lent heavily to firms in that sector. In addition, however, financial institutions purchase and hold foreign assets for the returns they provide. Because these returns are typically denominated in foreign currencies, a weak currency will raise the domestic currency value of such returns. It is not easy for financial institutions to balance these crosscutting considerations. What best suits the interests of financial institutions is the ability to buy foreign assets when the domestic currency is strong and repatriate the returns on these assets when the domestic currency has weakened. Because of these crosscutting interests, financial institutions "tend to be agnostic with respect to the level of the exchange rate" (Destler and Henning 1989, 132).

Bringing the two dimensions of exchange-rate policy together provides a full picture of sectoral preferences concerning that policy. The columns in Table 12.2 depict the degree of exchange-rate stability. The column labeled "High" denotes a fixed exchange rate (and thus no monetary policy autonomy), while the column labeled "Low" denotes a floating exchange rate (and thus full monetary policy autonomy). The rows in the table depict the level of the exchange rate. The row labeled "High" denotes a strong currency, the row labeled "Low" a weak currency. Each cell of the table thus represents a combination of the degree of exchange-rate stability and the level of the exchange rate.

Table 12.2
Sectoral Exchange-Rate Policy Preferences

		Preferred Degree of Exchange-Rate Stability	
		High	Low
Preferred Level of the Exchange Rate	High		Nontradable-goods industry *financial services*
	Low	Export-oriented industries	Import-competing industries *financial services*

Source: Based on Frieden 1991, 445.

We can place each sector in the cell corresponding to its exchange-rate policy preference. The "High–High" cell is empty; no sector desires a strong currency and a fixed exchange rate. The nontraded-goods sector and the financial services industry occupy the "High–Low" cell. Firms in the nontraded-goods sector want a strong currency to maximize their purchasing power, and they want a floating exchange rate so that the government can use monetary policy to manage the domestic economy. The financial services industry fits less clearly into this cell. Its preference for a floating exchange rate places it in the right column, but its agnosticism about the level of the exchange rate prevents us from assigning it definitively to the top row. Consequently, financial services appear in the top and bottom rows.

The export-oriented sector occupies the "Low–High" cell. Export-oriented firms want a weak currency to enhance their export competitiveness, and they want a stable exchange rate to minimize the disruptions caused by exchange-rate volatility. Because these industries are not heavily dependent upon the domestic economy, they are willing to sacrifice monetary policy autonomy to stabilize the exchange rate. Finally, the import-competing sector occupies the "Low–Low" cell. Firms in this sector want a weak currency to enhance their competitiveness against imports in the domestic market, and they want a floating exchange rate so that the government can use monetary policy to manage the domestic economy.

The political dynamics surrounding the sharp appreciation of the U.S. dollar in the early 1980s and its subsequent depreciation after 1985 nicely illustrate how these competing interest-group preferences seek to shape exchange-rate policy in the United States. (See Destler and Henning 1989; Frankel 1990.) The U.S. dollar appreciated by 50 percent between 1980 and 1985. Interest groups mobilized in an attempt to influence the Reagan administration's approach to both the level and the stability of the dollar. Export-oriented producers organized and lobbied for a weaker, more stable dollar. Farmers, for example, argued that the strong dollar was reducing their incomes, and they pressured the Reagan administration to bring the dollar down. Manufacturing industries, led by the Business Roundtable and the National Association of Manufacturers, also pressed for depreciation. The Business Roundtable put together a broad-based coalition of businesses, including representatives from Caterpillar, Ford, U.S. Steel, Honeywell, Motorola, IBM, and Xerox, to pressure the U.S. Treasury, the Federal Reserve, and Congress for policies to weaken the dollar.

The manufacturers also advocated measures to increase the stability of the dollar against the other major currencies. While few suggested that the United States return to a fixed exchange rate, most of the executives in the coalition welcomed the process of coordinated foreign exchange market intervention initiated by the 1985 Plaza Accord and encouraged the Reagan administration to pursue additional coordinated intervention. In addition, the group applauded the 1987 Louvre Accord, under which the United States, Japan, Germany, Great Britain, and France agreed to stabilize exchange rates at their current levels. Finally, the group encouraged the U.S. government to explore the possibility of implementing a target zone to bring stability to international monetary arrangements on a more permanent basis. Thus, just as the sectoral approach suggests, export-oriented producers pressured for a weak dollar and for greater exchange-rate stability.

POLICY ANALYSIS AND DEBATE

A Strong Dollar or a Weak Dollar?

Question

Should the United States pursue a strong dollar or a weak dollar?

Overview

At the close of 2000, the United States was registering the latest in a long series of record current-account deficits. The dollar was continuing to hold strong against the Japanese yen and the euro; in fact, it was near the top of a 70 percent appreciation against these currencies since the late 1990s. The newly elected Bush administration entered office determined to maintain this strong-dollar policy. Bush administration officials argued that a strong dollar was necessary to maintain foreign confidence and to attract foreign investment. Moreover, Treasury Secretary Paul O'Neill argued, the strong dollar reflected the strength of the American economy rather than express government policy.

Critics increasingly voiced opposition to the policy, arguing that the strong dollar was damaging the American economy and threatening the United States with a severe crisis. The overvalued dollar, they said, was devastating American producers by pricing American goods out of foreign markets and reducing the domestic price of imports. The resulting current-account deficit required the United States to import $2 billion of foreign capital each day. Moreover, the deficit was perilously near unsustainable levels, and if the government did not take steps to reduce it, the nation faced the possibility of a crisis generated by a rapid shift in market sentiment that would cause massive capital outflows and a sharp depreciation of the dollar. Critics called for the administration to abandon the strong dollar policy and adopt in its place a policy that engineered a gradual depreciation of the dollar to promote current-account adjustment and reduce the U.S. need to import foreign capital. What is the right value for the dollar?

Policy Options

- Pursue policies that keep the dollar strong against foreign currencies.
- Pursue policies that prevent the dollar from appreciating against foreign currencies.

Policy Analysis

- What are the costs and benefits to the United States of a weak dollar?
- What are the costs and benefits to the United States of a strong dollar?

Take a Position

- Which option do you prefer? Justify your choice.
- What criticisms of your position should you anticipate? How would you defend your recommendation against these criticisms?

Resources

Online: Do an online search for "strong dollar weak dollar". Look for C. Fred Bergsten's webpage at the Institute for International Economics (*http://www.IIE.org*). He writes regularly about dollar policy. See in particular his "The Correction of the Dollar and Foreign Intervention in the Currency Markets." Search also for Barry

Continued

Eichengreen's home page at the University of California at Berkeley. He has some interesting papers under his policy section. Nouriel Roubini's webpage has some useful links under his "Current Policy Topics."
In Print: Lawrence Lindsey, "In the Dollar We Trust," *The International Economy* 15 (March–April 2001): 6–9; 52; C. Fred Bergsten, "Strong Dollar, Weak Dollar," *International Economy* 15 (July–August 2001): 8-10; 40-41. Robert J. Aliber, "The Dollar's Day of Reckoning," *Wilson Quarterly* (Winter 2005): 14–24.

The financial services industry also exhibited the preferences highlighted by the sectoral approach. During the early 1980s, the industry displayed little concern about the dollar's appreciation. For the most part, it benefited from the falling prices of foreign assets that the strong dollar implied. To the extent that financial service firms voiced any concerns as the dollar appreciated, they focused on the impact the strong dollar was having on traded-goods industries in the United States (Destler and Henning 1989). Financial institutions also failed to register strong opposition to the Reagan administration's concerted effort to engineer a depreciation of the dollar after 1985. Thus, the financial sector was neither a strong supporter of the strong dollar nor a vocal opponent of a weaker dollar.

Financial services firms did react strongly, however, to the attempt by the traded-goods sector to pressure the Reagan administration to stabilize the dollar. The American Bankers' Association's Economic Advisory Committee argued that the G5 agreement to stabilize the dollar under the Louvre Accord was a mistake. In addition, the committee opposed broader international monetary reforms that would lead to the adoption of a target-zone system. Monetary policy, they argued, should not be dedicated to maintaining a stable exchange rate, and foreign exchange market intervention should be undertaken only in "exceptional circumstances." As the sectoral approach leads us to expect, therefore, the financial services sector was agnostic about the level of the exchange rate, but opposed to efforts to stabilize the dollar at a fixed exchange rate. American exchange-rate policy during the 1980s thus highlights the dynamics emphasized by the sectoral approach. The interests and power of two prominent sectors of the American economy—export-oriented producers and the financial services industry—shaped U.S. exchange-rate policy.

While the sectoral approach provides greater detail about governments' exchange-rate policies than does the partisan approach, it, too, has weaknesses. Three such weaknesses are most troublesome. First, the sectoral approach may overestimate the importance that export-oriented firms attach to exchange-rate stability. While exporters may be harmed by exchange-rate volatility, businesses can reduce their exposure to volatility by using forward markets to cover the risk they face. As a consequence, exchange-rate volatility may be less damaging in practice. Second, the model may overestimate the importance that the traded-good sector attaches to a weak currency. In an open economy, many firms import intermediate inputs. Because a weak currency raises the domestic currency price of these imports, it raises production costs. As a consequence, a portion of the gains that these firms realize from a weak currency is eliminated. Finally, the sectoral model tells us little about exchange-rate policy outcomes. Like the society-centered approach to trade policy, this model does not provide much help understanding which of the competing sectoral demands will ultimately be represented in exchange-rate policy. Insofar as we are interested in explaining policy outcomes, this shortcoming will remain an important weakness of the sectoral model.

Conclusion

Society-centered models of trade policy argue that domestic political pressures determine the monetary and exchange-rate policies that governments adopt. The three approaches presented in this chapter suggest that governments face a multitude of social pressures—from voters, from classes, and from sector-based interest groups. These pressures are transmitted to governments through multiple channels, including mass-based elections, class-based party systems, and interest-group lobbying. Social pressures can influence exchange-rate policy indirectly by shaping a government's macroeconomic policy objectives, and they can influence exchange-rate policy directly by shaping the choices that a government makes between a fixed or floating exchange rate and between a strong or weak currency. Rather than suggesting that monetary and exchange-rate policies are determined exclusively by one type of pressure or another, the society-centered approach suggests that they are influenced by a number of social pressures. One approach may be better suited to some countries than to others or to some periods than to others. A full understanding of how domestic politics influences monetary and exchange-rate policies, however, will probably require attention to all three approaches presented in the chapter.

Overall, however, the society-centered approaches to exchange-rate politics are susceptible to some of the same criticisms that have been directed toward society-centered approaches to domestic trade politics. Chapter 4 pointed to three specific criticisms: they don't explain outcomes; they omit the interests of noneconomic interest groups; and they assume that governments do not have independent preferences. How powerful are these criticisms? Let us look at each in turn. The claim that society-centered models tell us a lot about interests but little about outcomes is less powerful in the context of exchange-rate politics than in the context of trade politics. Two of the three models we examined provide explicit linkages between societal interests and policy outcomes. In the electoral model, outcomes result from government macroeconomic policy choices taken in reference to electoral concerns. In the partisan model, policy outcomes result from decisions made by the party that controls government. The sectoral approach is more vulnerable to this criticism, because, as has been noted, it convincingly accounts for interest-group preferences regarding monetary and exchange rate policy, but it tells us little about the process through which these competing interests are transformed into policy outcomes.

Society-centered models of exchange-rate and monetary policy are less vulnerable to the claim that they ignore the interests of noneconomic actors. While these models do exclude noneconomic interest groups, such interest groups appear to have less of a stake in monetary and exchange-rate policies than they have in trade policy. The exchange rate is a rather blunt policy instrument. A government cannot easily use exchange-rate policy to punish or reward specific foreign governments for their human-rights records or their environmental policies. For example, although the United States can deny China access to the U.S. market without disturbing its other trade relationships, the United States cannot easily alter the dollar's exchange rate against the yuan (the Chinese currency) without also altering the dollar's exchange rate against other currencies. For this reason, human-rights activists, environmental groups, and other noneconomic interest groups have not pressured governments to use exchange-rate policy to achieve specific foreign policy objectives. Thus, the omission of noneconomic interest groups from the society-centered approach may be less worrying in the context of exchange-rate and monetary policies than in that of trade policy.

Finally, our society-centered models of monetary and exchange-rate policy overstate the ability of domestic interest groups to influence policy and underestimate the importance of independent state action. A fairly large literature suggests that monetary and exchange-rate policies are heavily insulated from domestic pressure groups. (See, e.g., Krasner 1977; Odell 1982.) In the United States, for example, exchange-rate and monetary policy decisions are made by the Treasury Department, the Federal Reserve, and the White House, all of which are "well insulated from particular societal pressures" (Krasner 1977, 65). Moreover, in many countries, central banks operate with considerable independence from elected officials. Politically independent central banks can pursue monetary and exchange-rate policies free from interest-group pressures and partisan and electoral politics. In fact, over the last 15 years, more and more governments have granted their central banks greater political independence hoping to insulate monetary policy from social and more broadly political pressures. We take up this topic in the next chapter.

Key Terms

Aggregate Demand	Pocketbook Voters
Phillips Curve	Sociotropic Model

Web Links

Bradford DeLong, a professor of economics at the University of California, Berkeley, maintains a very useful website dedicated to macroeconomics. You can visit this site at *http://www.j-bradford-delong.net/Index.html.*

Suggestions for Further Reading

For a good introduction to the politics of macroeconomic policy, see William R. Keech, *Economic Politics: The Costs of Democracy* (Cambridge: Cambridge University Press, 1995). For a more advanced treatment, see Alan Drazen, *Political Economy in Macroeconomics* (Princeton: Princeton University Press, 2000).

For an in-depth and readable exploration of the development of Keynes's economic ideas, see Robert Skidelsky, *John Maynard Keynes: The Economist as Saviour, 1920–1937* (New York: Penguin Press, 1992).

Two excellent treatments of the impact of the interwar changes are Beth Simmons, *Who Adjusts: Domestic Sources of Foreign Economic Policy during the Interwar Period* (Princeton: Princeton University Press, 1994) and Barry J. Eichengreen, *Golden Fetters: The Gold Standard and the Great Depression, 1919–1939* (Oxford: Oxford University Press, 1992).

A detailed discussion of the partisan approach to exchange-rate politics can be found in Thomas Oatley, *Monetary Politics: Exchange Rate Cooperation in the European Union* (Ann Arbor: University of Michigan Press, 1997).

Two excellent readings on the sectoral approach to exchange-rate politics are Jeffry A. Frieden, "Invested Interests: the Politics of National Economic Policies in a World of Global Finance," *International Organization* 45 (Autumn 1991): 425–451; and Jeffry A. Frieden, "Monetary Populism in Nineteenth Century America: An Open-Economy Interpretation," *Journal of Economic History* 57 (June 1997): 367–395.

CHAPTER 13

A State-Centered Approach to Monetary and Exchange-Rate Politics

During 1999 and 2000, the European Central Bank (ECB) began raising interest rates in an attempt to stem the euro's depreciation against the dollar. European governments and many European business and labor groups complained strongly about the rising interest rates. In an already sluggish European economy, higher interest rates would only further depress growth, and a stronger euro would only make it more difficult for European firms to export. While the ECB may have heard these complaints, it did not respond to them. It continued to raise interest rates—six times, in fact, during the next 12 months—in order to achieve the economic objective it deemed most important: maintaining low inflation.

This episode, which did not even make the front page of major newspapers, reflects the revolutionary changes that have swept through monetary politics during the last 20 years. During the 1970s and 1980s, and even as late as the mid-1990s, European governments used monetary policy to pursue their particular economic policy goals. And as we saw in Chapter 12, government policy goals typically reflected the interests of domestic interest groups. In today's Europe, the European Central Bank sets interest rates, monetary policy is dedicated to achieving the ECB's primary objective, which is low inflation, and European governments can do little to change the ECB's policy. In a very short period, therefore, the EU has moved from a world in which governments retained full control over monetary policy to a world in which they have practically no control over this important policy instrument. Nor is the change restricted to Europe: governments throughout the world have handed monetary policy to politically independent central banks. Changes in the institutional framework governing monetary policy have in turn altered the way that domestic politics shapes monetary and exchange-rate policies.

This chapter examines the transformation from government to bank control through the lens of a state-centered approach to monetary and exchange-rate politics. While the approach is not often called a state-centered approach, it contains the central characteristic of such an approach: insulating policy makers from short-term political pressures can raise social welfare. We begin by examining contemporary economic theories which argue that political control of monetary policy diminishes social welfare by generating too much inflation. We then consider how, in theory, institutions that insulate monetary policy from politics, such as independent central banks and fixed exchange rates, can eliminate this inflation and thus raise social welfare. We next investigate how the emergence of independent central banks is likely to shape the domestic politics of monetary and exchange-rate policies. Finally, we conclude by looking at some weaknesses of this approach.

Monetary Policy and Unemployment

The state-centered approach is based on economic theories which have increasingly replaced the Keynesian models that dominated macroeconomic policymaking after World War II. The models we examined in Chapter 12, as well as the Keynesian economic theories upon which they are based, assumed that governments face a stable trade-off between inflation and unemployment. Governments can exploit this trade-off to guide the economy toward lower unemployment or lower inflation. Contemporary economic theory asserts that no such stable trade-off between inflation and unemployment exists. There is a trade-off in the short run, but a government cannot use monetary policy to reduce unemployment for any extended period without generating an ever-higher rate of inflation (Friedman 1968; Phelps 1968).

At the center of this theory is the claim that all countries have a **natural rate of unemployment,** the economy's long-run equilibrium rate of unemployment. That is, the natural rate of unemployment is the rate of unemployment to which the economy will return after a recession or a boom (Sachs and Larrain 1993). The natural rate of unemployment is determined by the economywide real wage, which is the wage at which all workers who want to work can find employment. The natural rate of unemployment is never zero and can in fact be substantially above zero. Every economy will always experience some unemployment. Some people will have left one job and be seeking another. New entrants into the labor market, such as recent high school and college graduates, will not find jobs immediately. Moreover, labor market institutions, such as labor unions and labor market regulations that govern minimum wages, hiring and firing practices, unemployment compensation, and other social welfare benefits, can raise the natural rate of unemployment substantially. These institutions can raise the economywide real wage, thereby reducing the demand for labor and raising the natural rate of unemployment. Because such institutions differ from one country to another, each country will have a distinct natural rate of unemployment.

Contemporary economic theory argues that a government cannot use monetary policy to move unemployment below or above the natural rate of unemployment for more than a short time. To understand this claim we must first look at how wage bargaining affects unemployment in the short run. We can then examine how monetary policy affects unemployment in the short run and in the long run. In the short run, such as a one- or two-year period, the unemployment rate is determined by the wage agreements concluded between unions and businesses. Suppose that, in the current

A CLOSER LOOK

The Natural Rate of Unemployment in the United States and the European Union

The natural rate of unemployment has traced very different paths in the United States and the European Union during the last 25 years. In the United States, the natural rate of unemployment rose during the 1970s, reaching a peak of about 6.4 percent in 1984. It has subsequently fallen steadily, so that by the late 1990s it stood at about 5.7 percent, with some estimates suggesting that it may be even lower (Gordon 1997). Economists point to three factors to account for the decline in the natural rate of unemployment since the mid-1980s. (See Stiglitz 1997.) The first is demographic change. The baby-boom generation now constitutes a larger share of the total American labor force. This makes the U.S. labor force older than it has been in the past, and mature workers typically have lower unemployment rates than the young. Second, economists point to a "wage aspiration effect." During periods of high productivity growth, workers get accustomed to large increases in real wages. When productivity slows, workers continue to demand such increases, pushing up both the real wage and unemployment. Workers moderate their wage demands only after they have become accustomed to the slower productivity growth. Such dynamics are believed to have contributed to the rise in the natural rate that followed the slowdown in productivity growth during the 1970s and early 1980s. The reduction in the natural rate since the early 1980s reflects the adjustment in workers' aspirations (Stiglitz 1997, 7). Finally, increased competitiveness in labor and product markets probably caused the natural rate to fall. Greater openness in trade has forced American firms to manage their labor costs in order to remain competitive. Declining union strength in the United States has reduced the bargaining power held by workers. Together, these developments have slowed the growth of real wages, causing the natural unemployment rate to fall.

The downward trend in the American natural rate of unemployment has led many economists to question the usefulness of the concept. If the natural rate can move so much, and if economists cannot predict where exactly it is at any particular moment, then it cannot be a useful guide for monetary policymakers. One prominent economist has challenged his colleagues: "Can you imagine a petition . . . calling on the Federal Reserve to raise interest rates sharply at the present 5.1 percent unemployment in order to ward off imminent inflation? If you cannot imagine such a thing . . . then we as a scientific profession have not advanced this concept to the point where it is suitable for practical use" (Galbraith 1997, 102). Others are not as concerned that the downward trend in the natural rate renders the concept less useful. As one such economist has written, "since 1960, inflation rose in 26 of the 32 quarters when the unemployment rate was below 5 percent, but inflation fell in 24 of the 27 quarters when unemployment was above 7 percent" (Stiglitz 1997, 5). The natural rate of unemployment thus does tell us something about the relationship between unemployment and inflation and therefore should guide the monetary policy decisions taken by the Federal Reserve.

Continued

In the European Union, the natural rate of unemployment has risen during the last 25 years. Prior to the first oil shock, unemployment in EU countries averaged less than 3 percent. It has since risen steadily, peaking at 11 percent in the mid-1980s before settling at somewhere around 9 percent (Bean 1994; Blanchard and Katz 1997, 66). The rise in the natural rate in the European Union has been attributed to the interaction between economic shocks and labor market institutions. Adverse economic shocks during the 1970s and 1980s raised the rate of unemployment. Productivity growth slowed and, in conjunction with the aspiration effect, led to rising real wages. High real interest rates resulting in part from the efforts by European governments to reduce inflation slowed economic activity and pushed unemployment up. Finally, there was a reduction in the demand for labor independently of these other developments and caused by a shift to more technology-intensive forms of production (Blanchard 1997).

Once unemployment had risen, labor market institutions limited the wage-based adjustments required to bring it back down. Labor unions, which have traditionally been very strong in many EU countries, kept real wages high by protecting workers from direct competition with nonunionized workers (OECD 1994, 11–12). Government labor market regulations, including laws that make it difficult to fire workers and generous unemployment compensation and other welfare benefits, also limited adjustment. These regulations discouraged firms from employing new workers and discouraged people from seeking work, because the benefits they got while unemployed allowed them to maintain a reasonable standard of living. Over time, many EU policies generated a large pool of long-term unemployed workers who lost job skills and consequently became less employable (Blanchard and Katz 1997, 68). In short, labor market institutions prevented workers who had lost jobs from competing for available jobs. As a result, higher unemployment failed to spark the wage adjustments needed to bring unemployment back down.

The apparent rigidity of European labor markets has gained increased importance as EU governments have implemented a monetary union. (See, e.g., Soltwedel et al. 2000.) Prior to the establishment of the monetary union, a government could respond to a country-specific shock that raised unemployment by expanding the money supply and devaluing the currency. Since this response is no longer possible, such shocks must now be adjusted through a reduction in wages. The need for wage-based adjustment under monetary union has led the EU Commission, as well as many EU governments, to begin to emphasize the need for reforms that impart greater flexibility to EU labor markets. Many EU governments have been slow to embrace far-reaching reform, however, in part because labor unions in their countries have been only reluctant participants in the reform process.

year, the economy is at its natural rate of unemployment and labor is bargaining with management to determine the real wage for the next year. This wage bargaining is complicated by inflation. Workers care about their real wage—the actual purchasing power of the money they are paid each week—but they are paid a nominal wage—a specific amount of cash per hour or per week. Because wage contracts usually fix wages for a particular period, typically from one to three years, the nominal wage embodied in a contract will lose purchasing power as prices rise over the life of the agreement. Because workers recognize that inflation will erode the value of their nominal wage, they will take inflation into account when negotiating their wage contracts. In other words, workers will seek nominal wage agreements that protect their desired real wage against the inflation they expect. If labor is seeking stable real wages for the next year, for example, but expects prices to rise by 4 percent in the course of the year, it will seek a 4 percent nominal wage increase.

How does labor know what inflation rate will prevail in the future? The obvious answer is that it doesn't. Instead, labor will formulate **expectations** about the future rate of inflation, which are essentially its "best guess" about the inflation rate during the period covered by the impending contract. In formulating these expectations, labor unions look at a variety of factors. They may look to the current government's track record; if inflation has persistently run at around 5 percent during the last few years, it might be reasonable to expect 5 percent inflation in the next few years. They may also look for evidence that the government is committed to reducing inflation in the future or, to the contrary, for evidence that the government is likely to produce higher inflation in the future. They may also take into account the partisan composition of the government or its position in the electoral cycle. Irrespective of the source, however, these expectations are likely to be imprecise.

When nominal wage agreements are based on an expected inflation rate that turns out to be mistaken, the real wage will rise or fall. If workers secure a nominal wage increase that is greater than the actual rate of inflation, then the real wage will rise by the difference between the nominal wage increase and the rate of inflation. So if a wage agreement raises nominal wages by 8 percent, but inflation is only 4 percent, then the real wage will rise by 4 percent. Conversely, if workers secure an agreement that raises their nominal wage by less than the actual rate of inflation, real wages will fall by the difference between the nominal wage increase and the rate of inflation. So if the wage agreement calls for a 4 percent nominal wage increase, but actual inflation is 8 percent, the real wage will fall by 4 percent.

Changes in the real wage in turn affect the short-run unemployment rate. An increase in the real wage makes labor more costly to employ. The demand for labor therefore falls, causing unemployment to rise. A reduction in the real wage makes labor less costly to employ. The demand for labor therefore rises, causing unemployment to fall. Thus, in the short run, unemployment rises above or falls below the natural rate of unemployment in response to changes in the real wage.

We can now examine how monetary policy affects unemployment in the short run and in the long run. In the short run, an *unanticipated* change in monetary policy that produces a rate of inflation different from the rate that unions expected and incorporated into their nominal wage contract, shifts unemployment above or below the natural rate. An unexpected *increase* in the rate of inflation generated by a monetary expansion will lower the real wage and reduce unemployment; an unexpected *reduction* in the rate of inflation caused by monetary contraction will raise the real wage and increase unemployment.

In the long run, however, these changes are reversed by labor market adjustments that push unemployment back to its natural rate. Suppose unanticipated inflation has reduced the real wage. As unemployment falls as a result, fewer people are available to work and businesses will have to compete against each other to attract new workers and to retain their current employees. This competition will cause real wages to rise, making it more costly to employ workers. As the real wage rises, the demand for labor falls and unemployment gradually returns to its natural rate.

Now suppose that lower-than-anticipated inflation has increased the real wage, causing unemployment to rise above the natural rate. Because unemployment has risen, a larger number of people are now competing for fewer jobs. Competition between workers for scarce jobs will cause real wages to fall, as each worker offers to accept employment at a real wage below those of other workers. As real wages are bid down, the unemployment rate returns to its natural rate. Over time, therefore, labor market adjustments bring the real wage back to the wage that clears the labor market, and the economy returns to its natural rate of unemployment. Thus, while an unanticipated change in monetary policy can move unemployment below or above the natural rate in the short run, the effects will be reversed over the long run. Therefore, governments cannot use monetary policy to reduce unemployment over the long run. Any monetary expansion will reduce unemployment for a short while, but eventually labor market adjustments will restore unemployment to its natural rate.

Moreover, a government determined to use monetary policy to keep unemployment below the natural rate for any lengthy period will have to continually increase the rate of inflation to do so. (This is called the **accelerationist principle.**) We can see why from a modified version of the **Phillips curve** (Figure 13.1). In this version, the economy is characterized by multiple Phillips curves. In each short-run period, policy makers face a trade-off between inflation and unemployment—the downward-sloping curves labeled T_1, T_2, and T_3 in the figure. Because there is no long-run trade-off between inflation and unemployment, the long-run Phillips curve is drawn as a vertical line that crosses the horizontal axis at the economy's natural rate of unemployment (U_n).

Now suppose that—from the natural rate of unemployment—point A on Phillips curve T_1—the government expands monetary policy in an attempt to push the rate of unemployment below the natural rate, say, to point U_b. Inflation rises, thereby reducing real wages and boosting employment. This effect in turn pushes the economy

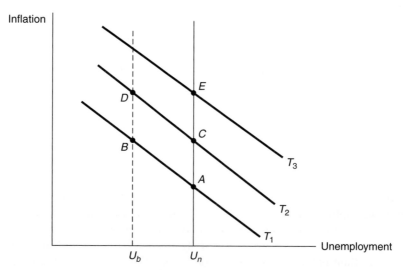

Figure 13.1   The Long-Run Phillips Curve.

along the short-run Phillips curve T_1 to point B. As workers and businesses react to the now-higher inflation, however, the real wage rises back to its initial level and unemployment return to its natural rate.

The inflation produced by the expansion is permanent, however; consequently, the government now faces a new short-run Phillips curve, labeled T_2. If the government wants to push unemployment below the natural rate again, it must expand the money supply once more. If so, then the resulting inflation reduces the real wage and causes unemployment to fall to point D. However, adjustments again restore the economy to its natural rate of unemployment at an even higher rate of inflation, point E on short-run Phillips curve T_3. Thus, if a government wants to keep unemployment below the natural rate for any extended period, it must continually increase the rate of inflation.

The experience of the United States since the early 1960s illustrates this dynamic at work. One can identify four distinct short-run Phillips curves for the United States between 1961 and 1999. (See Figure 13.2.) During the 1960s, the inflation–unemployment trade-off occurred within a fairly narrow range of relatively low inflation (an average of 3 percent). In the early 1970s, the American economy jumped to a new short-run Phillips curve that persisted until about 1983. The trade-off between inflation and unemployment is apparent on this new Phillips curve, but it occurs at a higher rate of inflation (which averaged about 8.2 percent throughout the period), without a corresponding decrease in the average level of unemployment. In fact, unemployment averaged 7.2 percent during this period, much higher than the level that prevailed during the 1960s.

The American economy moved to a third short-run Phillips curve between 1984 and 1994. Once again, the trade-off between inflation and unemployment is apparent

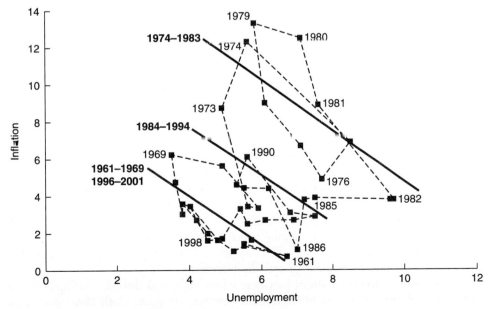

Figure 13.2 Phillips Curves in the United States, 1961–2001.
Source: Data From *Economic Report of the President,* 2002.

in this period, although now it takes place at a lower rate of inflation. Moreover, the reduction in inflation in this period did not cause unemployment to rise. In fact, average unemployment was lower during these ten years (6.5 percent) than in the previous ten years, precisely the opposite of what we would expect if a stable long-run Phillips curve trade-off were at work.

Finally, during the 1990s, the United States migrated to a fourth short-run Phillips curve, which coincides well with the curve that held during the 1960s. As was the case during the previous ten years, falling inflation did not raise unemployment relative to the earlier period. In fact, unemployment in this period was again lower, on average, than it had been during the previous ten years. The American experience during the last 40 years therefore illustrates the absence of a stable long-run trade-off between inflation and unemployment. Higher inflation during the 1970s did not reduce unemployment relative to the 1960s; lower inflation in the 1980s did not raise unemployment relative to the 1970s; and lower inflation in the 1990s did not raise unemployment relative to the 1980s.

The American experience was not unique, but was instead widely shared by most advanced industrialized countries. Average inflation rates in the European Union during the 1970s, rising to 11 percent, were more than twice as high as they had been during the 1960s. (See Table 13.1.) Some countries experienced much higher inflation than these averages suggest; Italy and Great Britain, for example, saw their inflation rates rise above 20 percent in the mid-1970s. Yet, this higher inflation failed to produce any sustained reduction in unemployment. In fact, unemployment rose almost continuously throughout the decade. (See Table 13.1.) Unemployment more than doubled in the European Union during the 1970s, jumping from 2.3 percent at the end of the 1960s to 5.4 percent in 1980. Thus, economic developments during the 1970s suggested that there was no stable trade-off between inflation and unemployment. Any gains in employment realized from monetary expansion were short term at best and were accompanied by a persistent increase in the rate of inflation.

All of this would be of little concern if inflation were innocuous. Inflation isn't innocuous, however, and may have a large negative impact on a country's economic performance. Inflation raises uncertainty among firms and unions, and this uncertainty can reduce investment and economic growth rates. Less investment and lower economic growth can in turn raise the natural rate of unemployment. The advanced industrialized countries provide some evidence about how inflation has affected economic performance during the last 26 years. Figure 13.3 illustrates the relationship between inflation and economic growth rates for 15 advanced industrialized countries over that period. Each point on the graph represents the average rate of inflation and the average rate of economic growth for one country between 1969 and 1995. The data suggest that countries with relatively high inflation rates have experienced lower economic growth, while countries with relatively low rates of inflation have had higher economic growth. Admittedly, this relationship is not very strong. In fact, Japan, which had one of the lowest rates of inflation and the fastest rate of economic growth of all the countries, is a bit of an anomaly. If we exclude Japan, the negative relationship between inflation and economic growth disappears.

A somewhat stronger pattern is evident when we look at the relationship between inflation and unemployment in these same countries (Figure 13.4). Here, each data point represents the average rate of inflation and the average rate of unemployment

Table 13.1

Inflation and Unemployment, 1960–1990 (period averages)

	1964–1970		1971–1980		1981–1990	
	Inflation	Unemployment	Inflation	Unemployment	Inflation	Unemployment
United States	3.0	4.2	7.4	6.4	4.2	7.1
Germany	3.7	0.7	5.3	2.2	2.8	6.0
France	4.4	2.0	9.9	4.1	6.3	9.3
Britain	4.2	1.7	14.0	3.8	6.5	9.7
Italy	4.5	5.0	14.8	6.1	10.4	9.5
Japan	5.4	1.2	7.6	1.8	1.4	2.5

Source: Commission of the European Communities.

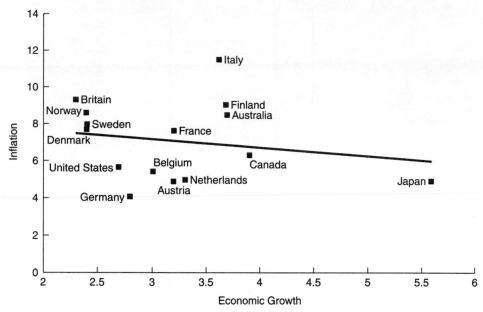

Figure 13.3 Inflation and Growth, 1969–1995.
Source: OECD.

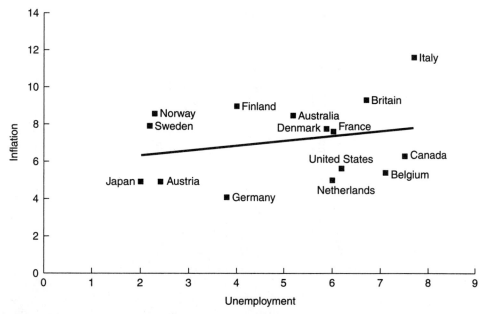

Figure 13.4 Inflation and Unemployment, 1969–1995.
Source: OECD.

for one country between 1969 and 1995. These data suggest that countries with high inflation have had relatively high unemployment rates, while countries with low inflation have had relatively lower unemployment rates. At the high end, inflation in Italy averaged just under 12 percent and unemployment just under 8 percent. At the low end, inflation in Japan averaged 4.9 percent, unemployment only 2 percent. Again, however, the relationship is not terribly strong.

Of course, the determinants of economic growth and unemployment are far more complex than this simple correlation suggests. It may be that once the other factors which determine economic growth and unemployment are taken into account, inflation has no impact at all. What does seem clear, however, is that high inflation has not been associated with *better* economic performance. There is no evidence that countries with higher inflation experienced stronger economic growth or lower unemployment. Consequently, economists argue that, because inflation provides no permanent gains in terms of higher employment or growth and carries potentially large costs in terms of fewer jobs and less growth, society is best served by monetary policies that consistently deliver low inflation.

The apparent collapse of a stable Phillips curve trade-off between inflation and unemployment during the 1970s, combined with innovative economic theories that reconceptualized the relationship between inflation, employment, and monetary policy, altered the way governments thought about monetary policy. The Keynesian strategies that most governments had adopted in the early postwar period were based on the assumption of a stable long-run trade-off between inflation and unemployment. As evidence accumulated that such a trade-off did not exist, and as economists developed new theories to explain why it should not exist, governments began to question the utility of Keynesian strategies. If monetary policy could not be used to maintain full employment, but only produced inflation, and if inflation in turn had a negative impact on economic performance, what good was served by continuing to pursue Keynesian strategies of demand management?

During the 1980s, governments increasingly concluded that the answer to this rhetorical question was "not much." And as they did, they began to abandon the Keynesian approach to macroeconomic management in favor of an alternative approach to monetary policy. In this alternative approach, the only proper objective of monetary policy was to achieve and maintain a very low and stable rate of inflation. The shift from Keynesian strategies to the pursuit of **price stability** occurred first in Great Britain, under the leadership of Margaret Thatcher, and in the United States at the tail end of the Carter administration. Governments in the other advanced industrialized countries adopted similar policies during the 1980s.

The Time-Consistency Problem

Although most governments were determined to achieve and maintain low inflation, few could easily do so. Expectations of high inflation were deeply embedded in society. By the 1980s, the ten-year history of high inflation had convinced workers and businesses to expect similarly high rates of inflation in the future. These expectations in turn shaped wage bargaining, giving inflation a momentum of its own. Expecting high inflation, unions demanded, and business provided, large annual nominal wage increases to keep pace. Governments then faced the unpleasant choice of delivering these high inflation rates or imposing high unemployment. In order to end inflation without generating a sharp increase in unemployment, each government would have to make a **credible commitment** to deliver low inflation. That is, each government would have to convince workers and businesses that it was truly determined to bring inflation down and keep it down.

Governments could not easily make credible commitments to low inflation, however, because they confronted time-consistency problems (Kydland and Prescott 1977). A **time-consistency problem** arises when the best course of action at a particular moment in time differs from the best course of action in general (Keech 1995, 38). Examinations in college courses offer an excellent example of the problem (Drazen 2000, 103). Professors are interested principally in getting their students to learn the material being taught in the course. Examinations are important only because they force students to study more than they would otherwise. As the semester begins, therefore, the professor's optimal strategy—that is, the best course of action in general—is to schedule a final exam. If no final exam is scheduled, most students will study little, but with the threat of a final exam, students will study harder and learn more from the course.

Once exam day arrives, however, the professor's optimal strategy is to cancel the exam. Because students expected an exam, they have studied hard and have learned as much about the material as they can. Giving the exam is pointless. Moreover, the professor is better off if she does not give the exam; she need not devote time to grading the exam and can use that time for other purposes. The students are also better off, for they are spared the time and the anxiety associated with taking the exam. Thus, the professor's optimal strategy at the beginning of the semester—to declare that a final exam will be given—is not her optimal strategy at the end of the semester. The professor, therefore, has time-inconsistent preferences.

Governments often have time-inconsistent monetary policy preferences. The government's optimal strategy this year is to declare that it will use monetary policy next year to maintain price stability. If workers believe that the government is committed to price stability, they will set nominal wages accordingly. Once next year's nominal wages are set, however, the government can use monetary policy to reduce the rate of unemployment. By raising inflation above the level that it had announced and upon which workers had based their nominal wage contracts, the government reduces real wages and raises employment. This decrease in unemployment can boost the government's popularity, making it more likely to win the next election. The government's monetary policy preferences, therefore, are not consistent over time. It has an incentive to convince wage bargainers that it is committed to low inflation, but then, once it has done so, it has an incentive to expand the money supply to reduce unemployment.

Because the government has time-inconsistent monetary policy preferences, wage bargainers have little incentive to believe any inflation target that the government announces. Imagine, for example, that you know that in every past semester your current professor has always announced at the beginning of the semester that there will be a final exam, but subsequently has always cancelled the exam. How credible would you find this professor's current beginning-of-the-semester promise to give a final examination? You would disregard the professor's promise because you recognize that he has an incentive to renege and because you have knowledge that he has reneged in the past. How much work would you then put into the course? Unless you were deeply interested in the subject, it is likely that you would work less hard in that class than in others in which you know that a final will be given.

The same logic applies to workers' response to government statements about inflation. Because workers recognize that the government has an incentive to renege on a promise to deliver low inflation, they will always expect the government to deliver higher inflation than it promises. These expectations of higher-than-announced inflation cause workers to seek nominal wage agreements that protect real wages from the inflation that they expect, rather than the amount that the government promises to deliver.

This interaction between wage bargainers and the government has perverse consequences for social welfare. Suppose the government truly intends to keep inflation next year at 2 percent and publicly announces its intention to do so. Workers disregard this promise, however, and expect the government to actually deliver 6 percent inflation during the next year. They then negotiate a nominal wage increase on the basis of this expectation. The government must now choose between two suboptimal monetary policy responses. On the one hand, the government can refuse to expand the money supply in response to the 6 percent wage increase and stick to its promise to deliver 2 percent inflation. If it does so, however, real wages will rise by 4 percent, and as a consequence, unemployment will rise. On the other hand, the government can expand the money supply in order to deliver the 6 percent inflation that labor anticipated but that nobody really wants. Thus, either inflation or unemployment will be higher than it would be if the government could make a credible commitment to low inflation.

Most European governments faced precisely this situation in the late 1970s. The ten-year history of high inflation generated expectations of continued high inflation in the future. Unions thus sought, and business generally provided, nominal wage increases based on the expectation of annual inflation rates of 8 to 10 percent. With these wage contracts in place, governments faced the unpleasant choice between delivering the high inflation that everyone expected but nobody really wanted or tightening monetary policy, reducing inflation, and raising unemployment substantially. Unwilling to embrace either option, many governments began to search for some way to make a credible commitment to price stability.

Commitment Mechanisms

Governments tried to establish a credible commitment to low inflation by creating **commitment mechanisms** in the form of institutions that tied their hands. Two institutions have been particularly prominent in this quest for a commitment mechanism: independent central banks and fixed exchange rates. In theory, both can provide a credible commitment by preventing the government from using monetary policy to achieve short-term objectives. In practice, however, only central-bank independence has actually done so.

Central bank independence is the degree to which the central bank can set monetary policy free from interference by the government. More specifically, central-bank independence is a function of three things: the degree to which the central bank is free to decide what economic objective to pursue, the degree to which the central bank is free to decide how to set monetary policy in pursuit of this objective, and the degree to which central bank decisions can be reversed by other branches of government (Blinder 1999, 54). A fully independent central bank has complete freedom to decide what economic goals to pursue, the capability of determining on its own how to use monetary policy to pursue those goals, and complete insulation from attempts by other branches of government to reverse its decisions.

Switzerland's central bank, the Swiss National Bank, provides a good illustration of a highly independent central bank (Eijffinger and Schaling 1993, 80–81). The National Bank Law that established the Swiss National Bank contains no provision whatsoever for allowing the government to influence monetary policy. In addition, the bank's principal policymaking body, the Bank Committee, is composed of 10 members who are selected by the Bank Council, a group of 40 individuals responsible for the management of the bank. Thus, the government has no direct role in selecting the people that make monetary policy decisions. As a consequence, the Swiss government cannot easily influence the monetary policies adopted by the Swiss National Bank, which thus controls Switzerland's monetary policy independently of the everyday vicissitudes of Swiss politics.

At the other end of the spectrum lies a fully subordinate central bank. Politically subordinate central banks implement monetary policy on behalf of, and in response to, the government, which determines the goals of monetary policy, instructs the central bank how to set monetary policy to achieve those goals, and can reverse the bank's decisions if they are contrary to the ones desired by the government. The Reserve Bank of Australia provides a good illustration of such a central bank (Eijffinger and Schaling 1993, 82–83). The Australian secretary of the treasury, a government minister, has final authority over monetary policy decisions and must approve any interest-rate changes that the bank may propose. In addition, one government official has a vote on the Reserve Bank Board, the principal monetary policy decision-making body. The Australian government thus has considerable control over the monetary policy decisions made by the Reserve Bank. As a result, Australian monetary policy can be strongly influenced by the government's political needs.

Granting the central bank independence solves the time-consistency problem by taking monetary policy completely out of politicians' hands. Monetary policy is no longer set by politicians motivated by short-run political considerations. Instead, appointed officials who cannot easily be removed from office set monetary policy, which is thus insulated from politics. Insulating monetary policy decisions from short-term political incentives makes it less likely that monetary policy will be directed toward short-term goals, such as a temporary increase in employment, and more likely that it will be oriented toward price stability. An independent central bank, therefore, can make a credible commitment to low inflation even though a government cannot.

The central bank's commitment to low inflation should in turn affect wage bargaining. Because the central bank is not motivated by political objectives, labor unions and businesses will believe that the central bank will deliver the inflation rate it promises to deliver. They will then negotiate next year's wage contract to embody this

POLICY ANALYSIS AND DEBATE

Central-Bank Independence and Democracy

Question
Should democracies grant central banks political independence?

Overview
As we have seen, governments have granted their central banks considerable independence during the last ten years. The justification for doing so lies in theories which assert that, by doing so, governments are able to commit to low inflation, which in turn generates better economic performance. Yet, granting the central bank independence is not costless. One important dimension of these costs is political. As Alan Blinder, former member of the Federal Reserve Board, has asked, "Isn't there something profoundly undemocratic about making the central bank independent of political control? Doesn't assigning so much power to unelected technocrats contradict some fundamental tenets of democratic theory" (Blinder 1999, 66)? Blinder has a point, for monetary policy is perhaps the single most important and single most powerful policy instrument at a government's disposal, and one might reasonably question the legitimacy of conferring such power on people that are not easily held accountable. In fact, it is surprising that democracies confer such independence. Could you imagine voters supporting a decision which allowed an institution that was independent of political control to determine income tax rates?

Blinder also highlights two factors that he thinks reduce the inconsistency between democracy and independent central banks. First, legislatures confer independence on central banks; thus, they can withdraw this independence. Accordingly, society retains some influence over monetary policy. Second, central bankers are typically appointed by elected officials and can be removed from office (or not reappointed) if they behave in a manner that is inconsistent with societal interests. Therefore, society sacrifices its ability to influence day-to-day decisions, but retains the ability to set the broad parameters within which monetary policy is made. Should society give up some of its political rights in exchange for the economic benefits that independent central banks are supposed to provide?

Policy Options
- Grant the central bank independence and allow it to set monetary policy without political interference.
- Assert political control over the central bank to ensure that monetary policy reflects the public interest.

Policy Analysis
- How important are the economic benefits that central-bank independence provides?
- How large are the political costs arising from central-bank independence?
- Are any other political institutions granted independence from electoral politics in democracies?

Take a Position
- Which option do you prefer? Justify your choice.
- What criticisms of your position should you anticipate? How would you defend your recommendation against these criticisms?

Continued

Resources

Online: Look for two readings focusing on the European Central Bank: Christa Randzio-Plath and Thomas Padoa-Schippo, "The European Central Bank: Independence and Accountability" (*http://www.zei.de/download/zei_wp/B00–16.pdf*), and Paivi Leino, "The European Central Bank and Legitimacy" (*http://www.jeanmonnetprogram.org/papers/00/001101.html*).

In Print: Alan Blinder, *Central Banking in Theory and Practice* (Cambridge, MA: MIT Press, 1999); Kathleen MacNamara and Sheri Berman, "Bank on Democracy: Why Central Banks Need Public Oversight," *Foreign Affairs* 78 (March–April 1999); Joseph E. Stiglitz, "Central Banking in a Democratic Society," *De Economist* 142 (2), 1998 : 199–226.

---

stated inflation target rather than their best guess of next year's inflation. As a consequence, they are more likely to establish a nominal wage that maintains the appropriate real wage. The result should be lower inflation, as well as less variation in the rate of unemployment and growth. Granting the central bank independence should lead to lower inflation, higher economic growth, and lower unemployment over the long run.

Do independent central banks actually have the economic consequences that are attributed to them in theory? There is some evidence that they do. Figure 13.5 depicts the relationship between central-bank independence and average inflation rates in 15 advanced industrialized countries between 1969 and 1995. The graph shows quite clearly that countries with more independent central banks (the countries located farther to the right along the horizontal axis) have experienced lower rates of inflation, on average, than countries with less independent central banks. Germany, Austria, and the United States, home to three of the most independent central banks in the advanced industrialized countries, have enjoyed substantially lower inflation than Italy and Britain, where politicians controlled monetary policy until quite recently.

Other evidence indicates, however, that the lower inflation enjoyed by countries with independent central banks may not have come without cost. Figure 13.6 suggests that countries with more independent central banks have experienced lower rates of economic growth, on average, than countries without independent central banks. Economic growth in Germany, for example, averaged 2.8 percent in the 26-year period from 1969 to 1995, compared with 3.6 percent average annual growth rates in Italy. A similar effect appears to exist for unemployment: Countries with independent central banks have had higher rates of unemployment, on average, than countries without independent central banks (Figure 13.7). Germany and the United States, for example, averaged higher unemployment over the 1969–1995 period than did Norway and Sweden, two countries in which governments retained control over monetary policy.

Thus, although independent central banks appear to reduce inflation, there is some evidence that they may also be associated with lower growth and higher unemployment. Once again, however, we should not conclude too much from these simple correlations. Economic outcomes are determined by a complex set of factors. Once these

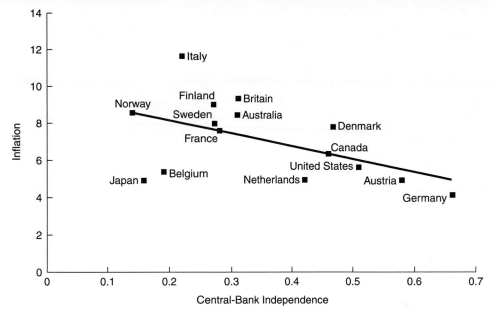

Figure 13.5   Central-Bank Independence and Inflation, 1969–1995.
Source: OECD and Cukierman 1992.

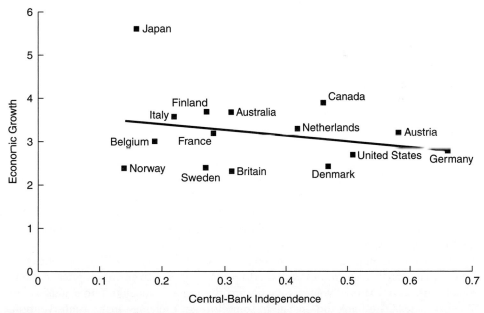

Figure 13.6   Central-Bank Independence and Economic Growth, 1969–1995.
Source: OECD and Cukierman 1992.

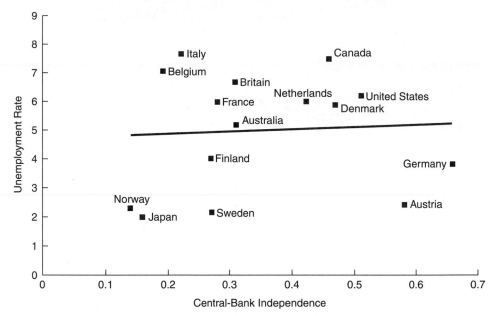

Figure 13.7   Central-Bank Independence and Unemployment, 1969–1995.
Source: OECD and Cukierman 1992.

other factors are taken into account, it may turn out that independent central banks do not have a negative impact on economic growth and the rate of unemployment. What does seem clear, however, at least for this set of countries, is that independent central banks have been better able to deliver low inflation than governments have.

In the early 1980s, however, few European governments had independent central banks. Consequently, they sought to establish a credible commitment by using the European monetary system as an alternative to central-bank independence (Giavazzi and Giovannini 1989; Oatley 1997). The EMS offered the possibility of a credible commitment to low inflation because it was centered upon the German central bank, the *Bundesbank,* the most independent central bank in the European Union. As a result, German monetary policy was little influenced by political pressure, and it could therefore commit to low inflation. Moreover, the *Bundesbank* had a strong record of delivering low inflation. In fact, German inflation was the lowest among all EU countries, averaging only 4.4 percent between 1975 and 1984 (Oatley 1997, 82). A fixed exchange rate with Germany, therefore, might allow the EU countries with high inflation to "import" both the *Bundesbank's* low inflation policy and its credible commitment to that policy.

Governments imported German monetary policy by pegging their currencies to the German mark. The *Bundesbank* used monetary policy to maintain price stability in Germany and was relatively passive toward the mark's exchange rate against other EU currencies. The bank did engage in some foreign exchange market intervention, but only reluctantly and only when required to do so by the system's rules. Other governments used their monetary policies to peg their currencies to the German mark. By pegging to the mark, governments enduring high inflation were forced to mimic the *Bundesbank*'s monetary policy. When the *Bundesbank* tightened that policy, other governments had to tighten their monetary policies in order to maintain their fixed exchange rates. As long as the *Bundesbank* continued to maintain low inflation in Germany, a fixed exchange rate inside the EMS would force other EU governments to pursue low-inflation monetary policies, too. By pegging to the mark, therefore, the high-inflation countries could "import" the *Bundesbank*'s low-inflation monetary policy.

In order to "import" the *Bundesbank* credible commitment to low inflation, however, unions and businesses had to believe that the government was determined to maintain its fixed exchange rate. If these social partners viewed the fixed exchange rate as an irrevocable commitment—one that the government would not alter, regardless of domestic economic developments—they would adjust their wage-bargaining behavior accordingly. Recognizing that their government was committed to the *Bundesbank*'s low-inflation monetary policy in order to maintain the fixed exchange rate, unions and businesses would reduce their estimates of future inflation rates. As these inflationary expectations fell, unions would seek smaller nominal wage increases. Thus, if a government could make a credible commitment to the fixed exchange rate, it could break the large nominal wage increases that were driving European inflation.

It proved very difficult for governments to demonstrate that they were irrevocably committed to a fixed exchange rate. The EMS did not take control of monetary policy away from the government and place it in the hands of appointed officials insulated from political pressures. Consequently, workers and businesses simply shifted their attention away from whether the government was committed to some inflation target and focused instead on whether the government was truly committed to its fixed exchange rate. Then, because EU governments retained full discretion over their currencies' exchange rates in the EMS, unions and businesses were never convinced that the government would not devalue within the system when it was politically convenient to do so. Governments gave them plenty of reason to be skeptical, as currency devaluations were quite common in the first seven years of the system's operation. Consequently, while EU governments did reduce inflation during the 1980s, and while the EMS facilitated this achievement by enabling countries with high inflation to "import" German monetary policy, there is little evidence that the fixed exchange rate provided a credible commitment to price stability. Instead, inflation fell because European governments accepted the higher unemployment that tight monetary policies generated in the context of large nominal wage increases.

EU governments' quest for a credible commitment to low inflation played an important role in the shift to, and the design of, economic and monetary union. The European Union's central bank, the European Central Bank (ECB), was established in January 1999 and is one of the world's most independent central banks. European governments participating in the EMU no longer have national monetary policies, a factor that greatly reduces their ability to determine national monetary policy. In addition, as a condition for membership in the EMU, EU governments have granted their own national central banks, which have become the operating agencies of the ECB, independence from politics. Finally, the laws governing the ECB and monetary policy in the European Union prohibit national governments from attempting to influence the vote of their respective national central-bank governors in the ECB, and they also prohibit the EU's Council of Ministers from attempting to influence ECB decisions. National governments in the EMU, therefore, are three times removed from monetary policy decisions: once by the EMU itself, a second time by domestic central-bank independence, and yet a third time by the rules governing decision making within the ECB.

The European Union's shift to highly independent central banking finds echoes in the rest of the advanced industrialized world. The American central bank, the Federal Reserve, has been highly independent since its creation. Other governments have reformed central bank laws to grant their banks greater independence. Japan moved to provide its central bank, the Bank of Japan, with greater independence in the mid-1990s. Great Britain granted its central bank, the Bank of England, full independence in 1997, even though it is not yet participating in the EMU. New Zealand granted its central bank greater independence in 1989. Thus, almost all central banks in the advanced industrialized world enjoy substantial independence, and most have gained this independence only recently. Independent central banks have directed monetary policy toward the maintenance of price stability, an objective that is often defined as about 1 to 2 percent inflation per year.

The last 25 years have thus brought fundamental changes to the politics of monetary policy. Throughout the advanced industrialized world, governments have abandoned the Keynesian strategies of demand management that dominated monetary policy in the early postwar period. As governments gradually, and in many cases grudgingly, accepted that there was no stable Phillips curve trade-off between inflation and unemployment that they could exploit for political advantage, they began to look for ways to tie their hands in order to reduce inflation and maintain price stability. The solution they adopted lay in granting political independence to their central banks, and allowing those banks to set monetary policy free of daily political interference. As a consequence, throughout the industrialized world, monetary policy is uniformly focused on a single economic objective: maintaining price stability.

Independent Central Banks and Exchange Rates

The creation of independent central banks will obviously have an impact on the way that domestic politics shapes monetary and exchange-rate policy. Yet, because the shift to independent central banks is such a recent phenomenon, it is not clear how the dynamics will change. We can, however, draw on the models we developed in Chapter 12 to speculate a bit about how such politics might evolve.

One possibility is that the politics of monetary and exchange-rate policies will be characterized by conflict between elected officials and central banks. Such conflicts may emerge because of three interconnected aspects of monetary and exchange-rate politics in this new institutional environment. First, although the institutional framework governing monetary policy has changed, interest-group preferences over monetary and exchange-rate policies have not. Interest groups, class and sector based, are still affected by monetary and exchange-rate policies in the ways we examined in Chapter 12. As a consequence, interest groups retain incentives to pressure the government and the central bank to adopt the monetary and exchange-rate policies they prefer. The emergence of independent central banks means only that these groups must pursue their goals through different channels.

Second, despite the creation of highly independent central banks, monetary policy is not perfectly insulated from political influence. Even as national governments have relinquished control over monetary policy to independent central banks, they have retained control over exchange-rate policy. In the United States, the Department of the Treasury, an executive-branch agency, takes the lead in setting exchange-rate policy for the dollar (Destler and Henning 1989). Treasury officials are responsible for negotiating currency agreements with foreign governments, and the Treasury makes decisions about when to engage in foreign exchange market intervention (although intervention per se is conducted by the New York Federal Reserve Bank). The Treasury's control over the dollar's exchange rate is not absolute, however. In general, the Treasury is reluctant to act without the consent of, or at least the absence of opposition from, the Federal Reserve. Moreover, although the Treasury can request the Federal Reserve to engage in foreign exchange intervention, it cannot order it to do so on its account. Thus, while the Treasury takes the lead in U.S. exchange rate policy, it has consistently sought cooperation with the Federal Reserve.

A similar split of authority is evident in the European Union. While the ECB controls monetary policy, the Council of Ministers has authority over the Euro's exchange rate against non-EU currencies. Article 109 of the Maastricht Treaty gives the Council of Ministers the authority to "conclude formal agreements on an exchange rate system . . . in relation to non-Community currencies," and it allows the Council to "adopt, adjust or abandon" specific parities within such a system. The treaty also gives the Council the authority to "formulate general orientations" for exchange-rate policy toward non-EU currencies (Gros and Thygesen 1998, 486–488; Henning 1997, 31–42). However, the treaty requires the Council of Ministers to consult with the ECB in making decisions in line with the authority granted it and to take into account the central bank's commitment to price stability.

Because monetary and exchange-rate policies are two sides of the same coin, government control of exchange-rate policy can be used to force the central bank to pursue the monetary policies that the government and its supporters desire. For example, some have argued that Helmut Schmidt, who was the German chancellor in the late 1970s and early 1980s, sought to create the European Monetary System in order to force the *Bundesbank* to pursue a more expansionary monetary policy (Oatley 1997). Fixing the German mark to the French franc, the Italian lira, and other EU currencies, Schmidt thought, would force the *Bundesbank* to intervene in the foreign exchange market. In most instances, this intervention would prevent the mark from appreciating inside the EMS and would therefore cause an expansion of the German money supply. The exchange rate commitment would thus force the *Bundesbank* to pursue a looser monetary policy than it wanted.

An identical logic can be applied to the contemporary international monetary system. A government or, in the case of the European Union, a group of governments that want a more expansionary monetary policy than the central bank is willing to adopt might use its control over exchange-rate policy to force the central bank to change its policy. Control over exchange rate policy, therefore, provides governments with a back door through which they can attempt to influence monetary policy. To the extent that they use this back door, they are likely to come into conflict with the central bank.

Such conflicts are most likely to arise when the central bank wants the exchange rate to move in one direction in order to maintain price stability, while the government wants the exchange rate to move in the other direction to satisfy demands made by important interest groups. Conflicts of this nature arose periodically between the German government and the *Bundesbank* prior to the creation of the EMU and emerged in the European Union in the fall of 1999 and summer of 2000. The euro depreciated sharply against the dollar and the yen in its first two years of existence. The ECB became concerned that the depreciation would generate inflation in the union as the price of traded goods rose in response to the euro's weakening. As Matti Vanhala, governor of the Bank of Finland, and therefore a member of the ECB's Governing Council, noted, the euro's weakness is "a bad thing from the point of view of the ECB's goals." The Bank of France's Jean-Claude Trichet echoed these concerns, emphasizing that the ECB needed to be "vigilant about inflation risks" arising from the euro's weakness (Barber 2000b, 9). The ECB tried to stem the euro's depreciation by raising interest rates. European governments were much less concerned about the euro's weakness and criticized ECB efforts to stabilize it. German Chancellor Gerhard Schroder, for example, stated that "the euro's low level [is] a cause for satisfaction rather than concern," because it increases German growth rates by making it easier for German companies to export (Barber 2000a, 8).

Similar dynamics emerged as the euro appreciated in 2004. European business associations began warning that too steep an appreciation would harm exporters (Major 2003, 7), and national politicians as well as EU officials began calling for the ECB to stem the currency's rise (Major 2004, 1). This time, European governments began to criticize the ECB for failing to cut interest rates. Some government officials, including the French finance minister, called for the ECB to take growth and unemployment rates, as well as inflation, into account when formulating monetary policy. He also suggested that the euro group, a committee composed of the finance ministers from euro-zone countries, be given a larger role in guiding ECB policy (Arnold and Parker 2004, 9). Such a development would represent a substantial reduction in the ECB's independence.

Such conflicts will not be simply between the government and the central bank: interest groups may exert pressures on whichever actor they believe is most likely to pursue their preferred policies. Thus, drawing on the sectoral model, we might expect firms in the traded-goods industries to exert pressure on the government for some form of exchange-rate arrangement because they benefit from a weak currency. Firms in the nontraded-goods sector, which benefit from a strong currency, might in turn become strong supporters of the central bank.

Of course, all of this is just speculation, as it remains difficult to distinguish clear patterns in the new institutional environment. What does seem clear, however, is that the political dynamics of monetary and exchange-rate policy have changed as governments have granted central banks greater political independence. Electoral, partisan, and sectoral interest-group pressures could rather easily influence the monetary and exchange-rate policies that governments adopted during the early postwar period. The granting of political independence to central banks makes it much more difficult for these groups to influence policy. Nevertheless, interest groups are still affected by monetary and exchange-rate policies in the ways detailed in the first half of this chapter. Consequently, these groups still have an incentive to try to influence those policies.

How they do so and the extent to which they are successful will become clear only as the future unfolds.

Conclusion

The state-centered approach to monetary and exchange-rate politics emphasizes the social-welfare-enhancing role of independent central banks. By taking monetary policy out of politics and placing it in the hands of officials tightly insulated from the push and pulls of politics, society enjoys lower inflation and better overall economic performance than it would enjoy if governments retained control of monetary policy. Governments have embraced this logic, abandoning activist monetary policies and allowing independent central banks to dedicate monetary policy to the maintenance of price stability.

Two principal criticisms can be advanced against this state-centered approach. First, it offers more of a prescriptive framework than an explanatory framework. The approach tells us that social welfare is greater with an independent central bank than with a politically controlled central bank, and on the basis of that claim, it suggests that governments should grant their central banks greater political independence. It tells us very little, however, about what factors motivate elected officials to create independent central banks. One might argue that governments create independent central banks to maximize long-term social welfare. Yet, such an explanation rests uneasily with the central logic of the time-consistency problem. After all, the entire rationale for central-bank independence rests on the claim that elected officials care more about short-term electoral gains than long-run social welfare. We thus need some explanation for why governments that are supposedly unconcerned with long-run welfare gains create central-bank institutions whose sole purpose is to raise long-run social welfare.

Nor does this state-centered approach explain how monetary authorities who are responsible for an independent central bank are likely to behave. While an independent central bank that gives priority to price stability may raise social welfare, little attention has been devoted to the question of whether the people who run the independent central bank actually have an incentive to give priority to price stability. Consequently, much work remains before this approach offers an explanation for the changes that have taken place in central-banking institutions since the early 1980s.

Key Terms

Accelerationist Principle

Central-bank Independence

Commitment Mechanism

Credible Commitment

Expectations

Natural Rate of Unemployment

Phillips Curve

Price Stability

Time-Consistency Problem

Web Links

Central banks in the advanced industrialized countries maintain websites with plenty of information about monetary and exchange-rate policy. Visit

The Federal Reserve Board: *http://www.federalreserve.gov/*.

The Bank of England: *http://www.bankofengland.co.uk/*.

The European Central Bank: *http://www.ecb.int/*.

The *Bundesbank*: *http://www.bundesbank.de/ind.ex_e.html*.

The Bank of Japan: *http://www.boj.or.jp/en/*.

Bank of France: *http://www.banque-france.fr./gb/home.htm*.

New York University maintains a website dedicated to the study of central banks. You can visit this site at *http://www.law.nyu.edu/centralbankscenter/*.

Suggestions for Further Reading

Perhaps the most comprehensive work on central-bank independence is Alex Cukierman, *Central Bank Strategy, Credibility, and Independence: Theory and Evidence* (Cambridge, MA: MIT Press, 1992). A good treatment of the politics of central banking in Western Europe before the EMU can be found in John B. Goodman, *Monetary Sovereignty: the Politics of Central Banking in Western Europe* (Ithaca, NY: Cornell University Press, 1992).

The classic statement of the time-consistency problem can be found in Finn Kydland and Edward C. Prescott, "Rules Rather than Discretion: The Dynamic Inconsistency of Optimal Plans," *Journal of Political Economy* 83: 473–91.

The best discussion of the European Monetary System as a commitment mechanism is found in Francesco Giavazzi and Alberto Giovannini, *Limiting Exchange Rate Flexibility in Europe* (Cambridge, MA: MIT Press, 1989). For a contrasting view, see Michele Fratianni and Jürgen von Hagen, *The European Monetary System and European Monetary Union* (Boulder, CO: Westview Press, 1992).

CHAPTER 14

Developing Countries and International Finance I: The Latin American Debt Crisis

D eveloping countries have had a difficult relationship with the international financial system. At the center of these difficulties lies a seemingly inexorable boom-
and-bust cycle. The cycle typically starts with changes in international capital markets
that create new opportunities for developing countries to attract foreign capital. Wanting to tap into foreign capital to speed economic development, developing countries
exploit this opportunity with great energy. Eventually, developing countries accumulate large foreign debt burdens that they cannot easily repay and are pushed toward
default. The looming threat of default frightens foreign lenders, who refuse to provide
additional loans to developing countries and who attempt to recover many of the loans
they had made previously. As foreign capital flees, the developing countries are pushed
into severe economic crises. Governments then turn to the International Monetary
Fund and the World Bank for assistance and are required to implement far-reaching
economic reforms in order to gain those organizations' aid. This cycle has repeated
twice in the last 25 years, once in Latin America during the 1970s and 1980s, and once in
Asia during the 1990s. A similar, though distinct, cycle continues to afflict sub-Saharan
Africa. The political economy of North–South financial relations focuses on this three-
phase cycle of overborrowing, crisis, and adjustment.

Each phase of the cycle is shaped by developments in the international financial
system and inside developing societies. Developments in the international financial
system, including changes in international financial markets, in the activities of the
International Monetary Fund and World Bank, and in government policies in the
advanced industrialized countries, powerfully affect North–South financial relations.
They shape the ability of developing countries to borrow foreign capital, their ability to
repay the debt they accumulate, and the economic reforms they must adopt when
crises strike. Events that unfold within developing countries determine the amount of
foreign capital that developing societies accumulate and influence how governments
and economic actors in those countries use their foreign debt. These decisions in turn
shape the ability of governments to service their foreign debt and therefore influence
the likelihood that the country will experience a debt crisis.

This chapter and the next examine the evolution of this cycle in North–South financial relations through the last 50 years. We begin with a short overview of international capital flows in order to understand why they are important for developing societies and how developing societies gain access to foreign capital. We then briefly examine the relatively stable immediate postwar period during which capital flows to developing countries were dominated by foreign aid and foreign direct investment. The rest of the chapter focuses on the first major financial crisis of the postwar period: the Latin American debt crisis of the 1980s. We examine how it originated, how it was managed, and its consequences, political and economic, for Latin America.

Foreign Capital and Economic Development

If a cycle of overborrowing, crisis, and adjustment has characterized the history of capital flows from the advanced industrialized countries to the developing world, why do developing countries continue to draw on foreign capital? Why do they not simply refrain from borrowing that capital, thus bringing the cycle to an end? Developing countries continue to draw on foreign capital because of the potentially large benefits that accompany its apparent dangers. These benefits arise from the ability to draw on foreign savings to finance economic development.

Investment is one of the most important factors determining the ability of any society to raise per capita incomes (Cypher and Dietz 1997, 239). Yet, investment in developing societies is constrained by a shortage of domestic savings (Bruton 1969; McKinnon 1964). Table 14.1 illustrates average savings rates during the last 40 years throughout the world. The most striking difference that the table highlights is between the high-income OECD countries and the world's poorest countries. On average, the high-income countries saved almost one-quarter of their national income each year between 1960 and 1999. In contrast, the least-developed countries have saved less than 10 percent of their national income per year. Even when a developing country has a high savings rate, as in East Asia and the Pacific and in Latin America, the low incomes characteristic of a developing society mean that the total pool of savings generated by even a high savings rate is small. The scarcity of savings limits the amount, and raises the cost of, investment in these societies.

Foreign capital adds to the pool of savings available to finance investment. The ability to import capital from the rest of the world, therefore, allows developing coun-

Table 14.1
Average Savings Rates as a Percent of GDP, 1960–1999

High-Income OECD	24.12
Least-Developed Countries	8.03
East Asia and the Pacific	31.43
Latin America and the Caribbean	21.1
Sub-Saharan Africa	17.73
South Asia	16.65

Source: World Bank, *World Development Indicators on CD-ROM,* 2001.

tries to invest more at lower interest rates than would be possible otherwise. Many studies have found a one-to-one relationship between foreign capital inflows and investment: one dollar of additional foreign capital in a developing country produces one dollar of additional investment. (See e.g., Bosworth and Collins 1999; World Bank 2001a.) Higher investment in turn promotes economic development. Indeed, a considerable body of research suggests that developing countries which have participated in international financial markets during the last 30 years have experienced faster economic growth rates than countries that have insulated themselves from international financial flows. (See IMF 2001; World Bank 2001a.) Although foreign capital does not always yield higher growth (see, e.g., Rodrik 1998a), a country that draws on foreign capital has the *opportunity* to reach a higher development trajectory. Many other factors, some of which lie inside developing countries and others that inhere in the international financial system, shape the extent to which a developing country can take advantage of this opportunity.

Foreign capital can be supplied to developing countries through a number of channels. The broadest distinction is between foreign aid and private capital flows. **Foreign aid,** or official development assistance, is foreign capital provided by governments in the advanced industrialized countries and by multilateral financial institutions such as the **International Bank for Reconstruction and Development** (IBRD), known more commonly as the **World Bank.** The largest share of foreign aid is provided as **bilateral development assistance**—that is, foreign aid granted by one government directly to another government. In 2003, the advanced industrialized countries together provided $50 billion of bilateral assistance to developing countries. The World Bank and other multilateral development agencies provided an additional $17 billion. The United States provided the most aid in absolute terms in 2003, about $16.2 billion (Figure 14.1). Japan, France, Germany, and Great Britain were the other large donors in absolute terms. The rankings change considerably when we measure aid as a share of the donor country's national income (Figure 14.2). By this measure, the smaller northern European countries are the most generous, dedicating between 0.6 and 1 percent of their total national incomes to foreign aid. The United States emerges as the least generous country, dedicating only 0.15 percent of its national income to foreign aid.

Foreign aid can be provided as a grant, which does not require repayment, or as a loan requiring repayment. Most bilateral aid is offered in grant form. Multilateral agencies provide all of their assistance as loans. These development loans are in turn divided into two categories. Under **nonconcessional lending programs,** the interest rate charged on a loan is close to market interest rates. Under **concessional lending programs,** interest rates are below market interest rates. In general, the world's poorest countries draw a higher proportion of their aid from concessional lending programs. In contrast, middle-income developing countries draw a higher proportion of their aid from nonconcessional aid programs.

Private capital flows transfer savings to the developing world through the activities of private individuals and businesses. Private capital can be transferred to developing countries in a number of ways. Commercial banks transfer capital by lending to private agents or governments in developing societies. Private capital is also transferred when individuals and large institutional investors purchase stocks traded in developing-country stock markets. Private capital can also be transferred through bonds sold by

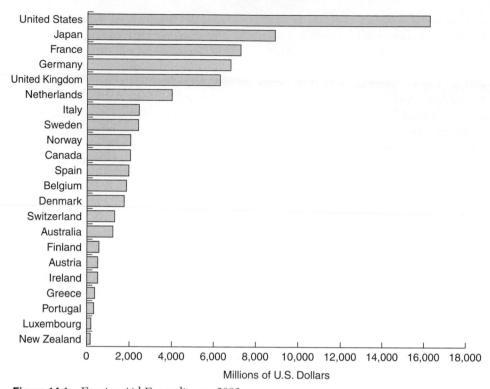

Figure 14.1   Foreign Aid Expenditures, 2003.
Source: OECD, *Statistical Annex of the 2004 Development Co-operation Report,* Table 4,
http://www.oecd.org/dataoecd/52/9/1893143.xls.

developing-country governments and businesses to individuals and private financial institutions in advanced industrialized societies. Finally, multinational corporations transfer capital each time they build a factory or some other facility in a developing country. The relative importance of each type of private capital flow has varied across time, as we shall see as we move through this chapter and the next.

These various private capital flows are usually divided into narrower categories. One such category distinguishes between debt-based flows and equity flows. Bank loans and bonds are debt-based instruments; each creates an obligation to repay either the commercial bank that made the loan or the bondholder. Stock purchases and foreign direct investments are equity flows; each confers an ownership stake in a specific business, and neither entails a repayment obligation. If a stock's value falls to zero, the stock's owner loses the investment. A second commonly used category distinguishes between fixed investment and portfolio investment. Fixed investment refers to foreign direct investments that create a fixed asset such as a factory or an office building. Bank loans, stock market transactions, and bond flows are **portfolio flows.** (They are called portfolio flows because they are the financial assets typically held in an investment portfolio.) Fixed investments are hard to withdraw from a developing country, whereas portfolio flows can be withdrawn rapidly by selling the stock or bond or by calling a loan.

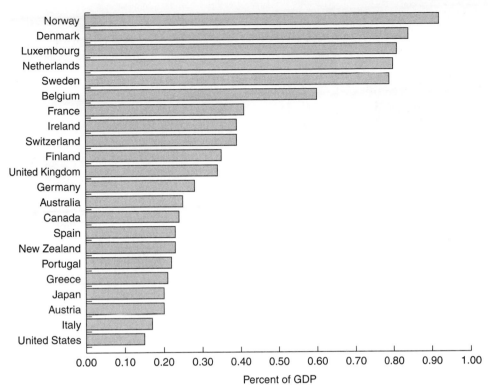

Figure 14.2   Foreign Aid Expenditures as a Share of GDP.
Source: OECD, *Statistical Annex of the 2004 Development Co-operation Report*, Table 4,
http://www.oecd.org/dataoecd/52/9/1893143.xls.

Throughout the postwar period, the advanced industrialized countries have maintained that developing countries should draw on private capital as much as possible.
Foreign aid is available only for worthwhile projects that private capital is unwilling to
finance. Consequently, private capital flows typically constitute somewhere between
two-thirds and three-quarters of all capital flows to the developing world. Yet, developing countries vary substantially in their ability to attract private capital inflows; thus,
some countries rely much more heavily than others on foreign aid. Figure 14.3 illustrates both points. East Asia and the Pacific, on the one hand, and Latin America and
the Caribbean, on the other, attract far more private capital than do the Middle East,
South Asia, and sub-Saharan Africa. Consequently, foreign aid constitutes a substantially larger share of foreign capital inflows in the Middle East, South Asia, and sub-
Saharan Africa. In fact, foreign aid accounts for half or more of all foreign capital flows
to these regions. In contrast, aid constitutes only about 10 percent of the foreign capital flowing into the other regions.

These different abilities to attract private capital reflect private lenders' need to
balance return against risk when investing in developing societies. On the one hand,
because savings are scarce, the return on an investment should be substantially higher
in these developing societies than it is in the advanced industrialized world. (Think

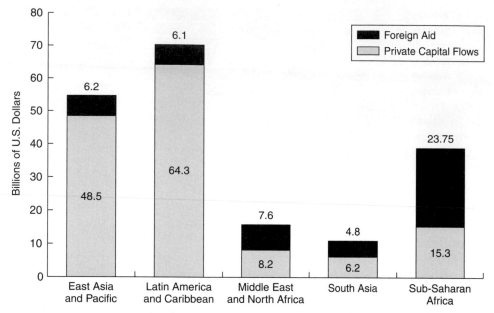

Figure 14.3   Private Capital and Foreign Aid Flows, 2003.
Source: Foreign aid flows from OECD, *Statistical Annex of the 2004 Development Co-operation Report,* Table 4, *http://www.oecd.org/dataoecd/52/9/1893143.xls*; private capital flows from World Bank, *Global Development Finance 2004,* Table B.36. *http://siteresources.worldbank .org/GDFINT2004/Home/20175282/gdf_statistical%20appendix.pdf.*

back to our discussion of comparative advantage.) Consequently, private lenders should earn a higher return on an investment in a developing country than on an equivalent investment in an advanced industrialized country. This acts to pull private capital in. On the other hand, foreign investment is risky. Private lenders face the risk of default—the chance that a particular borrower will be unwilling or unable to repay a debt. Private lenders also face political risk—the chance that political developments in a particular country will reduce the value of an investment. Political risk arises from political instability—coups, revolution, or civil war—and, less dramatically, from the absence of strong legal systems that protect foreign investment. When such risks are large, they substantially reduce an investment's expected return. This risk acts to push private capital away from a country. Indeed, such risks are one of (if not the) principal reasons why sub-Saharan Africa attracts so little private capital.

Developing societies import foreign capital, therefore, because it makes it possible to finance more investment at a lower cost than they could finance if they were forced to rely solely on their domestic savings. And while developing countries can import some capital through foreign aid programs, such programs are quite limited. Thus, if a developing society is to import foreign savings, it must rely on private capital. The desire to import foreign savings and the need to rely on private capital flows to do so creates difficulties for developing societies. For private capital never seems to flow to developing societies in a steady stream. Instead, financial markets shift from excessive concern about the risk of lending to developing societies to exuberance about the opportunities available in those societies and then back to excessive concern about the risk. As a consequence, a country that is unable to attract private capital one year is suddenly inundated with private capital the next, and then, just as suddenly, is shut out of global financial markets as private investors cease lending. The consequences are often devastating. We turn now to look at the first revolution of this cycle.

Capital Flows in the Early Postwar Period

The principal problem that most developing countries faced in the first 20 years following World War II was a shortage of foreign capital. Foreign aid and foreign direct investment were the principal sources of foreign capital for developing countries in the 1950s and 1960s, and neither was abundant. The United States was the only country capable of providing foreign aid. Western Europe was undergoing reconstruction following the Second World War, and this left no resources available to finance foreign aid programs. In fact, Western Europe was a large recipient of foreign aid, as most American aid was directed at postwar reconstruction until the end of the 1950s. Little aid was allocated to Latin America, because the American government believed that private markets would invest in the region. Most of sub-Saharan Africa remained part of colonial empires, the responsibility of the colonial power rather than of the broader international community. Thus, Africa attracted no foreign aid. World Bank lending to the developing world was also limited. It perceived its mission as providing loans at "close-to-commercial rates of interest to cover the foreign exchange costs of productive projects" (Mason and Asher 1973, 381). And most of its lending in this period also financed postwar reconstruction in Europe (Mason and Asher 1973).

Private capital flows were also quite limited, and they were dominated by foreign direct investment. The dominance of direct investment resulted from two considerations. First, many Latin American governments had defaulted on their foreign debt during the 1930s, and few lenders were willing to extend new loans to governments that had so recently defaulted. Second, the slow recovery of international financial markets in the immediate postwar period meant that few bank loans or bonds crossed international boundaries. To the extent that private investment flowed to developing countries at all during the 1950s, therefore, it tended to flow in the form of direct investment.

Governments in most developing countries were not content to rely so heavily on direct investment, which posed two problems for them from the perspective of developing countries' governments (Nurske 1967). First, most foreign direct investment was concentrated in primary commodities, particularly mining and petroleum, and thus did little to promote domestic manufacturing industries. This approach was inconsistent with the determination of developing countries to industrialize. Second, the slow growth of demand for primary commodities in the advanced industrialized world meant that the amount of investment made by MNCs in developing countries' primary-commodity sectors was likely to decline over time. Thus, while developing countries did not necessarily discourage private investment, they did not believe that it would help them achieve their development objectives.

Desiring additional foreign capital, but having little opportunity to borrow on private markets, developing countries pushed for expanded foreign aid programs. This

A CLOSER LOOK

The World Bank

The World Bank was created at the Bretton Woods conference in 1944 to finance development projects that could not attract private financing. The World Bank is owned and controlled by its member governments. Ownership is based on the shares that each country purchases upon joining, and the number of shares each country purchases is determined by its economic size. The Board of Governors, composed of representatives of all member countries, has ultimate decision-making authority, but responsibility for most of the Bank's operation rests with its executive directors, of which there are 24. Each of the Bank's five largest shareholders (the United States, Japan, Germany, France, and Great Britain) appoints its own executive director. The remaining executive directors are elected every two years to represent groups of countries. Decisions by the Board of Directors are made on a weighted voting scheme in which each country has votes equal to the number of shares it owns. Larger shareholders therefore have greater influence over World Bank decisions. The United States is the largest shareholder and hence has the most votes.

The World Bank functions like a private investment bank. It sells bonds to private investors and lends the resulting funds. It differs only in that its clients are restricted to developing-country governments. World Bank regulations limit the total amount the Bank can lend at any point in time to the combined total of its capital and reserves. This restriction ensures that the Bank always has the funds necessary to repay its bond-based debt. As a consequence, the World Bank is a very low risk borrower and pays very low rates of interest on the money it borrows. It can then pass these low interest rates on to the developing countries that borrow from it. World Bank loans typically carry maturities of 15 to 20 years and a 3- to 5-year grace period before repayment begins. Interest rates on World Bank loans are slightly higher than the interest rates the World Bank pays on its debt. Since its creation in 1945, the IBRD has loaned more than $360 billion to developing countries.

In 1960, the member governments created a new lending agency within the World Bank called the **International Development Association** (IDA). A concessional lending agency, the IDA provides development finance at below-market rates of interest. IDA lending terms are quite generous. Loans have maturities of 35 or 40 years, and most loans have a 10-year grace period before repayment begins. All IDA loans are made at zero interest rates. The IDA lent only to the poorest developing countries, however. Currently, a country must have a per capita income below $885 to qualify for IDA lending. The IDA lent a total of $107 billion to 109 developing countries between 1960 and 2001, and it lends an average of $6–7 billion per year. Most IDA loans are targeted at basic needs, including primary education, health services, and clean water and sanitation. In contrast to the IBRD, the IDA is funded by contributions from World Bank member countries. Historically, the United States has been the largest contributor, providing about 24 percent of all contributions to the IDA. Japan is a close second, having contributed about 22 percent of the total. Germany is the third-largest contributor, accounting for 11 percent of the total.

Continued

World Bank loans fall into two broad categories. Investments loans are long-term loans dedicated to "creating the physical and social infrastructure necessary for poverty reduction and sustainable development" (World Bank 2000a, 5). Such loans were originally oriented toward creating physical infrastructures—buying capital goods, constructing buildings, providing engineering assistance, and the like. Now investment loans are increasingly oriented toward what the World Bank calls institution building and social development. In Turkey, for example, the World Bank lent $300 million to support the Turkish government's plan to extend compulsory education from five to eight years. Other projects include urban poverty reduction, rural development, water and sanitation, natural resource management, and health. Investment loans have accounted for 75 to 80 percent of World Bank lending. Adjustment loans have become an important component of World Bank lending during the last 25 years. These short-term loans are advanced in support of structural reform. Adjustment loans seek to promote the creation of competitive market structures by supporting legal and regulatory reforms, the reform of trade and taxation policies, and the political reform of institutions (World Bank 2000a, 13). During the last 20 years, adjustment loans have accounted for between 20 and 25 percent of all World Bank lending.

pressure began to bear fruit in the late 1950s and early 1960s. The World Bank created the International Development Association (IDA) and began to provide concessional loans to many of its member governments. At the same time, a number of **regional development banks,** such as the Inter-American Development Bank, the Asian Development Bank, and the African Development Bank, were created to provide concessional lending on the model of the IDA. Advanced industrialized countries also expanded their bilateral aid programs during the 1960s. As a consequence, the amount of aid provided through multilateral development agencies increased fourfold between 1956 and 1970, while bilateral development assistance more than doubled during the same period. (See Table 14.2.) By the end of the 1960s, official development assistance to developing countries was almost twice as large as private capital flows.

The expansion of foreign aid programs during the 1960s reflected changing attitudes among governments in the advanced industrialized countries. These changing attitudes were in turn largely a product of the dynamics of decolonization. World Bank officials recognized that governments in the newly independent countries would have great difficulty borrowing on private capital markets and would be unlikely to qualify for lending under the World Bank's normal terms. The World Bank therefore began to reconsider its resistance to concessional lending. American attitudes toward foreign aid were also beginning to change in response to political concerns that arose from the process of decolonization. American policy makers believed that the rising influence of developing countries in the United Nations would eventually lead to the creation of an agency that offered development loans at concessional rates. The creation of such a UN agency could undermine the World Bank and weaken American influence over development lending. U.S. officials

Table 14.2
Financial Flows to Developing Countries, Millions of U.S. Dollars, 1956–1970

	1956	1960	1965	1970
Official Development Assistance				
Official Government Aid	2,900	4,236.4	5,773.1	6,587.4
Multilateral Organizations	272.5	368.5	312.9	1,176
OPEC				443.5
Private Finance				
Foreign Direct Investment	2,500	1,847.9	2,207.4	3,557.2
Portfolio Flows	0.0	408.2	836.0	777.0

Source: Wood, 1986, 83.

began to support a concessional lending agency within the World Bank, therefore, in order to prevent the creation of a rival within the United Nations, where developing countries had greater influence.

At the same time, during the late 1950s and early 1960s American policy makers increasingly came to view foreign aid as a weapon in the battle against the spread of Communism throughout the developing world. Nowhere was this more evident than in the Kennedy administration's "Alliance for Progress," which was designed to use U.S. government aid to promote socioeconomic reform in Latin America in order to prevent the spread of Cuban-style socialist revolutions throughout the region (Rabe 1999). These changes in attitude contributed to the tremendous growth of foreign aid programs during the 1960s.

Commercial Bank Lending and the Origins of the Latin American Debt Crisis

The composition and scale of foreign capital flows to parts of the developing world changed fundamentally during the 1970s. A trickle of private capital was transformed into a flood as commercial banks began lending heavily to a select group of developing countries, especially in Latin America. In the course of the decade, Latin American debt grew dramatically, as did the share of that debt owed to commercial banks. These dynamics culminated in a debt crisis in the early 1980s as Latin American governments proved unable to service their foreign debt and commercial banks thus ceased lending.

The changes in private capital flows to the developing world were driven by the interaction between developments within the international economy and dynamics internal to the political economy of import substitution industrialization. The two factors combined to generate an increase in developing countries' demand for, and commercial banks' willingness to supply, foreign capital. Growing demand for foreign capital in the developing world was generated by international and domestic developments. The most important international source of this greater demand lay in the sharp rise in the price of oil brought about in 1973. Higher oil prices cost developing countries about $260 billion during the 1970s (Cline 1984). Because most developing countries were oil importers, higher prices for their energy imports required them to reduce other imports, to raise their exports, or to borrow from foreign lenders to finance the larger current-account deficits they faced. Cutting imports was unattractive for governments deeply committed to ISI strategies. Increasing exports was also difficult, as import substitution had brought about a decline in the export sector in most countries. Consequently, the higher cost of oil widened current-account deficits throughout the developing world.

Import substitution industrialization also generated a growing demand for foreign capital. Most governments played a leading role in capital formation. Latin American governments were responsible for between one-third and one-half of total capital formation (Thorp 1999, 169). Governments created state-owned enterprises to drive industrialization, and they provided subsidized credit to targeted sectors. Reliance on both tools strengthened as governments shifted to secondary ISI. These strategies led to an expansion of government expenditures in connection with the initial investment and then in connection with continued subsidies to the unprofitable state-owned enterprises they created (Frieden 1981, 420). Government revenues failed to grow in line with these rising expenditures. As a consequence, budget deficits widened, reaching, on average in Latin America, 6.7 percent of GDP by the end of the 1970s. In some countries, deficits were even larger. Argentina's budget deficit rose to over 10 percent of GDP in the mid-1970s and remained above 7 percent of GDP until the early 1980s. Mexico's budget deficit increased in the early seventies and then exploded—to more than 10 percent of GDP—in the early 1980s. Governments needed to finance these deficits, which generated a demand for foreign capital.

The greater supply of foreign capital resulted from the oil shock's impact on commercial bank activity. The oil shock generated large current-account surpluses in the oil-exporting countries. Saudi Arabia's current-account surplus jumped from $2.5 billion in 1973 to $23 billion in 1974 and then averaged about $14 billion during the next three years. These surpluses, called **petrodollars,** provided the financial resources that developing countries needed to cover their greater demand for foreign capital. Commercial banks intermediated the flows, accepting deposits from oil exporters and lending the funds to other developing countries. The process came to be called **petrodollar recycling.**

Commercial banks loaned directly to governments, to state-owned enterprises, and to government-owned development banks. Most commercial bank lending was syndicated. In a **syndicated loan,** hundreds of commercial banks each take a small share of a large loan to a single borrower. Syndicated loans allow commercial banks to spread the risk involved in such large loans among a number of banks, rather than requiring one bank to bear the full risk that the borrowing country will default. Some banks involved in the syndicate were large and had considerable international experience; others were small and had little experience with international lending (Solomon 1999, 35).

These capital inflows generated a rapid expansion of foreign debt in developing countries. (See Table 14.3.) In 1970, the developing world as a whole owed only $72.7 billion to foreign lenders. By 1980, total foreign debt had ballooned to

Table 14.3
Developing-Country Foreign Debt, Billions of U.S. Dollars, 1970–1984

	All Developing Countries[1]	30 Most Heavily Indebted Countries[2]	7 Most Heavily Indebted Latin American Countries (See also remaining columns)	Argentina	Brazil	Chile	Colombia	Mexico	Peru	Venezuela
1970	72.7	65	28	5.8	5.7	3.0	2.2	7.0	3.2	1.4
1971	84.3	75	32	6.3	7.4	3.1	2.5	7.5	3.3	1.9
1972	98.7	88	39	6.8	11.5	3.5	2.8	8.2	3.5	2.5
1973	117.7	104	46	7.2	14.7	3.9	3.2	10.5	3.9	2.8
1974	147.1	129	60	7.6	22.0	5.2	3.3	14.0	5.2	2.7
1975	194.0	157	71	7.7	27.3	5.5	3.3	18.2	6.1	2.2
1976	235.6	192	89	9.3	33.3	5.6	3.8	24.0	7.6	4.9
1977	313.7	258	116	11.4	42.0	5.9	3.9	31.2	9.2	10.7
1978	391.7	317	142	13.3	54.6	7.4	5.1	35.7	9.7	16.6
1979	480.8	377	174	21.0	61.3	9.4	5.1	42.8	9.3	24.1
1980	586.7	461	214	27.2	71.5	12.1	5.9	57.4	9.4	29.3
1981	703.2	539	261	35.7	81.5	15.7	6.9	78.2	8.6	32.1
1982	809.9	606	294	43.6	93.9	17.3	8.7	86.1	10.7	32.2
1983	880.1	661	316	45.9	98.5	17.9	10.3	93.0	11.3	38.3
1984	921.8	686	328	48.9	103.9	19.7	12.0	94.8	12.2	36.9

[1]All 157 low- and middle-income countries as defined by the World Bank.
[2]Comprises Algeria, Argentina, Bolivia, Brazil, Chile, Colombia, Costa Rica, Cote d'Ivoire, Ecuador, Egypt, India, Indonesia, Jamaica, Malaysia, Mexico, Morocco, Nigeria, Pakistan, Peru, Philippines, South Korea, Sudan, Syria, Thailand, Turkey, Uruguay, Venezuela, Yugoslavia, Zaire, Zambia.
Source: World Bank, World Development Indicators on CD-ROM, 2001.

$586.7 billion. Most of this debt was owed by a small number of countries. The 30 most heavily indebted developing countries owed a total of $461 billion in 1980, close to 80 percent of the entire developing world's foreign debt. Latin American countries were among the largest borrowers. The foreign debt of the 7 most heavily indebted Latin American countries—Argentina, Brazil, Chile, Colombia, Mexico, Peru, and Venezuela—increased by a factor of ten between 1970 and 1982. By the early 1980s, these 7 countries accounted for about 80 percent of all Latin American debt and for about one-third of all developing-world foreign debt.

Initially, these capital inflows fuelled robust economic growth. The positive impact of commercial bank lending is quite clear in aggregate statistics for the period. In Latin America as a whole, economic growth averaged 5.6 percent per year between 1973 and 1980. Some Latin American countries grew at even faster rates. In Brazil, one of the largest borrowers, economic growth averaged 7.8 percent per year between 1973 and 1980, while Mexico, another of the large borrowers, realized an average rate of growth of 6.7 percent over the same period.

Behind this robust economic growth, however, lay some worrying trends. Debt problems begin to emerge when foreign debt grows more rapidly than the country's ability to service its debt. A country's **debt-service capacity**—its ability to make the payments of interest and principal required by the terms of the loan—is defined as the ratio of its debt service to its export revenues. As a country increases its foreign debt, it must also expand its exports to service the debt comfortably. Latin American governments did not expand their exports. Instead, foreign capital was invested in the nontraded-goods sector. Mexico, Argentina, and Venezuela, for example, created massive hydroelectric projects that were unnecessary, given realistic assessments of those countries' energy needs (Thorp 1999, 209). In addition, governments borrowed to buy military equipment, to pay for more expensive oil, and to subsidize consumer goods. Even when foreign capital was invested in the traded-goods sector, the preference for capital-intensive projects failed to generate exports. As a consequence, debt service grew faster than export revenues, causing debt service ratios to rise sharply (Table 14.4). In 1970, Latin American governments were using only 13 percent of their export revenues (on average) to service foreign debt. By 1978, debt service was consuming 38 percent of Latin America's export revenues. Debt-service ratios were even higher in Brazil, Chile, Mexico, and Peru, and rising ratios rendered Latin American countries vulnerable to international shocks.

Three such shocks hit Latin America hard in 1979 and the early 1980s. The first shock came from rising interest rates in the United States and Western Europe. The United States began raising interest rates in 1979 in an attempt to reduce inflation. Rising American interest rates were transmitted directly to Latin America, because two-thirds of Latin American debt carried variable interest rates. The ensuing higher interest rates on Latin American debt raised the cost of servicing the debt. The second shock came from the recession in the advanced industrialized world, caused by the higher interest rates. Recession reduced the demand for Latin American exports, causing their terms of trade to decline by 10 percentage points in the early 1980s (Cline 1984). Latin America's export revenues thus declined. By 1980, therefore, Latin American governments were facing larger debt-service payments and declining export earnings. As if this wasn't enough, oil prices rose sharply again in 1979, imposing a third shock.

Table 14.4
Debt Service Ratios in Latin America
[(Payments of Principal plus Interest)/Export Earnings], 1970–1984

	Argentina	Brazil	Chile	Colombia	Mexico	Peru	Venezuela	All Latin American Countries
1970	n.a.	n.a.	n.a.	28	n.a.	n.a.	4	n.a.
1971	n.a.	n.a.	n.a.	27	n.a.	n.a.	5	n.a.
1972	n.a.	n.a.	n.a.	26	n.a.	n.a.	8	n.a.
1973	n.a.	n.a.	n.a.	22	n.a.	n.a.	7	n.a.
1974	n.a.	n.a.	n.a.	21	n.a.	n.a.	5	n.a.
1975	n.a.	43	35	14	n.a.	n.a.	6	n.a.
1976	34	38	40	13	n.a.	n.a.	4	n.a.
1977	27	42	46	11	n.a.	53	8	27
1978	42	58	54	12	n.a.	50	9	38
1979	23	63	44	14	66	34	19	38
1980	37	63	43	16	44	45	27	36
1981	46	66	65	22	46	59	23	40
1982	50	82	71	30	51	49	30	47
1983	70	55	54	38	45	34	27	41
1984	63	45	60	30	45	30	25	39

n.a. = not available.
Source: World Bank, *World Development Indicators on CD-ROM*, 2001.

Many governments responded to these shocks by borrowing more from commercial banks. As a result, foreign debt jumped after 1979, rising from $481 billion in 1978 to $810 billion in 1982. Even more worrying, debt-service ratios rose sharply. (See Table 14.4.) For Latin America as a whole, debt service consumed almost 50 percent of all export earnings in 1982. Brazil's position was the most precarious, as debt service consumed more than 80 percent of its export revenues in 1982. Finally, an active debt-service crisis arose on August 18 of that year, when Mexico informed the United States government that it could not make its scheduled debt payment. (See Kraft 1984.) Mexico had in effect defaulted on its foreign debt. Commercial banks immediately ceased lending to Mexico and to other developing countries, fearing that Mexico's problems were not unique.

The abrupt cessation of commercial bank lending forced governments to eliminate the macroeconomic imbalances that their commercial bank loans had financed. Current-account deficits had to be eliminated because governments could not attract the capital inflows required to finance them. Budget deficits had to be reduced because governments could no longer borrow from commercial banks to pay for them. Rapid adjustment in turn caused economic activity to fall sharply throughout Latin America (Table 14.5.) The most heavily indebted countries suffered the worst. Argentina's economy shrank by 6 percent in 1981 and then by another 5 percent in 1982. Brazil's economy shrank by 4 percent in 1981 and then by another 3 percent in 1983. Mexico's economy shrank by 1 percent in 1982 and by another 3 percent in 1983. The end of capital inflows, therefore, brought an abrupt end to the economic boom of the 1970s.

Table 14.5
Economic Growth Rates (Percent) in Latin America, 1979–1983

	Latin America	Argentina	Brazil	Chile	Mexico	Peru	Colombia	Venezuela
1979	7	10	7	9	10	6	5	1
1980	9	4	9	8	9	3	4	−4
1981	−1	−6	−4	5	9	7	2	0
1982	−1	−5	1	−10	−1	−1	1	−2
1983	−2	4	−3	−4	−4	−12	2	−4

Source: World Bank, *World Development Indicators on CD-ROM*, 2001.

Commercial bank lending therefore proved a mixed blessing. On the one hand, it allowed many developing countries to finance the large current-account deficits generated by the oil shock. In the absence of these loans, governments would have been forced to reduce consumption sharply to pay for energy imports. Commercial bank loans also allowed developing countries to invest more than they could have otherwise. Private capital flows therefore relaxed many of the constraints that had characterized the foreign aid–dominated system of the 1950s and 1960s. On the other hand, the rapid accumulation of commercial bank debt rendered developing countries vulnerable to international shocks. As shocks hit, governments faced severe debt-service problems, causing commercial banks to stop lending and thereby precipitating a severe economic crisis. The management of this debt crisis dominated North–South financial relations throughout the 1980s.

Managing the Debt Crisis

By 1982, the 30 most heavily indebted developing countries owed more than $600 billion to foreign lenders. Few of these governments could service that debt. International power asymmetries shaped the management of this crisis. The creditor coalition, which included the commercial banks, the IMF, and the advanced industrialized countries, created an international **debt regime** that pushed the costs of the crisis onto the debtor countries by linking access to additional foreign capital to the adoption of market-oriented policy reforms.

The Debt Regime

The debt crisis was managed within a framework that reflected the interests of the creditors' coalition. This regime was based on a simple, if somewhat unbalanced, exchange between the coalition and the debtor governments. The heavily indebted countries were provided new loans and were allowed to reschedule their existing debt payments in exchange for implementing policy reforms.

The debt regime was based on the creditors' coalition's strongly held belief that developing countries eventually could repay their debt. The coalition initially diagnosed the debt crisis as a short-term balance-of-payments dilemma, or **liquidity**

problem. In other words, the creditors believed that high interest rates and falling export earnings had raised debt service above the debtor governments' current capacity to pay. Once this liquidity crisis eased as interest rates fell and growth resumed in the advanced industrialized world, developing countries could resume service.

This diagnosis shaped the creditors' initial response to the crisis. Because they believed that the crisis was a short-term liquidity problem, they prescribed short-term remedies. On the one hand, they required the debtor countries to reduce their expenditures by implementing macroeconomic stabilization programs. **Macroeconomic stabilization** was intended to eliminate the large current-account deficits in order to reduce the demand for external financing. The centerpiece of most stabilization programs was the reduction of government budget deficits. Balancing the government budget has a powerful effect on domestic economic activity, reducing domestic consumption and investment and thereby the demand for imports. The resulting unemployment would reduce wages, making exports more competitive. Exchange rate devaluation would further improve the balance of trade. The smaller current-account deficits that would follow would require smaller capital inflows. In the ideal world, stabilization would produce current-account surpluses.

On the other hand, the creditor coalition provided new loans and rescheduled existing debt in order to reduce the severity of the liquidity shortage. New loans were made available by the IMF and by commercial banks through a process called **concerted lending.** In 1983 and 1984, the IMF and commercial banks provided a total of $28.8 billion to the indebted governments (Cline 1995, 207). Developing countries were also allowed to reschedule existing debt payments. Debt owed to commercial banks was rescheduled in the **London Club,** a private association established and run by the large commercial banks. Rescheduling agreements neither forgave debt nor reduced the interest payments attached to the debt. They merely rescheduled the payments that debtor governments had to make, usually offering a grace period and extending the maturity of the debt. Access to both, however, was conditional on prior agreement with the IMF on the content of a stabilization package.

By 1985, the creditor coalition was revising its initial diagnosis. Latin American economies failed to recover as growth resumed in the advanced industrialized world. While creditors still believed that countries could repay their debt, they concluded that their ability to do so would require more substantial changes to their economies. Stabilization would not be sufficient. This new diagnosis generated a second, more invasive, set of policy reforms known as **structural adjustment,** premised on the belief that the economic structures developed under ISI had limited the ability of countries to expand their exports. Governments were too heavily involved in economic activity, economic production was too heavily oriented toward the domestic market, and locally produced manufactured goods were uncompetitive in world markets. This economic structure stifled entrepreneurship, reduced the capacity for economic growth, and limited the potential for exporting. Structural adjustment programs sought to reshape the indebted economies by reducing the role of government and increasing the role of the market. Reforms sought substantial market liberalization in four areas: trade liberalization, liberalization of foreign direct investment, privatization of state-owned enterprises, and broader deregulation to promote economic competition.

Structural adjustment programs were supported by additional financial support provided by the World Bank, new IMF programs, and commercial banks. Commercial

A CLOSER LOOK

The International Monetary Fund

The International Monetary Fund is based in Washington, DC. It has a staff of about 2,690, most of whom are professional economists, and a membership of 184 countries. The IMF controls $311 billion that it can lend to member governments facing balance-of-payments deficits. Two ruling bodies—the Board of Governors and the Executive Board—make decisions within the IMF. The **Board of Governors** sits at the top of the IMF decision-making process. Each country that is a member of the IMF appoints one official to the Board of Governors. Typically, the country's central-bank president or finance minister will serve in this capacity. The Board of Governors meets only once a year, however; therefore, almost all IMF decisions are actually made by the **Executive Board,** which is composed of 24 executive directors, each of whom is appointed by IMF member governments. Each of eight countries (the United States, Great Britain, France, Germany, Japan, China, Russia, and Saudi Arabia) appoints an executive director to represent its interests directly. The other 16 executive directors represent groups of IMF member countries. For example, Pier Carlo Padoan (an Italian) is currently the executive director representing Albania, Greece, Italy, Malta, Portugal, and Spain, while B. P. Misra (from India) is currently the executive director representing Bangladesh, Bhutan, India, and Sri Lanka. The countries belonging to each group jointly select the executive director who represents them. A managing director appointed by the Executive Board chairs the Board. Traditionally, the managing director has been a European (or at least non-American).

Voting in the Board of Governors and the Executive Board is based on a weighted voting scheme. The number of votes each country has reflects the size of its quota in the stabilization fund. The United States, which has the largest quota, currently has 371,743 votes (17.14 percent of the total votes). Palau, which has the smallest quota, currently has only 281 votes (.01 percent of the total votes). Many important decisions require an 85 percent majority. As a result, both the United States, with 17 percent of the total votes, and the EU (when its member governments can act jointly), with more than 16 percent of the total vote, can veto important IMF decisions. As a block, developing countries also control votes sufficient to veto IMF decisions. Exercising this developing-country veto requires a level of collective action that is not easily achieved, however. In contrast with other international organizations, therefore, the IMF is not based on the principle of "one country, one vote." Instead, it is based on the principle that the countries which contribute more to the stabilization fund have a greater say over how that fund is used. In practice, this means that the advanced industrialized countries have much greater influence over IMF decisions than developing countries have.

The IMF lends to its members under a number of different programs, each of which is designed to address different problems and carries different terms for repayments:

- Standby arrangements are used to address short-term balance-of-payments problems. This is the most widely used IMF program. The typical standby arrangement lasts 12–18 months. Governments have up to five years to repay loans under the program, but are expected to repay these credits within two to four years.

Continued

- The Extended Fund Facility was created in 1974 to help countries address balance-of-payments problems caused by structural weaknesses. The typical arrangement under this program is twice as long as a standby arrangement (three years). Moreover, governments have up to 10 years to repay loans under the program, but the expectation is that the loan will be repaid within 4.5 to 7 years.
- The Poverty Reduction and Growth Facility (PRGF) was established in 1999. Prior to that year, the IMF had provided financial assistance to low-income countries through its Enhanced Structural Adjustment Facility (ESAF), a program that financed many of the structural adjustment packages during the 1980s and 1990s. In 1999, the PRGF replaced the ESAF. Loans under the PRGF are based on a Poverty Reduction Strategy Paper, which is prepared by the borrowing government with input from civil society and other development partners, including the World Bank. The interest rate on PRGF loans is only 0.5 percent, and governments have up to ten years to repay loans.
- Two new programs were established in the late 1990s in response to financial crises that arose in emerging markets. The Supplemental Reserve Facility and the Contingent Credit Line provide additional financing for governments that are in the midst of or are threatened by a crisis and thus require substantial short-term financing. Countries have up to 2.5 years to repay loans under both programs, but are expected to repay within 1.5 years. To discourage the use of these programs, except in a crisis, both programs carry a substantial charge on top of the normal interest rate.

banks were asked to provide $20 billion of new loans over a three-year period in order to refinance one-third of the total interest coming due in the period. Multilateral financial institutions, particularly the World Bank, were asked to provide an additional $10 billion over the same period. In all cases, fresh loans from commercial banks hinged upon the ability of debtor governments to gain financial assistance from the IMF, and loans from the IMF and World Bank were contingent upon the willingness of governments to agree to structural adjustment programs.

This debt regime pushed the costs of the crisis onto the heavily indebted countries. Table 14.6 illustrates the economic consequences of the crisis for Latin America as a whole. Investment, consumption, and economic growth in the region all fell sharply after 1982. Indeed, by the end of the decade most of these indicators still had not recovered to their 1980 levels. The economic crisis hit labor markets particularly hard; unemployment rose and real wages fell by 30 percent over the course of the decade. Real exchange rates were devalued by 23 percent, on average, and by more substantial amounts in Chile (96 percent), Uruguay (70 percent), and a few other countries (Edwards 1995, 29–30). This adjustment brought a small increase in exports, a sharp reduction in imports, and an overall improvement in trade balances. From an aggregate $2 billion deficit in 1981, Latin America as a whole moved to a $39 billion trade surplus in 1984 (Edwards 1995, 23).

Latin American governments used these current-account surpluses for debt service. **Net transfers,** which measure new loans to a country minus interest-rate pay-

Table 14.6
Economic Conditions in Latin America, 1982–1990

	1980–81	1982	1983	1984	1985	1986–90
GDP[1]	100	95.6	91.3	92.2	92.7	94.1
Consumption[1]	77.0	74.0	70.3	70.4	69.9	71.6
Investment[1]	24.4	19.6	14.9	15.2	16.1	15.9
Unemployment[2]	6.7				10.1	8.0
Real Wages[3]	100.0				86.4	68.9
Imports[4]	−12.3	−9.7	−7.5	−8.0	−7.9	−9.2
Exports[4]	12.5	12.6	13.6	14.5	14.2	15.2
Net Transfers[4]	12.2	−18.7	−31.6	−26.9	−32.3	
Fiscal Deficit[5]	3.7	5.4	5.2	3.1	2.7	
Inflation	53.2%	57.7%	90.8%	116.4%	126.9%	

[1]As a percentage of 1980–81 GDP.
[2]Rate of open unemployment as a percentage of total labor force.
[3]Index of real wages in unemployment.
[4]$US billions.
[5]Percent of GDP.
Source: Thorp 1999; Edwards 1995, 24; Edwards 1989, 171.

ments made by this same country, provides a measure of the scale of this debt service. In 1976, net transfers for the 17 most heavily indebted countries totaled $12.8 billion, reflecting the fact that these countries were net importers of capital. Between 1982 and 1986, net transfers for these same 17 countries averaged $26.4 billion per year, reflecting the substantial flow of funds from the debtor countries to banks based in the advanced industrialized countries (Edwards 1995, 24). Thus, domestic economic adjustment generated the resources needed to service foreign debt.

The Sources of Bargaining Power

The creditors' coalition was able to push the costs of the debt crisis onto the debtor governments because it was better able to exploit its potential power than those governments were. Creditor power lay in the ability to control access to new financing. This control allowed the creditors to require debtor governments to adopt policy reforms in exchange for additional financing. Creating a creditor coalition to exploit this power was not a simple task, however. (See Lipson 1985.) It was certainly easy to deny new financial flows to the debtor governments. Commercial banks were unwilling to extend new loans after 1982, and the IMF would lend only in conjunction with stabilization agreements. In order to exploit this power, the creditors had to be willing to extend new funds, and that proved difficult, because of a free-rider problem. Each individual creditor recognized that debt service in the short run required additional financing and in the long run depended on structural reforms that governments would not implement without additional financing. But each individual creditor also preferred that other creditors provide these new loans. Thus, each creditor had an incentive to free ride on the contributions of the other members of the coalition.

POLICY ANALYSIS AND DEBATE

IMF Conditionality

Question
Should the IMF attach conditions to the credits it extends to developing countries?

Overview
IMF conditionality has long been a source of controversy. Critics of the practice argue that the economic policy reforms embodied in IMF conditionality agreements force governments to accept harsh austerity measures that reduce economic growth, raise unemployment, and push vulnerable segments of society deeper into poverty. Moreover, the IMF has been accused of adopting a "one size fits all" approach when designing conditionality agreements. It relies on the same economic model in analyzing each country, and it recommends the same set of policy changes for each country that comes to it for assistance. Consequently, critics allege, IMF policy reforms are often inappropriate, given a particular country's unique characteristics.

   The IMF defends itself by arguing that most developing-country crises share a common cause: large budget deficits, usually financed by the central bank. Such policies generate current-account deficits larger than private foreign lenders are willing to finance. Governments turn to the IMF only when they are already deep in crisis. Because most crises are so similar, the solution to them should also be similar in broad outline: governments must bring spending in line with revenues, and they must establish a stable base for participation in the international economy. And while the short-term costs can be high, the economy in crisis must be returned to a sustainable path, whether the IMF intervenes or not. Should the IMF require governments to implement policy reforms as a condition for drawing from the Fund?

Policy Options
- Continue to require conditionality agreements in connection with IMF credits.
- Abandon conditionality and allow governments to draw on the IMF without implementing stabilization or structural adjustment measures.

Policy Analysis
- To what extent are the economic crises which strike countries that turn to the IMF solely a product of IMF conditionality agreements?
- To what extend does conditionality protect the Fund's resources? What would happen to these resources if conditionality were eliminated?

Take a Position
- Which option do you prefer? Justify your choice.
- What criticisms of your position should you anticipate? How would you defend your recommendation against these criticisms?

Resources
Online: Do an online search for "IMF conditionality". Follow the links to some sites that defend conditionality and to some that criticize the practice. The Hoover Institution maintains a useful website that examines IMF-related issues. Search for "Meltzer Commission" to find some strong criticisms of the Fund's activities. The IMF explains and defends conditionality in a fact sheet. (Search "IMF facts conditionality".)

Continued

In Print: Joseph Stiglitz, "What I Learned at the World Economic Crisis," *The New Republic,* April 17, 2000, and *Globalization and Its Discontents* (New York: W.W. Norton and Company, 2002); Kenneth Rogoff, "The IMF Strikes Back," *Foreign Policy* (January–February 2003): 38–46; Graham R. Bird, *IMF Lending to Developing Countries: Issues and Evidence* (London: Routledge, 1995); Tony Killick, *IMF Programmes in Developing Countries: Design and Impact* (New York: Routledge, 1995).

Commercial banks had an incentive to free ride on IMF lending. Loans from the IMF would allow the debtor governments to service their commercial bank debt. If the IMF carried the full burden of new lending, commercial banks would be repaid without having to put more of their own funds at risk. Within the group of commercial banks involved in the loan syndicates, smaller banks had an incentive to free ride on the large banks. Smaller banks had much less at stake in Latin America than the large commercial banks had, because the smaller banks had lent proportionately less as a share of their capital. Consequently, default by Latin American governments would not necessarily imperil the smaller banks' survival. Thus, whereas the large commercial banks could not walk away from the debt crisis, the smaller banks could (Devlin 1989, 200–201). Smaller banks could refuse to put up additional funds knowing that the large banks had to do so. Once the large banks provided new loans, the small banks would benefit from the resulting debt service.

The effectiveness of the creditor coalition, therefore, hinged upon preventing free riding. The IMF played an important role in doing so. To prevent large commercial banks from free riding on IMF loans, the IMF refused to advance credit to a particular government until commercial banks pledged new loans to the same government. This linkage between IMF and private lending in turn encouraged the large commercial banks to prevent free riding by the small commercial banks. Because the large commercial banks were unable to free ride on the IMF, they sought to compel the small banks to provide their share of the new private loans. Large banks threatened to exclude smaller banks from participation in future syndicated loans—a potentially lucrative activity for the smaller banks—and threatened to make it difficult for the smaller banks to operate in the interbank market. American and European central-bank officials also pressured the small banks. Free riding thus became costly for the small banks.

The ability to solve the free-riding problems produced a unified creditors' coalition that controlled financial flows to Latin America. The IMF and the commercial banks advanced new loans to Latin American governments (although the commercial banks did so quite reluctantly), and all accepted a share of the risks of doing so. This united front allowed the creditors to reward governments that adopted a cooperative approach to the crisis with new financing and deny additional financing to governments that were unwilling to play by the creditors' rules.

In contrast, the debtor countries were unable to exploit their potential power. Debtor power lay in the threat of collective default. While each of the large debtors owed substantial funds to American banks—in 1982, for example, Mexico's debt to the nine largest American commercial banks equaled 44.4 percent of those banks' combined capital—no single government owed so much that a unilateral default would severely damage American banks or the American economy (Cline 1995, 74–75). Collective action could provide power, however. If all debtor governments defaulted, the capital of the largest American commercial banks would be eliminated, creating potentially severe consequences for the American economy. A credible threat to impose such a crisis might have compelled the creditors to provide more finance on easier terms, to demand less austerity, and perhaps to forgive a portion of the debt.

Yet, debtor governments never threatened a collective default (Tussie 1988). Latin American governments held a series of conferences in the early years of the crisis in order to discuss a coordinated response to it. Governments used these conferences to demand that the creditors "share responsibility in the search for a solution," and they demanded "equity in the distribution of the costs of adjustment," but they never threatened a collective default (Tussie 1988, 291). Argentina was the only country to adopt a noncooperative stance toward the creditors' coalition, and it tried to convince other Latin American governments to follow suit. Those governments, however, were unwilling to take a hard line; in fact, they encouraged Argentina to adopt a more cooperative stance (Tussie 1988, 288). Thus, instead of threatening collective default, debtor governments played by the creditors' rules.

Debtor governments never threatened collective default because they were caught in a prisoners' dilemma. While the threat of collective default could yield collective benefits, each government had an incentive to defect from a collective threat in order to seek a better deal on its own. The incentive to seek the best deal possible through unilateral action, rather than a reasonably good deal through collective action, arose because each debtor government believed that it possessed unique characteristics which enabled it to negotiate more favorable terms than would be available to the group as a whole. Mexico, for example, believed that it could exploit its proximity to the United States and its close ties with the U.S. government to gain more favorable terms. Brazil, which by 1984 was running a current-account surplus, believed that it could use this stronger position to its advantage in negotiations with its creditors (Tussie 1988, 288).

The bilateral approach embodied in the IMF and London Club framework reinforced these fears of defection. Because creditors negotiated with each debtor independently, they could adopt a "divide and conquer" strategy. They could offer "special deals" to induce particular governments to defect from any debtor coalition that might form. If one government did defect, it would gain favorable treatment, while the others would be punished for their uncooperative strategy. Punishment could include fewer new loans, higher interest rates and larger fees on rescheduled loans, and perhaps more stringent stabilization agreements. Thus, even though coordinated action among the debtor countries could yield collective gains, each individual government's incentive to seek a unilateral agreement dominated the strategy of a collective threat of default.

The debt regime reflected creditors' interests, therefore, because creditors were able to solve the collective action problem and develop a coordinated approach to the debt crisis and debtors were not. The creditors used their power to create a regime that pushed the costs of the debt crisis onto the heavily indebted countries. The regime was based on the dual premises that all debt would be repaid in the long run, but debt service would require the indebted governments to implement far-reaching economic policy reforms. Conditionality thus provided a powerful lever to induce developing countries to adopt economic reforms: Few developing countries could afford to cut themselves off completely from external financial flows. After 1982, these governments found that the price of continued access to international finance was far-reaching economic reform.

The Domestic Politics of Economic Reform

While the creditors' coalition established the structure for managing the debt crisis, used conditionality to promote economic reform, and set the parameters on the range of acceptable policies that could emerge from the reform process, the pace at which debtor governments adopted stabilization and structural adjustment programs was determined by domestic politics. Domestic politics caused most governments to delay implementing stabilization and structural adjustment programs.

Economic reform required governments to impose costs on powerful domestic interest groups. The need to impose these costs generated distributive conflict between those groups and thus delayed economic stabilization. Distributive conflict revolved around who would bear the costs associated with balancing the budget. To balance their budgets, governments had to make choices about which programs would be cut. Should the government reduce subsidies on basic consumption goods such as food or energy, or should it reduce credit subsidies to industry? In addition, governments had to decide which taxes were to be raised and upon which domestic groups the increases would fall. Each interest group lobbied the government to reduce expenditures on programs from which it did not benefit and impose higher taxes on other groups. This political dynamic generated a **war of attrition** between interest groups. Each group blocked meaningful policy reform because each believed that others would eventually agree to bear the costs of adjustment by accepting either large cuts to their favored programs or higher taxes (Alesina and Drazen 1991). This war of attrition drove the politics of stabilization throughout the early 1980s. The interest groups that had gained most from import substitution stood to lose the most from stabilization and structural adjustment. Import-competing firms that had benefited from government credit subsidies would be hit hard by fiscal retrenchment. State-owned enterprises would be particularly hard hit, as they would lose the government infusions that had covered their operating deficits during the 1970s. Workers in the urbanized nontraded-goods sector who had benefited from government subsidies of basic services, such as utilities and transportation, and essential food items would also be hit hard by budget cuts. Public-sector employees would suffer as well, as budget cuts brought an end to wage increases and forced large reductions in the number of government employees.

Unwilling to accept the reduction in income implied by fiscal austerity, interest groups blocked large cuts in government expenditures. In Brazil, for example, the military government attempted to implement an orthodox stabilization program in the early 1980s, but "both capitalists and labor in modern industry . . . demanded relief from austerity. So too did much of the urban middle class including government functionaries whose livelihood was imperiled by attacks on public spending" (Frieden 1991, 134). These groups shifted their support to the civilian political opposition, which took power from the military. Once in office, the new civilian government abandoned austerity measures. The Brazilian case was not unique: the import substitution coalition was well positioned to block substantial cuts in government programs in most heavily indebted countries.

The inability to reduce government expenditures resulted in high inflation throughout Latin America. Facing widening deficits and unable to reduce expenditures, many governments financed the resulting deficits through their central banks. Printing money to pay for government expenditures sparked inflation. Annual average inflation in Latin America rose from about 50 percent in the years immediately preceding the crisis to over 115 percent in 1984 and 1985 (Table 14.6.) Worse, these regionwide averages hide the most extreme cases. In Argentina, inflation averaged 787 percent per year during the 1980s. Brazil fared a little better, enduring average rates of inflation of 605 percent throughout the decade (Thorp 1999, 332). Bolivia's experience was the most extreme, with inflation rising above 20,000 percent in late 1985.

Even rapid inflation was insufficient to induce governments to cut expenditures. In Argentina, Brazil, and Peru, governments responded to high inflation with **heterodox strategies.** (See Edwards 1995, 33–37.) Advanced as an alternative to the orthodox measures embodied in IMF stabilization plans, heterodox strategies attacked inflation with government controls on wages and prices. The Argentinian and Brazilian plans illustrate the approach. In both programs, the government froze prices and wages in the public sector. Each government also introduced new currencies and established a fixed exchange rate. Initially, the programs appeared to work, as inflation dropped sharply in the first six months. Early successes were reversed, however, because neither government was willing to reduce government expenditures. In less than a year, inflation rates rose again and the programs were scrapped (Edwards 1995, 37).

It wasn't until the late 1980s that Latin America governments began to implement stabilization and structural adjustment programs. Governments reduced fiscal deficits and brought inflation under control. Macroeconomic stabilization provided a base upon which to begin structural reforms. Governments began to liberalize trade and privatize state-owned industries. Many governments also began to reduce their role in domestic financial systems and liberalize capital accounts as well (Edwards 1995, 212).

Three factors finally induced governments to implement reforms. First, the economic crisis altered the dynamics of interest-group politics. Key members of the import substitution coalition lost strength and faced higher costs from opposing reform. As a result, groups that had once been willing and able to block reform increasingly lost the capacity to do so. The economic crisis also caused "individuals and groups to accept [the fact] that their special interests need[ed] to be sacrificed . . . on the altar of the general good" (Williamson 1994, 19). Economic crisis thus created a new political consensus that the old order had failed and that reform was necessary. By weakening key interest groups and by forcing many of these same groups to redefine their interests, the severity of the economic crisis itself removed the political obstacles to reform.

Second, a new approach to the debt crisis initiated by the United States in 1989 created a greater incentive to adopt reforms. In March of 1989, the United States proposed a plan to encourage commercial banks to negotiate debt reduction agreements with debtor governments. Under this **Brady Plan** (named after Nicholas J. Brady, the secretary of the U.S. Treasury), debtor governments could convert their existing commercial bank debt into bond-based debt with a lower face value. The precise amount of debt reduction that each government realized would be determined by negotiations between the debtor government and its commercial bank creditors. To make the proposal attractive to commercial banks, the advanced industrialized countries and the multilateral financial institutions advanced $30 billion with which to guarantee the principal of these **Brady bonds.** This guarantee allowed commercial banks to exchange the uncertain repayment of a large bank debt for guaranteed repayment of a smaller amount of bond debt.

The Brady Plan strengthened the incentive to embark on reform by increasing the domestic benefits of reform. Large debt burdens reduced the incentive to adopt structural reforms because a significant share the gains from reform would be dedicated to debt service. Commercial banks would thus be the primary beneficiary of reform. It is not hard to see why domestic groups would be reluctant to accept costly reforms. Reducing the debt burden ensured that a larger share of the gains from reform would accrue to domestic groups and a smaller share would be devoted to debt service. As a result, the short-run costs of reform would be compensated for by gains over the long run. This plan created a greater incentive to accept the short-term costs that stabilization and structural adjustment entailed.

Mexico was the first to take advantage of the Brady Plan, concluding an agreement in July 1989. (See Cline 1995, 220–221.) The deal reduced Mexico's net transfers by about $4 billion, an amount equal to about 2 percent of Mexico's GDP. Reducing debt service allowed the Mexican economy to grow by 2 percentage points more than would have been possible without debt reduction (Edwards 1995, 81). By 1994, Brady Plan agreements covered about 80 percent of commercial bank debt and reduced debt service payments by about one-third (Cline 1995, 232).

Finally, as the economic crisis deepened, governments became more willing to recognize that the East Asian model offered lessons for Latin America. The Economic Commission on Latin America (ECLA) played an important role in prompting this recognition. (See Economic Commission for Latin American and the Caribbean 1985.) ECLA had begun to look closely at East Asia in the mid-1980s and was able to create a new consensus among Latin American governments that the East Asian model was relevant to Latin American development. As an ECLA study recommended in the late 1980s, "[T]he debt problem requires a structural transformation of the economy in at least two senses: the growth strategy needs to be *outward oriented* and largely based on a domestic effort to raise savings and productivity" (cited in Edwards 1995, 148). ECLA's transformation "was like 'Nixon in China.' When the institution that had for decades defended import substitution expressed doubts about its validity and recognized that there were lessons to be learned from the East Asian experience with outward-oriented policies, it was difficult to dismiss those doubts as purely neo-liberal propaganda" (Edwards 1995, 52).

The Latin American debt crisis was declared over in the mid-1990s (Cline 1995, 39). In hindsight, it is clear that the crisis was more than a financial one: it was a crisis of economic development strategy. The accumulation of foreign debt during the 1970s reflected developing countries' efforts to rejuvenate the waning energies of import substitution industrialization. Moreover, the crisis itself, and the debt regime through which it was managed, transformed developing countries' development strategies. Governments abandoned import substitution industrialization and adopted in its place market- and export-oriented development strategies. As a consequence, developing countries fundamentally altered their relationship with the international economy. The full implications of these changes are not yet clear.

Conclusion

The Latin American debt crisis illustrates the tragic cycle at the center of North–South financial relations. A growing demand for foreign capital generated in part by international events and in part by domestic developments combined with a growing willingness of commercial banks to lend to developing societies in order to generate large capital flows to Latin American countries during the 1970s. The resulting accumulation of foreign debt rendered Latin American societies extremely vulnerable to exogenous shocks. When such shocks hit in the late 1970s and early 1980s, governments found that they could no longer service their commercial bank debt, and commercial banks quickly ceased lending fresh funds. As the supply of foreign capital dried up, Latin American economies were pushed into crisis.

The Latin American debt crisis also forced governments in the advanced industrialized world to establish an international regime to manage the crisis. In the resulting debt regime, the IMF, the World Bank, and commercial banks provided additional financial assistance to the heavily indebted countries on the condition that governments implement stabilization and structural adjustment packages. This approach pushed most of the costs of the crisis onto Latin America. Moreover, the reforms it encouraged provoked far-reaching changes in Latin American political and economic systems. With a few changes that we will examine in the next chapter, this debt regime remains central to the management of developing-country financial crises.

Although the Latin American debt crisis is unique in many respects, in others it is all too typical. For while this crisis was the first of the postwar period, it would not be the last. In fact, crises have become increasingly common during the last 20 years, and the more recent ones share many of the central characteristics of the Latin American crisis and have been managed in much the same way. They have also generated much discussion about whether and how the international financial system should be reformed in order to reduce the number and severity of such crises. We examine these issues in Chapter 15.

Key Terms

Bilateral Development Assistance

Board of Governors

Brady Bonds

Brady Plan

Concerted Lending

Concessional Lending Programs

Debt Regime

Debt-Service Capacity

Debt-Service Ratio

Executive Board

Foreign Aid

Heterodox Strategies

International Bank for Reconstruction and Development

International Development Association

Liquidity Problem

London Club

Macroeconomic Stabilization

Net Transfers

Nonconcessional Lending Programs

Petrodollars

Petrodollar Recycling

Portfolio Flows

Regional Development Banks

Structural Adjustment

Syndicated Loan

War of Attrition

World Bank

Web Links

Perhaps the most useful site for global financial developments is maintained by Nouriel Roubini at the Stern School of Business at New York University. It can be found at *http://www.stern.nyu.edu/globalmacro/*.

Visit the World Bank at *http://www.worldbank.org*.

The IMF website provides useful information about stabilization and reform packages at *http://www.imf.org*.

The Organization for Economic Cooperation and Development maintains a web site on foreign aid. Visit *http://www.oecd.org/department/0,2688,en_2649_33721_1_1_1_1_1,00.html*, or do a Web search for "OECD Development Assistance Committee".

Suggestions for Further Reading

For a comprehensive history of the World Bank's first 20 years, see Edward S. Mason and Robert E. Asher, *The World Bank since Bretton Woods* (Washington, DC: The Brookings Institution, 1973), and Devesh Kapur, John P. Lewis, and Richard Webb, *The World Bank: Its First Half Century* (Washington, DC: Brookings Institution, 1997). For a critical perspective, see Kevin Danaher, ed., *50 Years Is Enough: The Case against the World Bank and the International Monetary Fund* (Boston: South End Press, 1994).

On the 1980s debt crisis and the politics of economic reform see Robert Devlin, *Debt and Crisis in Latin America: The Supply Side of the Story* (Princeton: Princeton University Press, 1989), Stephan Haggard and Robert Kaufman, eds., *The Politics of Economic Adjustment: International Constraints, Distributive Conflicts, and the State* (Princeton: Princeton University Press, 1992), and Robert Bates and Anne O. Krueger, eds., *Political and Economic Interactions in Economic Policy Reform* (Oxford: Blackwell, 1993).

Four short articles published in the IMF's journal *Finance Development* take a new look at the Washington Consensus; Jeremy Clift, "Beyond the Washington Consensus"; John Williamson, "From Reform Agenda to Damaged Brand Name"; Guillermo Ortiz, "Latin America: Overcoming Reform Fatigue"; and Trevor A. Manuel, "Africa: Finding the Right Path". All appear in *Finance and Development* 40 (September 2003), also available online at *http://www.imf.org/external/pubs/ft/fandd/2003/09/index.htm*.

CHAPTER 15

Developing Countries
and International Finance II:
A Decade of Crises

Private flows of capital to the developing world resumed in the early 1990s, but took a form different from their previous disposition. Traditional commercial bank loans such as those at the center of the Latin American debt crisis were increasingly accompanied, and in many instances surpassed, by bond and equity flows. The emergence of large and liquid private capital flows to developing countries contributed to a rash of crises during the decade. The crises began in Mexico in 1994 and continued, almost without interruption, until the Argentinean crisis of 2001–2002. In between, financial crises struck Asia, Russia, Brazil, and Turkey. Indeed, it is not too much of an exaggeration to suggest that, in hindsight, the decade was a period of continual crisis. As governments managed the fallout from one, another began to develop. Without exception, the domestic economic and political consequences of these crises was severe: economies collapsed, incomes fell sharply, and governments toppled.

The rash of financial crises encouraged governments to contemplate changing the crisis management system. As these new crises struck, governments turned to the debt regime established during the 1980s to manage them. As the scale and the consequences of the Asian crisis began to sink in, dissatisfaction with that regime grew. Some people argued that by applying the logic of stabilization and structural adjustment to Asia, the IMF had worsened the resulting economic crisis, pushing economies into deep recessions. They proposed that the IMF should change how it responds to crises. Others argued that the widespread belief that the IMF stood ready to "bail out" countries in distress itself encouraged the unsustainable private capital flows that created crises. These critics suggested that the IMF get out of the crisis management business altogether. Still others argued that developing countries should reintroduce controls to limit the volume of private capital flows. Criticisms prompted an extended discussion of what reforms could be adopted to reduce the frequency and severity of these new financial crises, as well to manage them more effectively. Yet, in spite of considerable discussion, little has come of these efforts. Consequently, we move into the 21st century facing the risk of additional crises.

We examine this decade of crisis and crisis management in this chapter. We begin by looking at the series of crises that struck during the 1990s, focusing deeply on the largest of them: the 1997 Asian crisis. We then examine how that crisis subsequently prompted considerable discussion about reforming the international financial system in order to alter how crises are managed and to try to reduce the frequency of such crises in the future. We then turn our attention to the other debt crisis that has dominated North–South relations during the last ten years, the one involving the world's poorest countries. The chapter concludes by drawing some more general lessons.

The Asian Financial Crisis

Developing countries attracted little new private capital during the 1980s. It was not until the end of the decade and after the reform process had begun to take root that private capital began flowing again to those countries. Private capital flows thus resumed in a changed environment. On the one hand, developing countries' policies toward private capital flows were radically different. While most governments had restricted such flows into and out of their economies in connection with import substitution, many dismantled these controls in connection with policy reforms implemented during the 1980s and early 1990s. Consequently, it became much easier for private individuals to move capital into and out of emerging markets. On the other hand, liberalization of financial markets in the advanced industrialized countries had decreased the relative importance of traditional bank loans and increased the importance of securities—stocks and bonds—as sources of financing. The growing importance of nonbank capital flows was reinforced by the lingering effect of the Latin American debt crisis; few banks were willing to lend to countries that had so recently defaulted.

These changes combined to alter the composition, as well as the scale, of private capital flows to the developing world. The importance of commercial bank lending diminished, while that of bond and equity flows increased. Most private capital flows to Latin America during the 1990s, for example, financed government and corporate bonds and purchased stocks in newly liberalized stock markets. By the mid-1990s, private capital flows to the entire developing world had risen to more than $200 billion per year, about 3 percent of these countries' GDP. (See Figure 15.1.) Asia was the largest recipient of capital inflows prior to 1997, accounting for almost 50 percent of total flows to all developing countries in the first half of the decade. Latin America was the second-largest recipient, obtaining between one-quarter and one-third of all flows to developing countries (IMF 2000).

The resumption of private capital flows generated one crisis after another. The growing importance of bond and equity flows, often referred to as **hot money** because they can be withdrawn from a developing country at the first hint of trouble, increased the volatility of private capital flows to these "emerging market" countries. Although developing countries have struggled with such volatility throughout the last hundred years, volatility increased during the 1990s compared with earlier periods (IMF 2001,

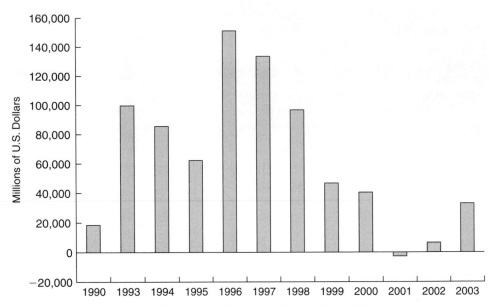

Figure 15.1   Private Capital Flows to the Developing World, 1990–2003
Note: Excludes foreign direct investment flows.
Source: World Bank, *Global Development Finance,* various issues.

163; World Bank 2001a). Historical evidence suggests that more volatile capital flows have been associated with lower economic growth rates over the long run (World Bank 2001a, 73). In addition, the record of the 1990s indicates that increased volatility of private capital flows is associated with more frequent financial crises that substantially reduce economic growth for a year or two.

Such financial crises became all too common during the 1990s. Mexico experienced the first one in late 1994. Four Asian countries—Indonesia, Malaysia, South Korea, and Thailand—had severe crises in the summer and fall of 1997. Brazil and Russia both experienced crises in 1998. Turkey and Argentina were struck by crises in 2000 and 2001. While each crisis was distinctive in some way, all shared important similarities. (See Table 15.1.) First, each of the countries struck by a crisis maintained some form of fixed exchange rate. In most instances, these governments maintained an adjustable rate, either in the form of a crawling peg or the slightly less restrictive crawling band. Second, each of the countries developed a heavy reliance on short-term foreign private capital inflows.

The combination proved perilous. Heavy dependence on short-term foreign capital required the continual rollover of foreign liabilities. The government's ability to roll over these liabilities depended critically upon its ability to maintain foreign investors' confidence in the country's commitment to the fixed exchange rate. In each crisis, events caused foreign investors to lose confidence in that commitment. The trigger for crisis varied. Sometimes it was a political shock, as in Mexico; sometimes it was an economic shock, as in Russia and Argentina; sometimes it was contagion from crises in

Table 15.1
A Chronology of Crises, 1994–2002

Mexico (December 1994–January 1995)

Exchange Rate: Crawling band pegged to the dollar.
Financing Problem: The Mexican government began issuing short-term debt linked to the U.S. dollar in April 1994 (Cetes, analogous to U.S. Treasury bonds) to reduce its interest rate. The value of the *Cetes* issued soon exceeded the central bank's foreign exchange reserves.
Trigger: Unrest in Chiapas province generated a speculative attack in early December.
IMF Support: Mexico secured credits for $48.8 billion, including $17.8 billion from the IMF and $20 billion from the U.S. government.
Fallout: The government devalued the peso by 15 percent on December 20 and then floated the peso on December 22. The peso depreciated from 3.64 per dollar to more than 7 per dollar. Mexico suffered a depression and severe banking problems that prompted government rescues.
Contagion: Speculative attacks spread throughout Latin America and Asia.

East Asia (July 1997–January 1998)

See details in this chapter.

Russia (August 1998)

Exchange Rate: Crawling band pegged to the dollar.
Financing Problem: The Russian government was paying very high interest rates on large short-term debt.
Trigger: Falling prices for oil (the country's major export) and weak growth generated speculative attacks. The government widened the ruble's band by 35 percent in August and then floated the ruble in early September. The ruble depreciated from 6.2 per dollar to more than 20 per dollar.
IMF Support: Russia secured IMF credits of $11.2 billion in July 1998.
Fallout: The government defaulted on its ruble-denominated debt and Soviet-era foreign debt and imposed a moratorium on private-sector payments of foreign debt. The economy fell into recession. Many Russian banks became insolvent.
Contagion. Speculative attacks spread to Latin America, hitting Brazil especially hard. The U.S. hedge fund Long Term Capital Management was pushed to the brink of bankruptcy and was rescued in an effort coordinated by the Federal Reserve Bank of New York.

Brazil (January 1999)

Exchange Rate: Crawling band pegged to the U.S. dollar.
Financing Problem: Growing government debt and a sizable current-account deficit generated large short-term external debt.
Trigger: The Russian crisis and the subsequent collapse of Long Term Capital Management generated speculative attacks between August and October of 1998. Attacks resumed in early 1999 when a state government defaulted on payments to the federal government. The *real* was devalued by 9 percent on January 13, 1999, and then floated on January 18. The currency depreciated from 1.21 per dollar to 2.18.
IMF Support: Brazil secured an IMF credit of $18 billion on December 2, 1998.
Fallout: Mild; growth strengthened in 1999 and 2000. The financial system suffered little.
Contagion: Brazil's devaluation contributed to recessions in Argentina and Uruguay and generated speculative attacks that forced Ecuador to float in February 1999.

Continued

Turkey (February 2001)

Exchange Rate: Crawling peg against the dollar and the German mark.

Financing Problem: Large government short-term debt and a large current-account deficit generated heavy dependence on short-term foreign capital.

Trigger: Concern about a criminal investigation into ten government-run banks in late November 2000 generated a speculative attack. Eight banks became insolvent and were taken over by the government. Investors lost confidence in February 2001 when conflict between the president and prime minister weakened the coalition government. The government floated the lira on February 22, and it depreciated from 668,000 per dollar to 1.6 million per dollar by October 2001.

IMF Support: Turkey secured an IMF credit of $10.4 billion on December 21.

Fallout: The Turkish economy contracted by 7.5 percent in 2001.

Contagion: None.

Argentina (2001)

Exchange Rate: Fixed to the U.S. dollar.

Financing Problem: Large government short-term debt.

Trigger: Speculative attacks against this peg emerged in 2000 and continued sporadically into 2001. The government introduced some exchange-rate flexibility in mid-2001, generating new speculative attacks. The government floated the peso in January 2002 and defaulted on its foreign debt.

IMF Support: Argentina secured a total of $40 billion in credits from the IMF and the advanced industrialized countries.

Fallout: Argentina's economy collapsed into deep depression.

Contagion: None.

Source: Compiled from information in Eichengreen (2001), Joint Economic Committee (2003), and material on the IMF website (*www.IMF.org*).

other regions. In all instances, however, the evaporation of foreign investors' confidence in the government's commitment to the fixed exchange rate triggered massive outflows of private capital that forced governments to devalue and (with the lone exception of Brazil) pushed the country into deep economic crisis. In many instances, the economic crisis toppled governments as well.

The Asian financial crisis of 1997 provides the clearest illustration of the challenges these countries faced. The Asian crisis illustrates how the new international financial crises differ from previous crises. At least three differences are worth emphasizing at the outset. First, the causes of the Asian crisis differed from the underlying causes of previous international financial crises. In contrast to the Latin American debt crisis, the Asian crisis had little to do with government borrowing, but originated instead in weak domestic banking sectors that had recently been liberalized and encouraged to intermediate between domestic and international markets. Second, the Asian crisis differed in scale from previous crises. The volume of capital outflows that Asian countries experienced and the size of the IMF-centered rescue packages that were provided to the countries in crisis were both unprecedented. Finally, the economic and political consequences of the crisis were far more severe than those of previous crises, with some countries suffering economic contractions worse than any experienced by any country since the Great Depression. What is most worrying about the Asian crisis is the possibility that it is not unique, but rather is the first of a new kind of international financial crisis that periodically will threaten the stability of the international financial system. We examine the Asian crisis in detail in this section, looking first at its origins and management and then turning to its impact on the broader international financial system.

The Asian crisis originated in political and economic dynamics within the four Asian countries that were hardest hit: Thailand, Indonesia, South Korea, and Malaysia. During the late 1980s and early 1990s, these Asian governments liberalized their financial markets to make it easier for domestic banks and firms to borrow on international financial markets. In Thailand, for example, the government created the Bangkok International Banking Facilities in 1992 in an attempt to make Thailand a banking center in Asia. The government hoped that Thai banks would borrow on international markets and then lend the funds obtained to borrowers across Asia. Financial liberalization throughout Asia thus enabled Asian banks to intermediate between international lenders and domestic borrowers. The incentive for such intermediation was powerful. Interest rates in international markets were considerably lower than interest rates inside Asian economies. Asian banks could thus borrow money at a relatively low rate of interest, such as 9 percent, from foreign commercial banks and then lend it to domestic borrowers at a much higher rate of interest, such as 12 percent.

This type of intermediation, however, was risky. Asian banks contracted short-term loans denominated in dollars and other foreign currencies from foreign banks and then offered these funds as long-term loans denominated in the domestic currency to local borrowers. Such transactions meant that Asian banks were exposed to two distinct kinds of risk. First, they faced **exchange-rate risk,** which arose from the possibility that the government would devalue the local currency. Were this to happen, the cost of servicing the dollar-denominated loans in the domestic currency would rise substantially. At the extreme, the domestic currency cost would rise above the payments that Asian banks were receiving from the businesses to which they had lent money. Asian banks were also exposed to the risk that foreign lenders would stop rolling over their short-term loans. Because Asian banks had borrowed on a short-term basis and then made long-term loans, they needed foreign commercial banks to renew the loans they had previously made. Each time a short-term loan was due, the foreign commercial bank would simply extend the loan for an additional 6 or 12 months. If foreign commercial banks suddenly became unwilling to continue this practice, the Asian banks would be forced to repay all of their short-term debt at once. Yet, because these funds were tied up in the long-term loans that the Asian banks had made to local borrowers, the Asian banks would be unable to raise the funds needed to repay their debts to foreign banks. Both risks proved important as the crisis unfolded.

The ability of Asian banks to intermediate safely between international and domestic financial markets was compromised by flaws in Asian countries' financial regulations. The central weakness was a problem called **moral hazard,** which arises when banks believe that the government will bail them out if they suffer large losses on the loans they have made. If banks believe that the government will cover their losses, they have little incentive to carefully evaluate the risks that are associated with the loans they make. If the loans are repaid, banks earn money. If the loans are not repaid, the government—and society's taxpayers—pick up the tab. In such an environment, banks have an incentive to make riskier loans than they would make in the absence of a guarantee from the government. This incentive arises because banks charge higher interest rates to high-risk borrowers. As a result, higher-risk loans, when they are repaid, yield higher returns than low-risk loans. A government guarantee thus creates a one-way bet for banks: lend heavily to risky borrowers and profit greatly if the loans are repaid, yet suffer little if they are not, because the government will bail them out. The danger is that the practice of lending heavily to high-risk borrowers makes a systemwide financial crisis more likely. Banks will lend too much to risky borrowers, and too many of these high-risk borrowers will default on their debt. Banks will therefore lose money, forcing the government to step in and bail them out. The government guarantee thus makes a financial crisis more likely.

Moral hazard was particularly acute in many of the Asian crisis countries. Financial institutions had close ties to governments, sometimes through personal relationships and sometimes through direct government ownership. In Indonesia, for example, seven state-owned banks controlled half of the assets in the banking system (Blustein 2001, 94), and relatives and close friends of Indonesian President Suharto controlled other financial institutions. In the past, such relationships had led governments to rescue banks and other financial institutions in distress. In Thailand, for example, the government rescued the Bangkok Bank of Commerce in 1996–1997 at the cost of $7 billion (Haggard 2000, 25). In Indonesia, two large corporate groups rescued Bank Duta (which held deposits from President Suharto's political foundations) after it had lost $500 million in foreign exchange markets. The corporate rescuers were in turn rewarded by the Suharto regime (Haggard 2000, 26). Given this history, foreign and domestic financial institutions participating in the Asian market had reason to believe that Asian governments would not allow domestic financial institutions to fail. This belief in turn led international investors to lend more to Asian banks, and Asian banks to lend more to Asian businesses, than either would have been willing to lend had Asian governments not rescued banks in the past.

In principle, governments can design financial regulations to prevent the risky lending practices to which moral hazard so often gives rise. Banking regulations established and enforced by government agencies can limit the activities that financial firms engage in and thereby confine the overall risk in lending portfolios. In the Asian crisis countries, however, such financial regulation was underdeveloped, and where it did exist, it was not effectively enforced. In Indonesia, for example, any regulator "who attempted to enforce prudential rules . . . was removed from his position" (Haggard 2000, 33). Nor was this kind of treatment restricted to civil servants: the managing director of the central bank was fired in 1992, and the minister of finance was fired in 1996 (Haggard 2000, 33). As Haggard notes, the more general problem lay in the "influence that business interests exercised over legislation, regulation, and the legal process" (Haggard 2000, 38). In other words, the same network of business–government relations that created the moral hazard problem in the first place also weakened the incentives that governments had to develop and enforce effective prudential regulations. As a consequence, there were few regulatory checks on the lending practices of Asian financial institutions.

This regulatory framework enabled Asian banks to accumulate financial positions that could not easily withstand the deteriorating economic conditions that Asian countries began to encounter in late 1996 and early 1997. Deteriorating economic conditions created domestic debt-service problems in two ways. First, Asian countries' exchange rates began to appreciate against the Japanese yen in the mid-1990s. Most Asian governments pegged their currencies to the dollar. When the dollar began to appreciate against the Japanese yen in the mid-1990s, Asian currencies rose in value along with it. Exchange-rate appreciation made it difficult for domestic firms to export to Japan, one of their major export markets, which in turn created debt-service problems for export-oriented firms. Second, real-estate prices began to fall in late 1996, creating debt-service problems for real-estate developers. In March, the Thai government purchased $4 billion of debt that property developers owed, but were unable to pay to domestic banks. By 1997, therefore, many of the Asian banks' largest domestic borrowers were struggling to service their debts. As a consequence, the number of **nonperforming loans**—loans on which interest payments had not been made for six months or more—held by Asian banks began to grow. Because domestic borrowers could not repay domestic banks, the domestic banks could not easily repay foreign banks. Domestic debt-service difficulties thus began to generate international debt-service difficulties.

Weaknesses in Asian financial systems became a source of general concern in the spring of 1997, when one of Thailand's largest financial institutions, Finance One, was discovered to be **insolvent;** that is, its total liabilities were greater than the value of its assets. The discovery that such an important financial institution was insolvent caused foreign banks to look much more closely at banks throughout Asia. Close inspection indicated that Finance One's situation was not unique; banks all over Asia were facing similar problems. In Thailand, the government suspended the operations of 16 of the nation's largest financial institutions, all of which were unable to raise the cash needed to continue operations. Deteriorating conditions in Asian financial systems and shifting international market sentiment combined to produce a panicked withdrawal of funds from Asian markets beginning in the summer of 1997. Foreign banks that had loaned heavily to Asian banks refused to roll over existing loans and demanded repayment of whatever loans they could. Funds also started flowing out of Asian stock markets.

The panic began in Thailand in May 1997, where it quickly consumed the Thai government's foreign exchange reserves and forced the government to float the baht. The panicked withdrawal of funds from Asia over the next six months struck practically every country in the region. After their experience with Thailand, financial markets shifted their attention to the Philippines, forcing the government to abandon its fixed exchange rate after only ten days. Attention then shifted to Indonesia and Malaysia in July and August, and governments in both countries responded to massive capital outflows by abandoning their fixed exchange rates and allowing their currencies to float. From there, speculation targeted Taiwan, forcing a devaluation of the Taiwanese dollar, and Hong Kong, where capital flight caused the Hong Kong stock market to lose about one-quarter of its value in only four days. The crisis moved to South Korea in November, forcing the government to float the won by the middle of the month. A total of $60 billion was pulled from the region in the second half of 1997, roughly two-thirds of all the capital that had flowed into the region the year before. An additional $55 billion was pulled out in 1998 (IMF 1999, 92).

As the crisis struck, Asian governments turned to the IMF for financial assistance. The Philippines was the first to do so, gaining a $1.1 billion credit on July 14. The Thai government turned to the Fund two weeks later and was provided $16 billion from the IMF and other Asian countries. Indonesia was able to hold out longer, turning to the IMF only in October and receiving a $23 billion package. South Korea received the most support from the international community, acquiring $57 billion from the IMF and other governments in early December. The sizes of these financial packages were historically unprecedented. The financial support offered by the IMF, other international financial institutions, and the advanced industrialized countries to the four countries most severely affected by the crisis—South Korea, Indonesia, Thailand, and Malaysia—totaled $117.7 billion.

As in earlier crises, financial assistance from the IMF was conditional upon economic reform. The reforms incorporated into IMF conditionality agreements in the Asian crisis targeted three broad areas: macroeconomic stabilization, reform of the financial sector, and structural reform. Macroeconomic stabilization programs were necessary, the IMF argued, to restore market confidence in the crisis countries and to stem the outflow of capital. Governments were urged to tighten monetary policy by raising interest rates in order to stem the depreciation of their currencies. Tighter fiscal policies were required to generate the financial resources needed to pay for restructuring of the financial sector. Financial sector reforms were based on three interacting components. First, governments were required to close insolvent financial institutions. In Thailand, for example, the government shut down 56 insolvent finance companies; the South Korean government closed nine large merchant banks; and the Indonesian government was required to close a large number of insolvent banks. Second, governments were asked to recapitalize weak financial institutions. Third, Asian governments were required to restructure their financial systems to improve the quality of financial intermediation. Restructuring entailed (1) redesigning financial regulations to promote better oversight, (2) ending close relationships between government officials and financial institutions, and (3) opening the domestic financial services industry to foreign financial institutions. Finally, the IMF required Asian governments to implement structural reforms, including trade liberalization, the elimination of domestic monopolies and other uncompetitive practices and regulations, and privatization of state-owned enterprises. In Thailand, structural reforms targeted the civil service and state-owned enterprises. In Indonesia, the IMF pressed the government to deregulate agriculture and reduce the monopoly position of the national agriculture marketing board. The Indonesian government was also pressed to privatize 13 state-owned enterprises and to suspend the development of auto and commercial aircraft industries.

The crisis had severe economic and political repercussions. The financial crisis and the implementation of IMF reform packages precipitated economic recessions throughout Asia. (See Table 15.2.) Indonesia experienced the biggest downturn, with economic output contracting by more than 13 percent in 1998. In most countries, the economic crisis hit the poor the hardest, and as a consequence, poverty rates throughout the region rose sharply. In Indonesia, the number of people living below the poverty line grew from 11 percent of the population prior to the crisis to 19.9 percent in 1998. In South Korea, the poverty rate rose from 8.6 percent of the population prior

Table 15.2
Economic Growth and Current-Account Balances in Asia

	1995	1996	1997	1998
	Economic Growth (annual percent change)			
Thailand	8.8	5.5	−0.4	−5.0
Indonesia	8.2	8.0	4.6	−13.7
South Korea	8.9	7.1	5.5	−5.8
	Current-Account Balance (percent of GDP)			
Thailand	−7.8	−7.9	−2.0	6.9
Indonesia	−3.2	−3.3	−1.8	1.6
South Korea	−1.9	−4.7	−1.9	7.3

Source: IMF Annual Report, 1999.

to the crisis to 19.2 percent in 1998. Deteriorating economic conditions sparked protest and political instability. Political unrest was most severe in Indonesia. Economic crisis sparked large scale opposition to the corruption, nepotism, and cronyism that had long characterized the Suharto government. As the crisis deepened, opposition to the Suharto regime grew, demanding fundamental political reforms and a reduction of basic commodity prices, particularly of energy and rice. Protests and opposition peaked in May 1998. Four students were killed by the military during an anti-Suharto demonstration at Triskati University on May 12, sparking even larger protests during the days that followed. By May 18, some of Suharto's close associates were asking that he step down from office, and on May 21 he did so. B.J. Habibie assumed the presidency following Suharto's resignation and began the task of economic and political reform.

The economic crisis sparked political change in Thailand as well. Thailand had begun constitutional reform in the early 1990s. Reform had then stalled under competing visions of how the new political institutions should be structured. A new constitution had been drafted in 1997 before the crisis, and its acceptance by the major societal groups was "propelled forward" by the economic crisis. As Haggard (2000, 94) notes, it is "highly doubtful that [this political reform] would have occurred in the way that it did in the absence of crisis circumstances." In addition, the government that had presided over the economy in the years leading up to the crisis was unable to maintain a majority coalition. It was replaced in November 1997 by a new government based on a five-party coalition dominated by the Democrat Party, the oldest political party in Thailand. The Democrat Party was "free of the more egregious patronage, pork-barrel spending, and corruption of its opponents" (Haggard 2000, 94). In Indonesia and Thailand, therefore, the economic crisis provoked a reaction against the corruption of previous governments, mobilized societal support for far-reaching constitutional reform, and brought to power groups committed to economic and political reform.

The years since the crisis have been characterized by political stabilization, gradual economic recovery, and mixed progress on the implementation of structural reform. Economic growth has resumed, and the most severe political instabilities had ended by 1999. What remains, however, is the daunting task of restructuring the domestic financial and corporate sectors. (See Lane et al. 1999.) This task requires governments to recapitalize weak banks and close insolvent ones. In addition, governments must find some way to reduce the burden of large debt loads on the corporate sector and to help banks cope with large burdens of nonperforming loans. Because of the close relations between business and government in many of these countries, this process of restructuring requires governments to impose substantial costs on politically important domestic actors. As a consequence, structural reform has progressed at different speeds, and with varying degrees of success, across the region.

Today, robust growth has returned to most of the Asian countries that were hard hit by the crisis, and as Anne O. Krueger, first deputy director of the IMF, has noted, the "turmoil of the late 1990s must be a distant memory" (Krueger 2004). Yet, it is important to recognize the many ways in which the Asian crisis continues to shape the international financial system. The crisis suggests that the opening of developing-country financial systems to international capital flows poses new challenges to the international financial system. The crisis also suggests that the stability of the contemporary international financial system depends in part upon the strength of banking systems in the developing countries that are tapping international financial markets. Finally, the crisis highlights weaknesses in the way that the advanced industrialized countries and the international financial institutions manage financial crises. These weaknesses raise concerns about the ability of governments and the IMF to manage future crises effectively and have given rise to extensive discussion about systemic reform.

Reforming the Crisis Management Regime

The Asian crisis forced governments in developing countries and in the advanced industrialized countries alike to reexamine their erstwhile beliefs about the benefits that developing countries realize from unrestricted capital flows and to reevaluate how financial crises are managed. How the Asian crisis will ultimately affect the international financial system depends upon what conclusions are drawn from this process of reevaluation, which is not yet complete.

The Asian crisis caused many academics and policymakers to reevaluate the benefits that developing countries realize from complete financial liberalization and unrestricted integration into the international financial system. As former World Bank chief economist Joseph Stiglitz has suggested, financial liberalization might expose developing countries to "unnecessary risks without commensurate returns" (Wessel and Davis 1998). Such concerns have been most strongly asserted by economist Jagdish Bhagwati of Columbia University. (See Bhagwati 1998b.) While the ability to draw on foreign savings can be beneficial, these critics argue, the benefits must be weighed against the costs that result from the crises that unrestricted capital flows seem to generate. Once one performs this balancing, say Bhagwati and others, one will find that there is little net gain from eliminating all capital controls and opening developing economies to increasingly volatile short-term capital flows. As a result, both "the weight of evidence and the force of logic," Bhagwati argues, "point . . . toward restraints on capital flows" (Bhagwati 1998b, 12).

A CLOSER LOOK

Crisis in Argentina

The long series of developing-world crises ended, at least for now, with a spectacular crisis in Argentina in 2001 and 2002. Argentina had been the poster child for neoliberal reform. It stabilized and restructured its economy during the early 1990s and subsequently experienced strong growth—indeed, among the strongest in all of Latin America (Krueger 2002). In 2001, Argentina collapsed in a severe economic and financial crisis. The economy shrank by a quarter between 1998 and 2002. Unemployment doubled, reaching 24 percent in 2002. Wages fell sharply, and the poverty rate doubled to more than 50 percent of the population. The economic crisis shook the political system. Argentineans took to the streets, banging on pots and pans in protest of government policy. More than 20 people were killed in these protests. The public and the collapsing economy toppled one government after another, as the country went through five presidents between mid-December 2001 and early January 2002. What went wrong?

Argentina's crisis resulted in part from the consequences of a previous government decision to fix the Argentinean peso to the U.S. dollar in order to control inflation (IMF 2003b). Argentina had been heavily indebted during the 1980s and was still struggling to implement economic reform in the early 1990s. This struggle manifested itself in part in hyperinflation, which peaked at 1,344 percent in 1990 (Joint Economic Committee 2003, 4). In 1991, Argentina passed the Convertibility Law, which established a fixed exchange rate: one peso equaled one dollar. The central bank was required to maintain sufficient dollars to guarantee this exchange rate. Thus, new pesos could be created only when the central bank had the dollars required to back them. Like EU governments, the Argentinean government believed that this fixed exchange rate would provide a credible commitment to low inflation that would break expectations of continued high inflation. Initially, the approach was quite successful; by 1994, inflation had fallen to 4 percent and remained quite low throughout the decade.

The Convertibility Law was less appropriate for the challenging international environment that Argentina confronted at the end of the decade. Having pegged to the dollar, Argentina's export competitiveness became linked to the dollar's strength in international markets. As the dollar appreciated in the late 1990s, the peso rose as well, pricing Argentina's exports out of foreign markets. Competitiveness was further diminished when Brazil devalued the real in late 1998. The overvalued peso, combined with rising global interest rates, pushed Argentina into recession in 1998.

The government could not use macroeconomic policy to stimulate the economy. Because monetary policy was maintaining the exchange rate, the government could not expand the money supply. Fiscal policy was also constrained (IMF 2003b). Government budget deficits throughout the 1990s had generated a government debt of about 50 percent of GDP, and much of this debt was denominated in foreign currencies. Fiscal expansion would require the government to borrow more, raising doubts about its ability to repay the debt. Borrowing would raise interest rates, thereby depressing economic activity. Fiscal expansion, therefore, was unlikely to promote growth. Instead, the government tried to balance the budget, which it hoped would

Continued

reduce interest rates and spark renewed growth. Balancing the budget proved difficult, however: politics prevented large expenditure cuts, and revenues fell as economic conditions deteriorated, thereby increasing the expenditure cuts needed to
balance the budget.

Facing few good options, the government began to introduce exchange rate flexibility in 2001, hoping that devaluing the peso would restore export competitiveness
and generate an export-led recovery. The peso's exchange rate peg was changed
from a pure dollar peg to a peg against the dollar and the euro. In June, the government created a separate lower exchange rate for exporters. This tinkering with the
exchange rate raised concerns in international financial markets that the government
was about to abandon the dollar peg. Such doubts pushed interest rates up (the yield
on a 10-year government bond denominated in dollars rose by 20 basis points, to
35 percent, during 2001) and caused dollars to flow out from Argentina (Federal
Reserve Board of San Francisco 2002). These dollar outflows quickly consumed
Argentina's foreign exchange reserves—almost 40 percent of the country's reserves
disappeared during the first seven months of 2001 (Eichengreen 2001, 11). Dollar
outflows made it costly to sustain the fixed exchange rate, for the government had to
contract the money supply, thereby placing strong downward pressure on the Argentinean economy.

Argentina turned to the IMF for assistance. The IMF responded by offering support in exchange for a government commitment to meaningful fiscal consolidation.
Working with the IMF and individual advanced industrialized countries, Argentina was
granted $40 billion of support in March 2000. The country returned to the IMF in Jan-
uary and September of 2001 in search of additional support. When the government
proved unwilling or unable to stabilize its fiscal position, the IMF cut off access to its
credits in December 2001. Unable to attract additional private funding and unable to
draw from the IMF, the government defaulted on $155 billion in government bonds.

Could Argentina have avoided this crisis? In hindsight, it seems that two policy
changes could have prevented the crisis. First, the government could have changed
its exchange rate arrangements during the late 1990s after inflation had come down.
Establishing a more flexible exchange rate would have enabled exports to recover,
and this could have reinvigorated the economy. Second, the government could have
consolidated its fiscal position during the 1990s. It could then have used fiscal policy
as the recession emerged. Domestic politics prevented both policy changes. The
Convertibility Law was popular; it was seen to have cut inflation and restored confidence in the peso. Changing the law would have thus cut against public opinion. Fiscal consolidation was limited by political opposition to the necessary expenditure
reductions.

This reevaluation of the costs and benefits of financial integration has led policymakers in two directions. First, governments and, to a lesser extent, the IMF have
begun considering whether capital controls might help reduce the volatility of financial
flows to developing countries. Policymakers have looked closely at the experience of
some developing-country governments that adopted capital controls designed to discourage short-term inflows without discouraging less volatile long-term lending and
foreign direct investment. (See Ariyoshi et al. 2000; Velasco and Cabezas 1998.) In
Chile, for example, the government requires a deposit with the central bank equal to

20 percent of the total investment and a stamp tax of 1.2 percent on inflows with maturities of less than one year. Medium- and long-term flows face no such deposit requirements or taxes (Velasco and Cabezas 1998, 147). Malaysia used similar measures in the early 1990s, limiting the amount of foreign deposits held by domestic banks, prohibiting the sale of short-term financial instruments to foreigners, and raising the cost of borrowing from foreigners. The country reimplemented these controls as the 1997 crisis struck (Eichengreen and Fishlow 1998, 63). Supporters of this approach argue that capital controls can reduce the likelihood of financial crises in part because they reduce the total volume of capital inflows and in part because they discourage the more volatile short-term flows while encouraging long-term inflows and foreign direct investment. Others are more skeptical, suggesting that the capital controls used by the Chilean government have had little impact on capital flows into and out of that country (Edwards 1999).

Second, policymakers have become much more aware of the importance of sound banking practices in developing countries. Thus, the IMF and the World Bank have been working with developing-country governments to reform banking regulation and to promote greater transparency in accounting practices. The hope is that such reforms will make it more difficult for banks in other developing countries to develop the financial positions that so weakened banks in Asia.

The Asian crisis has also sparked extensive discussions about reform of the international financial system. These discussions emerged in response to criticisms of the way the IMF responded to the crisis. (See Sachs, 1997; Krugman 1998; Stiglitz 2000, 2002; Blustein 2001.) The IMF was criticized for the specific contents of the conditionality agreements it negotiated with the countries in crisis. Many observers argued that macroeconomic stabilization programs were inappropriate for those countries. Macroeconomic imbalances were not at the base of the crisis; the crisis countries were running budget surpluses and had low inflation. In this context, macroeconomic stabilization not only failed to address the cause of the crisis, but, the critics contend, also pushed the countries involved into deep recessions (Krugman 1998). Rather than implement austerity measures, the crisis countries should have been encouraged to adopt "stable or even slightly expansionary" macroeconomic policies to counteract the macroeconomic consequences of the financial crisis (Sachs 1997).

Critics also argue that the IMF erred in forcing governments in the crisis countries to close banks. Forced closures, the critics contended, exacerbated fears about financial weaknesses in the crisis countries and, by doing so, precipitated additional financial panic. This problem was particularly acute in Indonesia, where bank closures led to banking crises as local depositors rushed to withdraw their funds. Finally, critics argue that many of the structural reforms that the IMF required had little direct bearing on the immediate problems that the Asian countries faced. As Paul Volcker, former chairman of the Federal Reserve Board, inquired after learning that the IMF had demanded that the Indonesian government dismantle its clove monopoly, "What [do] spice monopolies have to do with restoring financial stability" (cited in Blustein 2001, 212)? In short, critics argue that practically every aspect of IMF programs at the time was inappropriate. The programs worsened the economic situation of the countries affected, rather than restoring market confidence and cushioning the domestic economic fallout from the financial crisis.

POLICY ANALYSIS AND DEBATE

Capital Controls

Question

Should developing countries use capital controls to reduce capital flows?

Overview

The crises of the 1990s provoked a debate about whether developing countries should use capital controls to limit capital flows and thereby protect themselves from the risk of financial crises. Behind this disagreement lies a broader debate about the inherent stability (or instability) of financial markets. Some people argue that financial markets are inherently unstable, being prone to "manias, panics, and crashes (Kindleberger 2000)." Developing countries are particularly vulnerable to these perverse dynamics because they have weak financial institutions, thin (or illiquid) financial markets, and inadequate financial regulations. Consequently, developing countries should not be encouraged to integrate into the international financial system, but should instead tightly regulate the flow of capital into and out of their economies. In addition, governments should strive to attract foreign direct investment and other forms of long-term investments that will not expose them to the instabilities generated by short-term capital flows.

Others argue that financial markets are not inherently unstable. According to this group, financial crises such as those which struck during the 1990s are caused, not by perverse market behavior, but by bad government policies. Sometimes the bad policies are as simple as allowing too much foreign debt to be accumulated by the government. Sometimes the bad policies involve financial regulations that do little to promote prudent behavior by domestic financial institutions. Because financial crises result from bad policies, preventing crises does not require governments to insulate the national economy from the international financial system. Instead, to prevent crises, governments must simply adopt good policies. Should developing countries use capital controls to limit private capital inflows and outflows?

Policy Options

- Use capital controls to limit the volume of capital that can flow into and out of the national economy through private transactions.
- Liberalize the capital account and allow private individuals to engage in financial transactions with the rest of the world without restriction.

Policy Analysis

- What do developing countries give up by relying on capital controls?
- While capital controls may limit crises, do they also create any potential dangers?

Take a Position

- Which option do you prefer? Justify your choice.
- What criticisms of your position should you anticipate? How would you defend your recommendation against these criticisms?

Resources

Online: Do an online search for "capital controls developing countries". Follow the links to some sites that advocate the use of such controls and to some that criticize controls. Look in particular for Kenneth Rogoff's short article called "Straight Talk:

Continued

Rethinking Capital Controls" and Sebastian Edward's article "The Mirage of Capital Controls."

In Print: See the useful and entertaining exchange between Sebastian Edwards, "A Capital Idea?" *Foreign Affairs* 78 (May–June 1999): 18–22, and Jagdish Bhagwati, "The Capital Myth," *Foreign Affairs* 77 (May–June 1998): 7–12.

Other critics advance a more fundamental critique of the IMF, based on the logic of moral hazard. These critics claim that IMF financial assistance to countries in crisis makes future financial crises more likely. (See, e.g., International Financial Institution Advisory Commission 2000; Calomiris, 1998; Meltzer 1998.) At the core of this critique lies the recognition that IMF financial assistance to crisis countries allows governments to service foreign debt. "The IMF and the principal governments lend money to the Asian governments so that they can pay the interest on their existing banks loans or repay the principal. Extending credit helps the Asian banks avoid default, but the money goes to the foreign banks" (Meltzer 1998). IMF financial assistance, therefore, encourages foreign banks to believe that they can lend to developing countries without having to fear that borrowers in those countries will default. The expectation that the IMF will bail out crisis countries to prevent defaults in turn reduces the incentive of foreign banks to limit their lending to high-risk countries. In fact, the critics contend, the expectation of a bailout may even increase the incentive to lend to high-risk countries. Over time, foreign lending under the shadow of IMF bailouts will lead to more frequent financial crises that grow in scale. The Mexican crisis of 1994, critics point out, required a $40 billion bailout; the Asian crisis of 1997 required a $117 billion bailout. Critics contend that the next crisis is likely to be even larger (Meltzer 1998).

Widespread criticisms of the IMF's role in managing financial crises sparked a reform process christened "strengthening the international financial architecture." (See Eichengreen 1999; Goldstein 2003.) As one component of this reform process, advanced industrialized countries have been examining possible changes in two broad areas of IMF practices. First, discussion has focused on whether to reduce the scope and the detail of IMF conditionality agreements. There is widespread agreement that the IMF has over-extended itself in developing structural reform packages; the typical IMF agreement contains about 50 such reforms (Goldstein 2003.) Policymakers are discussing whether the IMF should "return to the basics" in designing conditionality agreements, focusing on macroeconomic stabilization and limiting structural reforms to clearly related areas. Second, discussions have concentrated on reducing the potential for moral hazard. The size of, and the interest rates attached to, IMF credits have been at the center of these discussions. There appears to be general agreement that the size of IMF loans must be reduced. Smaller loans would make it more difficult for private creditors to expect to be bailed out in the event of a crisis. There also appears to be agreement that the charges attached to IMF loans should be increased. Higher charges would raise the cost of turning to the IMF for assistance, perhaps giving governments greater incentive to manage their financial systems so as to avoid crises. While discussions about strengthening the international financial architecture have been continuing since 1998, they have yet to produce substantial results.

In the meantime, the participants in private capital markets appear to have drawn their own conclusions from the series of crises and made adjustments of their own. The composition of capital flows to the developing world has changed greatly in the years since the Asian crisis. (See Figure 15.2.) Flows of private debt-based capital (bank loans and bonds) have fallen sharply since 1997 and now constitute a small fraction of total flows. Direct investment flows have remained quite robust, however and, as a consequence, now make up the vast majority of flows to developing countries. The changing relative importance of these different types of capital flows reflects lessons drawn from the spate of recent crises by capital importers and lenders. Developing-country borrowers are increasingly wary of the negative risk associated with bank and bond-based capital flows. Consequently, demand for such flows has fallen. For their part, private lenders have become increasingly concerned about the risks they face when lending to these emerging markets and have pulled back. As a result, flows of private capital over the last few years are dominated by direct investment, which carries no obligation of repayment and cannot be transferred at the first sign of trouble. One might note the similarity between the current composition of private capital flows to the developing world and the composition that characterized the early postwar period.

The Heavily Indebted Poor Countries

Crises in the emerging market countries were not the only international financial problem to preoccupy governments during the last 15 years. Considerable attention has also been focused on the equally serious, if quite different, debt problem that

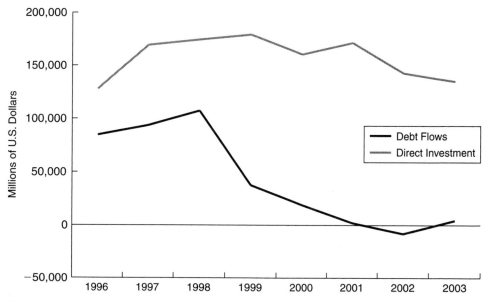

Figure 15.2   Private Capital Flows, 1996–2003.

plagues the world's poorest nations. Together, the world's poorest countries, the majority of which are located in Sub-Saharan Africa, owe about $200 billion to foreign creditors. Most of this debt is owed to official lenders—to the World Bank and the IMF or to governments in the advanced industrialized world. Payments to service this debt in 1999 (before the latest debt-relief initiative had taken effect) amounted to slightly more than $3 billion, a sum equal to 21 percent of government revenue and 15 percent of export earnings. The countries that owe this debt are poor. Roughly half of their combined population of 615 million people live on less than $1 per day, and for at least ten of these countries, per capita income was lower in 1999 than it had been in 1960.

These large debt burdens were accumulated, as large debt burdens had been accumulated in other countries, in response to internal and external dynamics. On the one hand, domestic political pressures encouraged governments to expand their expenditures well beyond their revenues. The expansion of the civil service and the creation of too many unproductive state-owned enterprises, combined with the excessive consumption expenditures of some authoritarian rulers, generated a large appetite for foreign capital. Official creditors sometimes collaborated in this perverse dynamic, providing loans because the borrowers were important political allies rather than because the projects they proposed represented a wise use of foreign funds. International factors also played an important role. The oil shocks of the 1970s, rising interest rates during the early 1980s, and declining terms of trade all generated a greater demand for foreign capital. As a consequence, the foreign debt owed by the 41 heavily indebted poor countries rose from $60 billion in 1980, to $105 billion by 1985, to $190 billion by 1990, and to almost $200 billion in 2000 (IMF 2000).

In absolute terms, Sub-Saharan Africa's total external debt is only a fraction of the debt incurred by Latin American governments during the 1980s or by Asia during the 1990s. Yet, measured as a share of GDP, this debt is almost as large as the debt that propelled Latin America into crisis in the early 1980s. And in many cases African debt-service ratios have been much higher than Latin America's 1980s ratios. Africa's total external debt in 1983 was 38 percent of GDP, compared with 48.1 percent in Latin America, while debt-service ratios for the African group stood at 34.7 percent in 1985 (Lancaster and Williamson 1986, 40–41). Debt-service ratios were even larger in some African countries. One study estimated that in 1985, on the basis of debt service ratios prior to debt rescheduling, the six African countries "most seriously affected" by the crisis had ratios ranging from a low of 47 percent in Zaire to a high of 123.9 percent in Sudan. Even in those six Sub-Saharan African countries judged by this same study to be only "moderately affected" by the crisis, debt-service ratios ranged from a low of 25.6 percent in Zimbabwe to a high of 45 percent in Uganda (Jaycox et al. 1986, 51). Thus, even though Africa's external debt was smaller in absolute terms than Latin America's debt, debt-service ratios for some African countries were higher than even the worst cases in Latin America.

Such heavy debt burdens have depressed economic growth in Sub-Saharan Africa. Facing large debt payments, governments are forced to devote a sizable share of their available domestic resources to debt service. These resources are therefore unavailable to finance domestic investment. The large debt burdens also make it impossible to attract new foreign capital. Private lenders are unwilling to lend to countries that are unable to service their existing debt, so private capital flows are not an option. Official lenders also are increasingly reluctant to offer new loans. As the scale of the debt problem grew, the World Bank and the IMF, as well as many of the bilateral donors, became increasingly focused on restructuring existing debt rather than on providing new loans, and any new loans that were forthcoming were typically offered primarily to facilitate debt service. As a consequence, large debts essentially forced countries to forgo access to fresh foreign capital.

The large debt burden also reduces the incentive that governments have to undertake economic reform. As we saw in the Latin American debt crisis, many of the economic gains from reform accrue to foreign lenders. Governments, as well as powerful interest groups, recognize this dynamic. Consequently, few are willing to accept the economic costs and the social disruption entailed by the fundamental economic reform necessary to climb back onto a sustainable platform. As a result, heavily indebted societies become trapped in poverty, unable to service their debt, unable to attract new foreign capital, and lacking the incentive to implement the painful reforms that could lead to a resumption of growth. Some argue that such debt-induced poverty traps are most likely in societies, like Sub-Saharan Africa, that suffer from "intrinsically low productivity" caused by geographic isolation, small internal markets, adverse ecologies (fragile soils, water stress, malaria), high fertility rates, and a recent history of civil or international war (Sachs 2002).

As the economy stops growing and begins to shrink, the government's ability to provide essential services declines. Health care and education, for example, are costly to provide, and spending on such services typically declines in heavily indebted countries. Governments also increasingly lack the resources required to maintain critical infrastructure, such as the transportation network (roads, rails, and ports). The declining quality of government services and the deteriorating infrastructure push the country even further behind. Declining health and education expenditures cause labor productivity to fall, while the deterioration of critical economic infrastructure renders the country even less attractive to foreign investors. These developments pose an additional burden that must be overcome in order to return to positive economic growth.

Because African debt is owed to official rather than private creditors, the African debt crisis emerged slowly instead of bursting suddenly onto the scene, like the crises in Latin America and Asia. African nations were not subject to the sudden shutoff of lending that happened in Latin America or to the sudden reversal of capital flows that struck East Asia. Instead, the African crisis developed slowly and steadily during the 1980s and continued to grow during the 1990s. As a consequence, the general public was slow to recognize the growing African debt problem. Instead, because Africa's debt never imperiled private lenders, its debt problem was managed by the advanced industrialized countries through low-profile negotiations throughout the 1980s and 1990s. It wasn't until the Jubilee 2000 movement that African debt was thrust into public view.

Governments managed the African debt crisis by using essentially the same negotiation and rescheduling process that was used to manage the Latin American debt crisis. African governments negotiated stabilization and structural adjustment packages with the IMF and World Bank, which then provided additional financial support, and existing debt was rescheduled. Because African governments' creditors were official lenders, however, rescheduling took place in the Paris Club rather than in the London Club. Created in 1956, the **Paris Club** brings the debtor government together with its creditor governments. The IMF and the World Bank, as well as the UNCTAD and the OECD, attend as observers. In the early years of the African crisis, 85–90 percent of a country's debt would be rescheduled under terms that provided a five-year grace period and a further five years for repayment. Paris Club agreements are conditional upon the debtor government's willingness to negotiate stabilization and structural adjustment programs with the IMF and World Bank (Lancaster and Williamson 1986, 42–43). Like the London Club reschedulings, Paris Club agreements were not originally intended to forgive debt. Instead, they were aimed at restructuring the payment schedule to provide the government a bit of breathing room.

By the late 1980s, the official creditors were concluding that the heavily indebted countries would never be able to repay their debts and that the level of debt service was having strongly deleterious consequences on those countries' economic performance. As this recognition took hold, governments began to offer debt reduction packages to the most heavily indebted poor countries. The Paris Club provided the forum for these debt reduction agreements. The first debt forgiveness terms were offered by governments in 1988. Under these terms, bilateral debt could be reduced by as much as one-third. In 1991, bilateral creditors expanded the terms to allow as much as a 50 percent debt reduction. The size of the debt reduction was further increased in 1994, with a maximum of a 67 percent reduction and a minimum of 50 percent. All of these initiatives focused on bilateral debts and excluded debt owed to multilateral organizations (the World Bank, the IMF, and regional development banks). Debt reduction was offered on a case-by-case basis through negotiations between the debtor government and its bilateral creditors in the Paris Club.

The results from these initial debt reduction programs were disappointing. In spite of reducing foreign debt by around $60 billion through this process, debt-service burdens actually increased for the poorest countries (IMF 2000; Easterly 2002, 125–126). Responding to pressure from a coalition of nongovernmental organizations and religious groups, the World Bank and the IMF launched the **Heavily Indebted Poor Countries** (HIPC) debt initiative in September 1996 in an attempt to reduce the weight of their debts. The initiative was expanded in 1999. Its most novel aspect was that, for the first time, debt owed to multilateral lenders would be reduced.

The HIPC initiative has limited country coverage. Only the world's poorest countries are eligible to participate. Moreover, the program is not intended to eliminate all foreign debt in these countries. Instead, the goal is to reduce foreign debt to sustainable levels. Sustainability has been defined as a foreign debt that allows a government to meet its debt-service obligations without the need for additional debt relief or further rescheduling within the Paris Club (Van Trotsenberg and MacArthur 1999). The IMF and the World Bank estimate that the typical country which completes the program will see its debt level reduced by two-thirds and its debt-service ratio cut in half.

Like other IMF and World Bank programs, the HIPC initiative involves a high degree of conditionality. The initiative is structured around a two-stage process. In the first stage, supposed to last no longer than three years, the government must work with domestic groups, the IMF, and the World Bank to develop a Poverty Reduction Strategy Paper (PRSP). The PRSP describes the macroeconomic, structural, and social policies the government will adopt in order to foster growth and reduce poverty. It also details how the government will use the resources freed up by debt service. During this stage, the government must establish a track record of implementing the strategy presented in the PRSP. At the end of the stage, the country reaches a "decision point" at which time the IMF and the World Bank conduct a debt-sustainability analysis to determine the country's eligibility for debt forgiveness. If the country's foreign debt is above 150 percent of its export earnings, the country is eligible, and the World Bank, the IMF, and bilateral creditors forgive enough of the country's debt to return it to a sustainable position. Once a country passes the decision point, it begins to receive debt relief in the form of lower debt-service payments.

The country then passes to the program's second stage, which is intended to enable the government to further demonstrate the strength of its commitment to the strategy established by its PRSP. "[T]he second period has no pre-determined length. It lasts until a government has satisfactorily implemented the key structural policy reforms agreed at the decision point, established macroeconomic stability, and adopted and implemented a poverty reduction strategy." Once the IMF and the World Bank conclude that the government has satisfactorily implemented its program, the country reaches the "completion point" and exits the HIPC initiative. Upon the country's reaching the completion point, the full amount of debt relief committed at the decision point is granted.

As of late 2004, fifteen countries had reached the completion point and been granted a total of $29 billion of debt forgiveness. (See Table 15.3.) Another 12 countries had progressed beyond the decision point and are anticipated to receive $27 billion of debt relief. According to the World Bank, total debt for the HIPC-eligible countries has fallen from $80 billion to $28 billion, while debt service has fallen from $4.9 billion to $2.6 billion. As a result, the World Bank argues, the foreign debt burden of the HIPC countries are now comparable to foreign debt burdens in other developing countries (World Bank 2004). Debt-to export ratios in both groups now stand at about 142 percent; debt-to-GDP ratios in both groups are around 35 percent. The World Bank claims that as debt burdens have fallen, government expenditures on poverty reduction programs have increased. In 1999, such expenditures accounted for only 5.5 percent of national income; by the end of 2003 they had risen to 7.3 percent. These expenditures are still lower than they are in other developing countries, but they appear to be moving in the right direction.

Many observers, including a large NGO-led movement, have argued that the HIPC initiative does not go far enough. (See, e.g., Roodman 2001; Birdsall and Williamson 2002.) Since the fall of 2004, a growing number of governments in the advanced industrialized countries have begun to reach the same conclusion. In September 2004, news of an American plan to forgive 100 percent of the debt owed by the HIPCs leaked out (Blustein 2004c). This proposal was subsequently discussed by the Group of Eight at the annual IMF–World Bank meetings in October. After the meetings, Gordon Brown, Great Britain's finance minister, claimed, "[T]here's a growing consensus that the next step is [to give poor countries] up to 100 percent debt relief" (Blustein 2004a). He further suggested that the only remaining issues were to work out of the details of how to achieve this aim.

Yet, there is considerable disagreement about the details. One important disagreement concerns how to finance 100 percent forgiveness. Almost all bilateral debt has already been forgiven. Consequently, almost all of the remaining debt is owed to multilateral lenders. Someone has to accept the costs arising from forgiving this debt. Either the multilateral lenders will have to accept these costs, or the advanced industrialized countries will have to advance funds to repay the multilaterals. The U.S. pro-

Table 15.3
Countries in the HIPC Initiative, January 2005

Countries Having Reached the Completion Point

Benin	Mali
Bolivia	Mauritania
Burkina Faso	Mozambique
Ethiopia	Nicaragua
Ghana	Niger
Guyana	Senegal
Madagascar	Tanzania
	Uganda

Countries at the Decision Point

Cameroon	Honduras
Chad	Malawi
Democratic Republic of Congo	Rwanda
The Gambia	São Tomé and Príncipe
Guinea	Sierra Leone
Guinea-Bissau	Zambia

Countries Not Yet at the Decision Point

Burundi	Liberia
Central African Republic	Myanmar
Comoros	Somalia
Republic of Congo	Sudan
Côte D'Ivoire	Togo
Lao PDR	

Source: World Bank 2004.

posal would have the multilateral institutions bear the costs. The World Bank and the IMF argue that they do not have the financial resources to wipe this debt off their books. Moreover, if they did use their resources to cancel the debt, a lesser amount of funds would be available for new loans to the middle-income countries and for future loans to the low-income countries. Asking the multilateral organizations to bear the costs of 100 percent forgiveness, therefore, would come at the expense of other things. Gordon Brown has proposed that the advanced industrialized countries put forward the funds required to repay debt owed to multilateral lenders. Other advanced industrialized countries have not been particularly enthusiastic about this approach.

Conclusion

At the beginning of the twenty-first century, developing countries are facing new challenges in managing their relationship with the international financial system. On the one hand, international financial integration over the last 20 years has greatly expanded developing countries' opportunities for attracting foreign capital. Yet, those countries seem incapable of escaping from a repeating cycle of overborrowing, crisis, and adjustment that lies at the center of their difficulties. As we have seen, this cycle typically starts with changes in international capital markets. Petrodollars increased the supply of foreign capital to many developing countries during the 1970s, and the dynamics of international financial integration increased the supply of foreign capital to Asian countries during the 1990s. Developing countries have exploited the opportunities presented by changes in international financial markets with great enthusiasm. By reducing the constraints imposed by limited savings and limited foreign exchange, foreign capital allows developing countries to invest more than they could if they were forced to rely solely upon domestic resources. The problem, however, is that developing countries eventually accumulate large foreign debt burdens that they cannot service and are pushed to the brink of default. Impending default causes foreign lenders to refuse additional loans to developing countries and to recall the loans they had made previously. Now shut out of international capital markets, developing countries experience severe economic crises and implement stabilization and structural adjustment packages under the supervision of the IMF and the World Bank. This cycle has repeated twice in the last 25 years, once in Latin America during the 1970s and 1980s and once in Asia during the 1990s. While the specific details of each cycle were distinctive, both cases were characterized by the same pattern of overborrowing, crisis, and adjustment.

These cycles are driven by the interaction between developments in the international system and those within developing countries. The cycle is driven in part by interests and institutions in the international system over which developing-country governments have little control. The volume and composition of capital flows from the advanced industrialized countries and the developing world have been shaped in large part by changes in international financial markets. The buildup of debt in Latin America during the 1970s was made possible by the growth of the Euromarkets and the large deposits in these markets made by OPEC members. The buildup of large foreign liabilities by many Asian countries resulted in part from the more general increase in international financial integration during the late 1980s. The ability to service foreign debt is also influenced by international developments. In the Latin American debt crisis, rising American interest rates and falling economic growth in the advanced industrialized world made it more difficult for Latin American governments to service their foreign debt. In the Asian crisis, the dollar's appreciation against the yen made it more difficult for Asian borrowers to service their debt. Finally, the advanced industrialized countries, the IMF, and the World Bank establish the conditions under which developing countries that are experiencing crises can regain access to foreign capital.

Interests and institutions within developing countries have also played an important role. Domestic politics influences how much foreign debt is accumulated and the uses to which it is put. In the 1970s, Latin American governments made poor decisions about how to use the foreign debt they were accumulating, thereby worsening their situation when the international environment soured. In Asia, governments failed to regulate the terms under which domestic banks intermediated between foreign and domestic financial markets, thereby weakening domestic financial systems and sparking an erosion of investor confidence in Asia. A country's ability to return to international capital markets following a crisis is contingent upon policy reform. Domestic politics often prevents governments from speedily implementing such reforms. Thus, while it might be tempting to place the blame for the cycle solely on the international financial system or solely on developing-country governments, a more reasonable approach is to recognize that these cycles are driven by the interaction between international and domestic developments.

Key Terms

Exchange-rate Risk

Heavily Indebted Poor Countries Initiative

Hot Money

Insolvent

Moral Hazard

Nonperforming Loans

Paris Club

Web Links

Perhaps the most useful site providing information on the Asian crisis, as well as on most contemporary issues in the international financial system, is the one maintained by Nouriel Roubini at the Stern School of Business at New York University. It can be found at *http://www.stern.nyu.edu/globalmacro/*.

The World Bank Website on the Heavily Indebted Poor Countries (HIPC) debt initiative can be found at *http://www.worldbank.org/hipc/*.

The IMF website on the HIPC initiative is at *http://www.imf.org/external/np/exr/facts/htpc.htm*.

Jubilee debt campaign websites can be found at *http://www.jubileeusa.org/jubilee.cgi* and *http://www.jubileedebtcampaign.org.uk*.

Suggestions for Further Reading

On the Asian financial crisis, see Stephan Haggard, *The Political Economy of the Asian Financial Crisis* (Washington, DC: Institute for International Economics, 2000); Paul Blustein, *The Chastening: Inside the Crisis That Rocked the Global Financial System and Humbled the IMF* (New York: Public Affairs, 2001); and Joseph E. Stiglitz, *Globalization and Its Discontents* (New York: W.W. Norton & Company, 2002).

An excellent examination of the politics of economic reform in sub-Saharan Africa is Nicolas Van de Walle, *African Economies and the Politics of Permanent Crisis, 1979–1999* (Cambridge: Cambridge University Press, 2001).

For the HIPC initiative, see Nancy Birdsall and John Williamson, *Delivering on Debt Relief: From IMF Gold to New Aid Architecture* (Washington, DC: Center for Global Development and Institute for International Economics, 2002), and David M. Roodman, *Still Waiting for the Jubilee: Pragmatic Solutions for the Third World Debt Crisis*, Worldwatch Paper 155 (Washington, DC: Worldwatch Institute, 2001).

CHAPTER 16

Globalization: Consequences and Controversies

The last 15 years have seen the emergence of a political backlash against globalization. This opposition has been most visible in a series of large protests, mostly peaceful, but sometimes violent, staged at annual meetings of the World Trade Organization, the Group of Eight, the International Monetary Fund and World Bank, and the World Economic Forum. Apart from the drama of public protest, the antiglobalization movement has articulated a number of criticisms of the global economy. The critique is multifaceted, ranging from the claim that globalization is widening income inequality to the assertion that it is contributing to the degradation of the natural environment. What binds together the many nongovernmental organizations and individuals that constitute the antiglobalization movement is opposition to a global economy that they believe ranks corporate and commercial interests over other concerns. As one scholar has written, "there is . . . an overarching umbrella uniting the backlash: opposition to corporate control of the global economy" (Broad 2002, 3). What binds the many reforms that the movement has proposed is the desire to shift this perceived balance so that other concerns are placed on an equal footing with corporate interests.

Defenders of globalization dispute all of these assertions and question the logic of the reforms the antiglobalization movement proposes. On the one hand, the defenders of globalization dispute most of the criticisms that are advanced. Globalization is the *solution* to the problems of income inequality and poverty, not their cause. And while working conditions in many developing countries are not up to Western standards, in most instances these factories offer the best opportunities that a worker in the developing world has ever had. Finally, the defenders of globalization recognize that economic activity has an impact on the natural environment, but claim that this impact can be positive as well as negative. On the other hand, the defenders question the rationale for the reforms proposed by the antiglobalization movement. Because they don't agree with the antiglobalization movement's criticisms, they see little need for reform. And even when they do see problems, they doubt that restricting trade is the most effective solution. Instead, they see such reforms as an effort to reconstruct protectionist practices and inject them into the global economy, a tactic that will reverse the gains which have been achieved.

Is there a right answer to this debate? At present, I don't think there is. What we do have, however, is an accumulating body of evidence which suggests that during the last 20 years the world has seen progress on every dimension that is at the center of the debate. For example, the number of people living in poverty has fallen, and global income inequality has ceased rising and has begun to fall; over time these factors should limit any negative impact that globalization has on the environment. At the same time, however, progress is slow: millions of people remain in poverty, and even those who have climbed out face a daily struggle. What is less clear, and where I think the debate is increasingly headed, is whether changes in the rules governing the global economy will hasten progress or whether instead they will merely slow what is already too slow improvement.

We examine this debate in this final chapter. We begin by defining globalization, discussing when it emerged, examining how it is reshaping national economies, and considering how far it has progressed. We then turn our attention to the controversies surrounding its consequences. We look first at the impact of globalization on the distribution of global income and global poverty. We then turn our attention to the "sweatshop problem." Our attention then shifts to the impact of globalization on the environment. Throughout, I attempt to present the most recent scholarly consensus on each issue and at the same time suggest that how we frame the issue plays an important role in shaping the conclusion we draw about the severity of the problem and the need for reform. We conclude by attempting to draw some broader conclusions from this discussion and consider whether and, if so, what kind of reforms to the global economy are required.

The Globalizing World Economy

As we have seen, governments have progressively eliminated policy barriers to trade during the last 50 years. The elimination of these barriers has been accompanied by a dramatic decrease in the cost of transportation and telecommunications (World Bank 1995). The cost of shipping goods by sea and by air has been cut in half since 1950. The cost of long-distance phone calls has fallen even more sharply: whereas it cost about $250 to make a three-minute call from New York to London in 1930, such a call now costs less than a dollar. Falling transport and telecommunications costs facilitate the creation of a global division of labor by making it cheaper to import and export intermediate inputs and to organize and manage production on a global scale. As political and technological barriers to international exchange have fallen, global economic activity has increased rapidly.

World trade has grown at historically unprecedented rates. Between 1950 and 2002, world trade grew at an average rate of 6 percent per year (Figure 16.1). What is perhaps more impressive than the simple growth of world trade, however, is the fact that international trade has consistently grown more rapidly than total world economic

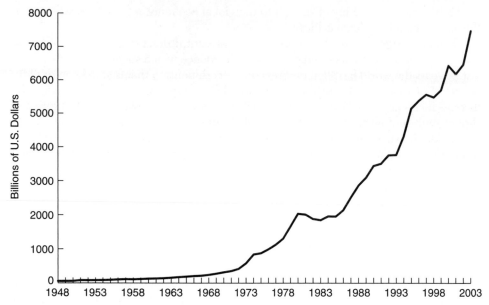

Figure 16.1   World Trade, 1948–2003.
Source: World Trade Organization.

production. Figure 16.2 charts the annual rate of growth of world exports and the annual rate of world economic growth. Looking at the two trends together indicates that in almost every year since 1950 world trade has grown at a faster rate than world economic output. Thus, year after year, a larger share of the world's economic output enters into international trade: each year, more of the world's total economic production is produced in one country and consumed in another. We saw that the number of MNCs operating in the global economy also increased sharply since 1980, and we saw in our discussion of the international financial system how the last 20 years have also brought dramatic growth of international financial flows.

The rapid growth of global economic exchange during the last 20 years has restructured the global economy. Trade theory tells us that countries which are open to international trade will specialize in goods that make intensive use of their abundant factors of production. In a fully open international economy, therefore, a **global division of labor** should emerge in which each country produces goods in which it has a comparative advantage and sheds industries in which it has a comparative disadvantage. Such a division of labor is emerging in the global economy. Although this division is far from complete, it is possible to identify four emerging tiers:

- The advanced industrialized countries hold a comparative advantage in capital and in human-capital-intensive goods. Producers in the advanced industrialized countries lead the world in the production of knowledge-intensive products, such as pharmaceuticals, computers and software, telecommunications equipment, commercial aircraft, and other research-intensive and high-technology products.

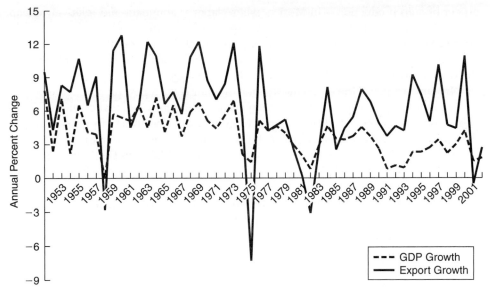

Figure 16.2   Growth of World Output and Trade.
Source: World Trade Organization.

- The Asian NICs—especially South Korea, Taiwan, Hong Kong, and Singapore—hold a comparative advantage in mature and relatively standardized capital-intensive goods, such as semiconductors and other computer components, automobiles, and steel. These countries have not yet become an important source of product or process innovation.
- The second wave of NICs, including Indonesia, Malaysia, Thailand, Mexico, and Argentina, hold a comparative advantage in labor-intensive goods, such as apparel, footwear, and the assembly of finished goods from components. These countries have not yet emerged as important international producers of capital-intensive goods, but are likely to make that transition relatively soon.
- Other developing countries hold comparative advantages in land-intensive primary commodities, such as fuel, minerals, and agricultural products.

This global division of labor emerges as firms begin, end, or relocate production in response to pressures exerted by international competition. An entrepreneur in Pakistan, for example, might recognize the opportunity to make a profit in the labor-abundant apparel industry and start a business to realize that profit. Conversely, an apparel producer in North Carolina might recognize that he cannot compete against apparel produced in developing countries like Pakistan, whereupon he stops producing clothes in North Carolina. These independent decisions cause apparel production to shift out of the United States and into Pakistan.

The relocation of production is also sometimes a consequence of MNCs' production decisions. Ford Motor Company, for example, may recognize that it needs to reduce its production costs in order to compete against Japanese producers in the American market. To do so, Ford may build an auto assembly plant—a labor-intensive aspect of auto production—in Mexico, where labor is abundant and relatively cheap. Ford's decision may therefore cause some aspects of auto production to shift out of the United States and into Mexico. The emerging global division of labor is the result of hundreds of thousands of such decisions taken by individuals and firms in response to the competitive challenges of the international economy.

In some respects, the emerging division of labor is not a new phenomenon. A division of labor also characterized the nineteenth century international economy. European countries specialized in manufactured goods, and what we now call the developing world specialized in raw materials. However, the contemporary division of labor differs from the late nineteenth century division of labor in two important ways. First, the contemporary division is more diverse than that of the nineteenth century. To the basic nineteenth century division between manufacturing and raw materials, the contemporary system adds divisions within manufacturing activity. Today we see some countries specializing in human-capital-intensive manufacturing, other countries specializing in capital-intensive manufacturing, and still others specializing in labor-intensive manufacturing.

Second, today's division is more international than that of the nineteenth century. During the nineteenth century, production "was primarily organized within national economies . . . production, plant, and firm were essentially national phenomena" (Hobsbawm 1989, 313). Today, production is increasingly an international phenomenon; the production of individual goods is being broken down and allocated to different regions of the globe. The personal computer is one example. The typical PC contains a microprocessor designed in the United States by Intel, Motorola, or Advanced Micro Devices (AMD). It contains a hard drive and memory chips that were likely produced in Taiwan or South Korea. The multiple components were probably assembled into a working PC in yet another location, perhaps Malaysia or Mexico. Thus, a personal computer and many of the other products that we use daily are no longer produced in a national economy. Instead, the production of many individual goods is organized globally.

National economies have thus become increasingly internationalized, and these international activities have in turn become increasingly woven into a deeply integrated web of trade and production relations. This is globalization. More concretely, **globalization** can be defined as an outcome and a process. As an outcome, globalization is a world economy in which government policies pose few barriers to, and technology enables, cross-border economic transactions. As a process, globalization consists of the flows of goods, services, people, capital, and technology that arise within this single world economy and the transformations of national economies that these flows produce.

How far has globalization progressed? There is disagreement among those who study the world economy. Some argue that globalization has fundamentally transformed the world economy as a whole and national economies individually. Robert Reich argues that "[w]e are living through a transformation that will rearrange the politics and economics of the coming century. There will be no national products or technologies, no national corporations, no national industries. There will no longer be national economies, at least as we have come to understand that concept" (1992, 3).

Others suggest that this transformation has already occurred. Business consultant and author Peter Drucker argues that "the talk today is of the 'changing world economy'. . . . The world economy is not 'changing'; it has already changed—in its foundations and in its structure—and in all probability the change is irreversible" (1986, 768).

Others are more skeptical. Robert Gilpin claims that "globalization is much more limited than many realize" (2000, 363). Skeptics point to the nineteenth-century global economy to buttress their counterarguments. In this first global economy, Gilpin argues, countries were more open to trade than they are today, and "although trade has grown enormously during the past half century, trade still accounts for a relatively small portion of most economies . . . [and] is still confined to a limited number of economic sectors. The principal competitors for most firms (with important exceptions in such areas as motor vehicles and electronics) are other national firms" (Gilpin 2000, 365). Even where globalization has progressed the furthest, in the "Triad" composed of Pacific Asia, the United States, and the European Union, national barriers continue to impose substantial obstacles to the international flow of goods and services (Gilpin 2000, 295).

It may be useful to look for middle ground in this debate. Economic processes are fundamentally changing the world economy. At the same time, it is important to recognize that globalization is limited in geographic scope, involving primarily the countries of the Triad. Globalization is limited in industrial scope as well, with some industries, such as electronics, being much more globalized than other industries, such as steel. As Peter Dicken observes, "although there are globalizing forces at work we do not have a fully globalized world economy. Globalization forces can be at work without this resulting in the all-encompassing end-state—the globalized economy—in which all unevenness and difference are ironed out, market forces are rampant and uncontrollable, and the nation–state merely passive and supine" (1998, 5). In short, while it is premature to proclaim a fully globalized world economy, and while nothing that is created by human activity is ever irreversible, it is also misleading to claim that nothing has changed.

This structural transformation of the world economy, together with the dynamics that characterize its operation, has generated a political debate about the economic, social, and political consequences of globalization. Does the global economy provide opportunities and rising incomes for the world's poor, or are the benefits captured solely by MNCs? Is globalization destroying the environment, and do global trade rules limit governments' capacity to use national regulations to prevent this damage? Does a global economy require global governance, and if so, what should the associated rules look like? More broadly, is globalization a good thing that should be supported, or is it something that should be resisted and reformed?

Each dimension of this debate raises complex issues that do not have simple answers. This inherent complexity grows when we attempt to look at all of the various strands of the debate together. How should we balance environmental damage against higher standards of living, for example? Yet, evidence and theory shed light on the central issues of the debate and help us clarify the costs and benefits in a way that may suggest certain conclusions and will at least help us understand where problems lie and why disagreement about the consequences of globalization are likely to persist.

Globalization and Income: Rising Poverty, Widening Inequality?

We start with a big—perhaps the biggest—question: how has globalization affected standards of living throughout the world? Is the recent period of intensified globalization associated with rising incomes and falling poverty, or has it instead been associated with widening global income inequality and rising poverty? Critics of globalization typically argue that globalization has brought rising inequality and poverty. For example, as Jay Mazur (president emeritus of the Union of Needletrades, Industrial and Textile Employees), wrote in *Foreign Affairs*, "globalization has dramatically increased inequality between and within nations" (Mazur 2000). Mazur's perspective is hardly unique; in fact, his assertion provides the foundation upon which most opposition to globalization is based. Is it an accurate characterization of the world over the last 20 years?

For the world as a whole, it is clear that globalization has been associated with rising incomes. The world economy grew by about 3.5 percent per year between 1960 and 2000, compared with only 1 percent per year in the mid-nineteenth century. As a consequence, total world income has risen much more rapidly during the last 40 years than it did during the nineteenth and the first half of the twentieth centuries. Faster growth has in turn brought large gains in per capita incomes, which rose from $667 in 1820 to $5,709 in constant 1990 dollars in 1998 (Maddison 2001, 264). Moreover, focusing only on the growth of income understates the gain, for it ignores the huge improvements in the quality of the goods we consume today. For instance, contrast long- distance travel today with long-distance travel in the mid-nineteenth century. Today's trip to Europe is more comfortable, is less costly, and takes much less time. Globalization, therefore, has been associated with an unprecedented increase in world income.

Of course, this much higher global income is not evenly distributed across individuals. Some societies enjoy vastly higher incomes than others, and some individuals within each society enjoy vastly higher incomes than others. So, while globalization has raised global income, it may also have caused global income to be so unequally distributed that only a very small fraction of the world's more than 6 billion people benefit from it. On one measure, globalization has been associated with precisely this effect. If we track the ratio of average income in the world's richest country to average income in the world's poorest country over the last 200 years, we see a dramatic widening of the gap between the richest and the poorest. (See Figure 16.3.) This state of affairs seems to support the claim that the benefits of globalization are unevenly distributed.

Yet, there are other ways of measuring the global distribution of income. In fact, a growing body of recent scholarship suggests that calculating the gap between richest and poorest is not an accurate way to measure the global distribution of income. (See, e.g., Firebaugh 2003; Dollar 2004; Bhalla 2002; Bourguignon and Morrisson 2002; Chen and Ravaillon 2001.) Ideally, we should gather data on incomes for every individual in the world. These data would allow us to calculate the distribution of income across the globe's 6 billion people. A growing body of research has begun to measure the distribution of global income with this approach. Because it is impossible to get

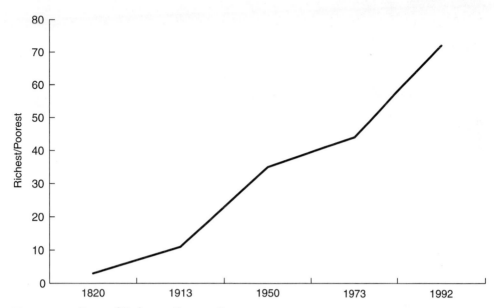

Figure 16.3 Ratio of Richest to Poorest Countries.
Source: United Nations, *Human Development Report* (New York: United Nations, 2004).

income data for every person in the world, researchers rely on surveys conducted on representative samples in each country. Enough such surveys have been conducted over a long-enough period of time to enable scholars to begin to produce a pretty clear picture of trends in global income inequality over time.

Researchers have pieced together data on global income inequality for the last 200 years. Figure 16.4 illustrates the trend they have uncovered by plotting the most common measure of income inequality—the Gini coefficient—for the period spanning 1820 to 1998. The **Gini coefficient** measures the concentration of global income. It ranges from a score of 0 to 1. A coefficient of 0 implies complete equality of income: every person has the same income. A coefficient of 1 implies complete inequality of income: one person has all income and everyone else has no income. Thus, the closer we get to 1, the more unequally distributed is global income. Tracing Gini coefficients across the last 200 hundred years reveals two clear trends. First, global income inequality increased steadily between 1820 and 1970. Second, something changed rather dramatically during the 1970s. This change caused the long term trend of growing inequality to stop and then begin to reverse itself. As a consequence, during the last 30 years global income inequality has begun to decrease. Global income remains very unequally distributed; in fact, global inequality is much greater than domestic income inequality in even the most unequal countries. Yet, the trend over the last 30 years is encouraging. Thus, intensified globalization during the last 20 years has *not* been associated with *widening* inequality, but has instead brought a moderate reduction in global income inequality.

This conclusion probably surprises you greatly. It becomes less surprising, I think, when you consider which countries have grown most rapidly during the last 25 years.

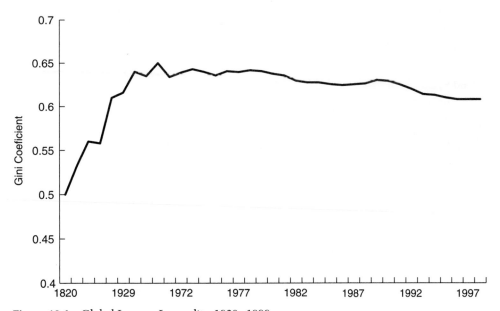

Figure 16.4   Global Income Inequality, 1820–1998.
Source: 1820–1970 from Bourguignon and Morrisson 2002; 1971–1998 from Sala-I-Martin 2002.

As Figure 16.5 illustrates, between 1960 and 1980 the world's richest societies grew faster than the poorest. Since 1980, however, the world's poorest societies have grown faster than the richest—indeed, more than twice as fast. China has been the fastest-growing economy in the world since the late 1970s, and India also has enjoyed rapid growth over the last 15 years. Thus, incomes in China and India have been catching up to incomes in the advanced industrialized world. China and India are home to one-third of the world's total population and account for a large percentage of the world's poorest individuals. Thus, as incomes in China and India converge toward incomes in the advanced industrialized world, global income inequality falls. Accordingly, some of the biggest beneficiaries of globalization over the last 20 years have been the world's poorest individuals.

As a consequence, the number of people living in poverty has fallen during the last 20 years. Recent research suggests that the absolute number of people living in poverty throughout the world fell by about 375 million between 1980 and 2000 (Bourguignon and Morrisson 2001; Chen and Ravallion 2002; World Bank 2002; Dollar 2004). As World Bank economist David Dollar (2004, 18) notes, this reduction in the number of people living in poverty is unprecedented. On some previous occasions, the *percentage* of the world's population living in poverty has fallen, but because population was growing so fast, the *absolute number* of people living in poverty rose. During the last 20 years, however, the absolute number of people living in poverty fell even while world population rose by 1.6 billion. In some countries, the reduction in poverty rates was substantial. The poverty rate in Vietnam was cut in half between 1988 and 1998, from 75 percent of the population to 37 percent (World Bank 2002, 50). India shows the same trend, with the poverty rate falling from 36 percent in 1993

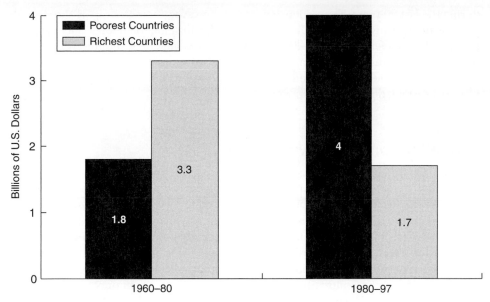

Figure 16.5 Growth Rates of Poorest and Richest Countries (weighted by population). *Source:* Dollar 2004, 15.

to 26–28 percent by 2000 (Deaton 2002). Thus, while far too many people remain deeply impoverished, their number has fallen, not risen, during the last 20 years.

Two points remain to be made. First, poverty has fallen the most in countries that have grown fastest during the last 20 years. It is quite clear, therefore, that "growth is good for the poor" (Dollar and Kraay 2001, 2004). In fact, on average, the incomes of the poorest segment of society rise as rapidly as average incomes in society as a whole. Thus, sustained 4 percent annual growth of average incomes will generate sustained 4 percent growth of the incomes of the poorest, demonstrating that reducing poverty depends importantly (though not solely) on raising growth rates. Second, and a bit more controversially, developing countries that have participated in the global economy have achieved more rapid growth than countries that have sheltered themselves from that economy. While the causal relationship between participation and growth is debated, there are no instances wherein countries that isolated themselves from the global economy have outperformed countries that integrated into the global economy. Hence, there is some evidence to suggest that the recent improvements in global income inequality and global poverty are a result of (i.e., caused by) globalization.

We see, then, that, rather than globalization giving rise to widening inequalities and increasing poverty, current research suggests the opposite conclusion: globalization has raised growth rates in the world's poorest societies, faster growth has reduced poverty, and the reduction in poverty has decreased global inequality. One need not accept the strongly optimistic version of this conclusion. One might instead conclude that emerging evidence indicates that global income remains very unequally distributed, but the trend of greater inequality has stabilized and poverty has begun to fall during the last 20 years. The evidence does not, however, seem to support the strongly pessimistic conclusion about the impact of globalization on global incomes and poverty. The evidence provides little support for the view that the intensification of globalization during the 1980s and 1990s or the widespread economic reforms that developing societies implemented during that period widened income inequality and caused a sustained rise in global poverty.

Globalization and "Sweatshops"

As millions of people pour into factories located in China, India, Bangladesh, and other developing societies to produce manufactured goods for consumers in the advanced industrialized countries, controversy has arisen around the conditions within which that work takes place. A large and increasingly powerful NGO-led movement dedicated to ending "sweatshops" in the developing world argues that these working conditions represent cold exploitation of developing-world workers by global capital. The group advocates enforceable global labor standards to improve conditions in developing countries' factories. After all, its members say, we have global rules to protect capital and intellectual property; why shouldn't we also have global rules to protect workers? Defenders of globalization dispute the basic premise and question the need for global labor standards.

Are factories in the developing world sweatshops, and will global labor standards improve conditions in these facilities? While the term "sweatshop" has no single definition, most definitions are a variation of the one advanced by Sweatshop Watch: "extreme exploitation, including the absence of a living wage or benefits, poor working conditions and arbitrary discipline" (Sweatshop Watch 2005). The claim that factories in the developing world are sweatshops seems simple and compelling. The wage discrepancy between developing countries and advanced industrialized world is very large. Table 16.1 illustrates this wage gap for a few industries. In all manufacturing industries, a typical worker employed by an MNC affiliate in an advanced industrialized country earns almost ten times as much as a typical worker employed by an MNC affiliate in a low-income country. The disparity is also apparent within specific manu-

Table 16.1
Annual Compensation by MNC Affiliates (Thousands of U.S. Dollars)

	High-Income Countries	Middle-Income Countries	Low-Income Countries
Manufacturing	45.0	14.1	4.9
Petroleum	72.8	30.7	25.4
Food	45.6	13.8	5.9
Primary and Fabricated Metals	38.6	18.0	13.8
Electronic and Electric Equipment	32.0	8.8	3.6

Source: Graham 2000, 92.

facturing industries. In the food-processing industry, for example, a worker employed by an MNC in the United States or Europe will earn just over $45,000 per year, while a worker employed by an MNC affiliate in a low-income country will earn slightly less than $6,000 per year.

The case seems even more compelling when one reads the litany of abuses that observers have cataloged. Researchers have documented numerous examples of four objectionable workplace practices during the last 15 years (Graham 2000, 99–104). First, many firms require their workers to work excessively long hours. In one Indonesian factory that produces shoes for Nike, for instance, employees reported working 11 hours per day, seven days a week (Connor 2002, 20). Often, such overtime is not compensated at a higher rate of pay. Second, workers are frequently forced to work in abusive environments that include exposure to toxic chemicals and other health and safety hazards, physical punishment for violations of workplace rules, and sexual harassment. Workers in a Chinese toy factory, for example, reported consistent chemical odors and paint dust in the air, which they suggested caused persistent headaches, dizziness, stomachaches, and nausea (National Labor Committee 2002, 17). Third, firms sometimes engage in bonded labor schemes under which a person "pledges his or her labor for a specified period of time in return for a loan" (Graham 2000, 103). Finally, many developing-country firms employ children. According to the International Labor Organization, more than 250 million children under the age of 14 are currently working.

Defenders of globalization argue that the comparison between wages paid to workers in the advanced industrialized world and wages paid in the developing world is misleading. On the one hand, workers in the advanced industrialized countries are more productive, on average, than workers in the developing world. Consequently, they should be paid more. On the other hand, it makes little sense to compare the wage earned by a worker in Vietnam with the wage earned by a worker in the United States. The Vietnamese worker has no opportunity to get the job in America. This comparison, therefore, doesn't accurately reflect the relative merits of the opportunities that workers in the developing world have. The appropriate comparison, defenders argue, is between the wages a Vietnamese worker is paid in a local factory that exports to the global economy with the income that same worker could earn from the other economic opportunities available to him or her.

One way to make this comparison is by contrasting the wages MNC affiliates pay workers in developing countries with the wages paid to these same workers by locally owned firms. Such a comparison is presented in Table 16.2. The data focus only on manufacturing industries, for, as we have seen, the wage gap is greatest there. If we divide the average wage paid by MNC affiliates by the average wage paid by local manufacturing firms, we obtain a ratio. When this ratio is greater than 1, MNC affiliates pay more than local firms; when it is less than 1, MNC affiliates pay less than local firms. The bottom row of the table clearly indicates that workers are paid more by MNC affiliates than they are by locally owned firms. Moreover, the premium rises as we move from high-income to low-income countries. A worker in a low-income country makes twice as much working for a foreign firm as he or she does working in a locally owned firm. Thus, while wages paid in export-oriented jobs in the developing world are far below wages paid in the West, these jobs pay more than other opportunities available to workers in developing countries.

Table 16.2
Compensation by MNCs and Local Firms

	High-Income Countries	Middle-Income Countries	Low-Income Countries
Average Compensation Paid by MNC Affiliate	32.4	9.5	3.4
Average Compensation Paid by Local Manufacturing Firm	22.6	5.4	1.7
Ratio	1.4	1.8	2.0

Source: Graham 2000, 94.

This conclusion is confirmed by a growing volume of survey and field research. The International Labor Organization (ILO) surveyed workers in developing countries and found that wages paid to workers in plants based in export-processing zones are higher than the wages available in the villages from which workers are typically recruited (ILO 1998). Again, jobs in export industries pay better than other alternatives. The ILO survey is in turn confirmed by field research conducted by a large number of scholars in numerous countries. (See Table 16.3.) The general point is quite clear: given the alternatives developing country workers have to choose from, a job in a factory engaged in production for export is typically the highest-paying option.

Finally, the point is brought home quite starkly by Nicolas Kristof, who relates the story of Nhep Chanda, "a 17-year-old girl who is one of hundreds of Cambodians who toil all day, every day, picking through the dump for plastic bags, metal cans and bits of food" (Kristof 2004, 19). She makes 75 cents a day. She's not scavenging through the dump because it's fun; she's doing it because it's her best available option. As Kristof notes, "For her, the idea of being exploited in a garment factory—working only six days a week, inside instead of in the broiling sun, for up to $2 a day—is a dream. 'I'd like to work in a factory, but I don't have any ID card, and you need one to show that you're old enough,' she said wistfully" (Kristof 2004, 19).

And what is true for wages is also true for the long hours that are typical of many developing-country factories. While NGOs place considerable emphasis on the long hours that are typical of factory work, in many instances these long hours constitute a shorter day than people are accustomed to working. Linda Lim (a professor at the University of Michigan) relates a conversation she had with a worker while in Vietnam studying conditions in Nike factories. This worker told her, "I am used to working 16 hours a day in our rice paddy, so 14 hours in the factory is not hard for me. It's just boring. But I don't mind. I always ask for overtime" (Lim 2000, 6). More broadly, Lim argues, workers often seek long hours: "If you ask workers their number one desire, it will almost invariably be for more overtime. . . . To put it simply, these workers are usually in the factories for a finite number of years and their number one goal is to maximize income during that time. And a higher wage, in my opinion, would do little to change that desire and motivation" (Lim 2000, 5–6).

Thus, defenders of globalization argue that what are unreasonable and intolerable working conditions from the vantage point of wealthy Americans are, from the vantage

Table 16.3
Pay in Export Jobs versus Pay from Other Opportunities

- In Vietnam, workers in foreign-owned and subcontracting apparel and footwear factories rank in the top 20 percent of the population by household expenditure (Glewwe 2000).
- In Vietnam, Nike subcontractor factories paid annual wages of $670 compared with an average minimum wage of $134 (Lim 2000).
- In Indonesia, Nike subcontractor factories paid annual wages of $720 compared with an average annual minimum of $241 (Lim 2000).
- In Bangladesh, legal minimum wages in export-processing zones are 40 percent higher than the national minimum for unskilled workers, 15 percent higher than for semiskilled workers working outside the export-processing zone, and 50 percent higher than for skilled workers working outside the zone (Panos 1999).
- In Bangladesh, garment workers earn 25 percent more than the country's average per capita income (Bhattacharya 1998).
- In Mexico, firms that exported 40 and 80 percent of their total sales paid wages that were at least 11 percent higher than the wages of non-export-oriented firms; companies that exported above 80 percent of their sales paid wages between 58 and 67 percent higher (Lukacs 2000).
- In the Philippines, workers reported themselves to be better off after finding employment in the export-processing zone during the 1990s. Forty-seven percent earned enough to have some savings, compared with 9 percent before employment in the zone (World Bank 1999, Appendix C).
- Footwear and apparel manufacturers in the countries that produce most such products for U.S. import pay higher wages and offer better working conditions than those available in local agriculture (U.S. Department of Labor 2000).
- The U.S. Chamber of Commerce found that in Shanghai, China, the 48 American companies surveyed paid an average hourly wage of $5.25, excluding benefits and bonuses (about $10,900 per year) Lukacs (2000).

Source: Compiled from Moran 2002; Lim 2001; and Brown, Deardorff, and Stern, 2003.

point of the world's poor, the best opportunity they have ever had to pull themselves out of poverty. Two dollars a day sewing shirts is not much to you and me. For people who would otherwise have to work even harder and even longer for even less money, it's a pretty good job. And while it is objectionable when we examine it up close, it is important to recognize that these factories are the sole reason why global income inequality has decreased and poverty has fallen by 375 million people during the last 20 years.

The antisweatshop movement responds by saying that even if this is all true, it would still be better to establish global rules that improved working conditions and wages in developing-world factories. Together with labor unions in the advanced industrialized countries, the antisweatshop movement has advocated linking developing countries' access to global markets to their adoption and enforcement of global labor standards. Two sets of standards have been proposed: a set of Core Labor Standards and a set of cash standards. **Core labor standards,** which are elaborated in the ILO's 1998 "Declaration on Fundamental Principles and Rights at Work," include freedom of association, the right to collective bargaining, the abolition of forced labor, the prevention of discrimination in employment, and a minimum age for employment. **Cash standards** focus on achieving specific workplace outcomes that affect labor costs. These standards include rules for maximum working hours and minimum wages, as well as for health and safety conditions in the workplace.

Defenders of globalization argue that the adoption of enforceable global labor standards might improve working conditions in the developing world, but it is more likely that such standards will push people in the developing world back into poverty. While global labor standards could bring meaningful improvements in wages or working conditions, they will also raise the cost of manufacturing production in developing societies. They might do so by raising labor costs directly through higher wages, or they might do so indirectly by requiring more costly production techniques and safety equipment in factories. Higher costs of production will make the developing world a less attractive place to invest. As a result, global standards will yield less investment, less production, and fewer jobs. The overall impact could be better jobs, but many fewer of them (Krugman 1997). If that is the result, then global labor standards will have pushed people in the developing world back into poverty.

Moreover, in order to enforce global labor standards, governments must be able to restrict trade with countries violating the rules. The desire to achieve effective enforcement is the primary impetus behind the effort to bring standards into the WTO (O'Brien et al. 2000, 87–88). And while in theory this seems perfectly reasonable, in practice it creates another instrument that governments in the advanced industrialized countries can use to keep developing-country imports out of their markets. As we have seen, protection is offered when a government needs to maintain the support of an important domestic industry. It is hard to believe that enforceable global labor standards won't be subject to this political dynamic, especially as they target foreign industries that compete against the most vulnerable industries in the advanced industrialized world. Protection of this sort would further reduce the incentive to invest in developing countries.

Such concerns are voiced by many economists and also by governments throughout the developing world. Developing countries see the effort to link labor standards to trade within the WTO as a new form of protectionism. As Martin Khor, the director of the Third World Network and a prominent critic of many other aspects of globalization, has argued, "developing countries fear that the objectives of the northern and the international trade unions, and of the developed country governments that back [the push for core labor standards] are mainly protectionist in nature, that they want to protect jobs in the North by reducing the low-cost incentive that attracts global corporations to the developing countries" (Khor 1999). Developing-country governments argue that the low wages paid to workers in their countries are not "exploitation." Low wages simply reflect the abundance of local low-skilled labor in the developing world. Linking trade to core labor standards merely punishes developing countries for capitalizing on this comparative advantage.

Moreover, defenders of globalization argue, standards are unnecessary because working conditions in the developing world will improve over time without them. Wages in all societies are linked to productivity. The wage differences we saw in Tables 16.1 and 16.2 and were caused, not by different labor market regulations, but from different levels of productivity. Wages are low in low-income countries because productivity is substantially lower in these countries. As productivity rises, wages will rise as well. Raising productivity takes time. The incomes currently being earned in low-skilled

POLICY ANALYSIS AND DEBATE

Labor Standards in the WTO

Question
How can working conditions in developing societies be improved?

Overview
The antisweatshop movement has advocated the development and enforcement of global labor standards to improve working conditions in developing countries. Some NGOs press for linking the Core Labor Standards to the WTO. Others want to go further, linking market access to the implementation and enforcement of so-called cash standards as well. Behind this push lies a concern that market-based development enables MNCs to profit, but creates few incentives for these firms to share the gains with workers.

Defenders of globalization argue that such standards would be counterproductive: the solution to poor working conditions lies in economic development that raises productivity in the developing world. The key to such productivity gains is continued participation in the global economy through exporting to, and attracting technology from, the advanced industrialized countries. Moreover, because enforceable labor standards will raise the cost of production in developing societies, such standards are more likely to reduce the number of jobs available to workers in the developing world than to improve conditions there. What should be done to improve working conditions in the developing world?

Policy Options
- Bring labor standards into the WTO and use the dispute settlement mechanism to ensure that developing countries enforce the standards.
- Liberalize trade in labor-intensive products in the advanced industrialized world in the belief that the resulting exports will improve working conditions in the developing world.

Policy Analysis
- What are the risks of relying on labor standards?
- What are the arguments against relying on markets to generate better working conditions?

Take a Position
- Which option do you prefer? Justify your choice
- What criticisms of your position should you anticipate? How would you defend your recommendation against these criticisms?

Resources

Online: Explore the material available on the National Labor Committee's website (*www.nlcnet.org*). Look also for an Oxfam-sponsored report entitled "We Are Not Machines." You might also do an online search for "sweatshops".

In Print: See the extended discussion of labor standards in Kimberly Ann Elliott and Richard Freeman, *Can Labor Standards Improve under Globalization?* (Washington, DC: Institute for International Economics, 2003); John Miller, "Why Economists

Continued

Are Wrong about Sweatshops and the Antisweatshop Movement," *Challenge* 46 (January–February 2003): 93–122; and Jagdish Bhagwati, *In Defense of Globalization* (New York: Oxford University Press, 2004).

manufacturing jobs are the necessary first step in this process. These higher incomes enable families to send their children to school rather than to work in the rice paddies (or to forage through the local dump). Education in turn qualifies these young people for employment in jobs demanding more skills and paying higher wages. Over time, society moves away from low-skilled, labor-intensive manufacturing.

The sweatshop debate thus raises complex issues that refuse to yield simple answers. Both groups want working conditions in the developing world to improve, but they offer fundamentally different approaches to that end. Moreover, each side in the debate is deeply skeptical of the remedy proposed by the other. The antisweatshop movement has little faith in the operation of the market; the defenders of globalization have little faith in the ability of governments to use regulations in a manner that yields welfare gains. Moreover, they argue that regulations often have consequences that cut against the antisweatshop movement's intended goals. Thus, one's stance in this debate reflects one's underlying beliefs about the benefits of markets and the ability of governments to regulate markets that are not easily altered, much less subject to negotiation and compromise. Regardless of where you stand, Paul Krugman's advice seems apt: the lives of millions of people are at stake in this debate. Consequently, it is critically important that remedies offered be the product of careful reflection about all of their potential consequences (Krugman 1997).

Trade and the Environment

Globalization has also generated controversy about its environmental consequences. This debate pits the environmental movement against the defenders of globalization. The debate over the environmental consequences of globalization is less sharp than the debate over sweatshops, however. The main reason is that there is greater consensus between the two groups about how to conceptualize the relationship between trade and the environment, and greater consensus about the impact of globalization on the environment generates smaller disagreement about how to manage the negative consequences that do exist. The differences between the two groups reflect different values and different evaluations of the appropriate solutions to the problems.

This current consensus is that globalization does not necessarily harm the environment, but can instead have either positive or negative environmental consequences. Globalization affects the environment in two ways. (See United Nations Environment Programme 2000, 35–40.) First, globalization has **scale effects** that arise from the expansion of economic activity. These scale effects can be positive or negative. Positive scale effects can arise from the diffusion of technology through trade and foreign investment and from the impact of rising incomes. As firms upgrade their technology, they consume fewer natural resources and generate less waste. Development can also improve the environment as individuals alter traditional practices. In poor societies, for example, people rely heavily on high-polluting fuels such as wood and coal to cook and heat. As incomes rise, people shift to cleaner fuels. Other positive effects stem from an apparent association between higher income and demand for a clean environment. This relationship may reflect a simple income effect: as people become wealthier, they can more easily afford the cost of environmental protection. Alternatively, it may reflect a change in values: as their material needs are satisfied, people begin to place greater value on the nonmaterial aspects of life associated with cleaner environments. In either case, rising incomes and more concern for the environment often go together.

Scale effects can also have negative environmental consequences. All economic activity has some impact on the environment. Economic activity requires natural resources and generates waste. As the scale of economic activity expands, the use of resources and the generation of waste will both increase. In addition, as incomes rise, consumption patterns can change in ways that harm the environment. For example, most Chinese now ride bicycles. Yet, as Chinese incomes rise, a larger percentage of the population will begin to drive cars. Consequently (assuming that the internal combustion engine remains predominant), CO_2 emissions will increase, with clear negative consequences for the global environment.

Globalization also has **structural effects** brought about by economic specialization within a global division of labor. These effects can also be positive or negative. If an economy has a comparative advantage in green industries, then specialization through trade will encourage it to shift out of polluting industries and into clean industries. If, by contrast, the country has a comparative advantage in dirty industries, then specialization through trade in these industries will lead to growing environmental problems. Many countries, for example, developed large aquaculture industries to produce shrimp for export. The shrimp ponds generated a large amount of waste that polluted local water supplies, lowered the water table, and thereby caused salt water to seep into the local supplies. The expansion of aquaculture damaged the surrounding mangrove forests (Bhagwati 2004b, 140).

Whether globalization has a positive or a negative impact on the environment, therefore, depends on whether the scale and structural effects are, on balance, positive or negative. Two different factors shape the balance between the positive and negative impact. First, for many (though not all) environmental problems, the balance is influenced by economic development. (See, e.g., Grossman and Krueger 1995; Frankel and Rose 2002.) At low income levels, environmental damage from economic activity is limited. As societies begin to industrialize and move from low- toward middle-income status, however, the negative scale and structural effects predominate and environmental damage worsens. As societies move from middle- to high-income status, the positive scale and structural effects begin to predominate. At high income levels, the positive effects outweigh the negative effects substantially. The result is an inverted-U shaped relationship between income levels and environmental damage. This shape is often called the **environmental Kuznets curve** (after Simon Kuznets, who posited a similar relationship between income levels and income distribution).

Government environmental regulations also play a critical role in influencing the balance between the positive and negative impact of globalization on the environment.

In most instances, the environmental consequences of economic activity are not taken into account through the market. In shrimp farming, for example, the private cost of production (building the ponds, feeding and harvesting the shrimp) was much lower than the social cost of production (the private costs plus the negative environmental consequences). Because shrimp farmers were able to impose these costs onto society as a whole, they expanded their production and caused more environmental damage than society would have accepted if the environmental costs had been incorporated into the economic picture.

Government regulations could reduce these negative environmental consequences by forcing shrimp farmers to take the environmental consequences of their activities into account. Such regulations could require farms to use the best available waste treatment systems, could raise the cost of water in response to fluctuations in the water table, and so on. By forcing the shrimp farmer to pay these social costs, environmental damage can be reduced. Thus, government regulation plays an important role in ensuring that scale and structural consequences are, on balance, positive rather than negative.

The mainstream environmental movement and the defenders of globalization largely agree on this conceptual framework. They disagree, however, in one very broad and one narrower way. First, each group holds a distinct philosophy about the place of humans in the natural world. Environmentalists believe that nature is autonomous and should be protected from human exploitation. Pro-globalizers believe that "nature is subordinate to humans" and should be used to raise our incomes (Bhagwati 2004b, 136–7). These different beliefs lead the two camps to weigh the income gains from globalization and the resulting environmental degradation quite differently. Environmentalists weigh the negative environmental consequences very heavily and the income gains from globalization less heavily. Pro-globalizers weigh the income gains from globalization heavily and the negative environmental consequences less so (Bhagwati 2004b, 136–137). Consequently, the two groups will always disagree about how much environmental damage they are willing to accept in order to achieve a given rise in income.

The two groups also disagree about whether current WTO rules limit governments' ability to use national regulations to achieve environmental goals. The environmental movement argues that WTO rules greatly complicate these efforts. One of the group's central concerns focuses on the environmental consequences of the somewhat obscure WTO term **like products.** WTO rules (GATT Articles I and III) require governments to treat "like products" identically. Historically, the main criterion for determining whether two items are like products is whether they can be substituted for one another in the marketplace (often called the market substitutability test). Consider, for example, two memory chips produced by different manufacturers. Suppose that both chips contain the same amount of memory, that both are produced to the same technical standards, and that both can be placed into the same expansion slot in a personal computer. Then, under the market substitutability test, the two memory chips are like products.

Environmental groups argue that the market substitutability test results in too broad a definition of "like products," with negative consequences for national environmental regulations. They argue that, in determining what makes products like and unlike, governments and the WTO should consider how the two products are made. Different production processes (known within the WTO as **process and production**

methods, or **PPMs**) can have very different environmental consequences. In the semiconductor industry, for example, one manufacturing process uses ozone-depleting chemicals while another process does not. Environmental groups argue that because our two hypothetical computer chips are produced through two different methods with two very different environmental consequences, they are not like products.

Yet, WTO rules often prevent governments from taking PPMs into account in determining whether two products are like. The two most well-known disputes in the GATT and WTO, the "tuna–dolphin case" and the "turtle–shrimp case," revolved around import bans adopted in pursuit of environmental goals. In both disputes, the central issue was whether the United States could discriminate between goods that differed only in the method used to harvest them. That is, could the U.S. import tuna and shrimp caught by using environmentally friendly techniques while banning imports of identical tuna and shrimp harvested with environmentally harmful techniques? In both cases, the WTO ruled that the American import bans violated WTO rules regarding PPMs and like products (though for different reasons—see this chapter's "Closer Look"). The environmental movement argues that if WTO rules allowed governments to take PPMs into account in determining like products, those governments could use trade restrictions to encourage the adoption of green production methods and discourage the use of harmful techniques.

The defenders of globalization are skeptical about the effort to widen the criteria for like products. At the broadest level, they question the need and the wisdom of pursuing environmental objectives through trade policy. Rather than trying to achieve environmental goals by restricting trade, they argue, it would be more effective to pursue those goals through environmental policy. As Bhagwati (2004b, 141) argues, "you cannot generally kill two birds with one stone." Thus, defenders of globalization maintain that the WTO should be used to achieve the income gains from globalization and environmental regulations should be used to safeguard the environment. There is simply no need to use trade restrictions to achieve environmental goals.

The environmental movement also argues that even when WTO rules do allow governments to restrict trade in pursuit of environmental goals, the burden of proof necessary to do so can be insurmountable. The WTO does allow governments to restrict trade in pursuit of an environmental goal. GATT Article XX, known as the general exceptions article, allows governments to restrict trade when doing so is "necessary to protect human, animal, or plant life or health" (Article XX(b)) . . . or when such measures relate "to the conservation of exhaustible natural resources if such measures are made effective in conjunction with restrictions on domestic production or consumption" (Article XX(g)). If a government invokes one of these exceptions, however, it must prove two things if challenged. First, it must prove that the trade restriction was in fact adopted to achieve goals set out in either XX(b) or XX(g), rather than being a form of disguised protectionism. Second, it must prove that the measure is consistent with the lead paragraph of Article XX, known as the *chapeau*. The *chapeau* states that a government can restrict trade "subject to the requirement that such measures are not applied in a manner which would constitute a means of arbitrary or unjustifiable discrimination between countries where the same conditions prevail, or a disguised restriction on international trade." The burden of proof required to restrict trade in pursuit of an environmental objective is thus quite high.

CLOSER LOOK

Environmental Disputes in the WTO

Two recent trade disputes involving American environmental regulations help illustrate how WTO rules can constrain governments' use of national environmental regulations. The first case involved an American decision to ban imports of tuna from Mexico, Venezuela, and Vanuatu. This dispute arose because U.S. regulations required the American tuna fleet to reduce the number of dolphins killed during tuna fishing. As a consequence, between 1960 and 1990 the number of dolphins killed by the American tuna fleet fell by 90 percent, from a high of about 500,000 per year (Vogel 2000, 353). Fishing fleets based in Mexico, Venezuela, and Vanuatu continued to kill dolphins at a much higher rate, however, and much of the tuna caught by these fleets was exported to the American market. The United States then banned tuna imports from those countries, hoping that the ban would encourage their governments to adopt regulations to protect dolphins.

The Mexican government filed a complaint with the GATT, arguing that the U.S. trade restriction represented a non-product-related PPM. The United States was prohibiting the import of a like product (tuna imported from Mexico was identical to tuna caught by the American fleet) because of the production process used in Mexico. The GATT dispute panel ruled in favor of Mexico, stating that while a country could impose whatever regulation it wanted within its own borders (as long as the regulation did not discriminate between domestic and foreign producers), it could not attempt to regulate the production methods used in other countries. Thus, the United States could not attempt to regulate how the Mexican fleet harvested tuna, and it could not make access to the American market contingent upon the adoption of dolphin-friendly techniques. Environmental groups claimed that this case reflected an antienvironment bias at the center of the GATT. As the Sierra Club stated, "Meeting in a closed room in Geneva . . . three unelected trade experts . . . conspired to kill flipper" (Vogel 2000, 353).

The second case involved the use of turtle-excluding devices, known as TEDs, on shrimp nets. This dispute originated in a law passed by the U.S. Congress in 1989 that required American shrimpers to use TEDs to prevent sea turtles from becoming entangled in shrimp nets. The United States then extended the regulation to foreign shrimpers in 1995. As a result, shrimp harvested in countries that did not require TEDs could not be sold in the United States. As in the tuna–dolphin case, the United States was restricting imports on the basis of a non-product-related PPM.

In October 1996, India, Pakistan, Malaysia, and Thailand, all of which were affected by the American regulation, initiated a dispute within the WTO. These governments argued that GATT rules prohibit the United States from restricting access to the U.S. market simply because their fleets used a different method to harvest shrimp. The initial WTO dispute panel ruled against the United States, as did the appellate body when the United States appealed. Some environmental groups argued that the decision in this case, like the decision in the previous tuna–dolphin case, reflected a willingness by the WTO to overturn environmental regulations in order to promote international trade. Charles Clarke of the World Wildlife Fund stated

Continued

that the decision "denies individual countries the right to restrict trade even when species, in this case sea turtles, are endangered and the complainant countries have signed international environmental agreements to protect them" (Zarocostas 1998).

The United States invoked Article XX(g) in the TEDs case, arguing that the U.S. ban on imported shrimp was legal because it attempted to conserve an exhaustible natural resource. The WTO Appellate Panel agreed with the American position, arguing that governments could use non-product-related PPMs to restrict trade in order to achieve an environmental objective. However, the Appellate Panel argued, trade restrictions imposed for this purpose must meet the conditions spelled out in the *chapeau* of Article XX. The Appellate Panel ruled that even while the U.S. import ban was consistent with Article XX, the U.S. had applied this ban in a discriminatory manner. The United States provided Caribbean nations with financial and technical assistance, as well as an extended transition period to help shrimpers adopt TEDs. The United States provided no such assistance to the Asian countries. As such, the U.S. ban discriminated between WTO members. For this reason, the U.S. trade restriction was found to be inconsistent with WTO rules.

The defenders of globalization argue that such stringent burdens of proof, while sometimes inconvenient, are necessary. Without stringent conditions, it would be too easy for governments to disguise simple protectionism as environmental safeguards (Esty 2001, 117). In banning shrimp and tuna imports, for example, was the U.S. government protecting dolphin and sea turtles, or was it protecting the American tuna fleet and American shrimpers against foreign competition? The world trade system needs rules that require a heavy burden of proof in order to prevent the widespread use of protectionist practices disguised as environmental safeguards. Relaxing these rules would result in large income sacrifices for uncertain environmental gains that could be as readily achieved with other methods.

Finally, the environmental movement is quite concerned about the potential for conflict between WTO rules and **multilateral environmental agreements** (MEAs)—international agreements between three or more governments dedicated to the achievement of a specific environmental objective. (See Table 16.4.) Potential conflict between MEAs and WTO rules arises because several MEAs contain trade restrictions that may violate WTO rules. Some MEAs encourage governments to restrict trade with nonmembers, thereby potentially violating the WTO's most-favored-nation clause. Other MEAs encourage governments to adopt different standards toward domestic and imported goods, thereby potentially violating the WTO's rule of national treatment. Many MEAs call upon governments to use trade sanctions to enforce the agreement, thereby raising the possibility of a violation of the most-favored-nation clause.

If a trade sanction is imposed to enforce one of these MEAs, could the sanctioned country use the WTO's dispute settlement mechanism to have the sanction removed? If so, wouldn't the WTO then undermine the goal of the MEA? Environmental groups argue that in order to prevent this possibility, the WTO should accept as a general principle that any trade restriction applied in connection with an MEA is fully consistent with WTO rules and beyond review by WTO dispute panels. (See, e.g., World Wildlife Fund 1999.)

Table 16.4
Multilateral Environmental Agreements

Agreement	Trade Provisions
Convention For the Protection of the Ozone Layer (Montreal Protocol)	• Requires governments to apply stricter trade provisions to nonparties than to parties to the agreement; in potential conflict with GATT Article I. • Regulates PPMs in potential conflict with GATT Article III. • Allows trade sanctions to enforce the agreement, in potential violation of GATT Article I.
Convention on International Trade in Endangered Species of Wild Fauna and Flora	• Requires governments to apply stricter trade provisions to nonparties than to parties to the agreement; in potential conflict with GATT Article I. • Requires licensing arrangements in potential conflict with GATT Article XI. • Allows trade sanctions to enforce the agreement, in potential violation of GATT Article I.
Convention on the Control of Transboundary Movements of Hazardous Wastes and Their Disposal	• Requires governments to apply stricter trade provisions to nonparties than to parties to the agreement; in potential conflict with GATT Article I. • Requires licensing arrangements in potential conflict with GATT Article XI. • Allows trade sanctions to enforce the agreement, in potential violation of GATT Article I.

In this matter, the defenders argue that WTO rules are not nearly as constraining as the environmental movement suggests. While the rules do require national environmental regulations to conform to a limited number of global principles, they hardly preclude the use of national environmental regulations or the provisions of international environmental agreements. The evidence behind this statement lies in the very fact that governments have negotiated a large number of MEAs and no government has been forced to remove a single environmental regulation as a result of a WTO dispute settlement ruling. Moreover, the potential for conflict between MEAs and WTO rules is only that: potential. To date, not a single WTO dispute has arisen from trade provisions contained in MEAs. Thus, the defenders of globalization argue, there is no need to change WTO rules in order to enable governments to safeguard the environment.

The emergence and subsequent evolution of this debate has pushed the WTO toward greater sensitivity to globalization's impact on the environment. While it is hard to characterize WTO rules as proenvironment, there is now a greater willingness to think about environmental concerns in interpreting WTO rules; a comparison of the tuna–dolphin and shrimp–turtle cases highlights this change. In addition, in 1995 the WTO created a **Committee on Trade and the Environment** (CTE). The CTE's mandate is "to identify the relationship between trade measures and environmental measures in order to promote sustainable development" and "to make appropriate recommendations on whether any modifications of the provisions of the multilateral trading system are required, compatible with the open, equitable and nondiscrimina-tory nature of the system." Since its creation, the CTE has examined a number of issues, including the relationship between the WTO and international environmental agreements; the feasibility of requiring environmental evaluations of trade agree-ments; the environmental impact of production subsidies, particularly in agricultural production and energy use; and other issues.

These changes within the WTO have led some commentators to suggest that while the environmentalists may have lost many of the individual battles, they have won the war to bring the environment into the world trade system (Weinstein and Charnovitz 2001). While this may be an overstatement, it does suggest that the debate over how globalization affects the environment, and the debate over how best to address these consequences, has evolved in a productive manner within the existing institutional framework. And because, at its core, environmentalists and the defenders of globalization will never fully agree on the balance to be struck between income gains and environmental degradation, perhaps that is the most we can hope to achieve.

Conclusion

The debate over globalization is a debate about how the income generated by global economic activity should be distributed. It is a debate about whether we should be willing to give up some of the income that globalization generates in order to achieve other goals, such as safeguarding the environment. Thus, current controversies over the consequences of globalization are the contemporary manifestation of the enduring battle between those who see themselves gaining from globalization and those who believe that they are losing from these dynamics.

The two camps engaged in this debate share a common objective: reducing global poverty through the sustainable exploitation of natural resources. But each side has a distinct approach to achieving this goal. These approaches themselves reflect the long-running debate about the relative merits of states and markets. The critics of globaliza-tion are quite skeptical of the market's ability to deliver sustained income gains for the majority of the world's population at a reasonable environmental cost. Consequently, they advocate a larger role for the state in redistributing income, protecting the poor, and safeguarding the environment. And few of these critics seem willing to question their implicit assumption that state power can achieve these goals without killing the golden goose that is generating the income they wish to redistribute.

Defenders of globalization, in contrast, are skeptical of the state's capacity to bring about positive change, particularly, but not exclusively, in the developing world. The defenders of globalization look at the history of import substitution industrialization and see far too many instances in which government intervention not only failed to reduce poverty, but in fact generated more poverty while also destroying the environment. (See, e.g., Lal 2004.) In contrasting that record to that of the last 20 years, the defenders of globalization conclude that markets will do what developing-country governments demonstrated they could not. And the defenders look at the history of protectionism in the advanced industrialized countries and ask why we should risk globalization's gains by creating global rules that make it easy for governments to impose new forms of protection. Because they have little faith in the state's ability to act in the "public interest," the defenders of globalization discount existing inequities and environmental damage and take refuge in the belief that these problems will take care of themselves as long as global income continues to rise.

What does this all imply for the future of globalization? I fear that the debate is having a corrosive effect on political support for globalization. One sees signs of eroding support within the American public. Public-opinion polls tracking attitudes about the global economy regularly indicate that the American public is uneasy about that economy. (See Scheve and Slaughter 2001.) The public fears that globalization is eliminating jobs and lowering wages in the United States; it fears that globalization is generating poverty and widening income inequalities; it fears that trade is destroying the environment. Since many of these fears are not supported by the evidence, these public-opinion polls suggest that globalization has a real public-relations problem that has been created in part by the antiglobalization movement and based on partially and, in many instances, factually incorrect claims.

This public-relations problem is a serious threat to globalization, for the United States remains the world's largest economy. As a consequence, there can be no globalization without American participation in, and support for, the global economic system. Yet, the U.S. government's support for globalization requires American voters to support the notion as well, and they seem to be unenthusiastic and perhaps even increasingly skeptical. Thus, the fate of the world's poor is in the hands of rather poorly informed American voters. Keep that in mind as you debate, discuss, and make decisions about how the global economy should be organized.

Key Terms

Cash Standards	Globalization
Committee on Trade and the Environment	Like Products
Core Labor Standards	Multilateral Environmental Agreements
Environmental Kuznets Curve	Process and Production Methods
Gini Coefficient	Scale Effects
Global Division of Labor	Structural Effects

Web Links

Visit the World Bank webpage on "Measuring Inequality": *http://web.worldbank.org/WBSITE/ EXTERNAL/TOPICS/EXTPOVERTY/EXTPA/0,,contentMDK:20238991~menuPK:492138~ pagePK:148956~piPK:216618~theSitePK:430367,00.html*.

There is a vast amount of material about sweatshops on the web. The National Labor Committee (*http://www.nlcnet.org*) is a good place to start.

Oxfam also provides a lot of online material concerning the relationship between globalization and development. Visit this organization at *http://www.oxfam.uk.org*.

You can also follow the WTO Committee on Trade and the Environment on the WTO website at *http://www.wto.org/english/tratop_e/envir_e/envir_e.htm*.

Suggestions for Further Reading

On global income inequality, the recent book by Glenn Firebaugh, *The New Geography of Global Income Inequality* (Cambridge: Harvard University Press, 2003), is probably the most thorough and the most accessible work on the subject.

On labor standards, the short book by Kimberly Ann Elliott and Richard Freeman, *Can Labor Standards Improve under Globalization?* (Washington, DC: Institute for International Economics, 2003) is excellent. A shorter argument in favor of standards can be found in John Miller, "Why Economists Are Wrong about Sweatshops and the Antisweatshop Movement," *Challenge* 46 (January–February 2003.): 93–122. Jagdish Bhagwati argues the opposite side in his *In Defense of Globalization* (New York: Oxford University Press, 2004).

On trade and the environment, see the now somewhat dated Daniel C. Esty, *The Greening of the GATT: Trade, Environment, and the Future* (Washington, DC: Institute for International Economics, 1994). A more recent treatment can be found in Brian Copeland and M. Scott Taylor, *Trade and the Environment: Theory and Evidence* (Princeton: Princeton University Press, 2003).

Glossary

Absolute Advantage The principle upon which Adam Smith first claimed that free trade benefits all countries. It holds that a country benefits from trade when it produces a particular good at a lower cost (in terms of labor input) than it costs to produce the good in any other country. By specializing in the production and export of this good and importing goods whose production costs are higher than in other countries, the country can consume more of both goods. In trade theories, this principle was later replaced by the principle of comparative advantage. (See comparative advantage, principle of.)

Accelerationist Principle A central component of monetarist theories and first stated by Milton Friedman in the 1960s, it claims that a government can keep unemployment below the natural rate of unemployment only if it is willing to accept a continually increasing rate of inflation. That is, the principle claims that there is no long-run Phillips Curve trade-off between inflation and unemployment. Such a trade-off exists only in the short run. This principle became widely accepted by governments and central bankers in the advanced industrialized countries during the 1980s, leading to the demise of Keynesian strategies of macroeconomic management. (See Keynesianism; Phillips curve.)

Antidumping Government investigations to determine whether a foreign firm is selling its products in international markets at a price that is below its cost of production. Under the rules of the international trade system, a positive finding in such an investigation allows the government to impose tariffs to offset the margin of dumping. (See dumping.)

Association Agreements Agreements between Eastern and Central European countries and the European Union following the collapse of the Soviet bloc in 1989. They removed barriers to trade in manufactured goods and established a framework for the progressive integration of Eastern and Western Europe.

Backward Linkages A term applied to the industrialization process that refers to instances when the creation of a domestic industry increases demand in domestic industries that supply inputs to the original industry. For example, the creation of a domestic auto industry may increase the demand for domestic auto parts such as batteries, glass, tires, etc.

Baker Plan Proposed in 1985 by Secretary of the U.S. Treasury James A. Baker, III, this plan attempted to resolve the developing-country debt crisis through a combination of economic adjustment and additional lending. Of particular significance, the plan linked access to financial assistance from the IMF, World Bank, and private lenders to the willingness of debtor governments to adopt structural adjustment programs.

Balance of Payments Adjustment The use of government policies to correct a balance-of-payments deficit or surplus.

Balance of Payments An accounting device that records a country's international transactions. The balance of payments is divided into two broad categories: the current account and the capital account.

Brady Plan Proposed in 1989 by Secretary of the U.S. Treasury Nicholas J. Brady, this plan attempted to bring the developing-country debt crisis to a close. It encouraged commercial banks to negotiate debt reduction agreements with debtor governments. To make the proposal attractive to commercial banks, the advanced industrialized countries and the multilateral financial institutions advanced $30 billion with which to guarantee the principal of the Brady bonds, as the new debt instruments came to be called.

Bretton Woods System   The international monetary system that was created in 1944 at Bretton Woods, New Hampshire. It was based on fixed-but-adjustable exchange rates in an attempt to provide a stable international monetary system and at the same time allow governments to use monetary policy to manage the domestic economy. The system collapsed in 1973 and represented the last time that governments attempted to create and maintain an international monetary system based on some form of fixed exchange rates.

Calvo Doctrine   Named after the Argentinean legal scholar Carlos Calvo, who first stated it in 1868, this doctrine argues that no government has the right to intervene in another country to enforce the private claims of that government's citizens. The doctrine was invoked by Latin American governments during the late 19 and early 20th century to challenge the right of governments to use diplomatic pressure and military force to protect foreign investments made by their citizens.

Capital Account   One of the two principal components of the balance of payments, it records all financial flows into and out of a particular country. Such financial flows include bank loans, equities (stocks and bonds), and foreign direct investment.

Central-Bank Independence   The degree to which a country's central bank can set monetary policy free from interference by the government. Typically considered to be a function of three things: the degree to which the central bank is free to decide what economic objective to pursue, the degree to which the central bank is free to decide how to set monetary policy in pursuit of this objective, and the degree to which central-bank decisions can be reversed by other branches of government. Contemporary economic theory argues that independent central banks are better able to deliver low inflation than are central banks controlled by the government.

Collective Action Problem   Applies to instances in which the action of a number of individuals is required to achieve a common goal. The problem arises because people will not voluntarily invest time, energy, or money to achieve a common goal, but will instead allow others to bear these costs. Because all members of the interested group act in the same way, insufficient time, energy, and money are dedicated to the achievement of the goal, and the goal is therefore not achieved. In international political economy, it has been used to understand interest-group formation, and in particular, why consumer interests are underrepresented in trade policy.

Common Agricultural Policy (CAP)   A set of policies used by the European Union to protect European farmers from farm products produced outside the union. These policies include production and export subsidies to support European farmers, as well as tariffs and quotas to limit imports of foreign agricultural products. The CAP is one of the most controversial aspects of the U.S.–EU trade relationship.

Comparative Advantage   First fully stated by David Ricardo in the early 19th century, this concept holds that a country has a comparative advantage in a good if it can produce that good more cheaply than it can produce other goods. By specializing in the production of goods in which it holds a comparative advantage and importing the other goods, the country can consume more of all goods. In contrast to Adam Smith, therefore, this principle states that a country need not have an absolute advantage in any good to benefit from trade. The principle provides a powerful justification for liberal international trade by asserting that all countries benefit from such trade.

Conditionality   Property applied to the terms governing transactions between the International Monetary Fund and member governments. In order to gain access to IMF financial resources, a government must agree to a set of policy changes designed to correct its balance-of-payments deficit. Typically, governments must tighten the money supply and reduce government spending. In more extreme cases, governments are also required to undertake structural reforms. (See macroeconomic stabilization; structural adjustment.)

Countervailing-Duty Investigation A government investigation used to determine whether a foreign government is subsidizing its national firms' exports directly or indirectly. Under the rules of the international trade system, a positive finding in such an investigation allows the government to impose tariffs to offset the subsidy.

Current Account One of the two principal components of the balance of payments. It records all payments between the country and the rest of the world in connection with goods, services, income earned on foreign investments, royalties, licenses, unilateral transfers by private individuals, government expenditures on foreign aid, and overseas military spending.

Customs Union A form of regional trading arrangement in which member governments eliminate all tariffs on trade between members of the union and create a common tariff that is imposed on goods entering any member country of the union from countries outside the union.

Debt-Service Capacity The ability of a country to make payments of interest and principal on foreign debt. Because debt service, especially in developing countries, must be made with foreign currencies, export earnings are a good measure of a country's debt-service capacity.

Debt-Service Ratio The percentage of a country's export earnings that must be devoted to payments of interest and principal on foreign debt. A high debt-service ratio means that a large share of the country's total export revenues must be used to make debt payments.

Devaluation A reduction in a currency's value within a fixed or fixed-but-adjustable exchange-rate system. Should be distinguished from depreciation, which is a change in a currency's value caused by foreign exchange market transactions. Thus, a floating currency may depreciate, but cannot be devalued.

Dispute Settlement Mechanism A quasi-judicial tribunal that is used to resolve trade disputes between WTO member governments.

Domestic Safeguards Clauses in the GATT that allow governments to temporarily suspend tariff reductions they have made previously when a domestic industry is being threatened by a sudden surge of imports.

Dumping The act of selling a good in a foreign market at a price that is either below the cost of production of the good or below the price at which the good sells for in the home market. Dumping is illegal under GATT rules, and governments are allowed to counter the practice by raising tariffs. (See antidumping investigation.)

East Asian Model A model in which economic development is conceptualized as a series of distinct stages of industrialization. In the first stage, industrial policy promotes labor-intensive light industry, such as textiles and other consumer durables. In the second stage, the emphasis of industrial policy shifts to heavy industries, such as steel, shipbuilding, petrochemicals, and synthetic fibers. In the third stage, governments target skill-intensive and research-and-development-intensive consumer durables and industrial machinery, such as machine tools, semiconductors, computers, telecommunications equipment, robotics, and biotechnology. Governments design policies and organizations to promote the transition from one stage to the other.

Economies of Scale Reductions in the unit cost of producing a good caused by increases in the number of goods produced. Economies of scale often arise from knowledge acquired in production. The existence of economies of scale in certain industries can provide a justification for welfare-enhancing industrial policy, as well as a rationale for strategic trade theory.

Enforcement Problem In the anarchic international state system, governments cannot be certain that other governments will comply with the trade agreements that they conclude. As a consequence, governments are reluctant to enter into such agreements. This problem complicates all forms of international cooperation and has been used to understand the need for the World Trade Organization.

Engel's Law   Law asserting that people spend smaller percentages of their total income on food and other primary commodities as their incomes rise. It was a central component of the Singer–Prebisch theory that formed a part of structuralism.

Eurodollars   Literally, dollar-denominated bank accounts and loans managed by banks outside of the United States. More broadly, the term refers to bank accounts denominated in currencies other than the currency issued by the government in the country in which the account is held.

European Monetary System (EMS)   Founded by European Community governments in 1979, the EMS was a fixed-but-adjustable exchange-rate system in which governments established a central parity against a basket of EU currencies called the European Currency Unit (ECU). Central parities against the ECU were then used to create bilateral exchange rates between all EU currencies. EU governments were required to maintain their currency's bilateral exchange rate within 2.25 percent of its central bilateral rate. In January 1999, monetary union replaced the EMS.

Exchange-Rate System   A set of rules that together specify the amount by which currencies can appreciate and depreciate in the foreign exchange market. Under a fixed exchange-rate system, the rules require governments to restrict currency movements to a narrow range around some central rate. In a floating exchange-rate system, governments can allow their currencies to move by as much as they desire.

Exchange Restrictions   Government regulations controlling the private use of foreign exchange. Used extensively by governments in the advanced industrialized countries under the Bretton Woods system to limit capital outflows.

Exon–Florio Amendment   An amendment to the United States 1988 Omnibus Trade Act that allows the executive to block foreign acquisitions of American firms for reasons of national security. More broadly, it highlights government concerns about the role foreign corporations play in the domestic economy.

Export-processing Zones   Industrial estates where the government provides land, utilities, transportation infrastructure, and, in some cases, buildings to the investing firms, usually at subsidized rates. They are often established by developing countries to attract foreign direct investments by MNCs.

Export-oriented Strategy   A development strategy in which emphasis is placed on producing manufactured goods that can be sold in international markets. Adopted by the East Asian NICs in the late 1950s to early 1960s after the gains from easy ISI had been exhausted. During the late 1980s, this strategy and the apparent Asian success based on it provided the foundation for the "Washington Consensus."

Factors   The basic tools of production, including labor, land, and capital.

Factor Endowments   The amount of land, labor, and capital a country has available. Countries have different relative factor endowments, and in the Hecksher–Ohlin model of international trade, these differences are the source of comparative advantage.

Factor Mobility   The ease with which factors of production can move from one industry to another. All factors are mobile in the long run, but many are relatively immobile in the short run. Different assumptions about the mobility of factors underlie two different political theories of trade politics. The factor model assumes a high degree of factor mobility, while the sectoral model assumes that at least one factor is immobile in the short run.

Factor Model   A political model which argues that the politics of trade policy is characterized by competition between labor and capital. Each of these two groups has a distinct trade policy preference because international trade has a differential effect on the groups' incomes. The scarce factor will be harmed by trade and therefore lobby for protection. The abundant factor will benefit from trade and therefore lobby for trade liberalization.

Factor Price Equalization (Stolper–Samuleson Theorem) In open economies, international trade will cause the price of the factors of production to equalize. In a two-country world, the price of each country's scarce factor will fall, while the price of each country's abundant factor will rise. Eventually, the price of labor will be the same in both countries and the price of capital will be the same in both countries.

Fast Track The domestic political process setting the terms under which the United States participates in international trade negotiations and ratifies the resulting agreements. Congress first grants the executive the authority to negotiate international trade agreements. Congress must then approve (by a simple majority and within 90 days) any trade agreement the executive concludes before the agreement can become law. Congress cannot amend the trade agreement. The 1974 Trade Act first instituted this procedure.

Fiscal Policy The use by the government of tax and spending policies to manage domestic demand. An expansionary fiscal policy will boost domestic demand, thereby raising economic output; a restrictive fiscal policy will reduce domestic demand, thereby lowering economic output.

Fixed Exchange-Rate System A system in which governments establish a central or official rate for their currency, usually expressed in terms of some standard, such as gold or another currency. Governments are required to use monetary policy and foreign exchange market intervention to maintain their currency within a band around the official rate.

Fixed-but-adjustable Exchange-Rate System A system in which governments establish a central or official rate for their currency against some standard, as in a fixed exchange-rate system, but are also allowed to change the official rate occasionally, usually under a set of well-defined circumstances.

Floating Exchange-Rate System A system in which governments do not establish a central or official rate for their currency and are under no obligation to engage in foreign exchange market intervention to influence the value of their currency. In this system, the value of one currency in terms of another is determined purely by the interaction between supply and demand in the foreign exchange market.

Foreign Aid (Official Development Assistance) Financial assistance provided to developing countries' governments by the advanced industrialized countries and by multilateral financial institutions such as the World Bank and the regional development banks in order to finance development projects. Foreign aid can be supplied as a grant (requiring no repayment) or a loan (requiring repayment). Loans can be offered on concessional terms (below market rates of interest) or nonconcessional terms (at market rates of interest).

Foreign Direct Investment A form of cross-border investment in which a resident or corporation based in one country owns a productive asset located in a second country. In most instances, such investments involve multinational corporations. This type of investment can involve the construction of a new, or the purchase of an existing, plant or factory.

Foreign Exchange Market The market in which national currencies are traded. It is through transactions in this market that the market exchange rates of the world's currencies are established. According to the Bank of International Settlements, more than $1 trillion worth of currencies are traded each day.

Foreign Exchange Reserves Government holdings of other countries' currencies.

Free-Trade Area A regional trading arrangement in which governments eliminate all tariffs on goods imported from other members, but retain independent tariffs on goods imported from nonmembers. (See also customs union and regional trade arrangements.)

GATT Part IV Added to GATT in 1964 in part as a result of developing countries' pressure. Contains three articles that focus on developing countries' trade problems. The three articles call upon the advanced industrialized countries to improve market access for commodity exporters, to refrain from raising barriers to the import of products that are of special interest to the developing world, and to engage in "joint action to promote trade and development."

General Agreement on Tariffs and Trade (GATT)   An international agreement concluded in 1947 establishing rules that regulate national trade policies. Between 1947 and 1995, GATT also was the principal international trade organization, providing a forum for trade negotiations, administering trade agreements, helping governments settle trade disputes, and reviewing national trade policies. In 1995, the last role was taken over by the World Trade Organization. Today, GATT continues to provide the core rules regulating national trade policies.

Generalized System of Preferences (GSP)   Part of the GATT concluded in the late 1960s under which advanced industrialized countries can allow manufactured exports from developing countries to enter their markets at preferential tariff rates. The GSP is therefore a legal exception to the GATT principle of nondiscrimination.

Global Division of Labor   One of the economic consequences of an open international trade system. Over time, trade will cause countries to specialize in producing goods that make intensive use of their abundant factors of production. Eventually, each country will produce goods in which it has a comparative advantage and shed industries in which it has a comparative disadvantage.

Group of 77   A coalition of developing countries established at the conclusion of the first UNCTAD conference in the early 1960s. Seventy-seven developing countries' governments signed a joint declaration that called for reform of the international trade system. The Group of 77 subsequently led the campaign for reform of the multilateral trade system during the next 20 years. (See UNCTAD and NIEO.)

Haberler Report   A study conducted under GATT supervision in the late 1950s and suggesting that the GATT-based trade system was relatively unfavorable to developing countries. The report altered the political dynamics of the international trade system by forcing the advanced industrialized countries to take the demands for reform made by developing countries more seriously.

Hecksher–Ohlin Model   A model of the determinants of comparative advantage which argues that comparative advantage arises from cross-national differences in factor endowments. A country's comparative advantage will lie in goods produced through heavy reliance on its abundant factors. Capital-abundant countries have a comparative advantage in capital-intensive goods, and labor-abundant countries have a comparative advantage in labor-intensive goods. (See factor endowments.)

Hegemony   A particular distribution of power in the international state system characterized by the existence of one country (a hegemon) whose power capabilities are substantially greater than the next-most-powerful country or countries. The relevant capabilities include economic power, measured as the size and technological sophistication of the economy and of military power. A prominent hypothesis, called hegemonic stability theory, links the openness and stability of the international economic system to the presence or absence of a hegemon.

Heterodox Strategies   An approach to macroeconomic stabilization adopted by some Latin American governments during the 1980s. Seen as an alternative to the orthodox approach advocated by the IMF, these strategies attempted to reduce inflation through government controls on wages and prices, rather than by restricting aggregate demand by reducing government budget deficits and slowing the rate of growth of the money supply. In most instances, they failed to stabilize the economy.

Horizontal Integration   A form of industrial organization that occurs when a corporation creates multiple production facilities, each of which produces the same good or goods. Many MNCs are horizontally integrated firms, producing the same product or product line in multiple factories based in different countries. Firms integrate horizontally to capture the full value of the intangible assets they control.

Import Substitution Industrialization (ISI)   An economic development strategy adopted in many developing countries after World War II in which states attempted to industrialize by substituting domestically produced goods for manufactured items that had previously been imported. The strategy proceeded in two stages. Under easy ISI, the focus was on creating simple consumer goods. In the second stage, the focus shifted to consumer durable goods, intermediate inputs, and the capital goods needed to produce consumer durables. Most governments have abandoned this approach since the mid-1980s in favor of an export-oriented strategy.

Industrial Policy   An assortment of government policies, including tax policy, government subsidies, traditional protectionism, and government procurement practices, used to channel resources away from some actors and industries and direct them toward those actors and industries which the government wishes to promote. The use of such policies is typically based on long-term economic development objectives defined in terms of boosting economic growth, improving productivity, and enhancing international competitiveness. The specific goals often are determined by explicit comparisons to other countries' economic achievements.

Infant-Industry Case for Protection   A theoretical justification for protection that applies to cases in which a country's newly created firms (infants) could not *initially* compete against foreign producers in an established industry, but would be able to do so eventually if they were given time to mature.

Intangible Asset   Something whose value is derived from knowledge or from skills or production processes of [a] firm. An intangible asset can be based on a patented process or design, or it can arise from production-specific know-how shared by workers in the firm. The inherent difficulty of selling or licensing this kind of asset provides an important rationale for horizontal integration.

Intellectual Property   Creations of the mind, such as inventions, literary and artistic works, symbols, names, images, and designs used in commerce. The protection of intellectual property is the subject of the Trade Related Intellectual Property Rights agreement negotiated as part of the Uruguay Round.

International Bank for Reconstruction and Development (IBRD or World Bank)   Established in 1944 at the Bretton Woods conference, the IBRD extends long-term loans to developing countries to finance physical and social infrastructure needed to reduce poverty and promote development. These loans are financed by bonds that the IBRD sells in private bond markets.

International Development Association (IDA)   Part of the World Bank group, the IDA was established in the early 1960s as a separate development lending agency. The IDA is a concessional loan agency; its loans have a longer time to maturity than standard IBRD loans have, and they carry 0 percent interest rates. These loans are financed by member government contributions. To be eligible for IDA lending, a country must have a per capita income of less than $885 per year.

International Monetary Fund (IMF)   Established at the Bretton Woods conference in 1944, the IMF was initially charged with helping governments finance and ultimately eliminate balance-of-payments deficits in order to maintain stable exchange rates. Since the shift to floating exchange rates in 1973, the IMF has become increasingly focused on the management of debt and balance-of-payments crises in developing countries. (See conditionality.)

Keynesianism   An approach to macroeconomic policy that places primary emphasis on using fiscal and monetary policies to manage domestic demand in order to maintain full employment. Named after John Maynard Keynes, who was the first to demonstrate that governments could use macroeconomic policies for this purpose. The approach was widely adopted by governments in the advanced industrialized countries following World War II, but lost favor during the 1980s.

Locational Incentives   Offered by governments to MNCs, locational incentives are designed to reduce the costs of, and thereby increase the return from, a particular investment. Governments offer them to induce MNCs to invest in their country rather than another.

London Club   A private association established and run by the large commercial banks engaged in international lending. Developing countries' governments that want to reschedule their commercial bank debt must work out the terms of a rescheduling agreement with the London Club.

Macroeconomic Policy   The use of fiscal and monetary policy to influence aggregate economic activity in the national economy, such as the rate of economic growth, the rate of inflation, and the level of unemployment. (See Keynesianism.)

Macroeconomic Stabilization   The correction, through various policy programs, of macroeconomic imbalances that are producing high and rising inflation. Most programs involve the reduction of a government budget deficit and a tight monetary policy. Most conditionality agreements with the IMF contain such a program.

Managed Float   A form of floating exchange-rate system in which governments occasionally intervene in foreign exchange markets to try to influence the value of their currency. Such interventions are voluntary and sometimes involve coordinated intervention by more than one country.

Maquiladora Program   An export-processing zone in northern Mexico established by the government in an attempt to encourage American manufacturing MNCs to create assembly operations.

Monetary Policy   Changes in the country's money supply undertaken in an attempt to manage aggregate economic activity. An expansionary monetary policy is typically associated with rising inflation, a restrictive monetary policy with falling inflation and rising unemployment.

Monetary Union   An exchange-rate system in which governments permanently fix their exchange rates and introduce a single currency. The European Union created a monetary union on January 1, 1999, and introduced a single currency—the euro—on January 1, 2002.

Moral Hazard   A consideration which arises when banks believe that the government will bail them out if they suffer large losses on the loans they have made. If banks believe that the government will cover their losses, they have little incentive to carefully evaluate the risks that are associated with the loans they make. If the loans are repaid, banks earn money. If the loans are not repaid, the government—and hence society's taxpayers—picks up the tab. In such an environment, banks have an incentive to make riskier loans than they would make in the absence of a guarantee from the government, thereby raising the likelihood of a crisis.

Most-Favored Nation   The central principle upon which the WTO is based, this rule requires that any advantage extended by one WTO member government to another also be extended to all other WTO members. The principle therefore prevents trade measures that discriminate between countries.

Multilateral Agreement on Investment (MAI)   A document negotiated by the advanced industrialized countries in the OECD between 1995 and 1997 that laid out international rules governing the treatment of MNCs by governments. Designed to promote investment liberalization based on the principles of national treatment and most-favored nation, the MAI was never concluded, because negotiations proved fruitless.

Multinational Corporation (MNC)   A company that has ownership and manages production facilities in two or more countries. There are approximately 63,459 parent firms that together own a total of 689,520 foreign affiliates. These parent firms and their foreign affiliates account for about 25 percent of the world's economic production and employ some 86 million people worldwide.

National Treatment   The second component of nondiscrimination in the GATT embodied in GATT Article III, as well as in the GATS and TRIPs agreements. National treatment requires governments to impose identical tax and regulatory policies on foreign and domestic like products. This principle thus prohibits governments from using taxes and regulatory policies to provide advantages to domestic producers over foreign producers.

Natural Rate of Unemployment   The economy's long-run equilibrium rate of unemployment, or the rate of unemployment to which the economy will return after a recession or a boom. The natural rate of unemployment is never zero and can in fact be substantially above zero.

New International Economic Order (NIEO)   A reform effort driven by the Group of 77 and adopted by the UN General Assembly in December 1974. It embodied a set of reform objectives that, if implemented, would have radically altered the nature and operation of the international economy by creating "development-friendly" trade rules and giving developing countries a larger role in the decision-making processes of the World Bank and International Monetary Fund. The NIEO was abandoned in the early 1980s.

Nontariff Barrier (NTB)   Any of a number of policy or structural impediments to trade other than tariffs. NTBs include such things as health and safety regulations, government purchasing practices, and retail and distribution networks. As quotas have been eliminated and tariffs reduced, NTBs have become one of the most important remaining obstacles to international trade and are thus an increasingly important issue in the WTO.

Nontraded-Goods Sector   Sector containing all economic activities that do not enter into international trade, either because the good is too costly to transport (e.g., houses or concrete) or because in some cases the good or service must be performed locally (e.g., the railway system, many public utilities, health care, auto repair, and the retail sector more generally). In addition, government employees, such as civil servants, teachers, and military personnel, also work in the nontraded-goods sector.

Official Development Assistance   See foreign aid.

Paris Club   An informal group composed of 19 permanent members, all of which are governments that hold large claims on other governments. Its primary role is to negotiate the rescheduling of these debts.

Performance Requirement   A target imposed on the local affiliate of an MNC by the host country government in order to promote a specific economic objective. If the government is trying to promote backward linkages, for example, it will require the local affiliate to purchase a specific percentage of its inputs from domestic suppliers. The use of these measures was somewhat constrained by the agreement on Trade Related Investment Measures negotiated during the Uruguay Round.

Phillips Curve   Curve that posits a trade-off between inflation and unemployment: governments can reduce unemployment only by causing higher inflation and can reduce inflation only by causing higher unemployment. Named after British economist A.W. Phillips, who was the first to pose such a relationship in 1958. The trade-off between inflation and unemployment is now seen to hold only in the short run. (See accelerationist principle.)

Plaza Accord   A pact reached in September 1985 under which the Group of Five agreed to reduce the value of the dollar against the Japanese yen and the German mark by 10 to 12 percent. This agreement is the most recent episode of a concerted attempt by the Group of Five to manage exchange rates.

Price Stability   Now commonly considered by governments to be the appropriate objective for monetary policy, it connotes a low and stable rate of inflation—about 1–2 percent per year.

Prisoners' Dilemma   A game-theoretic model often used to depict the difficulties that governments face when trying to cooperate in the global economy. Emphasizes the incentives that governments have to "cheat" on any international agreements into which they enter and shows how those incentives make governments reluctant to enter into cooperative agreements.

Reciprocal Trade Agreements Act   American trade legislation passed in 1934 under which Congress allowed the executive to reduce tariffs by as much as 50 percent in exchange for equivalent concessions from foreign governments. Created the institutional framework for reciprocal tariff reductions achieved under GATT following World War II.

Reciprocity   The central principle upon which bargaining within the WTO is based. The concessions that each government makes to its partners in multilateral trade negotiations are roughly the same size as the concessions it gains from its trading partners.

Regional Development Banks   Created in the 1960s to provide concessional lending on the model of the International Development Association. They include the Inter-American Development Bank, the Asian Development Bank, and the African Development Bank.

Regional Trading Arrangements (RTAs)   Trade agreements in which tariffs discriminate between members and nonmembers. While inherently discriminatory, RTAs are recognized as a legitimate exception to this principle under GATT Article XXIV. Sometimes called preferential trade arrangements. (See also customs union and free trade area.)

Rent   A higher-than-normal return on an investment. Rents are created by barriers to entry, which can result from monopolistic or oligopolistic market structures or government policies.

Rent Seeking   Efforts by private actors to convince politicians to enact policies that create rents they can capture. (See rent.)

Sectoral Model   A political model which argues that the politics of trade policy is characterized by competition between import-competing and export-oriented industries. Each industry has a distinct trade policy preference because international trade has a differential effect on the industries' incomes. Industries that rely heavily on the economy's scarce factor will be harmed by trade and therefore lobby for protection. Industries that rely heavily on the economy's abundant factor will benefit from trade and therefore lobby for trade liberalization.

Service   An economic activity, such as financial services, transportation, consulting and accounting, and telecommunications, that does not involve manufacturing, farming, or the extraction of resources.

Shock Therapy   A strategy for making a transition from a command economy to a market economy in which most of the components of a market economy are introduced as quickly as possible. Under this strategy, it is believed that within a year or two governments will create a stable macroeconomic environment, liberalize domestic prices, eliminate subsidies to enterprises, open the country to trade, and remove restrictions on private enterprise.

Singer–Prebisch Theory   Developed during the 1950s by Raul Prebisch and Hans Singer, it claimed that, because developing countries faced a secular decline in their terms of trade, participation in the GATT-based multilateral trade system would hamper their industrialization. The theory provided an intellectual justification for import substitution industrialization.

Smoot–Hawley Act   Trade legislation passed by the U.S. Congress in 1930 that raised the average American tariff to a historic high of almost 60 percent. Widely regarded to have contributed to the collapse of the world trade and monetary systems and deepened the global depression during the 1930s.

Specific Factor   A factor of production (labor, capital, or land) that is tied to a particular industry or sector and that cannot be easily or quickly moved to another sector. Indicates a low level of factor mobility (see factor mobility).

Speculative Attack   A spate of very large sales of one country's currency by private financial institutions, sparked by the belief that the government is about to devalue the currency. The huge volume of currency sales in recent speculative attacks has led some officials to conclude that fixed-but-adjustable exchange rates are no longer a viable policy option. Instead, governments must choose between a permanently fixed exchange rate and a floating exchange rate.

Sterilized Intervention   Foreign exchange market intervention that is not allowed to have an impact on the country's money supply. If a government sells foreign exchange to buy its own currency, thereby reducing the money supply, it will then buy government securities, thereby expanding the money supply. If a government sells its own currency and buys foreign currencies, thereby expanding its money supply, it will then sell government securities and buy its own currency, thereby reducing the money supply.

Stolper–Samuleson Theorem   See factor price equalization.

Strategic Trade Theory   Expands on the infant-industry case for protection by asserting that government intervention can help domestic firms gain international competitiveness in high-technology industries by providing means whereby those firms can overcome the competitive advantages enjoyed by established firms. The theory also suggests that governments can use trade policy to compete for valued industries. (See infant-industry case for protection.)

Structural Adjustment   Policy reforms designed and promoted by the World Bank and IMF that seek to increase the role of the market and reduce the role of the state in developing countries' economies. First emerged in connection with the Baker plan, but have subsequently become a standard component of IMF conditionality agreements.

Structuralism   A body of development economics that dominated the field in the early postwar period. It held that the shift of resources from agriculture to manufacturing associated with industrialization would occur only if the state adopted policies explicitly designed to bring it about. Structuralism provided the intellectual and theoretical justification for a large role for the state in the development process and for import substitution industrialization.

Syndicated Loan   A loan in which hundreds of commercial banks each take a small share of a large loan made to a single borrower. This arrangement allows commercial banks to spread the risk involved in large loans among a number of banks, rather than requiring one bank to bear the full risk that the borrowing country will default.

Target Zone   An exchange-rate system in which all currencies have an official rate surrounded by very wide margins within which the rate is allowed to fluctuate. When a currency moves outside the margins, the government is obligated to intervene in the foreign exchange market or alter domestic interest rates in order to bring the currency back inside. Such a system was discussed in connection with the Plaza Accord, but was never implemented.

Tariff Escalation   The practice of imposing higher tariffs on goods involving more processing. This practice, common in the advanced industrialized countries, makes it difficult for developing countries to export processed food to the industrialized countries. This barrier in turn makes it difficult for developing countries to diversify their exports away from commodities while still capitalizing on their comparative advantage.

Tariff Peaks   Tariff rates above 15 percent. Such rates apply to about 5 percent of the advanced industrialized countries' imports from all developing countries and to about 10 percent of their imports from the least-developed countries.

Tariffs   Taxes that governments impose on foreign goods coming into the country. This tax raises the price of the foreign good in the domestic market of the country imposing the tariff. While tariffs distort international trade, they are the least distortionary of all trade barriers.

Terms of Trade   The ratio of the price of a country's exports to the price of its imports. An improvement in a country's terms of trade means that the price of the goods it exports is rising relative to the price of the goods it imports, while a decline in a country's terms of trade means that the price of the goods it exports is falling relative to the price of the goods it imports. An improvement in its terms of trade makes a country richer, whereas a decline in its terms of trade makes it poorer.

Tobin Tax   A small tax on foreign exchange market transactions that is high enough to discourage short-term capital flows, but not high enough to discourage long-term capital flows or international trade. By discouraging short-term capital flows, countries gain a degree of macroeconomic policy autonomy.

Trade Openness   A standard measure of the degree to which a particular country is integrated into the world trading system. Openness is typically measured by dividing a country's total trade (its imports plus its exports) by its gross domestic product.

Trade Related Investment Measure (TRIMs)   A government policy toward foreign direct investment or MNCs that has an impact on the country's imports or exports. For example, domestic content or trade-balancing requirements force firms to import fewer inputs or export more output than they would in the absence of such regulations. The result is a distortion of international trade. Such measures are regulated under the WTO.

Unholy Trinity   Highlights the trade-offs that governments face when making decisions about fixed exchange rates, monetary policy, and international capital flows. Governments have three policy goals, each of which is desirable in its own right: (1) maintaining a fixed exchange rate, (2) having the ability to use monetary policy to manage the domestic economy, which we refer to as monetary policy autonomy, and (3) allowing financial capital to flow freely into and out of the domestic financial system, or capital mobility for short. The unholy trinity states that any government can achieve only two of these three goals simultaneously.

United Nations Conference on Trade and Development (UNCTAD)   First established in March 1964 in response to developing countries' dissatisfaction with GATT, this is a permanent UN body dedicated to promoting the developing countries' interests in the world trade system.

United Nations Resolution on Permanent Sovereignty over Natural Resources   Adopted by the UN General Assembly in 1962, this document recognizes the right of host countries to exercise full control over their natural resources and over the foreign firms operating within their borders extracting those resources. The resolution affirmed the right of host country governments to expropriate foreign investments and to determine the appropriate compensation in the event of expropriation.

U.S. Trade Representative   Established as the Special Trade Representative by Congress in the 1962 Trade Expansion Act and given its current name by Congress during the 1970s, this office sets and administers U.S. trade policy, is the nation's chief trade negotiator, and represents the United States in the WTO and other international trade organizations.

Vertical Integration   A form of industrial organization in which a single firm controls the different stages of the production process, rather than relying on the market to acquire inputs and sell outputs. A single corporation, for example, might own oil wells, the associated oil pipeline, the oil refinery, and a chain of gas stations. Difficulties inherent in long-term contracting create incentives for vertical integration.

Voluntary Export Restraints   A form of protectionism under which one country (or a number of countries) agrees to limit its exports to another country's market. Adopted by governments in order to circumvent GATT restrictions on the use of other types of protectionism, such as tariffs and quotas.

Washington Consensus, The   The collection of policy reforms advocated by U.S. officials and by the IMF and World Bank staffs as the solution to the economic problems faced by developing countries. The emphasis is on stabilization, structural adjustment, privatization, and market liberalization.

World Bank   See International Bank for Reconstruction and Development.

World Trade Organization   The principal international trade organization today that began operation in 1995. Located in Geneva, Switzerland, the WTO is a relatively small organization whose role includes administering trade agreements, providing a forum for trade negotiations, helping governments settle trade disputes, and reviewing national trade policies.

References

Aaronson, Susan A. 2001. *Taking Trade to the Streets: The Lost History of Public Efforts to Shape Globalization.* Ann Arbor: University of Michigan Press.

Abaroa, Patricia. 2004. "The International Investment Position of the United States at Yearend 2003," *Survey of Current Business* (July): 30–38. http://www.bea.doc.gov/bea/ARTICLES/2004/07July/0704_IIP.pdf (accessed January 12, 2005).

Aeppel, Timothy. 2003. "Dollar's Decline Is Mixed Blessing for Goods Makers," *Wall Street Journal* (December 19): A2.

AFL-CIO. 2001. "Global Fairness and the Free Trade Area of the Americas (FTAA)," http://www.aflcio.org/publ/estatements/feb2001/ftaa.htm.

Ake, Claude. 1981. *A Political Economy of Africa.* London: Longman.

Ake, Claude. 1996. *Democracy and Development in Africa.* Washington, DC: Brookings Institution.

Akehurst, Michael B. 1984. *A Modern Introduction to International Law,* 5th ed. Boston: Allen & Unwin.

Alesina, Alberto, and Alan Drazen. 1991. "Why are Stabilizations Delayed?" *The American Economic Review* 81 (December): 1170–88.

American Textile Manufacturers Institute. 2001. "Statement of the American Textile Manufacturers Institute to the Committee on Ways and Means, U.S. House of Representatives on President Bush's Trade Agenda" (March), http://www.atmi.org/NewsRoom/test030701.pdf.

Amsden, Alice H. 1979. "Taiwan's Economic History: A Case of *Etatisme* and a Challenge to Dependency Theory," *Modern China* 5 (July): 341–80.

Amsden, Alice H. 1989. *Asia's Next Giant: South Korea and Late Industrialization.* Oxford: Oxford University Press.

Amsden, Alice H., Jacek Kochanowicz, and Lance Taylor. 1994. *The Market Meets Its Match: Restructuring the Economies of Eastern Europe.* Cambridge: Harvard University Press.

Anderson, Kym. 1998. "Environmental and Labor Standards: What Role for the WTO?" in *The WTO as an International Organization,* edited by Anne O. Krueger. Chicago: The University of Chicago Press, 231–55.

Ariyoshi, Akira, Karl Habermeier, Bernard Laurens, Incitker-Robe, Jorge Iván Canales-Kriljenko, and Andrei Kirilenko. 2000. *Capital Controls: Country Experiences with Their Use and Liberalization.* Occasional Paper 190. Washington, DC: The International Monetary Fund.

Arnold, Martin, and George Parker. 2004. "French Minister Attacks ECB on Inflation," *The Financial Times* (June 10): 9.

Arulpragasam, Jehan, and David E. Sahn. 1994. "Policy Failure and the Limits of Rapid Reform: Lessons from Guinea," in *Adjusting to Policy Failure in African Economies,* edited by David E. Sahn. Ithaca: Cornell University Press, 53–95.

Asante, Samuel K.B. 1980. "United Nations Efforts at International Regulation of Transnational Corporations," in *Legal Aspects of the New International Economic Order,* edited by Kamal Hossain. London: Frances Pinter.

Åslund, Anders. 2002. *Building Capitalism: The Transformation of the Former Soviet Bloc.* Cambridge: Cambridge University Press.

Axelrod, Robert. 1984. *The Evolution of Cooperation.* New York: Basic Books.

Bael, Ivo van, and Jean Francois Bellis. 1990. *Anti-Dumpting and Other Trade Protection Laws of the EEC,* 2nd ed. Bicester: CCH Editions.

Bailey, Michael, Judith Goldstein, and Barry Weingast. 1997. "The Institutional Roots of American Trade Policy: Politics, Coalitions, and International Trade," *World Politics* 49 (April): 309–38.

Balassa, Bela and Associates. 1971. *The Structure of Protection in Developing Countries.* Baltimore: Johns Hopkins University Press.

Balcerowicz, Leszek. 1995. *Socialism, Capitalism, Transformation.* Budapest: Central European University Press.

Baldwin, Richard E. 1995. "A Domino Theory of Regionalism," in *Expanding Membership in the European Union,* edited by Richard E. Baldwin, Pentti Haaparanta, and Jaako Jiander. Cambridge: Cambridge University Press.

Baldwin, Robert. 1969. "The Case against Infant-Industry Protection," *The Journal of Political Economy* 77 (May–June): 295–305.

Baldwin, Robert E., and Christopher S. Magee. 2000. *Congressional Trade Votes: From NAFTA Approval to Fast-Track Defeat.* Washington, DC: Institute for International Economics.

Bank for International Settlements. 2005. *Triennial Central Bank Survey: Foreign Exchange and Derivatives Market Activity in 2004.* Basle: Bank for International Settlements.

Bank of Japan. 2000. "The Bank of Japan Law, preliminary translation by the Bank of Japan," http://www.boj.or.jp/en/about/bojlaw1.htm.

Barber, Tony. 2000. "Germans at Odds Over the Euro," *The Financial Times* (September 6): 8.

Barber, Tony. 2000. "Rift Emerges Over ECB's Euro Policy," *The Financial Times* (September 5): 9.

Barnett, Craig. 2004. "The Next Economy," *Foreign Policy* (September/October): 76–77.

Bates, Robert. 1997. *Open-Economy Politics: The Political Economy of the World Coffee Trade.* Princeton: Princeton University Press.

Bates, Robert. 1988. "Governments and Agricultural Markets in Africa," in *Toward a Political Economy of Development: A Rational Choice Perspective,* edited by Robert H. Bates. Berkeley: University of California Press.

Bates, Robert. 2001. *Prosperity and Violence: The Political Economy of Development.* New York: W.W. Norton and Company.

Bean, Charles. 1994. "European Unemployment: A Survey," *Journal of Economic Literature* 32 (June): 573–619.

Becker, Elizabeth. 2004. "U.S. and Europe Fail to Resolve Dispute on Aircraft Subsidies," *The New York Times* (October 1), C.5.

Berend, Ivan T. 1996. *Central and Eastern Europe, 1944–1993: Detour from the Periphery to the Periphery.* Cambridge: Cambridge University Press.

Berg, Andrew, Eduardo R. Borensztein, Ratna Sahay, and Jeromin Zettelmeyer. 1999. "The Evolution of Output in Transition Economies: Explaining the Differences," *IMF Working Paper No. 99/73.*

Bergsman, Joel, and Arthur Candal. 1969. "Industrialization: Past Success and Future Problems," in *The Economy of Brazil,* edited by Howard S. Ellis. Berkeley: University of California Press.

Bergsten, C. Fred, Thomas Horst, and Theodore H. Moran. 1978. *American Multinationals and American Interests.* Washington, DC: The Brookings Institution.

Bernanke, Ben S., Thomas Laubach, Frederic S. Mishkin, and Adam S. Posen. 1999. *Inflation Targeting: Lessons from the International Experience.* Princeton: Princeton University Press.

Bhagwati, Jagdish, and Hugh T. Patrick. 1990. *Aggressive Unilateralism: America's 301 Trade Policy and the World Trading System.* Ann Arbor: University of Michigan Press.

Bhagwati, Jagdish. 1978. *Anatomy and Consequences of Exchange Control Regimes.* Cambridge: Ballinger Publishing Company.

Bhagwati, Jagdish. 1982. "Directly Unproductive, Profit-Seeking (DUP) Activities," *Journal of Political Economy* 90 (October): 988–1002.

Bhagwati, Jagdish. 1988. *Protectionism.* Cambridge: MIT Press.

Bhagwati, Jagdish. 1998a. *A Stream of Windows: Unsettling Reflections on Trade, Immigration, and Democracy.* Cambridge: MIT Press.

Bhagwati, Jagdish. 1998b. The Capital Myth," *Foreign Affairs* 77 (May/June): 7–12.

Bhagwati, Jagdish. 2004. "Don't Cry for Cancún," *Foreign Affairs* 83 (Jan/Feb): 52–63.

Bhagwati, Jagdish. 2004. *In Defense of Globalization.* New York: Oxford University Press.

Bhalla, Surjit. 2002. *Imagine There's No Country: Poverty, Inequality, and Growth in the Age of Globalization.* Washington, DC: Institute for International Economics.

Bhattacharya, Debapriya. 1998. *Export Processing Zones in Bangladesh: Economic Impact and Social Issues.* Geneva: International Labor Office, Working Paper No. 80.

Binswanger, Hans P., and Klaus Deininger. 1997. "Explaining Agricultural and Agrarian Policies in Developing Countries," *Journal of Economic Literature* XXXV (December): 1958–2005.

Bird, Graham. 1987. *International Financial Policy and Economic Development.* London: MacMillan.

Birdsall, Nancy, and John Williamson. 2002. *Delivering on Debt Relief: From IMF Gold to a New Aid Architecture.* Washington, DC: Institute for International Economics.

Black, Robert, Stephen Blank, and Elizabeth C. Harrison. 1978. *Multinationals in Contention: Responses at Governmental and International Levels.* New York: The Conference Board.

Blanchard, Oliver. 1997. "The Medium Run," *Brookings Papers on Economic Activity* 2: 89–158.

Blanchard, Oliver, and Lawrence F. Katz. 1997. "What We Know and Do Not Know About the Natural Rate of Unemployment," *Journal of Economic Perspectives* 11 (Winter): 51–72.

Blinder, Alan S. 1999. *Central Banking in Theory and Practice.* Cambridge: MIT Press.

Bloch, Harry, and David Sapsford. 2000. "Whither the Terms of Trade? An Elaboration of the Prebisch-Singer Hypothesis," *Cambridge Journal of Economics* 24 (July): 461–481.

Block, Fred. 1977. *The Origins of International Economic Disorder: A Study of United States International Monetary Policy from World War II to the Present.* Berkeley: University of California Press.

Blustein, Paul. 2001. *The Chastening: Inside the Crisis That Rocked the Global Financial System and Humbled the IMF.* New York: Public Affairs.

Blustein, Paul. 2004a. "Debt Relief Plan Eludes IMF Group," *The Washington Post* (October 3): A28.

Blustein, Paul. 2004b. U.S. Files Grievance Over Airbus with WTO; E.U. Responds With Boeing Complaint," *The Washington Post* (October 7), E.01.

Blustein, Paul. 2004c. "U.S. Wants to Cancel Poorest Nations' Debt," *The Washington Post* (September 14). A0.

Boltuck, Richard, and Robert Litan. 1991. "America's Unfair Trade Laws," in *Down in the Dumps,* Boltuck and Litan, eds. Washington, DC: The Brookings Institution.

Borensztein, Eduardo, Mohsin S. Khan, Carmen Reinhart, and Peter Wickham. 1994. *The Behavior of Non-Oil Commodity Prices.* IMF Occasional Paper 112. Washington, DC: The International Monetary Fund.

Bosworth, Barry, and Susan M. Collins. 1999. "Capital Flows to Developing Economies: Implications for Saving and Investment," *Brookings Papers on Economic Activity* 1: 143–69.

Bottari, Mary. 2001. "NAFTA's Investor "Rights": A Corporate Dream, A Citizen Nightmare," *Multinational Monitor* 22 (April). http://www.essential.org/monitor/mm2001/01april/corp1.html.

Bourguignon, Francois, and Christian Morrisson. 2002. "Inequality Among World Citizens: 1820–1992," *American Economic Review* 82 (September): 727–744.

Brau, Edward H. 1986. "The Demand for External Finance," in *African Debt and Financing*, edited by Carol Lancaster and John Williamson. Washington, DC: Institute for International Economics.

Broad, Robin. 2002. *Global Backlash: Citizen Initiatives for a Just World Economy*. New York: Rowman and Littlefield, Inc.

Broadman, Harry G. 2004. "Global Economic Integration: Prospects for WTO Accession and Continued Economic Reforms," *Washington Quarterly* 27 (Spring): 79–98.

Bronfenbrenner, Kate. 1997. "We'll Close! Plant Closings, Plant-Closing Threats, Union Organizing and NAFTA," *Multinational Monitor* 3 (March): 8–13.

Brown, Archie, Michael Kaser, and Gerald S. Smith, eds. 1994. *The Cambridge Encyclopedia of Russia and the Former Soviet Union*, 2nd ed. Cambridge: Cambridge University Press.

Brown, Drusilla, Alan Deardorff, and Robert Stern. 2003. "The Effects of Multinational Production on Wages and Working Conditions in Developing Countries," *NBER Working Paper 9669*. Cambridge: National Bureau of Economic Research.

Brown, William A. 1950. *The United States and the Restoration of World Trade: An Analysis and Appraisal of the ITO Charter and the General Agreement on Tariffs and Trade*. Washington, DC: The Brookings Institution.

Bruton, Henry J. 1969. "The Two Gap Approach to Aid and Development: Comment," *American Economic Review* 59 (June): 439–46.

Bryant, Ralph. 1987. *International Financial Intermediation*. Washington, DC: The Brookings Institution.

Bulmer-Thomas, Victor. 1994. *The Economic History of Latin America since Independence*. Cambridge: Cambridge University Press.

Burritt, Chris. 1994. "N.C. Town That Lost Out on Mercedes Plant Lands Battery Factory," *The Atlanta Journal Constitution* (October 26): Section G, p.8.

The Business Roundtable. 1996. *Trade and Investment Reference Manual*. http://www.brtable.org/pdf/39.pdf.

Butler, Michael A. 1998. *Cautious Visionary: Cordell Hull and Trade Reform, 1933–1937*. Kent: The Kent State University Press.

Calomiris, Charles W. 1998. "The IMF's Imprudent Role as Lender of Last Resort," *The CATO Journal* 17 (Winter): 275–294.

Campos, R. G. de Oliveira, J. Haberler, J. Meade, and J. Tinbergen. 1958. *Trends in International Trade*. Geneva: GATT.

Cardoso, Fernando, and Enzo Faletto. 1979. *Dependency and Development in Latin America*. Los Angeles: University of California Press.

Casert, Raf. 2004. "Little Progress in Aircraft Talks; U.S., E.U. Butt Heads over Boeing and Airbus Subsidies," *The Washington Post* (September 17), E.03.

Caves, Richard E. 1996. *Multinational Enterprise and Economic Analysis*. Cambridge: Cambridge University Press.

Chen, Shaohua, and Martin Ravallion. 2001. "How Did the World's Poor Fare in the 1990s?" *Review of Income and Wealth* 47 (September): 283–300.

Chenery, Hollis. 1975. "The Structuralist Approach to Development Policy," *American Economic Review* 65 (May): 310–16.

Cline, William R. 1984. *International Debt: Systemic Risk and Policy Response*. Washington, DC: The Institute for International Economics.

Cline, William R. 1995. *International Debt Reexamined*. Washington, DC: Institute for International Economics.

Coalition Report to the World Trade Organization. 1999. "Technical Statement by United States Environmental Organizations," http://www.sierraclub.org/trade/summit/report.asp.

Cohen, Benjamin J. 1996. "Phoenix Risen: The Resurrection of Global Finance," *World Politics* 48 (January): 568–96.

Connor, Timothy. 2002. "We Are Not Machines: Indonesian Nike and Adidas Workers," http://www.maquilasolidarity.org/campaigns/nike/pdf/Wearenotmachines.pdf.

Conybeare, John. 1984. "Public Goods, Prisoners' Dilemmas and the International Political Economy," *International Studies Quarterly* 28: 5–22.

Corbo, Vittorio. 2000. "Economic Policy Reform in Latin America," in *Economic Policy Reform: The Second Stage,* edited by Anne O. Krueger. Chicago: University of Chicago Press.

Cordoba, Jose. 1994. "Mexico," in *The Political Economy of Policy Reform,* edited by John Williamson. Washington, DC: Institute for International Economics.

Cornelius, Wayne A., Ann L. Craig, and Jonathan Fox. 1994. *Transforming State-Society Relations in Mexico: The National Solidarity Strategy.* San Diego: Center for U.S.-Mexican Studies, University of California, San Diego.

Croome, John. 1995. *Reshaping the World Trading System: A History of the Uruguay Round.* Geneva: World Trade Organization.

Cukierman, Alex. 1992. *Central Bank Strategy, Credibility, and Independence: Theory and Evidence.* Cambridge: MIT Press.

Cypher, James M., and James L. Dietz. 1997. *The Process of Economic Development.* London: Routledge.

Dale, Reginald. 2001. "Emerging World Comes of Age at Doha," *International Herald Tribune* (November 30): 11.

Dam, Kenneth W. 1982. *The Rules of the Game: Reform and Evolution in the International Monetary System.* Chicago: University of Chicago Press.

Dam, Kenneth. 1970. *The GATT: Law and International Organization.* Chicago: University of Chicago Press.

Damian, Araceli. 2000. *Adjustment, Poverty, and Employment in Mexico.* London: Ashgate.

De Jonquieres, Guy. 2001. "All Night Haggling in Doha Ends in Agreement," *Financial Times* (November 15): 11.

De Rivero, Oswaldo. 1980. *New Economic Order and International Development Law.* Oxford: Pergamon Press.

De Vries, Margaret G., and J. Keith Horsefield. 1969. *The International Monetary Fund 1945–1969, Volume II: Analysis.* Washington, DC: The International Monetary Fund.

Deaton, Angus. 1999. "Commodity Prices and Growth in Africa," *Journal of Economic Perspectives* 13 (Summer): 23–40.

Deaton, Angus. 2002. "Is World Poverty Falling?" Finance and Development 39 (June): http://www.imf.org/external/pubs/ft/fandd/2002/06/deaton.htm.

Department of Labor. 2000. "Wages, Benefits, Poverty Line, and Meeting Workers' Needs in the Apparel and Footwear Industries of Selected Countries," *Bureau of International Labor Affairs.* http://www.dol.gov/dol/ilab/public/media/reports/oiea/wagestudy/main.htm.

Destler, I.M. 1986. *American Trade Politics: System Under Stress.* Washington, DC: Institute for International Economics.

Destler, I.M. 1995. *American Trade Politics,* 3rd ed. Washington, DC: Institute for International Economics.

Destler, I.M., and John Odell. 1987. *Anti-Protection: Changing Forces in United States Trade Politics.* Washington, DC: Institute for International Economics.

Destler, I.M., and C. Randall Henning. 1989. *Dollar Politics: Exchange Rate Policymaking in the United States.* Washington, DC: Institute for International Economics.

Destler, I.M., and Peter J. Balint. 1998. *The New Politics of American Trade: Trade, Labor, and the Environment.* Washington, DC: Institute for International Economics.

Devlin, Robert. 1989. *Debt and Crisis in Latin America: The Supply Side of the Story.* Princeton: Princeton University Press.

Dicken, Peter. 1998. *Global Shift: Transforming the World Economy,* 3rd ed. New York: Guilford Press.

Diebold, William Jr. 1952a. *The End of the ITO.* Princeton: Princeton Essays in International Finance, no. 16.

Dollar, David. 2004. "Globalization, Poverty, and Inequality," World Bank Research Working Paper 3333 (June): http://econ.worldbank.org/files/39000_wps3333.pdf (February 4, 2005).

Dollar, David, and Jakob Svensson. 1998. *What Explains the Success or Failure of Structural Adjustment Programs?* World Bank Policy Research Working Paper 1938. Washington, DC: The World Bank.

Dollar, David, and Aart Kraay. 2001. "Growth is Good for the Poor," *Development Research Group, The World Bank.* http://www.worldbank.org/research/growth/pdfiles/growthgood forpoor.pdf.

Dollar, David, and Aart Kraay. 2004. "Trade, Growth, and Poverty," *The Economic Journal* 114 (February): F22–F49.

Dollar, David, and Aart Kraay. 2002. "Spreading the Wealth," *Foreign Affairs* 91 (January/February): 120–133.

Doner, Richard, and Gary Hawes. 1995. "The Political Economy of Growth in Southeast and Northeast Asia," in *The Changing Political Economy of the Third World,* edited by Manochehr Dorraj. London: Lynne Rienner, 145–85.

Drazen, Allan. 2000. *Political Economy in Macroeconomics.* Princeton: Princeton University Press.

Drezner, Daniel. 2000. "Bottom Feeders," *Foreign Policy* 121 (November/December): 64–70.

Drucker, Peter. 1986. "The Changed World Economy," *Foreign Affairs* 64 (Spring): 768–791.

Dunning, John H. 1996. "Re-evaluating the Benefits of Foreign Direct Investment," in *Companies without Borders: Transnational Corporations in the 1990s,* edited by UNCTAD. London: International Thomson Business Press, 73–101.

Easterly, William. 2002. *The Elusive Quest for Growth: Economists' Adventures and Misadventures in the Tropics.* Cambridge: MIT Press.

Easterly, William, Norman Loayza, and Peter Montiel. 1997. "Has Latin American Post-Reform Growth Been Disappointing?" *Journal of International Economics* 43 (November): 287–311.

Economic Commission for Latin American and the Caribbean. 1985. *External Debt in Latin America: Adjustment Policies and Renegotiation.* Boulder: Lynne Rienner Publishers, Inc.

The Economist. 2002. "Out of Puff: A Survey of China," *The Economist* (June 15).

Edwards, Sebastian. 1999. "How Effective Are Capital Controls?" *Journal of Economic Perspectives* 13 (Fall): 65–84.

Edwards, Sebastian, ed. 1989. *Debt, Adjustment, and Recovery: Latin America's Prospects for Growth and Development.* New York: Basil Blackwell.

Edwards, Sebastian. 1995. *Crisis and Reform in Latin America: From Despair to Hope.* Oxford: Oxford University Press.

Eichengreen, Barry J. 1989a. "Hegemonic Stability Theories of the International Monetary System," in *Can Nations Agree? Issues in International Economic Cooperation,* edited by Richard N. Cooper, Barry Eichengreen, C. Randall Henning, Gerald Holtham, and Robert Putnam. Washington, DC: The Brookings Institution.

Eichengreen, Barry J. 1989b. "The Political Economy of the Smoot-Hawley Tariff," *Research in Economic History* Volume 13: 1–43.

Eichengreen, Barry J. 1994. *Golden Fetters.* Oxford: Oxford University Press.

Eichengreen, Barry J. 1996. *Globalizing Capital: A History of the International Monetary System.* Princeton: Princeton University Press.

Eichengreen, Barry J. 1999. *Toward A New International Financial Architecture: A Practical Post-Asia Agenda.* Washington, DC: Institute for International Economics.

Eichengreen, Barry J. 2001. "Crisis Prevention and Crisis Management: Any Lessons from Argentina and Turkey?" Background paper for the World Bank's Global Development Finance 2002. available at http://emlab.berkeley.edu/users/eichengr/policy/crisis101901 .pdf, accessed January 31, 2005.

Eichengreen, Barry J., and Albert Fishlow. 1998. "Contending with Capital Flows: What Is Different about the 1990s?" in *Capital Flows and Financial Crises,* edited by Miles Kahler. Ithaca: Cornell University Press.

Eichengreen, Barry J., and Charles Wyplosz. 1993. "The Unstable EMS," *Brookings Papers on Economic Activity* 1: 51–143.

Eijffinger, Sylvester, and Eric Schaling. 1993. "Central Bank Independence in Twelve Industrial Countries," *BNL Quarterly Review* 184 (March) 49–89.

Elliott, Kimberly Ann, and Richard Freeman. 2003. *Can Labor Standards Improve Under Globalization?* Washington DC: Institute for International Economics.

Ellman, Michael. 1989. *Socialist Planning.* Cambridge: Cambridge University Press.

Emerson, Michael. 1992. *One Market, One Money: An Evaluation of the Potential Benefits and Costs of Forming an Economic and Monetary Union.* Oxford: Oxford University Press.

Emminger, Otmar. 1977. *The D-Mark in the Conflict Between Internal and External Equilibrium, 1948–1975.* Princeton: Essays in International Finance.

Encarnation, Dennis J. 1989. *Dislodging Multinationals: India's Strategy in Comparative Perspective.* Ithaca: Cornell University Press.

Esty, Daniel C. 1994. *Greening the GATT: Trade, Environment, and the Future.* Washington, DC: Institute for International Economics.

Esty, Daniel. 2001. "Bridging the Trade-Environment Divide," *Journal of Economic Perspectives* 15 (Summer): 113–130.

European Bank for Reconstruction and Development. 1999. *Transition Report.* London: European Bank for Reconstruction and Development.

Faith, Nicholas. 1993. "Nothing Finer than a Plant in Carolina," *The Independent* (May 9): 14.

Federal Reserve Bank of New York. 2003. "U.S. Foreign Exchange Intervention," (October) http://www.ny.frb.org/about/fedpoint/fed44.html (accessed September 18, 2004).

Feldstein, Martin, and Charles Horioka. 1980. "Domestic Savings and International Capital Mobility," *Economic Journal* 90: 314–29.

Federal Reserve Board of San Francisco. 2002. "Learning from Argentina's Crisis," FRBSF Economic Letter Number 2002–31 (October 18). http://www.frbsf.org/publications/economics/letter/2002/el2002-31.pdf, accessed January 31, 2005.

Ferguson, Thomas. 1984. "From Normalcy to New Deal: Industrial Structure, Party Competition, and American Public Policy in the Great Depression," *International Organization* 38 (Winter). 41–94.

Finger, J. Michael. 1991. "Development Economics and the General Agreement on Tariffs and Trade," in *Trade Theory and Economic Reform: North, South, and East. Essays in Honor of Bela Balassa,* edited by Jaime de Melo and Andre Sapir. Oxford: Basil Blackwell, 203–23.

Finlayson, Jock A., and Mark Zacher. 1981. "The GATT and the Regulation of Trade Barriers: Regime Dynamics and Functions," *International Organization* 35 (Autumn): 561–602.

Firebaugh, Glenn. 2003. *The New Geography of Global Income Inequality.* Cambridge: Harvard University Press.

Fischer, Stanley. 2001. "Exchange Rate Regimes: Is the Bipolar View Correct?" *Journal of Economic Perspectives* (Spring).

Fish, M. Steven. 1998. "The Determinants of Economic Reform in the Post-Communist World," *East European Politics and Society* 12 (Winter): 31–78.

Flood and Garber. 1984. "Collapsing Exchange Rate Regimes: Some Linear Examples," *Journal of International Economics* 17: 1–13.

Frankel, Jeffrey A. 1990. "The Making of Exchange Rate Policy in the 1980s," *NBER Working Paper* #3539 (December).

Frankel, Jeffrey A. 1991. "Quantifying International Capital Mobility in the 1980s," in *National Saving and Economic Performance*, edited by Douglas Bernheim and John Sohover. Chicago: University of Chicago Press.

Frankel, Jeffrey A. 1997. *Regional Trading Blocs in the World Economic System*. Washington, DC: Institute for International Economics.

Frankel, Jeffrey A., and Andrew K. Rose. 2002. *Is Trade Good Or Bad For the Environment? Sorting Out the Causality*, NBER Working Paper 9201. Cambridge: National Bureau of Economic Research.

Frieden, Jeffry A. 1981. "Third World Indebted Industrialization: International Finance and State Capitalism in Mexico, Brazil, Algeria, and South Korea," *International Organization* 35 (Summer): 407–431.

Frieden, Jeffry A. 1988. "Sectoral Conflict and Foreign Economic Policy, 1914–1940," *International Organization* 42 (Winter): 59–90.

Frieden, Jeffry A. 1991. "Invested Interests: The Politics of National Economic Policies in a World of Global Finance," *International Organization* 45 (Autumn): 425–51.

Frieden, Jeffry A. 1991. *Debt, Development, and Democracy: Modern Political Economy and Latin America*. Princeton: Princeton University Press.

Frieden, Jeffry A. 1997a. "Monetary Populism in Nineteenth Century America: An Open-Economy Interpretation," *The Journal of Economic History* 57 (June): 367–95.

Frieden, Jeffry A. 1997b. "The Politics of Exchange Rates," in *Mexico 1994: Anatomy of an Emerging Market Crash*, edited by Sebastian Edwards and Moises Naim. Washington, DC: Carnegie Endowment for International Peace.

Frieden, Jeffry A. 1996. "The Impact of Goods and Capital Market Integration on European Monetary Politics," *Comparative Political Studies* 29 (April): 193–222.

Friedman, Milton. 1953. "The Case for Flexible Exchange Rates," *Essays in Positive Economics*. Chicago: University of Chicago Press.

Friedman, Milton. 1968. "The Role of Monetary Policy," *American Economic Review* 58 (March): 1–17.

Friman, H. Richard. 1988. "Rocks, Hard Places, and the New Protectionism: Textile Trade Policy Choices in the United States and Japan," *International Organization* 42 (Autumn): 689–723.

Fry, Maxwell. 1988. *Money, Interest, and Banking in Economic Development*. Baltimore: Johns Hopkins University Press.

Fu, Jun. 2000. *Institutions and Investments: Foreign Direct Investment in China during an Era of Reforms*. Ann Arbor: University of Michigan Press.

Funabashi, Yoichi. 1988. *Managing the Dollar: From the Plaza to the Louvre*. Washington, DC: Institute for International Economics.

Gable, Medard, and Henry Bruner. 2003. *Global Inc.: An Atlas of the Multinational Corporation*. New York: The New Press.

Galbraith, James K. 1997. "Time to Ditch the NAIRU," *Journal of Economic Perspectives* 11 (Winter): 93–108.

Garber, Peter M. 1993. "The Collapse of the Bretton Woods Fixed Exchange Rate System," in *A Retrospective on the Bretton Woods System: Lessons for International Monetary Reform*, edited by Michael D. Bordo and Barry Eichengreen. Chicago: University of Chicago Press.

Gardner, Richard N. 1969. *Sterling-Dollar Diplomacy: The Origins and the Prospects of Our International Economic Order*, new, expanded ed. New York: McGraw Hill Co.

Garnaut, Ross, and Yiping Huang, eds. 2001. *Growth Without Miracles: Readings on the Chinese Economy in the Era of Reform.* Oxford: Oxford University Press.

Garrett, Geoffrey. 1998. *Partisan Politics in the Global Economy.* Cambridge: Cambridge University Press.

Gaster, Robin. 1992. "Protectionism with Purpose: Guiding Foreign Investment," *Foreign Policy* 88 (Fall): 91–106.

Gereffi, Gary. 1990. "Paths of Industrialization: An Overview," in *Manufacturing Miracles: Paths of Industrialization in Latin America and East Asia,* edited by Gary Gereffi and Donald L. Wyman. Princeton: Princeton University Press.

Giavazzi, Francesco, and Alberto Giovannini. 1989. *Limiting Exchange Rate Flexibility in Europe.* Cambridge: MIT Press.

Gilligan, Michael. 1997. *Empowering Exporters: Reciprocity, Delegation, and Collective Action in American Trade Policy.* Ann Arbor: University of Michigan Press.

Gilpin, Robert. 1987. *The Political Economy of International Relations.* Princeton: Princeton University Press.

Gilpin, Robert. 2000. *The Challenge of Global Capitalism: The World Economy in the 21st Century.* Princeton: Princeton University Press.

Glewwe, Paul. 2000. "Are Foreign-Owned Businesses in Viet Nam Really Sweatshops?" in *University of Minnesota Extension Service Newsletter,* No. 701 (Summer). http://agecon .lib.umn.edu/mn/mae701.pdf.

Goldman, Marshall. 1991. *What Went Wrong with Perestroika.* New York: W.W. Norton & Co.

Goldstein, Judith. 1986. "The Political Economy of Trade: Institutions of Protection," *American Political Science Review* 80 (March): 161–84.

Goldstein, Morris. 2003. "IMF Structural Programs," in *Economic and Financial Crises in Emerging Market Economies,* edited by Martin Feldstein. Chicago: University of Chicago Press.

Goodman, John B., and Louis Pauly. 1993. "The Obsolescence of Capital Controls? Economic Management in an Age of Global Markets," *World Politics* 46 (October): 50–82.

Goodman, John B. 1992. *Monetary Sovereignty: The Politics of Central Banking in Western Europe.* Ithaca: Cornell University Press.

Gordon, Robert. 1997. "The Time-Varying NAIRU and its Implications for Economic Policy," *Journal of Economic Perspectives* 11 (Winter): 11–32.

Gowa, Joanne. 1983. *Closing the Gold Window: Domestic Politics and the End of Bretton Woods.* Ithaca: Cornell University Press.

Gowa, Joanne. 1988. "Public Goods and Political Institutions: Trade and Monetary Policy Processes in the United States," *International Organization* (Winter): 15–32.

Graham, Edward M. 1996. *Global Corporations and National Governments.* Washington, DC: Institute for International Economics.

Graham, Edward M. 2000. *Fighting the Wrong Enemy: Antiglobal Activities and Multinational Enterprises.* Washington, DC: Institute for International Economics.

Gray, Robin. 1985. "How Does the E.C. Set Trade Policy?" *Europe: Magazine of the European Community* 251 (September/October), 24–5.

Greenaway, David. 1983. *Trade Policy and the New Protectionism.* New York: St. Martin's Press.

Grimwade, Nigel. 2000. *International Trade: New Patterns of Trade, Production, and Investment.* London: Routledge.

Grindle, Merilee S. 1991. "The New Political Economy: Positive Economics and Negative Politics," in *Politics and Policy Making in Developing Countries: Perspectives on the New Political Economy,* edited by Gerald M. Meier. San Francisco: ICS Press, 41–67.

Gros, Daniel, and Niels Thygesen. 1998. *European Monetary Integration,* 2nd ed. New York: Longman.

Grosh, Barbara. 1994. "Through the Structural Adjustment Minefield: Politics in an Era of Economic Liberalization," in *Economic Change and Political Liberalization in Sub-Saharan Africa,* edited by Jennifer Widener. Baltimore: Johns Hopkins Press, 29–43.

Grossman, Gene, and Alan Krueger. 1995. "Economic Growth and the Environment," *Quarterly Journal of Economics* 110 (May): 353–377.

Grub, Phillip Donald, and Jian Hai Lin. 1991. *Foreign Direct Investment in China.* Westport: Quorum Books.

Gruber, Lloyd. 2000. *Ruling the World.* Princeton: Princeton University Press.

Haggard, Stephan. 1990. *Pathways from the Periphery: The Politics of Growth in the Newly Industrializing Countries.* Ithaca: Cornell University Press.

Haggard, Stephan. 2000. *The Political Economy of the Asian Financial Crisis.* Washington, DC: Institute for International Economics.

Haggard, Stephan, and Tun-jen Cheng. 1987. "State and Foreign Capital in the East Asian NICs," in *The Political Economy of the New Asian Industrialism,* edited by Frederic C. Deyo. Ithaca: Cornell University Press.

Haggard, Stephan, and Robert Kaufman, eds. 1992. *The Politics of Economic Adjustment: International Constraints, Distributive Conflicts, and the State.* Princeton: Princeton University Press.

Hall, Peter A. 1986. *Governing the Economy: The Politics of State Intervention in Britain and France.* Oxford: Oxford University Press.

Hall, Peter A. 1989. *The Political Power of Economic Ideas.* Princeton: Princeton University Press.

Hansen, Wendy. 1990. "The International Trade Commission and the Politics of Protectionism," *American Political Science Review* 84 (March): 21–46.

Harrison, Barbara. 1992. "Survey of Locating in North America," *Financial Times* (October 20): 38.

Harrison, Christopher S. 2004. *The Politics of International Pricing of Prescription Drugs.* Westport: Praeger.

Hart, Jeffrey. 1992. *Rival Capitalists: International Competitiveness in the United States, Japan, and Western Europe.* Ithaca: Cornell University Press.

Havrylyshyn, Oleh. 2001. "Recovery and Growth in Transition: A Decade of Evidence," *IMF Staff Papers* 48 (Special Issue): 53–87.

Havrylyshyn, Oleh, and John Odling-Smee. 2000. "The Political Economy of Stalled Reforms," *Finance and Development* 37 (September).

Hayes, John P. 1993. *Making Trade Policy in the European Community.* London: The MacMillan Press.

Heckscher, Eli. 1935. *Mercantilism.* London: Allen & Unwin.

Helleiner, Eric. 1994. *States and the Re-emergence of Global Finance: From Bretton Woods to the 1990s.* Ithaca: Cornell University Press.

Hellman, Joel S. 1998. "Winners Take All: The Politics of Partial Reform in Postcommunist Transitions," *World Politics* 50 (February): 203–34.

Henning, C. Randall. 1994. *Currencies and Politics in the United States, Germany, and Japan.* Washington, DC: Institute for International Economics.

Henning, C. Randall. 1997. *Cooperating with Europe's Monetary Union.* Washington, DC: Institute for International Economics.

Herbst, Jeffrey. 1993. *The Politics of Reform in Ghana, 1982–1991.* Berkeley: University of California Press.

Herring, Richard J., and Robert E. Litan. 1995. *Financial Regulation in the Global Economy.* Washington, DC: The Brookings Institution.

Hertel, Thomas W., and Will Martin. 2000. "Liberalising Agriculture Manufactures in a Millennium Round: Implications for Developing Countries," *World Economy* 23 (April): 455–469.

Hibbs, Douglas R. 1987. *The American Political Economy: Macroeconomics and Electoral Politics*. Cambridge: Harvard University Press.

Higashi, Chikara. 1983. *Japanese Trade Policy Formulation*. New York: Praeger.

Hillman, Arye. 1989. *The Political Economy of Protection*. New York: Harwood Academic Publishers.

Hilsenrath, Jon E. 2001. "Die-Hard Dollar Damages U.S. Exporters," *The Wall Street Journal*. (March 20): A2.

Hirschman, Albert O. 1958. *The Strategy of Economic Development*. New Haven: Yale University Press.

Hirschman, Albert O. 1971. "Ideologies of Economic Development," *A Bias for Hope: Essays on Development and Latin America*. New Haven: Yale University Press.

Hirschman, Albert O. 1968. "The Political Economy of Import-Substitution Industrialization in Latin America," *Quarterly Journal of Economics* LXXXII (February): 1–32.

Hiscox, Michael. 2002. *International Trade and Political Conflict: Commerce, Coalitions, and Mobility*. Princeton: Princeton University Press.

Hiscox, Michael. 2001. "Class versus Industry Cleavages: Inter-industry Factor Mobility and the Politics of Trade," *International Organization* 55 (Winter): 1–46.

Hobsbawm, Eric J. 1989. *The Age of Empire, 1875–1914*. New York: Vintage.

Hoekman, Bernard M., and Kostecki, Michel M. 1995. *The Political Economy of the World Trading System: From GATT to WTO*. Oxford: Oxford University Press.

Hopkins, Anthony G. 1979. *Two Essays on Underdevelopment*. Geneva: Graduate Institute of International Studies.

Horsefield, J. Keith. 1969. *The International Monetary Fund, 1945–1965: Twenty Years of International Monetary Cooperation, Volume I: Chronicle*. Washington, DC: International Monetary Fund.

Hufbauer, Gary, and Kimberly Elliott. 1994. *Measuring the Costs of Protection in the United States*. Washington, DC: Institute for International Economics.

Hymer, Stephen. 1976. *The International Operations of National Firms: A Study of Direct Foreign Investment*. Cambridge: MIT Press.

Ikenberry, G. John, David A. Lake, and Michael Mastanduno. 1988. "Introduction: Approaches to Explaining American Foreign Economic Policy," *International Organization* 42 (Winter): 1–14.

Ikenberry, G. John. 2000. "Don't Panic: How Secure is Globalization's Future?" *Foreign Affairs* 79 (May/June): 145–51.

International Financial Institution Advisory Commission. 2000. *IFIAC (Meltzer) Commission Report*, http://www.house.gov/jec/imf/meltzer.htm.

ILO. 1998. Labor and Social Issues Relating to Export Processing Zones. Geneva: ILO.

Inter-American Development Bank. 1997, *Latin America after a Decade of Reforms*. Washington, DC: Inter-American Development Bank.

International Monetary Fund. 1988. *Issues and Developments in International Trade Policy*. Occasional Paper 63. Washington, DC: International Monetary Fund.

International Monetary Fund. 1991. *Determinants and Systemic Consequences of International Capital Flows*, Occasional paper no 77. Washington, DC: The International Monetary Fund.

International Monetary Fund. 1999. *International Capital Markets: Developments, Prospects, and Key Policy Issues*. Washington, DC: The International Monetary Fund.

International Monetary Fund. 2000. *International Capital Markets: Developments, Prospects, and Key Policy Issues*. Washington, DC: The International Monetary Fund.

International Monetary Fund. 2001. "International Financial Integration and Developing Countries," *World Economic Outlook* (September): 143–171.

International Monetary Fund. 2002. *World Economic Outlook* (September). Washington, DC: The International Monetary Fund. http://www.imf.org/external/pubs/ft/weo/2002/02/index.htm.

International Monetary Fund. 2003a. "Classification of Exchange Rate Arrangements and Monetary Policy Frameworks," (December 31). http://www.imf.org/external/np/mfd/er/2003/emg/1203.htm.

International Monetary Fund. 2003b. "Lessons from the Crisis in Argentina," Policy Development and Review Department http://www.imf.org/external/np/pdr/lessons/100803.pdf, accessed January 31, 2005.

Ip, Greg. 2004. "Dollar's Decline Has Little Impact on Import Prices; While Euro-Zone Nations Feel Pressure, Trade Deficit Remains Unaffected So Far," *Wall Street Journal* (Jan 14): A1.

Irwin, Douglas. 1996. *Against the Tide: An Intellectual History of Free Trade.* Princeton: Princeton University Press.

Jabara, Cathy. 1994. "Structural Adjustment in a Small, Open Economy: The Case of Gambia," in *Adjusting to Policy Failure in African Economies,* edited by David E. Sahn. Ithaca: Cornell University Press, 302–331.

Jackson, John H. 1997. *The World Trading System: Law and Policy of International Economic Relations.* Cambridge: MIT Press.

Jaycox, Edward V. K., Ravi I. Gulhati, Sanjaya Lall, and Satya Yalamanchili. 1986. "The Nature of the Debt Problem in Eastern and Southern Africa," in *African Debt and Financing,* edited by Carol Lancaster and John Williamson. Washington, DC: Institute for International Economics.

Jenkins, Rhys. 1987. *Transnational Corporations and Uneven Development: The Internationalization of Capital and the Third World.* London: Methuen.

Johnson, Chalmers. 1982. *MITI and the Japanese Miracle: The Growth of Industrial Policy, 1925–1975.* Stanford: Stanford University Press.

Johnson, Leland L. 1967. *Economic Development and Cultural Change.* Chicago: The University of Chicago Press.

Johnson, Michael. 1998. *European Community Trade Policy and the Article 113 Committee.* London: Royal Institute for International Affairs.

Johnson, O.E.G. 1974. "Credit Controls as Instruments of Development Policy in the Light of Economic Theory," *Journal of Money, Credit and Banking* 6 (1): 85–99.

Joint Economic Committee, United States Congress. 2003. "Argentina's Economic Crisis: Causes and Cures," http://www.house.gov/jec/imf/06-13-03long.pdf, accessed January 31, 2005.

Jones, Geoffrey. 1996. *The Evolution of International Business: An Introduction.* London: Routledge.

Jones, Joseph M. 1934. *Tariff Retaliation: Repercussions of the Hawley-Smoot Bill.* Philadelphia: University of Pennsylvania Press.

Ka, Samba, and Nicolas Van de Walle. 1994. "Senegal: Stalled Reform in a Dominant Party System," in *Voting for Reform: Democracy, Political Liberalization and Economic Adjustment,* edited by Stephan Haggard and Steven B. Webb. Washington, DC: The World Bank.

Katzenstein, Peter J. 1977. "International Relations and Domestic Structures: Foreign Economic Policies of Advanced Industrialized States," *International Organization* 31 (Autumn): 1–45.

Keech, William R. 1995. *Economic Politics: The Costs of Democracy.* Cambridge: Cambridge University Press.

Kenen, Peter B. 1994. *The International Economy,* 3rd ed. Cambridge: Cambridge University Press.

Kenen, Peter. B. 1995. *Economic and Monetary Union in Europe: Moving beyond Maastricht.* Cambridge: Cambridge University Press.

Kennedy, Paul. 1988. *The Rise and Fall of the Great Powers*. New York: Random House.

Keohane, Robert O. 1980. "The Theory of Hegemonic Stability and Changes in International Economic Regimes, 1967–1977," in Ole Holsti, Randolph M. Siverson, and Alexander L. George, *Change in the International System*. Boulder: Westview Press.

Keohane, Robert O. 1984. *After Hegemony*. Princeton: Princeton University Press.

Keynes, John M. 1980. *The General Theory of Employment, Interest, and Money*. New York: Harcourt, Brace, and Jovanovich.

Khor, Martin. 1999. "How the South is Getting a Raw Deal at the WTO," in *Views from the South: The Effects of Globalization and the WTO on the Third World*, edited by Sarah Anderson. San Francisco: International Forum on Globalization, 41–49.

Killick, Tony. 1978. *Development Economics in Action: A Study of Economic Policies in Ghana*. London: Heinemann.

Kindleberger, Charles P. 1969. *Six Lectures on Direct Investment*. New Haven: Yale University Press.

Kindleberger, Charles P. 1974. *The World in Depression, 1929–1939*. Berkeley: University of California Press.

Kindleberger, Charles P. 2000. *Manias, Panics, and Crashes: A History of Financial Crises*. New York: Wiley.

King, Neil, Jr. 2004. "U.S., Europe Sue Each Other at WTO over Aircraft Subsidies; Boeing and Airbus Spar for Dominance in Sales; Brawl Could Rattle Industry," *The Wall Street Journal* (October 7), A.2.

Kobrin, Stephen. 1987. "Testing the Bargaining Hypothesis in the Manufacturing Sector in Developing Countries," *International Organization* 41 (Autumn): 609–638.

Kobrin, Stephen. 1998. "The MAI and the Clash of Globalizations," *Foreign Policy* 98 (Fall): 97–112.

Kock, Karin. 1969. *International Trade Policy and the GATT, 1947–1967*. Stockholm: Almqvist & Wiksell.

Kornai, Janos. 1992. *The Socialist System: The Political Economy of Communism*. Princeton: Princeton University Press.

Kraft, Joseph. 1984. *The Mexican Rescue*. New York: The Group of Thirty.

Kramer, Gordon. 1971. "Short-term Fluctuations in U.S. Voting Behavior, 1896–1964, *American Political Science Review* 65. 131–43.

Krasner, Stephen D. 1976. "State Power and the Structure of International Trade," *World Politics* 28 (April): 317–47.

Krasner, Stephen D. 1977. "United States Commercial and Monetary Policy: Unraveling the Paradox of External Strength and Internal Weakness," *International Organization* 31 (Autumn): 635–671.

Krasner, Stephen. 1985. *Structural Conflict: The Third World Against Global Liberalism*. Berkeley: University of California Press.

Kristof, Nicholas D. 2004. "Inviting All Democrats," *The New York Times* (January 14).

Krueger, Anne O. 1974. "The Political Economy of the Rent-Seeking Society," *The American Economic Review* 64 (June): 291–303.

Krueger, Anne O. 1985. "The Experience and Lessons of Asia's Super Exporters," in *Export-Oriented Development Strategies: The Success of Five Newly Industrializing Countries*, edited by Vittorio Corbo, Anne O. Krueger, and Fernando Ossa. Boulder: Westview Press, 187–212.

Krueger, Anne O. 1992. *The Political Economy of Agricultural Pricing Policy, Volume 5: A Synthesis of the Political Economy in Developing Countries*. Baltimore: Johns Hopkins University Press.

Krueger, Anne O. 1993a. *Political Economy of Policy Reform in Developing Countries*. Cambridge: MIT Press.

Krueger, Anne O. 1993b. "Virtuous and Vicious Circles in Economic Development," *American Economic Review* 83 (May): 351–355.

Krueger, Anne O. 1995. *American Trade Policy: A Tragedy in the Making.* Washington, DC: The AEI Press.

Krueger, Anne. O. 2002. "Crisis Prevention and Resolution: Lessons from Argentina," National Bureau Of Economic Research (NBER) Conference on "The Argentina Crisis," Cambridge (July 17), http://www.imf.org/external/np/speeches/2002/071702.htm.

Krueger, Anne O. 2004. "Lessons from the Asian Crisis," Keynote Address, SEACEN Meeting, Sri Lanka (February 12), available at http://www.imf.org/external/np/speeches/2004/021204.htm.

Krueger, Anne O., Maurice Schiff, and Alberto Valdes. 1991. *The Political Economy of Agricultural Pricing Policy,* five volumes. Baltimore: Johns Hopkins University Press.

Krugman, Paul. 1979. "A Model of Balance of Payments Crises," *Journal of Money, Credit, and Banking* 11 (August): 313–25.

Krugman, Paul. 1987. "Is Free Trade Passe?" *Journal of Economic Perspectives* 1 (Autumn): 131–44.

Krugman, Paul. 1996. "Are Currency Crises Self-Fulfilling?" *NBER Macroeconomics Annual,* 345–407.

Krugman, Paul. 1997. "In Praise of Cheap Labor: Bad Jobs at Bad Wages are Better than No Jobs at All," *Slate,* March 21.

Krugman, Paul. 1997. "What Do Undergrads Need to Know About Trade?" in *Pop Internationalism,* edited by Paul Krugman. Cambridge: MIT Press.

Krugman, Paul. 1998. "The Confidence Game: How Washington Worsened Asia's Crash," *New Republic Online* (October 5), http://www.thenewrepublic.com/archive/1098/100598/krugman100598.html.

Krugman, Paul R., and Maurice Obstfeld. 1994. *International Economics: Theory and Policy,* 4th ed. Reading: Addison Wesley.

Krugman, Paul R., and Maurice Obstfeld. 2003. *International Economics: Theory and Policy,* 6th ed. Reading: Addison Wesley.

Kydland, Finn, and Edward C. Prescott. 1977. "Rules rather than Discretion: The Dynamic Inconsistency of Optimal Plans," *Journal of Political Economy* 83: 473–91.

Lal, Deepak. 1983. *The Poverty of "Development Economics."* London: The Institute of Economic Affairs.

Lal, Deepak, and Hla Myint. 1996. *The Political Economy of Poverty, Equity, and Growth: A Comparative Study.* Oxford: Clarendon Press.

Lancaster, Carol, and John Williamson, eds. 1986. *African Debt and Financing.* Washington, DC: Institute for International Economics.

Lane, Timothy, Atish Ghosh, Javier Hamann, Steven Phillips, Marianee Schultze-Ghattas, and Tsidi Tsikata. 1999. *IMF-Suported Programs in Indonesia, Korea, and Thailand: A Preliminary Assessment.* IMF Occasional Paper 178. Washington, DC: International Monetary Fund.

La Porta, Rafael, and Florencio Lopez de Silanes. 1997. "The Benefits of Privatization: Evidence from Mexico," *NBER Working Paper* No. W6215 (October).

Lal, Deepak. 2004. *In Praise of Empires: Globalization and Order.* New York: Palgrave MacMillan.

Lardy, Nicholas R. 2002. *Integrating China into the Global Economy.* Washington, DC: Brookings Institution Press.

Lardy, Nicholas R. 1998. *China's Unfinished Economic Revolution.* Washington, DC: Brookings Institution Press.

Larson, Alan. 2002. "A New Negotiating Dynamic at Doha," *Economic Perspectives: An Electronic Journal of the U.S. Department of State* 7 (January): 6–8, http://www.usinfo.state.gov/journals/ites/0102/ijee/ijee0102.pdf.

League of Nations. 1944. *International Currency Experience: Lessons of the Interwar Period.* Geneva: League of Nations.

Leff, Nathaniel H. 1969. *Economic Policy-Making and Development in Brazil, 1947–1964.* New York: John Wiley & Sons, Inc.

Lekachman, Robert. 1966. *The Age of Keynes.* New York: Vintage.

Lewis, Arthur. 1954. "Economic Development with Unlimited Supplies of Labor," *Manchester School of Economic and Social Studies* 22: 139–91.

Lewis-Beck, Michael. 1988. *Economics and Elections.* Ann Arbor: University of Michigan Press.

Lim, Linda Y.C. 2000. "My Factory Visits in Southeast Asia and UM Code and Monitoring," September 6, http://www.fordschool.umich.edu/rsie/acit/ProViews.html.

Lim, Linda Y.C. 2001. *The Globalization Debate: Issues and Challenges.* Geneva: International Labour Organization.

Lindert, Peter H., and Jeffrey G. Williamson. forthcoming. "Does Globalization Make the World More Unequal?" in *Globalization in Historical Perspective,* edited by Michael Bordo, Alan M. Taylor, and Jeffrey G. Williamson. Chicago: The University of Chicago Press.

Lipson, Charles. 1985. *Standing Guard: Protecting Foreign Capital in the Nineteenth and Twentieth Centuries.* Berkeley: University of California Press.

Lipton, Michael. 1977. *Why Poor People Stay Poor: Urban Bias in Third World Development.* London: Temple Smith.

Little, Ian, Tibor Scitovsky, and Maurice Scott. 1970. *Industry and Trade in Some Developing Countries: A Comparative Study.* London: Oxford University Press.

Little, Ian. 1982. *Economic Development.* New York: Basic Books.

Liu, Paul K.C. 1992. "Science, Technology, and Human Capital Formation," in *Taiwan: From Developing to Mature Economy,* edited by Gustav Ranis. Boulder: Westview Press, 357–93.

Lohmann, Susanne, and Sharyn O'Halloran. 1994. "Divided Government and U.S. Trade Policy: Theory and Evidence," *International Organization* 48 (Autumn): 595–632.

Lora, Eduardo and Felipe Barrera. 1997. "A Decade of Structural Reform in Latin America: Growth, Productivity, and Investment Are Not What they Used to Be," Inter-American Development Bank, Office of the Chief Economist, Working Paper Green Series #350.

Low, Patrick, ed. 1992. *International Trade and the Environment.* Washington, DC: World Bank Discussion Papers, no. 159.

Lukacs, Aaron. 2000. *WTO Report Card III: Globalization and Developing Countries,* Trade Briefing Paper. Washington, DC: Center for Trade Policy Studies, Cato Institute, http://www.freetrade.org/pubs/briefs/tbp-010.pdf.

Lustig, Nora. 1998. *Mexico: The Remaking of an Economy,* 2nd ed. Washington, DC: Brookings Institution Press.

MacNamara, Kathleen. 1997. *The Currency of Ideas.* Ithaca: Cornell University Press.

Mackie, Thomas T., and Richard Rose, eds. 1991. *The International Almanac of Electoral History.* Washington, DC: Congressional Quarterly.

Maddison, Angus. 2001. *The World Economy: A Millennial Perspective.* Paris: Organization for Economic Cooperation and Development.

Magee, Stephen, William Brock, and Leslie Young. 1989. *Black Hole Tariffs and Endogenous Policy Theory.* Cambridge: Cambridge University Press.

Major, Tony. 2003. "ECB Plays Down Fears that Rising Euro Might Dent Growth in Zone," *The Financial Times* (October 10): 7.

Major, Tony. 2004. "ECB Shows Concern Over Euro," *The Financial Times* (January 9): 1.

Mann, Catherine. 2002. "Perspectives on the U.S. Current Account Deficit and Sustainability," *Journal of Economic Perspectives* 16 (Summer): 131–152.

Marer, Paul. 1974. "The Political Economy of Soviet Relations with Eastern Europe," in *Testing Theories of Economic Imperialism*, edited by Steven J. Rosen and James R. Kurth. Lexington, MA: Lexington Books, 231–60.

Marichal, Carlos. 1989. *A Century of Debt Crises in Latin America: From Independence to the Great Depression, 1820–1930.* Princeton: Princeton University Press.

Marston, Richard C. 1995. *International Financial Integration: A Study of Interest Differentials Between the Major Industrial Countries.* Cambridge: Cambridge University Press.

Martinussen, John. 1997. *Society, State, & Market: A Guide to Competing Theories of Development.* London: Zed Books.

Mason, David. 1996. *Revolution in East-Central Europe: The Rise and Fall of Communism and the Cold War.* Boulder: Westview Press.

Mason, Edward S., and Robert E. Asher. 1973. *The World Bank Since Bretton Woods.* Washington, DC: The Brookings Institution.

Mason, Mark. 1992. *American Multinationals and Japan: The Political Economy of Capital Controls, 1899–1980.* Cambridge: Harvard University Press.

Mastanduno, Michael. 1992. *Economic Containment: CoCom and the Politics of East-West Trade.* Ithaca: Cornell University Press.

Mazur, Jay. 2000. "Labor's New Internationalism," *Foreign Affairs* (January/February).

McDaniel, Douglas E. 1993. *United States Technology Export Control: An Assessment.* Westport: Praeger.

McEntee, Christopher. 1995. "Trends in the Region: States Evaluating Cost of Enticing Industry," *The Bond Buyer* (May 25): 20.

McIntyre, Ian. 1992. *Dogfight: The Transatlantic Battle Over Airbus.* Westport: Praeger.

McKinnon, Ronald L. 1964. "Foreign Exchange Constraints in Economic Development and Efficient Aid Allocation," *Economic Journal* 74 (June): 388–409.

McKinnon, Ronald L. 1993. *The Order of Economic Liberalization: Financial Control in the Transition to a Market Economy.* Baltimore: Johns Hopkins University Press.

Meltzer, Alan. 1998. "Asian Problems and the IMF," *The CATO Journal* 17 (Winter): 267–74.

Messerlin, Patrick A. 1999. *Measuring the Costs of Protection in Europe.* Washington, DC: Institute for International Economics.

Meunier, Sophie, and Kalypso Nicolaidis, 1999. "Who Speaks for Europe? The Delegation of Trade Authority in the EU," *Journal of Common Market Studies* 37 (September): 477–501.

Miller, John, 2003. "Why Economists Are Wrong About Sweatshops and the Antisweatshop Movement," *Challenge* 46 (January-February): 93–122.

Miller, Kenneth E. 1996. *Friends and Rivals: Coalition Politics in Denmark, 1901–1995.* Lanham: University Press of America.

Milner, Helen. 1988. *Resisting Protectionism: Global Industries and the Politics of International Trade.* Ithaca: Cornell University Press.

Mishel, Lawrence, Jared Bernstein, and John Schmitt. 2001. *State of Working America: 2000–01.* Ithaca: ILR Press.

Montiel, Peter, and Eduardo Fernandez-Arias. 2002. "Reform and Growth in Latin America: All Pain, No Gain?" IMF Staff Papers 48 (3): 522–546.

Moran, Theodore H. 1974. *Multinational Corporations and the Politics of Dependence: Copper in Chile.* Princeton: Princeton University Press.

Moran, Theodore H. 1999. *Foreign Direct Investment and Development: The New Policy Agenda for Developing Countries and Economies in Transition.* Washington, DC: Institute for International Economics.

Moran, Theodore H. 2002. *Beyond Sweatshops: Foreign Direct Investment in Developing Countries.* Washington, DC: The Brookings Institution.

Mühleisen, Martin, and Christopher Towe, eds. 2004. *U.S. Fiscal Policies and Priorities for Long-run Sustainability.* IMF Occasional Paper 227 (January). Washington, DC: The International Monetary Fund.

Multinational Monitor. 1999. "WTO and the Third World: On a Catastrophic Course: An interview with Martin Khor," *Multinational Monitor* 20 (October/November): 31–35.

Myerson, Allen R. 1996. "O Governor, Won't You Buy Me a Mercedes Plant?" *New York Times* (September 1): Section 3, p. 1.

The National Labor Committee. 2002. *Toys of Misery: A Report on the Toy Industry in China.* http://www.nlcnet.org/CHINA/1201/ToysOfMisery.pdf.

Naughton, Barry. 1995. *Growing Out of the Plan: Chinese Economic Reform, 1978–1993.* Cambridge: Cambridge University Press.

Nelson, Joan. 1992. "Poverty, Equity, and the Politics of Adjustment," in *The Politics of Economic Adjustment: International Constraints, Distributive Conflicts, and the State,* edited by Stephen Haggard and Robert R. Kaufman. Princeton: Princeton University Press, 221–69.

Nelson, Joan, ed. 1990. *Economic Crisis and Policy Choice: The Politics of Adjustment in the Third World.* Princeton: Princeton University Press.

Newhouse, John. 1982. *The Sporty Game.* New York: Knopf.

Nivola, Pietro S. 1993. *Regulating Unfair Trade.* Washington, DC: The Brookings Institution.

Nixon, Richard M. 1962. *Six Crises.* New York: Doubleday.

Nordhaus, William. 1989. "Alternative Approaches to the Political Business Cycle," *Brookings Papers on Economic Activity* 2: 1–68.

Nove, Alec. 1992. *An Economic History of the USSR 1917–1991,* 3rd ed. London: Penguin Books.

Nove, Alec. 1986. *The Soviet Economic System,* 3rd ed. Boston: Allen & Unwin.

Nugent, Neil. 1994. *The Government and Politics of the European Union,* 3rd ed. Durham: Duke University Press.

Nurske, Ragnar. 1967. *Problems of Capital Formation in Underdeveloped Countries and Patterns of Trade and Development.* Oxford: Oxford University Press.

O'Brien, Robert, Anne Marie Goetz, Jan Aart Scholte, and Marc Williams. 2000. *Contesting Global Governance: Multilateral Economic Institutions and Global Social Movements.* Cambridge: Cambridge University Press.

Oatley, Thomas. 1997. *Monetary Politics: Exchange Rate Cooperation in the European Union.* Ann Arbor: University of Michigan Press.

Oatley, Thomas. 1999. "How Constraining is Capital Mobility? The Partisan Hypothesis in an Open Economy," *American Journal of Political Science* 43 (October): 1003–27.

Oatley, Thomas. 2004. "Why is Stabilization Sometimes Delayed? Re-evaluating the Regime Type Hypothesis," *Comparative Political Studies* 37 (April): 286–312.

Obstfeld, Maurice. 1996. "Models of Currency Crises with Self-Fulfilling Features," *European Economic Review* 40: 1037–48.

Odell, John S. 1982. *U.S. International Monetary Policy: Markets, Power, and Ideas.* Princeton: Princeton University Press.

OECD. 1994. *The OECD Jobs Study: Evidence and Explanations.* Paris: Organization for Economic Cooperation and Development.

OECD. 1997. *Indicators of Tariff and Non-Tariff Barriers.* Paris: Organization for Economic Cooperation and Development.

O'Halloran, Sharyn. 1994. *Politics, Process, and American Trade Policy.* Ann Arbor: University of Michigan Press.

Okimoto, Daniel I. 1988. "Political Inclusivity: The Domestic Structure of Trade," in *The Political Economy of Japan. Volume 2: The Changing International Context,* edited by Takashi Onoguchi and Daniel I. Okimoto. Stanford: Stanford University Press.

Okomoto, Daniel. 1989. *Between MITI and the Market: Industrial Policy for High Technology.* Stanford: Stanford University Press.

Olson, Mancur. 1965. *The Logic of Collective Action.* Cambridge: Harvard University Press.

Orenstein, Mitchell A. 2001. *Out of the Red: Building Capitalism and Democracy in Postcommunist Europe.* Ann Arbor: University of Michigan Press.

Oye, Kenneth A. 1992. *Economic Discrimination and Political Exchange: World Political Economy in the 1930s and 1980s.* Princeton: Princeton University Press.

Oye, Kenneth A., ed. 1986. *Cooperation Under Anarchy.* Princeton: Princeton University Press.

Pae, Peter. 2004. "U.S. Embarks on Trade Fight with Europe: WTO Complaint by Washington Says Airbus Received Subsidies." *The Los Angeles Times* (October 7), C1.

Panos. 1999. *Globalization and Employment: New Opportunities, Real Threats.* Panos Briefing Paper No. 33 (May).

Pastor, Robert A. 1980. *Congress and the Politics of U.S. Foreign Economic Policy, 1929–1976.* Berkeley: University of California Press.

Pempel, T.J. 1977. "Japanese Foreign Economic Policy: The Domestic Bases for International Behavior," *International Organization* 31 (Autumn): 723–774.

Penrose, E.F. 1953. *Economic Planning for Peace.* Princeton: Princeton University Press.

Perkins, Nancy L. 1999. "The World Trade Organization Holds That Trade Barriers May, if Properly Designed and Applied, Be Used to Protect the Global Environment," *Legal Times* (February 8): 43.

Phelps, Edmund S. 1968. Money-Wage Dynamics and Labor-Market Equilibrium," *Journal of Political Economy* 76 (July–August): 678–711.

Phillips, Michael M., and Michael R. Sesit. 2001. "Dollar's Decline Could Give a Lift to Bush," *The Wall Street Journal* (August 16): A2.

Preeg, Ernest H. 1970. *Traders and Diplomats: An Analysis of the Kennedy Round of Negotiations under the General Agreement on Tariffs and Trade.* Washington, DC: The Brookings Institution.

Preeg, Ernest H. 1995. *Traders in a Brave New World: The Uruguay Round and the Future of the International Trading System.* Chicago: University of Chicago Press.

Prestowitz, Clyde V. 1989. *Trading Places: How We Are Giving Our Future to Japan and How to Reclaim It.* New York: Basic Books.

Public Citizen, Global Trade Watch. 1998. "School of Real Life Results" (December), http://www.citizen.org/pctrade/nafta/reports/5years.htm#job.

Public Citizen. 2001. *NAFTA Chapter 11 Investor-to-State Cases: Bankrupting Democracy: Lessons for Fast Track and the Free Trade Area of the Americas.* http://www.citizen.org/documents/ACF186.PDF.

Qian, Yingyi. 1999. "The Institutional Foundations of China's Market Transition," unpublished manuscript, http://www-econ.stanford.edu/faculty/workp/swp99011.html.

Rabe, Stephen G. 1999. *The Most Dangerous Area in the World: John F. Kennedy Confronts Communist Revolutions in Latin America.* Chapel Hill: University of North Carolina Press.

Rawski, Thomas G. 1999. "China's Move to Market: How Far? What Next?" Unpublished manuscript, http://www.pitt.edu/~tgrawski/paper99/rawski-cato.htm.

Ready, Kathryn J. 1993. "NAFTA: Labor, Industry, and Government Perspectives," in *The North American Free Trade Agreement: Labor, Industry, and Government Perspectives,* edited by Mario F. Bognanno and Kathryn J. Ready. Westport: Quorum Books.

Reich, Robert B. 1992. *The Work of Nations.* New York: Vintage Books.

Remmer, Karen L. 1986. "The Politics of Economic Stabilization: IMF Standby Programs in Latin America, 1954–1984," *Comparative Politics* 19 (October): 1–24.

Richardson, J. Henry. 1936. *British Foreign Economic Policy.* New York: The MacMillan Company.

Robison, Richard. 1986. *Indonesia: The Rise of Capital.* Sydney: Allen & Unwin.

Rodrik, Dani. 1994a. *Making Openness Work: The New Global Economy and the Developing Countries.* Washington, DC: Overseas Development Council.

Rodrik, Dani. 1994b. "The Rush to Free Trade in the Developing World: Why so Late? Why Now? Will It Last?" in *Voting for Reform: Democracy, Political Liberalization, and Economic Adjustment,* edited by Stephan Haggard and Steven B. Webb. Oxford: Oxford University Press, 61–88.

Rodrik, Dani. 1998a. "Who Needs Capital Account Liberalization?" in *Should the IMF Pursue Capital-Account Convertibility?* edited by Stanley Fischer et al. Essays in International Finance, 207. Department of Economics, Princeton University, Princeton, NJ.

Rodrik, Dani. 1998b. "Why Do More Open Economies Have Bigger Governments?" *Journal of Political Economy* 106 (5): 997–1032.

Rodrik, Dani. 1999. *Making Openness Work: The New Global Economy and the Developing Countries.* Washington, DC: Overseas Development Council.

Rodrik, Dani, and Francisco Rodríguez. 2001 "Trade Policy and Economic Growth: A Skeptic's Guide to the Cross-National Evidence" *NBER Macroeconomics Annual 2000,* eds. Ben Bernanke and Kenneth S. Rogoff. Cambridge: MIT Press.

Rogowski, Ron. 1989. *Commerce and Coalitions.* Princeton: Princeton University Press.

Roodman, David Malin. 2001. *Still Waiting For The Jubilee: Pragmatic Solutions For The Third World Debt Crisis.* Washington, DC: Worldwatch Institute.

Rosenstein-Rodan, Paul. 1943. "Problems of Industrialization of Eastern and South-Eastern Europe," *Economic Journal* 53 (June–Sept): 202–11.

Rowden, Rick. 2001. "A World of Debt," *The American Prospect,* vol. 12, no. 12 (July 2–July 16).

Ruggie, John. 1983. "International Regimes, Transactions, and Change: Embedded Liberalism in the Postwar Economic Order," in *International Regimes,* edited by Stephen D. Krasner. Ithaca: Cornell University Press.

Ryan, Michael P. 1998. *Knowledge Diplomacy: Global Competition and the Politics of Intellectual Property.* Washington, DC: The Brookings Institution.

Sachs, Jeffrey D. 1997. "The Wrong Medicine for Asia," *The New York Times* November 3.

Sachs, Jeffrey D. 1993. *Poland's Jump to the Market Economy.* Cambridge: MIT Press.

Sachs, Jeffrey D. 2002. "Resolving the Debt Crisis of Low-Income Countries," *Brookings Papers on Economic Activity* 1: 1–28.

Sachs, Jeffrey, and Felipe B. Larrain. 1993. *Macroeconomics in the Global Economy.* Englewood Cliffs: Prentice Hall.

Sachs, Jeffrey, and Charles Wyplosz. 1986. "The Economic Consequences of President Mitterrand." *Economic Policy* 1: 262–322.

Safarian, A.E. 1993. *Multinational Enterprises and Public Policy: A Study of Industrial Countries.* Brookfield: Edward Elgar.

Sala-I-Martin. 2002. *The Disturbing "Rise" of Global Income Inequality,* NBER Working Paper 8904. Cambridge, MA: National Bureau of Economic Research.

Sandler, Todd. 1992. *Collective Action: Theory and Applications.* Ann Arbor: University of Michigan Press.

Sanger, David E. 1998. "IMF Reports Plan Backfired, Worsening Indonesia Woes," *The New York Times* (January 14).

Sauvant, K.P., and V. Aranda. 1994. "The International Legal Framework for Transnational Corporations," in *Transnational Corporations: The International Legal Framework,* edited by A.A. Fatouros. London: Routledge.

Sazanami, Yoko, Shujiro Urata, and Hiroki Kawai. 1995. *Measuring the Costs of Protection in Japan.* Washington, DC: Institute for International Economics.

Scheve, Kenneth E., and Matthew J. Slaughter. 2001. *Globalization and the Perceptions of American Workers.* Washington, DC: Institute for International Economics.

Schiff, Maurice and Alberto Valdés. 1992. *The Plundering of Agriculture in Developing Countries.* Washington, DC: The World Bank.

Schott, Jeffrey J., and Jayashree Watal. 2000. "Decision-Making in the WTO," Institute for International Economics Policy Brief 00-2 (March) http://iie.com/publications/pb/pb00-2.htm (accessed March 30, 2005).

Schuknecht, Ludger. 1992. *Trade Protection in the European Community.* Reading: Harwood Academic Publishers.

Schwartz, Anna J. 1996. "U.S. Foreign Exchange Market Intervention Since 1962," *Scottish Journal of Political Economy* 43 (September): 379–97.

Schwartz, Anna J. 2000. *The Rise and Fall of Foreign Exchange Market Intervention,* NBER Working Paper 7751. Cambridge: National Bureau of Economic Research.

Scitovsky, Tibor. 1954. "Two Concepts of External Economies," *Journal of Political Economy* 62 (April): 143–51.

Scott, Robert. 2001. "Fast Track to Lost Jobs: Trade Deficits and Manufacturing Decline are the Legacies of NAFTA and the WTO," *Economic Policy Institute Briefing Paper* (October), http://www.epinet.org/briefingpapers/118/bp118.pdf.

Sell, Susan. 1998. *Power and Ideas.* Albany: SUNY Press.

The Semiconductor Industry Association. 2002. "What Is An Integrated Circuit?" http://www.semichips.org/ind_circuits.cfm.

Servan-Schreiber, Jean Jacques. 1968. *The American Challenge.* New York: Atheneum.

Shafer, Michael. 1983. "Capturing the Mineral Multinationals: Advantage or Disadvantage?" *International Organization* 37 (Winter): 93–119.

Shen, Raphael. 2000. *China's Economic Reform: An Experiment in Pragmatic Socialism.* Westport: Praeger.

Shirk, Susan. 1993. *The Political Logic of Economic Reform in China.* Berkeley: University of California Press.

Simmons, Beth A. 1996. "Rulers of the Game: Central Bank Independence during the Interwar Years," *International Organization* 50 (Summer): 407–43.

Simmons, Beth. 1994. *Who Adjusts? Domestic Sources of Foreign Economic Policy during the Interwar Years.* Princeton: Princeton University Press.

Simonsen, Mario Henrique, and Fundacao Getulio Vargas. 1988. "Brazil," in *The Open Economy: Tools for Policymakers in Developing Countries,* edited by Rudiger Dornbusch and F. Leslie C.H. Helmers. Oxford: Oxford University Press.

Skidelsky, Robert. 1994. *John Maynard Keynes: The Economist as Savior, 1920–1937.* London: Allen Lane, the Penguin Press.

Skidmore, Thomas E., and Peter H. Smith. 1989. *Modern Latin America,* 2nd ed. New York: Oxford University Press.

Slay, Ben. 1994. *The Polish Economy: Crisis, Reform, and Transformation.* Princeton: Princeton University Press.

Solinger, Dorothy J. 1991. *From Lathes to Looms: China's Industrial Policy in Comparative Perspective.* Stanford: Stanford University Press.

Solomon, Robert. 1977. *The International Monetary System, 1945–1976: An Insider's View.* New York: Harper & Row Publishers.

Solomon, Robert. 1999. *Money on the Move: The Revolution in International Finance Since 1980.* Princeton: Princeton University Press.

Soltwedel, Rudiger, Dirk Dohse, and Christiane Krieger-Boden. 2000. "European Labor Markets and EMU: Challenges Ahead," *Finance and Development* 37 (June): 37–40.

Spulber, Nicolas. 1968. "East-West Trade and the Paradoxes of the Strategic Embargo," in *International Trade and Central Planning: An Analysis of Economic Interactions,* edited by Alan A. Brown and Egon Neuberger. Berkeley: University of California Press, 104–26.

Stallings, Barbara. 1987. *Banker to the Third World: U.S. Portfolio Investment in Latin America, 1900–1986.* Berkeley: University of California Press.

Stein, Herbert. 1994. *Presidential Economics: The Making of Economic Policy from Roosevelt to Clinton.* Washington, DC: American Enterprise Institute.

Steinfeld, Edward S. 1998. *Forging Reform in Chine: The Fate of State-Owned Industry.* Cambridge: Cambridge University Press.

Stiglitz, Joseph. 1997. "Reflections on the Natural Rate Hypothesis," *Journal of Economic Perspectives* 11 (Winter): 3–10.

Stiglitz, Joseph. 2000. "The Insider: What I Learned at the World Economic Crisis," *The New Republic Online* (April 17), http://www.thenewrepublic.com/041700/stiglitz041700.html.

Stiglitz, Joseph. 2002. *Globalization and its Discontents.* New York: W.W. Norton.

Stolper, Wolfgang, and Paul Samuelson. 1941. "Protection and Real Wages," *Review of Economic Studies* 9: 58–73.

Stone, Randall W. 1996. *Satellites and Commissars: Strategy and Conflict in the Politics of Soviet-Bloc Trade.* Princeton: Princeton University Press.

Stopford, John M. 1996. "The Growing Interdependence Between Transnational Corporations and Governments," in *Companies without Borders: Transnational Corporations in the 1990s,* edited by UNCTAD. London: International Thomson Business Press, 255–79.

Summers, Lawrence H. 2000. "International Financial Crises: Causes, Prevention, and Cures," *American Economic Review* 90 (May): 1–16.

Sweatshop Watch. 2005. "Frequently Asked Questions," http://www.sweatshopwatch.org/swatch/questions/ (February 5, 2005).

Taylor, Michael. 1976. *Anarchy and Cooperation.* New York: Wiley.

Teece, David J. 1993. "The Multinational Enterprise: Market Failure and Market Power Considerations," in *The Theory of Transnational Corporations,* edited by John Dunning. New York: Routledge, 163–182.

Temin, Peter. 1996. *Lessons from the Great Depression.* Cambridge: MIT Press.

Thorp, Rosemary. 1999. *Progress, Poverty, and Exclusion: An Economic History of Latin America in the 20th Century.* Baltimore: Johns Hopkins University Press.

Todaro, Michael P. 2000. *Economic Development,* 7th ed. Reading: Addison-Wesley.

Tonelson, Alan. 2000. *Race to the Bottom.* New York: Westview Press

Toye, John. 1004. *Dilemmas of Development,* 2nd ed. Oxford: Blackwell.

Trebat, Thomas J. 1983. *Brazil's State-owned Enterprises: A Case Study of the State as Entrepreneur.* Cambridge: Cambridge University Press.

Triffin, Robert. 1960. *Gold and the Dollar Crisis.* New Haven: Yale University Press.

Tufte, Edward R. 1978. *Political Control of the Economy.* Princeton: Princeton University Press.

Tussie, Diana. 1988. "The Coordination of the Latin American Debtors: Is There a Logic behind the Story?" in *Managing World Debt,* edited by Stephanie Griffith-Jones. New York: St. Martin's Press.

Tyson, Laura D'Andrea. 1995. *Who's Bashing Whom? Trade Conflict in High Technology Industry.* Washington, DC: Institute for International Economics.

United Nations Commission on Transnational Corporations. 1983. *Transnational Corporations in World Development.* New York: United Nations.

United Nations Conference on Trade and Development. 1995. *World Investment Report: Transnational Corporations and Competitiveness.* Geneva: The United Nations.

United Nations Conference on Trade and Development. 1999. *World Investment Report: Foreign Direct Investment and the Challenge of Development.* Geneva: The United Nations.

United Nations Conference on Trade and Development. 2000. *World Investment Report: Cross-border Mergers and Acquisitions and Development.* Geneva: The United Nations.

United Nations Conference on Trade and Development. 2001. *World Investment Report: Promoting Linkages.* Geneva: The United Nations.

United Nations Conference on Trade and Development. 2004. *World Investment Report: The Shift Toward Services.* Geneva: The United Nations.

United Nations Environment Programme. 2000. *Environment and Trade: A Handbook.* New York: United Nations.

United Nations. 1964. *Towards a New Trade Policy for Development.* New York: United Nations.

U.S. Congress, Office of Technology Assessment. 1991. *Competing Economies: America, Europe, and the Pacific Rim, OTA-ITE-498* Washington, DC: U.S. Government Printing Office.

United States Government. 2002. *Economic Report of the President.* Washington, DC: Government Printing Office.

United States Government. 2004. *Economic Report of the President.* Washington, DC: Government Printing Office.

United States. Department of Labor. 2000. *Wages, Benefits, Poverty Line, and Meeting Workers' Needs in the Apparel and Footwear Industries of Selected Countries.* Washington, DC: Department of Labor http://www.dol.gov/ilab/media/reports/oiea/wagestudy/wagestudy.pdf (February 5, 2005).

United States Department of State. "Memorandum From Secretary of the Treasury Fowler to President Johnson, May 10, 1966," *Foreign Relations of the United States 1964–1968, Volume VIII: International Monetary and Trade Policy.* Washington, DC: GPO.

Van Trotsenberg, Axel, and Alan MacArthur. 1999. "The HIPC Initiative: Delivering Debt Relief to Poor Countries," http://www.worldbank.org/hipc/related-papers/hipc-initiative-feb99.pdf.

Varley, Pamela. 1998. *The Sweatshop Quandary: Corporate Responsibility on the Global Frontier.* Washington, DC: Investor Responsibility Research Center.

Velasco, Andres, and Pablo Cabezas. 1998. "Alternative Responses to Capital Inflows: A Tale of Two Countries," in *Capital Flows and Financial Crises,* edited by Miles Kahler. Ithaca: Cornell University Press.

Vernon, Raymond. 1971. *Sovereignty at Bay: The Multinational Spread of U.S. Enterprises.* New York: Basic Books.

Vernon, Raymond. 1998. *In the Hurricane's Eye: The Troubled Prospects of Multinational Enterprises.* Cambridge: Harvard University Press.

Viner, Jacob. 1960. *Studies in the Theory of International Trade.* London: Allen & Unwin.

Vogel, David. 2000. "International Trade and Environmental Regulation," in *Environmental Policy: New Directions for the Twenty-First Century,* edited by Norman J. Vig and Michael Kraft. Washington, DC: CQ Press.

Wade, Robert. 1990. *Governing the Market: Economic Theory and the Role of Government in East Asian Industrialization.* Princeton: Princeton University Press.

Wade, Robert. 1994. "Selective Industrial Policies in East Asia: Is *The East Asian Miracle* Right?" in *Miracle or Design? Lessons from the East Asian Experience,* by Albert Fishlow, Catherine Gwin, Stephan Haggard, Dani Rodrik, and Robert Wade. Washington, DC: Overseas Development Council, 55–79.

Wallach, Lori, and Michelle Sforza. 2000. *Whose Trade Organization? Corporate Globalization and the Erosion of Democracy.* Washington, DC: Public Citizen.

Warkentin, Craig, and Karen Mingst. 2000. "International institutions, the State, and Global Civil Society in the Age of the World Wide Web," *Global Governance* 6 (April–June): 237–55.

Waterbury, John. 1992. "The Heart of the Matter? Public Enterprise and the Adjustment Process," in *The Politics of Economic Adjustment: International Constraints, Distributive Conflicts, and the State,* edited by Stephen Haggard and Robert R. Kaufman. Princeton: Princeton University Press, 182–217.

Waters, Richard. 1996. "Bidding War Reaches New Heights," *Financial Times* (November 20): 5.

Weinstein, Michael M., and Steve Charnovitz. 2001. "The Greening of the WTO," *Foreign Affairs* 80 (November/December): 147–156.

Wessel, David, and Bob Davis. 1998. "Currency Controls are Getting a Hearing Amid the Asian Crisis," *The Wall Street Journal* (September 4).

Whalley, John. 1998. "Why Do Countries Seek Regional Trade Agreements?" in *The Regionalization of the World Economy,* edited by Jeffrey A. Frankel. Chicago: University of Chicago Press.

Wiarda, Howard J. 1994. "The U.S. Domestic Politics of the U.S.-Mexico Free Trade Agreement," in *The NAFTA Debate: Grappling with Unconventional Trade Issues,* edited by M. Delal Baer and Sidney Weintraub. Boulder: Lynne Rienner Publishers.

Wilkins, Myra. 1970. *The Emergence of Multinational Enterprise: American Business Abroad from the Colonial Era to 1914.* Cambridge: Harvard University Press.

Williams, Marc. 1991. *Third World Cooperation: The Group of 77 in UNCTAD.* London: Pintner Publishers.

Williamson, John, ed. 1990. *Latin American Adjustment: How Much has Happened?* Washington, DC: Institute for International Economics.

Williamson, John, ed. 1994. *The Political Economy of Policy Reform.* Washington, DC: Institute for International Economics.

Williamson, John. 1983. *The Exchange Rate System.* Washington, DC: Institute for International Economics.

Williamson, Oliver. 1985. *The Economic Institutions of Capitalism.* New York: Free Press.

Winham, Gilbert R. 1986. *International Trade and the Tokyo Round Negotiation.* Princeton: Princeton University Press.

Wood, Robert E. 1986. *From Marshall Plan to Debt Crisis: Foreign Aid and Development Choices in the World Economy.* Berkeley: University of California Press.

World Bank. N.D. "100 Percent Debt Cancellation? A Response from the IMF and the World Bank," http://www.worldbank.org/hipc/100_-_English.pdf.

World Bank. 1984. *Toward Sustained Development in Sub-Saharan Africa.* Washington, DC: The World Bank.

World Bank. 1989. *Sub-Saharan Africa: From Crisis to Sustainable Growth.* Washington, DC. The World Bank.

World Bank. 1991. *World Development Report: The Challenge of Development.* Oxford: Oxford University Press.

World Bank. 1993. *The East Asian Miracle: Economic Growth and Public Policy.* Washington, DC: The World Bank.

World Bank. 1994a. *Adjustment in Africa: Lessons from Country Case Studies.* Washington, DC: The World Bank.

World Bank. 1994b. *Adjustment in Africa: Reform, Results, and the Road Ahead.* Oxford: Oxford University Press.

World Bank. 1994c. *China: Internal Market Development and Regulation.* Washington, DC: The World Bank.

World Bank. 1995. *World Development Report.* Washington, DC: The World Bank.

World Bank. 1997. *Global Development Finance.* Washington, DC: The World Bank.

World Bank. 1999. The Philippines: The Case of Economic Zones. Washington, DC: The World Bank.

World Bank. 2000a. *Lending Instruments: Resources of Development Impact.* Washington, DC: The World Bank.

World Bank. 2000b. *Trade Blocs.* Washington, DC: The World Bank.

World Bank. 2001a. *Global Development Finance.* Washington, DC: The World Bank.

World Bank. 2001b. *Global Economic Prospects and the Developing Countries: Making Trade Work for the World's Poor.* Washington, DC: The World Bank.

World Bank. 2001c. *World Development Indicators.* Washington, DC: The World Bank.

World Bank. 2002a. "Financial Impact of the HPIC Initiative: First 25 Country Cases," http://www.worldbank.org/hipc/Financial_Impact_March0602.pdf.

World Bank. 2002b. *Globalization, Growth and Poverty: Building an Inclusive World Economy.* Washington, DC: The World Bank.

World Bank. 2002c. *Transition: The First Ten Years.* Washington, DC: The World Bank.

World Bank. 2004. "HIPC at a Glance," http://siteresources.worldbank.org/INTDEBTDEPT/DataAndStatistics/20263217/hipc-pages.pdf, accessed January 28, 2005.

World Trade Organization. 1995. *Trading Into the Future.* Geneva: The World Trade Organization.

World Trade Organization. 1998a. *Trade Policy Review, the European Union.* Geneva: The World Trade Organization.

World Trade Organization. 1998b. *Trade Policy Review, Japan.* Geneva: The World Trade Organization.

World Trade Organization. 2000a. *International Trade Statistics 2000,* http://www.wto.org/english/res_e/statis_e/chp_2_e.pdf.

World Trade Organization. 2000b. *Mapping of Regional Trade Arrangements.* WT/REG/W/41 11 October. Geneva: The World Trade Organization.

World Trade Organization. 2001. *Annual Report.* Geneva: The World Trade Organization.

World Wildlife Fund. 1999. *Trade Measures and Multilateral Environmental Agreements: Resolving Uncertainty and Removing the WTO Chill Factor,* Discussion Paper (November).

Zarocostas, John. 1998. "U.S. Loses Appeal on Saving Sea Turtles," *Journal of Commerce* (October 14): 1.

Index